Oracle WebLogic Server 12*c* Administration Handbook

About the Author

Sam R. Alapati is a manager and senior database architect at Cash America International in Fort Worth, Texas. Earlier, he worked with Miro Consulting, Inc., in New Jersey, as a senior technical director, as well as an Oracle database and Middleware administrator for the Boy Scouts of America, AT&T, and Oracle Corporation.

Sam has provided Oracle database, Oracle E-Business, and Oracle Fusion Middleware technology–related consulting services to several organizations, including some well-known Fortune 500 companies. Sam has worked on several WebLogic Server projects, including the installation, configuration, and tuning of production systems. He has also helped clients with architecting and capacity planning for major Oracle WebLogic Server environments. Sam is the author of several Oracle database administration books, a book on Java (*Java Masterclass: Java Exceptions, Assertions and Logging*), as well as the *OCA Oracle Application Server 10g Administrator Exam Guide* (for OCA certification), also published by Oracle Press.

About the Technical Editor

Scott Gossett is a technical director in the Oracle Engineered Systems organization with more than 25 years' experience specializing in Exadata, Oracle RAC, performance tuning, and high-availability databases. Prior to becoming a technical director, Scott was a senior principal instructor for Oracle Education for over 12 years, primarily teaching Oracle Internals, performance tuning, RAC, and database administration classes. In addition, Scott is one of the architects and primary authors of the Oracle Certified Masters Exam.

Scott has been a technical editor for 13 Oracle Press books and a coauthor for *Oracle Database 11g: The Complete Reference*.

Oracle Press™

Oracle WebLogic Server 12*c* Administration Handbook

Sam R. Alapati

New York Chicago San Francisco
Athens London Madrid Mexico City
Milan New Delhi Singapore Sydney Toronto

Cataloging-in-Publication Data is on file with the Library of Congress

McGraw-Hill Education books are available at special quantity discounts to use as premiums and sales promotions, or for use in corporate training programs. To contact a representative, please visit the Contact Us pages at www.mhprofessional.com.

Oracle WebLogic Server 12*c* Administration Handbook

1 2 3 4 5 6 7 8 9 0 DOC DOC 1 0 9 8 7 6 5 4

ISBN 978-0-07-182535-1
MHID 0-07-182535-5

Sponsoring Editor
Paul Carlstroem

Editorial Supervisor
Janet Walden

Project Manager
Preeti Longia Sinha, MPS Limited

Acquisitions Coordinator
Amanda Russell

Technical Editor
Scott Gossett

Copy Editor
LeeAnn Pickrell

Proofreader
Claire Splan

Indexer
Claire Splan

Production Supervisor
George Anderson

Composition
MPS Limited

Illustration
MPS Limited

Art Director, Cover
Jeff Weeks

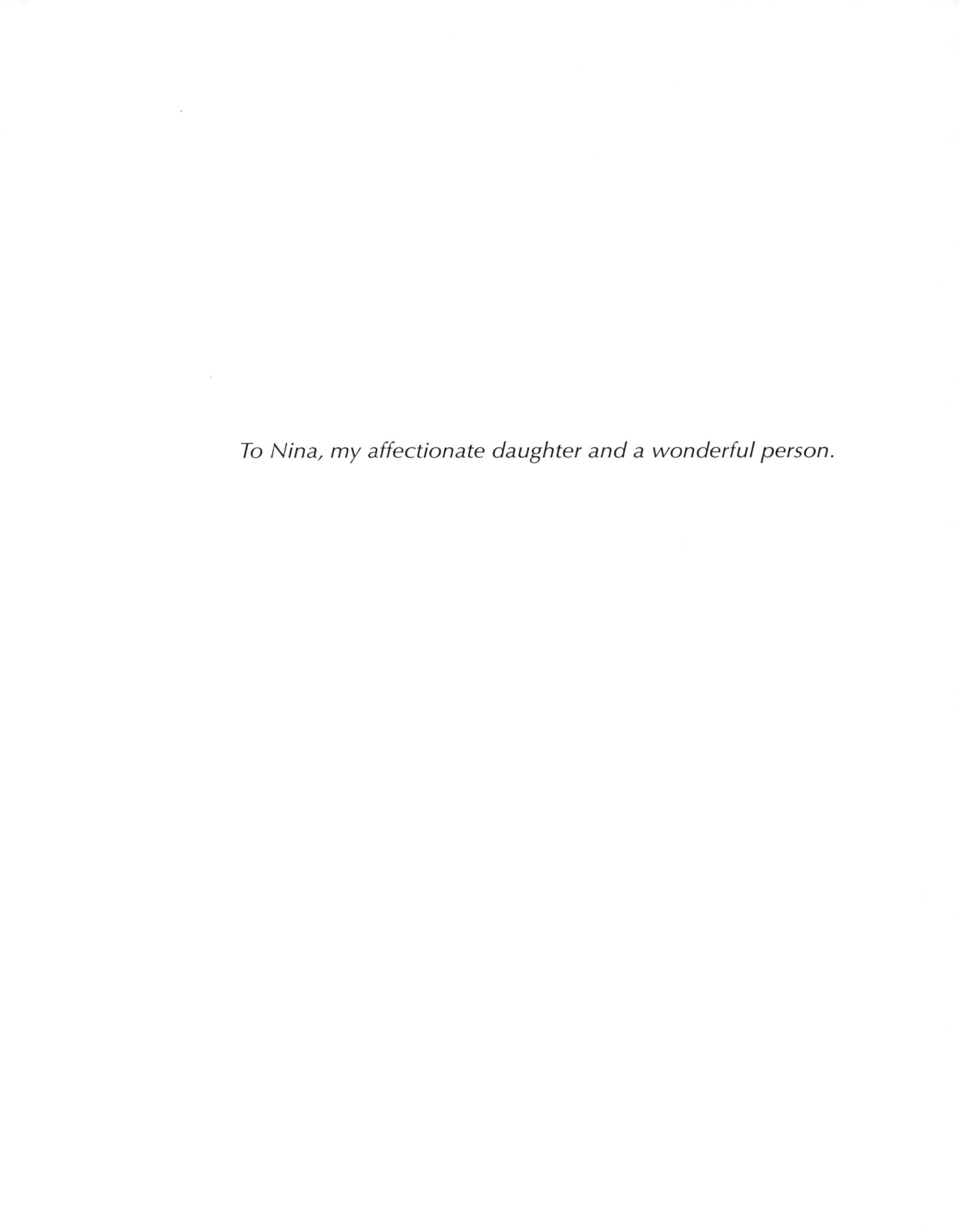

To Nina, my affectionate daughter and a wonderful person.

Contents at a Glance

Contents

Acknowledgments

I owe the successful completion of this book to the help and contributions offered by several people. I must first start with Paul Carlstroem, Senior Acquisitions Editor at McGraw-Hill Education, for his consistent support, encouragement, and uplifting comments throughout the writing of the this book. Paul is a great motivator who helped me stay on course through a tough writing process.

Amanda Russell, Editorial Coordinator, has been simply outstanding in the way she has managed this project from day one. Amanda's excellent project management skills and her support and understanding throughout the past several months made for an enjoyable writing project.

Although they weren't directly involved in the publication of this book, Tim Green and Wendy Rinaldi of McGraw-Hill have been extremely supportive and encouraged my writing projects for many years now. I owe both a deep debt of gratitude—I can repay their support by writing more books for them!

Scott Gossett did a superb job of carefully tech editing the entire book. Scott—thank you for all your hard work—as a result of your hard work in going through all the code, commands, and the screenshots in this book, I know things work as explained in this book!

The biggest personal thanks I owe to my family. I'd like to thank Valerie for all of her kind support throughout the course of writing this book. The twins, Nina (thank you again for your help with some of the figures in the book!) and Nicholas, and Shannon have been just as good as ever while I was busy writing away at home almost throughout this whole year (2013). Although I don't see them all the time, Keith, Shawn, and Dale have always been supportive and I wish to thank them. My biggest supporters and well wishers are my dear parents and brothers (and their families!), who have been a source of joy and happiness to me my entire life. I'd like to thank my father, Appa Rao; my mother, Swarna Kumari; my brothers, Siva Sankara Prasad and Hari Hara Prasad; as well as the rest of my family, Aruna, Vanaja, Ashwin, Teja, Aparna, and Soumya, for their support, affection, and kindness throughout my life.

Introduction

The main purpose of using Oracle WebLogic Server 12*c* is to deploy web applications. This book shows you how to install, configure, and manage Oracle WebLogic Server 12*c*, as well as how to deploy web applications with it and tune the performance of those applications. Oracle WebLogic Server 12*c* is the market-leading web application server and is fully compliant with the Java EE standards. The Java EE platform specifies the requirements that enable the building and supporting of scalable, secure, and robust enterprise Java applications. A Java EE–compliant web server provides all the necessary enterprise services, such as security and transaction management, to all the applications hosted by the application server. In addition, the applications must be built and packaged according to strict specifications to maintain portability across other Java EE–compliant web application servers. In fact, Oracle WebLogic Server offers several features beyond those specified by the Java EE standard, enabling you to build powerful enterprise solutions that make use of the latest technology.

Oracle WebLogic Server 12*c*, at its simplest, is just a Java program that supports a large number of essential services for running Java EE–based applications. By taking advantage of the services offered by the application server, Java applications don't have to worry about configuring database access, caching and concurrency, transaction management, security and messaging, and a bunch of other services necessary to support those applications. Because WebLogic Server and its various tools are Java programs, they run on all operating system platforms. In this book, I use a Windows 7 platform to explain how to manage and administer the Oracle WebLogic Server 12*c*. I use the Oracle WebLogic Server 12*c* (12.1.2) release, which was the latest version available during the writing of this book.

Oracle WebLogic Server 12*c* is the leading enterprise-ready Java Platform, Enterprise Edition (Java EE) application server. You can deploy just about any type of distributed application with WebLogic Server, including applications based on Service-Oriented Architecture (SOA). WebLogic Server provides a complete implementation of the Java EE 6 specification, which includes a rich set of APIs for creating distributed Java applications that let you access databases, messaging services, and external enterprise systems. WebLogic Server provides a comprehensive set of services for supporting Java EE applications based on standardized, modular components. Through its clustering capabilities, WebLogic Server enables enterprises to deploy mission-critical applications in a scalable and highly available environment. Oracle WebLogic Server 11*g* and Oracle WebLogic Server 12*c* have introduced several new diagnostic tools that allow system administrators to tune and monitor both the server environments as well as the deployed applications. Sophisticated security features protect access to services and secure data, and guard against attacks.

Although installing Oracle WebLogic Server 12*c* is easy, as is running web applications with it, at its heart it is an immensely complex application. The Oracle WebLogic Server 12*c* documentation is mostly complete and helpful, but it is humongous, and beginning WebLogic Server administrators often find it difficult to get the information they need to perform various tasks. The beginning user is often bewildered by the sheer number of new concepts he or she must assimilate in order to manage Oracle WebLogic Server 12*c* with confidence. Entire books can be written on individual topics such as WebLogic Server security. This book aims to clear the waters and provide the user with a way to understand basic WebLogic Server concepts such as configuration and administration of the server instances, deployment of web applications, security, performance, and many others.

Audience for This Book

Many books on architecting Java EE applications and writing Java code are available, but there are only two or so on configuring and managing Oracle WebLogic Server 12*c*. This book aims to take a beginning WebLogic Server user or administrator further than the rest of the books by providing both a simple explanation of the concepts as well as systematic instructions for performing numerous tasks that are part of WebLogic Server administration. Although Oracle's documentation is definitely a big help to users, having a single volume that explains key concepts and shows step-by-step procedures for configuring and managing various WebLogic Server services such as JMS and JDBC will be useful to many administrators and even some developers who need to manage WebLogic Server instances.

This book is designed primarily for those professionals tasked with managing WebLogic Server environments. These professionals may include full-time WebLogic Server administrators, other middleware administrators, or database administrators who are responsible for WebLogic Server installations. The book shows you how to create domains and deploy and migrate applications to production, as well as how to optimize the run-time environment. Developers who need to understand how WebLogic Server works and how to manage it in their environments will also find this book useful. Experienced WebLogic Server administrators will also find quite a bit of useful information in this book about newer topics such as the WebLogic Diagnostic Framework (WLDF).

In addition to providing a guide for WebLogic Server administrators, the book also serves as a handbook for developers and architects who work with WebLogic Server. For developers, the most useful topics might be how to manage the WebLogic Server instances, deploy applications, and configure connections to the database and other resources, whereas for architects, key topics might be WebLogic Server architecture, clustering, high availability, security, and performance tuning.

This book doesn't assume any prior knowledge of WebLogic Server or any other application server. It starts with the very basics and builds from there. Obviously, if you know a bit of the Java programming language and something about Java EE applications, you'll find it easier to work with middleware such as WebLogic Server.

Unlike normal web servers, a web application server such as Oracle WebLogic Server 12*c* hosts business logic for applications. A web application server not only hosts the web applications and web services you "deploy," but also provides you with a managed environment that handles transactions, database connections, messaging, security, and other tasks necessary for applications to do their jobs.

The book starts by describing basic Oracle WebLogic Server 12*c* concepts and terminology. Subsequent chapters explain how to manage WebLogic Server and how to configure domains. You'll learn how to configure custom networks, as well as JMS, JDBC, and JTA. You'll also learn how to diagnose problems by effectively using the powerful WebLogic Diagnostic Framework.

You'll learn how to create and manage domains, deploy applications in development and production environments, and how to secure your applications and the WebLogic Server environment. The book shows you how to manage the memory allocations to the server and how to diagnose and troubleshoot server performance issues using various techniques.

WebLogic Server is a huge, complex topic with numerous facets. The goal of this book is to make the task of WebLogic Server management easier by providing you the essentials of just about every important concept and technique you need to understand in order to manage WebLogic Server successfully.

The Background You Need

Because Oracle WebLogic Server deals with the support of Java-based web applications, the more you know about the Java EE platform, the better. The book doesn't actually require you to have any Java EE background—while some web application users may come from programming backgrounds, others don't. Therefore, the book assumes no Java programming knowledge on your behalf. This introduction to the book also provides a brief summary of the key Java EE application modules and applications that WebLogic Server hosts.

What the Book Covers

This book contains ten chapters, each of which provides a practical, hands-on explanation of a different facet of Oracle WebLogic Server 12*c* administration and management. Here's a synopsis of the book's contents:

Chapter 1 shows you how to install Oracle WebLogic Server 12*c* and provides an introduction to the main WebLogic Server management tools: the Administration Console, the WebLogic Scripting Tool (WLST), and the Node Manager.

Chapter 2 shows how to administer WebLogic Server instances and provides examples of the various ways to start and stop servers, and the different stages of a server's lifecycle.

Chapter 3 discusses the creation and configuration of WebLogic Server domains.

Chapter 4 introduces crucial WebLogic Server services such as JTA, JDBC, and JMS.

Chapter 5 shows how to configure key WebLogic Server features such as Work Managers and custom network channels.

Chapter 6 introduces the WebLogic Diagnostic Framework and also discusses the various ways you can monitor and troubleshoot a production system.

Chapter 7 shows you how to configure, create, and manage WebLogic Server clusters. You also learn how to perform both manual and automatic whole server migration and service migration.

Chapter 8 explains WebLogic Server application deployment concepts, including production deployment strategies to eliminate downtime during application deployment.

Chapter 9 introduces WebLogic Server security, including application and server security.

Chapter 10 offers a quick review of how to tune both WebLogic Server and the applications you host on the servers.

To really get what a web application server does, you need to understand the key components of Java EE applications, which I explain in the next section.

A Quick Introduction to Java EE Applications

You use Oracle WebLogic Server 12*c* to deploy web applications. Oracle WebLogic Server 12*c* implements the Java Platform, Enterprise Edition (Java EE) version 5.0 technologies. Java EE is a standard platform for developing enterprise Java applications, and all Java EE applications follow a standardized modular component architecture. WebLogic Server provides supporting services for these applications, so you don't have to program these services for each of your applications. Oracle WebLogic Server 12*c* supports all the Java EE applications and modules you wish to develop and run. These could be enterprise applications or web application modules such as servlets or JavaServer Pages (JSPs). The following sections describe each of the applications and modules supported by Oracle WebLogic Server 12*c*.

Web Application Modules

At its simplest, a web application can be just one servlet or JavaServer Page. A servlet is a Java program frequently used to generate dynamic web pages in response to client requests. JavaServer Pages are HTML-coded web pages that are translated or compiled into servlets. Note that both servlets and JSPs may need additional Java code called helper classes, which are deployed with the application.

Enterprise JavaBean Modules

Enterprise JavaBean (EJB) modules are server-side Java modules that implement business logic. There are three types of EJBs—session beans, entity beans, and message-driven beans—and they are defined here:

- **Session beans** These are used by a single client to execute a specific task and are nonpersistent; once they perform the tasks, they simply go away.
- **Entity beans** These are persistent beans that represent business objects based on a data store such as an Oracle database. Multiple clients can use the same entity bean.
- **Message-driven beans** These aren't associated with clients—rather, they handle messages and, in response to messages, assign instances of themselves to process messages.

Connector Modules

Connector modules, also known as resource adapters, enable Java EE applications to access a remote enterprise information system (EIS). You can use an EJB or a web application module such as a servlet or JSP to access EIS data and business logic.

Enterprise Applications

An enterprise application consists of one or more EJBs, web application modules, or connecter modules (resource adapters).

WebLogic Web Services

Web services are, simply put, web applications that deal with other applications, mainly located in the back end, such as CRM and order-processing applications. They don't interface with clients directly, as most web application modules such as EJBs and JSPs do. In the previous section, I defined an enterprise application as consisting of one or more EJBs, web application modules, or connector modules. You can also look at web services as another type of web application.

You can view the JSPs and servlets as supporting the presentation layer, and the EJBs and web services as supporting the business layer. JDBC and Java EE Connectors provide the back-end layer Java EE programming architectures. I understand that the introduction to web applications provided here is cursory, but once again, I'd like to remind you that the focus of this book is really on how to install, configure, manage, secure, and tune WebLogic Server—topics that are all explained in the following chapters!

CHAPTER 1

Installing Oracle WebLogic Server 12*c* and Using the Management Tools

The introduction to this book provided a quick outline of the Java Enterprise Edition (Java EE) and the nature of web applications for which you use Oracle WebLogic Server 12*c*. Since the primary goal of this book is for you to understand how to administer Oracle WebLogic Server 12*c*, let's begin by discussing key administration topics such as installing and upgrading Oracle WebLogic Server and becoming familiar with the administration tools you use day in and day out to manage the server. There are three major administrative tools that are going to be your day-to-day companions when managing Oracle WebLogic Server 12*c*: the Administration Console, the Node Manager utility, and the WebLogic Scripting Tool (WLST), which is based on the open source Jython language. This chapter briefly introduces these tools, and you'll learn how to use all three of these tools, as well as other WebLogic Server (this term is used as a synonym for Oracle WebLogic Server 12*c* throughout the rest of this book) management commands, in later chapters. In this and the next chapter, I make extensive use of the sample Oracle WebLogic Server 12*c* applications that you can install to learn various administrative and deployment-related concepts. This chapter introduces the Oracle WebLogic Server 12*c* sample domains that host the sample applications. This and other chapters use the sample domains to explain various Oracle WebLogic Server 12*c* management concepts. Before we start reviewing the installation, upgrading, and management of Oracle WebLogic Server 12*c*, however, let's review the Oracle WebLogic Server 12*c* product set as well as key terminology and important architectural concepts that illustrate how Oracle WebLogic Server 12*c* functions.

Oracle WebLogic Server: An Overview

Before you learn how to install, upgrade, and manage Oracle WebLogic Server, let's quickly review the set of Oracle WebLogic Server 12c products. Following that is a brief summary of key terminology that will help you understand the components of an Oracle WebLogic Server 12c domain, a collection of Oracle WebLogic Server instances and related resources and services that are managed together as a single unit.

Oracle WebLogic Server 12*c* Product Set

Oracle WebLogic Server 12*c* is a component of Oracle Fusion Middleware 12*c*, which consists of several Oracle products that span business intelligence, collaboration tools, content management, and integration services. The underlying application server supporting these middleware applications is Oracle WebLogic Server 12*c*. Products such as Oracle SOA Suite and Oracle Fusion applications rely on Oracle WebLogic Server 12*c* to run their code.

Oracle offers three distinct products as part of the Oracle WebLogic Server 12*c* application family:

- Oracle WebLogic Server Standard Edition (SE)
- Oracle WebLogic Server Enterprise Edition (EE)
- Oracle WebLogic Suite

Oracle WebLogic Server Standard Edition

The Oracle WebLogic Server Standard Edition (SE) is a full-featured application server, targeted for developers to aid in getting enterprise applications up and running quickly. Oracle WebLogic Server SE implements all the Java EE standards and offers management capabilities through the Administration Console.

Oracle WebLogic Server Enterprise Edition

Oracle WebLogic Server EE is the core application server designed for mission-critical applications that require high availability and advanced diagnostic capabilities. The EE version contains all the features of the SE version, of course, but in addition supports clustering of servers for high availability and the ability to manage multiple domains, plus various diagnostic tools.

Oracle WebLogic Suite

Oracle WebLogic Suite integrates the core WebLogic Server application server within the Oracle WebLogic Suite Java Infrastructure. The Oracle WebLogic Suite offers support for dynamic scale-out applications with features such as in-memory data grid technology and comprehensive management capabilities. It consists of the following components:

- Oracle WebLogic Server EE
- Oracle Coherence (provides in-memory caching)
- Oracle Top Link (provides persistence functionality)

This book deals exclusively with the Oracle WebLogic Server EE 12*c* product. (I refer to it simply as WebLogic Server in the rest of the book.) You manage WebLogic Server essentially the same way regardless of the operating system it is running on. This book uses examples run on a Windows installation of WebLogic Server; however, where necessary or relevant, certain tasks or commands are also shown for UNIX/Linux-based systems.

NOTE
WebLogic Server uses a configured pool of JDBC connections to interact with databases. You can use any RDBMS that supports a JDBC 2.0–compliant driver. This includes Oracle, IBM DB2, Microsoft SQL Server, MySQL, and other databases. The WebLogic Server installation includes an embedded database called Apache Derby. (Previously, Oracle shipped a different database by the name of PointBase.)

Terminology

Before we delve into the administration of WebLogic Server, I want to make sure you clearly understand the key terminology you're going to encounter throughout the book. Some of the WebLogic Server terms and definitions are obvious, but others aren't, such as the concept of a *machine,* for example.

WebLogic Server Instance

A *WebLogic Server instance* is a Java Virtual Machine (JVM) process that runs the Java code. The instance is the actively working component, receiving client requests and sending them on to the appropriate components, and sending the processed requests back to the originating clients. The server instance manages the resources necessary for applications, such as the JTA and JDBC services, to function. In each domain (to be explained in the following section), one instance serves as the Administration Server, which is your primary means of managing the domain. The rest of the WebLogic Server instances in a domain are called Managed Servers. If you have a domain with just one WebLogic Server instance, as is the case in a development environment, the single server instance functions as both the Administration Server and the Managed Server. Note that the terms *WebLogic Server* and *WebLogic instance* are often used interchangeably.

WebLogic Server Domain

A *domain* is a set of WebLogic Server instances (managed servers) that you manage with the Administration Server, which itself is nothing but another WebLogic Server instance, albeit a special one. Any configuration changes you make to a domain will apply to all members of that domain. Domains offer you ease of administration—for example, you can apply configuration changes on a domain-wide basis that apply to all the management servers that belong to that domain. Every domain has exactly one Administration Server, which is used to configure and manage that domain. In addition to the WebLogic Server instances, a domain also includes the application components that you deploy, as well as all the services required by the server instances of that domain. The Administration Server is usually referred to as the *Admin Server* for short.

A domain offers you the administrative ease you need to manage your WebLogic environment. A domain encompasses the Admin Server, Managed Servers (including those configured into WebLogic clusters), machines (servers), and all the services necessary to run your applications. The fact that a domain includes all the configuration data for the servers, deployments, and the physical network makes it easy to configure and manage complex, geographically dispersed WebLogic Server deployments. A domain lets you simultaneously deploy applications across multiple WebLogic Server instances located on heterogeneous servers and various networks, with different physical and network descriptions. Administering a domain makes it possible for you to configure high availability with the help of multiple WebLogic Server instances and administer various services spread across heterogeneous host servers.

The first step in using Oracle WebLogic Server to deploy applications is to create a domain. As mentioned earlier, a domain can just consist of a single Admin Server, with no Managed Servers at all, as is common in a development environment. A production cluster ranges over several physical machines to provide high availability and failover protection, but you can also configure a cluster on a single server for testing and development purposes. WebLogic Server stores the configuration information for a domain in the *config.xml* file, which is stored on the machine where the Admin Server runs and serves as the domain's configuration file. The domain also contains security settings, log files, and startup scripts for the Admin and Managed Servers that belong to that domain. The WebLogic Configuration Wizard and the WebLogic Domain Wizard offer you extremely easy ways to create domains, as well as the servers and clusters that belong to that domain.

NOTE
Each Managed Server contains a local copy of its domain configuration. Upon startup, it synchronizes its configuration with the Admin Server. Similarly, when you make domain configuration changes on the Admin Server, those changes are propagated to the Managed Server's configuration.

Administration Server

A *server* is an instance of WebLogic Server that runs in its own JVM, and the *Administration* (or *Admin*) *Server* is a special instance of WebLogic Server designed for managing the domain rather than running applications. There is a one-to-one relationship between domains and the Admin Server—an Admin Server belonging to Domain A can't manage Domain B.

You can deploy applications on the Admin Server, but unless you're operating in a purely developmental environment, use the Admin Server strictly for performing management tasks, not for deploying any applications. Although you can deploy applications on the Admin Server in a development environment, it's a best practice not to do so in a production environment. For one thing, you don't want application work to compete with administrative work in a production environment. You also want to firewall the Admin Server separately so external clients can't access it.

The Admin Server is critical to the functioning of a WebLogic Server domain because it manages the domain configuration, including the servers that are part of the domain, as well as all the applications and services you deploy to the various servers. Apart from this management of the domain configuration information, the Admin Server has all of the functionality of a Managed Server; in fact, an Admin Server runs the same code and is managed internally the same way as a Managed Server. The Admin Server hosts the *Administration Console,* which is a web application front end used for configuring, monitoring, and managing a domain. You can access the Administration Console with any supported browser that can access the Admin Server. All WebLogic system administration tools and APIs interact with the Admin Server. If you install the optional Node Manager service, the Admin Server communicates with the Node Manager service on each machine to talk to the Managed Servers running on that machine.

Managed Server

Managed Servers are the workhorses of WebLogic Server. Any additional servers you create after the creation of the default Admin Server are Managed Servers. The Managed Server contacts the Admin Server upon startup, to get its configuration and deployment settings. For this reason, you should always start the Admin Server before you start a Managed Server. Once a Managed Server starts running, it operates completely independently from the Admin Server.

Although you can deploy a Java EE application to the Admin Server itself, the recommended approach is to deploy applications to the Managed Servers. In a production environment, it's common to run multiple Managed Servers as part of a cluster. A Managed Server hosts your Java EE applications, as well as all related resources and services such as Java Database Connectivity (JDBC) connection pools and data sources, Java Transaction API (JTA) transaction services, and Java Messaging Service (JMS) connection factories that are necessary to support application deployments. On startup, a Managed Server contacts the Admin Server to retrieve any configuration changes since the Managed Server was last shut down. A Managed Server can continue to run, however, and it's even possible to start it in the absence of an Admin Server. Chapter 2 shows how you can start a Managed Server without a running Admin Server, in the special Managed Server Independence (MSI) mode. The MSI mode is enabled by default, and it allows the Managed Server to start using its locally cached configuration without having to contact the Admin Server for this information.

WebLogic Server Cluster

A *WebLogic Server cluster* is a group of WebLogic Server instances consisting of multiple Managed Servers that run simultaneously. The multiple Managed Servers work together to provide replication services for one another, and the Admin Server isn't generally a part of any cluster. Most production deployments use clusters to increase reliability and scalability through load distribution and high availability. To achieve the high availability capability, you deploy resources and services in a homogeneous fashion on each of the Managed Servers that are part of a cluster. Clusters host applications that respond to HTTP requests that are routed to the cluster through a hardware load balancer. You can also set up load balancing on a WebLogic Server instance or a third-party web server with the help of plug-ins supplied by WebLogic Server. The load balancer handles the HTTP requests after the requests pass through a firewall. Cluster members pass replicated copies of objects such as HTTP sessions among themselves to provide the failover capability for the cluster.

NOTE
The simplest domain will consist of just one server—the Admin Server. In a development environment, you can sometimes get by with such a simple setup and host all applications directly on the Admin Server without using a Managed Server or a cluster comprising several Managed Servers.

A WebLogic Server domain can consist of multiple Managed Servers that either are or are not part of a cluster, or it can consist of multiple clusters—just remember that even if you have multiple Managed Servers in a domain, you can avail yourself of WebLogic Server's high availability and load-balancing features only by deploying a cluster of servers. High availability lets you continue serving clients even when you experience a failure, such as a machine or WebLogic Server failure. WebLogic Server offers you many powerful features, including replication, failover, and the ability to migrate services so you have high availability for your system. Clusters provide load-balancing capabilities by letting you spread requests across the cluster members. Clusters also offer scalability by letting you easily add additional servers to the cluster to accommodate increased demand for WebLogic Server services. The important thing to understand here is that the cluster automatically provides these capabilities, so your users won't have to experience service disruptions. Each WebLogic domain may consist of multiple Java EE resources, such as JDBC connection pools and JMS servers, which the domain makes available to all the applications it hosts. Note that domain resources, like a JDBC connection pool, aren't shared across domains—each WebLogic domain must create its own set of resources. This requirement applies when dealing with clusters as well, which are treated as domain resources. A cluster's Managed Servers thus can't overlap domains and belong to more than one domain at the same time. Therefore, whenever you perform a failover within a cluster, you can fail over from one Managed Server to another Managed Server within the same domain but not to a Managed Server that belongs to a different domain.

How does one design a domain? Once you satisfy the simple requirement that you must install the same version of WebLogic Server for all the Managed Server instances in a cluster, it's easy to design a cluster. Although a WebLogic Server cluster can run entirely on a single machine, to take advantage of the high availability features, a cluster's member servers are typically installed on two or more physical machines. To increase a cluster's capacity, you can either add more Managed Server instances to the existing cluster architecture, or you can add more physical machines to the cluster, with the additional machines hosting new Managed Server instances, of course. Managed Servers can serve as backups for services such as JTA and JMS that another Managed Server in the same cluster hosts.

There's really no hard and fast rule for organizing your domains; one way to organize domains is to create separate domains to handle different types of work. For example, you can have one domain dedicated to online shopping and another to support your internal e-business operations. In general, you design domains based on your service needs, security requirements, and management considerations. You can also create separate domains for physically separate business locations.

It's sometimes easy to get confused as to how a cluster relates to a domain. Just remember that a domain is simply a set of WebLogic Server instances, some of which may be clustered and some not, and that a domain can contain multiple clusters.

Coherence Cluster

A domain may also include *Coherence Clusters,* which are groups of cluster nodes that share a group address to facilitate communication among the nodes. In addition, a WebLogic Server domain may also include a *Managed Coherence Cluster,* which is any WebLogic Managed Server assigned to a Coherence Cluster.

Machine

A *machine* in the WebLogic Server context is the logical representation of the computer that hosts one or more WebLogic Server instances (servers). The Admin Server uses the machine definitions that you create to start remote servers through the Node Managers that run on those servers. A machine could be a physical or virtual server that hosts an Admin or Managed Server that belongs to a domain. You'll see later in the book that you must define a machine first if you want the Admin Server to use the Node Manager service to monitor, start, and stop the Managed Servers running on a server. In a sense, a machine in a WebLogic Server environment is more or less equivalent to an instance of a Node Manager, and this is essentially the concept that a machine represents. WebLogic clusters make use of the machines you define in order to decide the optimal way to replicate session data on a different server that is part of a cluster.

Network Channels

Network channels are an optional feature that allows you to separate different classes of network traffic. You can make use of separate network channels to separate server and client traffic and direct it to different listening ports or addresses. If you need to allow both secure and nonsecure traffic on the same server, you can create multiple channels to support the diverse traffic with different security protocols. You can also use network channels to manage quality of service by using weighted, value-based priorities for different channels. This enables you to assign high-weighted values to faster channels that use faster network interface cards and dedicate them to the types of traffic that require faster throughput, for example. Network channels control all communication-related aspects such as listen addresses, protocols, and port numbers throughout the domain.

Node Manager

The *Node Manager* is an optional process that runs on a machine and manages the availability of all servers that run on that machine. Node Managers help you remotely start, stop, suspend, and restart Managed Servers. The Node Manager works with the Admin Server using a secure channel and lets you manage the availability, as well as monitor the health, of all Managed Servers in a single domain. The Managed Servers that the Node Manager controls can be independent servers or they can be members of a cluster. The Node Manager monitors remote Managed Servers and is capable of automatically restarting them when they fail. It also kills Managed Servers that exhibit unstable behavior. It is recommended that you install a Node Manager service on each machine that hosts a Managed Server. Managing the servers with Node Manager is actually a key requirement for configuring automatic server migration in a cluster following a server failure, as explained in Chapter 7. In Chapter 2, I explain how you can use Node Manager and the WebLogic Scripting Tool (WLST) together to perform various administrative tasks.

Virtual Host

A *virtual host* relies on the Domain Name System (DNS) to map hostnames to the IP address of a single server or a cluster of servers. By doing so, multiple domain names can be hosted on your server wherein different web applications can be assigned to different virtual hosts, effectively sharing all resources and being differentiated only by their hostnames.

Work Manager

A *Work Manager* helps you manage the WebLogic Server instance workload, specifically by letting you prioritize work execution, which you do by defining request classes and constraints. You can configure a Work Manager at the domain level (using a global Work Manager) or at the application or module level.

Services

Following are some of the main services used in a WebLogic environment:

- JDBC (Java Database Connectivity) enables Java programs to handle database connections established through connection pools.
- JMS (Java Messaging Service) is a standard API that enables applications to communicate through enterprise messaging systems.
- JTA (Java Transaction API) specifies standard Java interfaces between transaction managers and the parties in a distributed transaction system.

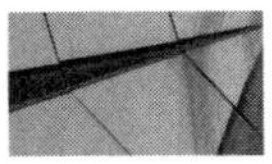

TIP
You can create Jolt Connection Pools to enable your applications to connect to Oracle Tuxedo domains. Jolt clients will then manage requests from your applications to the Oracle Tuxedo Services.

Deployment

When you want to make a Java EE application or a stand-alone application module available to users, you must first install those applications and modules in a WebLogic domain. Once you install the applications and modules, you must start those so the applications can begin processing user requests. *Deployment* is the process of installing the applications or modules and starting them so they are available to clients. Developers package applications for delivery to administrators, who then deploy the applications to WebLogic Server instances or clusters. Chapter 8 shows the various ways in which you can deploy applications to development and production environments by using the Administration Console, WLST, and the *weblogic.Deployer* utility.

NOTE
*Oracle WebLogic Server 12*c *fully supports Oracle Real Application Clusters (RAC). Chapter 4 shows you how to configure data sources to connect to Oracle RAC database services.*

Security Realm

You use security realms to protect WebLogic Server resources. A *security realm* is simply a logical container for your users, groups, roles, security policies, and security providers. It's the security realm that authenticates users and determines which resources they can access. WebLogic Server uses a default security realm named *myrealm*. In the default security realm, the Admin Server stores the domain security data in an LDAP server, but you can also choose an RDBMS store for this instead. The Managed Servers replicate this LDAP server, and when the Admin Server fails, it can use their copy of the LDAP server for providing security services to the deployed applications.

When you create a domain, the username/password credentials you provide are used by the Configuration Wizard to seed the security realm *myrealm*. The username you provide will be the initial administrative user in *myrealm*. When you start WebLogic Server, it uses the default security realm to authenticate usernames. You can configure the server to use other security realms, but you must always specify one of them as the default security realm.

If these simple definitions of the key WebLogic Server terminology don't satisfy your curiosity, not to worry—subsequent chapters discuss all these entities in great detail!

Important WebLogic Server Concepts

In order to fully comprehend how WebLogic Server works and to get the best performance out of it, it's important to understand several concepts. The most significant concepts are discussed in the following section.

Execute Threads and Queues

Understanding the internal architecture of Oracle WebLogic Server is important, particularly in terms of knowing how the server performs its work of satisfying user requests. When a client sends a request to WebLogic Server, the actual work to satisfy that request is performed by a Java thread called an *execute thread*. A user can submit work to WebLogic Server using an HTTP-based request to the servlet engine or a request for Remote Method Invocation (RMI) access to objects such as Enterprise JavaBeans (EJBs). When a server process starts, it binds itself to a port and assigns a *listen thread* to the port to listen for incoming requests. Once the request makes a connection, the server passes control of that connection to the *socket muxer*. The socket muxer reads requests off the socket and places the work requests into the self-tuning *execute queue* as they arrive. An idle execute thread will pick up a request from the execute queue and may, in turn, hand off the job of responding to those requests to special threads. The execute thread executes the requests and returns the responses.

Oracle WebLogic Server uses socket muxers, which are software modules, to read incoming requests on the server. Muxers read messages from the network, bundle them into a package of work, and queue them to the Work Manager, which then finds a thread on which to execute the work and makes sure the response gets back to the same socket from which the request came. There are two types of muxers—a Java muxer and a native muxer. A Java muxer uses pure Java to read data from the sockets, whereas the native muxers use platform-specific native binaries. By default, Oracle WebLogic Server uses the native muxer. This means that the *Enable Native IOP* parameter for the server is set to the value *SELECTED*. Note that with a native muxer, the server creates a fixed number of threads to read incoming requests, whereas with a Java muxer you can configure the number of threads in the Administration Console by modifying the *Percent Socket Readers* parameter. The native muxer allocates a certain percentage of the server threads to act as socket reader threads, which perform the pooling function, while the rest of the server threads are busy processing client requests. In general, you need to be careful about changing the number of socket reader threads. In many cases, the best optimization is to set it to 1.

You can tell if you're using a native muxer or a Java muxer by looking at the messages that involve the execute thread. If you're using the native muxer, the server error messages will refer to it as *weblogic.socket.EPollSocketMuxer,* whereas if you're using the Java muxer, you'll see *weblogic.socket.SocketMuxer* instead. Note that the *EPollSockerMuxer* is associated only with a JRockit JVM operating on a Linux server. You'll see the word *poll* in the case of a native muxer because it uses a polling mechanism to query a socket for data. Native muxers are seen as providing superior performance, especially when scaling up to large user bases, because they implement a nonblocking thread model. When administering WebLogic Server instances, you'll frequently encounter the so-called stuck thread situation, which occurs when a thread isn't returned to the thread pool within the timeframe you set for it (the default is 10 minutes). Resolution of stuck threads is a key component of WebLogic Server troubleshooting, and you'll notice that Oracle Support often asks for several server thread dumps when you open a service request. Chapter 6 shows you how to take a thread dump and analyze many performance issues on your own by identifying the resource contention leading to the stuck thread situation.

Implementing the JMX API and MBeans

WebLogic Server implements the system administration infrastructure with Oracle's Java Management Extensions (JMX). Implementing the JMX API involves using Java MBeans (*managed beans*) to model system administration tasks. If you understand MBeans and the JMX API, you can use them to create your own custom management tools. However, all administrative tools, such as the Administration Console, use the same MBeans and JMX API, so you don't have to reinvent the wheel by creating custom management tools. Although a WebLogic Server administrator doesn't need to know how to program the JMX API, it helps to understand the different types of MBeans and how the JMX API interacts with them.

WebLogic Server uses two basic types of MBeans—*configuration MBeans* and *runtime MBeans*—to configure, monitor, and manage the server and its resources.

- *Configuration MBeans* contain the configuration information for servers and resources that is stored in the domain's configuration files such as the *config.xml* file and other XML files. These are persistent MBeans, and the domain's configuration file, *config.xml,* stores the attribute values for these MBeans. Whenever you change a configuration attribute using a system administration tool such as the Admin Server, those changes persist in the *config.xml* file. Configuration values can also be set by modifying the startup scripts and adding additional arguments via the *-D* option in the Java startup command. The *config.xml* file automatically gets updated when you change any configuration settings. When a Managed Server starts, it contacts the Admin Server and gets a copy of the configuration details, which it stores in memory as configuration MBeans. Thus, all server instances in a domain have the same in-memory representation of the domain's configuration. Note that any attributes you change when starting a Managed Server won't affect the *config.xml* file, which is modified only if you change an attribute value on the Admin Server. When you shut down a server instance, all configuration MBeans hosted by that server are destroyed.
- *Runtime MBeans* help you monitor running server instances and contain attributes that hold run-time information for server instances and applications. Each of the server's resources updates the relevant runtime MBean following a change in its state. For example, the *ServerRuntimeMBean* is instantiated by the server when it starts and contains the run-time data for the server. Runtime MBeans consist only of run-time data and nothing else, and when you shut down the server, the run-time statistics in the *ServerRuntimeMBean* are destroyed, as is the case with all the other runtime MBeans.

MBean Servers act as containers for the various MBeans, and the servers create and provide access to the MBeans. Oracle provides three types of MBean Servers. The Admin Server hosts an instance of the Domain Runtime MBean Server, which manages the MBeans for domain-wide services. Both Managed Servers and the Admin Server host an instance of the Runtime MBean Server, which lets you configure server instances. The Admin Server also hosts the Edit MBean Server, which manages pending configuration changes. The Admin and the Managed Servers also can optionally host the JVM's Platform MBean Server, which controls MBeans that contain monitoring information for the JDK.

You can change most domain configuration attributes dynamically while the server instances are running. In cases where dynamic configuration of an attribute isn't possible, you must restart the server instance. Run-time values of the attributes you configure will reflect your changes immediately, and the values are persisted in the *config.xml* file.

Development and Production Mode

By default, WebLogic Server domains run in development mode using Oracle's Java Development Kit (JDK). In this mode, auto-deployment of applications is enabled and the Admin Server creates a *boot.properties* file automatically when you start it. You can also use the demo certificates for Secure Sockets Layer (SSL) without any warnings from WebLogic Server. The development mode is provided to get developers up and running quickly without having to worry about advanced deployment, configuration, or security issues.

In production mode, WebLogic Server defaults to using JRockit as the default JDK. In addition, you can't use the auto-deployment feature in production, and WebLogic Server issues warnings if you use the demo certificates for SSL. In production mode, you're also prompted for usernames and password when you start the instances.

It's easy to toggle between development and production modes, and you learn how to in Chapter 2.

Listen Ports and Listen Threads

Listen ports listen for connection requests, and, as connections come in, the listen thread assigned by the server to the listen port accepts the connection requests, establishes connections, and hands the requests over to the socket muxer.

By default, Oracle WebLogic Server uses two listen ports to listen to incoming requests for connections. The first listen port, which I'll call a *normal listen port,* accepts any type of request—administrative as well as user requests. The normal listen port accepts connections from various protocols such as HTTP, t3, IIOP, COM, LDAP, and SNMP. When you start a WebLogic Server instance, it starts listening on two different ports. The first one is a normal plaintext port, and the second is an SSL listen port that also accepts requests for connections from clients over protocols such as HTTPS, t3s, IIOPS, COMS, and LDAPS.

The second listen port is called an *administration port*. When you configure an administration port, the requests must use SSL, at which point you won't be able to direct any administrative requests to the normal port. Here's an informational message from the server when it starts. The message shows the two default listen ports in action:

```
<May 25, 2013 11:05:23 AM CDT> <Notice> <Server> <BEA-002613> <Channel
"Default" is now listening on 192.168.123.113:7001
for protocols iiop, t3, ldap, snmp,http.>
<May 25, 2013 11:05:23 AM CDT> <Notice> <Server> <BEA-002613> <Channel
"DefaultSecure[3]" is now listening on 192.168.232.1:7002 for protocols iiops,
t3s, ldaps, https.>
```

Although using the administration port is optional, note that you can start a server in the standby mode only if you use an administration port. In standby mode, the normal port will be unavailable, so you must use the administration port to manage the server. In addition, having two separate ports—one for administrative operations and the other for the application traffic—prevents a conflict between these two types of network traffic. In a production environment, you can thus ensure that critical administrative operations, such as starting and stopping servers or deploying applications, don't compete with the application traffic. The administration port accepts only secure SSL traffic, so all connections through this port will have to be authenticated. Note that only administrative users can authenticate on the administration port, and no administrative traffic is rejected on non-admin ports when you enable the administration port.

Choosing a JVM

To run Oracle WebLogic Server, you need a Java Virtual Machine (JVM). Oracle offers two types of JVMs for you when you install Oracle WebLogic Server—the Sun HotSpot JVM and the Oracle JRockit JVM. Oracle recommends that you use the JRockit JVM for production installations because of the many benefits it offers, including higher performance, increased scalability, and better manageability when compared to the Sun HotSpot JVM.

You configure the default JVM for a domain when creating a domain with the Configuration Wizard or with the WebLogic Scripting Tool (WLST). Of course, you can reconfigure the choice of a default JVM later on as well. If you choose Production Mode on the Configure Server Start Mode and JDK page during the Configuration Wizard's domain creation process, the choice of the JVM will default to the JRockit SDK. If you select Development Mode, on the other hand, your domain will be configured to use the Sun HotSpot SDK.

Changing the JVM after you create the domain is easy. Just set the *JAVA_VENDOR* environment variable in the *startWebLogic.cmd* script (or the *startWebLogic.sh* script in UNIX), as shown here:

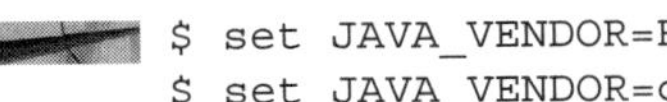

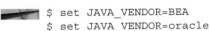

```
$ set JAVA_VENDOR=BEA                    /* For JRockit JVM
$ set JAVA_VENDOR=oracle                           /* for Oracle JVM
```

You can also set the value of the *JAVA_VENDOR* variable to Oracle in order to specify the JRockit JVM. You can confirm the JVM version the server is using by viewing the command window output after you start a WebLogic Server instance. Be sure to check the JRockit documentation for vendor-specific options if you're new to this JVM. You can use JRockit to run any applications that were created with the Sun HotSpot JDK.

Using Web Server Plug-Ins

Although WebLogic Server comes with a built-in web server, you can also use a third-party web server, such as the Apache HTTP Server, for example. Web servers can be used to field requests for simple, static HTML content; but dynamic content, such as that delivered by Java web applications developed as JSPs or servlets, are hosted on the WebLogic Server and the web server routes requests for the dynamic content to WebLogic Server. The web server can use a WebLogic proxy plug-in or the WebLogic Server–provided servlet named *HTTPClusterServlet* to direct servlet and JSP requests to the cluster. You must configure *HTTPClusterServlet* as the default web application on the proxy server machine if you want to use this instead of a proxy plug-in.

You can install a WebLogic plug-in on the web server, allowing it to talk to the applications running on WebLogic Server. Your WebLogic Server installation comes with plug-ins for the following web servers:

- Apache HTTP Server
- Microsoft Internet Information Server
- Oracle Java System Web Server

You can use a proxy plug-in to proxy requests from the web server to the clustered WebLogic Server instances to provide load-balancing and failover capabilities for those requests. You can configure the Secure Sockets Layer (SSL) protocol to secure data exchanged between the Apache HTTP Server Plug-In and WebLogic Server. Please refer to the Oracle WebLogic Server documentation on WebLogic Server plug-ins for more details about the various available plug-ins.

Although you can use WebLogic Server for its capabilities in hosting dynamic enterprise-level applications, you can also use it as a full-fledged web server capable of hosting high-volume web sites and server-static HTML files, servlets, and JSPs.

Management APIs

All the WebLogic Server administration tools and utilities you'll use to manage WebLogic Server call on various WebLogic application programming interfaces (APIs) to perform their tasks. Instead of relying exclusively on the management tools, you can also make use of the rich offering of WebLogic APIs to create your own custom management utilities. Here are brief descriptions of the key management APIs:

- **WebLogic Diagnostic Service APIs** These APIs support monitoring of the servers and the access and control of diagnostic data.
- **Java Management Extensions (JMX)** JMX is a public standard that you can use for monitoring and managing applications, devices, system objects, and service-oriented networks. WebLogic Server uses JMX-based services to manage its resources.
- **Deployment API** The deployment API enables the configuration and deployment of applications.
- **Logging APIs** Logging APIs help you write messages to log files and distribute those messages. WebLogic Server offers both the standard JDK logging APIs as well as the Jakarta-Log4J Project APIs.
- **Java EE Management API** This API enables you to create tools to discover resources such as connection pools and deployed applications.

Here are some things to note about the various management APIs:

- They implement and usually extend the relevant Java specification. For example, the deployment API implements the JSR-88 deployment specification.
- They enable you to integrate management tasks with other tools that comply with the same specification.
- The WebLogic Server administration tools, such as the Administration Console, use these APIs to perform various management tasks.

Installing Oracle WebLogic Server 12*c*

This section shows you how to install the latest release of WebLogic Server. As you'll see, the installation is remarkably easy. Of course, once you create your WebLogic Server domain, you'll need to configure it, and this could take a significant amount of time. Chapter 3 explains WebLogic Server domain configuration.

Although the installation steps and screenshots pertain to a Windows installation, they're similar to the installation steps you need to follow for a UNIX or Linux installation, except for a few operating system differences. All the scripts provided for starting and stopping the servers, for example, come in two versions—a Windows and a UNIX version. So the counterpart in UNIX for the Java Windows command script for starting a Managed Server, *startManagedWebLogic.cmd,* is the *startManagedWebLogic.sh* script.

NOTE

You can download the WebLogic Server installation files from the Oracle E-Delivery web site (http://edelivery.oracle.com) or from the Oracle Technology Network (OTN) web site.

Oracle offers Oracle WebLogic Server zip distribution, as in previous releases for development use, both for Windows and Linux (and Mac OS X) platforms. The zip distribution is intended purely for WebLogic Server development, and you must not use this in production environments. You can download both the generic installers and the zip distribution from the Oracle Technology Network site. Neither the generic installer nor the zip distribution includes a JVM/JDK. You can download installers with just Oracle WebLogic Server or one with Oracle Coherence and Oracle Enterprise Pack for Eclipse as well. Although it has a smaller footprint than the full-deployment version, note that the development-only installation doesn't come with the web server plug-ins, the Sun HotSpot or JRockit JDK, the sample applications, or the Derby database.

You can choose one of the following two generic self-extracting installer JARs for installing Oracle WebLogic Server 12*c* on any platform:

- ***wls_121200.jar*** Installs WebLogic Server and Coherence
- ***fmw_infra_121200.jar*** Installs WebLogic Server, Coherence, and infrastructure components for Fusion Middleware product platforms.

Let's turn to how you install Oracle WebLogic Server on a Windows system.

Installation Prerequisites

The installation procedures explained here are for the Windows platform, and they're mainly designed to get a working installation of WebLogic Server up and running so you can play with it. For example, the prerequisites for a basic installation require just 1GB of RAM and a 1 GHz processor. As for disk space for the installation, it takes about 2GB for the entire installation (including Oracle Coherence and Oracle Enterprise Pack for Eclipse). For actual production implementations, you must refer to the appropriate requirements.

A key requirement is that you must have a Java Development Kit (JDK) installed prior to the installation.

Installation Modes

There's more than one way to install WebLogic Server. The first and easiest method is to use the graphical mode, which is an interactive mode. The console mode is also an interactive mode, but it is run from the command line. The silent mode is a noninteractive mode of installation, where you can use a script or a text file when you need to install WebLogic Server on many hosts. The example that follows uses the graphical mode to install WebLogic Server.

In most operating systems, the installer will also automatically install the Java run-time JDKs. The two types of JDKs available are the Sun HotSpot JDK and the Oracle JRockit JDK. Oracle recommends that you use the JRockit JDK in production environments.

In this book, the installer used is named *wls_121200.jar*. Unlike in the previous release, WebLogic Server 12*c* doesn't include a JDK. Make sure you already have a JDK or download one from Oracle before you start the installation. You must do the following before you start the installation of WebLogic Server:

1. Install the JDK.
2. Set the *JAVA_HOME* variable to the path of the JDK you've installed.
3. Update the *PATH* environment variable to include both the *JAVA_HOME* and the *JAVA_HOME/bin* directories.

Installation Procedure

Follow these steps to install WebLogic Server:

1. Execute the following command to extract the jar file you've downloaded from the Oracle site and to launch the Oracle Fusion Middleware 12*c* Installer:

```
C:\Program Files\Java\jdk1.7.0_40\bin>java -jar c:\downloads\wls _121200.jar
Extracting files..............................................
```

2. On the Welcome screen, click Next to proceed with the installation.
3. The Installation Location Screen lets you enter the location where you want to install WebLogic Server. In this example, the location is C:\Oracle\Middleware. Click Next.
4. On the Installation Type screen, you have three choices: the WebLogic Server Installation, Coherence Installation, and Complete Installation. Select Complete Installation, as shown here. Note that this also includes the Server Examples, which contain several sample WebLogic Server domains that help you learn more about WebLogic Server application development and deployment. In a production environment, do not install the Server Examples, of course! Click Next.

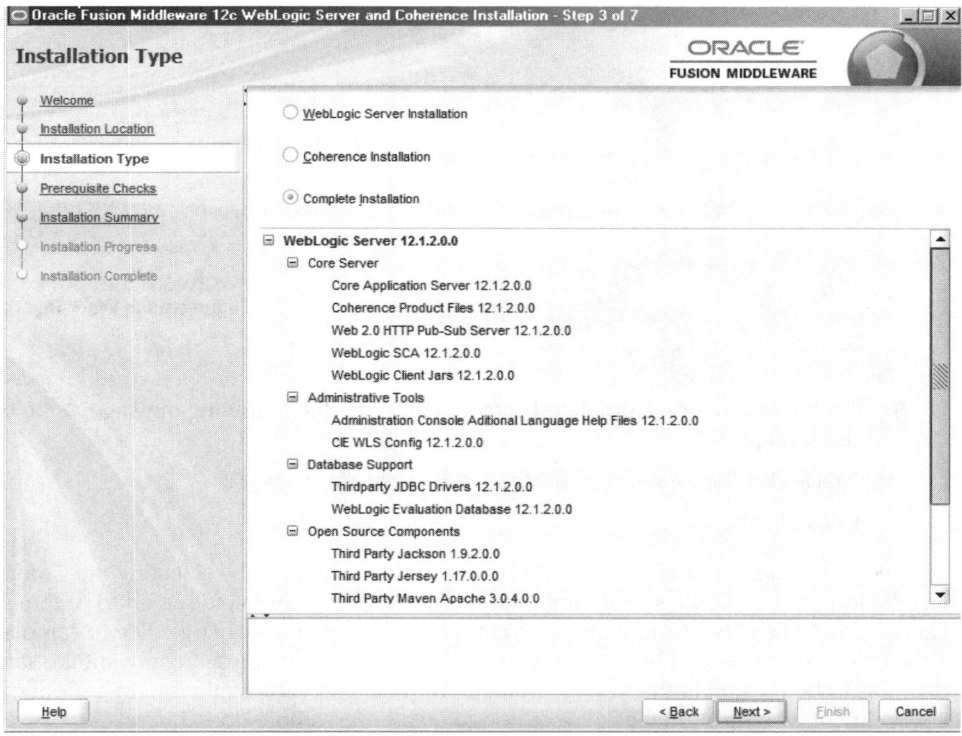

5. The Installation Summary shows all the products and features that will be installed. Click Install once you review the product and feature list.

6. The Prerequisite Checks page shows the status of the operating system certification check and the checking of the Java version used to run the installer. Once these two checks are successful, click Next.
7. You'll see the Installation Progress screen next, marking the progress of the installation. When this screen shows 100% completed, as shown here, click Next.

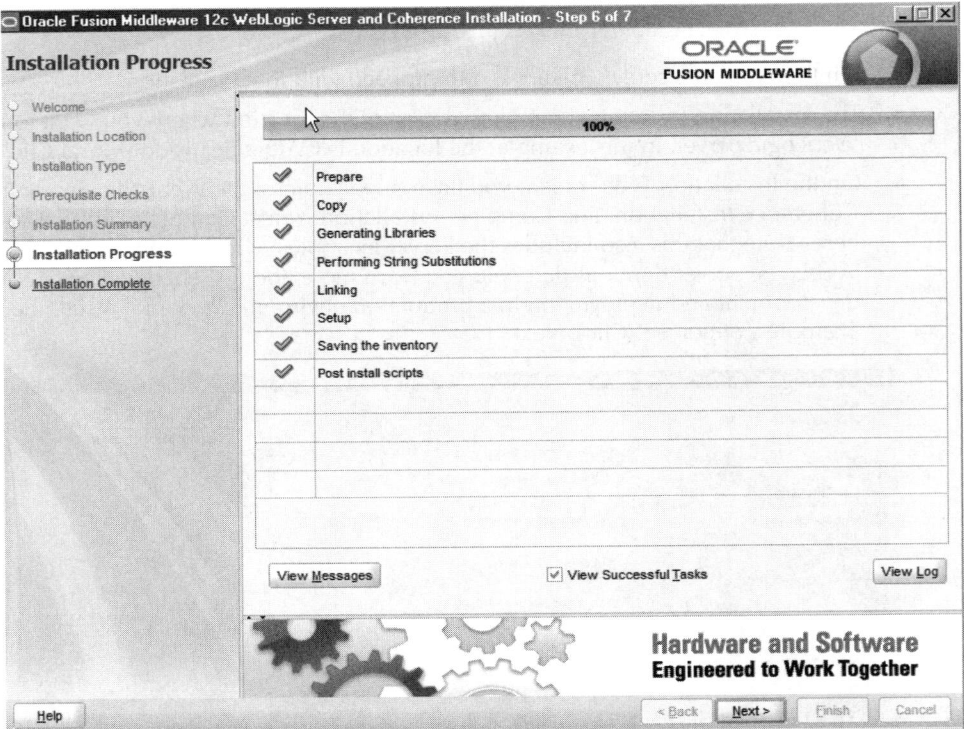

8. On the Installation Completed screen, you'll see the following message at the bottom of the screen:

   Oracle WebLogic Installation Completed Successfully.

   Click Finish.

Because you chose to install the WebLogic Server Examples (by selecting the Complete Installation option), you'll see an option on the Installation Complete screen to Automatically Launch The Quick Start Configuration Wizard to configure the WebLogic Server sample domains. This option is already prechecked, so you don't need to do anything if you want the sample domains to be created in the newly installed WebLogic Server installation. In a production environment, you must uncheck the option to create the sample domains.

For the sample domains, the SSL, Coherence, and Coherence Storage options are preconfigured and enabled by default and you can't change them. You must, however, specify the following settings for the sample domains:

- Administrative Server username/password
- Domain and application parent directories
- Listen port and listen address for the Administration Server
- SSL listen port and the Coherence listen port (if applicable)

Once the Quick Start Configuration Wizard starts, enter a password for the WebLogic Server on the first screen (shown here) and click Create.

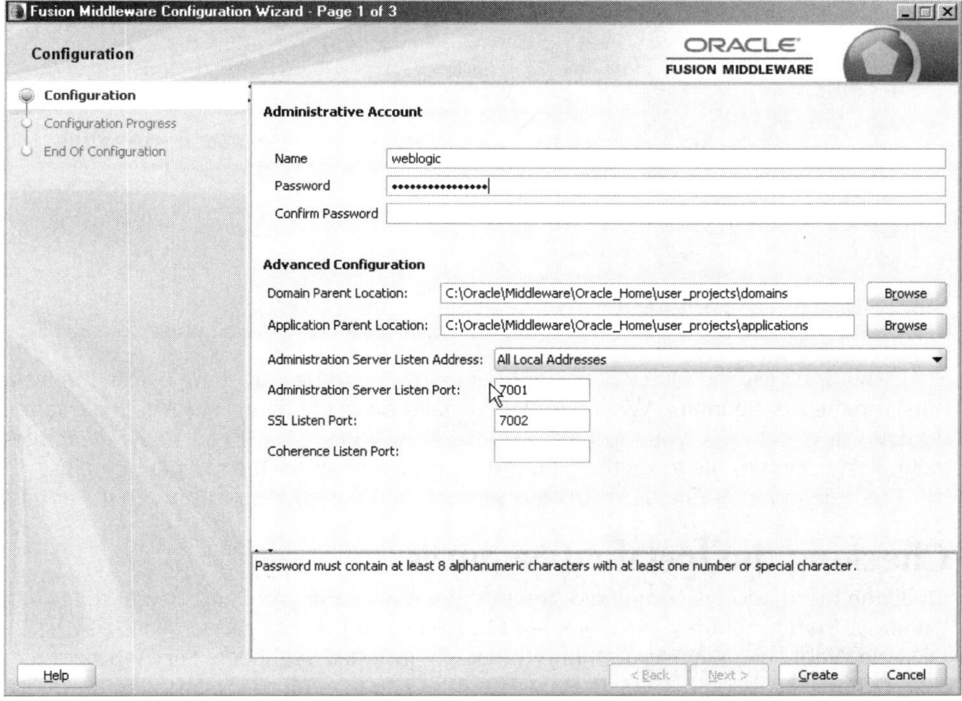

The Configuration Progress screen that displays next indicates that three example domains—*wl_server, medrec*, and *medrec-spring*—are generated by the Quick Start Configuration Wizard. Click Next.

The Configuration Success page shows the domain and application home information and the status for our three sample domains. Once you confirm that the status shows *Successful* for all three sample domains, click Finish. The following illustration shows the Configuration Details, indicating that all three of the sample domains have been successfully created. It also provides domain and admin location and the connection URL to the Administration Server for each of the three domains (remember that each WebLogic Server has its own separate Administration Server).

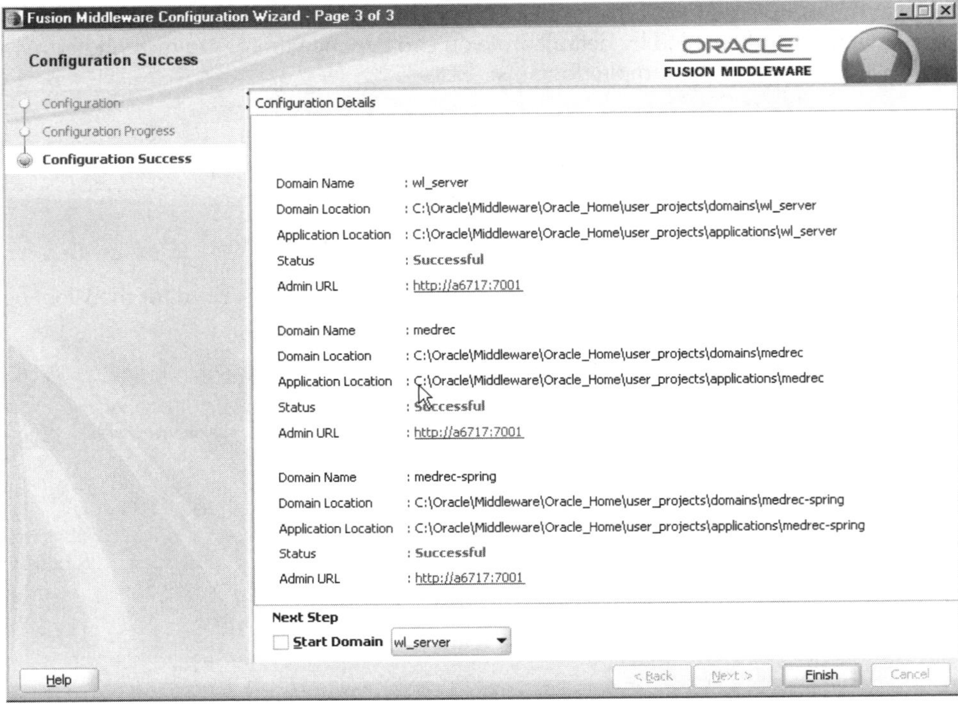

If you don't use the Quick Start Configuration Wizard by launching it from the installer, you must run the Configuration Wizard (or WLST) later on to configure the WebLogic sample domains. If you do this, you must also edit the EXAMPLES_HOME\wl_server\examples\src\examples.properties file to set the administrator credentials for the sample domains.

The installation of Oracle WebLogic Server 12*c* is complete at this point. It was easy, wasn't it?

Checking the Installed Features

Once the installation is completed, the installer places the WebLogic Server icons in the Windows Start program. Go to Oracle | Oracle Home | WebLogic Server 12*c* (12.1.2) for Eclipse | Oracle WebLogic, where you'll find the newly installed WebLogic Server program components under Oracle WebLogic. Click WebLogic Server 12*c* to explore the installed products, which are summarized next.

Online Documentation

This is a link to the Oracle WebLogic Server 12*c* documentation, so you have the relevant Oracle manuals at your fingertips.

Uninstall Oracle WebLogic

The Uninstall Oracle WebLogic option lets you access the Oracle Uninstaller to remove an existing WebLogic Server installation easily. The Uninstaller removes the entire WebLogic Server Platform installation with just a single click. On a Windows system, for example, the Uninstaller removes all files, shortcuts, Windows registry keys, and registry entries related to WebLogic Server.

Tools Under Tools, you'll find several important wizards. The Configuration Wizard helps you create a domain or modify and extend an existing domain. The Domain Template Builder helps you create domain templates that you can use with the Configuration Wizard to easily create new domains. A *domain template* provides preconfigured settings that include database components, services and security, and other environmental options. The Domain Template Builder also helps you create extension templates that you can use with the Configuration Wizard to update WebLogic domains. The new Reconfiguration Wizard helps you update an existing WebLogic Server installation to a new release. Finally, you can use the WebLogic Scripting Tool shortcut to start WLST; I discuss how to use WLST toward the end of this chapter, in the section titled "Using the WebLogic Scripting Tool (WLST)."

Reinstalling WebLogic Server

If you need to reinstall an identical version of WebLogic Server in the same location as a previously existing installation for any reason, first remove the previous installation by clicking the Uninstall Oracle Middleware shortcut under Start | Oracle| Oracle Home. This invokes the Oracle Uninstaller wizard, which leads you through the necessary steps to remove an installation. Make sure you stop all running WebLogic Server instances before you start uninstalling.

You can also manually start the deinstaller by going to the *ORACLE_HOME/oui/bin* directory and issuing the following command:

```
$ deinstall.cmd
```

Once the deinstaller completes its work, you must manually remove the ORACLE_HOME directory where you installed Oracle WebLogic Server. You can add new products to an existing installation, but you can't reinstall the same WebLogic Server release over an existing WebLogic Server installation of the same release.

Exploring the Installation Directories

Now that you've seen how easy it is to install WebLogic Server, let's explore the installation directories a bit. As I mentioned during the installation steps, you have two major home directories—Oracle Middleware Home and Oracle WebLogic Server Home. The Oracle Middleware Home directory is where all the WebLogic Server and other middleware product files are located—it's the top-level directory for all Oracle Fusion Middleware products, including the Oracle WebLogic Server. In this example here, there's only a single middleware product, which, of course, is Oracle WebLogic Server. During the installation, I chose C:\Oracle\Middleware as the Oracle Middleware Home directory, denoted by MW_HOME. WebLogic Server creates a directory called Oracle_Home under C:\Oracle\Middleware to serve as the Oracle Home directory. Remember, however, that, by default, the Oracle Installer installs WebLogic Server under the Middleware Home directory, but you are not required to install it here—you can choose to create the Oracle Home in any directory you choose, including a brand new directory for which you need only provide the name. The Installer will automatically create that directory for you. If you've installed and removed WebLogic Server earlier, Oracle recommends that you reuse the same directory for your new installation.

Table 1-1 shows the main directories under the Oracle_Home directory. Note that the last directory in the table is your WebLogic Server Home directory and that it's usually denoted by the environment variable *WL_HOME*.

Directory	Contents
coherence	Serves as Home directory for Oracle Coherence and contains the Coherence product files.
inventory	Contains information about the components, feature sets, and patches installed in this Oracle Home directory.
Install	Contains the installation-related files and scripts.
cfgtoollogs	Contains the installation and configuration log files.
OPatch	Contains *OPatch*, the new patching utility and supported files.
oracle_common	Directory that contains binary and library files for Oracle WebLogic Server.
Oui	Contains files use by the Oracle Universal Installer, including the deinstaller program.
user_projects	Serves as the standard location for WebLogic Server domains.
wl_server	Serves as the WebLogic Server Home directory, also known as WL_HOME. Contains the WebLogic Server product files.

TABLE 1-1. *The Oracle Middleware Home Directory*

Let's review what's been accomplished thus far: Following along with this example, you've successfully installed the Oracle WebLogic Server software, located in its Home directory, C:\Oracle\Middlware\wlserver_12.1. You don't have a custom domain yet, however, because you have to create it. The new server does include the three Oracle WebLogic Server sample domains because you chose to have the Installer create them during the server installation. You can't do a whole lot with this installation in terms of deploying applications and so on, until you create your own WebLogic Server domain. When you create a domain, you'll automatically have one Admin Server, and you can also create multiple Managed Servers or clusters to host your web applications. Chapter 3 is devoted to managing and configuring domains. In that chapter, you learn how to create domains and configure servers so you can get ready to deploy and run your web applications through Oracle WebLogic Server.

WebLogic Server Home

The WebLogic Server Home directory is simply the directory where we installed WebLogic Server, and, by default, it's located in the MW_HOME\wlserver directory. You refer to this directory as the WL_HOME directory, distinguished from the Oracle Middleware Home directory, which, in this example, is C:\Oracle\Middleware. Thus, the complete path of the WebLogic Server Home in this example is C:\Oracle\Middleware\wlserver.

Under the WebLogic Server Home (WL_HOME), you'll find the following directory structure:

- common
- modules
- plugins
- samples (if you chose to install the sample applications)

- server
- sip

The bin directory under the WL_HOME server directory contains the *startNodeManager* script to start the Node Manager. During the installation of WebLogic Server shown in this chapter, we chose to create the sample domains offered by Oracle. These are the *medrec, medrec-spring,* and *wl_server* domains. These domains are located under the user_projects directory, in the domains folder. The next section explores the contents of these domain directories, all of which have the same structure.

WebLogic Server Domain Directory

Each domain that you create will have the following directory structure, under the Oracle_Home/user_projects/domains directory:

- autodeploy
- bin
- common
- config
- console-ext
- init-info
- lib
- nodemanager
- security
- servers

Under the bin directory of each domain is where you'll find the various scripts to start and stop the Admin and Managed Servers, such as *startWebLogic.cmd* and *stopWebLogic.cmd*. Note that UNIX versions of these scripts are also located in this directory. The all-important domain configuration file, *config.xml,* is stored in the domains/config directory.

For now, it's enough to be aware of the basic structure of a WebLogic domain. Chapter 3 details how to configure a domain, and I will postpone the detailed examination of a domain directory's contents until that point.

The WebLogic Server Sample Applications

To demonstrate the basic features of the Administration Console, I'll use one of the three sample domains created during the installation when we chose to install the samples. The code examples provided by Oracle are located in various domains, all under the Oracle_Home\user_projects\domains directory. I understand that most readers don't need to install the sample applications because they already have a working knowledge of WebLogic Server. For those new to WebLogic Server, however, the sample applications will help you understand web applications, and the sample domains will help you learn how to administer and manage WebLogic Server.

NOTE
All the sample domains that the Configuration Wizard creates for you during the WebLogic Server installation (if you choose to install the samples) are located, by default, in the ORACLE_HOME\user_projects\domains directory (C:\Oracle\Middleware\Oracle_Home\user_projects\domains directory on my server, since ORACLE_HOME is defined as C:\Oracle\Middleware\Oracle_Home).You can specify alternative locations for the domain directories.

The WebLogic Server samples contain two different types of applications to familiarize you with Java EE applications and to help you understand how Oracle WebLogic Server works. The first set of applications is part of the domain named *wl_server,* and the domain's Admin Server is named Examples Server. The *wl_server* domain contains Oracle WebLogic Server API examples designed to show you how to implement Java EE APIs and related Oracle WebLogic Server features. Oracle also provides a web application called *examplesWebApp,* which includes several of these examples. In addition, there's a full-blown sample Java EE web application by the name of *Avitek Medical Records* as part of the domain named *medrec*. When you choose to install the examples, two versions of the Avitek Medical Records application are installed for you. The first one is the *MedRec* application designed to demonstrate various features of the Java EE platform. The second application, called *MedRec-Spring,* is the same as the MedRec application, but it is created using the Spring Framework and is part of the *medrec-spring* domain.

Oracle recommends that you start working with the *wl_server* domain to understand the basics of Java EE programming and WebLogic Server. If you're already familiar with both of these, check out the Avitek Medical Records and the Avitek Medical Records (Spring) sample applications. Both of these present realistic examples that show how to develop and deploy full-blown Java EE applications. The two applications also serve as great learning tools for Java EE developers and for WebLogic Server administrators who wish to understand application deployment concepts.

Key Environment Files

Let's take a close look at the key environment files you'll be using while managing your WebLogic Server. The two key WebLogic Server environment files in a Windows server are the *setDomainEnv.cmd* and the *setWLSEnv.cmd* files. These two files have similar counterparts in the UNIX environment, named, for example, *WLSEnv.sh* and so on.

The DomainEnv.cmd File

There's a *setDomainEnv.cmd* file for each domain you create with the Configuration Wizard. This script sets up the environment correctly so you can start WebLogic Server in a domain.

When you invoke the *setDomainEnv.cmd* file, it invokes the following variables before calling *commEnv* to set the other variables:

- **WL_HOME** The home directory of your WebLogic installation.
- **JAVA_VM** The desired Java VM to use. You can set this environment variable before calling this script to switch between Oralce and BEA or just use the default.
- **JAVA_HOME** Location of the version of Java used to start WebLogic Server. Depends directly on which JAVA_VM value is set by default or by the environment.
- **MEM_ARGS** The variable to override the standard memory arguments passed to Java.

- **PRODUCTION_MODE** The variable that determines whether Weblogic Server is started in production mode.
- **DOMAIN_PRODUCTION_MODE** Determines whether the workshop-related settings like the *debugger, testconsole,* or *iterativedev* should be enabled. You can only set these using the @REM command-line parameter named *production*. Specifying the *production* command-line parameter forces the server to start in production mode.
- **WLS_POLICY_FILE** The Java policy file to use. Set this environment variable to specify a policy file; otherwise, this script assigns a default value.

Other variables used in this script include

- **SERVER_NAME** Name of the WebLogic server.
- **JAVA_OPTIONS** Java command-line options for running the server (tagged on to the end of *JAVA_VM* and *MEM_ARGS*).
- **PROXY_SETTINGS** Tagged on to the end of the *JAVA_OPTIONS* variable; however, this variable is deprecated and should not be used. Use *JAVA_OPTIONS* instead.

The setWLSEnv.cmd File

The *setWLSEnv.cmd* script file configures the environment for development with WebLogic Server. It sets the following variables:

- **WL_HOME** The root directory of your WebLogic installation.
- **JAVA_HOME** Location of the version of Java used to start WebLogic Server. This variable must point to the root directory of a JDK installation and will be set for you by the Installer.
- **PATH** Adds the JDK and WebLogic directories to the system path.
- **CLASSPATH** Adds the JDK and WebLogic jars to the CLASSPATH.

Other variables that *setWLSEnv.cmd* takes are

- **PRE_CLASSPATH** Path style variable to be added to the beginning of the CLASSPATH.
- **POST_CLASSPATH** Path style variable to be added to the end of CLASSPATH.
- **PRE_PATH** Path style variable to be added to the beginning of the PATH.
- **POST_PATH** Path style variable to be added to the end of the PATH.

Starting the Examples Server

The Examples Server is the Admin Server for the *wl_server* domain. It contains basic web application examples. To launch the Examples Server, run the following two commands, the first to set up the environment and the second to start the WebLogic Server instance. Once you successfully run these two scripts, the Admin Server for the sample domain *wl_server* is started.

```
C:\Oracle\Middleware\Oracle_Home\user_projects\domains\wl_server\bin\setDomainEnv.
cmd
C:\Oracle\Middleware\Oracle_Home\user_projects\domains\wl_server\bin\startWebLogic
.cmd
```

The directory from which we start the Admin Server for the domain *wl_server,* C:\Oracle\Middleware\Oracle_Home\user_projects\domains\wl_server is also called the DOMAIN_HOME (for the server*wl_server*).

TIP
Because they're purely for learning purposes, do not install the WebLogic Server Examples on your production servers. Leaving them on a production server introduces vulnerabilities that can be exploited by hackers.

Once the Administration Server starts booting, you can follow the boot sequence in the command window that pops up. You'll also see a separate command window that shows the launching of the Derby database for the Examples Server. Once the Administration Server boots, you'll see the following in the command window:

```
...
.Calling setDomainEnv in this domain
Modifying classpath for the samples
Classpath has successfully been set to:
C:\Oracle\Middleware\Oracle_Home\user_projects\applications\wl_server\
examples\build\serverclasses;C:\Oracle\Middleware\Oracle_Home\
user_projects\applications\wl_server\examples\src;
C:\PROGRA~1\Java\JDK17~1.0_4\lib\tools.jar;
C:\Oracle\MIDDLE~1\ORACLE~1\wlserver\server\lib\weblog
...
C:\Oracle\MIDDLE~1\ORACLE~1\wlserver\server\lib\xqrl.jar;
C:\Oracle\Middleware\Oracle_Home\user_projects\applications\
wl_server\examples\build\clientclasses
Script has completed successfully
C:\Oracle\Middleware\Oracle_Home\user_projects\domains\wl_server>
```

Once the environment is set, execute the *startWebLogic.cmd* script to start the server:

```
C:\Oracle\Middleware\Oracle_Home\user_projects\domains\wl_server>start WebLogic.cmd

JAVA Memory arguments: -Xms256m -Xmx512m -XX:CompileThreshold=8000 -
XX:PermSize=128m  -XX:MaxPermSize=256m
...
CLASSPATH=C:\Oracle\Middleware\Oracle_Home\user_projects\
applications\wl_server\
***************************************************
starting weblogic with Java version:
java version "1.7.0_40"
 log file
C:\Oracle\Middleware\Oracle_Home\user_projects\domains\wl_server\
servers\AdminServer\logs\AdminServer.log is opened. All server side
log events will be written to this file.>
...
<Oct 19, 2013 11:16:27 AM CDT> <Notice> <WebLogicServer> <BEA-000331>
<Started the WebLogic Server Administration Server "AdminServer" for
domain "wl_server" running in development mode.>
```

```
<Oct 19, 2013 11:16:27 AM CDT> <Notice> <WebLogicServer> <BEA-000365>
<Server state changed to RUNNING.>
<Oct 19, 2013 11:16:27 AM CDT> <Notice> <WebLogicServer> <BEA-000360>
<The server started in RUNNING mode.>
$
```

In addition to the main Windows command console (don't close it or else your server instance will promptly die!) that displays the server lifecycle messages throughout the server's life, you'll also see another window that shows that the default Derby database server is also up and ready to receive requests. (You can change the database server to a different server, say Oracle Database 12*c*, later on in the process.) Here are the Derby server window's messages when it starts:

```
2013-10-19 11.05:00AMCDT: Security manager installed using the Basic server
security policy.
2013-10-19 11.05:00AMCDT: Apache Derby Network Server - 10.6.1.0 - (938214)
started and ready to accept connections on port 1527
```

Once you see that the WebLogic Server has started in RUNNING mode, the Examples Server is ready to use. Your browser will automatically launch at this point and display the Oracle WebLogic Server Samples Introduction Page, which is the gateway to the sample applications. If, for some reason, the browser doesn't automatically launch, you can go to the following URL to see the page:

```
http://localhost:7001/examplesWebApp/index.jsp
```

Note that port 7001 must be available for you to access the Administration Console for this domain. Remember that the default credentials to log into the Administration Console are *weblogic/welcome1*.

To launch one of the other sample applications, for example, the Avitek Medical Records Sample Application, run the following command, which starts the Admin Server for the *medrec* domain:

```
C:\Oracle\Middleware\Oracle_Home\user_projects\domains
\medrec\bin\startWebLogic.cmd
```

This command starts the application and displays the startup page. You can click the Start Using MedRec button to start the application. You can also start the Administration Console to manage the MedRec domain by clicking the Start The Administration Console button.

Stopping the Server

You can stop a running server by closing the command window or by pressing CTRL-C in the command window. In production environments, however, you use a shutdown script to stop the servers. You can use the following command script to shut down the Admin Server for the sample domain *medrec,* for example:

```
C:\Oracle\Middleware\Oracle_Home\user_projects\domains
\medrec\bin\stopWebLogic.cmd\medrec\bin\stopWebLogic.cmd
```

Note that you need to point your browser toward a different port number to access the Administration Console for each of these same servers. By default, the example domains run in the development mode. You can configure all servers in a domain to run in production mode by clicking Domain on the Administration Console Home page and checking the Production Mode box. You must first click the Lock & Edit button in the Change Center to activate the change. You must also restart the server so it can start in production mode. All servers in this domain will now run in production mode. Note that you can't toggle back to development mode once you enable production mode—you can disable the production mode only at the Admin Server startup command line by specifying the *-Dweblogic.ProductionModeEnabled=false* option.

Upgrading Oracle WebLogic Server

The latest version of Oracle WebLogic Server, as of the writing of this book, is the 12.1.2 release. You can upgrade to this release from earlier versions of WebLogic Server. When you upgrade Oracle WebLogic Server, not only must you install the new software, of course, but you also have to upgrade the security providers, the Node Manager, and the existing domains as well as any remote Managed Servers. If you're upgrading from WebLogic Server versions prior to WebLogic Server 10.3.1, you must follow a two-step process to upgrade to version 12.1.2:

1. First upgrade to WebLogic Server 10.3.6, using the instructions in the Oracle manual *Upgrade Guide to WebLogic Server 10.3.6*. As part of this, you must also run the WebLogic Server 10.3.6 Domain Upgrade Wizard to upgrade the domains.
2. Upgrade WebLogic Server 10.3.6 to WebLogic Server 12.1.2.

The following sections provide a summary of the upgrade procedures to upgrade from WebLogic Server installation release 10.3.6 to 12.1.1.

You must upgrade the WebLogic domain when you upgrade to WebLogic Server 12.1.2, by upgrading the domain directory on each computer in the domain. It's important to understand, however, that most Java EE applications, including web applications, EJBs, and so on, can be run without any modifications in the WebLogic Server 12.1.2 environment.

Before embarking on a major upgrade project, of course, you must verify that all components in your environment, such as databases, load balancers, and firewalls are compatible with WebLogic Server 12.1.2.

Upgrade Tools

What used to be called an upgrade of a domain in earlier releases is now called *reconfiguring a domain* in Oracle WebLogic Server 12.1.2, and in Oracle WebLogic Server 12*c*, the new Oracle Fusion Middleware Reconfiguration Wizard (hereafter called the Reconfiguration Wizard) has replaced the old Domain Upgrade Wizard. You can reconfigure a WebLogic domain using two methods:

- You can run the Reconfiguration Wizard.
- You can reconfigure a domain from the command line with the WebLogic Scripting Tool.

Oracle provides several reconfiguration templates for Fusion Middleware products to make upgrading WebLogic Server and Fusion Middleware installations easy. The Wizard applies the appropriate reconfiguration templates. The templates then update the domain version to the current version.

Oracle recommends that you use the WLST script to reconfigure a domain when you can't run the Reconfiguration Wizard for any reason.

Obviously, you don't have to use the Reconfiguration Wizard, but as with any GUI wizard, using it will certainly make life easier for you during an upgrade. You can, for example, manually upgrade a domain by installing the software for the current release, updating the domain script files to point to the new installation, and updating the CLASSPATH to remove outdated information. As you will see, the Reconfiguration Wizard can prevent many headaches with its automated approach to the upgrade.

Upgrade Procedures

When you upgrade to a newer release of WebLogic Server, in most cases, you don't have to upgrade the web applications you deploy. The latest release of WebLogic Server, 12.1.2, will work with all applications you created on earlier WebLogic Server releases. You do, however, have to upgrade several server components:

- Custom security provider
- Node Manager
- Domains
- Remote Managed Servers

In addition, you need to ensure that any external resources WebLogic Server connects to, such as an Oracle database, for example, are compatible with the new release. The following sections briefly describe the upgrade procedures. Before you start the actual upgrade process, however, do the usual due diligence effort, such as verifying the supported configurations and the compatibility of the various software applications, as well as doing an inventory of your current WebLogic Server environment. As with any upgrade of a server, back up your applications, shut down all running servers, and start by installing the new release of the Oracle WebLogic Server software.

As mentioned earlier, you may not have to do much to make your current applications run on the latest release of WebLogic Server. However, you must upgrade the security providers, the domain, the Node Manager, and the remote Managed Servers. The following sections briefly explain each in turn.

Upgrading the Security Provider

When upgrading the security providers, the Reconfiguration Wizard upgrades the JAR files for security providers so the providers can work under a 12.1.1 environment. If you're using a custom security provider in the 7.0 or 8.0 release, the Reconfiguration Wizard can upgrade those providers to run in a 12.1.1 environment as well.

Upgrading the Node Manager

Upgrade the Node Manager (on all machines where it currently runs) only if you intend to use any customized versions in the new environment. Otherwise, there's nothing for you to do here during an upgrade. Once the upgrade is completed, you must enroll the Node Manager with all machines, and Chapter 2 shows you how to do this.

Upgrading Existing Domains

Before upgrading any remote Managed Servers, upgrade the domain on the machine where the Admin Server resides. If you have any Managed Servers on the same server as the Admin Server, you don't have to upgrade them. Upgrading the domains updates the *config.xml* file—the key domain configuration file—and also updates persistent data in the JMS file stores.

Upgrading the Remote Managed Servers

During an upgrade, you need to upgrade just those Managed Servers that reside on remote servers. Before upgrading, you must first copy two important files (*config.xml* and *SerializedSystemIni.dat*) from the root directory of the original domain directory of the Admin Server to the root directory of the remote Managed Server domain.

If there's no Administration Server on the remote machine, you can use one of two methods to update the Managed Server domains on the remote machine:

- You can execute the *pack -managed=true* command to generate the domain template JAR and move the JAR to the remote machine, and then use the *unpack* utility to create the Managed Server domain (you'll learn about the pack/unpack commands in Chapter 3).
- Alternatively, you can use the WLST *writeTemplate* command to update the Managed Server domain on the remote machine. The WLST *writeTemplate* command has been modified in the WebLogic Server 12*c* release to work in the *online* mode, letting you update domains that run on remote machines using WLST instead of being limited to the *pack/unpack* utilities.

Reconfiguring a WebLogic Domain

Back up your domain before running the Reconfiguration Wizard, as the configuration process can't be reversed. To return the domain to its original state, you need the backup. The old Domain Upgrade Wizard automatically backed up the domain before starting the upgrade process, but with the Reconfiguration Wizard, you must back up the domain yourself.

Reconfiguring a domain is a long drawn-out affair, with multiple configuration screens and choices. You must consult the Oracle WebLogic Serve 12*c* documentation for the complete upgrade procedures. However, a summary of the upgrade process will help you understand the process, and that's what I provide next. Let's first review the domain upgrade process using the Oracle Middleware Reconfiguration Wizard. After that, you'll learn how to upgrade a domain using WLST.

Reconfiguring with the Reconfiguration Wizard

To upgrade a domain using the Reconfiguration Wizard, follow these general steps:

1. Start the Reconfiguration Wizard with the following command, after moving to the ORACLE_HOME\oracle_common\common\bin directory as shown here.

```
$ cd C:\Oracle\Middleware\Oracle_Home\oracle_common\common\bin>
$ C:\Oracle\Middleware\Oracle_Home\oracle_common\common\bin> reconfig.cmd
```

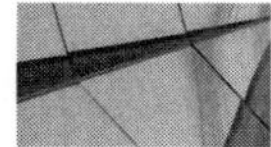

NOTE

*You can also run the Reconfiguration Wizard by going to Programs | Oracle |Oracle Home | WebLogic Server 12*c* | Tools | Reconfiguration Wizard. Once the Oracle Middleware Reconfiguration Wizard starts, it shows the Select Domain page.*

2. Specify the location of the domain you want to upgrade on the Select Domain page, shown here:

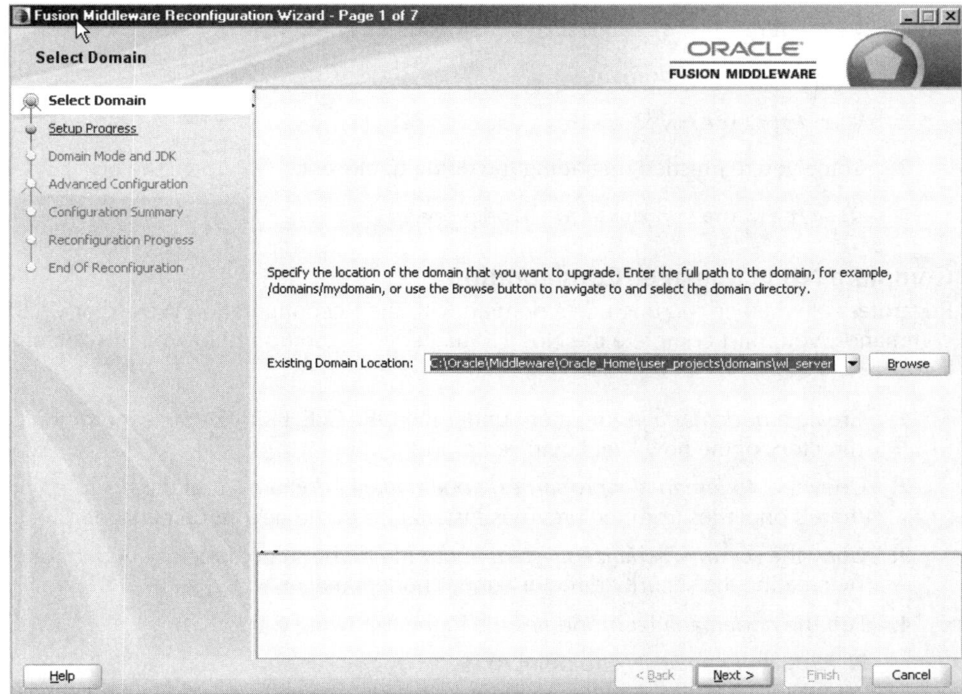

Click Next after ensuring that the full path to the domain directory of the domain you wish to upgrade is selected.

3. The Reconfiguration Setup Progress page shows the progress of the application of the reconfiguration templates. When the application of the templates is completed, click Next.
4. On the Domain Mode And JDK page, select the JDK you want the domain to use. Click Next.
5. (optional) Depending on your domain configuration, different additional screens may appear after this point.
6. On the Advanced Configuration page, check the boxes of all categories for which you want to perform configuration tasks. Click Next.
7. On the Configuration Summary page, review and then click Reconfig to complete the domain reconfiguration.
8. When you see the Reconfiguration Success page and the message "Oracle WebLogic Server Reconfiguration Succeeded," the domain has been updated successfully. Click Finish to exit the Reconfiguration Wizard.

Reconfiguring a Domain Using WLST

You haven't yet learned how to use the WLST scripting tool, but you will shortly! You can reconfigure a domain using WLST in offline mode.

Here's an example showing how to reconfigure a domain called *my _domain* with WLST:

1. Open the domain for upgrade: vb

```
wls:/offline> readDomainForUpgrade('c:/domains/my_domain')
```

2. Save the updated domain:

```
wls:/offline/my_domain> updateDomain()
```

3. Once you're finished upgrading the domain, close it:

```
wls:/offline/my_domain> closeDomain()
```

Complete Node Manager Configuration

Regardless of whether you upgrade a domain with the Reconfiguration Wizard or WLST commands, you must complete the Node Manager configuration following the domain update. Here are the steps:

1. Create a *nodemanager* directory under the ORACLE_HOME/oracle_common/common directory of the new WebLogic Server installation.
2. Copy the *nodemanager.properties, nodemanager.domains*, and the *nm_data.properties* (if there's one) files from the previous installation to the new nodemanager directory.
3. Copy the *security/SerializedSystemIni.dat* file to the same directory under nodemanager by creating the security directory under nodemanager.
4. Edit the *nodemanager.properties* file in the following way:
   - Update *DomainsFile* to point to ORACLE_HOME/oracle_common/common/nodemanager/nodemanager.domains file.
   - If the file contains a *javaHome* property setting, remove it.
   - Update *JavaHome* to point to the jre directory for the JDK that you're using for WebLogic Server 12.1.2.
   - Update *NodeManagerHome* to point to ORACLE_HOME/oracle_common/common/nodemanager.
   - Update *LogFile* to point to ORACLE_HOME/oracle_common/common/nodemanager/nodemanager.log.

If you're using your own security certificates, point to the location of those certificates in the *nodemanager.properties* file. If you are using the WebLogic Server demo certificate instead, run *Certgen* to create a demo keystore for the new installation.

Once you're all done, run *startNodeManager.cmd* from the ORACLE_HOME\wlserver\server\bin directory to ensure that the Node Manager starts.

Using OPatch to Patch Oracle WebLogic Server

In the previous release, you could patch Oracle WebLogic Server software with the Smart Update utility for both maintenance patches and maintenance packs. In WebLogic Server 12*c*, Smart Update isn't supported. You must use the *OPatch* utility to apply patches for Oracle WebLogic Server 12*c*.

TIP
You can use the Opatch *utility to patch not only WebLogic Server software, but also Oracle Fusion Middleware installations.*

You can find the *OPatch* utility in the ORACLE_HOME/Opatch directory. To view the list of commands available to you (on a Windows server), run the following command:

```
$ opatch.bat -help
```

Patching a WebLogic Server installation using *OPatch* is extremely simple. Here are the basic steps you must follow:

1. Get the patches you need to apply from the Oracle Support site.
2. Review the *README.txt* file for the patch to see what you need to do before applying a patch.
3. Check for any patch prerequisites with the following command:

   ```
   $ opatch apply /oracle/middleware/oracle_home/wl_server -report
   ```

4. Apply the patch with the *apply* command:

   ```
   $ opatch apply /oracle/middleware/wl_server/patches/15221446  /* patch number
   ```

   You can apply multiple patches with a single command, by specifying the *napply* option instead of the *apply* option.

5. Verify the patch application with the *lsinventory* command:

   ```
   $ opatch lsinventory
   ```

6. You can rollback a patch by using the *rollback* command:

   ```
   $ opatch rollback -id 15221446
   ```

   The *nrollback* option lets you rollback multiple patches with a single command.

Using the Administration Console

WebLogic Server offers a browser-based Administration Console to help manage a domain. The Admin Server hosts the Administration Console application, and you can access the Console from any browser that has network access to the Admin Server.

The Administration Console lets you administer your entire domain—the server instances, web applications, modules, and all the resources that the applications and modules need to use. Not only can you configure and monitor the servers, but also you can create new server instances with the Console. The Administration Console also helps you tune your applications. The Console makes performing various configuration and management tasks easy, without you're having to learn how to use the underlying JMX API, which is what you need to configure the domains manually. In Chapter 2, you'll learn the various ways in which you can start and stop WebLogic Server instances. The easiest, as well as the recommended way to manage your servers is through the Administration Console. You can even edit and save changes to the domain configuration file, *config.xml,* through the console. Throughout this book, you'll learn how to configure various aspects of WebLogic Server through the Administration Console.

This seems like the right place to point out that in Oracle WebLogic Server 12*c,* you can also manage Weblogic Server through Fusion Middleware Control. You can manage the following aspects of WebLogic Server through Fusion Middleware Control:

- Starting up and shutting down servers
- Clustering servers
- Managing WebLogic Server services, such as database connectivity (JDBC) and messaging (JMS)
- Deploying applications
- Monitoring server and application performance

TIP
If you're new to the Administration Console, it pays to check out the excellent help material you can access by clicking the How Do I link, where you'll find crystal clear steps for performing any task within the Administration Console.

Because the Administration Console is linked to a domain, until you create a domain, the Administration Console does not exist. When you create a domain, by default, a single Admin Server is created for you. It's the Admin Server that runs the web-based Administration Console that enables you to manage the entire domain. Thus, you must first start the Admin Server before you can access the Administration Console. Once you create a domain , you can access the Administration Console at the default port 7001, but you can also assign it any other free port number.

NOTE
You can disable the Administration Console by clearing the Console Enabled box on the Administration Console's configuration page for the Admin Server. If you do this, you can manage the domain only with management APIs.

Any configuration changes you make through the Administration Console will update the *config.xml,* which is the domain configuration file.

Logging In to the Administration Console

Once you've created a domain, launch the Admin Server first. Once the Admin Server is in running mode, you can access the Administration Console and manage the domain. Invoke the Administration Console by using the following URL:

```
http://localhost:7001/console
```

Note that 7001 is the default port that WebLogic Server uses. You can set the port to any valid port number you choose.

In the following example, as explained in the preceding section, let's use the Examples Server (Admin Server for the *wl_server* domain) provided by the Installer. Launch the Examples Server by going to Start | Oracle WebLogic | WebLogic Server 12cR1 | WebLogic Server. Because every domain will host its own Admin Server, if you are running multiple domains on your machine, each Admin Server will have to bind to a different port. For example, you can access the Administration Console for the *wl_server* domain using this address:

```
http://localhost:7001/console
```

Meanwhile, you can access the Administration Console for the *medrec-spring* domain by entering

```
http://localhost:7011/console
```

If you're using Secure Sockets Layer (SSL) to start your Admin Server, use *https* instead of *http,* as shown here, and note that you use a different port number from that of the non-SSL port:

```
https://localhost:7002/console
```

TIP

If you've configured a proxy server, configure your browser so it doesn't direct the Admin Server requests to the proxy. If you're running both the Admin Server and your web browser on the same server, make sure the requests are sent to the local host (or IP 127.0.0.1) and not to the proxy server.

The default administrative username for the Admin Server is *weblogic,* and the default password is *welcome1*. You may also log in later by choosing a username that you granted to a default global security role. If you grant the default global security role *Admin* to a user, for example, that user can perform any task using the Administration Console. If you gave another user a more limited security role, such as *Deployer, Monitor,* or *Operator,* the user won't be able to edit the configuration data; these users can only view, not modify, the configuration data.

On the Administration Console login page, shown in Figure 1-1, enter the default username and password (**weblogic** and **welcome1**, respectively), or for a custom domain, use the username and password combination you chose during domain creation. You can log out of the Console by clicking the Log Out button at the top of the right pane of the console.

Once you successfully log in to the Administration Console, you'll see the Home page, as shown in Figure 1-2. Notice that the Home page of the Administration Console contains two panes. Resources and servers are listed in the left pane. At the top of the right pane are the Log Out and Preferences buttons. When you click a server under a domain, the relevant configuration items will show up on the right; here, you can check or modify the server's configuration.

Navigating the Administration Console

The tree menu on the left pane of the Home page provides quick access to functionality that allows you to manage not only the servers and clusters but also the configuration of resources such as JMS servers and data sources. For example, by expanding wl_server | Services | Data Sources, you will see a complete list of data sources configured on this domain. At the top of the left pane, notice the Change Center, which helps you view and modify server configurations. Right underneath is the Domain Structure section. In this section, there are several key items that help you manage WebLogic Server. I explain these in the following sections.

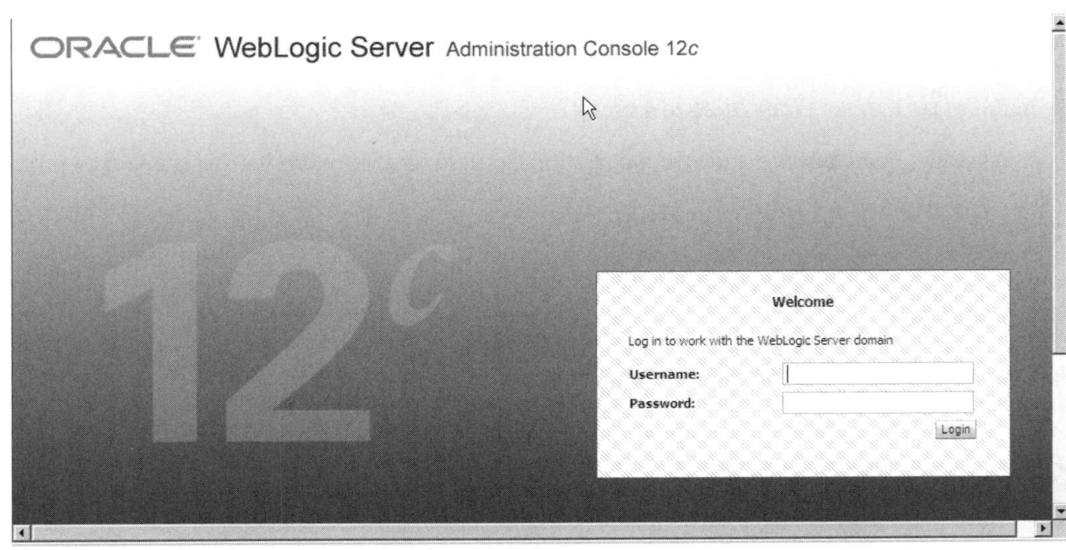

FIGURE 1-1. *The Oracle WebLogic Server Administration Console login page*

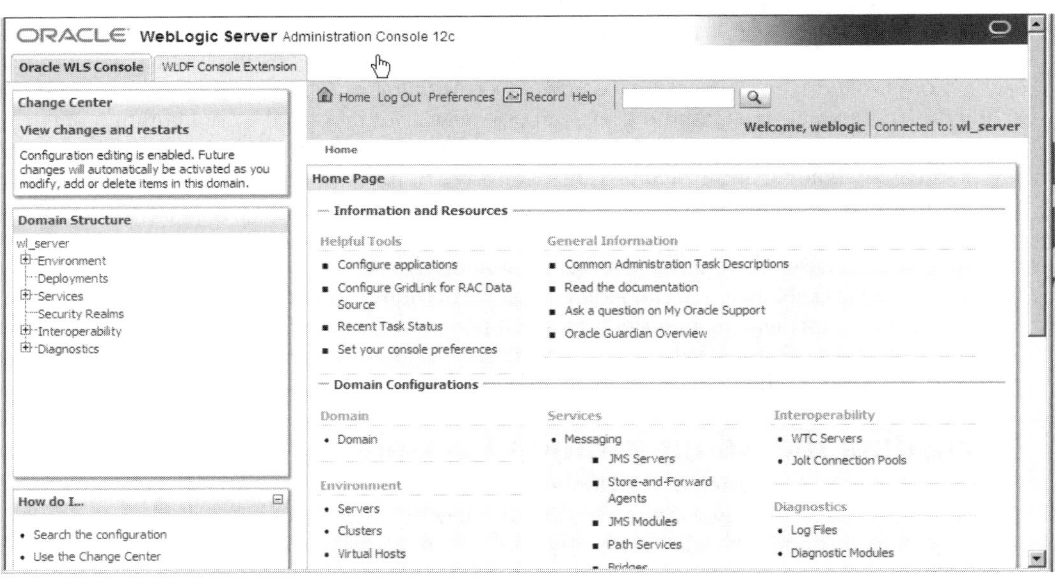

FIGURE 1-2. *The Administration Console Home page*

Environment

You'll find the following items under Environment:

- Servers
- Clusters
- Virtual Hosts
- Migratable Targets
- Coherence Servers
- Coherence Clusters
- Machines
- Work Managers
- Startup and Shutdown Classes

For example, if you click Servers, you'll then see in the right-hand pane the Configuration page for the lone server in the domain, *examplesServer,* which is the Admin Server for this domain (*wl_server*), as shown in Figure 1-3.

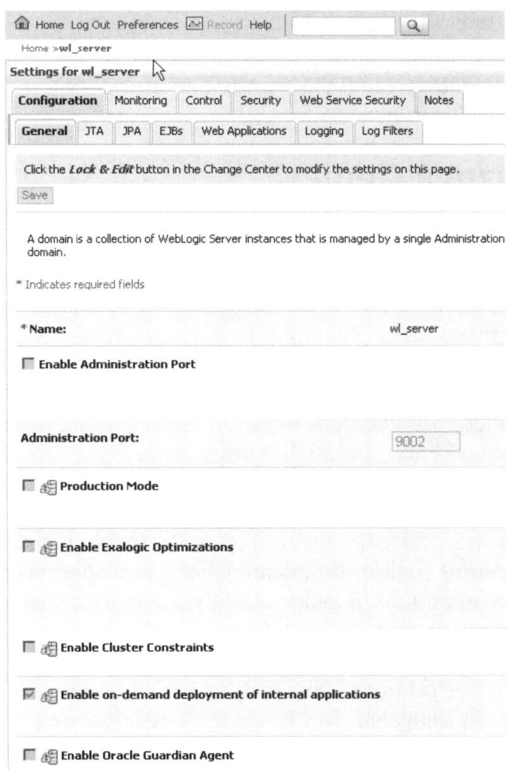

FIGURE 1-3. *The Configuration page for the Admin Server*

Deployments

This group takes you to the Deployments page, from where you can manage the enterprise applications or web modules you've deployed. You can start, stop, redeploy, or remove an application or module from this page.

Services

Important resources you can manage include messaging, which consists of Java Messaging Service (JMS) servers and JMS modules; Java Database Connectivity (JDBC) data sources; and Java Transaction APIs (JTA).

Security Realms

This group contains all security realms you have configured for this domain. Select a realm from under Security Realms in the left pane. When you do this, all the subnodes for all the security providers in a realm appear in the right pane, providing you access to a realm's users, groups, and roles. The Administration Console lets you configure any aspect of a security realm.

Interoperability

This group contains features that allow your applications to operate with Tuxedo Services, such as the WebLogic Tuxedo Connector and Jolt, a Java-based client that manages requests made to Oracle Tuxedo Services.

Diagnostics

This group contains diagnostic modules and diagnostic images (snapshots) to help manage the WebLogic Diagnostic Framework (WLDF). You can also configure Simple Network Management Protocol (SNMP) agents from here.

Using the Change Center

From the Administration Console's Change Center, you can lock a domain's configuration while you're changing any configuration attributes. By default, the Change Center is always enabled when you run a server in production mode and disabled in development mode. To make permanent configuration changes from the Administration Console, you must first obtain a lock, make your changes, and then activate them. By doing so, other accounts are prevented from making changes during your edit session, preventing conflicting or overlapping configuration changes.

Instead of making configuration changes piecemeal, you can make multiple changes and activate them all at once. You can click the View Changes and Restarts button to view all the pending changes that you have applied but not activated yet. The Change List page shows you all changes that are saved but not yet activated. By clicking the Restart Checklist tab, you can view the changes that have been activated but are waiting for a server restart before they become effective.

In development mode, the domain configuration locking feature is disabled by default; that is, the Automatically Acquire Lock And Activate Changes property is enabled. Automatic locking means you don't have to acquire a lock explicitly on the domain configuration before making any changes to it. In the top-left corner of the Administration Console, you'll see the following note: "Configuration editing is enabled. Future changes will automatically be activated as you modify, add or delete items in this domain." This means that when you make and save a configuration change, it's automatically activated. This is fine for a development environment, but for a production environment, you should always enable the locking feature. In fact, when you run the server in production mode, you don't have the option to set up automatic acquisition of configuration locks and activation of changes. The Automatically Acquire Lock And Activate Changes property is exclusive to servers running in development mode.

You can enable domain configuration locking by going to the right-hand pane of the Administration Console and clicking Preferences in the menu at the top of the page. At the bottom of the page, you'll see the box Automatically Acquire And Activate Changes. You can leave this box checked for a development domain so you can make quick configuration changes on the fly, but it should always be unchecked for a production domain. Clear this option and click Save. Once you click the Release Configuration button in the Change Center, the Lock & Edit button appears, as shown in Figure 1-4.

Once you enable domain configuration locking, you must use the Lock & Edit button to make any configuration changes, including editing, adding, or deleting any type of configuration attributes. The main purpose behind all this is to ensure that other sessions don't make configuration changes while you're trying to make changes. If you don't click the Lock & Edit button in the Change Center, the server won't even let you start the configuration process—the check boxes for selecting the server or a subcomponent you want to configure will be grayed out. Once you complete any configuration changes and save them, you must click the Activate Changes button to make those changes effective. As you'll see later, some configuration changes require that you restart the server.

To illustrate how to use the Lock & Edit feature, the following example shows you how to disable the Administration Console (something you may want to do to prevent access to the

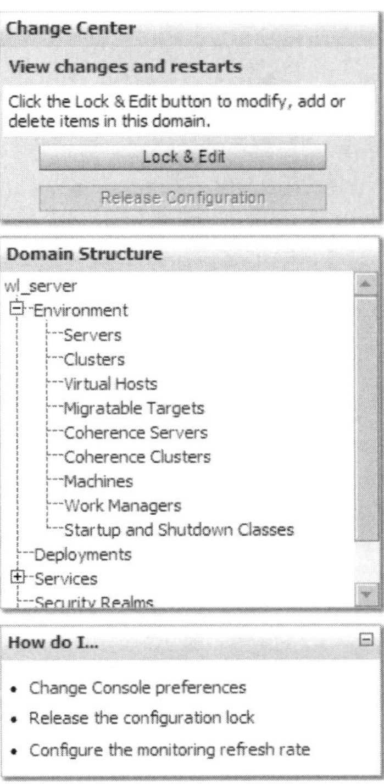

FIGURE 1-4. *The Change Center in the Administration Console*

Console in a production environment), which is a configuration change you can make from the Console:

1. Click Lock & Edit, as shown previously in Figure 1-4. This locks the configuration MBean hierarchy so you can make changes. Now the Lock & Edit button is grayed out, but the Release Configuration button becomes clickable so you can back out before you make your configuration changes.
2. In the Domain Structure section on the left, click the name of your domain—in the case of the Examples Server, this would be *wl_server*.
3. From the Configuration tab on the right pane of the Console, click the General tab and then click Advanced at the bottom of the page. Uncheck the Console Enabled option and click Save. When you click Save, you'll see the following message (in green) on the top of the page where you made the change, confirming that the change was successful:

   Settings Updated Successfully
4. Finally, you'll see two new buttons in the Change Center: Activate Changes and Undo All Changes, as shown in Figure 1-5. Click Activate Changes in the Change Center to make the change effective.

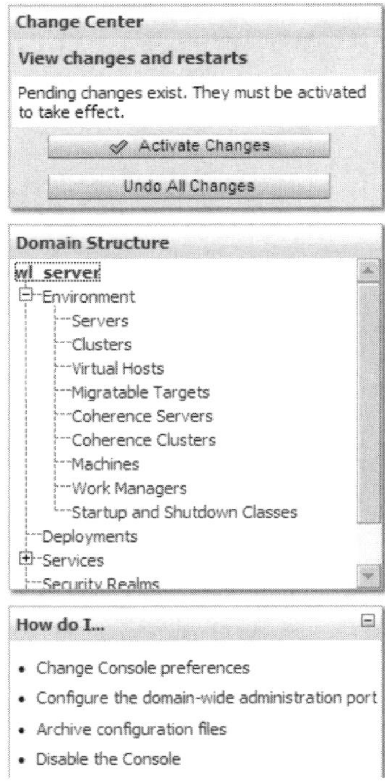

FIGURE 1-5. *The Activate Changes button in the Change Center*

After you click the Activate Changes button in the Change Center, you'll see the following message (in green) at the top of the right-hand pane:

All changes have been activated. However 1 item(s) must be restarted for the changes to take effect.

The reason the message states that "1 item(s) must be restarted" is because disabling the Console is a nondynamic change that requires a server restart.

NOTE
Some configuration changes are dynamic and, therefore, go into effect right away; other changes are nondynamic and require a server restart.

You'll also see the following in the command console, following the change you just made:

```
<Oct 25, 2013 1:37:51 PM CDT> <Warning> <Management> <BEA-141239>
<The non-dynamic attribute ConsoleEnabled on
weblogic.management.configuration.DomainMBeanImpl@d5bf4c12([wl_server])
has been changed. This may require redeploying or rebooting configured entities.>
<Oct 25, 2013 1:37:51 PM CDT> <Warning> <Management> <BEA-141238> <A non-dynamic
change has been made which affects the server examplesServer. This server must be
 rebooted in order to consume this change.>
```

Once you disable the Administration Console, you can reenable it only through the WebLogic Scripting Tool (WLST). Once the Admin Server is started, invoke WLST by navigating to Start | Programs | Oracle | Oracle Home | WebLogic Server 12c | Tools | WebLogic Scripting Tool and issue the following commands at the WLST command line:

```
Initializing WebLogic Scripting Tool (WLST)...
Jython scans all the jar files it can find at first startup.
Depending on the system, this process may take a few minutes to complete,
 and WLST may not return a prompt right away.
Welcome to WebLogic Server Administration Scripting Shell
Type help() for help on available commands
wls:/offline>
wls:/offline> connect("weblogic", "welcome1")
Connecting to t3://localhost:7001 with userid weblogic ...
Successfully connected to Admin Server 'examplesServer' that belongs
to domain  'wl_server'.
Warning: An insecure protocol was used to connect to the server.
To ensure on-the-wire security, the SSL port or Admin port should be
used instead.
wls:/wl_server/serverConfig> edit()
Location changed to edit tree. This is a writable tree with
DomainMBean as the root. To make changes you will need to start
 an edit session via
startEdit(). For more help, use help(edit)
wls:/wl_server/edit> startEdit()
Starting an edit session ...
Started edit session, please be sure to save and activate your changes
once you are done.
```

```
wls:/wl_server/edit !> cmo.setConsoleEnabled(true)
wls:/wl_server/edit !> save()
Saving all your changes ...
Saved all your changes successfully.
wls:/wl_server/edit !> activate()
Activating all your changes, this may take a while ...
The edit lock associated with this edit session is released
once the activation is completed.
```

Working with the Administration Console

You already know how to log into the Administration Console. The following sections show how to log out of the Console and to set Console preferences.

Logging Out of the Console

To log out of the Administration Console, click the Log Out button at the top of the right-hand pane. Logging out of the Administration Console doesn't affect the Admin Server. To log back in, use the URL for the console—http://*<hostname>:port*/console. When you shut down the Admin Server from the Administration Console, the Console immediately shuts down and won't be available until you manually restart the Admin Server. Once you restart the Admin Server, you can log back in to the Console by using the now familiar URL:

```
http://127.0.0.1:7001/console
```

Setting Console Preferences

You can set Administration Console preferences by clicking the Preferences button at the top of the right-hand pane. You can select several configuration-related properties from the Preferences page, including whether the server asks for confirmation of operations. You can also choose your preference for whether the server issues a warning message when a user logs out with an active domain configuration lock for a resource in place. Note that when this happens, other users won't be able to lock that resource for making their own configuration changes. The lock holder must either release the configuration changes or activate them first.

Changing the Console's URL

You can change the Console's URL (by default, http://localhost:7001/console) to a different URL. To change the Console's URL, on the Configuration page for the domain, click General and then Advanced at the bottom of the page. Enter the context path in the Console Context Path box. If you specify a new context path named *newconsole,* for example, you can then use the following URL to access the Console: http://localhost:7001/newconsole.

Changing the Listen Port and Listen Address

To change the listen port or listen address that you use to access the Administration Console, you must change those settings for the domain's Admin Server. You can change the following network-related configuration attributes from the Administration Console. Go to the Admin Server's Configuration page and click General. From this page, you can configure the following network-related settings:

- **Listen Address** This is the IP address or DNS name for the server.
- **Listen Port** Enter the default TCP/IP port for listening for non-SSL connection requests.

- **Listen Port Enabled** This lets you enable or disable the default non-SSL listen port.
- **SSL Listen Port** Enter the TCP/IP port on which to listen for secure SSL connection requests.
- **SSL Listen Port Enabled** If you haven't enabled the optional administration port, both application traffic and administrative traffic will go through the normal listen port and the SSL listen port. If you've enabled the administration port, then the administrative traffic will only go through the administrative port.

The preceding is a very brief summary of what you can do with the Administration Console. Throughout this book, you'll have plenty of chances to review the many capabilities of the Administration Console, as we discuss topics such as deployment, security, configuration management, and diagnostics.

A Brief Introduction to the Node Manager

The Node Manager, as mentioned earlier in this chapter, is a purely optional process (or daemon) that lets you remotely manage both the Admin Server and all Managed Servers within that domain. If you're in a production environment with high availability requirements, Oracle recommends that you use the Node Manager to manage the servers running on different machines. In Chapter 2, you'll find a detailed explanation of how to configure the Node Manager and how to manage servers using WLST and the Node Manager together.

Unlike the Admin Server, of which there's only a single instance running per domain, you must run the Node Manager on each of the servers (machines) on which you plan to run the Admin Server or one of the Managed Servers. You don't have to install the Node Manager separately—each installation of WebLogic Server comes with the Node Manager. You just need to start the Node Manager service or process on each of the machines running WebLogic Server instances. Thus, if you have WebLogic Server instances running on five different servers, you must have five Node Manager processes running, one per machine.

Oracle WebLogic Server offers you two types, or versions, rather, of the Node Manager—one a Java-based and the other a script-based version. Although both versions offer the same functions, you need to configure them differently. Also, different security considerations apply to the two versions, with the Java-based version offering you more security features than the script-based version. You can configure the Java-based Node Manager with the *nodemanager.properties* file, as shown in Chapter 2. The Java-based version allows you to use SSL, and the script-based version offers you the capability to manage servers over an SSH-enabled (or RSH-enabled) network once you copy the scripts to the remote servers.

You can run the Node Manager as a Windows service or an OS daemon so it automatically starts when you reboot the server. Chapter 2 shows you how to run the Node Manager as an operating system service, post installation. The Configuration Wizard gives you the option to install the Node Manager as an operating system service, which Oracle recommends you do. When you install the WebLogic Server software, choose the Java-based Node Manager if you're working on a Windows or a UNIX platform and wish to run the Node Manager as an operating system process.

NOTE
The Node Manager isn't supported on all platforms, so check the Oracle documentation to ensure it's supported on your platform.

The script-based Node Manager uses UNIX-style shell scripts, so you can run it only on UNIX and Linux systems. Oracle recommends that you run this version as an operating system service to enable automatic restarts.

Choosing between the Java-based and script-based versions of the Node Manager isn't really hard. Only the Java-based version works on a Windows system, so your choice on that platform is already made for you! Throughout this book, I use a Java-based Node Manager, as the examples are from a Windows environment. As for UNIX/Linux systems, you can use either version, with the script-based version being easier to configure from the security point of view. Other than this, the way the Node Manager interacts with server instances is essentially the same under the two versions.

Surprisingly, as critical as the Node Manager is for managing WebLogic Server, you really don't access the process directly. You access the Node Manager through either the Admin Server or the WLST scripting tool—both act as Node Manager clients. When you use the Admin Server as the client, you do so through the Administration Console. When you are using the Node Manager from the command line, you do so by first invoking WLST and using it as the interface to run Node Manager commands. For the script-based Node Manager, you can use an SSH client to connect to the Node Manager remotely.

You can perform the following functions by connecting with the Node Manager process through WLST:

- You can control the Admin Server by starting, stopping, and restarting the server with the Node Manager.
- The Node Manager can stop and start as well as suspend any Managed Server. When you start or stop a Managed Server through the Administration Console, the Admin Server first accesses the Node Manager, which, in turn, performs the actual task.
- The Node Manager also monitors the Managed Servers and tries to restart a failed Managed Server.

This chapter provides a very simple introduction to the Node Manager and its capabilities. Chapter 2 shows you how to work with the Node Manager to perform various administrative tasks.

Using the WebLogic Scripting Tool (WLST)

Most application servers provide you with a good scripting tool. For example, IBM's WebSphere has a scripting tool called *wsadmin* that is based on Jython, and JBoss has a similar scripting tool. Oracle WebLogic Server offers you a wonderful scripting tool called WebLogic Scripting Tool (WLST). WLST is a powerful tool, capable of performing several different types of administrative tasks for you, including configuration, management, and monitoring of tasks. As you'll see in Chapter 2, you can connect to Node Manager through the WLST interface to manage the server instances. For ease of use, you can use simple Jython scripts as wrappers for WLST commands.

You can use WLST in interactive mode by invoking it at the command line. You can also use it in batch mode by putting WLST commands in scripts, and you can embed WLST commands in Java code by importing *weblogic.management.scripting.utils.WLSTinterpreter* into your Java class.

Offline and Online WLST

You can use WLST in online mode by connecting to an active Admin or Managed Server. When connected to the Admin Server, you can use WLST to configure a domain. As is the case with the Administration Console, WLST in online mode acts as a Java Management Extensions (JMX) client that manages the domain's resources by modifying the server's Configuration MBeans. Thus, WLST offers you all the domain management configuration capabilities as the Administration Console.

In offline mode, WLST helps you extend a domain, create domain templates, and create domains with those templates. Because you aren't connected to an active Admin Server, you won't be able to modify domain configuration in offline mode. In offline mode, WLST acts as an interface to the Node Manager, and you can issue WLST commands to start and stop Managed Server instances without connecting to the Admin Server. Note that you can't start and stop Managed Servers through WLST without the Node Manager, however, as explained in Chapter 2.

CAUTION
Oracle recommends that you not use WLST in the offline mode to configure an active WebLogic domain. A running server ignores the offline commands, plus the Administration Console (and WLST online) can overwrite those commands.

Invoking WLST

In a Windows environment, you can invoke WLST through the Windows Start program and from the command line. The following sections show how to invoke WLST.

Starting WLST from the Start Program

You can invoke WLST in a Windows environment by simply selecting Start | Programs | Oracle | Oracle Home | WebLogic Server 12*c* | Tools | WebLogic Scripting Tool.

Invoking WLST from the Command Line

You can invoke WLST from the command line by using either the java *weblogic.WLST* command or the command script *wlst.cmd*. Before you can run the *weblogic.WLST* command, you must set the correct environment by issuing the *setDomainEnv.cmd* script, which is located in the WL_HOME\server\bin directory. In my case, this directory is C:\Oracle\Middleware\Oracle_Home\wlserver\server\bin, because the WL_HOME directory is defined as C:\Oracle\Middleware\Oracle_Home\wlserver on my Windows server. Once you set up the environment, you can invoke WLST with the Java command *weblogic.WLST,* located in the WL_HOME\common\bin directory:

```
C:\Oracle\Middleware\Oracle_Home\wlserver\server\bin>setWLSEnv.cmd
...
Your environment has been set.
```

Once the environment has been set, you are ready to invoke WLST with the Java command *weblogic.WLST*:

```
C:\Oracle\Middleware\Oracle_Home\wlserver\server\bin>java weblogic.WLST
Initializing WebLogic Scripting Tool (WLST) ...
Welcome to WebLogic Server Administration Scripting Shell
Type help() for help on available commands
wls:/offline>
```

Note that when you invoke WLST, by default, you're in offline mode. You can only issue certain commands in offline mode, such as those that create a new domain or domain template, for example. In offline mode, you can't view performance data pertaining to any domain resource or add and remove users. To issue any online commands, you must first connect to the Admin Server using the *connect* command. Once you use WLST to connect to an Admin Server, you can manage the configuration of the domain and view performance data. Although you can connect to a Managed Server through WLST, you can't modify the configuration for a Managed Server.

You can also invoke WLST by issuing the script *wlst.cmd* (*wlst.sh* in UNIX), as shown here:

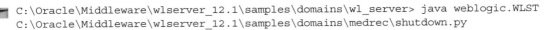

```
C:\Oracle\Middleware\Oracle_Home\\oracle_common\common\bin> wlst.cmd
CLASSPATH=C:\Oracle\MIDDLE~1\patch_wls1211\profiles\default\
sys_manifest_classpath\weblogic_patch.jar;
C:\Oracle\MIDDLE~1\patch_ocp371\profiles\default\sys_manifest_classpath\
weblogic_patch.jar;
C:\Oracle\MIDDLE~1\JROCKI~1.0-1\lib\tools.jar;
C:\Oracle\MIDDLE~1\WLSERV~1.1\server\lib\weblogic_sp.jar;
C:\Oracle\MIDDLE~1\WLSERV~1.1\server\lib\weblogic.jar;
C:\Oracle\MIDDLE~1\modules\features\weblogic.server.modules_12.1.1.0.jar;
C:\Oracle\MIDDLE~1\WLSERV~1.1\server\lib\webservices.jar;
C:\Oracle\MIDDLE~1\modules\ORGAPA~1.1/lib/ant-all.jar;
C:\Oracle\MIDDLE~1\modules\NETSFA~1.0_1/lib/ant-contrib.jar;
C:\Oracle\MIDDLE~1\utils\config\10.3\config-launch.jar;
C:\Oracle\MIDDLE~1\WLSERV~1.1\common\derby\lib\derbynet.jar;
C:\Oracle\MIDDLE~1\WLSERV~1.1\common\derby\lib\derbyclient.jar;
C:\Oracle\MIDDLE~1\WLSERV~1.1\common\derby\lib\derbytools.jar;
Initializing WebLogic Scripting Tool (WLST)...
Welcome to WebLogic Server Administration Scripting Shell
Type help() for help on available commands
wls:/offline>
```

Note that you use the *wlst.cmd* script from the ORACLE_HOME\oracle_common\common\bin directory and not a directory specific to any particular WebLogic Server domain.

Using WLST in Script Mode

Although you can use WLST in interactive mode to make configuration changes quickly in a development environment, WLST offers limited scripting language features and is cumbersome to use in a real-life WebLogic environment. You can use WLST scripts to automate server configuration and application deployment. A WLST script is a text file with the *.py* extension, and it includes WLST commands. WebLogic Server provides online and offline sample WLST scripts. For example, the Oracle-provided sample WLST script *clusterMedRecDomain.py* lets you create a WebLogic cluster with three Managed Servers. Similarly, the sample script named *basicWLSDomain.py* lets you create a simple WebLogic domain for development purposes, using the Oracle-supplied Basic WebLogic Server Domain template. You'll find both of these scripts and a few others in the WL_HOME\common\templates\scripts\wlst directory (C:\Oracle\Middleware\Oracle_Home\wlserver\common\templates\scripts\wlst in my case).

You can invoke a WLST script (*.py*) by providing the name of the script as an argument to the java *weblogic.WLST* command, as shown here:

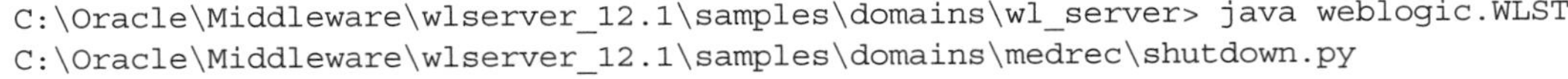

```
C:\Oracle\Middleware\wlserver_12.1\samples\domains\wl_server> java weblogic.WLST
C:\Oracle\Middleware\wlserver_12.1\samples\domains\medrec\shutdown.py
```

Here are the contents of the *shutdown.py* script:

```
import os
if os.environ.has_key('wlsUserID'):
    wlsUserID = os.environ['wlsUserID']
if os.environ.has_key('wlsPassword'):
    wlsPassword = os.environ['wlsPassword']
connect(  url='t3://LOCALHOST:7001', adminServerName='examplesServer')
shutdown('examplesServerMedRecServer','Server', ignoreSessions='true')
exit()
```

Alternatively, you can first invoke WLST and specify the *execfile* command to execute the *shutdown.py* script.

```
wls:offline>
execfile('C:\MyOra\Middleware\Oracle_Home\wlserver\samples\domains\medrec\shutdown
.py')
```

If you're embedding WLST commands in a shell script or a Windows command script, invoke WLST with the *wlst.cmd* script (WL_HOME\common\bin\wlst.cmd). Doing this ensures that all the environment variables are set correctly. WebLogic Server also allows you to write all the WLST commands you enter during an interactive session to a file that you can later run as a WLST script. Simply issue the *startRecording* command to record all your interactive commands and issue the *stopRecording* command to stop the capturing of the commands, as shown here:

```
wls:/test_domain/serverConfig>
startRecording('C:\Oracle\Middleware\wls_12.1\test\test.py')
Started recording to C:\Oracle\Middleware\wls_12.1\test\test.py
```

Issue the WLST commands you want to capture in *test.py*. Once you're done, stop the recording of the commands by issuing the *stopRecording* command:

```
wls:/test_domain/serverConfig> stopRecording()
Stopped recording to C:\Oracle\Middleware\wls_12.1\test\test.py
wls:/test_domain/serverConfig>
```

You can edit the *test.py* file and execute it as a WLST script.

Connecting to a WebLogic Server Instance

In the offline mode, you aren't connected to a running server. Use the *connect* command to connect to the Admin Server, as shown here:

```
wls:/offline> connect()
Please enter your username :weblogic
Please enter your password :
Please enter your server URL [t3://localhost:7001] :
Connecting to t3://localhost:7001 with userid weblogic...
Successfully connected to Admin Server 'examplesServer' that belongs to
domain 'wl_server'.
Warning: An insecure protocol was used to connect to the server.
```

```
 To ensure on-the-wire security, the SSL port or Admin port
 should be used instead.
wls:/wl_server/serverConfig>
```

In the example, you'll notice a warning because I'm not using a secure port such as the administration port or an SSL port. Oracle recommends that you use either SSL or the administration port in a production system. You can ignore this warning in a development environment.

TIP
To view the help topics, type ***help*** *at the WLST command line. You must specify an argument for the* help *command; for example,* help(connect) *will give you information about using the* connect *command.*

You can also directly specify the administrator's credentials at the command line, as shown here:

```
wls:/offline> connect('weblogic','welcome1','t3://localhost:7001')
Connecting to WebLogic Server instance running at t3://localhost:7001 as
username weblogic...
Successfully connected to Admin Server 'ExamplesServer' that belongs to
domain 'examples'.
wls:/mydomain/serverConfig>
```

As you can see, I had to supply the user credentials (the same ones used for the Administration Console) to connect to the Admin Server. Oracle recommends that you do this only when using WLST in interactive mode. The default behavior is for WLST to see if you have created a "user configuration file" to store the encrypted credentials and a "key file" with which the server can decrypt the credentials. If you start WLST from the domain directory from which you started the Admin Server, it can use the *boot.properties* file to get the encrypted credentials. (The *boot .properties* file is discussed in Chapter 2.)

When you use WLST in scripts, it's safer not to use the clear text credentials in the script. You can use the *storeUserConfig* command to store the credentials in an encrypted form, following which you can specify the name of the user configuration file instead of the credentials. Here's how to do this:

```
wls:/offline> connect(userConfigFile='C:\Oracle\test\myuserconfigfile.secure',
userKeyFile='C:\Oracle\test\myuserkeyfile.secure')
Connecting to t3://localhost:7001 with userid username ...
Successfully connected to Admin Server 'AdminServer' that belongs to domain
'examples'.
wls:/examples/serverConfig>
```

In order to use the *userConfigFile* option, you must first issue the *storeUserConfig* command to create a user configuration file and its key file. The configuration file contains the encrypted credentials, and the key file contains the key the server uses for encrypting and decrypting the credentials. Here's an example that shows how to do this:

```
wls:/test_domain/serverConfig>
storeUserConfig('C:\MyOra\myuserconfigfile.secure',
'C:\Oracle\test\myuserkeyfile.secure')
Creating the key file can reduce the security of your system if it is not
kept in a secured location after it is created. Do you want to create the
key file? y or n   y
Please confirm user config key creation: y or n   y
The username and password that were used for this current WLS connection are
stored in C:\MyOra\mysuserconfigfile.secure and
C:\Oracle\test\myuserkeyfile.secure
wls:/test_domain/serverConfrg>
```

Once you generate the user configuration file and the key file, you can supply the names of these two files instead of entering administrator credentials on the command line.

Disconnecting from the Server

You disconnect from a server by issuing the *disconnect* command, as shown here:

```
wls:/wl_server/serverConfig> disconnect()
Disconnected from WebLogic Server: examplesServer
wls:/offline>
```

To exit from WLST, use the *exit* command:

```
wls:/offline> exit()
Exiting WebLogic Scripting Tool.
C:\MyOra\Middleware\wlserver_10.3\samples\domains\medrec >
```

By default, the server outputs all WLST messages or output to standard output, that is, to the screen. You can redirect all the messages to any file you wish by using the *redirect* command:

```
wls:/wl_server/serverConfig> redirect
('C:\Oracle\Middleware\wl_server_12.1\logs\wlst.log')
```

Using the Help Command

WLST has numerous commands that you can use in your daily work. You can check out these commands and their syntax using the *help* facility. Here's a listing of all the *help* facility commands.

```
wls:/wl_server/serverConfig> help()
WLST is a command line scripting tool to configure and administer WebLogic
Server. Try:
    help('all')             List all WLST commands available.
    help('browse')          List commands for browsing the hierarchy.
    help('common')          List the most commonly used commands.
    help('control')         List commands for controlling the domain/server.
    help('deployment')      List commands for deploying applications.
    help('diagnostics')     List commands for performing diagnostics.
    help('editing')         List commands for editing the configuration.
    help('information')     List commands for displaying information.
    help('lifecycle')       List commands for managing life cycle.
```

```
help('nodemanager')      List commands for using Node Manager.
help('offline')          List all offline commands available.
help('online')           List all online commands available.
help('storeadmin')       List all store admin commands.
help('trees')            List commands use to navigate MBean hierarchy.
help('variables')        List all global variables available.
```

Key WLST Command Groups

As I mentioned earlier, WLST offers a large number of commands to help perform various management and programming tasks. Here's a brief description of the key WLST command types. Note that you can execute some commands only in offline mode and others in online mode.

Lifecycle Commands

You can use the lifecycle commands to manage the lifecycle of both the Admin and the Managed Servers. WLST offers the *start, startServer, suspend, resume,* and *migrate* commands to control a server lifecycle. Here are examples showing how to suspend and resume the Admin Server instance:

```
wls:/wl_server/serverConfig> suspend('examplesServer')
..Server examplesServer suspended successfully.
wls:/wl_server/serverConfig> resume('examplesServer')
Server examplesServer resumed successfully.
wls:/wl_server/serverConfig>
```

Node Manager Commands

You can use the Node Manager commands to start, stop, and monitor server instances. Before you can use Node Manager to manage server instances, you must connect WLST to the Node Manager using the *nmConnect* command. The *nmStart* command lets you start a server instance with the help of the Node Manager. Here's how you use the *nmConnect* command to connect to the Node Manager from WLST. First, make sure that the Node Manager is running; if not, you can start it from the Windows Start command.

```
wls:/myserver/serverConfig> nmConnect('weblogic', 'welcome1', 'localhost',
'7011', 'medrec',
'C:\Oracle\Middleware\user_projects\domains\medrec','ssl')
Connecting to Node Manager Server ...
Successfully connected to Node Manager.
```

Chapter 2 explains other important Node Manager–related commands such as *nmDisconnect, nmEntroll,* and *nmkill.*

Deployment Commands

Deployment commands such as *deploy, undeploy, startApplication,* and *stopApplication* enable you to deploy, undeploy, and redeploy applications; update deployment plans; as well as start and stop applications. Here's how you execute the *deploy* command:

```
wls:/test_domain/serverConfig/Servers> deploy('myApp',
'C:\Oracle\myApps\demos\app\myApp.ear',targets='ManagedServer1',
planPath='C:\Oracle\myApps\demos\app\plan\plan.xml',timeout=120000)'
```

In this example, the *myApp* application is packaged in the form of a Java EAR file, *myApp.ear*. The server targets this application to the Managed Server named *ManagedServer1* using the deployment file in C:\Oracle\myApps\demos\app\plan\plan.xml. The server will wait for 120,000 milliseconds for the deployment to finish.

Editing Commands

You can use commands such as *get, set, edit, startEdit, stopEdit, save,* and *activate* to view and edit the MBean domain configuration hierarchy. You can edit and modify a domain's configuration in both offline and online modes. Oracle recommends that you change only the Admin Server's domain configuration MBeans, and not those of the Managed Servers, to avoid ending up with an inconsistent configuration. As you may recall, domain configuration changes are synchronized between the Admin Server and the Managed Server. You can, however, view the hierarchy for the Managed Server MBeans. Note that you must connect to the Admin Server before editing any of the configuration beans. Here's a simple example that shows how to use the *startEdit, stopEdit,* and *activate* commands:

```
wls:/wl_server/edit> startEdit(30000, 60000)
Starting an edit session ...
Started edit session, please be sure to save and activate your changes once
you are done.
wls:/wl_server/edit !> stopEdit()
Sure you would like to stop your edit session? (y/n)
y
Edit session has been stopped successfully.
wls:/wl_server/edit !> activate(200000, block='true')
Activating all your changes, this may take a while ...
the edit lock associated with this edit session is released once the
activation is completed.
Action completed.
wls:/wl_server/edit>
```

Diagnostic Commands

Diagnostic commands such as *exportDiagnosticData* and *getAvailableCapturedImages* help you work with diagnostic data stored in the WebLogic Diagnostic Framework (WLDF) data stores. Chapter 6 shows how to use key WLST diagnostic commands.

Summary

This chapter introduced you to key WebLogic Server concepts and terminology. You learned how to install WebLogic Server, as well as how to upgrade it using the new Oracle Fusion Middleware Reconfiguration Wizard. The chapter also introduced you to the key WebLogic Server administrative tools such as the Administration Console, Node Manager, and WLST. WLST is an extremely powerful tool, capable of assisting with a wide variety of administrative tasks. I've attempted merely to introduce you to the WLST interface in this chapter. Chapter 2 shows you how to use WLST to manage a server's lifecycle. Similarly, other chapters show how you can effectively use the many powerful, yet easy-to-use WLST commands to perform other types of management tasks.

Now that you have a basic understanding of WebLogic Server, let's learn how to use WLST and Node Manager commands together to manage servers in the next chapter. Chapter 2 also explains the various server run states and how to manage them.

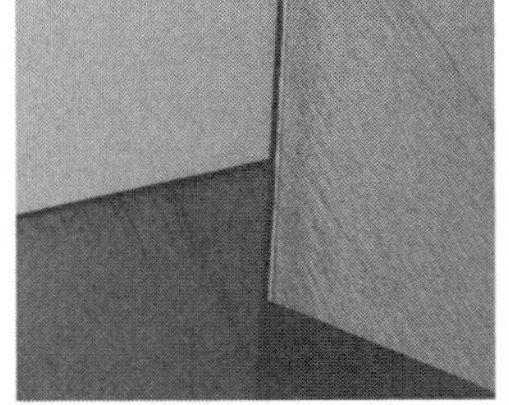

CHAPTER 2

Administering WebLogic Server Instances

The first chapter of this book introduced you to the Administration Console, the WebLogic Scripting Tool (WLST), and the Node Manager, three very important management tools for handling day-to-day administrative tasks as well as for performing various server configuration tasks. This chapter shows you how to manage WebLogic Server using these tools and other management APIs offered by WebLogic Server. The chapter explains the WebLogic Server lifecycle, from startup to shutdown. Ant tasks help you perform many management and configuration tasks. This chapter shows you how to build simple Ant-based scripts to manage WebLogic Server. The chapter also reviews the Node Manager and WLST tools at a deeper level and shows you how to configure the Node Manager for use with Managed Servers. You'll also learn how to use WLST and the Node Manager together to manage the WebLogic Server lifecycle efficiently. This chapter also seeks to enhance your understanding of the role of the Administration Console in WebLogic Server management. Dealing with server failures is, of course, a critical issue, and the chapter shows you how to handle an Admin Server failure as well as how to run the Managed Server in the Managed Server Independence (MSI) mode.

Let's start this chapter with a quick review of both the Admin Server and Managed Servers.

Managing the Servers

You can start, stop, and manage a running WebLogic Server instance using multiple tools—you can use the Node Manager, WLST, and command-line scripts to start and stop the server instances. This chapter is devoted mainly to explaining, in detail, the various server management commands as well as dealing with server failures. To start this chapter off right, let's review two basic types of WebLogic Server instances—the Admin Server and the Managed Server.

Administration and Managed Servers

Each WebLogic Server domain has a minimum of one server. If you only have a single server, as is often the case in development environments, then you use that server for both management purposes and for deploying applications. In production environments, however the norm is to use multiple Managed Servers, usually organized into a cluster for providing load balancing, high availability, and scalability benefits. In the following sections, let's revisit the two types of servers—the Admin Server and the Managed Server—that you must manage in a WebLogic Server environment.

Admin Server

Although you can deploy web applications through the Admin Server, its main purpose is to act as the central command center for managing all domain resources, including the configuration of the servers. The Admin Server maintains the configuration files for the domain and distributes the configuration updates to the Managed Servers. When the Admin Server notifies the Managed Servers of any domain configuration changes, the Managed Servers update their local config directory, thus ensuring that they always cache a current copy of their configuration. Because you need the Admin Server to manage the entire domain, in a production environment, you always run the Admin Server by itself on a separate physical machine and run the Managed Servers on their own machines. In addition, you protect and secure the Admin Server carefully to ensure that it is up at all times.

As you learned in Chapter 1, you can manage the Admin Server through WLST commands, the Administration Console, or a custom JMX client.

Managed Servers

The Managed Servers host your web applications, web services, and the resources necessary to support these applications and services. Although the Admin Server and the Managed Server both maintain copies of the domain's configuration, you can modify the configuration only through the Admin Server, not from the Managed Servers.

Upon starting, a Managed Server connects to the Admin Server and synchronizes its domain configuration document with the Admin Server's copy of the domain configuration file. The Managed Server also gets its security data from the Admin Server. If you configure SSL for a Managed Server, however, it uses its own SSL-related files such as the certificate files.

Admin Server Failures and the Managed Servers

Let's say you have the Admin Server and multiple Managed Servers all running on the same physical or virtual machine. What happens to the Managed Servers if the Admin Server fails and you're unable to start it for some reason? The Managed Servers will continue to run, despite the failure of the Admin Server—you just won't be able to modify the Managed Server's configuration because there's nothing to manage it with! The last section of this chapter shows you how to set up the Managed Servers to run independently of the Admin Server. If the Managed Servers are part of a cluster, all the load balancing and high availability features of that cluster remain intact, even in the absence of the Admin Server.

Can you start a Managed Server if the Admin Server is not running? Turns out that you can—the Managed Server is said to be in Managed Server Independence (MSI) mode when it runs in the absence of the Admin Server. The Managed Server, instead of contacting the running Admin Server for the domain configuration, simply uses its own local copy of the configuration files to look up the startup configuration. Once it boots, it attempts to connect to the Admin Server at periodic intervals. Once you bring the Admin Server online, the Managed Server makes contact with it and synchronizes its configuration files with those of the Admin Server. This is possible only if the Admin Server and the Managed Server share the domain directory, in which case the configuration files need not be distributed, or if the Managed Server has already been started once and has successfully downloaded a copy of the configuration.

Selecting the Start Mode for a Server

Before we start discussing the actual startup and shutdown procedures for a server instance, it's important to understand that you can choose to start a server in two different modes—production or development mode. The default mode is development mode. When you enable production mode, a number of configuration attributes will have different default values from those in a server running in development mode. Here's a summary of how key configuration attributes vary in a server running in production mode:

- The servlet engine will not check for servlet changes.
- When using 8.1 executed threads, the default pool size changes from 15 to 25.
- Log files roll over at 5MB instead of 5KB.

NOTE

In the current release, when you run a WebLogic server instance in production mode, by default, the server rotates its server log file whenever the file grows to 5000 kilobytes in size. WebLogic Server also sets a threshold size limit of 2,097,152KB before it forces a hard rotation to prevent the log file from reaching an excessively large size.

- Log files will not automatically be started in a new file.
- The server uses a larger memory buffer for the log files.
- The domain log messages are buffered.
- SNMP requires MD5 authentication.
- Server start timeouts go from 30 seconds to 2 minutes.

You can use one of the following methods to select the domain's startup mode:

- In the start script for the Admin Server, add the following line:

  ```
  set STARTMODE=
  ```

  Set the value of the *startmode* attribute to *true* if you want to run a server in production mode. By default, the server runs in development mode, so you can leave the *startmode* attribute blank or specify the value *false,* if you want to run the server in development mode. The default start scripts provided by Oracle are the *startWebLogic.cmd* (Windows) and *startWebLogic.sh* (UNIX) scripts; they are located in your domain home directory. For example, in the case of the *wl_server* domain, the startup script *startWebLogic.cmd* for the domain's Admin Server is located in the C:\Oracle\Middleware\wlserver_12.1\samples\domains\wl_server directory. The startup scripts contain commands that allow you to specify several startup options in addition to the run mode.
- You can also specify the development or production run mode by setting the *ProductionModeEnabled* flag to *false* or *true* with the *-D* option, when starting the server with the *weblogic.Server* command:

  ```
  java -ms200m -mx200m -classpath $CLASSPATH
       -Dweblogic.Name=myserver
       -Dweblogic.ProductionModeEnabled=false
       -Dweblogic.management.username=myUserName
       -Dweblogic.management.password=myPassword
       weblogic.Server
  ```
- Another method is to enable production mode for all the servers in a domain in the Administration Console by navigating to Home | Domain | Configuration | General and checking the Production Mode check box. You must restart the Admin Server after saving this change. Just remember that you can't disable production mode from the Administration Console.

If you find that even after setting the *production_mode* attribute to the value *false* in the *setDomainEnv.cmd* (or *setDomainEnv.sh*) file and restarting the servers, the Admin Server continues to run in production mode, check your *config.xml* file for the domain and remove the entry for the production mode. The entry will be in the following format:

```
<production-mode-enabled>true</production-mode-enabled>
```

You can make this change directly in the *config.xml* file or edit the file from the Administration Console. You can check the mode in which a server started by viewing the output generated by the server in the command window following a server startup. You'll see the following lines right after the server starts:

```
JAVA Memory arguments: -Xms256m -Xmx512m -XX:CompileThreshold=8000 -XX:PermSize=
128m -XX:MaxPermSize=256m
WLS Start Mode=Development
```

You can find out which JVM the server is using by viewing the messages generated in the command window by the server as it is starting:

```
starting weblogic with Java version:
java version "1.6.0_29"
Java(TM) SE Runtime Environment (build 1.6.0_29-b11)
Java HotSpot(TM) Client VM (build 20.4-b02, mixed mode)
```

Configuring Class Caching

WebLogic Server allows you to use class caching to reduce the search time for classes and thus the server startup time. You can use class caching only in development mode, however. The server uses an invisible file to store all class definitions and loads these definitions from the cache file each time you restart the server. The server invalidates the cache once you make any changes to the system class path.

To enable class caching, first set the *CLASS_CACHE* environment variable to *true* in the *startWebLogic.cmd* scrip by adding the following to the script:

```
set CLASS_CACHE=true
if "%CLASS_CACHE%"=="true" (
    echo Class caching enabled...
    set JAVA_OPTIONS=%JAVA_OPTIONS% -Dlaunch.main.class=%SERVER_CLASS%
    -Dlaunch.class.path="%CLASSPATH%"
    -Dlaunch.complete=weblogic.store.internal.LockManagerImpl
    -cp %WL_HOME%\server\lib\pcl2.jar
    set SERVER_CLASS=com.oracle.classloader.launch.Launcher
)
```

Setting the Environment Variables

Before you can start or stop your WebLogic Server instances, you need to do something else first—you must set the necessary environment variables for WebLogic Server to run. You must do this prior to running any WLST or Node Manager commands. On a Windows system, for example, you can set the environment variables by running *setDomainEnv.cmd,* as shown here:

```
C:\Oracle\Middleware\Oracle_Home\wlserver\server\bin>setWLSEnv.cmd
```

The *setWLSEnv.cmd* script is located in the WL_HOME\server\bin directory, and, in my environment, this translates to C:\Oracle\Middleware\Oracle_Home\wlserver\server\bin.

Every domain has its own copy of the *setDomainEnv.cmd* script. The Configuration Wizard creates the *setDomainEnv.cmd* (and *setDomainEnv.sh*) file when you create the domain. The command file sets some required environment variables, such as the WebLogic and Java home directories, the maximum and minimum memory allocations for the Java heap size, and log file configuration. For example, here is a list of some key environment variables that are set in the script:

```
set WL_HOME=C:\Oracle\Middleware\wlserver_12.1
set BEA_JAVA_HOME=C:\Oracle\Middleware\jrockit_160_29_D1.2.0-10
```

```
set SUN_JAVA_HOME=C:\Oracle\Middleware\jdk160_29
set JAVA_HOME=%JAVA_HOME%
set SAMPLES_HOME=%WL_HOME%\samples
set DOMAIN_HOME=C:\Oracle\Middleware\wlserver_12.1\samples\domains\wl_server
set DERBY_FLAG=true
set enableHotswapFlag=
set PRODUCTION_MODE=
if "%PRODUCTION_MODE%"=="true" (
      set debugFlag=false
      set testConsoleFlag=false
      set iterativeDevFlag=false
      set logErrorsToConsoleFlag=false
)
if "%JAVA_VENDOR%"=="Sun" (
      set WLS_MEM_ARGS_64BIT=-Xms256m -Xmx512m
      set WLS_MEM_ARGS_32BIT=-Xms256m -Xmx512m
) else (
      set WLS_MEM_ARGS_64BIT=-Xms512m -Xmx512m
      set WLS_MEM_ARGS_32BIT=-Xms512m -Xmx512m
)
```

Note that the *setDomainEnv.cmd* file calls *commEnv.cmd* from the $WL_HOME\common\bin directory. The *commEnv.cmd* file contains common environment variables for the WebLogic environment, such as *MW_HOME,* which is the common directory for all Oracle Fusion Middleware installations, as well as *COHERENCE_HOME* and *ANT_HOME*, the Ant home directory.

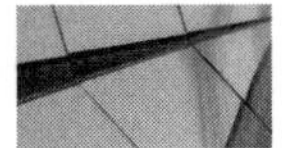

NOTE
The startWebLogic.cmd *script automatically calls the* setDomainEnv.cmd *script, as shown by the following line in the* startWebLogic.cmd *script:*

```
call "%DOMAIN_HOME%\bin\setDomainEnv.cmd" %*
```

Thus, you don't need to set your environment explicitly if you run the startWebLogic.cmd script *directly.*

Here's how you run the *setDomainEnv.cmd* script from the domain directory for the same domain *medrec:*

```
C:\Oracle\Middleware\Oracle_Home\user_projects\domains\medrec\bin\setDomainEnv.cmd
```

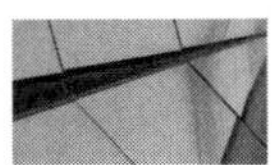

TIP
You can use the commEnv *command to configure your environment for doing simple development, as it will create a class path and path that allow you access to the version of WebLogic Server you're using. From there, you can simply execute the* java weblogic.Server *command in an empty directory, and it will create a whole new domain for you without using any extra tools. You'll see an example in Chapter 3.*

Configuring Server Instances with the Administration Console

When you create a domain with the help of the Configuration Wizard, you can configure several settings such as the listen address and the port numbers for both the Admin and the Managed Servers. You can configure administrative access to the server, for example, to a port that is firewalled.

Note that you can choose to use SSL and select an SSL listen port. You can also enable SSL later through the Administration Console's Configuration page for the Admin Server. The Configuration page in the Administration Console lets you configure all properties for an Administration Server, including the listen address and listen port. You access the Configuration page by selecting the domain name in the left-hand pane of the console and then clicking the Configuration tab in the right-hand pane. Figure 2-1 shows the Configuration page for the Admin Server.

For example, in the left-hand pane, click the domain (e.g., *wl_server*). This takes you to the settings page for the domain (Settings For wl_server in this example), in which any setting applies to all Managed Servers hosted on the domain. Here is a summary of some of the key configuration attributes at the domain level.

Administration Port You can enable SSL for the domain-wide port by selecting that option here. If you decide to enable the administration port, it will apply to the entire domain, so make sure you configure SSL for all the Managed Servers as well. Once you enable the administration port, an administrator can't log in through the normal port. Also, the administration port allows only administrative connections and not application connection requests. If you don't specify the administration port, you can't start a server instance in the STANDBY state.

Settings for wl_server
Configuration
Monitoring
Control
Security
Web Service Security
Notes
General
JTA
JPA
EJBs
Web Applications
Logging
Log Filters
Save
A domain is a collection of WebLogic Server instances that is managed by a single Administration Server. Use this page to configure administrative options that apply to all servers in the current domain.
* Indicates required fields
*Name:
wl_server
The name of this WebLogic Server domain. More Info...
Enable Administration Port
Specifies whether the domain-wide administration port should be enabled for this WebLogic Server domain. Because the administration port uses SSL, enabling the administration port requires that SSL must be configured for all servers in the domain. More Info...
Administration Port:
9002
The common secure administration port for this WebLogic Server domain. (Requires you to enable the administration port.) More Info...
Production Mode
Specifies whether all servers in this domain run in production mode. Once enabled, this can only be disabled in the admin server startup command line. More Info...

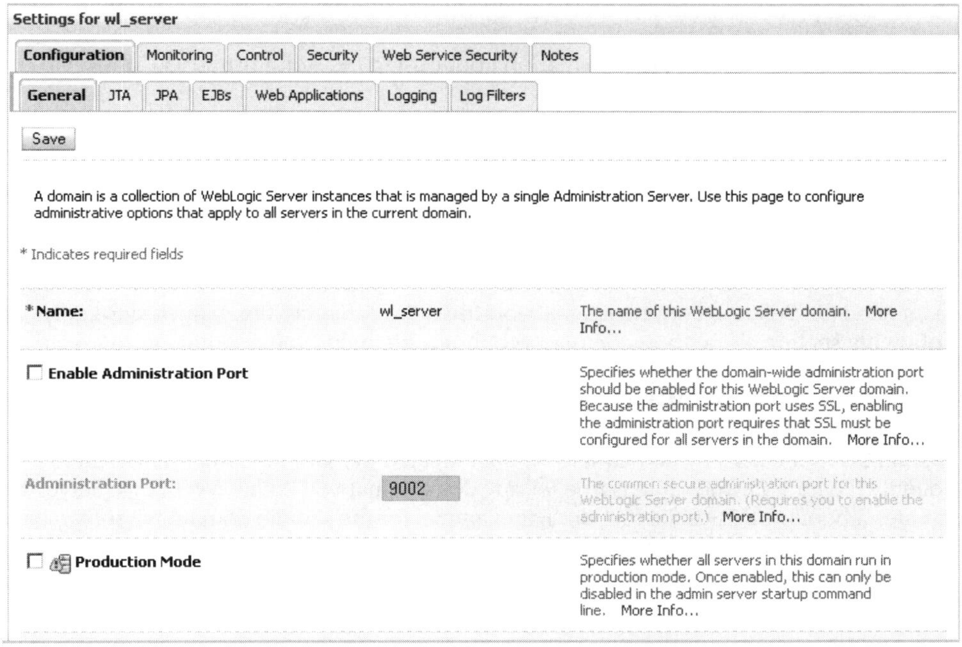

FIGURE 2-1. *The Configuration Wizard's Configuration page for the Admin Server*

Production Mode You can choose whether you want to run the domain in production mode. As shown elsewhere in this chapter, you can specify the start mode on the command line as well. If you set the start mode through the Administration Console, you must bounce the server for the change to take effect. Note that setting the start mode at the domain level means that this setting will be enforced for all Managed Servers in the domain.

Enable Exalogic Optimizations The Enable Exalogic Optimizations attribute is pertinent only to cases where you are configuring domains for Oracle Exalogic. The optimizations offer superior thread management and reduced contention for locks. Set this only when running on Exalogic, as that is the only place that it will provide value. For more information on Oracle Exalogic, go to www.oracle.com/us/products/middleware/exalogic/index.html.

Enable Cluster Constraints By selecting this configuration option, you're specifying that any deployments you target to a cluster will succeed only if all servers in that cluster are running. If you don't check this option, by default, deployment is attempted only on the reachable servers and not all server members of a cluster.

Console Enabled By default, the Admin Server always deploys the Administration Console. By unchecking this option, you can choose not to deploy it.

Console Session Timeout This attribute sets the timeout interval for the Administration Console. The default interval is 3600 seconds.

Administration Protocol This option lets you choose the default protocol if you enable the administration port. If a request through the administration port doesn't specify a protocol, the server uses this default protocol.

Chapter 3 provides more information about using the Administration Console to configure servers.

Providing User Credentials

When you start an Administration Server or when you start a Managed Server with the *java weblogic.Server* command, the server prompts you for a username and a password. It doesn't prompt you for the credentials when you use the Node Manager to start Managed Servers, however. To avoid having to specify the username and password credentials each time you start your servers, Oracle recommends that you use a boot identity file, named *boot.properties*. The following section shows how the boot properties file helps you and how to re-create the file.

Creating a Boot Identity File

In the sample domains from Chapter 1, you didn't have to specify credentials when starting the Admin Server because, when Oracle Installer created the sample domains, it created a default boot identity file for you. The same is true for any domain that you create; WebLogic Server automatically creates a boot properties file for you. For example, for the sample domain wl_server, the *boot.properties* file is located under the C:\Oracle\Middleware\wlserver_12.1\samples\domains\wl_server\servers\examplesServer\security directory. Here are the contents of the *boot.properties* file:

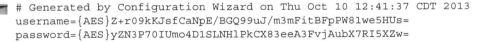

```
# Generated by Configuration Wizard on Thu Oct 10 12:41:37 CDT 2013
username={AES}Z+r09kKJsfCaNpE/BGQ99uJ/m3mFitBFpPW81we5HUs=
password={AES}yZN3P70IUmo4D1SLNHlPkCX83eeA3FvjAubX7RI5XZw=
```

As you can see, the username and passwords are in an encrypted form—the *boot.properties* file contains the encrypted credentials, with the encryption key itself stored in the *SerializedSystemIni.dat* file. Apparently the name for this file was chosen with the intention of obfuscating its contents—however, over time, the contents of the file have become widely known. Note that you can't directly substitute these encrypted values with plaintext values to change the user credentials. There's a different way to modify the encrypted credentials, as shown in this section.

If your *boot.properties* file is in place, when you start a server, WebLogic Server doesn't require you to input the administrator username and password. If, for some reason, WebLogic Server can't see the *boot.properties* file, it prompts you to provide those credentials before it can start the server:

```
<Oct 14, 2013 8:37:11 AM CDT> <Info> <Security> <BEA-090065> <Getting boot
 identity from user.>
Enter username to boot WebLogic server: weblogic
Enter password to boot WebLogic server:
<Oct 14, 2013 8:37:42 AM CDT> <Notice> <WebLogicServer> <BEA-000365>
<Server state changed to STARTING.>
<Oct 14, 2013 8:37:42 AM CDT> <Info> <WorkManager> <BEA-002900>
<Initializing self-tuning thread pool.>
...
```

Once again, the default username is weblogic and the default password is welcome1.

Creating the boot identity file is easy. If the file doesn't exist, you can simply add the following two lines in a text file named *boot.properties* and place it in the directory specified earlier:

```
username=username
password=password
```

You must specify the same credentials that are currently in place when you create a boot identity file. Make sure there are no leading or trailing blanks in the two lines. Save the *boot.properties* file and restart the server. The server uses the credentials you specified in the *boot.properties* file and automatically overwrites the plaintext credentials with encrypted versions. All you're doing by creating the *boot.properties* file is avoiding the prompts for the credentials when you start a server. Note that you can only specify current passwords in the *boot.properties* file you create; you can't specify a new set of credentials by simply creating a new *boot.properties* file. The reason you can't specify a new set of values for the username and password directly in the *boot.properties* file is because those values must be identical to those of an existing account in the Authentication provider for your default security realm. Furthermore, the user must have a role that enables the user to start a server.

You can always specify a non-default *boot.properties* file by providing the location for the file in the *weblogic.Server* start command. Add the following to the start command to point to a location that you wish to specify:

```
-DWeblogic.system.BootIdentityFile=<filename>
```

If you are using the *startWebLogic* script to start the servers, add the following *JAVA_OPTIONS* attribute to the script, to point to an alternative location for the *boot.properties* file:

```
JAVA_OPTIONS=-Dweblogic.system.BootIdentityFile=C:\temp\boot.properties
```

What happens if you use a *boot.properties* file but, for some reason, the server can't access it, say because it was accidentally deleted? The server still starts, but it now prompts you for the username and password. Because the *boot.properties* file allows you to log in without producing the administrative credentials, in a production system, there's a risk of someone being able to start the servers without the appropriate credentials. To prevent this, you can make the *boot.properties* file disappear after you start the server by adding the following to either the *weblogic.Server* start command or the *startWebLogic.cmd* script (as the value for the *JAVA_OPTIONS* attribute):

```
-Dweblogic.system.RemoveBootIdentity=true
```

Logging in Through a New Administrator Account

Suppose you forgot your user credentials and enter incorrect credentials when trying to start the Admin Server, in this case, through a WLST *startserver* command. Here's the error message that follows:

```
wls:/offline>
startServer('AdminServer','wl_server','t3://localhost:7001','weblogic','welcome2')
Starting weblogic server ...
WLST-WLS-1371305204890: <Oct 15, 2013 9:06:49 AM CDT> <Notice> <Security> <BEA-
090082> <Security initializing using security realm myrealm.>
WLST-WLS-1371305204890: <Jun 15, 2013 9:06:49 AM CDT> <Critical> <Security> <BEA-
090402> <Authentication denied: Boot identity not valid; The user name and/or
password from the boot identity file (boot.properties) is not valid. The boot
identity may have been changed since the boot identity file was created. Please
edit and update the boot identity file with the proper values of username and
password. The first time the updated boot identity file is used to start the
server, these new values are encrypted.>
WLST-WLS-1371305204890: <Oct 15, 2013 9:06:49 AM CDT> <Critical> <WebLogicServer>
 <BEA-000386> <Server subsystem failed. Reason:
weblogic.security.SecurityInitializationException: Authentication denied: Boot
identity not valid; The user name and/or password from the boot identity file
(boot.properties) is not valid.
```

You have lost the administrator password, and now you can't access the system. Not to worry! You can still log in to the WebLogic Server by creating a new administrator account. The following steps describe how to add a new WebLogic username and password in the Administrators group:

1. Shut down the WebLogic Server instance, if it's running:

   ```
   stopWebLogic.cmd/* in UNIX, stopWebLogic.sh
   ```

2. Set the environment:

   ```
   setDomainEnv.cmd            /* in UNIX, setDomainEnv.sh
   ```

3. Because it's a critical file, back up the *DefaultAuthenticatorInit.ldift* file under the \ security directory. For example:

   ```
   C:\Oracle\Middleware\oracle_home\user_projects\domains\wl_server\security
   ```

4. Change to the \security directory. For example:

   ```
   cd C:\Oracle\Middleware\wlserver_12.1\samples\domains\wl_server\security
   ```

5. Run the following command:

```
java weblogic.security.utils.AdminAccount newAdmin newPassword .
```

For example:

```
java weblogic.security.utils.AdminAccount weblogic2 welcome2 .
```

Note that the period (.) at the end of the command is *not* a typo—you need it. The command will re-create the *DefaultAuthenticatorInit.ldif* file.

6. Change to the following directory (or equivalent), where the LDAP files are located:

```
C:\Oracle\Middleware\oracle_home\user_projects\domains\wl_server\servers\
examplesServer\data\ldap
```

7. Remove the following file:

```
del DefaultAuthenticatormyrealmInit.initialized
```

The server will automatically re-create this file when you reboot the Admin Server.

8. Start the Admin Server and provide the new user credentials:

```
cd C:\Oracle\Middleware\oracle_home\user_projects\domains\wl_server
startWebLogic.cmd
```

Once the console login window appears, log in with your new credentials. Once you log in, you'll notice that there are two administrative users in the wl_server domain now—*weblogic* and the new *weblogic2* user. If you've lost the password for the weblogic user, you can change it at this point.

Changing the Weblogic User Password Through the Console

You can change the password of any user, including the user *weblogic,* from the Administration Console. Here's an example that shows how to change the password for the user named *weblogic,* which is the name for the default administrator for a domain.

1. In the left-hand pane of the Administration Console, click Security Realms.
2. In the right-hand pane, on the Summary Of Security Realms page, click the realm Myrealm, which is the default realm for a server.
3. Click Users And Groups, and then select the user *weblogic*.Click Passwords.
4. Enter a new password and confirm it.
5. Click Save.

Before you can log into the Administration Console or perform any command-line administrative tasks with the new password, you must do one more thing—edit the *boot.properties* file, as shown earlier, and enter the username (**weblogic**) and the new password. As mentioned earlier, WebLogic Server encrypts those credentials for you when you start the server the next time. You're now ready to use the new password for the administrative user *weblogic*.

Managed Servers use the same password as that of the domain's Admin Server. If you change the Admin Server password through the Administration Console, that password is automatically transmitted to all the Managed Servers in the domain.

Using the Node Manager to Manage Servers

Before discussing how to start and stop WebLogic Server instances, let's review the critical role the Node Manager plays in administering instances, as well as how to configure the Node Manager and check its logs. The Node Manager helps you remotely control WebLogic Server instances. If you connect to the Node Manager through WLST, you can start, stop, and monitor the Admin Server. It's important to understand that, unlike the Admin Server, the Node Manager is not associated with any domain. Because most production WebLogic environments are spread over multiple machines and servers, the Node Manager utility helps you remotely manage the servers. If high availability is a requirement, it is strongly recommended that you use the Node Manager because starting servers with the Node Manager is a prerequisite for certain high availability operations such as a whole server migration. You install the Node Manager service on each machine where you have a WebLogic Server instance running. A Node Manager service running on a machine can manage servers belonging to multiple domains; therefore, you need to install just one Node Manager service on each machine that runs a WebLogic Server instance.

You can use a Java-based or a script-based Node Manager on a UNIX or Linux system. On a Windows system, Oracle supports just the Java-based Node Manager. Although the Java-based Node Manager provides better security than the script-based version, in terms of operational features, there's no difference between the two types of Node Managers. The advantage in using the script-based Node Manager is that it can help you remotely manage the server if you've configured your network to use SSH.

Node Manager Capabilities

You can invoke the Node Manager, which is a Java-based stand-alone tool, explicitly from the command line as well as implicitly through the Administration Console. As you recall, you must install the Node Manager (installed automatically when you install WebLogic Server) on each machine that runs the Admin and Managed Servers. On the server where the Admin Server runs, you can connect to the Node Manager through WLST, which acts offline as an interface to the command-line Node Manager.

You can use WLST offline commands to start and stop the Admin Server after first connecting to the Node Manager. In the WLST online mode, you can start Managed Servers and stop server instances that you had started with the Node Manager. When you use WLST with the Node Manager, WLST acts as a Node Manager client. The Node Manager can act both as a client of the Admin Server as well as a service that controls the Admin Server. Here's a description of the key Node Manager capabilities:

- The Node Manager can control the Admin Server because it can start, stop, and monitor the Admin Server through the WLST interface.
- The Admin Server acts as a client of the Node Manager when you start or stop Managed Servers from the Administration Console. To start or stop a Managed Server from the Administration Console, you access the Node Manager indirectly through the Admin Server.
- The Node Manager makes remote administration of the Managed Servers through the Administration Console possible. Once you start a Managed Server with the Node Manager, you can stop it from the Administration Console. If the Node Manager service is down, you can't shut down or restart a Managed Server from the Administration Console.
- You can start and stop the Managed Servers with the Node Manager, even when the Admin Server is down for some reason. This default behavior is explained later in this chapter in the section "Managed Server Independence (MSI) Mode."

- The Node Manager monitors the health of the servers and kills any servers that report a health state of "failed." It also automatically restarts a failed server instance by default.
- The Node Manager can migrate whole servers in a WebLogic cluster, as explained in Chapter 7.
- If you configure service migrations (see Chapter 7), the Node Manager runs a pre-migration script on the new machine that hosts the server before the service migration begins and runs the necessary post-migration script from the current location of the service.

You can use a single Node Manager process on each of a domain's machines that host one or more Managed Servers. This is called a *per-host* configuration of the Node Manager. The default Node Manager in Oracle WebLogic Server 12*c* is called a *per-domain* model. When you use the Node Manager to start a server, it creates a separate process for that server instance that is identical to the one created when you execute the *startManagedWebLogic.cmd* script manually. Because the Node Manager doesn't control the Admin Server itself, you won't need the Node Manager to run on any machine hosting an Admin Server unless you also have one or more Managed Servers running on that machine. Remember, a Node Manager isn't associated with a specific domain—you can have just a single Node Manager on a machine work with multiple Managed Servers belonging to different domains.

When you use the *per host* Node Manager, how does the Node Manager know which domains to manage? All the domain information is specified in the *nodemanager.domains* file, which is located in the Node Manager home directory for a WebLogic Server installation: WL_HOME\common\nodemanager. When you start a Node Manager service, you can view the following in the boot sequence:

```
INFO: Loading domains file:
C:\Oracle\MIDDLE~1\WLSERV~1.1\common\NODEMA~1\nodemanager.domains
<Oct 15, 2013 9:12:32 AM> <INFO> <Loading identity key store:
FileName=C:\Oracle\MIDDLE~1\ORACLE~1WLSERV~1.1\server\lib\DemoIdentity.jks,
 Type=jks, PassPhraseUsed=true>
Oct  15, 2013 9:12:32 AM weblogic.nodemanager.server.SSLConfig loadKeyStoreConfig
```

The informational message "Loading domains file" shows the boot process reading the domain information from the *nodemanager.domains* file, which contains entries that specify the domain directory for each domain the Node Manager controls.

TIP

It's a best practice to move the Node Manager configuration file out of the installation directory in a production environment. Although WebLogic Server creates the user_projects directory under the installation directory, you must move that elsewhere as well, as writing changes to installation directories is never a good idea.

Remember that when you start the Managed Servers through the Administration Console (recommended), Node Manager automatically restarts those servers when they crash. If you shut down the Managed Servers yourself through the Administration Console or WLST, the Node Manager considers this normal and doesn't attempt to launch the Managed Servers.

Default Node Manager Configuration in WebLogic Server 12c

In Oracle WebLogic Server 12*c*, Oracle is using, for the first time a per-domain model for Node Manager. A per-domain model means that, by default, when you create a domain, there's a domain-specific version of Node Manager exclusively for that domain.

When you create a domain, WebLogic Server uses the security credentials you supply for the server (Admin server) to create the *nm_password_properties* file. This file is created in the directory ORACLE_HOME\user_projects\domains\domain_name directory. In addition, the Configuration Wizard also creates the *nodemanager.domains* file for you under the same nodemanager directory. Domain-specific scripts to start and stop the Node Manager, as well as scripts to install Node Manager as a Web Service, are located in the ORACLE_HOME\user_projects\domains\domain_name (DOMAIN_HOME) directory.

NOTE
The default Node Manager configuration as described here doesn't allow you to edit the DOMAIN_HOME\nodemanager contents, which is the NodeManagerHome *location.*

When you create a domain using the Configuration Wizard or through WLST offline commands, you have to choose between a *PerDomain* or a *CustomLocation* for the Java-based Node Manager. The *PerDomain* configuration is really the same as the default configuration, with the difference that it lets you choose unique Node Manager credentials. The *CustomLocation* option–based Node Manager also runs on a per-domain basis, but you can select a unique location for the *NodeManagerHome* variable.

What all this means is that, unlike prior releases of Oracle WebLogic Server, by default, you must use a domain-specific Node Manager. The old configuration model of a per-host Node Manager is still available, and all the usual scripts are still in the WL_HOME\server\bin directory (in my case, this directory is C:\Oracle\Middleware\Oracle_Home\wl_server\server\bin directory). You can't just decide that you want to use a per-host Node Manager, however, without some additional work on your part! To access the Node Manager functionality as in the earlier releases and continue to use the Node Manager service on a per-host basis, you must explicitly configure it by following these steps:

1. Create a *nodemanager.domains* file listing all the domains you want this Node Manager to control and place it in the ORACLE_HOME\oracle_common\common\nodemanager directory. Alternatively, you can use WLST's *nmEnroll* command to register all the domains with Node Manager.
2. You can use the demo Identity and Trust keystores for development and testing purposes, but you need to create them with the *CertGen* and the *ImportPrivateKey* utilities, as shown here:
   a. Set up the environment:

   ```
   $ WLS_HOME\server\bin\setWLSEnv.cmd
   ```

   b. Generate a certificate and a private key:

   ```
   java utils.CertGen -keyfilepass DemoIdentityPassPhrase -certfile democert
   -keyfile demokeyYou can use the fully qualified DN host name by adding the
   -cn option to
   the previous command:
   ```

```
java utils.CertGen -keyfilepass DemoIdentityPassPhrase -certfile democert -keyfile
demokey -cn abc.oracle.com
```

c. Import the private key and the certificate generated in the previous step:

```
java utils.ImportPrivateKey -keystore DemoIdentity.jks -storepass
DemoIdentityKeyStorePassPhrase -keyfile demokey -keyfilepass
DemoIdentityPassPhrase -certfile democert.pem -keyfile demokey. pem -alias
 demoidentity
```

d. Finally, you must copy the *DemoIdentity.jks* keystore to the NodeManagerHome security directory.

Starting the Node Manager

The following examples show you how to start the Java-based Node Manager in a Windows environment. You can start this type of Node Manager with the *weblogic.NodeManager* executable, as shown here, after first setting the environment:

```
$ cd  C:\Oracle\Middleware\oracle_home\wlserverserver\bin
$ C:\Oracle\Middleware\Oracle_Home\wlserver\server\bin>setWLSEnv.cmd
…
Your environment has been set.
C:\Oracle\Middleware\Oracle_Home\wlserver\server\bin>java weblogic.NodeManager
C:\Oracle\Middleware\Oracle_Home\wlserver\server\bin>
C:\Oracle\Middleware\Oracle_Home\user_projects\domains\wl_server\bin>startNodeMana
ger.cmd
NODEMGR_HOME is already set to
C:\Oracle\MIDDLE~1\ORACLE~1\USER_P~1\domains\WL_SER~1\NODEMA~1
C:\Oracle\Middleware\Oracle_Home\user_projects\domains\wl_server\bin>set
 CLASSPATH=.;
C:\PROGRA~1\Java\JDK17~1.0_4\lib\tools.jar;
C:\Oracle\MIDDLE~1\ORACLE~1\wlserver\server\lib\weblogic_sp.jar;
C:\Oracle\MIDDLE~1\ORACLE~1\wlserver\server\lib\weblogic.jar;
C:\Oracle\MIDDLE~1\ORACLE~1\wlserver\server\lib\webservices.jar;
C:\Oracle\MIDDLE~1\ORACLE~1\oracle_common\modules\org.apache.ant_1.7.1/lib/ant-
all.jar;
C:\Oracle\MIDDLE~1\ORACLE~1\oracle_common\modules\net.sf.antcontrib_1.1.0.0_1-
0b2/lib/ant-contrib.jar;
C:\Oracle\MIDDLE~1\ORACLE~1\wlserver\modules\features\oracle.wls.common.nodemanage
r_1.0.0.0.jar;
C:\Oracle\Middleware\Oracle_Home\user_projects\domains\wl_server\bin>if not "" ==
"" set CLASSPATH=;.;
C:\PROGRA~1\Java\JDK17~1.0_4\lib\tools.jar;C:\Oracle\MIDDLE~1\ORACLE~1\wlserver\se
rver\lib\weblogic_sp.jar;
C:\Oracle\MIDDLE~1\ORACLE~1\wlserver\server\lib\weblogic.jar;
C:\Oracle\MIDDLE~1\ORACLE~1\wlserver\server\lib\webservices.jar;
C:\Oracle\MIDDLE~1\ORACLE~1\oracle_common\modules\org.apache.ant_1.7.1/lib/ant-
all.jar;
C:\Oracle\MIDDLE~1\ORACLE~1\oracle_common\modules\net.sf.antcontrib_1.1.0.0_1-
0b2/lib/ant-contrib.jar;
C:\Oracle\MIDDLE~1\ORACLE~1\wlserver\modules\features\oracle.wls.common.nodemanage
r_1.0.0.0.jar;
```

```
C:\Oracle\Middleware\Oracle_Home\user_projects\domains\wl_server\bin>if not "" ==
"" set CLASSPATH=.;
C:\PROGRA~1\Java\JDK17~1.0_4\lib\tools.jar;
C:\Oracle\MIDDLE~1\ORACLE~1\wlserver\server\lib\weblogic_sp.jar;
C:\Oracle\MIDDLE~1\ORACLE~1\wlserver\server\lib\weblogic.jar;
C:\Oracle\MIDDLE~1\ORACLE~1\wlserver\server\lib\webservices.jar;
C:\Oracle\MIDDLE~1\ORACLE~1\oracle_common\modules\org.apache.ant_1.7.1/lib/ant-
all.jar;
C:\Oracle\MIDDLE~1\ORACLE~1\oracle_common\modules\net.sf.antcontrib_1.1.0.0_1-
0b2/lib/ant-contrib.jar;
C:\Oracle\MIDDLE~1\ORACLE~1\wlserver\modules\features\oracle.wls.common.nodemanage
r_1.0.0.0.jar;;
C:\Oracle\Middleware\Oracle_Home\user_projects\domains\wl_server\bin>cd
C:\Oracle\MIDDLE~1\ORACLE~1\USER_P~1\domains\WL_SER~1\NODEMA~1
C:\Oracle\MIDDLE~1\ORACLE~1\USER_P~1\domains\WL_SER~1\NODEMA~1>if not "" == "" if
not "" == "" goto runNMWithListenAddressAndPort
C:\Oracle\MIDDLE~1\ORACLE~1\USER_P~1\domains\WL_SER~1\NODEMA~1>if not "" == ""
goto runNMWithListenAddress
C:\Oracle\MIDDLE~1\ORACLE~1\USER_P~1\domains\WL_SER~1\NODEMA~1>if not "" == ""
goto runNMWithListenPort
C:\Oracle\MIDDLE~1\ORACLE~1\USER_P~1\domains\WL_SER~1\NODEMA~1>"C:\PROGRA~1\Java\J
DK17~1.0_4\bin\java.exe" -client -Xms32m -Xmx200m -XX:MaxPermSize=128m -
XX:+UseSpinning -Dcoherence.home=C:\Oracle\MIDDLE~1\ORACLE~1\coherence -
Dbea.home=C:\Oracle\MIDDLE~1\ORACLE~1 -
Dweblogic.RootDirectory=C:\Oracle\MIDDLE~1\ORACLE~1\USER_P~1\domains\WL_SER~1 -
Xverify:none -
Djava.endorsed.dirs=C:\PROGRA~1\Java\JDK17~1.0_4\jre\lib\endorsed;C:\Oracle\MIDDLE
~1\ORACLE~1\oracle_common\modules\endorsed "-
Djava.security.policy=C:\Oracle\MIDDLE~1\ORACLE~1\wlserver\server\lib\weblogic.pol
icy" "-Dweblogic.nodemanager.JavaHome=C:\PROGRA~1\Java\JDK17~1.0_4"
weblogic.NodeManager -v
Java HotSpot(TM) Client VM warning: ignoring option UseSpinning; support was
removed in 7.0_40
<Oct 19, 2013 5:20:32 PM CDT> <INFO> <Loading domains file:
C:\Oracle\Middleware\Oracle_Home\user_projects\domains\wl_server\nodemanager\nodem
anager.domains>
<Oct 19, 2013 5:20:33 PM CDT> <INFO> <Upgrade> <Setting NodeManager properties
version to 12.1.2>
<Oct 19, 2013 5:20:33 PM CDT> <INFO> <Upgrade> <Saving upgraded NodeManager
properties to
'C:\Oracle\Middleware\Oracle_Home\user_projects\domains\wl_server\nodemanager\node
manager.properties'>
<Oct 19, 2013 5:20:33 PM CDT> <INFO> <Loading domains file:
C:\Oracle\Middleware\Oracle_Home\user_projects\domains\wl_server\nodemanager\
nodemanager.domains>
<Oct 19, 2013 5:20:33 PM CDT> <INFO> <Loading identity key store:
FileName=C:\Oracle\Middleware\Oracle_Home\user_projects\domains\wl_server\security
\DemoIdentity.jks, Type=jks, PassPhraseUsed=true>
<Oct 19, 2013 5:20:33 PM CDT> <INFO> <Loaded NodeManager configuration properties
from
```

```
'C:\Oracle\MIDDLE~1\ORACLE~1\USER_P~1\domains\WL_SER~1\NODEMA~1\nodemanager.proper
ties'>
Node manager v12.1.2

Configuration settings:
NodeManagerHome=C:\Oracle\Middleware\Oracle_Home\user_projects\domains\wl_server\n
odemanager
ListenAddress=localhost
ListenPort=5556
ListenBacklog=50
SecureListener=true
AuthenticationEnabled=true
NativeVersionEnabled=true
CrashRecoveryEnabled=false
JavaHome=C:\PROGRA~1\Java\JDK17~1.0_4
StartScriptEnabled=true
StopScriptEnabled=false
StartScriptName=startWebLogic.cmd
StopScriptName=
CoherenceStartScriptEnabled=false
CoherenceStartScriptName=null
LogFile=C:\Oracle\Middleware\Oracle_Home\user_projects\domains\wl_server\nodem
anager\nodemanager.log
LogLevel=INFO
LogLimit=0
LogCount=1
LogAppend=true
LogToStderr=true
LogFormatter=weblogic.nodemanager.server.LogFormatter
DomainsFile=C:\Oracle\Middleware\Oracle_Home\user_projects\domains\wl_server\nodem
anager\nodemanager.domains
DomainsFileEnabled=true
StateCheckInterval=500
UseMACBroadcast=false
DomainRegistrationEnabled=false
DomainsDirRemoteSharingEnabled=false
RotatedFileCount=7
FileSizeKB=500
NumberOfFilesLimited=false
RotationTimeStart=00:00
RotationType=bySize
FileTimeSpan=24
FileTimeSpanFactor=3600000
ProcessDestroyTimeout=20000
Domain name mappings:

wl_server -> C:\Oracle\Middleware\Oracle_Home\user_projects\domains\wl_server
<Oct 19, 2013 5:20:33 PM CDT> <INFO> <WebLogic Server 12.1.2.0.0 Fri Jun 7
15:16:15 PDT 2013 1530982 WLS_12.1.2.0.0_GENERIC_130607.1100>
<Oct 19, 2013 5:20:33 PM CDT> <INFO> <Secure socket listener started on port 5556,
host localhost/127.0.0.1>
```

The Java *weblogic.NodeManager* command accepts optional arguments. You can override existing properties by specifying the arguments with the *-D* option, as shown in this example:

```
java %JAVA_OPTIONS% -D[server_property=value] -D[nodemanager_property=value]
weblogic.NodeManager
```

Standard Java arguments, such as memory settings, can be passed in the command line. Valid *server_property* arguments include *bea_home*, which points to the Oracle WebLogic Server home, and *java.security.policy*, which is the path to the security policy file for a machine. Every other property is a *nodemanager_property*, which can be passed on the command line, as shown in the following example that sets the listen address and listen port:

```
java -Xms=256m -Xmx=512m
-Djava.security.policy="C:\Oracle\MIDDLE~1\ORACLE_HOMEWLSERV\server\lib\
weblogic.policy"
-Dbea_home="C:\MyOra\MIDDLE~1\WLSERV~1.3" -DListenAddress="localhost"
-DListenPort="5556" weblogic.NodeManager
```

Any Node Manager property you configured in the *nodemanager.properties* configuration file doesn't need to be specified as a command-prompt argument, as those settings will take effect by default.

NOTE
The Node Manager not only starts the Managed Servers under normal conditions, but also starts it under unexpected conditions when the servers fail. You can configure it to start failed servers automatically.

Instead of using the *weblogic.NodeManager* executable directly on the command line, you can simplify matters by using a script that sets the required environment variables before executing the *weblogic.NodeManager* command. WebLogic Server provides the *startNodeManager.cmd* script (the *startNodeManager.sh* script in UNIX) for you. You'll find this script in the WL_HOME\server\bin directory. Here's how you invoke *startNodeManager.cmd* to start the Node Manager from the command line:

```
C:\Oracle\Middleware\Oracle_Home\wlserver\server\bin> startNodeManager.cmd
...
INFO: Loading domains file:
C:\Oracle\MIDDLE~1\WLSERV~1\common\NODEMA~1\nodemanager.domains
...
Configuration settings:

NodeManagerHome=C:\Oracle\MIDDLE~1\Oracle~1\WLSERV~1\common\NODEMA~1
ListenAddress=
ListenPort=5556
ListenBacklog=50
SecureListener=true
AuthenticationEnabled=true
NativeVersionEnabled=true
CrashRecoveryEnabled=false
JavaHome=C:\Oracle\MIDDLE~1\JDK160~1\jre
```

```
StartScriptEnabled=true
StopScriptEnabled=false
StartScriptName=startWebLogic.cmd
StopScriptName=
LogFile=C:\Oracle\MIDDLE~1\Oracle~1\WLSERV~1\common\NODEMA~1\nodemanager.log
LogLevel=INFO
LogLimit=0
LogCount=1
LogAppend=true
LogToStderr=true
LogFormatter=weblogic.nodemanager.server.LogFormatter
DomainsFile=C:\Oracle\MIDDLE~1\Oracle~1\WLSERV~1.1\common\NODEMA~1\nodemanager.dom
ains
DomainsFileEnabled=true
StateCheckInterval=500
UseMACBroadcast=false
DomainRegistrationEnabled=false
DomainsDirRemoteSharingEnabled=false
Domain name mappings:
wl_server -> C:\oracle\middleware\oracle_home\wlserver_12.1\common\bin
my_domain -> C:\oracle\middleware\oracle_home\user_projects\domains\my_domain
medrec-spring -> C:\oracle\middleware\wlserver\samples\domains\medrec-spring
medrec -> C:\Oracle\Middleware\wlserver_12.1\samples\domains\medrec
<Jun 15, 2013 9:12:33 AM> <INFO> <Secure socket listener started on port 5556>
Jun 15, 2013 9:12:33 AM weblogic.nodemanager.server.SSLListener run
INFO: Secure socket listener started on port 5556
```

Oracle recommends that you configure a nondefault port number and listen address for production environments. The other Node Manager environment variables that you can set at the command line or in the start file are *WL_HOME*, *PATH*, *CLASSPATH*, and *JAVA_HOME*.

TIP
You can also launch the Node Manager from WLST if you're automating server management.

By default, the Node Manager start script launches the service in the WL_HOME\common\nodemanager directory, which serves as the working directory for Node Manager. Log files for the Node Manager service are stored in this directory. You can change the default location of this directory by setting the value of the NODEMGR_HOME variable in the Node Manager start script.

Stopping the Node Manager

The simplest way to shut down the Node Manager is to just close the command shell in which it runs. Here's what you'll see if you press CTRL-C in a running Node Manager window:

```
INFO: Secure socket listener started on port 5556
Terminate batch job (Y/N)? y
C:\Oracle\Middleware\wlserver_12.1\server\bin>
```

You can also invoke the WLST *stopNodeManager* command in online or offline mode. The command stops a running Node Manager process. This method won't work with the scripted version of Node Manager, however. Here's an example that shows how to use the *stopNodeManager* command in WLST:

```
C:\Oracle\Middleware\Oracle_Home\wlserver\common\bin>wlst.cmd
CLASSPATH=C:\Oracle\MIDDLE~1\patch_wls1211\profiles\default\sys_manifest_classpath
\weblogic_patch.jar;
C:\Oracle\MIDDLE~1\patch_ocp371\profiles\default\sys_manifest_classpath\weblogic_p
atch.jar;
C:\Oracle\MIDDLE~1\JROCKI~1.0-1\lib\tools.jar;
C:\Oracle\MIDDLE~1\WLSERV~1.1\server\lib\weblogic_sp.jar;
C:\Oracle\MIDDLE~1\WLSERV~1.1\server\lib\weblogic.jar;
C:\Oracle\MIDDLE~1\modules\features\weblogic.server.modules_12.1.1.0.jar;
C:\Oracle\MIDDLE~1\WLSERV~1.1\server\lib\webservices.jar;
C:\Oracle\MIDDLE~1\modules\ORGAPA~1.1/lib/ant-all.jar;
C:\Oracle\MIDDLE~1\modules\NETSFA~1.0_1/lib/ant-contrib.jar;;
C:\Oracle\MIDDLE~1\utils\config\10.3\config-launch.jar;
C:\Oracle\MIDDLE~1\WLSERV~1.1\common\derby\lib\derbynet.jar;
C:\Oracle\MIDDLE~1\WLSERV~1.1\common\derby\lib\derbyclient.jar;
C:\Oracle\MIDDLE~1\WLSERV~1.1\common\derby\lib\derbytools.jar;;
Initializing WebLogic Scripting Tool (WLST) ...
Welcome to WebLogic Server Administration Scripting Shell
Type help() for help on available commands
wls:/offline>
wls:/offline>
nmConnect('weblogic','welcome1','localhost','5556','wl_server','C:\Oracle\Middlewa
re\Oracle_Home\samples\domains\wl_server','ssl')
Connecting to Node Manager ...
<Jun 4, 2013 10:08:53 AM CDT> <Info> <Security> <BEA-090905> <Disabling CryptoJJCE
Provider self-integrity check for better startup performance. To enable this
check, specify -Dweblogic.security.allowCryptoJDefaultJCEVerification=true>
<Jun 4, 2013 10:08:53 AM CDT> <Info> <Security> <BEA-090906> <Changing the default
Random Number Generator in RSA CryptoJ from ECDRBG to FIPS186PRNG. To disable this
change, specify -Dweblogic.security.allowCryptoJDefaultPRNG=true>
Successfully Connected to Node Manager.
wls:/nm/wl_server>
wls:/offline> stopNodeManager()
Stopped Node Manager Process successfully
wls:/offline> NMProcess: Stopped draining NMProcess
NMProcess: Stopped draining NMProcess
wls:/offline>
```

For the previous *stopNodeManager* command to work, however, you must have started Node Manager originally with the *startNodeManager* command. If you try to shut down the Node Manager with the *stopNodeManager* command when you haven't started the Node Manager with the *startNodeManager* command, you'll get the following error:

```
wls:/nm/wl_server> stopNodeManager()
Traceback (innermost last):
  File "<console>", line 1, in ?
  File "<iostream>", line 340, in stopNodeManager
```

```
Use dumpStack() to view the full stacktrace
        at weblogic.management.scripting.ExceptionHandler.handleException
(ExceptionHandler.java:59)        at
weblogic.management.scripting.WLSTUtils.throwWLSTException(WLSTUtils.
java:181)        at
weblogic.management.scripting.NodeManagerService.nmQuit(
NodeManagerService.java:504)
        at sun.reflect.NativeMethodAccessorImpl.invoke0(Native Method)
        at
sun.reflect.NativeMethodAccessorImpl.invoke(NativeMethodAccessorImpljava:39)
        at
sun.reflect.DelegatingMethodAccessorImpl.invoke(DelegatingMethodAccessorImpl.java:
25)
        at java.lang.reflect.Method.invoke(Method.java:597)

weblogic.management.scripting.ScriptException:
weblogic.management.scripting.ScriptException: Error occurred while performing
startNodeManager : Problem stopping the Node Manager. : Disabled command: QUIT
Use dumpStack() to view the full stacktrace
wls:/nm/wl_server>
```

However, you can successfully stop the Node Manager process, even if you haven't started the Node Manager with the *startNodeManager* command, provided you've specified the property *QuitEnabled=true* when starting the Node Manager. You can specify the *QuitEnabled* property in the *nodemanager.properties* file. Once you do this, you can start the Node Manager as a Windows service and stop the service remotely via WLST.

Monitoring the Node Manager Logs

You can view the Node Manager logs directly by examining the log files or using the Administration Console.

The nodemanager.log File

The Node Manager log file is under the Node Manager home directory (WL_HOME\common\nodemanager) and is named *nodemanager.log*. Because you need only a single Node Manager per machine, this log file contains logs for all the domains managed by the Node Manager on that machine. Note that the script-based Node Manager doesn't have an analogous log file. You can also view the Node Manager logs for a server by using the WLST *nmServerLog* command. The command to view the Node Manager logs after connecting to it in WLST is as follows:

```
wls:/wl_server/serverConfig> nmConnect('weblogic', 'welcome1', 'localhost','5556
','wl_server','C:\Oracle\Middleware\Oracle_Home\user_projects\domains\wl_server','
ssl')
Connecting to Node Manager ...
...
Successfully Connected to Node Manager.
wls:/wl_server/serverConfig> nmLog()
<Oct 15, 2013 9:12:31 AM> <INFO> <Loading domains file:
C:\Oracle\MIDDLE~1\WLSERV~1.1\common\NODEMA~1\nodemanager.domains>
```

```
<Oct 15, 2013 9:12:32 AM> <INFO> <Loading identity key store:
FileName=C:\Oracle\MIDDLE~1\WLSERV~1.1\server\lib\DemoIdentity.jks, Type=jks,
PassPhraseUsed=true>
...
wls:/wl_server/serverConfig>
```

Note that this command won't work with the scripted version of Node Manager.

Checking the Node Manager Logs from the Administration Console

You can access the Node Manager log files from the Administration Console by navigating to Home | Machines | *(your machine name)* | Monitoring | Node Manager Log. This allows you to view the console output for the Node Manager instance configured for each of the machines in the domain.

Running the Node Manager as a Windows Service

You may want to create the Node Manager as a Windows service so it can restart the Managed Servers when they crash. Oracle recommends that you create this service. Here are the steps for configuring the Node Manager as a Windows service if you didn't do so during the installation process:

1. Configure the Node Manager properties file (*nodemanager.properties*).

   Edit the *nodemanager.properties* file in the WL_HOME/common/nodemanager directory by setting the following two properties:

   - *CrashRecoveryEnabled=true*
   - *StartScriptEnabled=true*

2. Execute the following Windows command file:

   ```
   C:\Oracle\Middleware\wlserver_12.1\server\bin>installNodeMgrSvc.cmd
   ...
   Oracle Enterprise Pack for Eclipse NodeManager (C_Oracle_Middleware_wlserver_12.1)
   installed.

   C:\Oracle\Middleware\Oracle_Home\wlserver\server\bin>ENDLOCAL
   C:\Oracle\Middleware\Oracle_Home\wlserver\server\bin>
   ```

When you execute this file, Windows creates a new service called "Oracle Enterprise Pack for Eclipse NodeManager (C_Oracle_Middleware_wlserver_12.1)" In your case, the name of this service might be different, based on which installation type you chose for WebLogic Server. By default, Node Manager uses the Windows Local System Account to log in. To enable a different account to start the Node Manager service, double-click the new Windows service you just created and click the Log On button. Here, you can provide the credentials for running the Node Manager service, as shown in Figure 2-2.

Once you create the Node Manager as a Windows service, you can test the service by invoking the Windows Task Manager and killing the Java processes associated with a Managed Server. (This is a simulation of a Managed Server failure.) You'll notice that those Java processes reappear right away, showing that the Node Manager is indeed restarting them following their failure. This only works if three conditions are met. The *CrashRecoveryEnabled* parameter is set (see the next section); the Managed Server (or Admin Server) was started by the Node Manager; and the following JVM properties for the Managed Server are set: *-Xrs* for the Oracle HotSpot VM. or -Xnohup for Oracle JRockit JVM (see the next section).

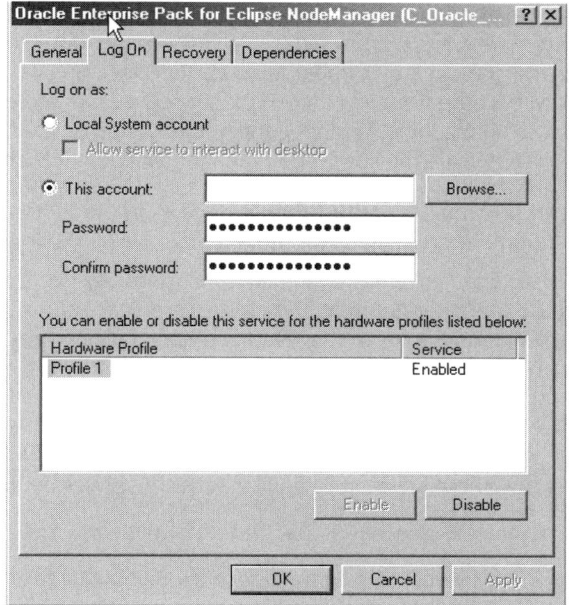

FIGURE 2-2. *Providing credentials for the Node Manager service*

Oracle recommends that you create a Node Manager Windows service on a Windows system or run it as an operating system service in UNIX. When you want to configure the Node Manager to receive requests from a remote system, you must first uninstall the default Node Manager service by executing the *uninstallNodeMgrSvc.cmd* script (in the same directory as the *installNodeMgrSvc.cmd* script) and specify the listen address and listen port settings.

NOTE
In previous releases of WebLogic Server, the default value for the startScriptEnabled *parameter was* false, *but it has been changed in the 12*c *release to* true.

On a UNIX server, you can use start and stop scripts to start Managed Servers or to perform tasks such as unmounting a remote disk at shutdown time, for example. The start and stop scripts should be placed in the DOMAIN_HOME\bin\service_migration directory. To use a start script to specify any special startup actions, change the *StartScriptEnabled* property to *true* in the *nodemanager.properties* file. You can also specify your own start script name by setting the *StartScriptName* property in the same file.

Configuring the Node Manager

Although this section reviews the configuration of only the Java-based Node Manager, most of the discussion applies to the script-based version of the Node Manager as well. You can customize the Node Manager by editing the *nodemanager.properties* file, which is the configuration file for the

Node Manager. You can also set the configuration properties on the command line when you invoke the Node Manager. You'll find the *nodemanager.properties* file in the WL_HOME/common/nodemanager directory, which is considered the Node Manager home directory. Note that the Node Manager is outside any domain and is under the common directory, which is directly underneath the WL_HOME directory, because a single Node Manager service can serve multiple domains that have servers running on a given machine. You'll see the *nodemanager.properties* file only after starting Node Manager the first time. Here are the key Node Manager configuration attributes you must be aware of:

- ***AuthenticationEnabled*** If the value is set to *true,* Node Manager checks the credentials against the domain credentials (in the example here, weblogic/welcome1).
- ***CrashRecoveryEnabled*** You can enable this property (set it to the value *true*) to ensure that the Node Manager automatically restarts servers after a crash. For the Node Manager to restart the Admin Server or the Managed Server following a crash, you must have started the Admin Server with the Node Manager and the Managed Servers with the Admin Server (either through the Administration Console or through the WLST interface). By default, crash recovery is disabled. If you're using the script-based Node Manager instead of the Java-based Node Manager discussed here, you can specify the following line in the Node Manager script to configure automatic restarts of servers by the Node Manager:

  ```
  wlscontrol.sh -d domain_name CRASHRECOVERY
  ```

- ***QuitEnabled*** If you set this parameter to *true,* you can stop the Node Manager remotely.
- ***DomainFileEnabled*** If you set the name of the *nodemanager.domains* file with the *DomainsFile* property, Node Manager uses that file to read the names as well as the domain directories of the domains it must support. If you set the *DomainFileEnabled* property to *true,* the Node Manager reads the file you specified with the *DomainsFile* parameter. By default, the Node Manager assumes the domain of the current directory or that of the WL_HOME directory.

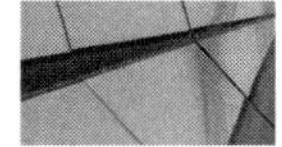

NOTE
The Configuration Wizard automatically creates the nodemanager.domains *file when you create a domain with it, but you can also manually add a domain to the file. For each domain, there's an entry in the file, in the format* domain-name=domain-directory.

- ***StartScriptName*** This specifies the name of the script that starts a server, such as *startWebLogic.sh* or *startWebLogic.cmd*.
- ***StartScriptEnabled*** This specifies whether the provided start script will be started after the reboot of the physical server.
- ***LogFile* and *LogLevel*** This specifies the location of the log file and the server logging severity levels.
- ***ListenPort*** By default, the Node Manager uses port 5556, but you can change it to any port you wish.

By default, Oracle-configured Node Manager startup scripts and install scripts set all the necessary variables for Node Manager and they set it up to listen on the default address, localhost. You can edit the *nodemanager.properties* file to have the Node Manager start listening on a different address. You do this by setting the *LISTEN_ADDRESS* variable to the host you want and the *LISTEN_PORT* variable to the port you want.

Alternatively, you can request that Node Manager start listening on a nondefault server and or port by passing the server and port values when you start the Node Manager service with the *startNodeManager* script, as shown here:

```
$ startNodeManager.cmd my_server 7777
```

You can specify the Node Manager properties on the command line or in the *nodemanager.properties* file. The values you specify on the command line will override those you specify in the *nodemanager.properties* file. By default, this file is created in the directory specified in *NodeManagerHome*, where *NodeManagerHome* usually is designated as *ORACLE_HOME\user_projects\domains\domain_name\nodemanager*. If you haven't defined *NodeManagerHome*, the *nodemanager.properties* file is created in the current directory. Each time Node Manager starts, it looks for the *nodemanager.properties* in the current directory and creates the file if it's not present in that directory, and you won't be able to access this file until Node Manager has started at least once.

You can view the current properties of the Node Manager running on any server by opening the *nodemanager.properties* file, as shown here:

```
#Sat Oct 19 15:26:15 CDT 2013
DomainsFile=C\:\\Oracle\\MIDDLE~1\Oracle~1\WLSERV~1\\common\\NODEMA~1\\nodemanager
.domains
LogLimit=0
PropertiesVersion=10.3
DomainsDirRemoteSharingEnabled=false
javaHome=C\:\\Oracle\\MIDDLE~1\\JOracle~1\\ROCKI~1.0-1
AuthenticationEnabled=true
NodeManagerHome=C\:\\Oracle\\MIDDLE~1\\ORACLE~1\\WLSERV~1\\\common\\NODEMA~1
JavaHome=C\:\\Oracle\\MIDDLE~1\\JROCKI~1.0-1\\jre
LogLevel=INFO
DomainsFileEnabled=true
StartScriptName=startWebLogic.cmd
ListenAddress=
NativeVersionEnabled=true
ListenPort=5556
LogToStderr=true
SecureListener=true
LogCount=1
DomainRegistrationEnabled=false
StopScriptEnabled=false
QuitEnabled=false
LogAppend=true
StateCheckInterval=500
CrashRecoveryEnabled=false
StartScriptEnabled=true
LogFile=C\:\\Oracle\\MIDDLE~1\\ORACLE~1\\WLSERV~1\\common\\NODEMA~1\\nodemanager.l
og
LogFormatter=weblogic.nodemanager.server.LogFormatter
ListenBacklog=50
```

You must configure the following JVM properties for all Managed Servers in a domain that are under a Node Manager's control if you've automated the Node Manager startup by configuring it as a Windows service:

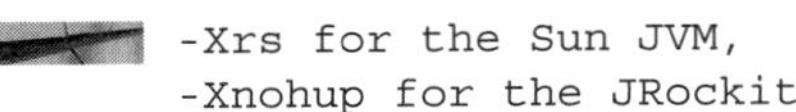

```
-Xrs for the Sun JVM,
-Xnohup for the JRockit
```

Now let's recap all the steps needed to allow the Node Manager to restart a failed Managed Server automatically:

1. In the *nodemanager.properties* file, ensure the *CrashRecoveryEnabled* property is set to *true* as follows:

   ```
   CrashRecoveryEnabled=true
   ```

   For example, the *nodemanager.properties* file is in the following location in my installation:

   ```
   C:\Oracle\Middleware\Oracle_Home\wlserver\common\nodemanager\
   nodemanager.properties
   ```

2. For the Managed Server that you want to configure to restart automatically, add the *-Xrs* (for Java Hotspot VM or *-Xnohup* (for Oracle JRockit JVM) arguments to your startup script. For example, edit the following startup script for the Examples Server:

   ```
   C:\Oracle\Middleware\Oracle_Home\wlserver\samples\domains\wl_server\bin\
   startManagedWebLogic.cmd
   ```

   Add the *-Xrs (or -Xnohup)* argument at the end of *JAVA_OPTIONS* as follows:

   ```
   set JAVA_OPTIONS=-Dweblogic.security.SSL.trustedCAKeyStore="
   C:\Oracle\Middleware\Oracle_Home\wlserver\
   server\lib\cacerts" %JAVA_OPTIONS% -Xrs
   ```

3. Start the Managed Server using the Node Manager, or start it from the Administration Console. For example, the following commands start the Examples Server, which is technically an Admin Server, from the Node Manager:

   ```
   C:\Oracle\Middleware\Oracle_Home\wlserver\common\bin>wlst
   wls:/offline> nmConnect('weblogic', 'welcome1', 'localhost', '5556',
   'wl_server', '
   C:\Oracle\Middleware\Oracle_Home\user_projects\domains\wl_server','ssl')
   Connecting to Node Manager ...
   Successfully Connected to Node Manager.
   wls:/nm/wl_server>wls:/nm/wl_server> nmStart('examplesServer')
   Starting server examplesServer ...
   ```

4. In the Windows Task Manager, locate the *java.exe* process with the largest memory, and manually kill it.

At this point, the process will automatically restart immediately and the Managed Server will fully start shortly thereafter.

The Node Manager Domains File

If you've configured a per-host Node Manager instead of the per-domain Node Manager, when the Configuration Wizard creates various domains on a server, it records that domain information (the domain name and directory) in the *nodemanager.domains* file, located under the WL_HOME\common\nodemanager directory. Here are the contents of the *nodemanager.domains* file in my installation, where I have the three sample domains and a domain I've created (test_domain):

```
#Domains and directories created by Configuration Wizard
#Sat Oct 19 10:58:18 CDT 2013
wl_server=C:\Oracle\Middleware\Oracle_Home\user_projects\\domains\\wl_server
medrec-
spring=C\:\\Oracle\\Middleware\\Oracle_Home\\user_projects\\domains\\medrec-spring
medrec=C\:\\Oracle\\Middleware\\Oracle_Home\\user_projects\\domains\\medrec
```

When Node Manager starts, it reads the *nodemanager.domains* file to get the domain name and domain directory for all domains on that host.

You can also see the domains by reviewing the last part of the output printed to the terminal when you start Node Manager:

```
Domain name mappings:

wl_server -> C:\Oracle\Middleware\user_projects\domains\wl_server
medrec-spring -> C:\Oracle\Middleware\user_projects\domains\medrec-spring
medrec -> C:\Oracle\Middleware\user_projects\samples\domains\medrec

<Oct 19, 2013 11:19:46 AM> <INFO> <Secure socket listener started on port 5556>
Oct 19, 2013 11:19:46 AM weblogic.nodemanager.server.SSLListener run
INFO: Secure socket listener started on port 5556
```

Configuring Node Manager Using WLST Offline

You can use WLST offline commands to configure the following Node Manager configuration tasks.

- Set the Node Manager username and password
- Set Node Manager properties
- Set the Node Manager type

The following examples show how to use WLST to configure these Node Manager properties:

```
# set the Node Manager listen address and listen port.
cd('/')
cd('NMProperties')
set('ListenAddress','localhost')
set('ListenPort',7001)
# Set the Node Manager username and password.
cd('/')
cd('SecurityConfiguration/domain_name')
```

```
set('NodeManagerUsername','username')
set('NodeManagerPasswordEncrypted','password')

# Set the Node Manager type to custom location type and set the custom location
Node Manager home.
setOption('NodeManagerType','CustomLocationNodeManager')
setOption('NodeManagerHome','C:/mydomains/nodemanager')
```

Key WLST Node Manager Commands

The Node Manager helps you remotely control WebLogic Server instances. WLST Node Manager commands help you access the Node Manager features. Following are examples that explain, from a day-to-day operational standpoint, how to use the most important WLST Node Manager commands.

Connect to Node Manager

Assuming the Node Manager is already running (for example, started from the Windows service), you need to connect to the Node Manager using the *nmConnect* command before you run any of the Node Manager WLST commands. Note that you must specify a domain name (*wl_server* in this example) when you connect to the Node Manager.

```
C:\Oracle\Middleware\Oracle_home\wlserver\common\bin>wlst.cmd
...
Initializing WebLogic Scripting Tool (WLST) ...
Welcome to WebLogic Server Administration Scripting Shell
Type help() for help on available commands
wls:/offline>
wls:/offline> nmConnect('weblogic', 'welcome1', 'localhost', '5556', 'wl_server',
'C:\Oracle\Middleware\Oracle_Home\wlserver\samples\domains\wl_server','ssl')
Connecting to Node Manager ...
Successfully Connected to Node Manager.
wls:/nm/wl_server>
```

In a production environment, you must first execute the *nmEntroll* command to enroll the machine on which the Node Manager is running before executing the *nmConnect* command to connect to the Node Manager. By executing the *nmEnroll* command, you ensure that the Node Manager credentials are available to the Managed Servers that the Node Manager manages. You run the *nmEnroll* command only once on each machine in a WebLogic domain.

NOTE
The nm_password. properties *file contains the Node Manager credentials that WebLogic Server uses to authenticate the connections between the Node Manager and a client such as the Admin Server.*

Check Node Manager Version

You can find the Node Manager version with the *nmVersion* command:

```
wls:/nm/wl_server> nmVersion()
The Node Manager version that you are currently connected to is 10.3.
wls:/nm/wl_server>
```

Check Node Manager Connection Status

Invoke the *nm* command to find out if WLST is currently connected to the Node Manager:

```
wls:/nm/wl_server> nm()
Currently connected to Node Manager to monitor the domain wl_server.
```

Start a Server

Execute the *nmStart* command to start a server in the current WebLogic domain with Node Manager. Here's an example:

```
wls:/nm/wl_server> nmStart()
Starting server wl_server ...
Successfully started server wl_server ...
```

In this example, the *nmStart* command was issued without any arguments. You can, however, specify the *serverName* argument to indicate the name of the server you want to start. For example, to start the Managed Server *MyManagedServer1,* issue the command in the following way:

```
nmStart('MyManagedServer1')
```

You can start the Admin Server and the Managed Servers with the *nmStart* command. Make sure the *boot.properties* file exists before you issue this command. You also have the option of specifying the user credentials with the *nmStartprops* argument after first connecting to the Node Manager. Here's an example:

```
prps = makePropertiesObject("username=weblogic, password=welcome1")
nmStart("medrecServer", props=prps)
```

Enroll a Machine

Use the *nmEnroll* command to enroll the machine on which WLST is running after first connecting to the Admin Server. WLST doesn't need to connect to Node Manager to run this command. The *nmEnroll* command lets the Node Manager running on a machine manage servers in a specific domain. Here's an example:

```
wls:/nm/wl_server> nmStart()
Starting server myserver ...
Error Starting server myserver: weblogic.nodemanager.NMException:
Exception while starting server 'myserver'
wls:/nm/wl_server> connect()
Please enter your username :weblogic
Please enter your password :
Please enter your server URL [t3://localhost:7001] :
Connecting to t3://localhost:7001 with userid weblogic ...
Successfully connected to Admin Server 'examplesServer' that belongs to
domain 'wl_server'.
Warning: An insecure protocol was used to connect to the server. To ensure
on-the-wire security, the SSL port or Admin port should be used instead.
wls:/wl_server/serverConfig> nmEnroll()
Enrolling this machine with the domain directory at . ...
```

```
Successfully enrolled this machine with the domain directory at
C:\Oracle\Middleware\Oracle_Home\wlserver\common\bin\..
wls:/wl_server/serverConfig>
```

You run this command the first time you use the Node Manager—once for every domain. This command updates the *nodemanager.domains* file and also downloads the *nodemanager .properties* file from the Admin Server.

Disconnect from the Node Manager

Execute the *nmDisconnect* command to disconnect WLST from the Node Manager session:

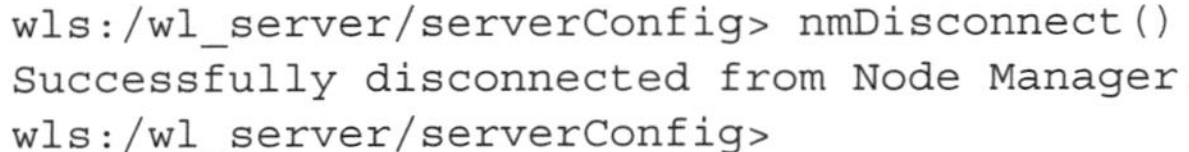

```
wls:/wl_server/serverConfig> nmDisconnect()
Successfully disconnected from Node Manager.
wls:/wl_server/serverConfig>
```

Lifecycle of WebLogic Server Instances

When you start a WebLogic Server instance, the instance transitions through several distinct "states." In most cases, you issue just the simple *start* command, which brings the instance to a RUNNING state, where it is ready to accept requests. However, it is possible to bring the server instance to a state that's not quite in the RUNNING mode.

So you can clearly understand the various states a server instance can transition through or remain in, I've broken the various states into two different groups and discuss them in the next two sections.

The STARTING, STANDBY, and RUNNING States

When it's not running, a WebLogic Server instance is in the SHUTDOWN state. Note that the various server lifecycle states described here could be transitional or permanent states, based on the type of startup or shutdown commands you issue. Following a *startup* command, the server instance transitions from the SHUTDOWN state through the following states or stages of the server lifecycle:

- **STARTING** When you issue any type of *startup* command (there are three different startup commands, as you'll see in the next section), the server instance transitions from the SHUTDOWN to the STANDBY state. During the STARTING state, the instance reads the domain configuration data from its config directory. The Managed Servers, however, get their configuration data from the Admin Server. In this state, the instance starts the basic services such as the kernel and execute queues, the container service for logging, and the Node Manager service (not the same as the Node Manager but a service that the Admin Server uses to talk to the Node Manager). The server also deploys applications during this phase.
- **STANDBY** In the STANDBY state, the server instance allows you to issue just two administrative requests: you can move the server state to either the RUNNING or SHUTDOWN state. Normally, the server instance automatically transitions through the STANDBY state to the next state, unless you explicitly start the instance in the standby mode. When you intentionally start it in the STANDBY mode, the instance stays in the STANDBY state until you move it into the RUNNING state. You have this option so you can keep a ready standby server instance on hand to meet your high availability requirements. Note that all ports are closed in this state, but you can quickly transition to a RUNNING state from here, so this state could be used to keep a server in a hot STANDBY mode.

- **ADMIN** The ADMIN state permits only administrative tasks such as deploying applications, with those applications being able to process requests only from users with the *Admin* and *AppTester* roles. Obviously, you can use this capability following deployment of an application to test your application one last time, as explained in Chapter 8. Note that while you can launch the Administration Console at this point, only requests from clients with the *Admin* role are entertained. Running a server in the ADMIN state is also useful when trying to diagnose problems with a troublesome application. You can move the server to the ADMIN state when things go awry and then connect to it with JMX (or even a debugger) to see what may have caused the problem.
- **RESUMING** This is a purely transitional state that the server instance goes through after it transitions automatically through the ADMIN state or you issue the *resume* command after first placing the instance in the STANDBY or ADMIN state. You can change this state from the command line or through the Administration Console.
- **RUNNING** This, of course, is the final state that the server instance reaches, after you issue either a *startup* command or the *resume* command to move the server out of the ADMIN or STANDBY state. In the RUNNING state, the server can accept and service client requests for its services.

Startup Options

You can start a WebLogic Server instance in different modes so the server will reach a different end state after the startup command. Here are your options:

- **Normal start mode** When you issue the normal startup command (*startserver* or *nmStart*, both of which are explained in this chapter), the server instance will transition through the following stages, which you can observe in your command window:

  ```
  SHUTDOWN > STARTING > STANDBY > ADMIN > RESUMING > RUNNING
  ```

  Here are the informational messages following the startup of a server, showing how the server is transitioning through the various startup transitional stages:

  ```
  ************************************************
  starting weblogic with Java version:
  java version "1.6.0_29"
  Java(TM) SE Runtime Environment (build 1.6.0_29-b11)
  Oracle JRockit(R) (build R28.2.0-79-146777-1.6.0_29-20111005-1808-windows-ia32,
  compiled mode)
  Starting WLS with line:
  C:\Oracle\MIDDLE~1\ORACLE~1\JROCKI~1.0-1\bin\java -jrockit
    -Xms512m -Xmx512m -Dweblogic
  ...
  <Oct 15, 2013 11:19:14 AM CDT> <Notice> <WebLogicServer> <BEA-000365>
  <Server state changed to STARTING.>
  <Oct 15, 2013 11:19:14 AM CDT> <Info> <WorkManager> <BEA-002900>
   <Initializing slf-tuning thread pool.>
  <Oct 15, 2013 11:19:29 AM CDT> <Notice> <WebLogicServer> <BEA-000365>
   <Server state changed to STANDBY.>
  <Oct 15, 2013 11:19:29 AM CDT> <Notice> <WebLogicServer> <BEA-000365>
   <Server state changed to STARTING.>
  ```

```
<Oct 15, 2013 11:20:29 AM CDT> <Notice> <WebLogicServer> <BEA-000365>
 <Server state changed to ADMIN.>
<Oct 15, 2013 11:20:29 AM CDT> <Notice> <WebLogicServer> <BEA-000365> <Server
state changed to RESUMING.>
<Oct 15, 2013 11:20:30 AM CDT> <Notice> <WebLogicServer> <BEA-000331>
<Started the WebLogic Server Administration Server "examplesServer"
for domain "wl_server" running in development mode.>
<Oct 15, 2013 11:20:30 AM CDT> <Notice> <WebLogicServer> <BEA-000365>
<Server state changed to RUNNING.>
<Oct 15, 2013 11:20:30 AM CDT> <Notice> <WebLogicServer> <BEA-000360>
<The server started in RUNNING mode.>
```

NOTE
By default, when you issue a startup command, the server starts in RUNNING mode. You can specify a different state for the startup command by setting the ServerMBean.StartupMode *attribute through the java weblogic.Server startup command, by using a WLST command or by configuring it in the Administration Console.*

- **STANDBY mode** You can also start a server in STANDBY mode, wherein the server will pass through the following states:

  ```
  SHUTDOWN > STARTING > STANDBY
  ```

  You can move to the RUNNING state directly with the startup command, or you can get there from an ADMIN or STANDBY state by issuing the *resume* command. Similarly, you can move to the SUSPENDING (or FORCE_SUSPENDING) state from the RUNNING state by issuing a *suspend* (or *force suspend*) command.
- **Start in ADMIN mode** You can start an instance in the ADMIN mode to transition the instance from the SHUTDOWN to the ADMIN state. The instance goes through the following states:

  ```
  SHUTDOWN > STARTING > STANDBY > ADMIN
  ```

- **Resume the instance** You can issue the *resume* command from either the STANDBY or the ADMIN state. The server processes through the following states:

  ```
  STANDBY > ADMIN > RESUMING > RUNNING
  ```

The SHUTDOWN, SUSPENDING, and FAILED States

Just as you use the startup and *resume* commands to place the server in the final RUNNING state, you can use a set of commands to shut down or suspend the server. In addition, the server could also end up in the FAILED state. Here's a brief description of these server states:

- **SHUTDOWN** You can issue either the *shutdown* or the *force shutdown* commands to shut down a server. The server stops accepting any type of requests at this point. The graceful *shutdown* command stops the server from accepting new requests and ensures that it completes processing all outstanding requests. In a clustered environment, the command will cause the load balancer to redirect requests to the server to other server instances. This leads to the secondary server taking over and finding a new backup server. This is quite different from server behavior when you use the *force shutdown* command to shut down an unresponsive server. The Node Manager in this case may just issue a kill directive, and requests are *not* redirected to a different server.

- **SUSPENDING** When you issue a *shutdown* command, the server moves through the SUSPENDING state after first gracefully suspending several subsystems and services and then completing all in-flight work. You can also force the server to *remain* in a suspended mode by issuing the *suspend* command. The FORCE_SUSPENDING state is similar to the SUSPENDING state—the only difference is that the server abandons in-flight work. The server reaches the FORCE_SUSPENDING transitional state when you issue a *force suspend* or a *force shutdown* command.
- **FAILED** Obviously the FAILED state is not something you want to see because it means there's a problem, such as inadequate memory or stuck JVM threads, that has caused the server to go into the FAILED state. In this state, the server can't, of course, entertain any requests from clients or administrators. Here's what you'll see in your command window, following a failure:

```
<Oct 15, 2013 11:49:04 AM CDT> <Notice> <WebLogicServer> <BEA-000365> <Server
 state changed to FAILED.>
<Oct 15, 2013 11:49:04 AM CDT> <Error> <WebLogicServer> <BEA-000383> <A critical
 service failed. The server will shut itself down.>
<Oct 15, 2013 11:49:04 AM CDT> <Notice> <WebLogicServer> <BEA-000365> <Server
state changed to FORCE_SHUTTING_DOWN.>
```

Self-Health Monitoring

WebLogic Server offers built-in server health monitoring to enhance the availability of a domain's servers. Subsystems of a server instance, such as the JMS services, for example, monitor their own health status, in this case by monitoring the JMS thread pool. Other subsystems monitor both the WebLogic Server's internal thresholds as well as any user-defined thresholds and statistics, such as, for example, the execute thread statistics. When the monitoring system of a server subsystem such as JMS concludes that it's not running in a reliable fashion, it designates the server's status as "failed." The server instance continuously monitors the state of all registered subsystems, and when a critical subsystem shows a FAILED state, the server instance changes its own run status to FAILED, indicating that it can't handle critical requests from the applications it hosts.

If you configure the Node Manager on all the machines in your environment, the Node Manager will try to reboot failed servers automatically, thus enhancing the uptime of your domain components without your intervention.

How the Server Deals with the FAILED State

How a server instance deals with a FAILED state depends on when exactly the server enters the FAILED state. Following a failure condition, the server could end up in either the SHUTDOWN or the ADMIN state. If it reaches the FAILED state before it enters the ADMIN state, the server will shut itself down (SHUTDOWN state). If you have enabled the administration port, the server will return to the ADMIN state if it fails after successfully transitioning through the ADMIN state. Note that you can configure the server such that it always shuts down, even after passing the ADMIN state, instead of reverting to the ADMIN state following a failure condition.

Shutdown Command Options

As with the startup options, you have several options available to shut down a server instance, as described here:

- **Normal shutdown** When you issue the *stopWebLogic.cmd* or *stopWebLogic.sh* command, the instance will gracefully handle all in-flight work and shut itself down by passing through the following phases:

  ```
  RUNNING > SUSPENDING > ADMIN > SHUTTING_DOWN > SHUTDOWN
  ```

- **Suspend** You issue the *suspend* command to move a server instance from the RUNNING to the ADMIN state. All in-flight work is handled properly, and the server passes through the following phases:

  ```
  RUNNING > SUSPENDING > ADMIN
  ```

- **Force suspend** This command will achieve the same result as the *suspend* command, but in-flight work will be abandoned.

NOTE
When you start the Admin Server, one of the first things it does is to start the Node Manager service—this service doesn't actually start the Node Manager; it reports all changes in the Admin Server run state to the Node Manager.

Controlling Graceful Shutdown

When you issue either a normal shutdown or a *suspend* command, the server gracefully handles the sessions it's processing work from. By default, the HTTP sessions can stay alive for one hour before the sessions time out. You can configure the duration of the shutdown process by setting the following attributes of the ServerMBean:

- ***Ignore sessions during shutdown*** Following your *shutdown* or *suspend* command, all HTTP sessions are immediately dropped by the instance if you enable this attribute.
- ***Graceful shutdown timeout*** You can specify a duration within which the server will gracefully shut down, failing which it will perform a forced shutdown.

You can configure both of these attributes through the Administration Console from the Server Name | Control | Start/Stop page.

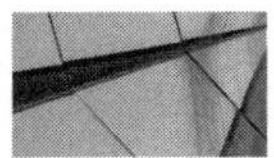

NOTE
WebLogic Server uses a lock file to prevent you from starting the server if it's already running. Thus, you'll see the following error when you try to start an already-running server:

```
weblogic.management.ManagementException: Unable to obtain lock on C:\Oracle
\Middleware\Oracle_Home\user_projects\domains\wl_server\servers\examplesServer\
vtmp\examplesServer.lok. Server may already be running
```

In this case, your attempt to start the server results in the server shutting itself down in the FAILED state. This doesn't impact the server that is already running, however.

Starting and Stopping WebLogic Server

You can start and stop the Admin and Managed Servers in many different ways. You can use

- A startup and shutdown script
- A Java command from the command line
- Ant *wl_server* tasks
- The Administration Console
- WLST by itself
- WLST in combination with the Node Manager

Regardless of the method you choose to start a WebLogic Server instance, you're essentially initializing a JVM within which the Admin Server or the Managed Server will run. Oracle recommends that you employ the WLST and the Node Manager together to manage both the Admin and Managed Servers. On a day-to-day basis, you'll use the Administration Console in most cases, which makes your life easy. In the following sections, I describe the various start/stop methods in detail. Before I review the various ways to stop and start servers, let's review server messages and logs.

Server Messages

When a server instance starts and when it shuts down, it puts out various types of messages. In fact, these messages are ongoing throughout a server's lifetime. Many of these messages are purely informational, in which case they are denoted by the word *<Notice>*. Certain messages are intended as cautions, and they include the word *<Warning>* as part of the message. Both types of notices also state the relevant area they are dealing with, such as Server, Log Management, or Security. Here are some examples, showing both types of messages sent by the server instance:

```
<Oct 15, 2013 10:55:57 AM CDT> <Notice> <LoggingService> <BEA-320401>
<The log file has been rotated to
C:\Oracle\Middleware\wlserver_12.1\samples\domains\wl_server\servers\
examplesServer\logs\access.log00002. Log messages will continue to be logged in
C:\Oracle\Middleware\Oracle_Home\user_projects\domains\wl_server\servers\
examplesServer\logs\access.log.>

<Oct 15, 2013 10:56:22 AM CDT> <Notice> <WebLogicServer> <BEA-000331>
<Started the WebLogic Server Administration Server "examplesServer"
 for domain "wl_server" running in development mode.>

<Oct 15, 2013 10:56:08 AM CDT> <Warning> <Munger> <BEA-2156203> <A version
attribute was not found in element "web-app" in the deployment descriptor
C:\Oracle\Middleware\Oracle_Home\samples\server\examples\build\mainWebApp/WEB-
INF/web.xml. A version attribute is required, but this version of the WebLogic
Server will assume that the latest version is used. Future versions of WebLogic
Server will reject descriptors that do not specify the Java EE version. To
eliminate this warning, add an appropriate "version=" to element "web-app"
in the deployment descriptor.>
```

Obviously, you must pay close attention to all the warning messages, although you can generally safely ignore most of them.

Server Logs

On a Windows server, the server lifecycle messages are shown in the command window that pops up automatically when you start a server from the Windows Programs button or with a startup command. Of course, you must keep this command window running because killing the window will also kill the server instance itself. You can view the entire log file of the server instance in the WL_HOME\domains\<*domain_name*>\servers\log directory. In the case of the sample AdminServer instance in the wl_server domain on my server, the log files are located in the C:\Oracle\Middleware\Oracle_Home\user_projects\domains\wl_server\servers\AdminServer\logs directory.

WebLogic Server retains older log files by appending a numbered suffix such as 00005 at the end of the filename. Note that you have separate log files for both the domain and the server. In addition, subsystems such as JDBC and JMS have their own separate log files. There are two log files, one named after the domain itself and the other named after the server. Once you restart a server, the current "live" log file is the one with the highest number at the end, for example, MedRecServer.log00009. The current log file is the log the server writes to after it rolls over the previous log file once it exceeds the maximum size set for it. Chapters 3 and 6 contain detailed explanations of log formats and other aspects of log management.

Using a Startup Script to Start and Stop Servers

You can use startup scripts to start either the Admin or the Managed Servers. In the examples in this book, during installation, WebLogic Server places scripts to start and stop the Admin and the Managed Servers under each sample domain it creates. You can use these scripts to manage the server startup and shutdown out of the box when administering the sample domains used in this book.

Starting the Admin Server with a Startup Script

For any of the sample domains, use the Oracle-provided *startWebLogic.cmd* script to start the Admin Server for that domain. The startup scripts for both the Admin and the Managed Servers are located in the domain directory. Here's an example that shows how to start the Admin Server for the sample wl_server domain.

```
C:\Oracle\Middleware\wlserver_12.1\samples\domains\medrec>\startWebLogic.cmd
```

TIP

Instead of using commands, you can configure the Admin Server to start whenever the server launches. Note that I said the Admin Server specifically, *because you can't start the Managed Server in this manner. This method might work in many cases, however, because you really don't need a separate Managed Server in a developmental environment—you can deploy your applications directly through the Admin Server in such an environment.*

In a UNIX system, you use a shell script instead, such as *startWebLogic.sh* to start your servers. The *startWebLogic.cmd* (and the *startWebLogic.sh*) startup script invokes the *setDomainEnv.cmd* first to set the environment, and then it invokes another *startWebLogic.cmd* script under the ~\bin subdirectory, which subsequently executes the *java weblogic.Server* command to actually start the server. The *java weblogic.Server* command launches a JVM that will run the WebLogic Server instance.

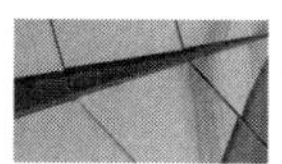

NOTE
You can also create your own custom script for starting an Admin Server.

On a Windows server, you can also start the Admin Server by going to the Start menu and clicking the Start Admin Server button located under the domain name (Start | WebLogic Server | User_projects | *domain_name* | Start Admin Server). Doing this also executes the same *weblogic .Server* command that's run by the *startWebLogic.cmd* script. When you create a domain through the Configuration Wizard (explained in Chapter 3), the Wizard adds the command to start the Admin Server to the Start menu.

Starting the Managed Server with a Script

You can start the Managed Servers in your environment by invoking an Oracle-provided script that is automatically created when you use the Configuration Wizard to create a Managed Server. The script name is *startManagedWebLogic,* and the script doesn't need the Node Manager. The script invokes the *java weblogic.Server* class through a Java command.

NOTE
If you use the Configuration Wizard to create a domain, it ensures that all the files you need for starting the server are already present.

Although not required, before you start a single Managed Server or a cluster, it is recommended that you first start the Admin Server. Use the *startManagedWebLogic.cmd* script in a domain's bin directory to start a Managed Server. For a UNIX system, you use the *startManagedWebLogic.sh* script instead. Note that on a UNIX server, you must also provide values for the *SERVER_NAME* environment variable and, optionally, the *ADMIN_URL* environment variable, as shown here:

```
$ startManagedWebLogic.sh SERVER_NAME {ADMIN_URL}
```

Here's an example:

```
$ startManagedWebLogic.sh MyManagedServer1 http://myhost:7001
```

Note that if you have multiple Managed Servers that are not part of a cluster, you must execute the *startManagerWebLogic.cmd* script multiple times, passing the name of a different Managed Server each time. In the following example, I start the Managed Server ManagedServer1 using the *startManagedWebLogic.cmd* script:

```
C:\Oracle\Middleware\Oracle_Home\user_projects\domains\test_domain\bin>startManage
dWebLogic.cmd ManagedServer1.JAVA Memory arguments: -Xms256m -Xmx512m -
XX:CompileThreshold=8000 -XX:PermSize=128m -XX:MaxPermSize=256m
WLS Start Mode=Development
CLASSPATH=C:\Oracle\MIDDLE~1\patch_wls1211\profiles\default\sys_manifest_classpath
<Oct 17, 2013 12:53:41 PM CDT> <Notice> <WebLogicServer> <BEA-000365> <Server
state changed to RUNNING.>
```

```
<Oct 17, 2013 12:53:41 PM CDT> <Notice> <WebLogicServer> <BEA-000360> <The
server started in RUNNING mode.>
```

As with the Admin Server, once you see the "Server started in RUNNING mode" message, it means the Managed Server has completed its boot sequence and is waiting to process requests. The following message in the Windows command line shows where to find the log file that contains information about the events that occur during the server's lifecycle:

```
<Oct 17, 2013 12:52:57 PM CDT> <Notice> <Log Management> <BEA-170019>
<The server log file
C:\Oracle\Middleware\user_projects\domains\test_domain\servers\ManagedServer1
\logs\ManagedServer1.log is opened. All server side log events will be
written to this file.>
```

Using Scripts to Shut Down Servers

WebLogic Server also provides the *stopWebLogic.cmd* and *stopWebLogic.sh* scripts to help you shut down the Admin and Managed Servers. These scripts are located in the same directory as the startup scripts. The *stopWebLogic.cmd* script, for example, shuts down the Admin Server and, as the following line in the script shows, calls the WLST script *shutdown.py*:

```
%JAVA_HOME%\bin\java -classpath %FMWCONFIG_CLASSPATH% %MEM_ARGS% %JVM_D64%
%JAVA_OPTIONS% weblogic.WLST shutdown.py
```

When invoking WLST through a script, do so with the *wlst.cmd* (*wlst.sh* in UNIX) script file. This way, the necessary environment variables for WLST are automatically set. You'll find the *wlst.cmd* and the *wlst.sh* scripts in the WL_HOME\common\bin directory. Note that when you stop the Admin Server through the *stopWebLogic.cmd* script, the command invokes WLST:

```
Stopping Weblogic Server...
Initializing WebLogic Scripting Tool (WLST) ...
Welcome to WebLogic Server Administration Scripting Shell
Type help() for help on available commands
Connecting to t3://MIROPC61:7001 with userid weblogic ...
```

When you stop a server through the Windows Programs facility, behind the scenes, WebLogic Server utilizes WLST to stop the server, as shown in the following output when you click the Stop Examples Server button:

```
Stopping Weblogic Server...
Initializing WebLogic Scripting Tool (WLST) ...
Welcome to WebLogic Server Administration Scripting Shell
Type help() for help on available commands
Connecting to t3://a6717:7001 with userid weblogic ...
Successfully connected to Admin Server 'examplesServer' that belongs to domain
'wl_server'.
Warning: An insecure protocol was used to connect to the server.
To ensure on-the-wire security, the SSL port or Admin port should be used
instead. Shutting down the server examplesServer with force=false while
 connected to examplesServer ...
Disconnected from weblogic server: examplesServer
```

```
Exiting WebLogic Scripting Tool.
Done
Stopping Derby Server...
Derby server stopped.
C:\Oracle\Middleware\Oracle_Home\user_projects\domains\wl_server>
```

You have a similar shutdown script, named *stopManagedWebLogic.cmd,* for the Managed Servers as well. Both the Admin and the Managed Servers use the same Python script named *shutdown.py.*

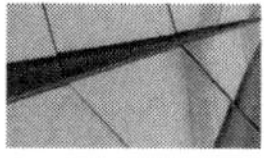

NOTE
You can embed a WLST script in Ant with the <wlst> *Ant task. This is a great solution for automating server control in testing and development environments.*

Startup and Shutdown Scripts

You can write startup and shutdown scripts to enable the server to perform additional tasks when starting or shutting down. WebLogic Server invokes the shutdown scripts when you shut down servers from the Administration Console or with the *java weblogic.Server* command.

Using the java weblogic.Server Command

If you are dealing with a development environment, you can execute the *java weblogic.Server* command directly to start the Admin Server (the *weblogic.Server* class is the main Java class for any WebLogic Server instance). You can invoke *java weblogic.Server* directly on the command line or incorporate it in a startup script. You can issue the command *java weblogic.Server -help* to learn which options you can add to the *weblogic.Server* command.

NOTE
If you choose a product directory that's different from the Oracle Middleware home directory, the java weblogic.Server *command won't work.*

Here are the steps for executing the *java weblogic.Server* command:

1. Set up your environment:

```
WL_HOME\server\bin\setWLSEnv.cmd          /* setWLSEnv.sh in UNIX
```

NOTE
For the remainder of the book, MW_HOME refers to the Middleware home of your WebLogic Server installation, such as C:\Oracle\Middleware, and WL_HOME refers to the home directory of your WebLogic Server installation, such as C:\Oracle\Middleware\wlserver_12.1.

You can also set the class path for the server by using the *-classpath* argument in your startup command. Whether you use the *setWLSEnv.cmd* or specify the class path in the startup command, Oracle strongly recommends that you include the following two jar files in your class path for the JVM:

- WL_HOME\server\lib\weblogic_sp.jar
- WL_HOME\server\lib\weblogic.jar

NOTE
You can also use the weblogic.Server *command-line option to create and configure a domain, as discussed in Chapter 3.*

2. Move to the root of the WebLogic Server domain directory:

```
WL_HOME\samples\domains\wl_server
```

3. Start the Admin Server by executing the following command:

```
$java weblogic.Server
```

4. Start a Managed Server by executing the following command. Note that you must add the option *-Dweblogic.management.server* to the *weblogic.Server* command; otherwise, the command will start the Admin Server.

```
$java -Dweblogic.Name=managed-server-name
-Dweblogic.management.server=url-for-Administration-Server weblogic.Server
```

For example, if your domain name is wl_server and the Managed Server's name is examplesManagedServer, enter the following command:

```
$java -Dweblogic.Name=examplesManagedServer
-Dweblogic.management.server=localhost:7001 weblogic.Server
```

To start a Managed Server with the *java weblogic.Server* command, you must first start the Admin Server.

The default protocol is HTTP. You can specify HTTPS, t3, or the t3s protocol as well. You must specify the Admin Server's SSL port after enabling SSL on both the Admin and Managed Servers if you plan to use the secure ports, t3s, or HTTPS.

NOTE
If you enable the administration port for the domain's Admin Server, all Managed Servers must also use SSL. You must then specify a secure protocol (HTTPS instead of HTTP) and the administration port when you start any Managed Servers, as shown here:

```
-Dweblogic.management.server=https://admin_server:administration_port
```

Chapter 3 shows how to enable the administration port.

In the previous examples, the *java weblogic.Server* command was issued from the WL_HOME\samples\domains\wl_server directory to start the Admin and the Managed Server that belong to that domain. What happens when you issue the *java weblogic.Server* command without the *-Dweblogic.Domain=<value> (WebLogic domain name)* option and the *-Dweblogic. Name=<value> (WebLogic server name)* option depends on whether there's a *config.xml* file in the *<domain_name>*\config directory, as explained in the following two sections.

The config.xml File Exists

When you execute the *java weblogic.Server* command from the domain directory (for example, WL_HOME\samples\domains\wl_server directory for the wl_server domain) without specifying the server name, WebLogic Server starts the server instance if that's the only instance defined in the *config.xml* file. If you've defined multiple instances in the *config.xml* file, the search is made in the following order:

1. If the *config.xml* file defines an Admin Server, the command looks for a server with that name.
2. If there's no Admin Server definition in the *config.xml* file, then the command looks for the configuration for a server named *myserver* and starts the *myserver* instance if it finds its configuration in the *config.xml* file.
3. If the *config.xml* file contains no reference to a server with the name *myserver*, the command gives you an error message.

TIP

Oracle recommends that you use the java weblogic.Server *command only for starting development environments and not production environments because it won't run from a directory that is outside the Middleware home directory. Also, the server run time won't recognize any patches*

The config.xml File Doesn't Exist

If the *config.xml* file doesn't exist in the directory from which you issue the *weblogic.Server* command, WebLogic Server prompts you to find out if you want it to create the file, as shown here:

```
C:\Oracle\Middleware\Oracle_Home\wlserver\server\bin>setWLSEnv
Your environment has been set.
C:\Oracle\Middleware\Oracle_Home\wlserver\server\bin>java weblogic.Server
<Oct 15, 2013 11:13:56 AM CDT> <Info> <Security> <BEA-090905> <Disabling CryptoJ
JCE Provider self-integrity check for better startup performance. To enable this
check, specify -Dweblogic.security.allowCryptoJDefaultJCEVerification=true>
<Oct 15, 2013 11:13:56 AM CDT> <Info> <Security> <BEA-090906> <Changing the
default Random Number Generator in RSA CryptoJ from ECDRBG to FIPS186PRNG. To
disable this change, specify -Dweblogic.security.allowCryptoJDefaultPRNG=true>
<Oct 15, 2013 11:13:56 AM CDT> <Info> <WebLogicServer> <BEA-000377> <Starting
WebLogic Server with Java HotSpot(TM) Client VM Version 20.4-b02 from Sun
Microsystems Inc..>
C:\Oracle\Middleware\Oracle_Home\wlserver\server\bin\config not found
No config.xml was found.
Would you like the server to create a default configuration and boot? (y/n): y
```

When you respond with a *Y*, WebLogic Server creates a new domain configuration named *mydomain*. WebLogic Server does the following when you choose to create the default configuration:

- Generates a new domain named *mydomain* and a domain directory under the directory from which you issued the *java weblogic.Server* command.
- Creates an administrative user with the username and password you supply and stores the user definition and related security data in the domain_name\security files named *DefaultAuthenticatorInit.ldift* and *DefaultRoleMapperInit.ldift,* and in the *SerializedSystemIni.dat* file.
- Stores an encrypted form of your credentials in the *boot.properties* file so you don't have to specify login credentials when the server is instantiated in the future.
- Creates the *startWebLogic.cmd* and *startWebLogic.sh* scripts to manage the startup of the Admin Server.
- Boots the Admin Server *myserver* for the new domain *mydomain* in development mode.

As the discussion here shows, if you attempt to start the Admin Server or the Managed Server from an alternate location, WebLogic Server may not be able to find the appropriate configuration file and thus prompts for the creation of the *config.xml* file. You can also see how easy it is to create a new domain just by issuing the *java weblogic.Server* command.

NOTE
You can start a lightweight WebLogic Server instance without EJBs, JCA, and JMS by changing to the DOMAIN_HOME\bin directory and running the following commands:

```
$setDomainEnv.cmd
$java weblogic.Server -DserverType="wlx"
```

Configuring Server Attributes with weblogic.Server

In the previous sections, I showed how to execute *weblogic.Server* from the command line without really providing any configuration options for the servers. In more real-world cases, however, you often need to specify some configuration options, and it's easy to do so with *weblogic.Server*. The following sections describe the key server configuration attributes you can specify with *weblogic.Server* when you start a server.

Specifying JVM Parameters

You can specify the following options to configure the server's JVM:

- ***Classpath*** If you haven't set the environment variable *CLASSPATH,* the server uses the value you set for the *classpath* option. The information you need to provide for this option is explained earlier in this chapter in the section "Using the *java weblogic.Server* Command."
- ***-Xms and -Xmx*** These options enable you to specify the minimum and maximum values for the Java heap space. To avoid adversely impacting performance due to the frequent resizing of the Java heap by the JVM, Oracle recommends using the same values for the maximum and minimum settings, for example, *-Xms1024m* and *-Xmx1024m* (set the memory values in megabytes). Setting these attributes is discussed in greater detail in Chapter 10.

Specifying Directories and Domains

You can also use the *-D* option at the command line to specify the location of various directories and the domain name. You can do this if you have multiple installations of WebLogic Server on the same machine. For example, the following option specifies the location of the WebLogic home directory:

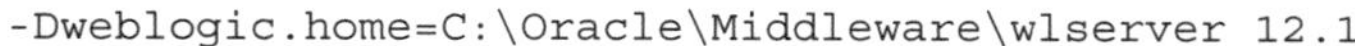

```
-Dweblogic.home=C:\Oracle\Middleware\wlserver_12.1
```

Overriding Server Configuration

When invoking the *weblogic.Server* Java class from the command line, you can use various options for temporarily overriding a server's configuration. The server uses these configuration values only once at startup time but it doesn't modify *config.xml*. You'll also see the older values in the Administration Console when you check these attributes. Thus, when you restart the server, it uses the older values stored in *config.xml*. You've already encountered one of these options, the *-Dweblogic.management.server* option, which you use when starting a Managed Server. Some of the other options you can specify at the command line are

- ***-Dweblogic.management.username=*<username>** This option lets you specify credentials that override those in the *boot.properties* file. You must ensure that the user belongs to a proper role with permissions to start servers. The *-Dweblogic.management.password* option similarly enables you to specify a password, overriding the values specified in the *boot.properties* file.
- ***-Dweblogic.home=*<WL_HOME>** This option lets you specify the WebLogic Server home.
- ***-Dweblogic.Domain=*<domain>** This option lets you specify the domain name (when creating a domain).
- ***-Dweblogic.Stdout=*<filename>** This option lets you redirect server standard output to a file.
- ***-Dweblogic.security.SSL.ignoreHostnameVerification=true*** The server will not verify hostnames when acting as an SSL client, which lets you use the demonstration digital certificates installed by Oracle. In a production environment, don't use the demo digital certificates or turn off hostname verification.
- ***-Dweblogic.management.startupMode=*<mode>** The default running mode for a server is the RUNNING state. You can specify either STANDBY or ADMIN as the value for this option.

Remember that any options you specify using the various *-Dweblogic.management* options don't affect the values in the *config.xml* file. To make your changes persist, you can manually edit the *config.xml* file. The recommended approach is to do your edits through the Administration Console or through WLST, however.

Using the Ant Tool to Manage Servers

Oracle WebLogic Server provides you with the Ant tool and a set of Ant tasks. Ant is a Java-based tool that provides features similar to the *make* command in UNIX, and it is used primarily to build Java applications. In addition, Ant offers several built-in tasks to compile, package, test, and deploy Java applications. Ant uses XML build files and lets you perform many tasks such as starting servers; building jar, war, and ear files; and deploying the applications. You can access the Ant manual at ant.apache.org/manual/index.html. Here are some of the most useful WebLogic Server Ant tasks:

- ***wl_server*** Lets you start, shut down, or connect to a WebLogic Server instance
- ***wlcompile*** Lets you invoke the *javac* complier to compile Java applications
- ***wlconfig*** Configures a WebLogic Server domain
- ***wldeploy*** Performs *wl.deployer* functions
- ***wlpackage*** Packages split development directory applications as ear files that you can deploy

WebLogic Server offers a predefined WLST Ant task in the version of Ant that ships with WebLogic. This Ant task lets you run WLST commands or scripts from within an Ant build file. You can specify WLST commands directly inside the build file by specifying the *<script>* tags. Here's a simple example that shows how to run a WLST command from an Ant script:

```
<target name="appserver.connect">
    <wlst debug="false" failOnError="true">
      <script replaceProperties="true">
        connect("${wls.username}", "${wls.password}",
        "${wls.admin.url}")
      </script>
    </wlst>
</target>
```

You can execute this task by typing **ant** at the command line in the staging directory or by typing **ant appserver.connect**. If you want to specify WLST commands within a WLST (Python) script, use the *fileName* attribute, as shown here:

```
<target name="mywlsttest">
    <wlst filename="./mytest.py"
debug="false" failOnError="true">
      </wlst>
</target>
```

In the short introduction to Ant that follows, I use the wl_server task to show how you can manage server instances.

Checking to See If Ant Is Installed

Although you can download and install Ant yourself, the WebLogic Server installer does install Ant by default. To check if Ant exists in your installation, do the following:

1. Set the environment:

```
C:\Oracle\Middleware\Oracle_Home\user_projects\domains\wl_server>setDomainEnv.cmd
Modifying classpath for the samples
...
Script has completed successfully
```

2. Type **ant** at the command line:

```
C:\Oracle\Middleware\Oracle_Home\user_projects\domains\wl_server>ant
Buildfile: build.xml does not exist!
Build failed
C:\Oracle\Middleware\Oracle_Home\wlserver\samples\domains\wl_server>
```

If you see this output, it means Ant is correctly installed and is working correctly on your system. By default, Ant looks for a file named *build.xml*—if it finds it, it runs the *build.xml* file; otherwise, it returns the "Build failed" message.

Ant Build Files

An Ant build file has one *project* and at least one *target,* where targets consist of *task* elements. A target is simply the task or tasks you want to execute, and a task is defined as the actual code you want to execute. You must specify three attributes for a project: the name of the project (*name*), the default target (*target*) to use, and the base directory from which to figure the path (*basedir*). You specify *properties* to customize the build process or to provide shortcuts for frequently used strings. You specify properties with name/value pairs.

How to Start a Server with an Ant Program

The following examples show how to build simple *build.xml* files to start a server. In the first example, I just use the wl_server target with no additional attributes to start the Admin Server for the sample *medrec* domain:

```
<project name="AntExample" >
  <target name="wlserver-default">
    <wlserver/>
  </target>
</project>
```

Save the *build.xml* file in the *medrec* domain directory (C:\Oracle\Middleware\wlserver_12.1\samples\domains\medrec). Type **ant** at the command line. (Make sure you've run *setDomainEnv.cmd* first so you don't have to point to the Ant installation.)

```
C:\Oracle\Middleware\Oracle_Home\user_projects\domains\medrec>ant
Buildfile: build.xml

BUILD SUCCESSFUL
Total time: 0 seconds
```

The "Build Successful" message means that the *build.xml* file was syntactically correct and that Ant has successfully executed the commands therein.

The following Ant *build.xml* file connects to the running server:

```
<project name=AntExample" >
  <target name=connect-server>
    <wlserver host=localhost" port="7012" username="weblogic" password="welcome1"
action="connect"/>
  </target>
</project
```

To execute this new target, simply run the following command:

```
C:\Oracle\Middleware\Oracle_Home\user_projects\domains\medrec>ant connect-server
Buildfile: build.xml
connect-server:
BUILD SUCCESSFUL
```

These simple examples offer merely a flavor of Ant tasks. You can create Ant tasks not only to connect to a server, but also to perform a wide array of tasks, including deploying your applications.

Managing Servers from the Administration Console

You can't start the Admin Server from the Administration Console because the Admin Server must be started before you can access it; however, you can shut down the Admin Server from the console. When you shut down the Admin Server from the Administration Console, you lose the connection to the console right away, as shown here on the web page that was hosting the console prior to the shutting down of the Admin Server:

```
Server Shutdown
The administration server is shutting down, and the console is no longer
available. You will have to manually start the Administration Server using the
node manager or a command line to continue administering this domain.
Once the server is restarted return to the Home page.
```

You can start and shut down the Managed Servers from the Administration Console, as explained in the following sections, but first I'll show you how to configure a Managed Server to communicate with the Node Manager. By default, the Node Manager can't communicate with the Managed Server, as it does with the Admin Server. To administer Managed Servers remotely through the Administration Console, you must, of course, first start the Node Manager service on each machine that hosts a Managed Server. Before you can use the Node Manager to control the Managed Servers, you must first configure the physical (or virtual) server hosting the Managed Server(s) as a *machine*. Second, you must assign each of the Managed Server instances to that machine. The process is not nearly as hard as it sounds, as the following sections demonstrate.

Configuring the Host as a WebLogic Server Machine

Before you can start using the Node Manager to administer Managed Servers remotely, you must first configure the physical or virtual server hosting those Managed Servers as a WebLogic Server machine. Once you do this, you must assign the Managed Servers to that machine. Why do you need to do this? Because doing so tells WebLogic Server that the Managed Servers are running on a specific physical (or virtual) server and that it should treat those servers as being under the control of the Node Manager running on that server or machine. It also allows you to associate servers and Managed Servers with a specific Node Manager service. Let's first find out how to go about configuring a host server as a WebLogic machine; the next section will show you how to assign various Managed Servers to this machine.

Use the Administration Console to configure the host server as a machine in a WebLogic Server domain. Here's how:

1. In the Change Center of the Administration Console, click Lock & Edit.
2. In the left-hand pane, expand Environment and select Machines.

3. Click New and enter a name for the machine in the Name field. You can assign any name you wish to the machine.
4. Click OK and select the new machine's name in the Machines table.
5. Select the Node Manager tab.
6. You can accept the values that are filled in for the Listen Address (IP address or DNS name) and Listen Port fields. The Node Manager uses this port to listen for incoming requests, and, by default, Oracle uses port number 5556.
7. Click Save.
8. Activate your changes by clicking Activate Changes in the Change Center.

Now that you've completed the process of configuring a specific host as a machine, let's turn to how you assign a Managed Server to this machine so the Node Manager can start and stop the Managed Server.

Assigning WebLogic Server Instances to a Machine

Once you configure the host server as a machine, you then assign the Managed Server instances to the new machine. Follow these steps.

1. Click Lock & Edit in the Administration Console's Change Center.
2. In the left-hand pane, expand Environment and select Servers. Select the name of a Managed Server you want to assign to your new machine.
3. In the right-hand pane, select Configuration | General.
4. In the Machine field, select the new machine you just created.
5. Click Save.
6. Activate your changes by clicking Activate Changes in the Change Center.

TIP

You can also associate a Managed Server with a machine when you use the Configuration Wizard to create the Managed Server. The Wizard also lets you configure a machine and set the Node Manager listen address and listen port.

You've completed the two-part process: configuring a server as a machine and assigning Managed Servers to a machine. Now you're ready to use the Node Manager to administer the Managed Server. You can do this through the Administration Console or through WLST Node Manager commands. Before you run off to administer your Managed Servers with the Node Manager and the Administration Console, let's review how to configure the Managed Servers to work with the Node Manager.

Configuring Managed Servers to Work with the Node Manager

Once you've set up your machines and assigned all your Managed Servers to those machines, you need to do one other thing: configure the Managed Servers to work with the Node Manager. First, you can configure the startup settings for Managed Servers you want the Node Manager to manage remotely. In the Administration Console, in the left-hand pane, select Environment | Servers and click the name of the Managed Server you want to configure. In the right-hand pane, click Configuration |

Server Start. Doing this takes you to the startup settings for the Managed Server. From this page, you can configure the class path, as well as several home directories, as summarized here:

- **Java Home** The path to the Java Home directory on the machine running the Node Manager.
- **Java Vendor** The Java vendor (Oracle for example) to use when starting a Managed Server.
- **BEA Home** The Oracle WebLogic home directory to use when starting this Managed Server.
- **Root Directory** By default, the Managed Servers use the domain directory as their root directory. You can specify an alternative root directory for the Managed Server here.
- **Class Path** The Java class path to use when starting this particular Managed Server.
- **Arguments** The arguments you wish to specify with the *java weblogic.Server* command, such as memory heap, garbage collection, and class path settings for the Node Manager to use in starting this Managed Server.
- **Security Policy File** The security policy file directory and filename on the server hosting the Node Manager during the startup of this Managed Server.
- **Username/Password** The username and password credentials that the Node Manager uses during server startup. By default, the Domain Wizard uses the name you provided when creating the domain, and the Administration Console uses the username you used to log into it. You can provide a different username from the Administration Console.

Configuring How Node Manager Handles Server Failures

In the Settings For *<Managed_Server_Name>* page, click the Health Monitoring tab. From here, you can configure how frequently the Node Manager checks the Managed Server's health, as well as specify whether the Node Manager automatically restarts a failed Managed Server. Additionally, you can set the frequency with which the servers themselves perform a self-health check. Here are the options you can set from this page:

- **Health Check Interval** The frequency with which the server checks its own health—if it perceives a failure, it automatically changes the server run state to FAILED.
- **Auto Kill If Failed** Lets you specify whether a Node Manager should automatically kill a server in a FAILED state.
- **Auto Restart** Enables you to configure the automatic restart of a server after a crash.
- **Restart Interval** The maximum time interval during which the Node Manager can keep trying to restart a failed server.
- **Max Restarts Within Interval** Number of times the Node Manager can try a restart operation within the duration specified by the Restart Interval attribute.
- **Restart Delay Seconds** The gap between restart attempts.

You can view the current settings for all Node Manager–related properties for a Managed Server that belongs to a domain, such as my test domain *my_domain*, by going to the MW_HOME\user\projects\domains\my_domain\servers\My_ManagedServer_1\data\nodemanager directory and viewing the *startup.properties* file for the Managed Server, as shown here (each Managed Server has one of these *startup.properties* files):

```
#Server startup properties
#Sat  Oct 19 12:56:49 CDT 2013
```

```
SSLArguments=-Dweblogic.security.SSL.ignoreHostnameVerification\=false -
Dweblogic.ReverseDNSAllowed\=false
RestartMax=2
RestartDelaySeconds=0
RestartInterval=3600
AdminURL=http\://192.168.56.1\:7001
AutoRestart=true
AutoKillIfFailed=false
```

When you make configuration changes in the Administration Console, WebLogic Server writes those changes to the *nodemanager.properties* file. You can change this file manually, but the recommended approach is to do it via the Console. When you first start a Managed Server through the Node Manager, the Node Manager creates several directories for logs and other things and stores the configuration and *boot.properties* files therein, as shown here in an excerpt from the Node Manager's log file:

```
<Oct 19, 2013 8:26:41 AM> <INFO> <Secure socket listener started on port 5556>
<Oct 19, 2013 12:39:29 PM> <INFO> <wl_server> <ManagedServer1>
<Creating directory
 "C:\Oracle\Middleware\wlserver\common\bin\servers\ManagedServer1\logs">
<Oct 19, 2013 12:39:29 PM> <INFO> <wl_server> <ManagedServer1> <Creating directory
 "C:\Oracle\Middleware\wlserver\common\bin\servers\ManagedServer1\security">
<Oct 19, 2013 12:39:29 PM> <INFO> <wl_server> <ManagedServer1> <Creating
directory
"C:\Oracle\Middleware\wlserver\common\bin\servers\ManagedServer1\data\
nodemanager">
<Oct 19, 2013 12:39:29 PM> <INFO> <wl_server> <ManagedServer1> <Creating directory
"C:\Oracle\Middleware\wlserver\common\bin\servers\ManagedServer1\tmp">
<Oct 19, 2013 12:39:29 PM> <INFO> <wl_server> <ManagedServer1> <Creating directory
"C:\Oracle\Middleware\wlserver\common\bin\servers\domain_bak">
<Oct 19, 2013 12:39:29 PM> <INFO> <wl_server> <ManagedServer1> <Creating directory
 "C:\Oracle\Middleware\wlserver\common\bin\servers\domain_bak\config_prev">
<Oct 19, 2013 12:39:29 PM> <INFO> <wl_server> <ManagedServer1> <Boot identity
properties saved to
"C:\Oracle\Middleware\wlserver\common\bin\servers\ManagedServer1\data\nodemanager\
boot.properties">
<Oct 19, 2013 12:39:29 PM> <INFO> <wl_server> <ManagedServer1> <Startup
configuration properties saved to
"C:\Oracle\Middleware\wlserver\common\bin\servers\ManagedServer1\data\nodemanager\
startup.properties">
<Oct 19, 2013 12:39:29 PM> <INFO> <wl_server> <ManagedServer1> <Server error log
also redirected to server log>
<Oct 19, 2013 12:39:29 PM> <INFO> <wl_server> <ManagedServer1> <Starting WebLogic
server with command line:
C:\Oracle\Middleware\wlserver\common\bin\bin\startWebLogic.cmd >
<Oct 19, 2013 12:39:29 PM> <INFO> <wl_server> <ManagedServer1> <Working directory
is 'C:\Oracle\Middleware\wlserver\common\bin'>
<Oct 19, 2013 12:39:29 PM> <INFO> <wl_server> <ManagedServer1> <Server output log
file is 'C:\Oracle\Middleware\wlserver\common\bin\servers\ManagedServer1\logs\
ManagedServer1.out'>My_ManagedServer_1\data\nodemanager\startup.properties">
```

Starting a Managed Server from the Console

Before you can start a Managed Server from the Administration Console, make sure that you first start the Node Manager service. If you're using a Windows server, all you have to do is to click the Node Manager button under the Start Programs menu in a Windows Server. If the Node Manager is not running, an attempt to start a Managed Server from the Administration Console will result in an error. Once you start the Node Manager, follow these steps to start a Managed Server for the Administration Console:

1. Select Servers by expanding Environment in the left-hand pane of the console.
2. Select Control in the right-hand pane.
3. Select the Managed Server you want to start in the Summary Of Servers page, as shown in Figure 2-3.
4. Click Start.

You'll see the following informational message (in green) at the top of the Summary Of Servers page: "A request has been sent to the Node Manager to start the selected servers." The Node Manager will then boot the selected Managed Server on the machine that hosts the server.

NOTE
You can stop, suspend, and resume a Managed Server from the Administration Console, provided you have already started the Node Manager service, configured a machine, and associated the Managed Server with that machine.

Summary of Servers

Configuration | **Control**

Use this page to change the state of the servers in this WebLogic Server domain. Control operations on Managed Servers require starting the Node Manager. Starting Managed Servers in Standby mode requires the domain-wide administration port.

Customize this table

Servers (Filtered - More Columns Exist)

Start | Resume | Suspend | Shutdown | Restart SSL — Showing 1 to 2 of 2 Previous | Next

	Server	Machine	State	Status of Last Action
☐	examplesServer(admin)		RUNNING	None
☑	ManagedServer1	Machine1	SHUTDOWN	None

Start | Resume | Suspend | Shutdown | Restart SSL — Showing 1 to 2 of 2 Previous | Next

FIGURE 2-3. *Starting a Managed Server from the Administration Console*

Once you click the Start button on the Summary Of Servers page to start a Managed Server, the server instance starts booting. Wait for a few seconds and check the Managed Server's status in the State column of the Server State table or just refresh the page you're on—you'll see the State column transitioning from the initial SHUTDOWN state to STARTING before finally finishing in the RUNNING state. The Managed Server is now ready and at your command.

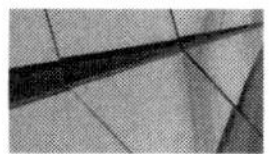

TIP

You can start a Managed Server in STANDBY mode only if you've configured a domain-wide administration port. You'll learn how to configure the administration port in Chapter 3, which discusses the creation and configuration of WebLogic domains.

Shutting Down a Managed Server from the Administration Console

To shut down a Managed Server, select the server you wish to shut down from the left-hand pane of the console under the Servers table. In the right-hand pane (named the Summary Of Servers page), select Control | Start/Stop, and select the server name from the Server Status table. You can choose between a graceful shutdown (When Work Completes) and a forced shutdown (Force Shutdown Now).

You can always shut down the Admin Server from the Administration Console, but this also makes the Console inaccessible because the Admin Server hosts the Console. You can also kill the JVM for a WebLogic Server instance by using the *kill* command after identifying the server process with the *ps* command in UNIX or the Task Manager on a Windows system. The WebLogic Server instance is the Java process that generally uses the most memory.

Using WLST Without the Node Manager

You can't start or stop a Managed Server with WLST without first connecting to the Node Manager. However, you can use WLST commands to start the Admin Server without the Node Manager running. The following example shows how to start the Admin Server for the *medrec* domain after invoking WLST with the *java weblogic. WLST* command. (In a Windows server, you can simply execute the WebLogic Scripting Tool command from the Start menu.) Make sure you set the environment by running the *setDomainEnv.cmd* script before you do this.

```
C:\Oracle\\Middlewar\Oracle_Home\user_projects\domains\medrec\bin>setDomainEnv.cmd
C:\Oracle\Middleware\Oracle_Home\user_projects\domains\wl_server>java
weblogic.WLST
wls:/offline>
wls:/offline>
startServer('examplesServer','wl_server','t3://localhost:7001','weblogic',
'welcome1','C:\Oracle\Middleware\wlserver_12.1\samples\domains\wl_server',
'false',60000,jvmArgs='-XX:MaxPermSize=512m, -Xmx512m, -XX:+UseParallelGC')

Starting weblogic server ...
Server started successfully.
wls:/offline> exit ()
```

Exiting from WLST won't shut down the Admin Server. In other words, the Admin Server runs independently of WLST.

Once you start the Admin Server, as shown here, WLST is still in the offline mode because it hasn't connected to the server yet—you can connect to the Admin Server with the *connect* command:

```
wls:/offline> connect('weblogic','welcome1','t3://localhost:7001')
Connecting to t3://localhost:7001 with userid weblogic ...
Successfully connected to Admin Server 'examplesServer' that belongs to
domain 'wl_server'.
Warning: An insecure protocol was used to connect to the server.
To ensure on-the-wire security, the SSL port or Admin port
should be used instead.
wls:/wl_server/serverConfig>
```

Once you're connected to the Admin Server, you can issue various lifecycle commands to control the servers. Note that Oracle recommends that you enable the administration port when issuing any administrative commands. You can issue WLST lifecycle commands to check the status of the server (*state* command), suspend the server (*suspend* command), and resume the server's operation (*resume* command), as shown in the following examples:

- Check the state of the server:

  ```
  wls:/wl_server/serverConfig> state('examplesServer')
  Current state of 'examplesServer' : RUNNING
  wls:/wl_server/serverConfig>
  ```

- Suspend the server:

  ```
  wls:/wl_server/serverConfig> suspend('MedRecServer', block="true")
  Server examplesServer suspended successfully.
  ```

- Check the state of the server after suspending it:

  ```
  wls:/wl_server/serverConfig> state('examplesServer')
  Current state of 'examplesServer' : ADMIN
  ```

- Resume the operation of the server:

  ```
  wls:/wl_server/serverConfig> resume ('examplesServer') ,"block=true")
  Server (examplesServer' resumed successfully.
  ```

- Check the state of the server again:

  ```
  wls:/wl_server/serverConfig> state(' ('examplesServer')) /* check state again
  Current state of ' (examplesServer': RUNNING
  ```

On occasion, you may encounter an error message such as the following when starting up the Admin Server:

```
<Error> <HTTP> <Servlet: AppManagerServlet" failed to
preload on startup in Web Application:consolehelp.
WLST-WLS-1289076763292: java.lang.OutOfMemoryError: PermGen space
WLST-WLS-1289076763292: at java.lang.ClassLoader.defineClass1(Native Method)
```

The Java permanent generation (PermGen) space stores metadata such as classes and is independent of the Java heap space. This error usually occurs when resources aren't released immediately following a restart of the Admin Server. You'll find that this error usually doesn't occur once you switch to the Oracle JRockit JVM implementation from the default Oracle Java VM.

Stopping Servers with WLST Commands

You can stop an Admin Server through WLST without the Node Manager, as shown here:

```
wls:/medrec/serverConfig> shutdown()
Shutting down the server examplesServer with force=false while connected to
MedRecServer ...
Disconnected from weblogic server: examplesServer
wls:/offline>
```

By default, the *shutdown* command shuts down the server to which it is connected. It is an online command, so you must first connect to the Admin Server. The WLST *shutdown* command lets you shut down any Managed Server instance once you connect to the Admin Server or shut down even the Admin Server itself. If you connect to a Managed Server, you can shut down only that particular Managed Server. By default, the *shutdown* command waits until all in-flight work is completed, so this is a graceful command. All active sessions must complete before the server shuts down; however, you can specify the option *force=true* to shut down the server without waiting for active sessions to finish their work (the default value is *false*). You can also use the *shutdown* command to shut down a cluster by specifying the value *cluster* for the *entityType* argument (the default value for this attribute is *server*).

Using WLST with the Node Manager

Although there are multiple ways to start and stop the WebLogic Servers, in practice, you'll mostly use WLST and the Node Manager together to manage the server instances. WLST can act as a client of the Node Manager when you connect it to the Node Manager on a specific host and use the Node Manager to control the Admin and Managed Servers running on the machine where the Node Manager is running. WLST can also work as a client of the Admin Server by connecting to the Admin Server (and not to the Node Manager) to control Managed Servers throughout the domain. In the latter case, the Admin Server uses the Node Managers running on each of the machines in the domain to control the Managed Servers running on that machine. Thus, in this case, there's an indirect connection between WLST and the Node Manager, which is much simpler than connecting to each Node Manager running in the domain and also cuts down on the connection overhead. This approach is generally best, as you can manage the entire domain by simply connecting to the domain's Admin Server with WLST—however, if the Admin Server isn't running, you need to know how to work with just WLST and the Node Manager.

Using WLST and Node Manager Without the Admin Server

To control the servers on any machine, WLST can directly connect to the Node Manager running on that machine. This comes in handy when the Admin Server isn't running for some reason, as the Admin Server isn't needed for WLST and the Node Manager to work together to start the servers. You can also use this technique to start the Admin Server on a remote machine. Here are the steps to connect WLST to the Node Manager and start servers (the domain name is *medrec*):

1. Start WLST:

```
C:\Oracle\Middleware\Oracle_Home\user_projects\domains\medrec\bin>setDomainEnv.cmd
C:\Oracle\Middleware\Oracle_Home\user_projects\domains\medrec>java weblogic.WLST
Initializing WebLogic Scripting Tool (WLST) ...
```

```
Welcome to WebLogic Server Administration Scripting Shell
Type help() for help on available commands
wls:/offline>
```

2. Start the Node Manager with the WLST command *startNodeManager* if you haven't configured the Node Manager to start automatically with the host computer:

```
wls:/offline> startNodeManager()
Launching NodeManager
...
NMProcess: INFO: Secure socket listener started on port 5556
Successfully launched the Node Manager.
The Node Manager process is running independent of the WLST process.
Exiting WLST will not stop the Node Manager process. Please refer
to the Node Manager logs for more information.
The Node Manager logs will be under
C:\Oracle\Middleware\Oracle_Home\user_projects\domains\wl_server\.
Node Manager starting in the background
wls:/offline>
```

3. Connect WLST to the Node Manager (the domain name is *wl_server*) using the WLST command *nmConnect*:

```
wls:/offline> nmConnect('weblogic', 'welcome1', 'localhost', '5556',
'wl_server',
'C:\Oracle\Middleware\Oracle_Home\user_projects\domains\wl_server,''ssl')
Successfully Connected to Node Manager.
wls:/nm/wl_server>
```

4. Check the status of the Node Manager again with the *nm* command if you want to verify that WLST has connected successfully to the Node Manager:

```
wls:/nm/wl_server> nm()
Currently connected to Node Manager to monitor the domain medrec.
Successfully Connected to Node Manager.
```

NOTE
By default, the Node Manager automatically restarts Managed Server instances that were directly or otherwise killed.

Once you've connected to the Node Manager through WLST, use the *nmStart* command to start the Admin Server (MedRecServer for the *medrec* domain) with the Node Manager:

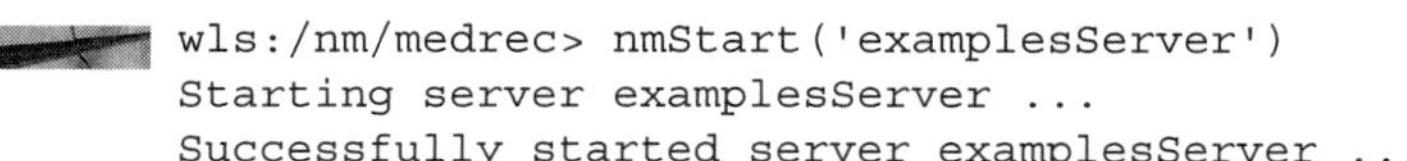

```
wls:/nm/medrec> nmStart('examplesServer')
Starting server examplesServer ...
Successfully started server examplesServer ...
```

Check the status of the MedRecServer with the *nmServerStatus* command:

```
wls:/nm/medrec> nmServerStatus('examplesServer')
RUNNING
:
```

You can execute the *nmKill* command to kill either an Admin Server or a Managed Server, as shown here:

```
wls:/nm/medrec> nmKill('examplesServer')
Killing server examplesServer ...
Successfully killed server examplesServer ...
```

Note that you must first run the *nmEnroll* command before running the *nmConnect* command. The *nmEnroll* command ensures that each Managed Server in the domain has the correct Node Manager credentials. You must first connect to a running WebLogic Server before you can execute the *nmEnroll* command, as shown by this error message:

```
wls:/offline> nmEnroll('C:/MyOra/Middleware/wlserver_12.1/common/nodemanager')
You will need to be connected to a running server to execute this command
```

First, connect to the Admin Server with the *connect* command, and then execute the *nmEnroll* command:

```
wls:/offline> connect('weblogic','welcome1','t3://localhost:7001')
Connecting to t3://localhost:7001 with userid weblogic ...
Successfully connected to Admin Server 'examplesServer' that belongs to domain
'wl_server'.
Warning: An insecure protocol was used to connect to the server. To ensure on-the-
wire security, the SSL port or Admin port should be used instead.
wls:/wl_server/serverConfig>
nmEnroll('C:\Oracle\Middleware\Oracle_Home\wl_server\common\nodemanager')
Enrolling this machine with the domain directory at
C:\Oracle\Middleware\Oracle_Home\wl_server\commonnodemanager ...
Successfully enrolled this machine with the domain directory at
C:\Oracle\Middleware\Oracle_Home\wlserver\common\nodemanager.
wls:/wl_server/serverConfig>
```

You need to run the *nmEnroll* command only once for each domain. Note that you must run the *nmEnroll* command on each machine where the Node Manager runs, and you must also run it for each domain running on a machine. Once you run the *nmEnroll* command on a machine, it creates the *nm_password.properties* file with the Node Manager username and password. This file exists under the domain's DOMAIN_HOME\config\nodemanager directory. These credentials are not the same as those for the Admin Server. The Node Manager credentials are used only to authenticate connections between the Node Manager and its clients, such as the Admin Server. There is a separate *nm_password.properties* file for each machine, but the credentials can be different on each machine. Once the *nm_password.properties* file is created, you can modify the Node Manager credentials from the Administration Console. You can also edit the credentials manually in the file, but make sure you restart the Node Manager after you do so.

The Node Manager can use its own properties set in the *nodemanager.properties* file to start a Managed Server. These properties are specified in the server *startup.properties* file in the DOMAIN_HOME\servers\<*server_name*>\data\nodemanager directory. The file contains several properties that enable you to configure the Node Manager to restart automatically failed Managed Servers:

- ***RestartMax*** Sets the maximum number of times the Node Manager attempts to restart a server
- ***RestartDelaySeconds*** Sets the interval between restart attempts

- ***AutoRestart*** Specifies whether the Node Manager can automatically restart the server when the server fails
- ***AutoKillIfFailed*** Specifies whether the Node Manager should kill the server if it shows a FAILED health status

However, to ensure that servers start reliably, you should specify the startup arguments for Managed Servers in the Administration Console by going to the Servers | *<Managed Server>* | Configuration | Server Start page for each of the Managed Servers in your domain.

You can also start a Managed Server without an Admin Server using WLST and the Node Manager together. Once you connect to the Node Manager from WLST, issue the *nmStart* command and specify the name of the Managed Server you want to start, as shown here:

```
wls:/nm/wl_server> nmStart('ManagedServer1')
```

As you can see, you use the same command, *nmStart,* to start either the Admin Server or a Managed Server. You can use the *nmStart* command when you want to restart a Managed Server in the absence of a running Admin Server. You can kill a server with the *nmKill* command when you're connected to the Node Manager from WLST.

Using WLST and the Node Manager with the Admin Server

When you use WLST as a client of the Admin Server, the Node Manager must be running, but you don't connect WLST to the Node Manager with the *nmConnect* command, as is the case when WLST runs as a client of the Node Manager. Instead, you connect WLST to the Admin Server instance and the Admin Server will contact the Node Manager on behalf of WLST. Here are the steps to start a Managed Server with the Node Manager:

1. Start WLST:

```
C:\Oracle\Middleware\Oracle_Home\user_projects\domains\medrec>java weblogic.WLST
```

2. Start the Node Manager:

```
wls:/offline> startNodeManager()
Launching NodeManager ...
```

3. Start the Admin Server for the domain:

```
wls:/offline> startServer('MedRecServer','medrec','t3://localhost:7011',
'weblogic','welcome1','C:\Oracle\Middleware\Oracle_Home\user_projects
/domains/medrec','true',60000,'false')
Starting weblogic server ...
```

4. Connect WLST to the Admin Server:

```
wls:/offline> connect("weblogic",'welcome1',"t3://localhost:7011")
Connecting to t3://localhost:7011 with userid weblogic ...
Successfully connected to Admin Server 'MedRecServer' that belongs to domain
'medrec'.
```

Note that you can also connect by issuing the *connect* command without any arguments. You'll be prompted for the credentials and the URL for the Admin Server you're connecting to:

```
wls:/offline> connect()
Please enter your username :weblogic
Please enter your password :
Please enter your server URL [t3://localhost:7001] :t3://localhost:7011
Connecting to t3://localhost:7011 with userid weblogic ...
Successfully connected to Admin Server 'MedRecServer' that belongs
to domain 'medrec-spring'.

Warning: An insecure protocol was used to connect to the
server. To ensure on-the-wire security, the SSL port or
Admin port should be used instead.

wls:/medrec-spring/serverConfig>
```

Note that you must run WLST from the same domain as the one the Admin Server belongs to.

5. Start a Managed Server with the WLST *start* command:

```
wls:/medrec/serverConfig> start('ManagedServer1')
```

The *start* command shown here starts the Managed Server named ManagedServer1.

You can specify four arguments with the *start* command: The *type* argument specifies the type of server—the default value is *server,* so you don't have to specify this when starting a server. To start a cluster, you specify the value *Cluster* for the server argument, for example, *start('MyCluster', 'Cluster').* The optional *url* argument defaults to *t3:\\localhost:7001,* so you must supply the correct listen address and listen port in your own case. The last argument, *block,* which has a default value of *true,* specifies whether WLST should block user interaction until the server is fully started.

Note that when you connect WLST to the Admin Server, WLST loses the connection to the WebLogic server if you shut down the Admin Server:

```
wls:/medrec/serverConfig> WLST lost connection to the WebLogic Server that you
were connected to, this may happen if the server was shut down or partitioned.You
will have to re-connect to the server once the server is available.
Disconnected from weblogic server: AdminServer
```

Setting Up a WebLogic Server Instance as a Windows Service

All the examples thus far have shown you how to start the WebLogic Server instances using various methods so you can familiarize yourself with the startup options. More realistically, however, you probably want to set up the WebLogic Server instances as a Windows service so the servers can automatically start up following a reboot of the machine hosting the WebLogic Servers.

Setting Up the Service

Oracle WebLogic Server provides a WebLogic Windows service program called *beasvc.exe*. You can execute this program from within a script or call on the master script provided by Oracle for this purpose. Called the *installSvc.cmd* script, it is a wrapper for *beasvc.exe*. Follow these steps to set up a WebLogic Server instances as a Windows service. This example shows how to start an Admin Server as a Windows service.

1. Change to the WL_HOME\server\bin directory.
2. Create a text file with the following contents and name it *createSvc.cmd*:

```
echo off
SETLOCAL
set DOMAIN_NAME=medrec
set USERDOMAIN_HOME=C:\Oracle\Middleware\Oracle_Home\user_projects\domains\medrec
set SERVER_NAME=MedRecServer
set PRODUCTION_MODE=false
set JAVA_VENDOR=sun
set JAVA_HOME=C:\Oracle\Middleware\jdk160_21
set MEM_ARGS=-Xms1024m -Xmx1024m
call """C:\Oracle\Middleware\Oracle_Home\wlserver\server\bin\installSvc.cmd
ENDLOCAL
```

NOTE:
Once you create a Windows service, WebLogic Server adds a registry entry in the Windows Registry under HKEY_LOCAL_MACHINE\SYSTEM\CurrentControlSet\Services, with the server name and startup options.

3. Execute the *createSvc.cmd* script from the WL_HOME\server\bin directory. You should see the following message, indicating the service was successfully created:

```
$ beasvc medrec_ MedRecServer installed.
```

4. Go to Administrative Services | Services after opening the Windows Control Panel. You'll see a new service whose name starts with *beasvc* (in this case, the name will be *beasvc medrec_medrecserver*). Right-click this service, start it, and configure it to run automatically after a server boot.

The following options in the automatic service creation script you created are purely optional:

- ***JAVA_OPTIONS*** Sets Java options to the Java arguments you specify for the JVM
- ***JAVA_VM*** Sets the Java Virtual Machine you want to use
- ***MEM_ARGS*** Sets the minimum and maximum memory arguments you want to pass to the JVM, for example, *MEM_ARGS=-Xms1024m -Xmx1024m*

Setting Up the Managed Server as a Windows Service

The example in the previous section shows how to set up the Admin Server as a Windows service. You can set up a Windows service for all your Managed Servers as well. However, because you want your Managed Servers to start after the Admin Server (so they can contact the Admin Server to retrieve their configuration data), you must add the following arguments to the line that invokes the *beasvc* utility in the *installSvc.cmd* script (*:"%WL_HOME%\server\bin\beasvc"* ...):

```
-depend: "beasvc medrec_MedRecServer"
-delay:     "1600"
```

The argument *-depend* refers to the Admin Server that starts before the Managed Server. The *-delay* argument specifies the amount of time (in milliseconds) that the Admin Server has to complete its startup cycle. In this case, after adding our two arguments, *beasvc* will be invoked in the following manner by the *installSvc.cmd* master script:

```
"%WL_HOME%\server\bin\beasvc" -install
-svcname:"beasvc %DOMAIN_NAME%_%SERVER_NAME%"   / * points to the
Managed Server you are starting with this script
-depend: "beasvc medrec_MedRecServer" /* points to the domain Admin Server
-delay:     "1600"
```

Remember that your own script, *createSvc.cmd,* calls the *installSvc.cmd* script at the very end of the script.

The master script provided by Oracle, *installSvc.cmd* in the WL_HOME\server\bin\ directory, is similar to the script I used to create a Windows service. Don't change the master script itself—instead, write a simple custom script such as the one shown in the preceding example. The only time you may want to edit the master script is if you're using a nondefault JVM. In such a case, you must edit the *installSvc.cmd* script by setting values for the *JAVA_HOME* and *JAVA_VENDOR* variables to point to the nondefault JVM.

Remember that the previous example set up a service for an Admin Server. You set up a Windows service for a Managed Server in the same fashion, but with an extra argument to specify the hostname and listen port for the Admin Server, as shown here:

```
set JAVA_OPTIONS=-Dweblogic.management.server=http://adminserver:7501
```

Starting and Stopping the Service

Once you create a Windows service for the server startup, the servers will start automatically following a restart of the Windows server. You can also stop and restart the service from the Services Control Panel, which you can access by selecting Start | Settings | Control Panel | Services. Locate the Windows service name, which takes the format *beasvc <domain name>_<Managed Server name>* (for example, *beasvc medrec_MedRecServer*), and start or stop the service.

Changing Startup Credentials for a Service

When installing a Windows service, you can either configure things such that the service retrieves usernames and passwords from the *boot.properties* file or from the Windows registry. In my example, WebLogic Server encrypts the credentials in the Windows registry. If you need to change these credentials, you must first uninstall the service (see the following section). Once you do this, edit the *createSvc.cmd* script and reset the *WLS_USER* and *WLS_PW* directives. Finally, create a new service by executing the *createSvc.cmd* script.

To avoid having to remove and reinstall a Windows service each time you need to change some credentials, use a boot identity file. This lets you change login credentials and bypass the username/password prompts.

Removing a Service

You can remove a Windows service by calling the *uninstallSvc.cmd* script, as shown here:

```
cd C:\Oracle\Middleware\Oracle_Home\wlserver\server\bin
set DOMAIN_NAME=medrec
set SERVER_NAME=MedRecServer
call C:\Oracle\Middleware\Oracle_Home\wlserver\server\bin\uninstallSvc.cmd
```

You should see a message indicating that the service was successfully removed.

Dealing with WebLogic Server Failures

As with any type of server instance, the Oracle WebLogic Server is susceptible to failures, whether due to a power failure or a faulty hardware component. Even if you're running a clustered environment for high availability, you must expect to deal with the occasional WebLogic Server failure. WebLogic Server does offer you several ways to monitor application workload and avoid failures due to an overload caused by either an unexpected spike in web traffic or maxed-out resources. The built-in overload protection capabilities are explained in Chapter 5. Chapter 7 discusses how to fail over to another server in a cluster following a server failure without interrupting your service levels. This section shows you how to deal with the occasional failure of either the Admin Server or the Management Server.

A note on how to interpret server exit codes when trying to restart a failed or stopped server: When you terminate a server process (Managed or Admin Server), the process terminates with an exit code of zero. This happens even if you shut down the server forcefully. Sometimes, the server shuts itself down when it detects stuck threads or a low memory situation, and it will do so with an exit code greater than 0. You can safely restart the server following such a shutdown. If the server fails to start normally by not transitioning to the starting state, it issues a negative exit code. In this case, you must first fix the problem that prevented the server from starting before trying to restart it.

Note that an Admin Server automatically detects any running Managed Servers and, thus, following the failure of the Admin Server, you don't have to reboot the running Managed Servers; they can happily continue running until you restart the Admin Server, at which time the Admin Server will resume managing the state of the Managed Servers under the domain that it was managing prior to its failure (or shutdown). When it restarts, the Admin Server waits for the Managed Servers to connect again.

Starting a Failed Admin Server

The procedures for starting a failed Admin Server depend on whether you can reuse the same IP address as that of the failed server or not. The following sections explain how to deal with both scenarios—when you can reuse the IP address and when you can't do so. Regardless of the scenario, the procedure to restart a failed Admin Server is fairly easy.

Using the Same IP Address

If the original machine on which the failed Admin Server ran is still available, all you have to do is restart the Admin Server as usual.

Using a Different IP Address

Sometimes you may not be able to reuse the same IP address following an Admin Server failure. If you can't use the original server, you must first install WebLogic Server on a different machine. Once the installation completes, restore all the application files from a backup or by accessing storage mounted on a Network File System (NFS). Make sure all the configuration files as well as the application files are placed in the same directories that they occupied on the original machine.

Restarting a failed Admin Server on a different machine with a new IP address is just about as easy as when you can reuse the IP address—it requires just one additional step. Perform the same procedures, as in the case where you reuse the IP address, and update the domain's *config.xml* file with the new IP address. You can do this manually or use WLST offline.

Here's the *config.xml* server attribute that you need to change:

```
<server>
  <name>AdminServer</name>
...
  <listen-address>192.168.0.20</listen-address>
</server>
```

The *listen-address* parameter may also be a hostname reference. You can then restart the Admin Server as usual.

Moving an Access or Network Tier Server to a Different Machine

If you have to restart a server instance on a different machine, you can do so easily as long as you don't change your domain configuration. If the network configuration is modified on the new machine, you must update your domain network configuration through the Administration Console before restarting the server, as shown here:

1. Start the configuration session by clicking the Lock & Edit button.
2. In the left-hand pane, select Environment | Servers.
3. Choose the name of the server in the right-hand pane.
4. Modify the listen address and port settings using the Configuration | General tab.
5. Modify any network channels that you may have configured, from the same location.
6. Activate your changes by clicking the Activate Changes button.

You can now restart the Managed Servers on the new servers by following the normal steps in restarting a failed access or network tier server.

How the Managed Servers Handle an Admin Server Failure

When the Admin Server fails, Managed Servers will continue to run without any problem, servicing the deployed applications as usual. The Managed Servers will frequently attempt to reconnect to the Admin Server. These connection attempts are made simultaneously on all the URLs available to the Managed Servers, thus allowing themselves to connect to the Admin Server regardless of which URL the Admin Server uses to come back online again. Note that if the Admin

Server is restarted with a different IP address, a Managed Server may or may not be able to connect to it. The Managed Server can connect to the Admin Server successfully only if you've specified a DNS name for the Admin Server URL, which enables the mapping of this URL to more than one IP address. You must provide this DNS name when starting the Managed Server, as shown here:

```
-Dweblogic.management.server=protocol://wlsadminserver:port
or
startManagedWebLogic.cmd managed_server_name protocol://wlsadminserver:port
```

Just how frequently does the Managed Server attempt to reconnect to a failed Admin Server? This depends on the setting of the *AdminReconnectIntervalSeconds* attribute, which is set to 10 seconds by default.

NOTE
You handle Managed Server failures the same way in clustered environments as you do in nonclustered environments.

Managed Server Independence (MSI) Mode

If a Managed Server goes down while the Admin Server is running, restarting it after fixing the problem that caused it to shut down is easy. You can use any of the server startup methods I discussed earlier to start the Managed Server. If the Admin Server is also down, however, what happens to the Managed Server? You'll be happy to learn that you can restart a failed Managed Server, regardless of the status of the Admin Server. When you start or restart a failed Managed Server in the absence of a running Admin Server instance, you are running the Managed Server in the Managed Server Independence (MSI) mode. MSI helps you avoid a single point of failure for the Admin Server, something that is critical in a production environment.

When a Managed Server starts in the MSI mode, it reads its configuration and security information directly, instead of contacting the Admin Server first. It reads the *config.xml* file from its own local config directory and the security-related files, *SerializedSystemIni.dat* and *boot .properties,* from its security directory. In fact, you can even copy these files from the Admin Server directories to the Managed Server directories if necessary. If the Managed Server is running on the same machine as the Admin Server, the two servers will share the same root directory, which, by default, is the directory from where the startup script for the server is executed. In such a case, the Managed Server will, of course, easily find the necessary files to start in the MSI mode. If not, you need to make those files available to the Managed Server by copying them from a backup and placing them in the root directory.

NOTE
Managed Server Independence (MSI) Mode is enabled by default. You can disable it from the Administration Console.

Once you select the Server for which you want to do this from the left-hand pane, go to the Configuration | Tuning tab in the right-hand pane. Here, click Advanced, and you can deselect the Managed Server Independence Enabled option from under the Advanced Options list. When you opt out of the default MSI behavior, even when all the necessary configuration or security files are available to it, a Managed Server can't start if the Admin Server is down. Once a Managed Server starts in the MSI mode, it will run in that mode until it's successful in connecting to a running Admin Server again.

Although you can service all deployed applications with the Managed Servers running in MSI mode, you must be aware of a few things:

- You can't change the configuration of the Managed Servers once you start them in MSI mode.
- The Managed Servers deploy applications from their staging directories.
- You can't use the Node Manager to start a Managed Server running in MSI mode—you must manually start the Managed Server on the machine that hosts it.

NOTE
You can start a Managed Server in MSI mode only if it has been started at least once by the Admin Server. The very first time you start a Managed Server, it must be able to contact the Admin Server.

- The Managed Server only writes log messages to their local files and not to the domain log file because there's no Admin Server to write the forwarded messages from the Managed Servers to the domain log file.

Deleting Servers

On occasion, you may need to delete an Admin Server and replace it with a different Admin Server with a different name. You can do this using the Administration Console and WLST together, as I explain here:

1. Click Lock & Edit in the Administration Console's Change Center.
2. Shut down all Managed Servers. The Admin Server must be running.
3. Invoke WLST:

```
C:\Oracle\Middleware\Oracle_Home\user_projects\domains\medrec>java weblogic.WLST
```

4. Run the following series of commands:

```
connect()
edit()
startEdit()
cmo.setAdminServerName("newAdminServer")
activate()

shutdown()
exit()
```

5. Copy the Admin Server data to the new Admin Server. For example, if the original Admin Server was called MedRecServer and you renamed it to newAdminServer, copy the contents from DOMAIN_HOME\servers\MedRecServer to DOMAIN_HOME\servers\newAdminServer.

6. Start the new Admin Server after first setting its new name.

```
set SERVER_NAME=newAdminServer
startWebLogic.cmd
```

   If you run into startup errors, confirm that there are no references to MedRecServer in *config.xml* or *setDomainEnv.sh*.

7. Start the Administration Console. The Servers page will now show the name of the new Admin Server.

Summary

This chapter introduced you to the management of WebLogic Server instances through WLST and the Node Manager. You also learned about the various server run states and how to transition through them. The next chapter shows you how to create and configure a WebLogic domain.

CHAPTER 3

Creating and Configuring WebLogic Server Domains

The first two chapters of this book provided you with an introduction to managing server cycles using various tools such as the Administration Console, WLST, and the Node Manager. This chapter explores the concept of a WebLogic Server domain and shows you how to create domains using various methods. The chapter also explains, in detail, key domain configuration topics such as how to configure virtual hosts and how to configure a persistent WebLogic store for saving information such as diagnostic data. The chapter also discusses how to safeguard critical domain data by backing up the data. In addition, the chapter explains how to use WebLogic Server as a web server. Oracle WebLogic Server is a huge topic that really includes not only the configuration of the Admin and Managed Servers and domains but also various services such as JDBC and JMS. WebLogic Server's immense functionality and wide array of supported features mean that you need to understand how to configure a very large set of services and features. Thus, although formally this is the chapter where I discuss WebLogic Server domain configuration, you really should consider the entire book to be about Oracle WebLogic Server configuration.

Structure of a WebLogic Server Domain

Understanding a domain lies at the heart of mastering the use of WebLogic Server. WebLogic Server uses the concept of domains to organize the WebLogic Server instances into a coherent group, configure the environment, deploy applications, and implement security across the entire environment. In a typical enterprise-wide deployment of WebLogic Server, you'll have multiple server instances on various hosts, each possibly running on a different network and with a different configuration. Your domains may have multiple clusters as well as independent Managed Servers. The hosts may belong to various operating systems, and the applications may have to traverse diverse networks. Although the Java EE specification provides standard enterprise APIs for architecting applications, it lets each application server vendor (such as Oracle, for example) implement its application deployment methods, high availability, failover features, and many other administrative procedures using proprietary methods. In fact, these value-added capabilities are how vendors distinguish themselves, and WebLogic Server has the richest set of capabilities among all application servers.

An Oracle WebLogic Server domain is a set of one or more Oracle WebLogic Server instances (and other resources) that work together to serve web applications. Each domain must have a WebLogic Server instance called the Administration Server, or the Admin Server, as it's usually called. In addition to the Admin Server, you can have one or more Managed Servers in a domain. The Admin Server is really meant for configuration purposes only; it is the Managed Servers that host and run the various web applications. In a development environment, you can keep things simple by having just one server instance in your WebLogic Server domain—the mandatory Admin Server, on which you can deploy your applications. In this case, the single server instance will perform the management and configuration duties, as well as host all the applications. Of course, in a production setup, you must run with multiple management servers, whose job it'll be to host and run the web applications.

A domain is a grouping of instances, and you can have different groupings of instances depending on the architecture you choose to implement. Just a reminder: WebLogic Server refers to a running Admin or Managed Server as an instance because that's really what the servers are. Each server (Admin or Managed Server) is an instance of the WebLogic Server and runs in its own Java Virtual Machine (JVM) and with its own configuration.

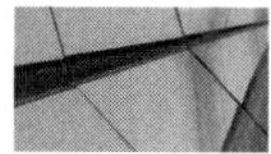

NOTE
If you have a single WebLogic Server instance in a domain, that instance will perform double duty as both an Admin Server and a Managed Server—that is, you perform all work, including domain configuration and hosting all of your applications, through this single server.

A domain is a logical construct, consisting of a set of servers, network and application resources, and related services, as well as security policies. The Admin Server is in charge of the entire domain configuration, and you perform all administrative tasks for that domain through this server. Understanding that a domain is not limited to a single physical server is important; in production environments, domains are usually spread across multiple physical servers. A domain can also contain one or more clusters, and you can run both clusters of servers and independent servers as part of the same domain.

All of the following configurations are valid WebLogic Server domains:

- **MyDomain1** Admin Server plus three Managed Servers, each running on a separate Windows or UNIX server
- **MyDomain2** Admin Server plus one cluster consisting of three Managed Servers, with the three members of the cluster running on three different Windows or UNIX servers
- **MyDomain3** Admin Server plus three Managed Servers, all running on the same Windows or UNIX Server
- **MyDomain4** Admin Server plus three Managed Servers running as part of a cluster, along with two independent (noncluster) Managed Servers

To aid your understanding of WebLogic Server domains, I'll review the role of a WebLogic instance, an Admin Server, a Managed Server, and a cluster in the following sections.

WebLogic Server Instances

Each WebLogic Server domain has a single server instance that serves as the Admin Server. The Admin Server maintains the domain's configuration information. If you're working in a development environment, you don't need any other server instances besides the Admin Server because you can deploy all applications on the Admin Server itself. Although you can do the same in a production environment (that is, use just one Admin Server and nothing else), Oracle strongly recommends that you use one or more Managed Servers, running on their own or as part of a cluster, to deploy your applications. Thus, the Admin Server is dedicated to performing configuration and administrative tasks only and not any deployment functions. You use the Admin Server as the central location from which you configure and manage all the remaining resources in a domain. Managed Servers are the actual workhorses in any domain because these servers host applications, web services, and the necessary resources such as JDBC connection pools to support the applications and web services.

When you create a domain, you automatically have an Admin Server, and when you're working in a development environment, you can start deploying your Java EE applications on that single Admin Server. Remember that although you deploy applications on Managed Servers, you can make any configuration- or deployment-related actions only through the Admin Server. Each WebLogic Server domain has its own Admin Server. Thus, if you have multiple domains in your environment, in order to connect to the Administration Console for a domain, you must use a different port number for each of the domains because the different Admin Servers can't use the same port number.

NOTE
Oracle recommends that you create a Node Manager service on each of the machines that hosts a Managed Server in your environment. The Node Manager helps administer Managed Servers on remote machines and can automatically start failed servers. You don't need the Node Manager on a machine that runs the Admin Server unless that server also happens to run one or more Managed Servers.

WebLogic Server Clusters

A WebLogic Server cluster, as explained in Chapter 1, is a set of two or more Managed Servers running as a single unit to provide scalability and high availability for your applications. Because a cluster has multiple Managed Servers, the failure of a single Managed Server belonging to a cluster won't cause any disruption because the other members of the cluster will continue to serve the web applications without any problem. In addition to failover, clusters also provide load-balancing capabilities.

Just as an Oracle Real Application Clusters (RAC) setup provides various benefits, such as high availability for the Oracle Database, a WebLogic Server cluster provides the following key benefits:

- Scalability by taking advantage of parallel processing of your needs
- Reliability through replication
- Availability through redundancy

WebLogic clusters provide application failover by replicating session state and maintaining copies of objects on all the cluster members. In addition, WebLogic Server provides for the automatic migration of services such as JMS services and JTA Transaction Recovery Services, which must always be available. Migration can be configured through the migration of an entire server (called *whole server migration*) or by migrating individual services (called *service-level migration*).

Domain Resources

Configuring a WebLogic Server domain includes configuring various resources for Managed Servers that are part of the domain, as well as configuring several services that support the applications you deploy on the Managed Servers. Managed Server resources include the machine definitions (see Chapter 2), network channels (see Chapter 4), and virtual hosting (see the section "Configuring Virtual Hosts" later in this chapter). In addition to these server resources, web applications may use some or all of the following resources and services:

- Security providers
- Resource adapters
- Diagnostic and monitoring services
- JDBC data sources
- Database or disk-based file persistent stores
- Work managers

In addition to the servers, the definition of a domain includes all the Java EE services and resources to support the applications and services hosted by the Managed Servers. The domain-wide resources include the machines that host the various servers, as well as any network channels you may configure. In addition, each domain's Managed Servers host other resources and services, which may be deployed to either individual servers or an entire cluster. These resources that you can assign to a server or cluster include all the application components, of course, such as EJBs, enterprise applications, and Java EE connectors. In addition, they include the JDBC connection pools, JMS servers, and any virtual hosts you may configure.

Domain Restrictions

The following restrictions apply to any WebLogic Server domain you may create:

- You can't name your domain "weblogic" because that name is reserved.
- You can't name a server, machine, cluster, virtual host, or any other resource the same name as that of the domain to which it belongs. These are targetable entities, and sharing names would lead to ambiguity.
- When naming an Admin or Managed Server, remember that its name must be unique in each WebLogic Server deployment, even if the server belongs to different domains.
- Each domain must have its own Admin Server.
- A cluster has a one-to-one relationship with a domain—it can't straddle multiple domains.
- You can't share a configured resource such as a JDBC connection pool among domains—each domain must have a complete set of its own resources to support applications.

Domain Directories

When you create a domain, WebLogic Server will create a new domain directory under the WL_HOME\user_projects\domains directory. Of course, this is the default behavior, which you can change by specifying a different directory during the domain creation process. For example, if you create a new domain and name it *MyDomain,* WebLogic Server will create a new directory named MyDomain, as shown here:

```
WL_HOME\user_projects\domains\MyDomain
```

The directory MyDomain, which contains data and information pertaining to the domain *MyDomain,* is called the *domain directory.*

Although the installer creates the sample domains in the installation directory, the recommended practice is always to select a different location for a domain directory, a location that's not under the installation directory. By doing this, you avoid mixing user data with the installed products, which is always a bad practice. Selecting a directory that is not in the installation directory makes backing up these directories and avoiding collisions with other users on the same machine easier. Creating domains under the installation directory would also make it difficult to migrate forward your domains as you install later versions of the product.

Following is a brief summary of a domain directory's contents, which are stored in various subfolders.

The Domain Root Directory

Each WebLogic Server instance, including the Admin Server, stores a copy of the domain's configuration files in a root directory. For the Admin Server, the domain directory always serves as the root directory as well. You can also let the Managed Servers use the domain directory as their root directory (the default), or you can specify a different root directory for the Managed Server instances. If your Admin Server and Managed Servers run on different machines, you'll have to create a root directory for the Managed Servers on the machines where those servers are running. When the Managed Server starts, it writes the configuration information from the domain directory to its own root directory and will continue to write run-time data to the root directory throughout the life of the Managed Server.

A domain can have multiple root directories, one for each of the Managed Servers, or you can choose to use the same root directory for multiple servers. You can configure several WebLogic Server instances, running on different server machines, to use the same root directory if you wish. By default, WebLogic Server looks for *config.xml* in the config directory from which you started the server. If *config.xml* is in this directory, the server deems it the root directory. You can ask a server to use a different directory as the root directory by using a command-line argument, as shown here:

```
java -Dweblogic.RootDirectory=C:\Oracle\Middleware\wlserver_12.1\user_projects
\domains\MyDomain weblogic.Server
```

If you don't supply a root directory for the Node Manager, it creates the following root directory on each server where it runs:

```
WL_HOME\common\nodemanager
```

You can choose to specify a root directory for the Node Manager by navigating to the Environment | Servers | *<server_name>* | Configuration | Server Start page in the Administration Console.

The root directory is where a server stores its working copy of the domain configuration files and run-time data. The Admin Server also stores security resources such as the default embedded Lightweight Directory Access Protocol (LDAP) server under the root directory. The Admin Server uses the domain directory as its root directory and so does the Managed Server, but you can assign a different directory as the root directory for the Managed Server if you wish. If you start a Managed Server from a machine that doesn't share a file system with the Admin Server's host, the Managed Server will create a root directory on the server it runs by copying the data from the Admin Server's host machine.

The location of the Managed Server's root directory is determined by whether you started the server with the Node Manager. If you used the Node Manager to start the Managed Server, the server root directory will be on the same machine where the Node Manager process runs. The server will use any root directory you might have specified in the Administration Console in the Environment | Servers | *<server-name>* | Configuration | Server Start page as the server's root directory. If no directory was specified as a root directory in the Administration Console, the server's root directory will be WL_HOME\common\nodemanager. If you've started the Managed Server directly through a script (instead of through the Node Manager), unless you specify the root directory by specifying the *Dweblogic.RootDirectory=path* option in your startup command, the Managed Server's root directory will be the current or working directory from which you started the server.

TIP
Oracle recommends that you do not use the WebLogic Server installation directory as the server root directory.

Organization of a Domain Directory's Contents

By default, WebLogic Server creates a domain directory for each domain you create, under the MW_HOME\user_projects\domains directory. Under each domain's home directory (domain

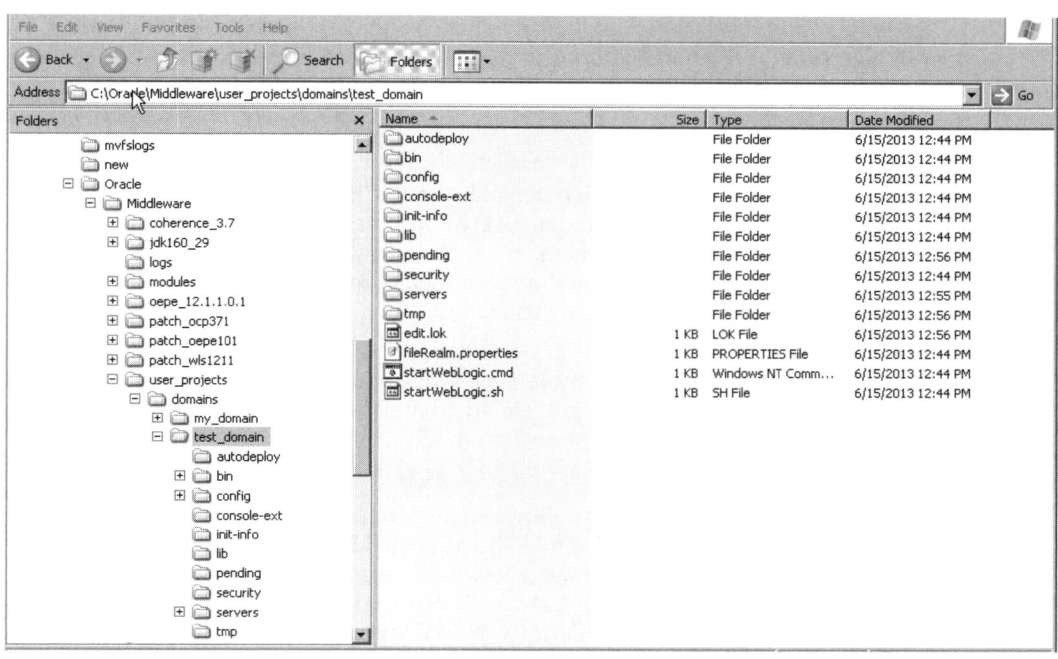

FIGURE 3-1. *A domain's directory structure*

directory), you'll find several folders, the most important of which are briefly described here. Figure 3-1 shows the domain files under the domain directory on a Windows server.

- **autodeploy** In a development environment, the server will automatically deploy any applications or modules you place here. You must run the server in development mode for it to take advantage of the automatic deployment feature.
- **bin** Contains the start and stop scripts, such as *startWebLogic.cmd* (and *startWebLogic.sh*).
- **common** Contains common files.
- **config** Contains the key domain configuration file, *config.xml*. Under the \config directory, you'll also find various folders such as security, which contains a security provider configuration extension for each of the security providers in the domain's current realm. The \diagnostics subdirectory contains the system modules for instrumentation in the WebLogic Diagnostic Framework (WLDF). Similarly, the JDBC folder contains global JDBC system modules, and the JMS folder contains JMS system modules. The \deployment subdirectory under the config directory serves as the staging area for applications deployed in the "staging" mode (see Chapter 8). You shouldn't directly handle the applications in this subdirectory—it is meant for the WebLogic deployment software. The startup directory contains system modules with startup plans, which are used to generate shell scripts that can be run during the server startup process.
- **console-ext** Contains any Administration Console extensions you've created.

- **configArchive** Contains versioned jar files that contain a domain's previous configuration. Each time you activate changes, the server changes the pending changes in a version jar file named *config.jar#n*, where *n* is an increasing number. Once the default number of maximum versions is reached, the server deletes the oldest versioned archive.
- **init-info** Contains the WebLogic domain provisioning files; this is a read-only directory.
- **lib** Contains the jar files, which you place in this directory so they are available to all applications running on the domain's server instances. Note that jar files placed here are not distributed to Managed Servers in the same way that applications (WAR, EAR, and EJB JAR applications) are. Either the \lib directory must be on a shared file system, or the contents must be copied to each "machine."
- **pending** Temporarily contains any configuration files involved in a configuration change that has been made but not activated yet. Once you activate the changes, the "pending" configuration files in this directory are automatically removed by WebLogic. This only applies when the server is in production mode.
- **security** Holds security-related files such as *SerializedSystemIni.dat*.
- **servers** Contains a separate subdirectory for each of the WebLogic instances in your domain, including both Admin and Managed Servers. For example, if you wish to examine the logs of the Managed Server My_ManagedServer1, you go to the DOMAIN_HOME\servers\My_ManagedServer1\logs directory and review the file *My_ManagedServer1.log*. In the DOMAIN_HOME\servers*<AdminServer_name>*\security directory, you'll find the server's *boot.properties* file. In the DOMAIN_HOME\servers\My_ManagedServer1\cache\EJBCompilerCache directory, you'll find the compiled EJBs hosted by that server. The DOMAIN_HOME\servers\My_ManagedServer1\data\ldap directory stores the WebLogic Server's embedded LDAP database, and the DOMAIN_HOME\servers\My_ManagedServer1\data\store directory holds the default persistent store for the Managed Server.

Note that the autodeploy, configArchive, console-ext, and pending directories are only present for an Admin Server and not for Managed Servers.

Understanding Domain Configuration Changes

The *config.xml* file is the key domain configuration file for WebLogic Server. The following section explains the nature of the *config.xml* file, as well as how to modify it by making configuration changes through the Administration Console and WLST. This section also introduces you to the run-time and configuration management beans (MBeans) that enable the management of domain configuration. You'll also learn how to record audit information relating to configuration changes.

The Domain Configuration File: config.xml

Each WebLogic Server domain contains a central configuration file called *config.xml,* which is stored in the DOMAIN_HOME\config directory. Both the Admin Server and the Managed Servers derive their run-time configuration information from the *config.xml* file. In addition to the *config.xml* file, there are subsidiary configuration files. Note that each server in a domain maintains its own copy of the domain configuration documents. Here are the contents of a typical *config.xml* file:

```
<?xml version="1.0" encoding="UTF-8" ?>
- <domain xsi:schemaLocation="http://xmlns.oracle.com/weblogic/security/wls
…
<name>my_domain</name>
  <domain-version>12.1.1.0</domain-version>
- <security-configuration
xmlns:xacml="http://xmlns.oracle.com/weblogic/security/xacml"
xmlns:pas="http://xmlns.oracle.com/weblogic/security/providers/passwordvalidator">
  <name>my_domain</name>
- <realm>
  <sec:authentication-provider xsi:type="wls:default-authenticatorType" />
- <sec:authentication-provider xsi:type="wls:default-identity-asserterType">
  <sec:active-type>AuthenticatedUser</sec:active-type>
  </sec:authentication-provider>
  <sec:role-mapper xsi:type="xacml:xacml-role-mapperType" />
  <sec:authorizer xsi:type="xacml:xacml-authorizerType" />
  <sec:adjudicator xsi:type="wls:default-adjudicatorType" />
  <sec:credential-mapper xsi:type="wls:default-credential-mapperType" />
  <sec:cert-path-provider xsi:type="wls:web-logic-cert-path-providerType" />
  <sec:cert-path-builder>WebLogicCertPathProvider</sec:cert-path-builder>
  <sec:name>myrealm</sec:name>
- <sec:password-validator xsi:type="pas:system-password-validatorType">
  <sec:name>SystemPasswordValidator</sec:name>
  <pas:min-password-length>8</pas:min-password-length>
  <pas:min-numeric-or-special-characters>1</pas:min-numeric-or-special-characters>
  </sec:password-validator>
  </realm>
  <default-realm>myrealm</default-realm>
  <credential-
encrypted>{AES}oBM/cndX0/ik44E8rDaaNPF0GcoatNLs1T1rieIEZMtV1anGMpBFKeMX4MUyWn0tK/n
kW5iy7U8p9zGLzjzpRxkJcnUM7XmKFUYAWxRk7b0EXAve9TwqWuMndtB/erQe</credential-
encrypted>
  <node-manager-username>weblogic</node-manager-username>
  <node-manager-password-
encrypted>{AES}X2ThzZVpZwyqOrwPVKmY0Ffy9xbdDW+OO2Ry5D66/lw=</node-manager-
password-encrypted>
  </security-configuration>
- <server>
  <name>AdminServer</name>
  <machine>My_Machine_1</machine>
  <listen-address />
  </server>
- <server>
  <name>My_ManagedServer_1</name>
  <machine>My_Machine_1</machine>
  <listen-port>7003</listen-port>
  <listen-address />
  </server>
```

```
- <embedded-ldap>
  <name>my_domain</name>
  <credential-
encrypted>{AES}0kqK4xPk1ZPuIJ5Sa1azPEqAajquFwGFL1/xB7KLFLmPhf1QqFR3uacoLEC/pL6G<
/credential-encrypted>
  </embedded-ldap>
  <configuration-version>12.1.1.0</configuration-version>
- <machine>
  <name>My_Machine_1</name>
- <node-manager>
  <name>My_Machine_1</name>
  <listen-address>localhost</listen-address>
  </node-manager>
  </machine>
  <admin-server-name>AdminServer</admin-server-name>
  </domain>
```

The *config.xml* file contains information pertaining to two distinct types of configuration data—environmental and application related. Environmental configuration information pertains to system resources such as JDBC data sources and network addresses. It's mostly the WebLogic Server system administrator's job to configure the system parameters using the Administration Console, WLST, or JMX APIs. The responsibility for configuring the application-related configuration information lies with the application developers. The way the application development team configures the application components depends on the type of application component. For example, JMS and JDBC modules are simply handed over to the WebLogic Server administrators for deployment. Other types of components may contain optional programs and configuration information stored in the form of Extensible Markup Language (XML)–based descriptors. When an application is deployed in a domain, the application components are linked to the environment-related resource definitions.

JMS and JDBC are discussed in Chapter 4, so the discussion in the previous paragraph is probably a bit too early—for now, the most important thing to remember is that two types of entities are configured: (1) JVMs (server instances and the network endpoint information) and (2) resources, which are either user applications or the system resources that they use. The latter of these two mostly exist in external archives and descriptors, and the *config.xml* file describes how the latter are mapped onto the former at run time.

Each Managed Server and Admin Server creates an in-memory representation of the configuration information in the *config.xml* file. Each Managed Server also keeps a copy of the domain's *config.xml* file, but the Managed Server can't modify the file. The Managed Servers also keep a copy of the subsidiary configuration files. An interesting point to remember is that *config.xml* is a *sparse representation* of a server's configuration. It contains only those configured entities that have been explicitly changed from their default values. This is important because it allows the system to evolve in the future if defaults change. As a rule of thumb, you should configure explicitly only what is absolutely necessary and leave the rest of the parameters at their default values.

Modifying Domain Configuration

You can use either the Administration Console or WLST offline commands to make configuration changes to a WebLogic Server domain. Although the *config.xml* file can be modified through XSLT or an XML parser application, you should instead use the Administration Console or WLST to modify a domain's configuration.

Before I delve into how to make configuration changes and how a domain handles configuration changes, let's review how WebLogic Server uses what are known as *management beans,* or *MBeans.*

How a Domain Manages Changes

WebLogic Server uses two types of MBeans: runtime MBeans and configuration MBeans.

- **Runtime MBeans** These MBeans are read-only and are designed for monitoring a domain. They contain the configuration created from the *config.xml* file by a server. The runtime MBeans are held in memory for the use of the running WebLogic Server instance and contain information about the run-time state of the server instance and its resources. The runtime MBeans don't persist this information in the *config.xml* file, however. When a server shuts down, all run-time information about the server contained in the runtime MBeans is removed.

  WebLogic Server uses different runtime MBeans to monitor various resources. For example, it instantiates a *ServerRuntimeBean* when you start a WebLogic Server instance and loads it with the current run-time information. Although the runtime MBeans are not editable, a resource updates the data in these MBeans when the resources change their state. Thus, runtime MBeans always hold information about the current state of the server and all of its resources. Runtime MBeans have "operations" performed on them, and this allows you to control the server's running state. These run-time operations don't result in changing the configuration of the domain, though.

- **Configuration MBeans** These are editable MBeans that enable you to modify the configuration and persist them to the *config.xml* file. For domain configuration, it's the configuration MBeans that are crucial. These beans help configure both servers as well as all the server resources because they represent the information stored in domain configuration files such as the *config.xml* file. Note that the configuration MBeans hold configuration information for only those services (JDBC, JMS, and so on) that you target at the system level, but not those services you include as modules within individual applications. The configuration MBeans provide an in-memory representation of a domain's configuration.

Lifecycle of MBeans

WebLogic Server instantiates various runtime MBeans, such as the *ServerRuntimeMBean,* when you start a new instance. Resources that use these MBeans will subsequently update them with their current run status. The resources will also destroy the runtime MBeans relevant to their operation when you shut down the server or the server crashes.

A configuration MBean follows a different lifecycle than that of a runtime MBean. The purpose of a configuration MBean is to provide an in-memory copy of the domain configuration for each server that runs in that domain. WebLogic Server uses a set of read-only and a set of editable configuration MBeans. When you start a Managed Server, it first contacts the Admin Server to get all the changes that may have occurred while the Managed Server was shut down. It updates its local copies of the domain configuration files (including the *config.xml* file) with the new data. Once it updates the configuration files, the server instantiates the configuration MBeans, which reflect the data from the *config.xml* and other configuration files. For example, if the *config.xml* states that the listen port is 7002, the configuration MBean will have the same value for its *ListenPort* attribute.

The Admin Server maintains two sets of configuration MBeans and configuration files. The first set of configuration MBeans and configuration files are read-only and represent the current configuration of the domain. The second set of MBeans is editable and relates to a corresponding set of "pending" configuration files. The configuration MBeans that represent the configuration information in the *config.xml* and other configuration files are read-only and thus not editable by a JMX client. The Admin Server instantiates a set of editable configuration MBeans based on a set of editable domain configuration files that it maintains in the config\pending directory. When JMX clients make a configuration change, they actually modify these editable configuration MBeans. Once a client modifies these editable configuration MBeans, the Admin Server copies the changes to the pending configuration files in the DOMAIN_HOME\pending directory. Once you click the Activate Changes button in the Change Center of the Administration Console, for example, the configuration changes you made are made part of the read-only configuration files and MBeans.

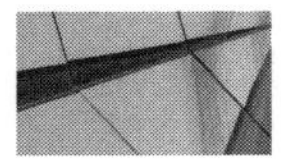

NOTE
You can avoid the potential inconsistency in the configuration of Managed Servers by disabling the Managed Server Independence (MSI) mode feature.

One useful way to think of this is that the MBeans provide a JMX view onto the configuration documents that are stored in the domain configuration. They are, in many ways, even more helpful, as they provide a complete picture, including the default values that are being used at run time.

MBean Servers

MBean Servers act as containers for MBeans, and the Admin Server's JVM maintains the following three MBean Servers:

- **Domain Runtime MBean Server** Contains MBeans for providing domain services such as JDBC data sources and JMS servers, as well as application deployment. For example, the *ServerLifecycle* and *ClusterLifecycle* MBeans allow you to monitor and manage domain-wide entities.
- **Edit MBean Server** Exposes the *ConfigurationManagerMBean,* which performs the locking and activating of configuration changes through the Administration Console. The Edit MBean Server hosts the pending configuration MBeans.
- **Runtime MBean Server** Contains MBeans that help with the monitoring and controlling of running server instances. In the current release, Oracle actually uses the "platform" MBean Server provided by the JVM as a repository for the runtime MBeans. Because Oracle uses the platform MBean Server, you can see the standard VM MBeans in the same location, which makes programming monitoring functionality for a specific VM easier.

There's a Runtime MBean Server running on every Managed Server as well.

JMX clients interface with the single-service MBean for each of the three servers to gain access to the MBeans contained in each of the servers. For example, a JMX client uses the *RuntimeServiceMBean* as an entry point MBean to access runtime MBeans and active configuration MBeans. Similarly, the clients access the *DomainRuntimeServiceMBean* for accessing the MBeans hosted by the Domain Runtime MBean Server for domain services. Finally, the *EditServiceMBean* allows clients access to the editable configuration MBeans managed by the Edit MBean Server. JMX clients are required to use the credentials of users defined in the domain's security realm in order to connect to any of the MBean Servers.

How MBeans Are Organized

WebLogic Server uses a hierarchical system to organize its MBeans inventory. At the top of the MBean hierarchy is the *DomainMBean,* which is analogous to the root directory. Underneath this root directory are MBean *types* such as the *LogMBean,* for example. You can think of MBean types as subdirectories in the hierarchy of MBeans. You can have the domain as the type or a server as the type. Under each MBean type, such as the *ServerMBean,* are MBean instances, which correlate to a server instance such as an Admin Server or a Managed Server. Under each of the MBean instances are the actual attributes and operations that you can view or modify with WLST commands. The hierarchical system of organizing the MBeans means that you can use filesystem commands such as *ls, cd,* and *pwd* to move around in the hierarchy, just as you would in a UNIX or Linux file system. Note that configuration MBeans are a direct reflection of the XML hierarchy in the *config.xml* file.

Following is how the WebLogic Server organizes its MBeans in a hierarchy of types=>instances=>attributes (and operations).

```
Domain MBean (root)
    |---MBean type (ServerMBean)
                   |----MBean instance(My_AdminServer)
                             |----MBean attributes and operations (StartupMode)
                   |----MBean Instance(Managed_Server1)
                             |----MBean attributes and operations (AutoRestart)
```

You, as an administrator, don't have to know anything further about how to work with MBeans and the MBean Servers directly. You can use a JMX client such as the Admin Server or WLST to edit the configuration MBeans. When you make a configuration change through the Administration Console, for example, the console, which is a JMX client, modifies the configuration MBeans and instructs the Admin Server to save those changes. Note that the server doesn't directly modify the configuration file, such as the *config.xml* file—it saves the changes in the pending configuration files for the domain, which are stored in the domain's pending directory. The Administration Console (or any other JMX client you may be using) will then update the read-only configuration files and configuration MBeans for all servers as part of the change activation process.

Accessing MBeans Through WLST

You can use WLST, which is a JMX client, to interact with a server's in-memory MBeans. The MBeans offer a management interface so WLST can manage various server resources. Using WLST, you can connect to an Admin Server to manage a domain's configuration and check how various server resources are performing. You can connect to a Managed Server and view performance data, but you can't modify its configuration through WLST. You can view and modify the configuration data stored in the *config.xml* file through WLST offline commands (without connecting to the server); however, Oracle recommends that you don't do this because if the server is running and you modify the *config.xml* file with a WLST offline command, not only will the running server ignore those changes, but also any changes made through the Administration Console will overwrite those changes. Also, since WebLogic Server doesn't store most of the default configuration values in the *config.xml* file, you can't access many management objects through WLST offline commands.

WLST provides a layer above the standard Jython interpreter, which provides a directory navigation paradigm that is familiar to most users and especially those administrators who are used to scripted configuration. You can use WLST online commands to access the hierarchy of a server's MBeans. You can use various commands to navigate the MBean hierarchy and query the runtime MBeans, as well as the editable copies of all domain configuration MBeans. When you use WLST to connect to a server instance, WLST connects to the *DomainMBean,* which is the root of the MBean hierarchy. WLST uses a variable named *cmo* (configuration management object) to represent the current management object. You can use the *cmo* variable to query (get) or modify (set) a management object's attributes. The value of the *cmo* at any given moment is the same as the current WLST path. You can change directories with the *cd* command, and this resets the value of the *cmo* object to that of the new WLST path. Thus, when you change directories by moving to the Servers/ManagedServer1 directory, as shown in the following example, the *cmo* changes to an instance of the *ServerMBean* from the previous *cmo* of the *DomainMBean*.

```
wls:/offline> connect('weblogic','welcome1')
Connecting to t3://localhost:7001 with userid weblogic ...
Successfully connected to Admin Server 'TestServer' that belongs to domain 'test
_domain'.

Warning: An insecure protocol was used to connect to the
server. To ensure on-the-wire security, the SSL port or
Admin port should be used instead.

wls:/test_domain/serverConfig> cmo
[MBeanServerInvocationHandler]com.bea:Name=test_domain,Type=Domain
wls:/test_domain/serverConfig> cd('Servers')
wls:/test_domain/serverConfig/Servers>
wls:/test_domain/serverConfig/Servers> cd('ManagedServer1')
wls:/test_domain/serverConfig/Servers/ManagedServer1>

wls:/test_domain/serverConfig/Servers/ManagedServer1> cmo
[MBeanServerInvocationHandler]com.bea:Name=ManagedServer1,Type=Server
wls:/test_domain/serverConfig/Servers/ManagedServer1>
```

You can return to the parent directory (and the parent MBean) by executing the *cd* command, as shown here:

```
wls:/mydomain/serverConfig/Servers/myserver/Log/myserver> cmo
MBeanServerInvocationHandler]mydomain:Name=myserver,Server=myserver,Type=Log
wls:/mydomain/serverConfig/Servers/myserver/Log/myserver> cd('..')
wls:/mydomain/serverConfig/Servers/myserver/Log>
wls:/mydomain/serverConfig/Servers/myserver/Log> cmo
[MBeanServerInvocationHandler]mydomain:Name=myserver,Type=Server
```

Use the *ls* command to view the attributes and operations, as well as all child MBeans, from any directory you happen to be in. Here's how you execute the command:

```
wls:/offline> connect('weblogic','welcome1')
wls:/test_domain/serverConfig/Servers> ls()
dr--   ManagedServer1
dr--   TestServer
wls:/test_domain/serverConfig/Servers>
```

You can view all the directories under a server, say TestServer in this example, by doing the following (I'm showing only a partial list of directories here):

```
wls:/test_domain/serverConfig/Servers> cd('TestServer')
wls:/test_domain/serverConfig/Servers/TestServer> ls()
```

```
dr--   Cluster
dr--   CoherenceClusterSystemResource
dr--   DataSource
dr--   DefaultFileStore
dr--   ExecuteQueues
dr--   JTAMigratableTarget
dr--   Log
dr--   Machine
dr--   OverloadProtection
dr--   ReliableDeliveryPolicy
dr--   ServerDebug
dr--   ServerDiagnosticConfig
dr--   ServerStart
...
wls:/test_domain/serverConfig/Servers/TestServer>
```

The *serverRuntime* command is a WLST tree command that takes you to the root of the *ServerRuntimeMBean* hierarchy. This hierarchy stores all the runtime MBeans for the server to which you've connected with WLST. Here's how you execute the command:

```
wls:/test_domain/serverConfig/Servers/TestServer> serverRuntime()
Location changed to serverRuntime tree. This is a read-only tree with
ServerRuntimeMBean as the root.
For more help, use help(serverRuntime)
wls:/test_domain/serverRuntime>
```

Note that prior to executing the *serverRuntime* command, you were at the serverConfig directory, which is the root of the configuration MBean hierarchy. This is the default tree where you land when you first connect to a running server with WLST. You can issue the *ls* command to view the various runtime MBeans:

```
wls:/test_domain/serverRuntime> ls()
dr--   ApplicationRuntimes
dr--   AsyncReplicationRuntime
dr--   ClusterRuntime
dr--   ConnectorServiceRuntime
dr--   DefaultExecuteQueueRuntime
dr--   EntityCacheCumulativeRuntime
dr--   EntityCacheCurrentStateRuntime
dr--   EntityCacheHistoricalRuntime
dr--   ExecuteQueueRuntimes
dr--   JDBCServiceRuntime
dr--   JMSRuntime
dr--   JTARuntime
...
wls:/test_domain/serverRuntime>
```

When you issue the *serverRuntime* command, it places WLST at the *ServerRuntimeMBean,* which is the root of the server runtime MBean hierarchy. You can view all the server configuration attributes when you issue this command. You can also issue the *domainRuntime* command to go to the root of the domain-wide management objects, which is *DomainRuntimeMBean*. Note that you can execute either the *domainRuntime* or the *serverRuntime* command after you connect to the Admin Server. You can issue only the *serverRuntime* command after you connect to a Managed Server.

Note that to connect to the WebLogic MBean Server, a JMX client such as WLST must supply valid credentials, meaning credentials that are defined in the domain's security realm. (Security realms are discussed in Chapter 9.) There are four default global security roles in the security realm: *Admin*, *Deployer*, *Operator*, and *Monitor*. Whereas a user with any of the roles can view all unencrypted attribute values, only a user with the *Admin* role can modify the attributes (as well as view encrypted attribute values). These roles also allow for a standard distribution of responsibilities, where *Deployers* are allowed to create new deployable entities (application and system resources) and *Operators* are allowed to start and stop server instances. *Monitors* can only view the system state and report information. An *Admin* can do any of these and also define and configure new server instances.

Using the Lock & Edit Mechanism in the Administration Console

When you make configuration changes through the Administration Console, you're changing the editable configuration MBeans. Changing configuration is a two-step process: you must first obtain a lock on the configuration MBean edit tree by using the Lock & Edit feature in the Administration Console. The lock ensures that your changes are saved to the *config.xml* file and other configuration files in the domain directory. Once you make your changes, you must then activate the changes. Once you activate the configuration changes, all running servers will update their own copy of the domain's *config.xml* file as well as their read-only configuration MBeans. This completes the configuration change process.

All this may seem like unnecessary overhead for making domain configuration changes, but there's important reasoning behind this. A key feature of the domain configuration process is the ability to stage and validate groups of changes for your production environment. Most IT operations require a closely controlled rollout process for introducing updates to the production environment. Changes to the domain configuration or the introduction of new application versions require coordinating multiple changes. For instance, when deploying a new application, you need to configure new server instances, deploy new JDBC connection pools, and deploy one or more application archives. With WebLogic Server, all of these changes can be staged in the pending directory with a series of edit/save cycles and then activated at a scheduled time. WebLogic Server's configuration mechanism helps you by ensuring that the application of changes is all or none across the domain.

As you learned in Chapter 2, the Change Center of the Administration Console lets you lock pending configuration changes so that another user can't change the configuration while you're still in the process of modifying a domain's configuration. However, after you obtain a configuration change lock by clicking the Lock & Edit button in the Change Center, you can open a WLST session to edit that session's configuration changes.

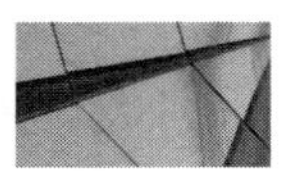

TIP

You can make unlimited configuration changes by obtaining a single lock and activate all your changes at once. You can configure a timeout period to limit the amount of time the Administration Console holds a lock you placed in the Change Center.

— Change Center Preferences

☐ **Warn If User Holds Lock** — Causes a warning message to be issued when a user logs out, indicating that the user is currently the owner of the domain configuration lock. More Info...

Activation Timeout: 300 — The time(in seconds) after which an activation task should timeout. Value of -1 indicates the task will not timeout. 0 indicates asynchronous activation. Default value is 300 seconds. More Info...

☐ **Warn User Before Taking Lock** — Causes a warning message to be issued when a user attempts to take the domain lock, indicating that another user is currently the owner of the domain configuration lock. More Info...

☐ **Automatically Acquire Lock and Activate Changes** — Automatically acquire the lock that enables configuration editing and automatically activate changes as the user modifies, adds and deletes items (for example, when the user clicks the Save button). This feature is not available in production mode. More Info...

FIGURE 3-2. *Enabling configuration locking in the Administration Console*

When you run a server in development mode, the configuration locking feature is disabled—that is, by default, all the configuration changes you make are automatically activated by the Console. The feature is automatically enabled in production mode. If you want to use the configuration locking feature, you must explicitly enable it. Here are the steps to do so:

1. In the right-hand pane of the Administration Console, click Preferences.
2. Select User Preferences.
3. Deselect Automatically Acquire Lock And Activate Changes.
4. Click Save.

Figure 3-2 shows how to enable the configuration locking feature through the Administration Console. To enable the Lock & Edit feature, you must make sure to uncheck the Automatically Acquire Lock And Activate Changes box. Once you enable the locking feature, you must start any configuration changes by first clicking the Lock & Edit button and then save those changes before clicking the Activate Changes button to make the changes take effect.

NOTE
Dynamic configuration changes you make through the Administration Console come into effect right away; nondynamic changes require you to restart the servers.

Tracking Changes with Configuration Auditing

Whenever you change the configuration of any domain resource on any server, the Admin Server issues relevant log messages recording those changes, even in cases where the configuration attempts are unsuccessful. However, the Admin Server writes those changes to its own log file on the server where it's running, not to the domain-wide message log. You can set up domain configuration auditing, consisting of an audit trail of all domain configuration changes, by enabling the WebLogic Auditing Provider. The Provider will also write the changes as audit events in its own security log.

Enabling Configuration Auditing with the Administration Console

You can use the Administration Console to set up configuration auditing by following these steps:

1. Click Lock & Edit in the Change Center of the Administration Console.
2. In the left-hand pane, select the domain you want to configure (for example, wl_server).
3. Select Configuration | General.
4. Click Advanced at the bottom of the General page.
5. Select from the following four configuration auditing methods:
   - **None** No auditing of configuration events.
   - **Change Log** Write configuration events only to the Admin Server log.
   - **Change Audit** Direct events to the Security Audit Framework and let the Auditing Provider handle the configuration events.
   - **Change Log and Audit** Send configuration event information to both the Admin Server log and the Auditing Provider.
6. Click Save and activate changes by clicking Activate Changes in the Change Center.

Making a Domain Read-Only

In a production environment, you may wish to ensure that no one can edit the domain configuration by making run-time changes. You can set the appropriate attributes of the *JMXMBean* to disable the WebLogic editing service. The *EditMBeanServerEnabled* attribute of the *JMXMBean* controls whether JMX clients can access the runtime MBeans as well as read-only configuration MBeans when connecting to a server's Domain Runtime MBean Server. Here's how to use this attribute to disable configuration editing of the Examples Server domain:

1. Make sure the Admin Server is running.
2. Open a command prompt, and set the environment with the following command:

```
C:\MyOra\Middleware\wlserver_10.3\samples\domains\wl_server\bin>setDomainEnv.cmd
```

3. Start WLST and connect to the Admin Server:

```
C:\MyOra\Middleware\wlserver_10.3\samples\domains\wl_server>java
weblogic.WLST
wls:/offline> connect('weblogic','welcome1')
```

4. Execute the following commands to start a WLST editing session:

```
wls:/wl_server/serverConfig> edit()
wls:/wl_server/edit !> startEdit()
```

5. Change the directory to the JMX directory:

```
wls:/wl_server/edit !> cd('JMX/wl_server')
```

6. Set the *EditMBeanServerEnabled* attribute of the *JMXMBean* to false:

```
wls:/wl_server/edit/JMX/wl_server !> set('EditMBeanServerEnabled','false')
```

7. Activate the changes you made and exit WLST:

```
wls:/wl_server/edit/JMX/wl_server !> activate()
wls:/wl_server/edit/JMX/wl_server !> exit()
```

Following this change, JMX clients, such as the Administration Console and WLST in online mode, can't modify the domain configuration. The example here showed how to control the Edit MBean Server (a type of JMX server); you can control each of the other MBean Servers in the same way. You can change the domain configuration with WLST offline commands. As stated earlier, however, Oracle recommends that you do not use WLST offline commands to modify the domain configuration.

Controlling the Logging of Configuration Changes

You can set several options with the *weblogic.Server* command to control the way servers log configuration changes. For example, by setting the following option, you can specify that the server write the domain configuration auditing messages just to the Admin Server log:

```
-Dweblogic.domain.ConfigurationAuditType="log"
```

By default, WebLogic Server saves all server log files in the DOMAIN_NAME\servers\<*server_name*>\logs directory. You can change the default server log filename and its location by following these steps. Figure 3-3 shows the relevant page in the Administration Console.

1. Click Lock & Edit in the Change Center.
2. In the left-hand pane, expand the Environment group and select Servers.
3. Click the name of the server in the Servers table.
4. Select Logging | General.

Rotation
Rotation type: By Size
Criteria for moving old log messages to a separate file. More Info...
Rotation file size: 500
The size (1 - 65535 kilobytes) that triggers the server to move log messages to a separate file. The default is 500 kilobytes. After the log file reaches the specified minimum size, the next time the server checks the file size, it will rename the current log file as SERVER_NAME.lognnnnn and create a new one to store subsequent messages. (Requires that you specify a file rotation type of Size.) More Info...
Begin rotation time: 00:00
Determines the start time (hour and minute) for a time-based rotation sequence. More Info...
Rotation interval: 24
The interval (in hours) at which the server saves old log messages to another file. (Requires that you specify a file rotation type of TIME.) More Info...
Limit number of retained files
Indicates whether to limit the number of log files that this server instance creates to store old messages. (Requires that you specify a file rotation type of SIZE or TIME.) More Info...
Files to retain: 7
The maximum number of log files that the server creates when it rotates the log. This number does not include the file that the server uses to store current messages. (Requires that you enable Number of Files Limited.) More Info...

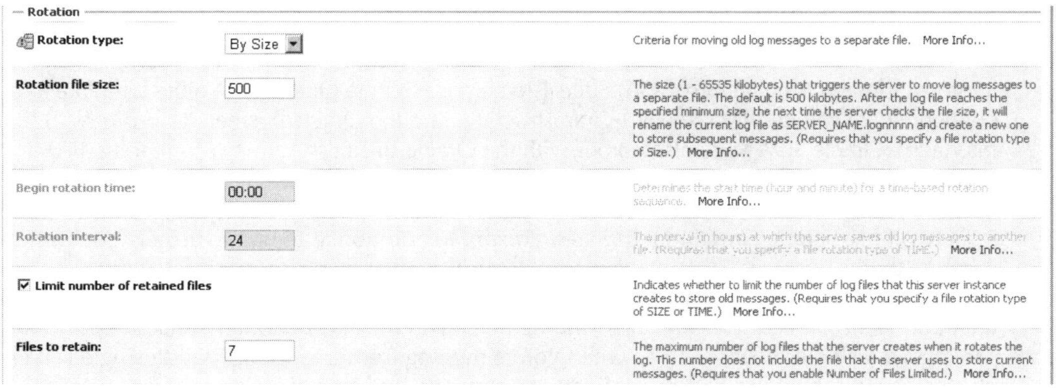

FIGURE 3-3. *Configuring the logging settings for a server*

5. Enter the new name for the log file and, if necessary, a new path in the Log File Name field.
6. Click Save and activate your changes by clicking the Activate Changes button in the Change Center.

You must also restart the server for it to start writing messages to the new log file.

Creating Domain Templates

A domain template is simply a jar file with all the resources (and applications) you need to create a WebLogic domain. A domain template is especially handy when you need to create new domains on a machine that doesn't share file systems with the servers hosting other WebLogic Server domains. You can use the Domain Template Builder, a graphic tool, to build or extend a domain. WebLogic Server uses three types of templates: domain templates, extension templates, and a Managed Server template. You use the first two to create and extend a domain. The third type of template (the Managed Server template) is only for use with WebLogic Server's *pack* utility when creating a Managed Server domain on remote machines. The WebLogic Server installation includes several domain-creation as well as extension templates, including the basic WebLogic Server Domain template, which the Configuration Wizard uses, by default, when you use the Wizard to create a new domain.

Instead of using the default WebLogic Server templates, you can create your own custom templates. Creating a custom template isn't hard—you can use either an existing domain or a template as the source for your custom templates. For example, you can choose a specific domain as the basis for a custom template. If you want that domain to serve as a model for other domains you're planning to create, you can then use the new custom template for creating additional domains with the Configuration Wizard, the *unpack* utility, or WLST commands.

Templates Offered by WebLogic Server

Oracle WebLogic Server provides several predefined domain templates, and you can find them in the WL_HOME\common\templates\wls directory (in my case, the directory is C:\oracle\middleware\oracle_home\wl_server\common\tempaltes\wls). For example, the Basic WebLogic Server Domain template is a simple domain template that helps configure an Admin Server and a default security realm. You must create and configure all other servers, services, and applications after you create this domain. The WebLogic Advanced Web Services template, an extension template, includes resources necessary for advanced web service implementations. If you're using Fusion Middleware products, you should know that almost all of them come with WebLogic domain or extension templates, so you can configure WebLogic Server for each Fusion Middleware product. For example, Oracle Service-Oriented Architecture (SOA) Suite 12*c* comes with the Oracle SOA Suite template to help configure data sources, JMS, the SOA infrastructure, and the Oracle business-to-business (B2B) user interfaces. Oracle SOA Suite also comes with the Oracle Business Activity Monitoring (BAM) template to configure the Oracle BAM Server and the Oracle BAM Web Applications tier.

Any template, whether it's a default Oracle template or one you create yourself, contains at least two files—*config.xml* and *template-info.xml*. In addition, a template usually contains several other XML files, such as *jdbc.xml, jmx.xml, security.xml,* and *startscript.xml.* If you're using a Fusion Middleware product template, it will also contain a *database.xml* file for configuring JCBC data connections. The *config-groups.xml* file helps you move functionally related applications and services in a single move, such as when you're moving from a topology with a single server to a cluster. This file contains all the applications, services, and mappings among the various components of a domain. When you create a domain with any of the templates offered by Oracle, the template creates all the necessary directories such as bin, config, security, nodemanager, and so on. You can review the *readme.txt* file that's part of each of these directories to understand what's either stored already, or will be stored, in that directory.

The following sections show you how to create a custom domain and a custom extension template with the Domain Template Builder.

Creating a Custom Domain Template

Follow these steps to create a custom domain with the Domain Template Builder:

1. Go to the MW_HOME\wl_server_12.1\common\bin directory and start the Domain Template Builder by executing the *config_builder.cmd* command (use the *config_builder.sh* command in UNIX/Linux environments):

```
C:\Oracle\Middleware\wlserver_12.1\common\bin>config_builder.cmd
```

2. On the Create A New Template screen, select the Create A Domain Template option. This option allows you to define all a domain's resources, including servers, services, applications, environment, and operating systems. Click Next.
3. On the Select A Template Domain Source screen, shown in Figure 3-4, you must decide between choosing an existing domain or a domain template as the source for your new domain. This page has two tabs—the Select A Domain tab and the Select A Template

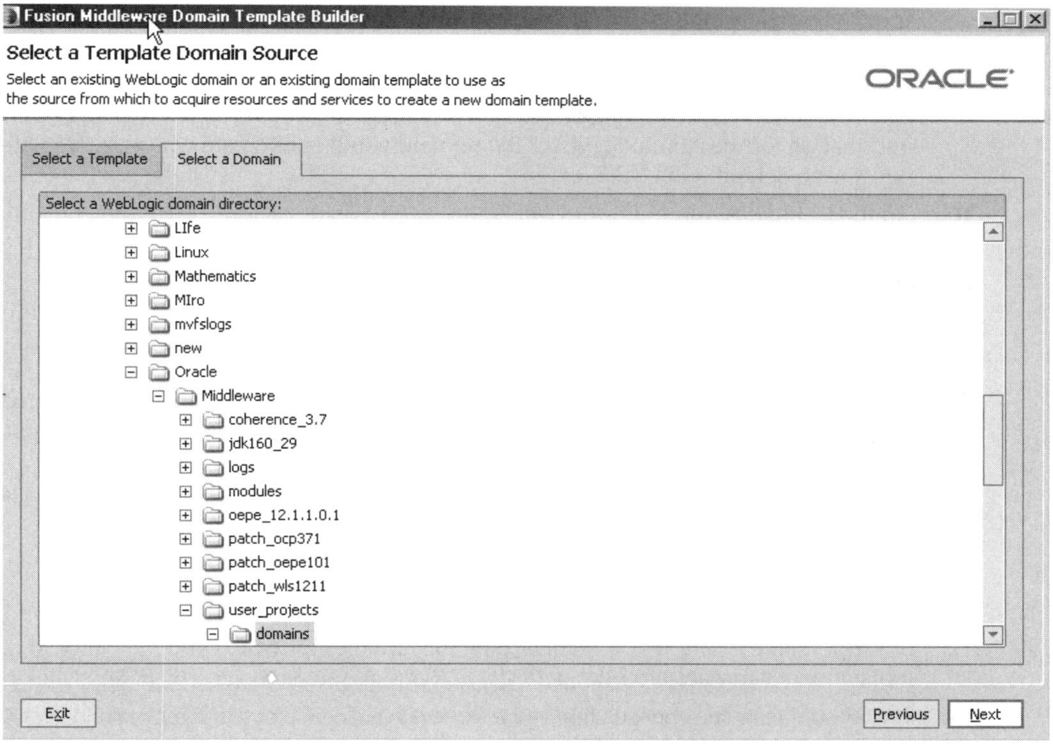

FIGURE 3-4. *Choosing between an existing domain and a domain template*

tab—to help you choose between an existing domain and a domain template. Thus, if you already have a well-configured domain, you can create a custom template that allows you to re-create this domain. To do this, choose the Select A Domain tab. (You don't actually have to click it because it's selected for you by default.) Domains are identified by the blue folder icon in front of the domain directory folder name. Click Next after you select the source domain or a source domain template.

4. On the Describe The Template screen, enter a name for the domain template and, optionally, a brief description of the template. Click Next.
5. On the Specify Template JAR Name and Location screen, you can optionally change the template JAR name and location. Accept the defaults and click Next.
6. If you are presented with the Add or Omit Applications screen, this is where you can choose which applications are included in your custom template. By default, all applications are selected. Click Next.
7. In most cases, you don't have to do anything on the Add Files screen. Because I selected the domain *MyDomain* as the source for the new domain template, the Template Builder Wizard, by default, will include several files automatically. These files include the bin and lib directories and all files from the root directory with the extensions *.cmd, .sh, .xml, .properties,* and *.ini*. The *config.xml* file for the source domain for the new template is also part of the file list. If you select an existing template rather than an existing domain as the source for the new template, the Wizard picks up all files from the source template automatically. Click Next.
8. The Add SQL Files screen lets you add optional SQL scripts to the new template. In this context, *SQL scripts* refer to any scripts you wish to run in the RDBMS that you choose to use with the new domain, which you plan to create with this domain template. Click Next.
9. On the Configure The Administration Server screen, provide listen address and listen port information for the Admin Server of the domain you'll later create with this template. Accept the default and click Next.
10. On the Configure Administrator User Name and Password screen, enter the credentials for the default administrator for the new domain you'll create with the template. Click Next.
11. On the Specify Start Menu Entries screen, you can optionally specify any Windows Start Menu options. Note that if you've selected an existing template as the source for this new custom template, the Wizard displays all Start menu options from the template you chose. In my case, since I'm using an existing domain as the source, I must define the Start menu entries myself. For example, I can specify the *startWebLogic.cmd* command as a Start menu option. If you choose to do so as well, click Add, provide a Shortcut link name, and then under Program, select *startWebLogic.cmd*. Click Next.
12. By default, the Domain Template Builder will replace hardcoded environment variables in various scripts and files with what are called *replacement variables*. You can use the Prepare Scripts And Files With Replacement Variables screen to replace any hardcoded variables that the Domain Template Builder hasn't already replaced. The Domain Template Builder offers replacement variables for any string you want to replace in a file or script. Some examples of the environment variables for which you may have to choose replacement variables are *JAVA_HOME, SERVER_NAME,* and *LISTEN_PORT.* Click Next.
13. Review your template configuration in the Review WebLogic Domain Template and click Create.
14. Click Done on the Creating Template screen once you see the message "Template Creation Successful."

The custom domain template you've just created will be stored in a new directory called user_domains under the MW_HOME directory. (The Domain Template Builder automatically creates this directory for you when you create your first custom domain. You'll find a new domain template named *my_domain_12.1.1.0* in this domain.) You can now use this domain template to create a new domain with the Configuration Wizard. In the Select Domain Source screen (the second screen) of the Configuration Wizard, choose the Base This Domain On An Existing Template option, browse to the user_domains directory, and select the custom domain template. Your new domain will be an exact replica of the source domain on which your custom domain template is based.

Creating a Custom Extension Template

The previous section showed you how to create a custom domain template. You basically follow the same procedures to create a custom extension template. After you invoke the Domain Template Builder, on the Create A New Template screen, select Create An Extension Template instead of Create A Domain Template. On the Select A Template Domain Source screen, pick a WebLogic domain or an extension template as the source for your new custom extension template. Figure 3-5 shows the Select A Template Domain page, listing all available domain templates and extension templates. The remaining steps (4–14) are analogous to the steps described in the previous section for creating a new domain template.

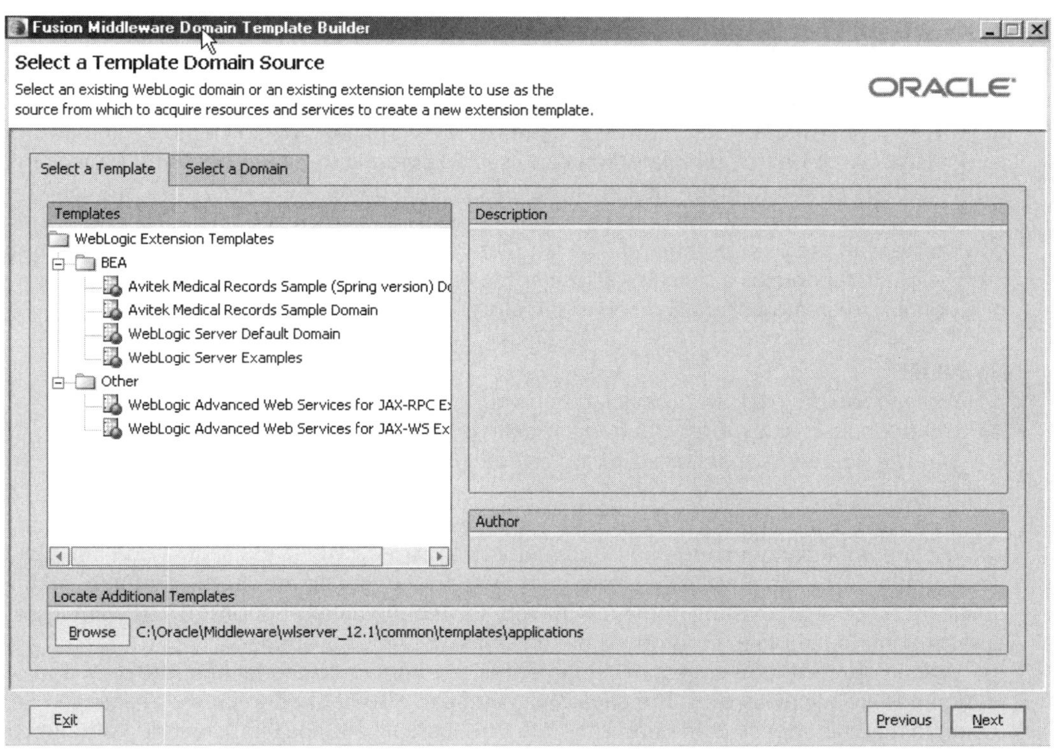

FIGURE 3-5. *The Select A Template Domain Source screen*

Using Server Templates

If you have a number of servers with a common set of attributes, you can use *server templates* to define the common attributes to apply to different server instances. You use server templates primarily for creating dynamic clusters, which are explained in Chapter 7.

When you define a server template, you specify the common attributes for a group of server instances. You can then specify the server template for each server instance in order to specify the configuration for the server instance. You can always override attribute values in the server template by directly configuring the server instance. The values you set for any individual server configuration will override the default values and the values you set in a server template. You can define macros for any string attributes in a server template.

The following is a brief summary of the steps to create two server instances by specifying their common attributes with a server template:

1. Create a server template and name it **my-cluster-server-template**.
2. Set all of the common attributes in the server template my-cluster-server-template.
3. Create server instances **my-server1** and **my-server2** and assign the my-cluster-server-template to both the server instances.
4. Specify any server specific attributes you wish to configure for a server.

Creating Templates with the pack and unpack Commands

As described previously, you can use the Domain Template Builder to create highly customized templates of your own by using either an existing domain or a template as the source. If you don't require a lot of customization, however, there's an even simpler way to create a template, as well as domains based on that template. You can use two commands called *pack* and *unpack* to create simple templates and domains quickly from the command line itself. The *pack* command helps you create a template, and the *unpack* command helps you create a domain from the templates you create with the *pack* command. The template that the *pack* command creates contains a *.jar* archive file that contains a snapshot of the entire domain or a subset of it. You can use the subset of a domain to create a Managed Server directory hierarchy on a remote host.

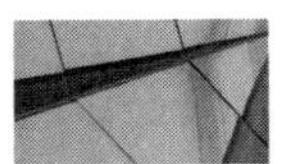

NOTE
You can use the pack *and* unpack *commands to create a full WebLogic Server domain or a subset of a domain that you can use to create a Managed Server domain directory on remote machines.*

If you create a domain template based on an existing template with the *pack* command, you can use the *unpack* command, the Configuration Wizard, or WLST to create a domain with the new template. The templates you create with the *pack* command are mostly useful for taking a quick snapshot of an existing domain with very few configuration options. If you want a real custom domain template, consider using the Domain Template Builder.

When you want to migrate a development or test domain to production, the *pack* and *unpack* commands are handy as well. The *pack* command can also be used to create a Managed Server template that the *unpack* command can then use to create a Managed Server domain directory on a remote machine.

Using the pack Command

The *pack* command's syntax is as follows:

```
pack -domain=domain -template=template -template_name="template_name"
[-template_author="author"][-template_desc="description"] [-managed=true|false]
[-log=log_file] [-log_priority=log_priority]
```

Here's an example that shows how to create a subset of a domain, which you can then use to create a Managed Server domain directory on a remote machine. Note that I specify the *managed=true* option to specify that the template is for creating a Managed Server on a remote machine. This example shows how to use the *pack* command to do this. Execute the command from the WL_HOME\wlserver_12.1\common\bin directory:

```
C:\Oracle\Middleware\wlserver_12.1\common\bin>pack
-domain=C:\ORACLE\MIDDLEWARE\USER_PROJECTS\DOMAINS\my_domain -
template=c:\oracle\middleware\user_templates\wl_server_12.1.1.0.jar
-template_name="My WebLogic Domain Template"
-managed=true
<< read domain from "C:\Oracle\Middleware\user_projects\domains\my_domain"
>>  succeed: read domain from
"C:\Oracle\Middleware\user_projects\domains\my_domain"
<< set config option Managed to "true"
>>  succeed: set config option Managed to "true"
<< write template to "C:\Oracle\Middleware\user_tempaltes\wl_server_12.1.1.0.jar"
...

>>  succeed: write template to
"C:\Oracle\Middleware\user_templates\wl_server_12.1.1.0.jar"
<< close template
>>  succeed: close template
```

In this example, the *pack* command saves the template you've created, *mytemplate.jar,* in the WL_HOME\user_templates directory. The reason for storing the templates here is that, for most domains, users will need all of the extra start scripts, security, and other files. You need to be careful when using the *pack* and *unpack* commands with domains other than the Fusion Middleware domains because they can pull in all of the jar files and the like.

Using the unpack Command

Use the *unpack* command to create a full domain or a subset of the domain to create a Managed Server domain directory on a remote machine. In addition to using the templates you create with the *pack* command, you can use the *unpack* command to create domains from templates you've created with the Domain Template Builder or WSLT. In fact, you can use the *unpack* command with any domain templates, including the default templates that come with the WebLogic Server installation.

Following is the syntax for the *unpack* command.

```
unpack -template=template -domain=domain [-user_name=username]
[-password=password] [-app_dir=application_directory]
[-java_home=java_home_directory] [-server_start_mode=dev|prod] [-log=log_file]
[-log_priority=log_priority]
```

Here's an example that shows how to execute the *unpack* command:

```
C:\Oracle\Middleware\wlserver_12.1\common\bin>unpack
-template=c:\oracle\middleware\user_tempaltes\wl_server_12.1.1.0.jar -
domain=C:\ORACLE\MIDDLEWARE\USER_PROECTS\DOMAINS\my_domain2
<< read template from "C:\Oracle\Middleware\user_tempaltes\wl_server_12.1.1.0.jar"
>>  succeed: read template from
"C:\Oracle\Middleware\user_tempaltes\wl_server_2.1.1.0.jar"
<< set config option DomainName to "my_domain"
>>  succeed: set config option DomainName to "my_domain"
<< write Domain to "C:\Oracle\Middleware\user_projects\domains\my_domain2"
...
>>  succeed: write Domain to
"C:\Oracle\Middleware\user_projects\domains\my_domain2"
<< close template >>  succeed: close template
C:\Oracle\Middleware\wlserver_12.1\common\bin>
```

The domain you create with the *unpack* command contains all the application and resource files for the domain, as well as the start scripts and several security and configuration files. When you execute the *unpack* command with a Managed Server template, the Managed Server domain directory will contain a start script and the *config_bootstrap.xml* file, which is based on the *config.xml* file for the original domain. You'll see new entries for the domain you created with the *unpack* command in both the WL_HOME\common\nodemanager\nodemanager.domains file and a new domain directory for the domain under the MW_HOME\user_projects\domains directory.

In the Oracle WebLogic Server 12*c* release, persistent stores aren't included in a packed domain. An empty file store directory is created in the target system if a file store is located in the source domain. The template generated by the *pack* command will, however, include the deployment plans located in external directories. The *unpack* command copies these deployment plans in the following standard location:

```
domain_home/config/deployments/deployment_name/plan
```

Finally, the Node Manager configuration is preserved for both managed and nonmanaged modes if the Node Manager type is either *DomainNodeManager* or *CustomLocationNodeManager*.

Creating a WebLogic Server Domain

As in the case with the configuration and management of a WebLogic Server domain, you can create a domain using several methods: you can use the WebLogic Configuration Wizard, the WLST commands, or the command-line utility *weblogic.Server* to create a domain. You may recall from Chapter 2 that the *weblogic.Server* Java class is the main class for a WebLogic Server instance and that you can invoke this command through scripts, operating system shell commands, or the Node Manager. Your actual choice of a domain creation tool depends on whether you prefer a graphical or command-line interface, and whether you need to automate the domain creation process.

Using the weblogic.Server Command

Although you can easily create a WebLogic Server domain by invoking the *weblogic.Server* command, you must be aware that this is a limited method in that you can create only a single server instance with this approach. You can't create any Managed Servers, nor can you modify an existing domain with this command. The following example shows how to create a domain using the *weblogic.Server* command:

1. Run the command *setWLSEnv.cmd* to set up the necessary environment variables:

```
C:\Oracle\Middleware\wlserver_12.1\server\bin>setWLSEnv.cmd

CLASSPATH="C:\Oracle\MIDDLE~1\patch_wls1211\profiles\default\sys_manifest_class
path\weblogic_patch.jar;
C:\Oracle\MIDDLE~1\patch_oepe101\profiles\default\sys_manifest_classpath\weblogic_
patch.jar;
C:\Oracle\MIDDLE~1\patch_ocp371\profiles\default\sys_manifest_classpath\weblogic_
patch.jar;
C:\Oracle\MIDDLE~1\JDK160~1\lib\tools.jar;
C:\Oracle\MIDDLE~1\WLSERV~1.1\server\lib\weblogic_sp.jar;
C:\Oracle\MIDDLE~1\WLSERV~1.1\server\lib\weblogic.jar;
C:\Oracle\MIDDLE~1\modules\features\weblogic.server.modules_12.1.1.0.jar;
C:\Oracle\MIDDLE~1\WLSERV~1.1\server\lib\webservices.jar;
C:\Oracle\MIDDLE~1\modules\ORGAPA~1.1/lib/ant-
all.jar;C:\Oracle\MIDDLE~1\modules\NETSFA~1.0_1/lib/ant-contrib.jar;"

PATH="C:\Oracle\MIDDLE~1\patch_wls1211\profiles\default\native;C:\Oracle\MIDDLE~
…
Your environment has been set.
C:\Oracle\Middleware\wlserver_12.1\server\bin>
```

2. Create a directory with the same name as the domain you wish to create (*test_domain* in my example):

```
C:\Oracle\Middleware\wlserver_12.1\server\bin>mkdir
c:\oracle\middleware\user_projects\test_domain
```

3. Change to the new directory and run the following *java weblogic.Server* command to create the domain:

```
C:\Oracle\Middleware\wlserver_12.1\server\bin>cd
c:\oracle\middleware\user_projects\test_domain
C:\Oracle\Middleware\user_projects\test_domain>java -Dweblogic.Domain=test_domain
-Dweblogic.Name=TestServer -Dweblogic.management.username=weblogic -
Dweblogic.management.password=welcome2 -Dweblogic.ListenPort=7022 weblogic.Server

<Jul 2, 2013 10:18:46 AM CDT> <Info> <Security> <BEA-090905> <Disabling Cryp
toJ JCE Provider self-integrity check for better startup performance. To enable this
check, specify -Dweblogic.security.allowCryptoJDefaultJCEVerification=true>
<Jul 2, 2013 10:18:46 AM CDT> <Info> <Security> <BEA-090906> <Changing the default
 Random Number Generator in RSA CryptoJ from ECDRBG to FIPS186PRNG. To disable
this change, specify -Dweblogic.security.allowCryptoJDefaultPRNG=true>
<Jul 2, 2013 10:18:46 AM CDT> <Info> <WebLogicServer> <BEA-000377> <Starting
WebLogic Server with Java HotSpot(TM) Client VM Version 20.4-b02 from Sun
Microsystems Inc..>
C:\Oracle\Middleware\user_projects\test_domain\config not found

No config.xml was found.
Would you like the server to create a default configuration and boot? (y/n): y
<Jul 2, 2013 10:26:09 AM CDT> <Info> <Management> <BEA-140013>
<C:\Oracle\Middleware\user_projects\test_domain\config not found>
<Jul 2, 2013 10:26:12 AM CDT> <Info> <Management> <BEA-141254> <Generating new
 domain directory in C:\Oracle\Middleware\user_projects\test_domain.>
```

```
<Jul 2, 2013 10:26:19 AM CDT> <Info> <Management> <BEA-141255> <Domain generation
completed in 7,663 milliseconds.>
<Jul 2, 2013 10:26:20 AM CDT> <Info> <Management> <BEA-141107> <Version: WebLogic
Server Temporary Patch for 13340309 Thu Feb 16 18:30:21 IST 2012
WebLogic Server Temporary Patch for 13019800 Mon Jan 16 16:53:54 IST 2012
WebLogic Server Temporary Patch for BUG13391585 Thu Feb 02 10:18:36 IST 2012
WebLogic Server Temporary Patch for 13516712 Mon Jan 30 15:09:33 IST 2012
WebLogic Server Temporary Patch for BUG13641115 Tue Jan 31 11:19:13 IST 2012
WebLogic Server Temporary Patch for BUG13603813 Wed Feb 15 19:34:13 IST 2012
WebLogic Server Temporary Patch for 13424251 Mon Jan 30 14:32:34 IST 2012
WebLogic Server Temporary Patch for 13361720 Mon Jan 30 15:24:05 IST 2012
WebLogic Server Temporary Patch for BUG13421471 Wed Feb 01 11:24:18 IST 2012
WebLogic Server Temporary Patch for BUG13657792 Thu Feb 23 12:57:33 IST 2012
WebLogic Server 12.1.1.0  Wed Dec 7 08:40:57 PST 2011 1445491 >
<Jul 2, 2013 10:26:21 AM CDT> <Notice> <WebLogicServer> <BEA-000365> <Server
state changed to STARTING.>
```

Once you answer yes (*Y*) to the questions whether you'd like to create a default configuration, WebLogic Server creates the configuration and instantiates the new domain, named *MyDomain*. Here's a summary of the configuration:

- The *config.xml* file is created for the new domain.
- There's one server—the Admin Server—named NewServer.
- The domain uses the default security realm, which is named *myrealm*.
- There is one admin user named weblogic (password is welcome1).
- The listen address of the Admin Server is localhost, port 7022. (You can also use the IP address of the host or the DNS name of the host.)

You can use the *boot.properties* file to bypass the prompt for a login credential when starting the server. You can use *the startWebLogic.cmd* (Windows) and the *startWebLogic.sh* (UNIX) scripts to start the server.

Using the Configuration Wizard to Create a Domain

Probably the easiest way to create a domain is through the Configuration Wizard. When you install WebLogic Server and choose to create the sample applications and domains, the Oracle Installer invokes the Configuration Wizard to create the various domains. The Configuration Wizard uses default templates to create or extend an existing domain. If you add a Managed Server or some other service to a domain, you've extended the domain. A template is simply a jar file that contains the necessary scripts and files WebLogic Server needs to create or extend domains.

There are three basic types of templates: domain templates that help create an entire domain, extension templates that add to the functionality of a domain, and Managed Server templates that help you take a subset of resources from a domain as a model to use in a Managed Server on a remote server. You can create the first two types of templates with the Domain Template Builder, and you can create all three types with the *pack* utility. Regardless of how you create a template, you can use the Configuration Wizard to create a domain or extend an existing domain. The Configuration Wizard will, by default, use the set of predefined domain template (the basic WebLogic Server domain template) and extension templates that comes with the WebLogic Server installation. Once you learn how to create your own templates, whether with the Domain Template Builder or with the *pack* command, you can substitute those templates for the default templates. Note that a domain template will enable you to create an Admin Server and define infrastructure components and general environmental variables for the domain. The Configuration Wizard uses the extension templates when you extend the basic domain by adding a Managed Server. You can use the Configuration Wizard to create a domain with just an Admin Server or a domain that includes additional Managed Servers or even a cluster. In addition, you can customize a domain by configuring JDBC settings, for example, to point to a different database rather than the default database (Apache Derby database) used by the domain and extension templates.

You can always start the Configuration Wizard in graphical mode on a Windows system. On a UNIX system, however, not all consoles support a graphical mode Configuration Wizard. If a UNIX console can't start the Configuration Wizard in graphical mode, it starts the Wizard in console mode by default.

1. The Configuration Wizard can be started in one of two ways on Windows:
   - Click the Windows shortcut at Start | Programs | Oracle | OracleHome | WebLogic Server 12*c* | Tools | Configuration Wizard.
   - Change to the following directory at the command prompt and execute the *config.cmd* file directly:

   ```
   cd C:\MyOra\Middleware\wlserver_10.3\common\bin
   config
   ```

2. On the Create Domain screen, you can choose to create a new domain or extend one. Because you're creating a new domain here, select Create A New Domain, as shown in Figure 3-6.
3. On the Templates screen, shown in Figure 3-7, you can choose one of the following two options:
   - Create Domain Using Product Templates
   - Create Domain Using Custom Template

   You can select the Create Domain Using Custom Template option if you want to base the new domain on a custom template instead of letting WebLogic Server choose its own default domain-creation template. Note that if you've already installed other Oracle Fusion Middleware products, such as the Oracle SOA Suite, you'll see additional products from those installations on this screen. Click Next.
4. Specify the login credentials for this new domain on the Administrator Account screen and click Next.
5. On the Domain Mode And JDK screen, shown in Figure 3-8, select the domain startup mode (development or production), as well as the JDK for the domain startup mode you choose. You can select one of the JDKs listed by the installer or specify a different JDK of your own. If you choose your own JDK, you must create the startup scripts for it yourself. If you choose an installer-offered JDK, the Configuration Wizard creates the server startup scripts to invoke the JDK. Click Next.
6. The Configure JDBC Data Sources screen appears only if you have already installed products such as Oracle SOA Suite 12*c*. Certain components such as Oracle SOA Suite

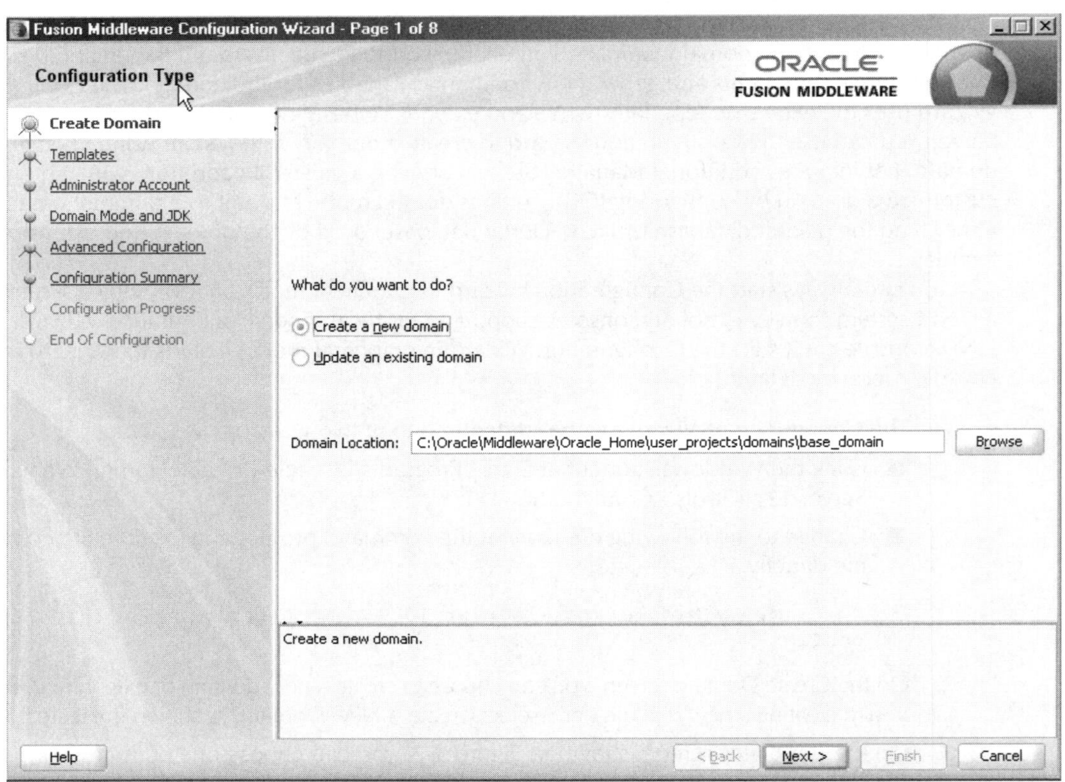

FIGURE 3-6. *Selecting the configuration type in the Configuration Wizard*

need to use the Oracle Fusion Middleware Repository Creation Utility (RCU) to load database schemas. If your domain contains a product such as Oracle SOA Suite, you need to configure the database schemas here. If your deployment needs the schemas' configuration, you must select all the tables and specify the database and service, the hostname, and the port for connecting to the database where the schemas are stored. You can choose one or several databases to store the various schemas. You can also specify the same or a different password for the schema owners. The Configuration Wizard will test your connections using the schema passwords you've chosen if you click the Test Component Schema button. Click Next when you've completed configuring the schemas.

The Configure RAC Multi Data Sources screen appears only if you have already installed products such as Oracle SOA Suite. If you do configure data sources, you'll have the opportunity to test those connections by clicking the Test Connection button. You may also have to click the Run Scripts button if any products you've already installed, such as SOA, include SQL files that need to be run. Once you finish running the necessary scripts, click Next.

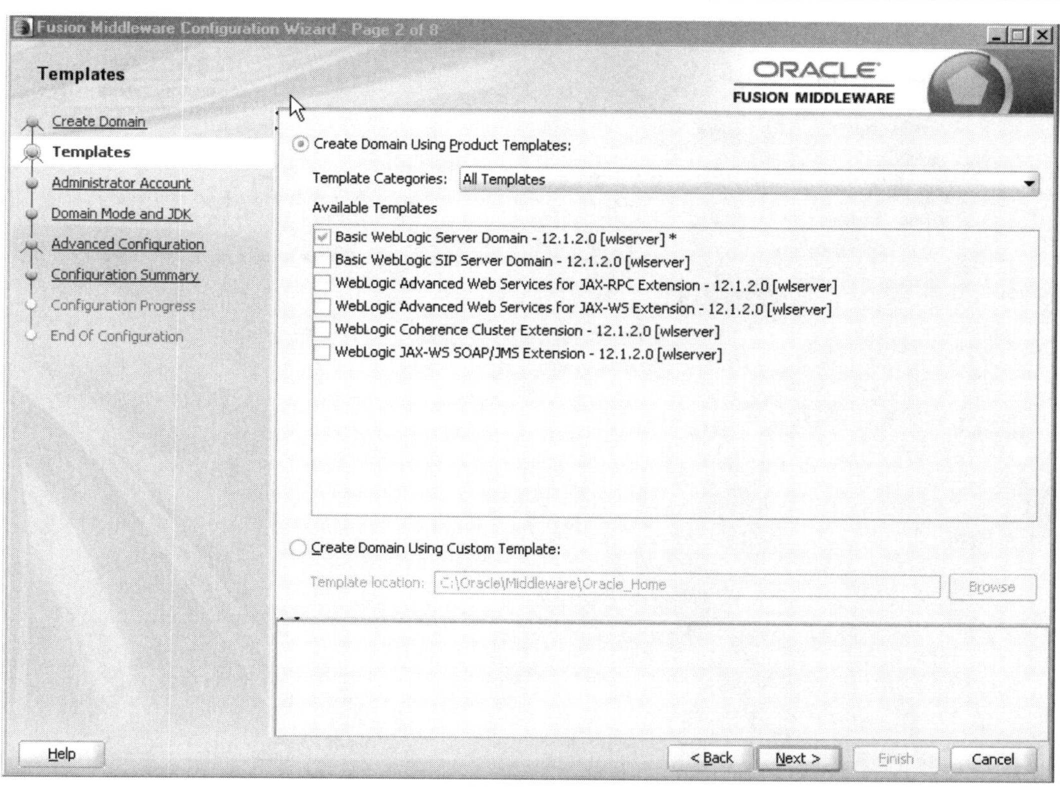

FIGURE 3-7. *The Templates page*

7. If the Configure Keystore Credentials screen appears, a component may require that you set a keystore password. Enter the passwords that you want to use for the keystore, and click Next.
8. On the Advanced Configuration screen, you may perform certain advanced configuration tasks such as modifying the Admin Server and Managed Server configuration settings and configuring the Node Manager. For example, you can select a specific Managed Server and set its listen address, listen port, and SSL listen port, as well as enable SSL communications for this server. In addition, you can configure an RDBMS as a data source for security products from this screen. You can also add (or delete) Managed Servers, clusters, and machines to the domain, as well as add Managed Servers to an existing cluster. Depending on what options you choose, you will navigate through additional screens. Select each check box you need and click Next.
9. The Configuration Summary appears next. You can drill down to an individual item's configuration details by clicking that item in the Domain Summary pane on the left side of the screen. Review the domain configuration settings, and click Create once you're satisfied with the settings.

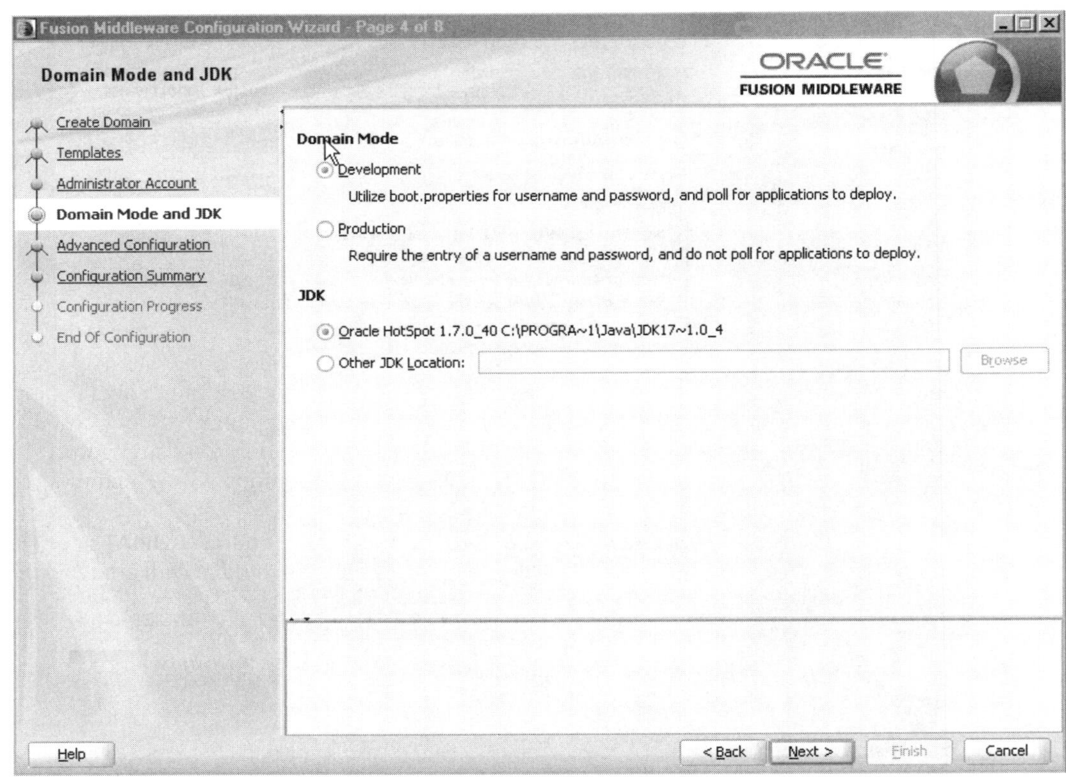

FIGURE 3-8. *Selecting the domain startup mode and the JDK*

10. You'll see the Configuration Progress screen next, showing you the progress of the domain creation. Click Next when the domain creation process is completed. Figure 3-9 shows the Configuration Success screen that follows a successful domain creation. Click Finish.

Note that by checking the box named Start Admin Server on the Configuration Success page, you can optionally choose to start the Admin Server for your new domain. If you do so, you can log into the Administration Console at this point. Selecting this option does not auto-start the Admin Server every time the machine boots up; it is intended only as a one-time startup after creating the domain.

Extending Domains

In the previous section, you learned how to configure a new domain with the Configuration Wizard. Once you create a domain, you can continue to use the Wizard to extend it. Oracle WebLogic Server uses extension templates to enable the extension of existing domains. The Wizard automatically accesses the default extension templates, but you can create your own extension templates with WLST or the *pack* utility. In addition, Oracle uses special extension

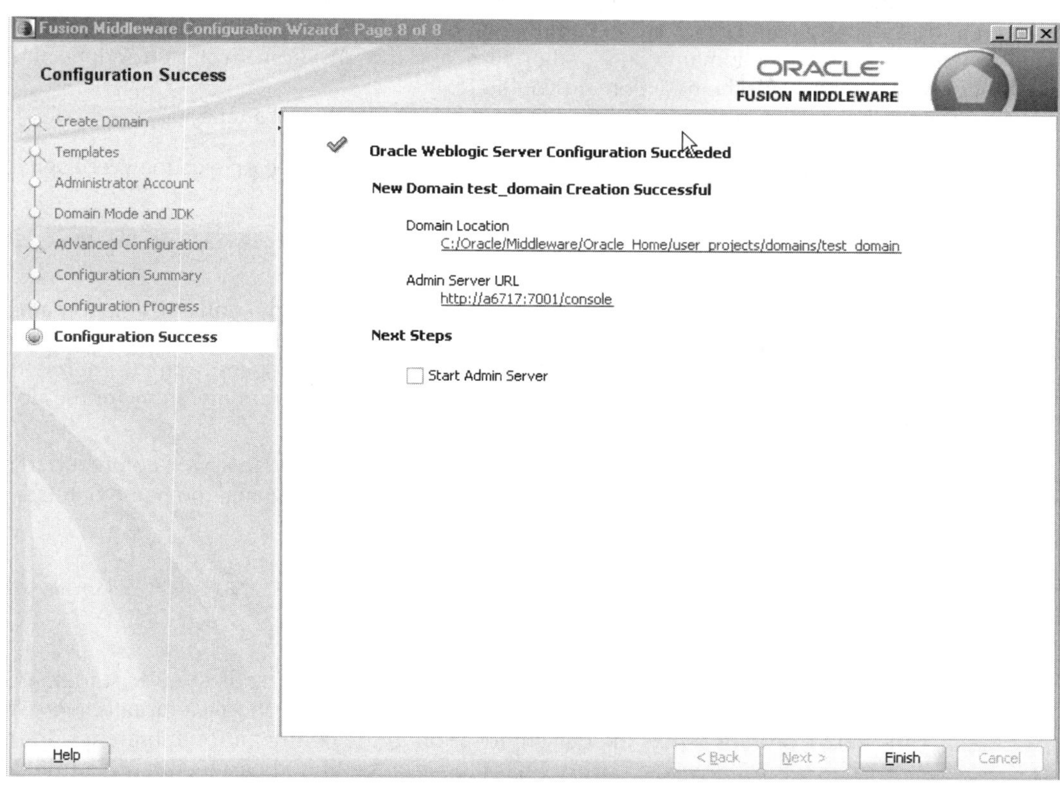

FIGURE 3-9. *A successful domain creation*

templates for various Fusion Middleware products. If you want to add more Managed Servers, add members to an existing cluster, change the JDBC data sources, or change the JMS file store configuration, use the Configuration Wizard.

To extend a domain using the Configuration Wizard, simply select the Extend An Existing WebLogic Domain option on the Welcome screen, instead of Create A New WebLogic Domain. The only new configuration screen you'll encounter is the third screen, Select Extension Source. Here, you can choose between using a preexisting Oracle extension template or specify an existing one. Once you select the extension template, the rest of the screens are identical to those that you navigate through when configuring a new domain.

Creating a Domain with WLST Commands

You can easily create a domain using the WLST offline command *createDomain* (preceded by a couple of other WLST commands, as you'll see shortly). Recall that a WLST offline command means you don't need to connect to a running WebLogic Server instance. You can also choose to modify existing WebLogic domains using WLST commands. The resulting domains would be the same as the ones you can create with the Configuration Wizard.

You can use either a domain template or an existing WebLogic domain as the source when creating a domain with WLST offline commands. The domain template is simply a jar file that contains the necessary domain configuration files, applications, domain startup scripts, and security information for the new domain you'll create.

Follow these steps to create a new domain using WLST offline commands:

1. Execute the *readDomain* command, as shown here, to open an existing WebLogic domain:

```
wls:/offline>readDomain('C:/Oracle/Middleware/user_projects/domains/base_domain')
wls:/offline/base_domain>
```

   In this example, I show how to create a new domain based on an existing domain—thus, I start with the *readDomain* WLST command. This command opens the domain *base_domain* for updating. Note that the WLST prompt changes from wls:/offline to wls:/offline/base_domain—this is the root of the configuration hierarchy for the domain *base_domain*.

   If you wish to use an existing template instead, use the *readTemplate* command to read a template. The *readTemplate* command takes just one parameter, the name of the template you want to use:

```
wls:/offline>
readTemplate('C:/Oracle/Middleware/Oracle_Home/wlserver/common/templates/wls/wls_
starter.jar')
wls:/offline/wls_starter>
```

   In the example shown here, the *readTemplate* command reads the *wls_starter.jar* domain template in order to create a new domain based on this template. Note that the WLST prompt shows the current location in the configuration hierarchy—in this case, it's wls:/offline/wls_starter. This is the configuration bean hierarchy for the domain template you wish to use, and you can now interact with the configuration MBean using WLST commands. Remember in Windows, you must use forward slashes or double backslashes in your directory names; for example, they must either be specified as C:\\Oracle\\Middleware\\wlserver_12.1\\common\\templates\\domains \\wls_starter.jar or C:/Oracle/Middleware/wlserver_12.1common/templates/domains/ wls_starter.jar.

   Just to reemphasize, I'm creating the new domain using an existing domain as the basis, not a template. Thus, I'll have to create a template before I create the domain, as the following steps explain.

2. Execute the *writeTemplate* WLST command to write the current domain configuration to a specific domain template.

```
wls:/offline/base_domain>writeTemplate('C:\Oracle\Middleware\
user_templates\MyBaseTemplate.jar')
wls:/offline/base_domain>
```

   WebLogic Server writes the domain configuration to the *MyBaseTemplate.jar* template. You can now use this template to create a new WebLogic domain.

3. Once you write the domain configuration to your new template *MyBaseDomain.jar*, you must issue the following command to close the domain. Otherwise, you'll receive an error stating that a domain (or a template) is open.

```
wls:/offline/base_domain>closeDomain()
wls:/offline>
```

Similarly, if you've issued the *readTemplate* instead of the *readDomain* command, you must issue the *closeTemplate* command at this stage to proceed to the next step where you create the domain:

```
wls:/offline/base_domain>closeTemplate()
```

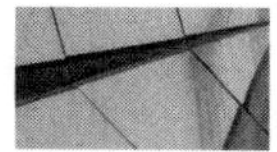

NOTE
The writeTemplate *command does provide similar functionality as the* pack *command, but you only create an Admin Server template with the* writeTemplate *command.*

4. Now that you have written the existing domain information to a template, you're ready to use that template to create a new domain using the *createDomain* command. Here's the syntax for the *createDomain* command:

```
createDomain(domainTemplate, domainDir, user, password)
```

Domain names must include only alphanumeric characters, hyphens (-), or underscore characters (_), and must contain at least one letter or digit. Here's the actual command for our example:

```
wls:/offline>
createDomain('C:/Oracle/Middleware/user_templates/wl_server_12.1.2.0.jar','C:/Orac
le/Middleware/user_projects/domains//my_domain1','weblogic','welcome1')
wls:/offline>
```

This command creates a new WebLogic Server domain using the template you created earlier and sets the default credentials to weblogic/welcome1. You won't receive any confirmation that the domain has been created, but the absence of any error messages means that the domain was successfully created. If you go to the domain directory you've specified for the new domain (C:\Oracle\Middleware\user_projects\domains\my_domain2), you'll see a new domain directory with the name my_domain2. You can start using the new domain now. Note that the *createDomain* WLST command works essentially the same as the *unpack* command.

At this point, you can start the Admin Server of your new domain by double-clicking C:\Oracle\Middleware\user_projects\domains\new_base_domain\startWebLogic.cmd (or using other startup methods discussed in Chapter 2), navigating to the Administration Console at http://localhost:7001/console, and logging in as the "weblogic" user.

When you create a domain with WLST commands, you can modify the domain configuration for the domain you're creating. You can review some of the current configuration settings after you issue the *readDomain* command, followed by the *ls* command, as shown here (in a shortened form of the actual output):

```
wls:/offline>readDomain('C:/Oracle/Middleware/user_projects/domains/my_domain2')
wls:/offline/my_domain2>ls()
drw-   AnyMachine
...
-rw-   Active                                        false
-rw-   AdminServerName                               My_AdminServer
-rw-   AdministrationMBeanAuditingEnabled            false
-rw-   AdministrationPort                            9002
wls:/offline/my_domain2>
```

Using the WLST set Command to Modify Domain Configuration

At this juncture, it's a good idea to learn how to modify the new domain's configuration with the *set* command and to finalize your updates with the *updateDomain* command. Here's a simple example that shows how to change the listen port of the Admin Server on your newly created domain with the *set* command:

```
wls:/offline>readDomain('C:/Oracle/Middleware/Oracle_Home/user_projects/domains
/my_domain2')
wls:/offline/my_domain2>cd('Server/AdminServer')
wls:/offline/my_domain2/Server/AdminServer>set('ListenPort',7777)
wls:/offline/my_domain2/Server/AdminServer>updateDomain()
wls:/offline/my_domain2/Server/AdminServer>closeDomain()
wls:/offline>
```

Note that I used the *cd* command to move to the Admin Server first. I then issued the *set* command with the new listen port and finally issued the *updateDomain* command to update the *config.xml* file for this domain. The *updateDomain* command updates and saves the domain configuration—the command automatically updates the domain's *config.xml* file. You must first open the domain configuration for editing with the *readDomain* command before you can issue the *updateDomain* command. When you've completed editing the domain configuration, issue the *closeDomain* command, which closes the domain for editing purposes. If the Admin Server was running, it must be restarted for the listen port change to take effect. At this point, once the Admin Server is started, the Administration Console is accessible at the new port on http://localhost:7777/console.

The WLST *set* command, when used in the offline mode, sets the value of specific configuration attributes and writes the new values to the domain's configuration files. You can issue multiple *set* commands in a row to update several configuration attributes, or you can use a script to execute a series of configuration changes, especially when you want to update a number of domains. Instead of executing the *set* command, you can also use the *cmo* (current management object) variable to set attribute values, as shown here:

```
wls:/offline/new_base_domain/Server/AdminServer>cmo.setListenPort(7666)
wls:/offline/new_base_domain/Server/AdminServer>updateDomain()
```

The effect of using the *set* or the *cmo.setattrName(value)* commands is the same: if you look in the MW_HOME\user_projects\domains\<*domain_name*>\config directory, you'll see that, in addition to the *config.xml* file, you now also have a file named *backup_config.xml* as well. Whenever you make a change to the *config.xml* file through WSLT or the Administration Console, the existing *config.xml* is saved in a backup file named *backup_config.xml, backup_config1.xml,* and so on.

Using the configToScript Command

Instead of using commands such as *createDomain* and the rest, you can simply use the WLST command *configToScript* to re-create domains. The command works with WLST in either the offline or online mode. The script reads a domain and converts the config directory into an executable WLST script, producing a Python file (*.py*) that you can then run on a different server. Because the script requires a running instance, it automatically starts the instance if it's not currently running. Here's the syntax of the *configToScript* command:

```
configToScript([configPath], [pyPath], [overwrite], [propertiesFile],
[createDeploymentScript])
```

When you execute the *configToScript* command, it creates a WLST script to re-create the domain, as well as a properties file that you can edit to update any security-related files containing encryption and key information.

Here's an example that shows how to execute the *configToScript* command. Make sure you specify the domain directory for the domain you want to use for creating the *config.py* file—by default, WLST looks for the *config.xml* file in the directory from which you started it.

```
wls:/offline>
wls:/offline>
configToScript('C:\oracle\middleware\user_projects\domains\my_domain')
configToScript is loading configuration from
C:\Oracle\Middleware\Oracle_Home\user_projects\
domains\my_domain\config\config.xml ...
Completed configuration load, now converting resources to wlst script...
Creating the key file can reduce the security of your system if it is not kept
 in a secured location after it is created. Creating new key...
Using existing user key file...
Using existing user key file...
Using existing user key file...
Using existing user key file...
Using existing user key file...
Using existing user key file...
Using existing user key file...
Using existing user key file...
Using existing user key file...
Using existing user key file...
Using existing user key file...
Using existing user key file...
Using existing user key file...
Using existing user key file...
configToScript completed successfully The WLST script is written to
```

```
C:\oracle\middleware\user_projects\domains\my_domain\config\config.py and the
properties file associated with this script is written to
C:\oracle\middleware\user_projects\domains\my_domain\config\config.py.properties
WLST found encrypted passwords in the domain configuration.
These passwords are stored encrypted in
C:/oracle/middleware/user_projects/domains/my_domain/config/c2sConfigwl_server and
C:/oracle/middleware/user_projects/domains/my_domain/config/c2sSecretwl_server.
 WLST will use these password values  while the script is run.
wls:/offline>
```

The command creates the *config.py* script and saves it in the *config* directory of the domain. When you execute the *config.py* script, WLST connects to a running server and run the commands in the *config.py* script to create the server resources. If a server isn't running, WLST will start a server using the values in the properties file, run the script commands to create various resources, and when it finishes, shut down the server.

Selecting the Startup Mode for the WebLogic Domain

You can start the WebLogic domain in either of two modes—development or production. Development mode doesn't involve a strict configuration of the domain, whereas production mode requires a more rigorous configuration of security.

NOTE
If you want to auto-deploy your applications, you must start the WebLogic domain in development mode.

Here are the key differences between using development mode and production mode:

- **Deploying applications** Only development mode lets you automatically deploy applications, which is done by deploying applications placed in the DOMAIN_HOME\autodeploy directory. If you start the domain in production mode, you have to use one of the standard deployment techniques: using the WebLogic server Administration Console, WSLT, or the *weblogic.Deployer* command.
- **JDBC system resource** Development mode allows you 15 connections by default, whereas production mode has capacity for 25 connections.
- **SSL** In development mode, you can use the demonstration digital certificates and the demonstration keystores. Using the same under production mode will result in a warning.
- **FastSwap** You can use the FastSwap feature, which lets you shorten your application development cycle only in development mode. Chapter 8 (which covers deploying applications) explains the FastSwap feature in detail.
- **Rotating log files** Each time you restart the WebLogic server instance in development mode, the server rotates the log file and also renames it once it reaches a size of 500KB. A WebLogic Server running in development mode can store only a specific number of log files by default, whereas in production mode the server can create an unlimited number of log files.

Advanced Domain Configuration Options

In the previous section, you learned how to create a simple WebLogic domain, mostly with default values for all servers and services. This section briefly describes how to configure various settings such as those for the Admin and Managed Servers. It also discusses some important configuration options, such as creating custom file- and JDBC-based persistent stores that you'll need for storing JMS messages, among other things.

Configuring the Admin Server

Following is a brief description of the key configuration parameters for the Admin Server. You'll find these options on the Configure The Admin Server screen when creating a domain.

- **Name** This mandatory field helps identify the Admin Server, and you must provide a unique name for it when you have multiple domains.
- **Listen address** You can select either All Local Addresses or Localhost as the value for the listen address parameter. If you want the server instance to be available to both local and remote processes, choose All Local Addresses as the value for the listen address parameter. If you want only local processes running on the same server to be able to connect to the server instance, select Localhost as the listen address. Note that you can provide either an IP address or a DNS name for the listen address parameter.
- **Listen port** The port value you specify for the listen port parameter is for nonsecure (normal) connections using HTTP and t3. The default value of the listen port is 7001.
- **SSL enabled** By checking this box, you can enable the SSL listen port.
- **SSL listen port** This option lets you specify a port for secure SSL connections if you chose to enable SSL connections (see the previous bullet). The default port for SSL connections is 7002.

NOTE
The range of port numbers for the localhost is 1 to 65000. If you choose 80 as the value for the localhost port number, you can omit the port number from the URL used in an HTTP request (http://localhost:portnumber/test.html).

Configuring Managed Servers

Creating and configuring a Managed Server using the Configuration Wizard is easy. Invoke the Configuration Wizard (with the *config.cmd* script) and select the Update An Existing Domain option on the Configuration Type screen. Click Next twice. Then on the Advanced Configuration screen, select Managed Servers, Clusters And Coherence. On the Managed Servers screen, click Next and then select the Add option to create a new Managed Server.

The process for creating a Managed Server is very similar to the one for creating the Admin Server, which you learned in the previous section, wherein you configure things such as the listen address, listen port, SSL listen port, and SSL enabled settings, for example.

Cloning a Managed Server

In Oracle WebLogic Server 12*c*, you can *clone* a new Managed Server from an existing Managed Server. Accessing this new cloning function is simple, which you'll find very handy when you're creating multiple Managed Servers in your environment.

You can access the Cloning function through the Configuration Wizard. Once you invoke the Wizard, select the following options to clone an existing Managed Server:

1. On the Configuration type screen, select Update An Existing Domain.
2. On the Advanced Configuration screen, select Managed Servers, Clusters And Coherence.
3. On the Managed Servers screen, click the existing server name to activate the Clone button (when the screen first appears, it's grayed out).
4. Click Clone on the Managed Servers screen to create an identical Managed Server as the existing Managed Server, but with a different listen port, of course.
5. On the Assign Servers To Machines screen, make sure the new clone Managed Server that appears in the left pane is moved to the right pane to assign the server to the machine.

In addition to using the Configuration Wizard, you can also use WLST commands to clone an existing Managed Server.

Configuring Clusters

If you choose to add at least one Managed Server, the Configuration Wizard will show you the Clusters screen, shown in Figure 3-10, through which you can add, delete, and configure a cluster. Click Add on the Clusters screen to create a new cluster. Here are the cluster configuration attributes you must configure:

- **Cluster Name** You must select a unique valid name consisting of a character string.
- **Cluster Address** You must provide the address of all the Managed Servers in the cluster using either a DNS name that maps to multiple IP addresses or a comma-separated list of DNS names (or IP addresses) and ports associated with those DNS names, for example, prod1:7001,prod2:7001).

Assigning Managed Servers to Clusters

If you choose to create one or more clusters, you'll see the Assign Servers To Clusters screen. You can assign Managed Servers to the cluster you select in the Cluster pane of this screen. Note that you can only assign Managed Servers to a cluster because an Admin Server of a domain is not part of a cluster. Of course, you can also remove an assigned Managed Server from a cluster on the same screen.

Configuring Machines

As explained in Chapter 2, you need to first define (create) a machine if you want the Node Manager to start remote Managed Servers. In addition, the concept of a machine helps WebLogic Server determine the best servers in a cluster to handle various domain-wide tasks. You must configure machines for each server where you're running a Node Manager process. Chapter 2

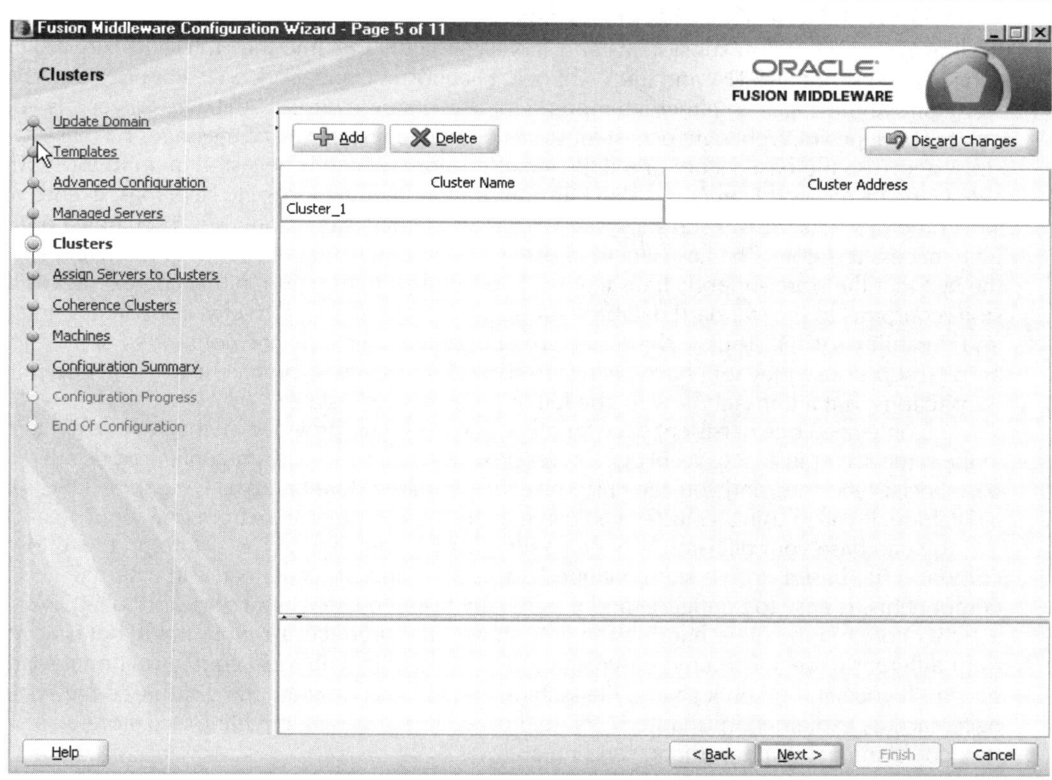

FIGURE 3-10. *Configuring a WebLogic cluster using the Configuration Wizard*

also showed you how to create a machine using the Configuration Wizard, in which you select the Machine tab (Windows) and click Add to add a machine definition. You specify a machine name, as well as the Node Manager listen address (the default is localhost) and listen port (the default is 5556). On UNIX servers, there are additional configuration items relating to the UNIX group ID (UNIX GID). Click Next after you've configured the settings.

Once you configure a machine, the next step is to assign the WebLogic Server Managed Server instances to that machine. Chapter 2 showed you how to assign WebLogic Server instances to a machine. You must do this for each WebLogic Server instance you want to assign to a machine.

Targeting Deployments to Clusters or Servers

The Target Deployments To Clusters Or Servers screen appears only if you use a template you've created that contains Java EE applications or libraries. Chapter 8 shows you how to deploy applications to WebLogic Servers. The next screen, Target Services To Clusters Or Servers, is similar—you'll see this during configuration only if your template includes any Java EE libraries.

Configuring a Persistent Store

Several WebLogic Server subsystems and services, mainly JMS and the Store-and-Forward (SAF) service agents, but also JTA and the WebLogic Diagnostic Framework (WLDF), need a persistence store to save messages on either a temporary or a permanent basis. WebLogic Server lets you create two types of WebLogic persistent stores to enable the storing of messages by these subsystems—a file-based store or a JDBC-enabled store, which is persisted in an RDBMS. The WebLogic Diagnostic Framework (WLDF) can use the persistent store to save logs, events, and the server metrics it harvests. Each subsystem that uses the persistent store uses a separate connection ID to access the store. The key benefit of using a persistent store is better performance, as well as the fact that the store supports transactions. Supporting a transaction in this context means the store conforms to the standard database transaction properties—atomicity, consistency, integrity, and durability (ACID). Thus, if the server goes down unexpectedly, the committed transactions aren't lost because they will have been stored on disk already—you may lose the uncommitted transactions, but a transaction won't be left in an incomplete state.

You only need one persistent store for all your subsystems, provided all the systems are targeted to the same server instance. WebLogic Server provides a ready-to-use, preconfigured default file-based persistent store, and you can customize the file-based store or create a separate JDBC store in a database. If you're using a cluster, you can migrate the persistent store from one server to another.

You can base your decision between a file-based system and a JDBC store on the following criteria: A file-based store is self-contained on a server and isn't connected to external components, is easy to configure, and is generally faster to use when compared to a JDBC store. A JDBC store, on the other hand, is innately slower and produces network traffic but is accessible from different servers. For a file-based store to be shareable, you must configure it on a shared file system. If you set it up on a shared file system, you can also migrate the disk-based file system, if necessary, as explained in Chapter 7. Note, however, that storing the file-based store on a shared disk could impact its performance and reliability.

Creating a Custom File-Based Store

Here are the steps for creating a custom file-based store:

1. Click Lock & Edit in the Change Center of the Administration Console.
2. Select Persistent Stores after expanding Services in the left-hand pane.
3. On the Summary Of Persistent Stores page, click New | Create FileStore.
4. On the Create A New File Store page, enter the name of the file store you want to create, the directory where you want the file store to reside (for example, C:\Oracle\Middleware\user_projects\domains\new_base_domain\servers\AdminServer\data\store\MyFileStore), and the server where you want to deploy the file store. If you're targeting your persistent file store to a migratable target, ensure that all members of the migratable target can access the directory you specify. Click OK when done.
5. Click the name of the new persistent store on the Summary Of Persistent Stores page.

   (Optional) Specify the following advanced parameters from the File Store | Configuration page: an optional logical name for the store, as well as Synchronous Write Policy options to specify how the persistent store writes messages and other data to disk.
6. Click Save and activate the persistent store by clicking the Activate Changes button in the Change Center of the Console.

You need to restart the server only if you're modifying the configuration of a persistent store, but not when you initially create it.

Creating a JDBC-Based Persistent Store

The process of creating a JDBC-based persistent store is similar to creating a file-based store, but there are a few extra steps, such as setting up the connections to the database. Here are the steps:

1. Click Lock & Edit in the Change Center of the Administration Console.
2. Select Persistent Stores from Services in the left-hand pane.
3. Click New | Create JDBCStore on the Summary Of Persistent Stores page.
4. On the Create A New JDBC Store page, shown in Figure 3-11, enter the name of the store and the target server for the store. For Data Source, you can select a configured JDBC data source or a multi data source. For now, select a JDBC data source by clicking the Create A New Data Source button. Enter a name, a JNDI (for example, **jdbc/db/MyFileStore**), and a database type (for example, Oracle). On the next screen, choose a database driver, such as Oracle's Driver (Thin) for Service Connections, after which you will be required to enter your database connection properties, including database name, hostname, port, database username, and password. You must ensure that all servers in a migratable target can access this data source if you're targeting a migratable target. You can also specify a prefix name to use for table names if you want to use them with multiple instances. Click OK when you're done.

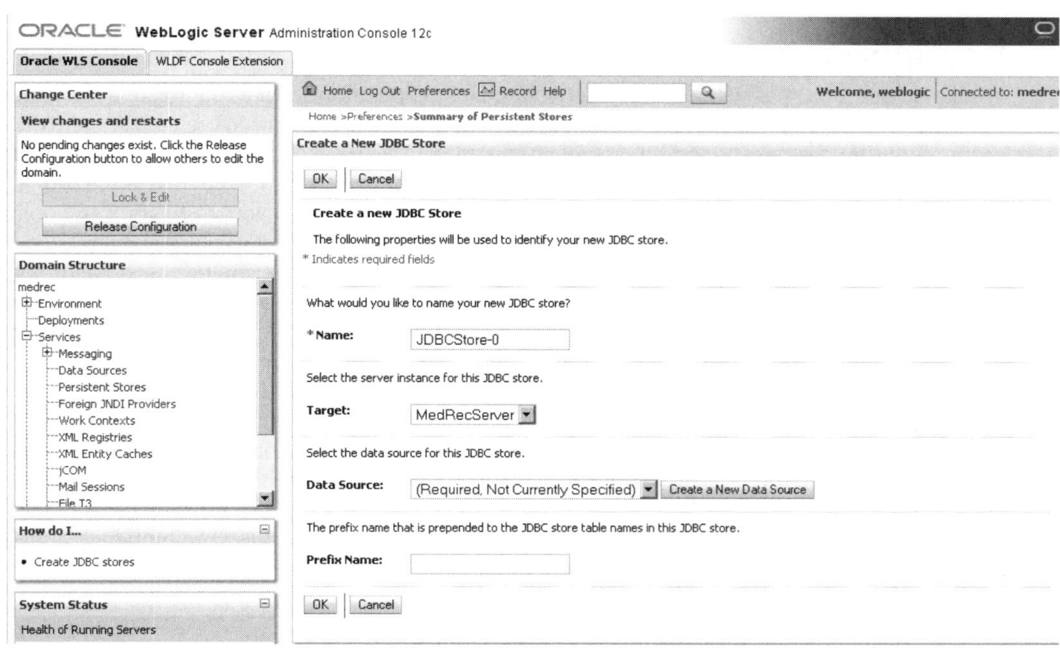

FIGURE 3-11. *Creating a new JDBC store*

NOTE

You must use a JDBC data source that uses a non-XA JDBC driver and not one that supports global transactions. Subsystems that use the JDBC store, such as JMS, have the necessary X/Open Architecture (XA) capabilities. Chapter 4 discusses transactions and JDBC drivers.

5. From the Summary Of Persistent Stores page, select the JDBC store you've just created. Click the JDBC Store | Configuration tab and update optional advanced parameters such as the logical name for the JDBC store. You can also select the Create Table From DDL File option to create the store's backing store, named WLStore, if there isn't one. You can also specify JDBC tuning parameters such as the maximum number of inserts and deletes per batch, but Oracle recommends that you leave these parameters alone unless Oracle Support requests that you modify them.
6. Click Save and then click the Activate Changes button in the Change Center of the Console.

You don't have to restart the server unless you've reconfigured your current JDBC store.

Configuring Server Environments

Deploying enterprise applications through WebLogic Server means you have to configure a bunch of things after you successfully complete the WebLogic Server installation. This chapter reviews some of the essential items you must configure, including the network, the configuration of WebLogic Server as a web server, proxying, and the WebLogic persistent store for using services such as JMX. Later chapters will show you how to configure other important things such as Work Managers, for example.

Configuring the Network

WebLogic Server comes with a default network channel and allows you to configure a dedicated administration channel for administrative traffic. In addition, you can configure custom network channels. Using custom channels, you can configure your network to meet your domain's needs by configuring different network interface cards (NICs) and port numbers. You can use these multiple channels to separate external client traffic from internal server traffic. If you wish, you can configure the network so that client traffic is handled by a dedicated NIC. All this promotes stability, performance, and the ability to handle various types of network failures, including the failure of a NIC. Network channels also enable you to configure different protocols and security requirements based on web traffic. You can use custom network channels to create complex network configurations that use different protocols for different listen addresses and ports, all on the same machine.

A network channel simply defines network connections for WebLogic Server instances by allowing you to specify attributes such as the network protocol, listen address, and listen port, as well as connection properties. Note, however, that the network channels and their configuration can have a huge bearing on service levels. Custom network channels certainly are an important WebLogic Server feature for production environments because you can customize channels for specific application requirements as well as scheduled and unscheduled maintenance activity. Custom network channels are discussed, in detail, in Chapter 5.

The Default Network Channel

You only need to configure basic attributes for your development server's Managed Servers. The two basic network attributes are the listen address and listen port.

Every WebLogic Server domain has a default channel that is generated automatically by WebLogic Server. The default channel provides a single listen address, one port for HTTP (nonsecure) communication (7001 by default), and one port for HTTPS (secure) communication (7002 by default). You can configure the listen address and listen port using the Configuration | General page of the Managed Server in the Administration Console; the values you assign are stored in attributes of the *ServerMBean* and *SSLMBean*.

The default network channel continues to exist, even when you create multiple custom network channels. However, remember that the default network channel is sufficient only for development and test servers, and not for a production environment, for various reasons. By default, WebLogic Server uses the nonsecure default protocol specified for the default channel to send nonsecure communications relating to session information to members of a cluster. Thus, if you want to disable the default channel, ensure that you create an alternative custom network channel that uses a nonsecure protocol. The other alternative is to create a special replication channel for cluster communications such as these.

The Administration Channel

You can have WebLogic Server create a separate administration channel by enabling an administration port. By default, the server has only the default channel running on the default listen port (7001). When you enable the optional administration port, a Managed Server will subsequently only use this port to communicate with the Admin Server—thus the name *administration channel*. You can start a Managed Server in the standby state only if you've configured the administration port. Once you set up an administration port, all administration traffic will flow through this port, with the other ports handling the application traffic. Thus, you can separate these two types of traffic by enabling the administration port, thereby letting the server create the administration channel for you.

The administration port you enable accepts only secure SSL traffic. Also, all connections to the server via the administration port must be authenticated. Just remember that the administration port you configure applies to the entire domain and not to any individual members of the domain. Therefore, when you set the administration port for one Managed Server in a domain, you must go ahead and enable the port for all other Managed Servers as well.

The Administration Port and SSL Once you enable the administration port, regardless of how you start a Managed Server, you must connect to the Admin Server through an SSL connection. In addition, following the enabling of the administration port, you can only connect to the Administration Console through the administration port. By default, SSL is disabled. You can also enable it from the Administration Console's Server | Configuration | General page by checking the SSL Listen Port Enabled check box. WebLogic Server uses demo certificate files for SSL communication, but you can configure SSL for production with a different set of security settings. Once you configure an administration port, you have two default listen ports for each server instance: the default listen port and the default SSL listen port. You must always keep the default non-SSL port because the server uses it if it can't bind to the administration port you've configured.

NOTE
Oracle WebLogic Server strongly recommends enabling the administration port. Besides separating administration and user traffic, the administration port is a prerequisite if you want to start a server in standby mode.

Configuring the Administration Port Before you enable the administration port, ensure that all servers in the domain support the SSL protocol. You must also enable (and disable) the administration port simultaneously for all the servers of a domain as well. Because you can't dynamically enable the administration port on a Managed Server, you must restart the Managed Servers once you enable the administration port for each server in the Administration Console.

Follow these steps to configure a domain-wide administration port:

1. Click Lock & Edit in the Change Center of the Administration Console.
2. Shut down all the domain's Managed Servers.
3. Under Domain Structure in the left-hand pane, select the domain for which you want to enable the administration port.
4. Go to Configuration | General.
5. Check the Enable Administration Port check box.
6. Enter the SSL port number for the administration port in the Administration Port field.
7. Click Save, and activate your changes by clicking the Activate Changes button in the Administration Console.
8. Start all the domain's Managed Servers.
9. As this is a nondynamic change, restart the Admin Server for the change to take effect.

Remember that you must now use the administration port to connect to the Administration Console. If you try to connect to the Console using the HTTP port and protocol (for example, http://localhost:7777/console), you will get the following message in your browser:

```
Console/Management requests or requests with <require-admin-traffic> specified
to 'true' can only be made through an administration channel
```

In addition, since Managed Servers must use the administration port now, you must specify the HTTPS protocol and the new administration port when starting a Managed Server, as shown here:

```
-Dweblogic.management.server=https://hostname:admin_port
```

If you aren't using a start script or command-line option, but instead are using the Node Manager to start your Managed Servers, you don't have to change anything: the Node Manager automatically uses the administration port if it's enabled.

Once you've configured the administration port, your server will have two default ports: a non-SSL listen port and an SSL listen port. You may disable either of these if you want to do so for some reason—you just can't disable both at the same time. To disable (and reenable) the listen ports, go to the Administration Console's Environment | Servers | Configuration | General page, and deselect or select Listen Port Enabled or SSL Listen Port Enabled. You can disable the verification of hostnames if the hostname in the URL is different from the hostname in an Admin Server's certificate by entering the following:

```
-Dweblogic.security.SSL.ignoreHostnameVerification=true
```

Note that you're supposed to use this feature only in a development or testing environment. Production configurations must use real certificates, but that's a lot of overhead for setting up a development or testing environment.

If you want the Managed Server to use the administration channel during a reboot, use the following option at the command line when you start a Managed Server:

```
-Dweblogic.admin.ListenAddress=<addr>
```

By doing this, you'll ensure that the Managed Server starts using the administration channel upon restarting.

Configuring WebLogic Server as a Web Server

By now, you are well aware that Oracle WebLogic Server is a powerful Java EE–compliant application server capable of supporting multiple web applications by serving dynamic content through servlets, JSPs, and custom tag libraries. You can also use WebLogic Server as a full-fledged HTTP server, serving static content such as HTTP pages, applets, and multimedia files, just like a normal web server. WebLogic Server provides all the standard web server features such as virtual hosts, which enable a single server or cluster to host multiple web sites, with each logical web server having a distinct hostname. You use the Domain Name Service (DNS) to map all the virtual hosts to the same IP address and enable a single web application to use these multiple virtual web sites. This section shows you how to configure the web server and the HTTP protocol.

Configuring the Listen Port

The default listening port on which the WebLogic Server listens for HTTP requests is port 80. When using this default port number, HTTP requests can leave out the port number, as in http://hostname/intro.html, instead of http://hostname:portnumber/intro.html, for example. The issue of setting port numbers is slightly more complex on a UNIX server than on a Windows server. If you want to use a port number under 1025 on a UNIX system, you must start the server as a privileged user, which leaves you vulnerable from a security viewpoint. By setting the *weblogic.system.enableSetGID* and the *weblogic.system.enableSetUID* properties to *true,* however, you can make the server switch its UNIX ID to a nonprivileged user account after initially binding to port 80, for example. WebLogic Server then uses the nonprivileged user account and group by setting the properties *weblogic.system.nonPrivUser* and *weblogic.system.nonPrivGroup*.

Here's how to configure the listen port through the Administration Console. The Managed Server can be running or shut down. If it's shut down, you need to restart it to use the listen port you've configured. Follow these steps in the Administration Console to configure a listen port for a server:

1. Click Lock & Edit in the Change Center of the Administration Console.
2. Select Servers from Environment in the left-hand pane.
3. Click the name of the server for which you want to configure the listen port.
4. Select Configuration | General.
5. Enter the value in the Listen Port box for the non-SSL listen port and/or the SSL listen port.
6. Click Save and then click the Activate Changes button in the Change Center of the Console.
7. Restart the server(s) for which you've changed the listen port number.

These steps work in a Windows installation. If you are running WebLogic Server under a Linux or UNIX-based operating system, additional steps are required to bind to the operating system username and group. To do so, in the left-hand pane, expand Environment and click Machines. If the machine is of type UNIX Machine, then you should select the Enable Post-Bind

UID and Enable Post-Bind GID check boxes, and enter the corresponding Post-Bind UID and Post-Bind GID to which you want the WebLogic Server web server to bind. By default, this is set to the UNIX user "nobody" and group "nobody."

Overriding Network Configuration with Command-Line Options

When starting a server from the command line, you may specify some options to override the configuration stored on the *config.xml* file. When you do so, the server will run with the options you've set until you restart the server. Changing any configuration settings (dynamic changes) through the Administration Console or through WLST won't affect these options until you restart the server. When you specify options at the command line by using the *-Dweblogic* option, the server instance initializes the configuration MBeans based on the configuration in the *config.xml* file, but for the duration of the server's lifecycle it substitutes the values in the file with those you manually specify.

When do you specify configuration options at the command line to override the settings in the *config.xml* file? You do so when you want to use a different set of values temporarily for configuration properties for testing or other purposes. For example, if you need to troubleshoot SSL issues, you may add the *-Dssl.debug=true* and *-Dweblogic.security.SSL.verbose=true* arguments during the course of the troubleshooting. This allows you to make temporary configuration changes without having to modify the *config.xml* file.

It's important to understand that you can't query the Administration Console to check any configuration values you've set on the command line to override the values in the *config.xml* file. Instead, use WLST to find the temporary configuration changes by interrogating the server's local configuration MBean. Here's an example that shows how to verify the attribute values you've set from the command line:

```
C:\Oracle\Middleware\Oracle_Home\wlserver\server\bin>java weblogic.WLST
wls:/offline> connect ('weblogic','welcome1','t3://localhost:7003')
Connecting to t3://localhost:7003 with userid weblogic ...
Successfully connected to managed Server 'My_ManagedServer_1' that belongs
to domain 'My_domain'.
wls:/My_domain/serverConfig> cmo.getAdministrationPort()
7001
wls:/My_domain/serverConfig> cd ('Servers/My_AdminServer/Log/My_AdminServer')
wls:/My_domain/serverConfig/Servers/My_AdminServer/Log/My_AdminServer>
cmo.getStdoutSeverity()
'Notice'
```

The WLST command *getStdoutSeverity* shows the current severity level of messages that the server prints to standard output. In this example, it is set to *Notice*. You can use the logging settings to change the severity level from the command line temporarily.

You can temporarily override the *config.xml* file values by setting command line values for server communications (port and host), SSL, security, messages and logging, clusters, deployment, and other server configuration options. This section shows some examples of how you can override the server communication and SSL configuration settings in the *config.xml* file. Note that setting configuration options in this way should not be a routine practice in your environment. In general, individual teams should lay out clear rules about which part of the WebLogic Server configuration is managed in which configuration artifacts. Moving the configuration to scripts would make for a great deal of confusion.

Server Communication Here are a few examples of the options that can be set at the command line to configure server communications:

- *-Dweblogic.management.server=[protocol://]Admin-host:port* /* overrides the administrator port setting.
- *-Dweblogic.ListenAddress=host* /* overrides the host address where the instance listens for requests.
- *-Dweblogic.ListenPort=portnumber* /* overrides the plain-text listen port.
- *-Dweblogic.ssl.ListenPort=portnumber* /* overrides the SSL listening port.

SSL Any options that you start with the *-Dweblogic.security.SSL* option modify the *weblogic .management.configuration.SSLMBean*, which is the MBean that represents a server's SSL configuration. Here's an example:

```
-Dweblogic.security.SSL.ignoreHostnameVerification=true /* disables host name
 verification
```

You can enable SSL for a server instance named My Server by issuing the following command when you start that server:

```
java -Dweblogic.Name=MedRecServer
        -Dweblogic.ssl.Enabled=true weblogic.Server
```

Note that the Administration Console won't show you any values that you set at the command line.

HTTP Tunneling

Normal HTTP connections are stateless and provide a two-way connection between server and client. HTTP tunneling is a way of allowing direct RMI access via port 80 and the HTTP protocol. This allows an EJB or JMS client to have access to service interfaces in JNDI without making a direct t3 connection. HTTP tunneling is commonly used to allow an applet to gain access to such functionality. You can simulate HTTP tunneling using a t3 protocol to set up a connection to tunnel through an HTTP connection for supporting stateful connections. By default, HTTP tunneling is disabled on a server, and you can turn it on in the Administration Console. You do this by going to Servers | Protocols | General and checking the Enable Tunneling check box. By doing this, you specify that tunneling should be enabled for this server for the t3, t3s, HTTP, HTTPS, IIOP, and IIOPS protocols. You can also configure two attributes that control tunneling behavior: the *tunneling client ping* attribute and the *tunneling client timeout* attribute. The *tunneling client ping* attribute determines the time within which a server must respond to a client request. The *tunneling client timeout* attribute determines how long a server must wait after a client request before concluding that the client connection is dead and terminating it. Oracle recommends that you leave these attributes at their default settings.

Setting a Default Web Application

A web application that you designate as a default application will field all HTTP requests that don't resolve to another application. The default application doesn't use its name inside the URL, as other web applications on the server do. In our sample wl_server domain, for example, the default application is named DefaultWebApp. For example, if there's a request for the file *stores.jsp* under the document root, the requestor can access it through the URL http://localhost:port/stores.jsp. If a client request uses a URL that doesn't resolve to any of your deployed applications, WebLogic Server forwards the request to your default application.

If you haven't configured a default application or if the resource isn't in the default web application, the user will receive an "HTTP 404, Resource Not Found" error. Setting up a default web application is simple. Use the context root in the *application.xml* or *weblogic.xml* file to set a web application as a server's default application. Just set the context root to / and set the context path in the *weblogic.xml* descriptor for the default web application as shown here:

```
<weblogic-web-app>
  <context-root>/</context-root>
</weblogic-web-app>
```

Of course, you must make sure you have deployed the web application to a server or a virtual host.

Preventing POST Denial of Service Attacks

You can set up the WebLogic Server so it prevents POST denial-of-service requests, which are designed to overwhelm a web server by sending enormous amounts of data in an HTTP post request with the intention of causing disruption by overloading the server. You can set the following attributes in the Administration Console for both normal and virtual servers to prevent these types of attacks.

The *PostTimeoutSecs* attribute controls the time the server pauses in between the receiving of chunks of HTTP POST data. The *MaxPostTimeSecs* attribute sets the maximum time a server may continue to receive POST data. Finally, the *MaxPostSize* attribute limits the number of bytes in a single POST method HTTP request. This can be configured via the Administration Console by navigating to Server | Protocols | HTTP. Note that Oracle recommends that you leave the default settings on for all three attributes.

Configuring HTTP Logging

HTTP access logging is highly useful for tracking HTTP transactions conducted by a web server. By default, WebLogic Server logs are in what is known as the *common log format,* the syntax of which is shown here:

```
host RFC931 auth_user [day/month/year:hour:minute:second
UTC_offset] "request" status bytes
```

A few observations about the common log format are in order. The *RFC931* attribute shows the IDENTD information returned for remote clients, but WebLogic Server doesn't support the identification of users. The *auth_user* contains a value only if the remote client authenticated with a user ID. The *request* attribute shows the first line of the client's HTTP request, and the *status* attribute shows the HTTP status returned by the server, if available.

WebLogic Server also supports the *extended log format,* which is a new logging standard specified by the World Wide Web Consortium (W3C). You can customize logging information with the extended log format by setting various attributes and selecting the exact type and even order of the logging information. Setting up the extended log format for all logging files is easy. Simply change the Format attribute to Extended on the HTTP tab in the Administration Console. You can specify various directives in the extended log format-enabled log file to tell the server which types of information it should record in the log files.

TIP
You can specify different logging attributes for each server or for each virtual host.

In the next section, I show how to enable and configure HTTP logging, specify the location and names of the log files, and change the way the server rotates the log files.

Configuring the HTTP Logs

By default, WebLogic Server stores all HTTP logs in the directory as server logs in the WL_HOME\user_projects\domains\<*domain_name*>\servers\<*server_name*>\logs directory. Follow these steps to configure HTTP access logs for a server or virtual host:

1. Click Lock & Edit in the Change Center of the Administration Console.
2. Select Servers from the left-hand pane, after expanding the Environment tab.
3. Click the server name from the Servers table.
4. Select Logging | HTTP.
5. Check the HTTP Access Log File Enabled box.
6. Enter a path and filename for the access log in the Log File Name field. This can be a relative directory, such as logs\access_log.txt, or a fully qualified directory, such as C:\Oracle\Middleware\user_projects\domains\base_domain\servers\AdminServer\logs\access_log.txt.

   If you want the server to affix a date and timestamp to the log files it rotates, enter the date and format variables surrounded by percentage (%) characters, as shown in this example:

   ```
   access_%yyyy%_%MM%_%dd%_%hh%_%mm%.log
   ```

   If you don't specify a date and timestamp, the server simply renames the older rotated logs with a serial number, such as *access.log00099*, for example.
7. In the Rotation File Size field, select the size to which the log file can grow before it's rotated by the server—that is, start writing to a new log file after archiving the filled-up (or timed-out) log file. The new file, meaning the current log file, will always have the simple name *access.log*, with no date, timestamp, or serial number.

   You can do the following on this page:

   - Choose to limit the maximum number of old log files the server retains by specifying a value in the Limit Number Of Retained Files check box.
   - Specify that the server not wait until the current log reaches its maximum capacity, but instead write to a new file after a specific time interval. You can do this by choosing By Time in the Rotation Type list box and entering the time interval in the Rotation Interval field.
   - Specify the log archive directory location in the Log File Rotation Directory field.
8. If you want to specify the extended log format for the log files instead of the default common log format, click Advanced at the bottom of the page and select the Extended format in the Format drop-down list. You can specify the fields for the extended log format by selecting Extended Logging Format Fields on this page.

9. Click Save and activate the logging changes you made by clicking the Activate Changes button in the Change Center.

Note that you must restart the server for the logging changes to take effect.

Proxying Requests to Other Web Servers

If you choose to set up the WebLogic Server as your main web server, you can configure it to act as a proxy for other web servers such as an Apache web server on the same or a different machine. WebLogic Server can then pass on specified HTTP requests to the other web server based on the URL of the HTTP request.

Unlike the rest of the web server configuration, you must configure proxying within the web application itself, not on WebLogic Server. Use the *HttpProxyServlet* provided by WebLogic Server and configure it within a web application that you've deployed on the WebLogic Server that you want to proxy HTTP requests. The *HttpProxyServlet* receives HTTP requests and sends it to the proxy URL you've configured, but the client response is sent through the WebLogic Server.

You must use the default web application on a server instance to set up web server proxying. Note that you set up proxying by configuring various things in the web application's deployment descriptor, named *web.xml*. (Deployment descriptors are discussed in detail in Chapter 8.) A sample *web.xml* extract showing how you actually configure the web application for proxying is included in Listing 3-1. Follow these steps to set up proxying to a different web server such as an Apache web server:

1. First, register the proxy servlet *HttpProxyServlet* in the application's *web.xml* file.
2. Specify the URL of the server to which you want the HTTP requests to be proxied.
3. By default, the proxy will use one-way SSL. Optionally, set up two-way SSL by configuring several *<keystore>* initialization parameters that include the specification of your certificate and key.
4. Configure the *<servlet-mappng>* element to map the *HttpProxyServlet* to a specific URL using the *<url-pattern>* element. Note that you can set this element to "/" so that WebLogic Server can proxy all requests it can't resolve to the remote server. If you do this, however, also map the extensions, such as *.jsp,* for example.
5. Finally, deploy the application you've configured for proxying to the Managed Server that will redirect the client requests to the Apache or another web server.

Listing 3-1 shows part of a *web.xml* file that configures the web application to use the proxy servlet *HttpProxyServlet*.

Listing 3-1 *Configuring a Web Application for Proxying*

```
<web-app>
  <servlet>
    <servlet-name>ProxyServlet</servlet-name>
    <servlet-class>weblogic.servlet.proxy.HttpProxyServlet</servlet-class>
    <init-param>
      <param-name>redirectURL</param-name>
      <param-value>server:port</param-value>
    </init-param>
  </servlet>
  <servlet-mapping>
```

```
    <servlet-name>ProxyServlet</servlet-name>
    <url-pattern>/</url-pattern>
  </servlet-mapping>
  <servlet-mapping>
    <servlet-name>ProxyServlet</servlet-name>
    <url-pattern>*.jsp</url-pattern>
  </servlet-mapping>
  <servlet-mapping>
    <servlet-name>ProxyServlet</servlet-name>
    <url-pattern>*.htm</url-pattern>
  </servlet-mapping>
  <servlet-mapping>
    <servlet-name>ProxyServlet</servlet-name>
    <url-pattern>*.html</url-pattern>
  </servlet-mapping>
</web-app>
```

Configuring the WebLogic Server Proxy Plug-Ins

Although you can, technically speaking, use WebLogic Server itself as a full-featured HTTP server, remember that its main purpose is to host dynamic web applications. You're better off using a dedicated web server for serving the static content and passing requests for JSPs and servlets to the WebLogic Server. In this type of configuration, a dedicated web server such as Apache HTTP Server, which serves as your primary HTTP server, is said to act as a proxy for the WebLogic Server instances. Note that a proxy web server is by no means necessary in your environment—if your applications mostly serve dynamic content such as JSPs and servlets, you may not need a web server to act as a proxy. WebLogic Server offers server proxy plug-ins for web servers, including Oracle HTTP Server, Apache HTTP Server, Microsoft Internet Information Server, and Oracle Java System Web Server. Note that, in most cases, this is the primary mechanism for managing clusters of HTTP sessions.

The proxy plug-ins give HTTP servers the ability to communicate with WebLogic Server instances. The plug-ins allow the web server to proxy requests that need dynamic functionality to the WebLogic Server. When a user directs an HTTP request to the web server, it serves any static pages that are necessary to satisfy the request and forwards the requests for dynamic pages to WebLogic Server, which processes those requests using servlets or JSPs. The WebLogic Server instance doesn't have to run on the same host as the web server.

The following sections shows you how to install and configure an Apache web server plug-in to proxy requests to WebLogic Server.

NOTE
By default, the plug-ins don't support two-way SSL, but you configure them so they request the client certificate, which they then pass along to the WebLogic Server instance.

Installing the Apache Web Server Plug-In

When you configure an Apache HTTP Server plug-in, you treat the plug-in like any other Apache module the web server loads when it starts. You can configure plug-in proxy requests to the WebLogic Server by proxying requests based on all or part of the request URL (proxying by path), or on the MIME type of the requested file. You can also specify a combination of the path and the MIME type, if you wish.

In releases prior to Oracle WebLogic Server 12*c,* you didn't have to download the Apache plug-in separately, as it was bundled with WebLogic Server. WebLogic Web Server Plugins 12.1.2 is now a downloadable option, separate from WebLogic Server. Access the Oracle WebLogic Web Server Plugins page using the following URL:

www.oracle.com/technetwork/middleware/ias/downloads/wls-plugins-096117.html

The full name for the plug-in is Oracle WebLogic Server Proxy Plug-In 12*c* for Apache HTTP Server. Using this plug-in, the Apache HTTP Server proxies incoming HTTP requests to the back-end WebLogic Managed Servers or clusters.

Because you are installing the plug-in as an Apache module and linking it as a dynamic shared object (DSO), you don't have to recompile the Apache web server.

Follow these steps to install the Apache HTTP Server plug-in:

1. Select the appropriate plug-in shared object file from the downloaded plug-in zip distribution. For Apache HTTP Server 2.2.*x* running on Windows 64-bit, locate the lib*mod_wl_.so* file under C:\myhome\weblogic-plugins-12.1.2, which serves as the PLUGIN_HOME (location where I extracted the plug-in zip file) in my example. The WebLogic proxy module for Apache HTTP 2.4 is named *mod_wl_24.so.*
2. Before you install the *mod_wl_.so* plug-in, you must ensure the *mod_so.c* module is enabled in the Apache server so you can install *mod_wl_22.so* as a dynamic shared object. You can verify this by executing this command:

   ```
   APACHE_HOME\bin\apachectl -l
   ```

   In the previous command, APACHE_HOME is the directory containing your Apache HTTP Server installation. In some installations of Apache, you may have to run the following command instead:

   ```
   APACHE_HOME\bin\httpd -l
   ```

   If you don't see *mod_so.c* as an enabled module, you must recompile the Apache server with the appropriate options (by including the *-enable-module=so* option).
3. Copy the *mod_wl_.so* file to the APACHE_HOME\modules directory.
4. Add the following to the *httpd.conf* file for the Apache server (you may want to first copy the current *httpd.conf* file), located under APACHE_HOME\conf:

   ```
   LoadModule weblogic_module  C:\myhome\weblogic-plugins-12.1.2\lib\mod_wl_so
   ```

   Optionally, you can define parameters in the Location block (for proxying by path) or the IfModule block (for proxying by MIME type). Here are examples for both:

   ```
   <Location  /mywebapp>
      SetHandler weblogic-handler
   </Location>

   <IfModule mod_weblogic.c>
      WebLogicHost wls-host
      WebLogicPort wls-port
   </IfModule>
   ```

If you're using Apache 2.4.*x*, in the *httpd.conf* file, the *LoadModule* line should look like this:

```
LoadModule weblogic_module  C:\myhome\weblogic-plugins-12.1.2\lib\
mod_wl_24.so
```

Include %PLUGIN_HOME\lib in the *PATH*, as shown here:

```
set PATH=c:\myhome\weblogic-plugin-12.1.2\lib:...
```

Alternatively, you can copy the contents of the lib directory to APACHE_HOME\lib, or you can edit APACHE_HOME\bin\apachectl to include the PLUGIN_HOME\lib directory in the path.

5. Check the syntax of the modified *httpd.conf* file:

```
APACHE_HOME\bin\apachectl -t
```

In some installations of Apache, you may have to run the following command instead:

```
APACHE_HOME\bin\httpd -t
```

6. Restart WebLogic Server and the Apache HTTP Server.

You should see the default page you defined for the default web application of your WebLogic Server instance.

Configuring the Apache Plug-In

Once you install the Apache plug-in, you must configure it so it routes requests to the appropriate WebLogic Server instance. The previous section described how to install the Apache HTTP Server plug-in so the Apache server loads the WebLogic plug-in library as an Apache module. Here is how you configure it:

1. Go to the APACHE_HOME\conf directory and open the *httpd.conf* file for editing.
2. Add the following IfModule block to the bottom of the file to specify which application requests the module must handle:

```
<IfModule mod_weblogic.c>
  WebLogicHost myweblogic.server.com
  WebLogicPort 7011
  MatchExpression *.jsp
</IfModule>
```

Note that the *MatchExpression* line in the IfModule block is optional—it specifies that all MIME type *.jsp* files must be proxied. Use the IfModule block to specify any parameters that apply to proxying by MIME type.

3. Use the Location block to specify parameters that apply to proxying by path. When you use the Location block, you must also use the *SetHandler* statement within that block to specify the handler for the Apache HTTP Server plug-in module. Here's an example:

```
<Location /weblogic>
  SetHandler weblogic-handler
  PathTrim /weblogic
</Location>
```

The *PathTrim* parameter shows the URL string that's trimmed from the beginning, before the Apache web server passes on a request to the Oracle WebLogic Server.

Configuring Virtual Hosts

You use virtual hosting to define multiple hostnames for a server or cluster to use. You can use DNS to specify multiple hostnames that map to a single IP address of WebLogic Server. You then designate which virtual host will serve the various web applications. The key here is that, as far as the browser is concerned, it doesn't see the individual machines that are behind the firewall or in the cluster; it sees the "virtual host" that hosts the application. Virtual hosting thus enables you to maintain multiple hosts on a single machine. Virtual hosts are useful for load balancing purposes, especially in a clustered environment. You can avail yourself of many more configuration possibilities by setting up virtual hosts. There's no limit on the number of virtual hosts you can set up, and you can specify separate HTTP parameters for each virtual host, settings that will override the server's settings. Remember that you can set up virtual hosts for a single WebLogic Server or for a cluster of servers.

NOTE
If you target a virtual host to a WebLogic cluster, it will apply to all cluster members.

Setting up virtual hosting in your environment involves, of course, creating the virtual host itself, but, in addition, there are multiple actions you must take to make applications use that virtual host. Here are the actions you must perform in order to enable virtual hosting of your web applications:

1. Create a virtual host.
2. Configure HTTP for the virtual host.
3. Target virtual hosts to servers.
4. Target the web applications to the virtual host.

The following section shows you, in detail, the steps to take to perform each of these actions through the Administration Console.

Creating a Virtual Host

Here's how to create a virtual host:

1. Select Virtual Hosts from the Environment group in the left-hand pane of the Administration Console.
2. Click New.
3. On the New Virtual Host page, enter the name for the virtual host you want to create. Click OK.
4. On the Summary Of Virtual Hosts page, select the virtual host you created.
5. On the Configuration | Logging page, follow the same steps from here on as you did when configuring a regular server for logging (see the earlier section "Configuring HTTP Logs").

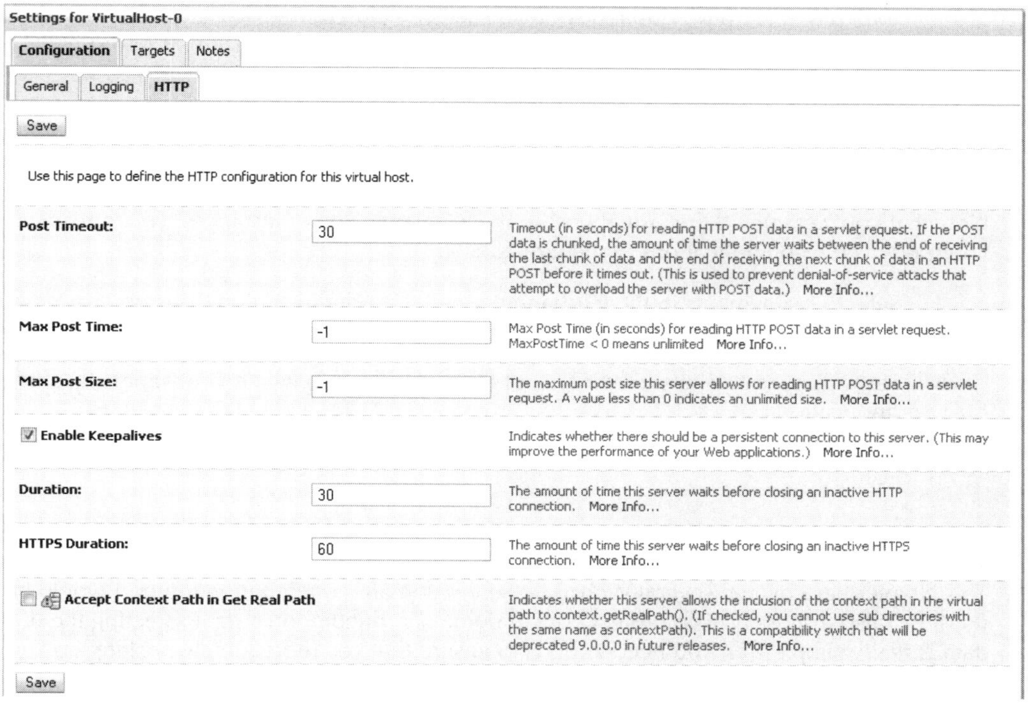

Settings for VirtualHost-0

Configuration | Targets | Notes

General | Logging | HTTP

Save

Use this page to define the HTTP configuration for this virtual host.

Post Timeout:	30	Timeout (in seconds) for reading HTTP POST data in a servlet request. If the POST data is chunked, the amount of time the server waits between the end of receiving the last chunk of data and the end of receiving the next chunk of data in an HTTP POST before it times out. (This is used to prevent denial-of-service attacks that attempt to overload the server with POST data.) More Info...
Max Post Time:	-1	Max Post Time (in seconds) for reading HTTP POST data in a servlet request. MaxPostTime < 0 means unlimited More Info...
Max Post Size:	-1	The maximum post size this server allows for reading HTTP POST data in a servlet request. A value less than 0 indicates an unlimited size. More Info...
☑ **Enable Keepalives**		Indicates whether there should be a persistent connection to this server. (This may improve the performance of your Web applications.) More Info...
Duration:	30	The amount of time this server waits before closing an inactive HTTP connection. More Info...
HTTPS Duration:	60	The amount of time this server waits before closing an inactive HTTPS connection. More Info...
☐ **Accept Context Path in Get Real Path**		Indicates whether this server allows the inclusion of the context path in the virtual path to context.getRealPath(). (If checked, you cannot use sub directories with the same name as contextPath). This is a compatibility switch that will be deprecated 9.0.0.0 in future releases. More Info...

Save

FIGURE 3-12. *Configuring HTTP settings for a virtual host*

Configuring HTTP for the Virtual Host

The next step is to configure the HTTP settings for the virtual host. The settings are similar to what you would configure for a real host:

1. Select Virtual Host from the Environment tab in the left-hand pane of the Administration Console.
2. On the Virtual Hosts page, select the virtual host you want to configure.
3. Select Configuration | HTTP and set the following attributes: Post Timeout, Max Post Time, Max Post Size, Enable Keepalives, Duration, HTTPS Duration, and Accept Context Path In Get Real Path. You'll find explanations for each of these attributes on the Console page. Figure 3-12 shows the HTTP settings page for the new virtual host. Click Save when done.

Targeting Virtual Hosts to Servers

Servers must be assigned to virtual hosts to take advantage of virtual hosting capabilities. Here is how to target virtual hosts to servers:

1. Select Virtual Hosts by expanding the Environment group in the left-hand pane of the Administration Console.
2. Select the name of the virtual host on the Summary Of Virtual Hosts page.

3. Select Targets and choose either independent servers or clusters. This is where you want to deploy your new virtual host. If you select a cluster, the virtual host is enabled for all servers that are part of that cluster, but you can specify only a subset of those clusters if you wish.
4. Click Save.

Targeting Web Applications to the Virtual Host

Now that you've targeted the virtual host to the WebLogic Server instances, you're ready to target your deployed web applications to the virtual host:

1. Select Deployments in the left-hand pane of the Administration Console.
2. On the Summary Of Deployments page, select the web application.
3. Select Targets and select the name of the virtual host to which you want to deploy the application.
4. Click Save.

Protecting Domain Data

This chapter has covered several WebLogic Server domain configuration topics. I would be remiss if I didn't also discuss how to protect critical domain configuration data. Protecting the domain data is really simple—all you need to do is to ensure that you're frequently backing up key server configuration and security files (and directories). Without an Admin Server, you can't manage your running Managed Servers. You must, therefore, protect all critical domain configuration data so you can recover it in the event of server failures. You must periodically archive the domain configuration and save it to disk or tape. You can also copy all domain configuration data to a different "standby" server, which can act as a backup server. Chapter 2 showed you how to restart an Admin Server on a different machine following a server failure. You need access to the machine where the Admin Server was running to get the configuration files. If the machine itself is unreachable, then you can only restart the Admin Server by restoring good backups of the configuration and security files on the new server(s). Thus, a good backup policy for the domain configuration files is highly critical. The following sections explain the various configuration and security files that you must back up regularly.

You must protect a domain's configuration files by specifying a backup scheme for your WebLogic Server configuration files. You'll need the backups if your configuration files get corrupted for some reason. The configuration files also come in handy when you decide to return to an older configuration after testing some configuration changes. You can use either WLST or the Administration Console to specify the archiving of the configuration files.

Backing Up a Domain's config.xml File

By default, WebLogic Server backs up the critical *config.xml* file and renames it to a different name, such as *backup_config1.xml, backup_config2.xml,* and so on. This way, if you ever have to revert to an older configuration state, you can simply rename the appropriate *backup_config#.xml* file to *config.xml* and restart the Admin Server. If you make a series of configuration changes and make a mistake somewhere along the way, your Admin Server may not boot up the next time.

You can simply restore the domain to its last known good configuration by using the automatically backed up configuration files. To provide additional security, you can make your own backups of the backed-up configuration files and save them to tape or disk.

Backing Up the Security Data

If you don't have the security data, you can't restart the Admin Server on a different machine. In addition to the *config.xml* file, you must also back up the *boot.properties* file. If you aren't using an RDBMS for storing the security data, WebLogic Server stores the security realm and other settings in the default embedded LDAP server. The Admin Server acts as the master for the LDAP data, and the Managed Servers read the security data when they initially connect to the Admin Server. A server's LDAP data is in the MW_HOME\user_projects\domains\\<*domain_name*>\servers\\<*AdminServer_name*>\data\ldap directory. By default, WebLogic Server backs up the LDAP data into a zip file named *EmbeddedLDAPBackup.zip* and stores it in the \ldap\backup subdirectory. The server creates a new zip file with the LDAP data whenever you change any security-related data. You can use this backup file for restoring the contents of the default LDAP server, but backing up the ldap directory in its entirety on a periodic basis is advisable. WebLogic Server automatically propagates all security changes to the Managed Servers when you make those changes through the Administration Console. Therefore, you don't have to back up the security data on the Managed Servers separately.

TIP

If you want to return to the initial default security settings, all you have to do is remove the security directory. When you restart the Admin Server, it automatically creates a new security directory and creates new security files with the default security settings.

You must also include the security directory (MW_HOME\user_projects\domains\\<*domain_name*>\security) in all your backups of WebLogic Server because that directory includes the critical *SerializedSystemIni.dat* file, which the Admin Server requires for startup. In addition, backing up all security certificates, keys, and keystores is a good idea if you've configured your servers with SSL. Once you have an effective backup policy in place, you can easily restore failed servers. Please refer to Chapter 2 for details about restoring a failed Admin Server and how to run a Managed Server in the absence of the Admin Server.

You can use utilities such as *jar, copy,* and *xcopy* to back up domains. However, the *pack* and *unpack* commands are also useful for performing quick backups and restores. As you know by now, the template archives that the *pack* command creates can contain either an entire domain or part of it. Once you create a domain's archives with the *pack* command, you can use the *unpack* command to re-create a domain or part of it on another machine.

Summary

This chapter showed you how to create a domain using different methods. You also learned how to configure a domain, create virtual hosts, and backup domain data. With this background, it's time now to start looking at how to configure WebLogic Server resources such as JDBC, JMS, and JTA, which are the main topics in the next chapter.

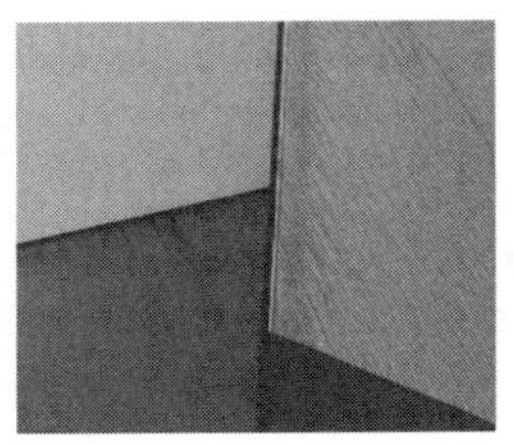

CHAPTER 4

Configuring Naming, Transactions, Connections, and Messaging

Middleware products such as Oracle WebLogic Server 12c provide multiple services to help perform various enterprise business functions. These services include the following:

- **Naming** Finding a resource by name instead of location
- **Transactions** Support for transactional Java applications
- **Database connectivity** The ability to access an RDBMS such as the Oracle Database
- **Messaging** Sending and receiving messages among applications

In addition to these services, there are other services such as security, for example, which is discussed in Chapter 9. This chapter focuses on the four main middleware services: naming and directory services, transaction support, database connectivity services, and messaging services. For naming services, WebLogic Server uses the Java Naming and Directory Interface (JNDI) protocol. For transaction services, WebLogic Server implements (and extends) the Java Transaction API (JTA). You configure database connectivity by configuring JDBC data sources and then targeting those resources to the servers in a domain. For messaging, WebLogic Server implements the Java Messaging Service (JMS) API. The loose coupling of the WebLogic Server in a three-tier system with various application components in the provisioning of the persistence services enhances the reliability of the middleware server by limiting the impact of individual service failures on the various tiers.

NOTE
The chapter describes the most important JNDI, JTA, JDBC, and JMS concepts. Although this chapter shows you how to configure several aspects of these services, a complete discussion of all the configuration attributes for each of the numerous configurable topics is outside the scope of this book. Please refer to the Oracle WebLogic Server documentation for complete configuration details for a specific item.

This chapter strives to provide you with a basic understanding of how Oracle WebLogic Server uses JNDI, JTA, JDBC, and JMS to make it easy for clients to find objects based on their given names and provide reliable database connections, transaction support, and messaging services for enterprise applications. Each of these is a huge topic by itself. Although the sheer number of configuration options for each of these major services might, at times, be overwhelming, this chapter shows you how to configure the most important components of these services. It also shows you how to monitor JTA, JDBC, and JMS services. The chapter ends with a brief review of how to configure WebLogic Server JavaMail.

JNDI and Naming and Directory Services

The first concept you must grasp with regard to the configuration of database connections or messaging services is the *Java Naming and Directory Interface (JNDI)*. JNDI is part of the Java platform. It provides a standard interface to connect to various naming and directory services such as DNS and LDAP. Java applications use naming services to find objects in data sources and the JMS. It's much easier for applications to find objects based on meaningful JNDI names rather than using the actual resource names. WebLogic Server JNDI lets clients access the WebLogic Server naming services to access and retrieve various objects such as data services from that namespace.

JNDI permits any service provider implementation to plug into its framework because it is independent of specific implementation of a directory or naming service. JNDI is implemented through the *javax.naming, javax.naming.directory, javax.naming.ldap,* and *javax.naming.event* core JNDI packages. Oracle WebLogic Server 12*c*'s implementation of JNDI makes objects accessible and retrievable in the WebLogic namespace and also allows clients access to WebLogic Server naming services.

JNDI Architecture

JNDI provides the main naming and directory service used by all Java EE resources, applications, and clients. Not only can developers use JNDI to locate the various objects and services registered in various Java EE services, but also they can register their own objects with the JNDI tree. JNDI is a standard Java EE mechanism that clients can use to publish, locate, and retrieve objects to access naming and directory servers. In order to locate various objects, you first bind them to a distributed directory service using JNDI. Clients then locate and retrieve those objects from the JNDI tree. For example, when you deploy an EJB, it's bound to a JNDI name and made available in the global JNDI tree. The same is true of any services such as a JDBC data source. Java clients use these JNDI names to gain access to the resource. You can bind all Java EE resources such as JTA transactions, JDBC data connections, JMS connection factories, and Remote Method Invocation (RMI) objects in the JNDI tree.

JNDI is hierarchical in structure—it represents a hierarchy of *context* objects. Objects are bound into and retrieved from a specific context in that hierarchy. The root of that hierarchy for a given user is *InitialContext* and is acquired in a context-sensitive way.

JNDI uses an open architecture that allows different implementations of directory services. These implementations map JNDI calls to their implementation of the directory services. JNDI offers a standard interface for these directory services, and Oracle WebLogic Server 12*c* offers a powerful implementation of JNDI that lets you use naming and directory features for any type of Java EE application.

Note that the JNDI framework in a clustered environment is common to all the cluster members. The JNDI tree is applicable to the entire cluster, and it holds the information for all objects that use the JNDI bindings. WebLogic Server's implementation of JNDI transparently replicates the cluster-wide JNDI tree to each cluster member, with each cluster member holding a local copy of the JNDI tree, but to the client, the cluster-wide tree appears as a single global tree. Although the JNDI tree is replicated over the cluster, you can, however, add bindings for specific resources to the local JNDI tree of a cluster member, making those resources available to only a specific cluster member. WebLogic Server JNDI supports two types of objects (and services)—replicated and pinned objects. A pinned object is available to the entire cluster but is bound to just one member of the cluster, whereas a replicated JNDI object is replicated to all members of a cluster.

Oracle WebLogic Server 12*c* implements RMI to complement its JNDI implementation. The RMI framework is a standard Java EE technology that lets Java clients access remote objects through the use of stubs. The stubs proxy requests to the remote objects and return necessary values. You can create your own RMI stubs, such as cluster-aware RMI stubs for a WebLogic cluster, for example. Because these stubs are cluster aware, they provide transparent load balancing and failover capabilities to the clients. The key point here is that when an object is registered in JNDI, the WebLogic implementation often replaces it with a stub that is "cluster aware." When retrieving the object, the client gets that stub along with information that help it find its replicated backup in the event of a failure.

Viewing the WebLogic Server JNDI Tree

Every WebLogic Server has a local JNDI tree, to which you bind Java EE resources such as the JDBC data sources, JMS connection factories, and so on. When you deploy a Java EE application, WebLogic Server automatically creates a JNDI name for the application and binds it to the JNDI tree of the server. You can load various Java EE services such as JDBC data sources, EJBs, and JMS in the JNDI tree through the Administration Console. All you have to do is provide a name in the JNDI Name attribute field when you create any Java EE service or component. Once you load the object, JNDI provides a path to this object, and you can view the object in the JNDI tree.

You can view the local JNDI tree for a server from the Administration Console. Use the following steps to view the JNDI tree:

1. In the left-hand pane, click Servers after expanding the Environment group.
2. In the right-hand pane, click the name of the server whose JNDI tree you wish to view.
3. In the Settings For <Server Name> (for example, Settings For examplesServer) page, you'll see a link named View JNDI Tree at the top of the page. Click this link.

The JNDI tree for this server will appear in a new tree, as shown in Figure 4-1.

You can navigate to the JNDI tree from the left panel of the JNDI Tree window. For example, you can click JDBC and then click the data source name to see the data source's bindings in the JNDI tree. Figure 4-1 shows the details for the bound object named *examples-dataSource-demoPool*. The binding name of an object in the JNDI tree shows the location of the data

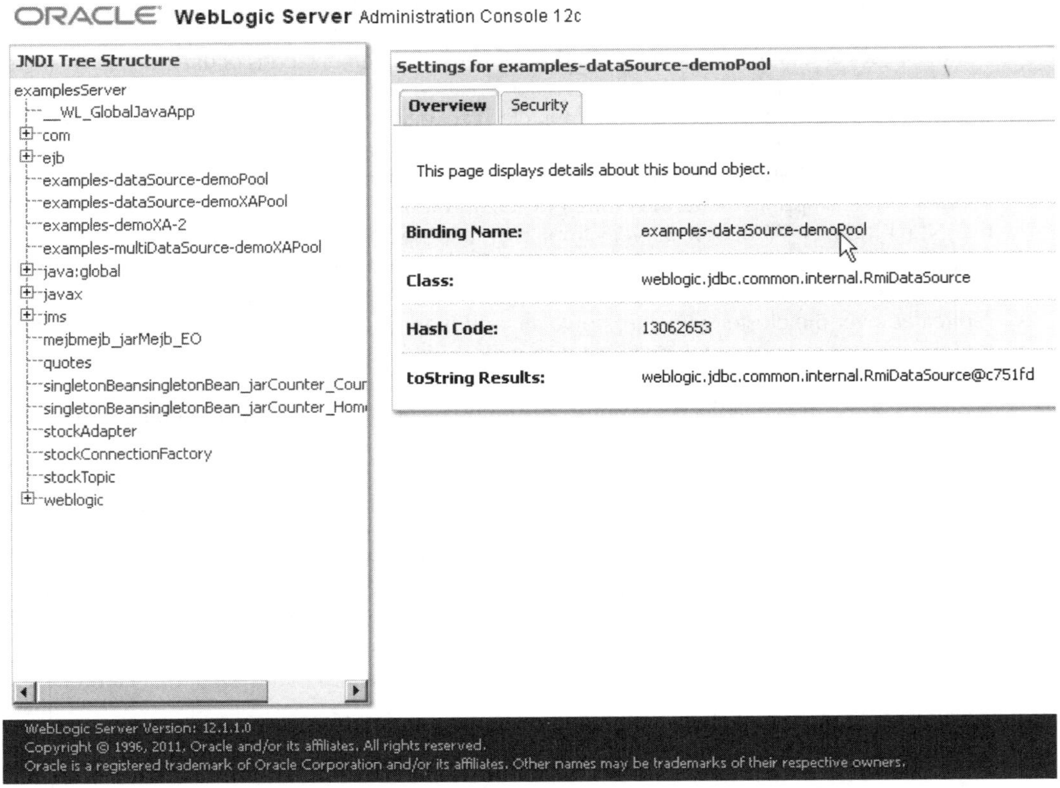

FIGURE 4-1. *The WebLogic Server JNDI tree*

source in the JNDI tree. By default, the name of the data source is the same as its JNDI name (JNDI path). An application that looks up the JNDI path gets the *java.sql.DataSource* instance that corresponds to that data source.

Using JNDI to Connect a Java Client to a Server

Before a client can use JNDI to access various WebLogic Server resources such as data sources, you must load those objects into the server's JNDI tree. JNDI services enable the applications to access service providers, such as a naming or directory service or an LDAP directory. Applications use a context as a sort of link to a JNDI service provider. For a Java client to access the WebLogic Server JNDI tree, it needs to get an object reference for a remote object by first establishing an initial context (using the *javax.naming.InitialContext* class) that represents the context root of the server. The client uses the initial context to specify various environmental properties to identify the server and the connection for logging into WebLogic Server. Using this context, the client can then look up the named object in the JNDI tree.

Using InitialContext to get a WebLogic Context Reference

WebLogic Server provides an *InitialContext* implementation through its JNDI Service Provider Implementation (SPI) to enable connections from remote Java clients. Developers can set the environment properties for client application connections to customize the *InitialContext,* either by using a hash table or the *set* methods of the environment objects. Here are the properties that the developer must use to customize the *InitialContext* by defining various environmental properties (there are several additional optional properties as well) that specify how the *WLInitialContextFactory* creates the context:

- ***Context.INITIAL_CONTEXT_FACTORY*** Specifies the fully qualified name of the class to be used in the JNDI context. To access the WebLogic JNDI tree, you must specify the class name *weblogic.jndi.WLInitialContextFactory*.
- ***Context.PROVIDER_URL*** Specifies the URL of the WebLogic Server where the JNDI tree is located. The default is t3://localhost:7001.
- ***Context.SECURITY_PRINCIPAL*** Specifies the user defined in a WebLogic Server security realm. The default is the *guest* user if the thread isn't associated with a WebLogic Server user already.
- ***Context.SECURITY_CREDENTIALS*** Specifies the password for the user defined in the *Context.SECURITY_PRINCIPAL* property.

It should be noted here that, when creating the *InitialContext,* you are establishing a network connection to the server/cluster and that the connection and any objects that are acquired from JNDI in this case are associated with the *SECURITY_PRINCIPAL* property.

You can also specify additional properties to determine how objects bind to a cluster-wide JNDI tree. Some bindings may not be replicated across each server within the cluster. Developers can create a context with a hash table that specifies the environment properties by passing the hash table as a parameter to the constructor for *javax.naming.InitialContext* class. Here's an example that shows how to obtain a WebLogic initial context by using the *javax.naming.InitialContext* class:

```
import javax.naming.*;
private static InitialContext ctx = null;
```

```
public static InitialContext getInitialContext( ) throws NamingException {
  if (ctx == null) {
    Hashtable env = new Hashtable();
    env.put(Context.INITIAL_CONTEXT_FACTORY,
            "weblogic.jndi.WLInitialContextFactory");
    env.put(Context.PROVIDER_URL,
            "t3://testserver:7001");
    ctx = new InitialContext(env);
  }
  return ctx;
}
```

Alternatively, you can use a WebLogic environment object implemented by the helper class *weblogic.jndi.environment* to create a context. For example, you can create an *InitialContext* with default values for all properties, as shown here:

```
Environment env = new Environment();
Context ctx = env.getInitialContext();
```

And here's how you create the security context with the JNDI environment object:

```
weblogic.jndi.Environment environment = new weblogic.jndi.Environment();
environment.setInitialContextFactory(
  weblogic.jndi.Environment.DEFAULT_INITIAL_CONTEXT_FACTORY);
environment.setProviderURL("t3://myhost:7001");
environment.setSecurityPrincipal("guest");
environment.setSecurityCredentials("guest");
InitialContext ctx = environment.getInitialContext();
```

Using InitialContext to Look Up Values in the JNDI Tree

Once an application obtains the initial context, it can look up objects that are bound in that context. Here's an example that shows how to look up a data source and user transaction and use them to create JDBC connections to a data source:

```
javax.naming.Context ctx = null;
javax.transaction.UserTransaction tx = null;
javax.sql.DataSource ds = null;
java.sql.Connection con = null;
try {
  ctx = new InitialContext(env) ;
  //Look up the TxDataSource
  ds = (DataSource) ctx.lookup("myTxDs");
  //use the JNDI tree to initiate a new JTA transaction
  tx = (UserTransaction) ctx.lookup("java:comp/UserTransaction");
  //initiate the transaction
  tx.begin( );
  con = ds.getConnection( );
  //perform your JDBC updates here. . .
  //commit the transaction
  tx.commit( );
```

```
}
catch (Exception e) {
  // exceptions code goes here
}
finally {
  try {
    if (ctx ! = null) ctx.close( );
    //release other JDBC resources here
    }
  catch (Exception ignored) {}
  }
```

In general, you don't access JDBC connections and the transaction manager from a remote client. In most cases, those are retrieved from a local *InitialContext* that is created when an EJB or servlet is initialized. Note that the local lookups from JNDI have now commonly been replaced by "injecting" references with annotations.

Clustered JNDI

WebLogic Server provides cluster-wide JNDI services to support deployment of objects in a clustered environment. Whenever you add a WebLogic Server instance to a cluster, the server's JNDI tree is merged with that of the cluster and the merged JNDI tree is propagated automatically to all members of that cluster. To reduce the potential network traffic due to the replication and synchronizing of the JNDI tree, WebLogic Server lets developers specify which objects of the JNDI tree the server must replicate to the cluster JNDI tree. You can do this by specifying the *REPLICATE_BINDINGS* property for the initial context factory, *weblogic.jndi.WLInitialContextFactory*. Of course, the fewer the objects you specify for replication, the fewer load balancing and failover capabilities the server will have.

WebLogic Server also uses RMI stubs to decrease the network traffic due to the replication of the JNDI tree across a cluster. Instead of replicating the actual objects, the server replicates the RMI stubs, which are very compact, thus reducing the network traffic. However, large custom objects must be replicated completely to the cluster members. To reduce the network traffic for replicating large custom objects, developers can write RMI proxies for the custom objects or pin the custom object to one of the cluster's servers. They can also deploy the custom object separately to each cluster member. It's important to note here that most of the time the replication happens implicitly when you deploy an EJB or an RMI object to a cluster. The WebLogic Server machinery takes care of the replication on behalf of the user.

Configuring Transactions

Enterprise applications use the concept of a transaction to enforce transactional integrity. In a distributed environment that depends on the interconnections among numerous components such as servers, networks, databases, and application servers, a failure in any component can potentially mess up the business logic embedded in the Java applications. Fortunately, developers don't have to program all the transactional details. Because WebLogic Server supports the well-known Java Transaction API (JTA), all the developer has to do is use transactional commands to control transactions from the Java applications. Note that a *transaction* is defined as any logical set of operations and thus can apply to a JDBC database operation, a JMS messaging operation, or any similar set of operations that involves the use of transactions.

Transactions and the ACID Test

A transaction is simply a set of operations that together comprise a logical unit of work. If all the operations succeed, the results of the transaction are committed or written to the database. If any of the operations fail, the operation as a whole fails, and the results are rolled back and not recorded in the data store. It's common to describe the characteristics of a transaction by referring to the well-known ACID properties of transactions. Here's what the ACID acronym stands for:

- **Atomic** All operations must succeed or fail as one unit.
- **Consistent** Regardless of the fate of the transaction (success or failure), the database must be left in a consistent state.
- **Isolated** Multiple transactions must not "step" on each other by adversely affecting each other's work.
- **Durable** All successful transactional changes must be recorded permanently in the database.

Types of WebLogic Transactions

There are two types of transactions: local or global. A *local* transaction involves a connection to just a single resource such as a JDBC database connection or a JMS queue. The *javax.transaction* package implements JTA for local transactions. A *global,* or *distributed,* transaction involves multiple resources, not all of which need to be of the same type. For example, a global transaction may include several database resources, or it can include one database resource and a JMS resource. Both of these are global transactions because they involve multiple resources. The Java package *javax.transaction.xa* contains the API for managing distributed transactions. A local resource needs just a resource manager, whereas a global transaction requires a transaction manager as well. Thus, the JTA architecture looks like the following:

Java App=>Transaction Manager=>Resource Manager=>Resource

Transactions and the Two-Phase Commit

A global (distributed) transaction uses the so-named *two-phase commit* protocol to handle transactions that involve multiple resources. During the first phase, changes to a resource are transmitted to the resources and written to a transaction log file. During the second phase, the transaction manager asks all resources to commit the changes, provided all resources have assured the transaction manager that they can successfully complete their portion of the transaction. If any of the resources reports that it can't successfully complete its part of the transaction, the transaction manager rolls back the entire transaction. WebLogic Server uses the well-known XA interface to implement the two-phase commit mechanism.

Configuring WebLogic JTA

Configuring the JTA properties for Oracle WebLogic Server 12*c* is easy. Simply select the default Oracle Thin (XA) driver when you create a data source. The Oracle Thin (XA) driver supports global transactions. It should be noted that XA transactions are fairly expensive when compared to localized transactions. They are an important part of some applications that require accessing multiple resources but should only be used when really necessary.

When you configure the transaction properties for a data source, you're actually configuring the WebLogic JTA properties. You can configure WebLogic Server transactions by setting options at the domain level or at the server level. Domain-level options, which include most of the key JTA configuration choices, apply to all servers in a domain. Any settings you specify for monitoring and logging will apply to individual servers. In the following section, let's briefly review the configuration options for WebLogic JTA at the domain level.

Configuring Domain JTA Options

You can configure a domain's JTA configuration options through the Administration Console by following these steps:

1. Click Lock & Edit in the Change Center of the Administration Console.
2. In the left-hand pane, under Domain Structure, click the domain name (wl_server in my example).
3. On the Settings For wl_server page, click JTA (you are already in configuration mode).
4. On the transaction Configuration page, shown in Figure 4-2 (not all options can be seen), you can set various domain-level transactions options. Here are the key domain-level transaction options:
    - **Timeout Seconds** Specifies the maximum amount of times a transaction can remain in the first phase of a two-phase commit transaction. Once this time limit is reached, the server rolls back the transaction. The minimum value is 1 second, and the default is 30 seconds.
    - **Abandon Timeout Seconds** Specifies the maximum time period for which the transaction manager will attempt the completion of the second phase of the two-phase commit transaction. The server abandons the transaction and rolls it back once it exceeds the timeout interval.
    - **Max Transactions** Specifies the maximum number of active transactions on a single server. The minimum is 1 transaction, and the default is 10000 transactions.
    - **Enable Two Phase Commit** Lets you select the two-phase commit protocol for transactions spanning multiple resource managers (a database and a JMS queue, for example). This option is already selected in my example since I chose the XA-enabled driver earlier.

Once you configure WebLogic JTA, the system manages transactions using the JTA API and the WebLogic JTA extensions. Following are some of the important points to keep in mind regarding the configuration of JTA options.

- The configuration settings for JTA (transactions) are applicable at the domain and cluster level:
    - At the domain level, the attributes you set will apply to all servers in a domain. These settings are superseded by any settings at the cluster level.
    - At the cluster level, attribute settings apply to a cluster within a domain. These settings supersede any settings at the domain level.
- Monitoring tasks for JTA are performed at the server level.
- Configuration settings for participating resources (such as JDBC data sources) are on a per configured object basis and apply to all instances of a particular object.

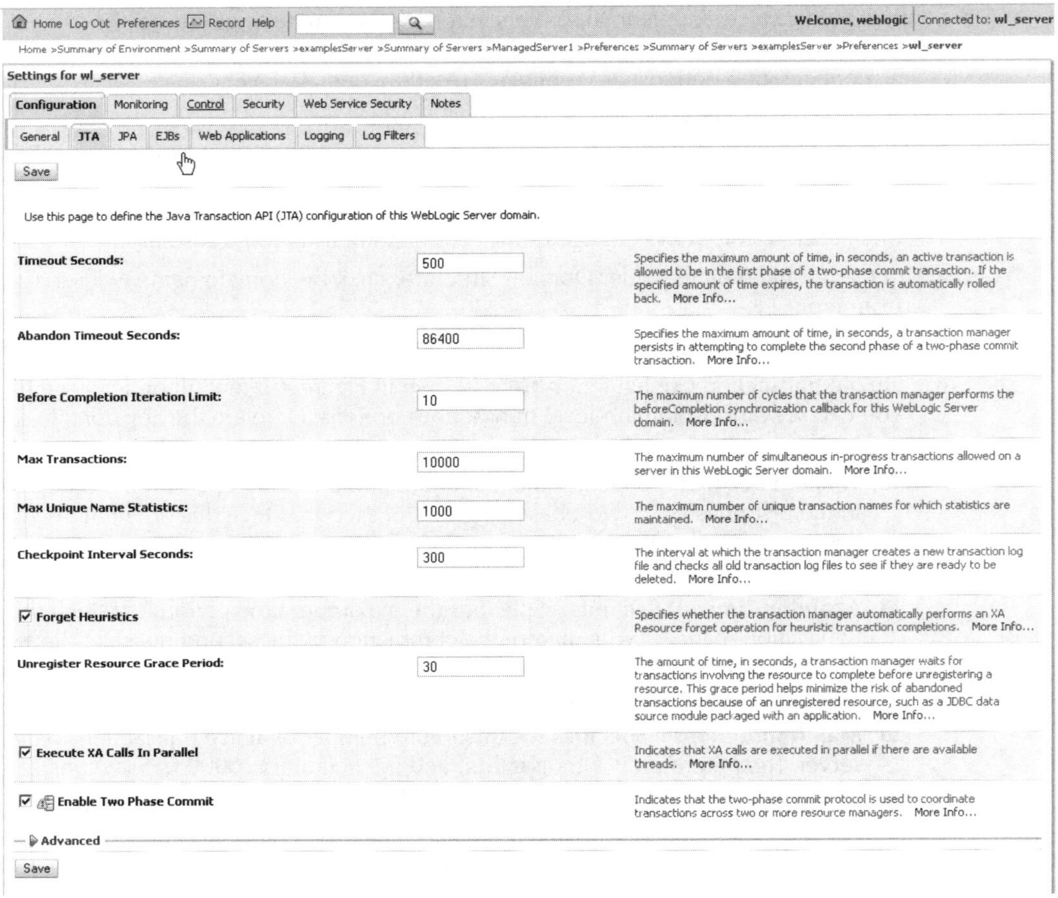

FIGURE 4-2. *Setting domain-level options for JTA*

Configuring the Default Persistent Store

If you haven't configured a custom persistent store (see Chapter 3 for details about configuring a custom file-based and a JDBC-based persistent store), the JMS server uses the default persistent store for the Managed Server to support persistent messaging. The JMS server stores the critical transaction logs that the server uses for recovering in-flight transactions in this persistent store. You don't really need to configure this default persistent store; however, in a clustered environment, you must enable the migration of the Transaction Recovery Service to handle a server failure. Migrating the Transaction Recovery Service involves specifying a location on a shared storage system available to all the cluster members.

Configuring Transaction Options for Data Sources

Transaction protocols for JDBC data sources control how WebLogic Server handles connections during transactions. You can configure transaction options for JDBC data sources by following these steps:

1. Click Lock & Edit in the Change Center of the Administration Console.
2. In the left-hand pane, expand Services and select Data Sources.
3. Select the data source name on the Summary Of JDBC Data Sources page.
4. Click the Transaction tab.
5. The Settings For <*data source-name*> page lets you define transaction options for this JDBC data source. By default, the Supports Global Transactions option is enabled, which is what you want. Because my data source uses an XA JDBC driver, connections will automatically support the two-phase commit protocol. If you use a non-XA JDBC driver, you can select from three transaction processing options: Logging Last Resource, Emulate Two-Phase Commit, and One-Phase Commit. Since I chose an XA JDBC driver, none of these transaction options are available; the transactions will automatically use the two-phase commit protocol. If you use a non-XA JDBC driver for your data source and the data source supports global transactions, you need to select one of the transaction protocols I mentioned earlier. Even if you aren't using an XA-aware JDBC driver, select the Supports Global Transactions option because this allows non-XA transactions participating in a JTA transaction to get the appropriate transactional semantics. Both the Emulate Two-Phase Commit and the Logging Last Resource transaction options ensure that non-XA JDBC connections can participate in global transactions. The One-Phase Commit option restricts applications to just a database resource (no JMS).

NOTE
It should be noted that the Logging Last Resource (LLR for short) is a very important optimization for many applications, especially those that combine JMS and JDBC. This approach allows the user to turn what would be an XA transaction into one that is local to a single database and get the same transaction guarantees much more efficiently.

Monitoring Transaction Services

You can monitor all server transaction activity from the Administration Console. You can check on the total number of active transactions as well as the number of transactions that were committed or rolled back, transactions that were abandoned, and similar details about current server transactions. You can also find the average commit time for transactions from the Console, and you can also roll back or commit active transactions.

To view a summary of all transaction information for all the resources running on a specific WebLogic Server instance, click the server in the left-hand pane of the console and select Monitoring | JTA in the right-hand pane. Figure 4-3 (not all options appear in the figure) shows the JTA Monitoring page for a server, and the important monitoring information is explained here:

- **Transactions Total Count** Shows the total number of processed transactions since server startup and includes committed as well as any rolled-back transactions.
- **Transactions Committed Total Count/Transactions Rolled Back For Timeout Total Count** Shows the total number of committed and rolled-back transactions since server startup. You can also view the number of transactions rolled back due to transaction timeouts, resource errors, system errors, and application errors.

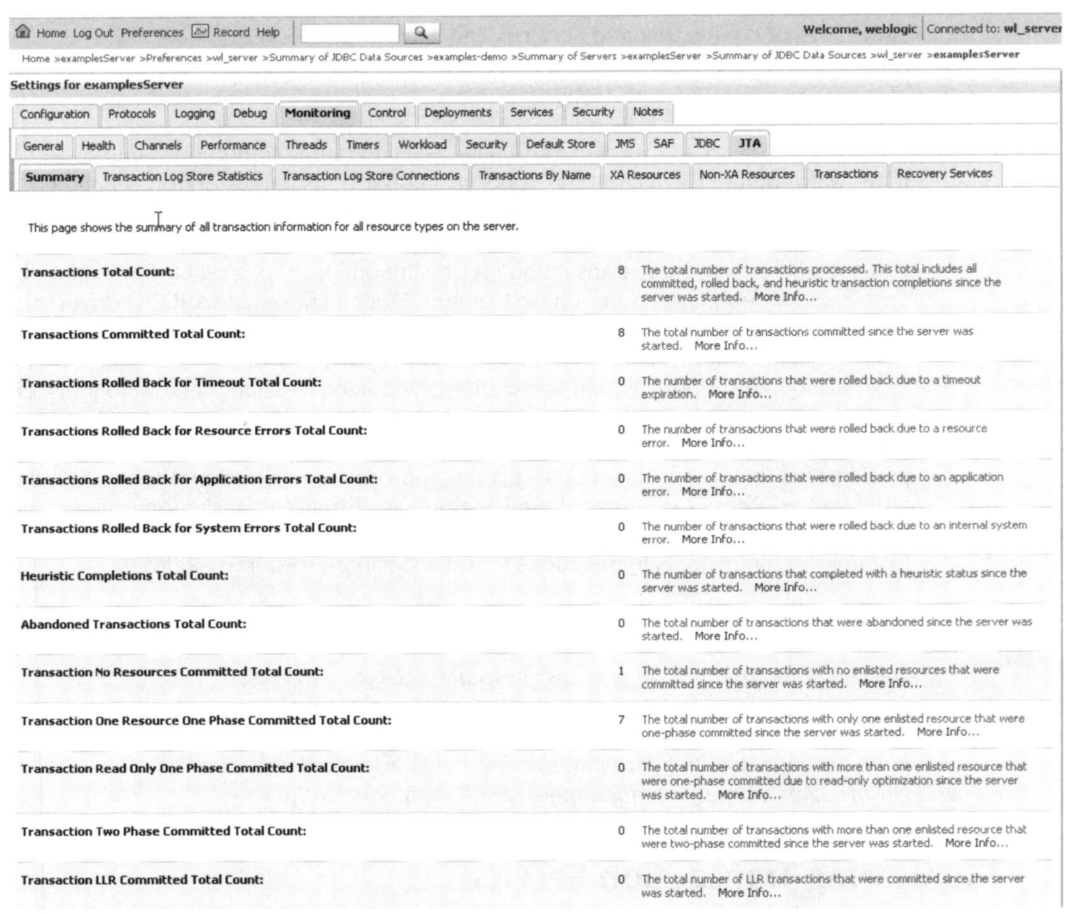

FIGURE 4-3. *The JTA monitoring page*

- **Abandoned Transactions Total Count** Number of transactions abandoned since server startup.
- **Transaction Two Phase Committed Total Count** Shows the number of transactions with multiple resources that successfully used the two-phase commit protocol.

The previous monitoring properties show transactions at an aggregate server level. You can also view the statistics for a specific transaction by selecting Environment | Servers | Monitoring | JTA | Transactions By Name. The resulting page shows all the named transactions being managed by the server. The name of a transaction is the name defined by the application that starts a transaction. Each transaction also has a transaction ID that's assigned by the transaction manager. For each named transaction in the table, you can view information such as total commits and rollbacks, application rollbacks, system rollbacks, timeout rollbacks, resource rollbacks, and the number of abandoned transactions.

NOTE
The server message log contains just the information about the operation of the server instance. You won't find JMS messages and JTA transactional messages in the server message log. You use separate log files for these messages. You can configure the JMS log files by going to Services | Messaging | JMS Servers | <JMS Server Name> | *Logging. The JMS log file has a name such as* jmsServers/MedRecJMSServer/jms.messages.log.

Transaction Logs and Transaction Recovery

WebLogic Server maintains transaction logs (referred to as *tlog* files), but these are quite different from normal server logs. The server uses the transaction logs to track all current transactions. WebLogic Server only records information about uncommitted transactions in the transaction log. When a server restarts after a failure, it uses the information in the transaction log to recover transactions. When you restart an instance, the server uses the transaction log files to perform the second phase of a two-phase commit transaction that was interrupted by the server failure. Using the transaction information from the transaction logs, the server makes an attempt to complete all in-flight, uncommitted transactions from the time the server failed.

WebLogic Server creates transaction logs for each server in a domain and stores the logs in the following directory: WL_HOME*<domain-name>*\server*<server_name>*\logs. The transaction logs are named in the following format: *<server-name>.nnnn.tlog*, for example, *myserver.0009.tlog*. You can't inspect the transactions log directly, as they aren't readable by humans. WebLogic Server automatically deletes the transaction logs when it deems them unnecessary—of course, you must leave the transaction logs strictly alone! If a transaction is corrupted, however, you may have to delete the transaction logs (online) to remove the phantom transactions. If you set too high a transaction timeout value, the transaction logs tend to be large. If you see many transaction log files, it's because there are many transactions that are still running in the server. In order to ensure that the highly critical transaction logs are protected, you must first make sure there's plenty of free space in the file system holding the transaction logs and you must try to store the log files on highly available file systems such as a storage area network (SAN) storage system.

Because the transaction logs aren't in a directly readable format, WebLogic Server provides a tool that helps you decrypt the log files. You can find this in the modules directory (MW_HOME/modules) in the module named *com.bea.core.tranasaction_3.0.0.0.jar*. To use this tool, execute the following command from the location of the log files:

```
WL_HOME\<domain-name>\server\<server_name>\logs> java weblogic.transaction
.internal.TransactionLoggerImpl <server-name>
```

Note that the transaction log file keeps track of the XA transaction IDs for all of the outstanding transactions and which external resources were involved. The process of recovery involves reconnecting to all of those managed resources and telling them what to do with each of the outstanding requests.

The transactions you need to worry about are the ones that were "in flight" when the server went down. Let's say that the server was updating a record for a particular user in the database. If that record is locked, it will remain locked until that server (or an alternate server that also has access to the associated transaction log) can be brought up to verify its state.

Note also that in certain architectures transactions can easily span multiple service instances. Say, for example, there is a web application tier sitting in front of a services tier that is represented by EJBs or web services or that hosts a JMS queue connected to an MDB. Each of these servers will have its own transaction log containing information about the transactions it was executing. The "coordinator" of the transaction is the server on which the transaction was first started, and the crashed server must coordinate with that server to make sure everything is consistent—that is, that the ACID properties of the transactions are maintained.

When you reboot a server after a crash, WebLogic's Transaction Recovery Service automatically recovers any pending transactions that are logged in the transaction log. The transaction manager tries to commit or roll back all transactions that were ready to commit or roll back prior to the server crash. The service abandons a transaction only if the transaction timed out. If you can't restart the server quickly, you can copy and move the transaction logs to the new server so it can process the in-flight transactions that are recorded in the log. If this is a clustered server, you can migrate the Transaction Recovery Service to a different member of the cluster, where that server will then try to commit or roll back the in-flight transactions.

Configuring Database Connections

WebLogic Server uses a standard JDBC API to enable connections to a relational database. The JDBC specification supports transactions, statement caching, connection pooling, and many other features. WebLogic's services such as the Java Persistence API (JPA), container-managed entity beans, persistent messages, and others rely on the JDBC API. JDBC drivers provide an implementation of the standard JDBC API and enable the actual connectivity to a relational database.

In order to configure database connectivity to an Oracle (or any other) database, you first configure a JDBC data source. Once you do this, you can deploy the JDBC resource to one or more servers in a WebLogic domain, which allows all applications deployed to that server to have access to this data source. For clusters, you can create a *multi data source* and deploy it to the cluster. Multi data sources are used when you need load balancing or failover protection—in fact, you must specify either load balancing or failover as a choice when configuring a multi data source. Multi data sources contain more than one data source, and they are bound to the JNDI tree just as a single data source is. In addition to the simple data sources (called *generic* data sources) and multi data sources, you can also create a *GridLink data source*. Note that GridLink data sources are specific to Oracle RAC.

When you start the server that already contains a data source or when you create a new data source instance, a pool of database connections is created for each data source you've configured. Applications then request a database connection by looking up the data source in the JNDI tree. Once an application is finished with the database connection, it terminates its connection by calling the *connection.close* method, following which that connection is returned to the connection pool of that data source. The preceding describes the traditional way of obtaining a data source object by looking up the JNDI tree of the server. In most new applications, the data source is injected by the container, as shown here:

```
// inject data source
@Resource(mappedName="jdbc/MyDataSource")
Private javax.sql.DataSource datasource;
```

NOTE
In the case of JPA, the data source is referenced in the persistence.xml file. In most cases, the taking and releasing of the connection is taken care of by the container, using resource injection.

Each JDBC connection generally represents a separate network connection to the database that must be established and authenticated. This is a very expensive proposition, and the whole point of the connection pool is to avoid having to pay this cost on every operation. The downside is that there's some cost in maintaining each connection to the database (in terms of using up database resources and bumping up against the maximum number of processes limit in a database), memory overhead in the server, network overhead to support unused connections, and so on. The connection pool is a shared resource, and, for many applications, this can become a bottleneck because it limits the number of concurrent requests.

Another advantage of maintaining connection pools is to control the number of connections to the database; otherwise, a large number of connections can overload and freeze the database if your front-end application has a sudden spike in activity that the database can't handle.

JDBC Architecture

WebLogic Server's JDK provides JDBC version 4. JDBC is implemented with the help of two core packages: *java.sql*, which is the Core API, and *javax.sql*, which is the optional package API. These two packages enable JDBC to provide low-level RDBMS access to Java classes and interfaces. The *java.sql* package contains the classes and interfaces that let you make database connections and run SQL commands, whereas the *javax.sql* package contains the classes and interfaces that let you use data sources, pooled connections, and distributed transactions.

Using WebLogic JDBC Drivers

Before you configure database connectivity, you must ensure you have the necessary JDBC drivers. A JDBC driver manages the exchange of information between Java programs and an RDBMS such as Oracle, which come with built-in network libraries that help communicate with the database over a network. The network libraries, which are shipped as dynamic link libraries (DLLs) on a Windows platform, offer superior performance when working with a specific RDBMS because they're optimized for that individual database. However, directly accessing the network libraries of a specific RDBMS means that you'll have to rewrite the database connectivity–related code for each database because it's custom tailored for each database.

Database drivers abstract the network functionality by using a high-level API that works with the lower level network library APIs. A developer can thus use the same application with multiple types of RDBMSs by employing the appropriate database drivers. JDBC is analogous to the well-known ODBC standard and is designed to help Java developers work with relational databases in the same, consistent manner. JDBC is exclusive to Java applications.

There are four types of JDBC drivers, and they are briefly explained here:

- **Type 1 driver** The Type 1 drivers are also called *JDBC-ODBC bridges* because they connect Java applications and ODBC drivers. These drivers offer slower performance than the other drivers because of the multiple driver layers, but they allow Java applications standardized access to ODBC resources such as Microsoft SQL Server and Microsoft Access.

  Java App⇔Type 1 Driver⇔ODBC Driver⇔Network Libraries⇔RDBMS

- **Type 2 driver** The Type 2 drivers bypass the ODBC layer and thus offer better performance than Type 1 drivers. You must install them on the server where WebLogic Server runs.

  Java App⇔Type 2 Driver⇔Network Libraries⇔RDBMS

- **Type 3 driver** When you use Type 3 drivers, you install them on the middleware server, which lets you avoid having to install the drivers on the client machines.

  Java App⇔Type 3 Driver⇔Middleware Interface⇔Database Driver⇔RDBMS

- **Type 4 driver** Also referred to as "thin" drivers. These are vendor (database) specific and don't require any network libraries. Type 4 drivers offer the best performance but aren't portable—you need to use the appropriate Type 4 driver for each database.

  Java App⇔Type 4 Driver⇔RDBMS

JDBC Drivers Offered by WebLogic Server

WebLogic Server comes preinstalled with several JDBC drivers. Oracle ships the following types of data drivers with WebLogic Server:

- Oracle Thin driver (XA and non-XA)
- Oracle Type 4 JDBC drivers from DataDirect for the DB2, Informix, Microsoft SQL Server, and Sybase
- Third-party JDBC drivers for MySQL (non-XA)

Because WebLogic Server already comes with drivers for Oracle Database, you don't have to install any special drivers for Oracle databases. You don't have to specify any of these drivers in the server's classpath either since they're part of the *weblogic.jar* manifest file, which is used for starting the server. However, if you install other third-party drivers to enable connections to other RDBMSs, you need to modify your WebLogic Server startup scripts so the system classpath includes the JDBC driver libraries. The Oracle Type 4 JDBC drivers are optimized for Java and offer top-notch performance for the four databases listed here. Oracle automatically installs the Type 4 JDBC drivers when you perform a complete (instead of a custom) installation of WebLogic Server. The Type 4 drivers are located in the WL_HOME\server\lib folder (the files have the prefix *DDJDBC*). The Oracle Thin driver (*ojdbc6.jar*), also a Type 4 driver, which I use in this book, is installed automatically as well, in the WL_HOME\server\lib directory. You'll also find copies of the Oracle and MySQL Thin drivers in the WL_HOME\server\ext\jdbc\oracle (and mysql) directories.

TIP
You can replace the default Thin drivers for Oracle and MySQL with any different driver by simply replacing the driver file (for example, ojdbc6.jar *for the Oracle Thin driver) in the WL_HOME\server\lib directory. Alternatively, you can just add the name of the new driver file to your* CLASSPATH *variable when starting the server.*

You can use the Oracle Thin driver in debug mode by adding the *ojdbc6_g.jar* (for JDK 6) at the beginning of the CLASSPATH. You'll find the two files in the WL_HOME\server\ext\jdbc \oracle\12c folder.

Both Type 2 and Type 4 drivers allow Java applications to directly connect to a database; however, for a Type 2 database, you must also install client-side network libraries. You use JDBC drivers mostly to make a direct connection to a database from Java applications deployed on WebLogic Server. You can use third-party JDBC drivers, but you must ensure the drivers are thread-safe and support JDBC transactions.

Transactions

As mentioned earlier, a transaction consists of one or more database operations that form a logical unit of work. A transaction is successful only if all the operations that comprise that transaction are successful. If any operation within a transaction fails, the entire transaction is deemed a failure and is rolled back; that is, the transaction isn't committed to the database. The database will only record the results of a successful transaction.

Statements

You issue a SQL statement to either query the database or to add, delete, or modify data stored in the database tables. In order to issue a SQL statement from a Java program, you create a statement object from an open connection. You can execute simple SQL statements using a basic statement object through the *java.sql.Statement* interface. You can also execute prepared statements through the *java.sql.PreparedStatement* interface for processing precompiled SQL statements. Once you create either a simple statement object or a *PreparedStatement* object, you call the object's methods to define your SQL statements, execute them, and retrieve the results.

ResultSets and RowSets

You use the *java.sql.ResultSet* interface to retrieve the results of a SQL statement. You can navigate only once over the contents of a *ResultSet*. However, you can use a *RowSet* to traverse a set of results multiple times, in any order you please. A *RowSet* combines connections, statements, and *ResultSets* with a single interface—the *RowSet*—and is thus easier to use.

Enabling XA in the Database

You must perform some special steps to enable recovery of Oracle resources following a reboot after a crash. Although the database handles XA database transactions fine, you must perform these steps to enable the WebLogic Server transaction manager to perform a crash recovery of an XA resource. Here are the steps:

1. Log in to the Oracle database as the user sys:

```
SQL> connect sys/<password> as sysdba
```

2. Execute the following script:

```
SQL> @$ORACLE_HOME/rdbms/admin/xaview.sql
```

3. The *xaview.sql* script creates the necessary views to perform a recovery scan of prepared statements. Execute the following commands to grant various permissions on the views:

```
SQL> grant select on v$xatrans$ to public;
SQL> grant select on pending _trans$ to public;
SQL> grant select on dba_2pc_pending to public;
SQL> grant execute on dbms_system to <user>;
```

Data Sources

WebLogic Server maintains a pool of reusable physical database connections to minimize the overhead involved in connecting to a database. All the connections in a pool connect to the same database and use the same username and password for the connections. In order for a Java application to talk to a database, it must first open a connection to the database. Java programs open a connection by using the *java.sql.Connection* interface. Once the application opens a connection, it can then create statement objects and manage transactions. Clients obtain a *Connection* object when they request a connection from the connection pool. A *Connection* object is a logical representation of the actual physical database connection. WebLogic maintains the pooled connections as a collection of *PooledConnection* objects. Behind the scenes WebLogic associates the client's *Connection* object to a *PooledConnection* object.

You can create a direct connection to a database directly from within the application code. However, this isn't recommended since the application will then be responsible for closing the connections after completing its work and too many open connections can exhaust the number of processes the database can handle.

WebLogic Server data sources help separate database connection information from your application code. Data sources make applications portable and offer an easy way to configure and secure database connections. A data source is a Java EE standard approach to connecting to a database and represents a pool of database connections. The *data source* is simply a mapping of a logical name to the connection pool and thus offers a way for requests to access the underlying connection pool easily. Applications don't have to know the underlying database setup or the actual connection properties because the data source abstracts all those connection details. When you deploy a data source through an application module, target a data source, or start an instance, WebLogic Server creates the pool of database connections specified by the data source. Java applications perform a lookup of the JNDI tree to find the data source and request database connections using the *getConnectionMethod.* Once the application finishes using that connection, the connection goes back to the data source's connection pool. As a WebLogic administrator, you must configure JDBC data sources and target or deploy these JDBC resources to various servers in a domain.

Once you configure a data source, the connections will be automatically active when you start the server. You can configure the server to launch a specific number of connections each time it starts. WebLogic Server will always maintain this minimum number of database connections for applications to connect to databases. WebLogic Server uses the WebLogic Pool Driver to maintain the pool of database connections. This Pool Driver is compatible with all WebLogic and third-party JDBC drivers. Applications or server-side components such as EJBs and servlets request a new connection from the WebLogic Pool Driver and not from the JDBC driver. It's the Pool Driver's job to open new connections (up to the maximum number that you configured) and to return unused connections to the connection pool.

WebLogic Server offers three main types of data sources that you can configure:

- **Generic data source** Lets you configure basic connection pools.
- **Multi data source** You can create a multi data source by combining multiple generic data sources, so as to provide load balancing and failover capabilities. When an application looks up the JNDI tree and requests a database connection, the multi data source determines which specific (generic) data source to assign to that connection. You can configure the selection of the individual data sources by choosing a load balancing or failover algorithm.
- **GridLink data source** This type of data source is designed to offer failover support for an Oracle RAC–based connection.

You can use the Administration Console to create and configure each of these three types of WebLogic Server data sources.

Understanding WebLogic JDBC Configuration

An interesting thing to note about JDBC resources is that both system administrators and developers can create a JDBC resource, but the deployment and management (how to modify it) depends on who creates the resource. A system administrator can create a JDBC module, called a *system module,* using the Administration Console or WLST. A developer can also create a JDBC module, called an *application module,* with a tool that allows the creation of the necessary XML descriptor file and add the JDBC module to the packaged application, which is then deployed by the administrator.

The choice of how a resource is scoped is mostly a decision about whether the resource and its connection pool are to be shared across multiple applications. Note that this has implications for whether XA is used as well. For a self-contained application where there are multiple modules using the same data source, it often makes sense to keep the connection information together with the application. This saves the administrator the extra step of having to configure and deploy it separately.

If you're deploying multiple applications and each of those applications needs to manipulate different tables in the same database or manipulate tables that are storing JMS messages, then deploying a system resource probably makes the most sense. Conveniently, the format is the same for both system and application modules. Note that SOA code that takes advantage of data sources must have that data source preconfigured on the server. It cannot be bundled with the code.

XML files store the JDBC configuration details and conform to the *jdbc-data-source.xsd* schema. If you're creating multiple JDBC data sources, each of these data sources is represented by a separate XML file. A multi data source needs only a single XML file. The application JDBC modules are similar to Java EE modules and can be included in a Java EE application as any other module or deployed separately by themselves.

Using a JDBC System Module

When a WebLogic Server administrator creates a JDBC resource, WebLogic Server creates a JDBC module in the domain directory and updates the *config.xml* file with a *JDBCSystemResource* element that points to the new JDBC resource. As you can see in the extract from the *config.xml* file shown in the following listing, the *<jdbc-system-resource>* element includes the name of the JDBC XML file, *MedRec-jdbc.xml,* within the *<descriptor-file-name>* element. The *<target>* element shows the server (MedRecServer) to which the JDBC resource is targeted:

```
<jdbc-system-resource>
  <name>MedRecGlobalDataSourceXA</name>
  <target>MedRecServer</target>
  <descriptor-file-name>jdbc/MedRec-jdbc.xml</descriptor-file-name>
</jdbc-system-resource>
<jdbc-system-resource>
  <name>JDBC Data Source-0</name>
  <target>MedRecServer</target>
  <descriptor-file-name>jdbc/JDBC_Data_Source-0-3407-jdbc.xml</descriptor-file-
name>
</jdbc-system-resource>
```

And here's the actual XML file, *MedRec-jdbc.xml,* that contains the JDBC connection attributes, such as the JDBC driver parameters, connection pool parameters, and data source parameters:

```
<?xml version='1.0' encoding='UTF-8'?>
<jdbc-data-source xmlns="http://xmlns.oracle.com/weblogic/jdbc-data-source"
xmlns:sec="http://xmlns.oracle.com/weblogic/security"
xmlns:wls="http://xmlns.oracle.com/weblogic/security/wls"
xmlns:xsi="http://www.w3.org/2001/XMLSchema-instance"
 xsi:schemaLocation="http://xmlns.oracle.com/weblogic/jdbc-data-source
http://xmlns.oracle.com/weblogic/jdbc-data-source/1.0/jdbc-data-source.xsd">
  <name>JDBC Data Source-0</name>
  <jdbc-driver-params>
    <url>jdbc:oracle:thin:@miropc61.miro.local:1521:orcl1</url>
    <driver-name>oracle.jdbc.xa.client.OracleXADataSource</driver-name>
```

```
    <properties>
      <property>
        <name>user</name>
        <value>hr</value>
      </property>
    </properties>
    <password-
encrypted>{AES}9JbZiiRt0l2Dq7GWYngvIxsykaTqhZnnzNbVGO8Ed88=</password-
encrypted>
  </jdbc-driver-params>
  <jdbc-connection-pool-params>
    <test-table-name>SQL SELECT 1 FROM DUAL</test-table-name>
  </jdbc-connection-pool-params>
  <jdbc-data-source-params>
    <global-transactions-protocol>TwoPhaseCommit</global-transactions-protocol>
  </jdbc-data-source-params>
</jdbc-data-source>
```

When an administrator creates a JDBC module, that module is available to all servers and clusters of that domain, and therefore, you can consider the system module a global module. Any application you deploy on the same server targets (Managed Servers, clusters) will have the JDBC module available for its use. The system administrator has full control over the system modules—the administrator can delete or modify them without hindrance. When a JDBC application module is available, it must always be targeted to specific servers. A JDBC application module can be added as a packaged module to an enterprise application. You can bundle the packaged module with an EAR (or exploded directory) and refer to them in a deployment descriptor such as *weblogic-application.xml*. Application scoping of JDBC resources can make things easier in situations where the resources are associated with only one application. You can also deploy a JDBC application module to a specific server or cluster, and the module is called a *stand-alone module*.

Earlier you saw how the *config.xml* file maps the *JDBCSystemResource* element to the JDBC XML file. This file shows how to configure a single data source. Let's examine the JDBC XML file closely in order to understand how to specify values of all the elements in that file. Each *<jdbc-data-source>* element in a JDBC XML file includes values for the driver, connection pool, XA, and connection parameters. If you're configuring a multi data source JDBC connection, you also need to include the algorithm type and data source list parameters, as you'll see when I show how to configure a multi data source JDBC connection.

The example shown earlier described the basic configuration elements of a data source, which could have been created by a system administrator or a developer. The JDBC application module and system module are similar XML files that contain configuration information for a single or multi data source. What are the advantages of using a system module? If a developer creates a JDBC system module, he or she can include the module as a package module inside an Enterprise Application Archive (EAR) file or as part of an exploded EAR directory. The developer decides if the JDBC module is specific to only a certain application or if it can be used by all applications. Here are the advantages to using a system module:

- You can ensure that your application always has access to the necessary data sources.
- It makes migrating applications to various environments easier, as you do not need to reconfigure JDBC when you move between environments.
- The administrator can modify configurations but can't delete an application JDBC module.

When you use a packaged JDBC module, the modules are deployed along with the main enterprise application, but you can also deploy a stand-alone JDBC module, where you make the module available to a specific target. Stand-alone JDBC modules make it easier to move the JDBC configuration among various domains. Note, however, that if you deploy a stand-alone JDBC application module, you must use the Administration Console or a JSR-88–compliant tool to update the configuration of the module—you can't use WLST to modify or reconfigure the application module.

Creating a Generic Data Source

This section first shows you how to create a generic data source using the Administration Console. You can also create data sources with WLST scripts. Several configuration aspects are similar for a generic data source, a multi data source, and a GridLink data source. Once we finish creating a generic data source, I'll explain the relevant features that you need to configure for the GridLink and the multi data sources.

1. In the Change Center of the Administration Console, click Lock & Edit.
2. In the left-hand pane of the console, expand Services and select Data Sources.
3. On the Summary Of JDBC Data Sources page, click New. You'll see a drop-down list with three options: Generic Data Source, GridLink Data Source, and Multi Data Source, as shown in Figure 4-4. Select Generic Data Source.
4. On the Create A New JDBC Data Source page, in the Name box, enter a name for the new JDBC data source. In this example, the name of the data source is MyDataSource1. Also enter a JNDI name in the JNDI Name box, such as *examples-dataSource-demoPool,* for example. Select the RDBMS you want to connect to in the Database Type drop-down list. I chose Oracle because I want to set up a data source to connect to an Oracle database. Click Next.
5. On this page, you need to select the database driver to connect to the database. I chose the Oracle Driver (Thin XA), which is the default driver. Figure 4-5 shows how to select the database driver. If you select a third-party JDBC driver that doesn't come with the WebLogic Server installation, you must first install that driver before you can select it on this page. Click Next.
6. On the Transaction Options page, I didn't need to do anything because I chose an XA driver earlier. The Oracle XA JDBC driver I chose automatically supports global transactions and uses the two-phase commit protocol. For this driver, you can't configure any other options, such as Logging Last Resource, for example—those options are only shown if you choose a non-XA JDBC driver. Click Next.
7. On the Connection Properties page, shown in Figure 4-6, you enter the database name, host name, port, and database user credentials. Select the database username that you want to use to connect to the database. You can test the database connection on the Test Database Connection page by clicking Test Configuration at the bottom of the page. The Console tests the connection using the default query *"select 1 from dual"* (for Oracle databases) and shows the message "Connection Test Succeeded" at the top of the page if your connection test works. Click Next.
8. On the Select Targets page, you'll see a list of all the servers in that domain. Select the server or cluster to which you want to deploy your new data source. You can choose not to deploy the data source at this point and instead deploy it at a later time. In the case of

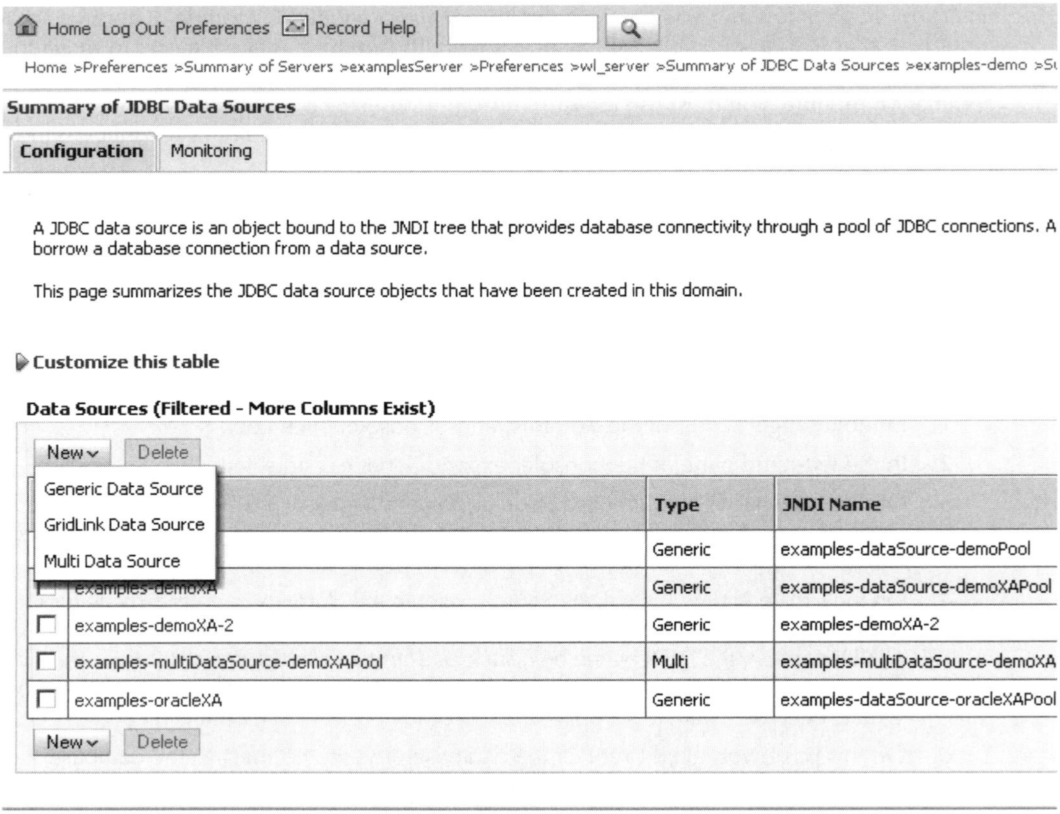

FIGURE 4-4. *Selecting a data source type*

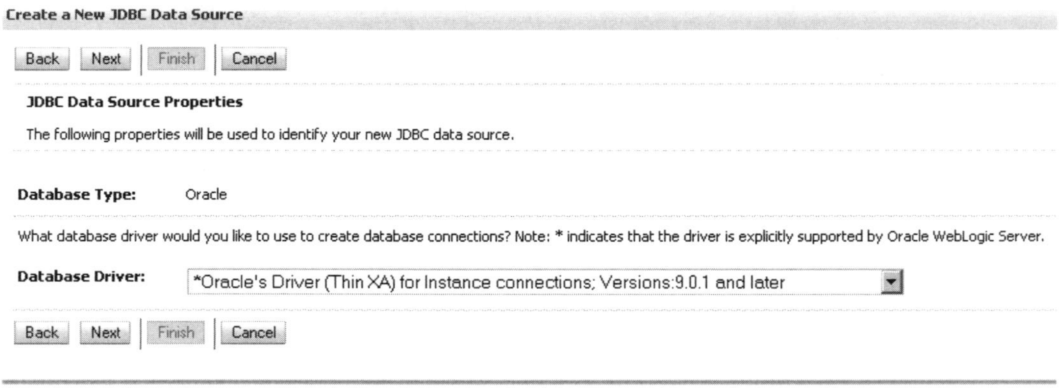

FIGURE 4-5. *Selecting the database driver for the data source*

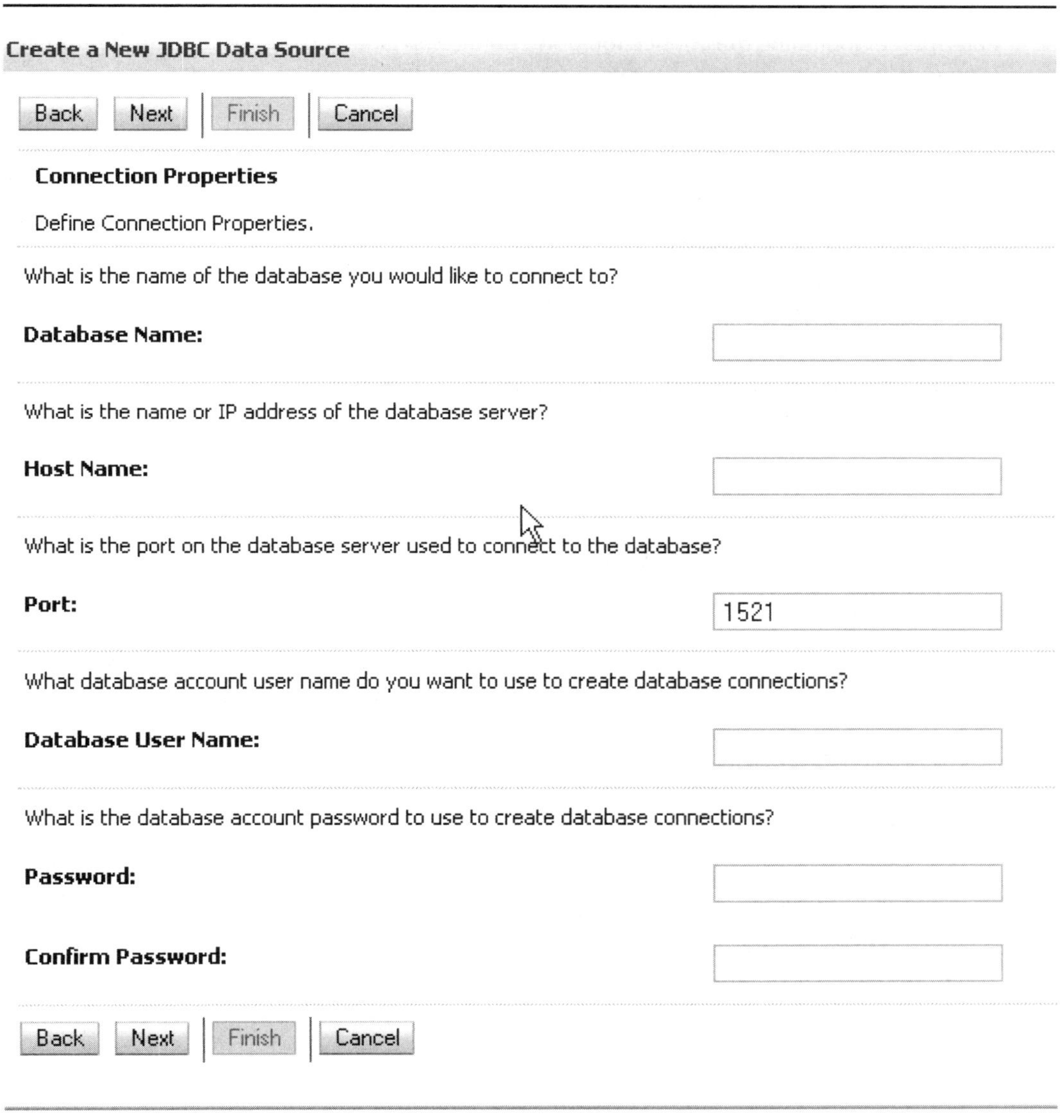

Create a New JDBC Data Source

Back Next Finish Cancel

Connection Properties

Define Connection Properties.

What is the name of the database you would like to connect to?

Database Name:

What is the name or IP address of the database server?

Host Name:

What is the port on the database server used to connect to the database?

Port: 1521

What database account user name do you want to use to create database connections?

Database User Name:

What is the database account password to use to create database connections?

Password:

Confirm Password:

Back Next Finish Cancel

FIGURE 4-6. *Setting connection properties for the data source*

a cluster, you can choose to target a data source separately to each Managed Server in that cluster or target it directly to the cluster. In the latter case, the data source is aware of the cluster and redirects client requests for database connections to one of the Managed Servers in that cluster. Click Finish.

9. Activate the changes (even if you're not deploying the data source right now) by clicking Activate Changes in the Change Center of the Console.

When you deploy a data source to a single server, WebLogic Server creates an instance of the data source, including the connection pool, on the server. If you deploy to a cluster instead, the server creates an instance of the data source on each of the server's members.

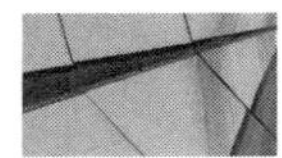

NOTE
You can set a value for the JDBCLoginTimeoutSeconds *attribute on the* ServerMBean, *to prevent the server from "hanging" indefinitely when it's starting if the database is unavailable or unreachable.*

Configuring a Multi Data Source

Because a multi data source provides failover and load balancing among multiple data sources, you must first create the generic data sources that will comprise the multi data source. Once you create the generic data sources, target them to the same target where you want to configure and deploy a multi data source. The multi data source can then provide failover and load balancing among the multiple generic data sources you've created.

Once you create multiple generic data sources, create a JDBC multi data source by following these steps:

1. Click Lock & Edit in the Change Center of the Administration Console.
2. In the left-hand pane of the Console, expand Services and select Data Sources.
3. Click New and select Multi Data Source on the Summary Of Data Sources page.
4. In the Configure The Multi Data Source page, enter a unique name for the new multi data source and a JNDI name (i.e., the JNDI path), where the data source will bind in the JNDI tree. Finally, select an algorithm type by choosing between two options: Failover and Load Balancing. This algorithm determines the primary purpose of the multi data source. The Failover option sends connection requests to the database by trying each data source in the ordered list of data sources sequentially, starting with the first data source. You must enable the Test Reserved Connections option on the data source if you choose the failover algorithm. The server knows which connection the multi data source will use by testing the connections. The Load Balancing option, on the other hand, evenly distributes connection requests among all the individual data sources, using a round-robin scheme. Click Next.
5. On the Select Targets page, select the servers (or clusters) where you want to deploy the multi data sources. You must have previously deployed the individual data sources to the same targets. Click Next.
6. On the Select Data Source Type page, select XA Driver and click Next.
7. On the Add Data Sources page, shown in Figure 4-7, select all the data sources you created earlier. Click Finish. Doing this deploys the new multi data source definition to the targets you've specified in the previous steps.
8. Activate the changes by clicking the Activate Changes button in the Change Center of the Console.

Using a GridLink Data Source

A GridLink data source lets you provide connectivity between WebLogic Server and an Oracle RAC database service, which is targeted to an Oracle RAC cluster. Database services are abstractions for workloads with common characteristics. A GridLink data source is independent of

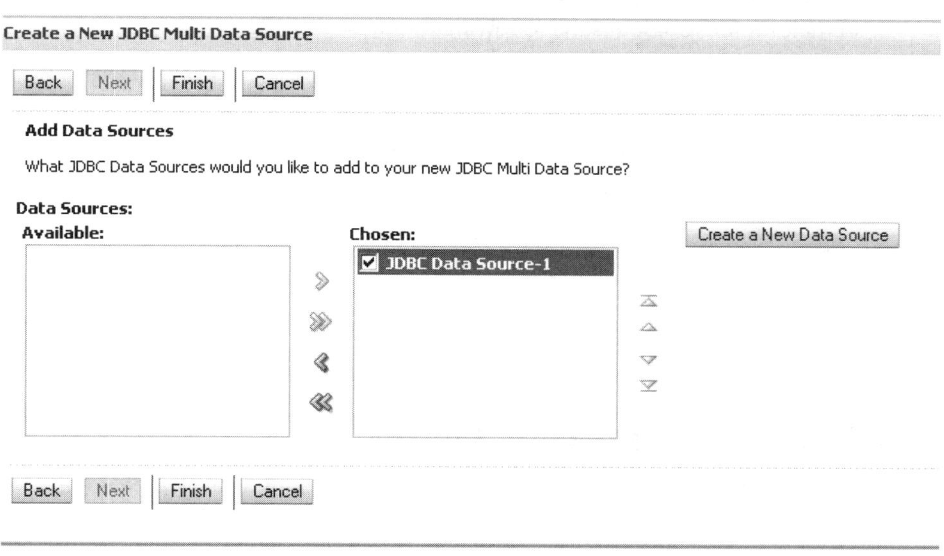

FIGURE 4-7. *Adding a JDBC data source to the new multi data source*

the number of nodes in a RAC cluster. You can use Oracle Single Client Access Name (SCAN) addresses to configure both the Transparent Network Substrate (TNS) and Oracle Notification Service (ONS) listeners. Using a SCAN address means that you don't need to change anything when you add or remove nodes from the RAC configuration.

GridLink data sources offer the following benefits:

- **Load balancing** A GridLink data source uses Fast Application Notification (FAN) events issued by the database to implement run-time load balancing by distributing database connection requests to the Oracle RAC instances. Run-time load balancing helps balance work among the various RAC instances, enhancing both performance and scalability.
- **Fast connection failover** GridLink data sources use the Oracle RAC Fast Connection Failover feature to rapidly detect instance failures. Using ONS, a GridLink data source can quickly remove invalid data connections from the connection pool, thus ensuring that the remaining connections are all valid.
- **Graceful handling of database outages** GridLink data sources let the application server gracefully handle both planned and unplanned outages. If the outage is planned, the data sources allow all current transactions to complete. If the outage is unplanned, the data sources roll back the transactions that are in the midst of execution.

Creating a GridLink data source is essentially similar to how you create a generic data source, with some additional steps to configure the connection properties and ONS client configuration details. Here are the additional steps you must follow to create a GridLink data source:

1. **GridLink data source connection Properties Options page** On this page, enter either the complete JDBC URL or let the assistant generate the URL based on the host and port

pairs you provide. Whether you provide the complete JDBC URL or WebLogic Server creates it for you, it has the following format:

```
jdbc:oracle:thin:@(DESCRIPTION=(ADDRESS_LIST=(ADDRESS=(PROTOCOL=TCP)
(HOST=dbhost1)(PORT=1521))(ADDRESS=(PROTOCOL=TCP)(HOST=dbhost2)(PORT=1521))
(ADDRESS=(PROTOCOL=TCP)(HOST=dbhost3)(PORT=1521)))
(CONNECT_DATA=(SERVICE_NAME=orcl)))
```

You can alternatively enter a SCAN address such as the following:

```
jdbc:oracle:thin:@(DESCRIPTION=(ADDRESS_LIST=(ADDRESS=(PROTOCOL=TCP)
(HOST=dbhost.myCompany.com)(PORT=1521)))(CONNECT_DATA=(SERVICE_NAME=orcl)))
```

2. **ONS Client Configuration page** Here you can choose to subscribe to Oracle FAN events by selecting Fan Enabled. Under ONS Nodes, you can provide a comma-separated list of ONS listener addresses and ports for handling ONS-based Oracle FAN events.

Configuring a JDBC Data Source

In the preceding sections, you learned how to create a generic data source, a multi data source, and a GridLink data source. This section shows you how to configure JDBC data source properties through the Administration Console. Following are the configuration pages you need to use when configuring JDBC data sources via the Administration Console:

- General
- Transactions
- Connection Pool
- Diagnostics
- Identity
- Targets
- Security

The following sections explain how to configure each of these areas. Note that to configure the various options for a JDBC data source, you must follow these steps:

1. Expand Services in the left-hand pane of the Administration Console and select Data Sources.
2. On the Summary Of JDBC Data Sources page, select the specific data source you'd like to configure, for example, *examples-dataSource-demoXAPool*.
3. You'll then view and configure the general configuration options for this data source on the Settings For *examples-demoXA* page. You can click the various tabs such as Connection Pool, Transaction, Diagnostics, Security, and so on, to configure each of these for the data source you've selected.

Here are the key data source configuration options for each of the areas listed earlier.

Configuring General Options

General configuration options for a data source (accessed by clicking the General tab on the Settings For <*data source-name*> page) include the following:

- **Name** This is the name for the data source and is a required parameter.
- **JNDI Name** The JNDI name is identical to the JDBC name, but you can specify multiple JNDI names on separate lines, as a list. This is a required parameter.
- **Row Prefetch Enabled** Selecting this option lets the server send multiple rows to the client during each server access—obviously, you want to enable row prefetching to enhance database access performance. Remember, though, that when you run the client and WebLogic Server in the same JVM, row fetching isn't enabled. Row prefetching is disabled by default.
- **Row Prefetch Size** Of course, you only need to worry about the size of the rows that you want to prefetch if you've enabled row prefetching. Using this parameter, you can set the number of rows to prefetch for each server access by an external client. You can accept the default value or raise it using a trial-and-error process to settle on a size that maximizes performance. The default value of this parameter is 48 rows.
- **Stream Chunk Size** Enables you to specify the data chunk size (in bytes) for streaming data types that are sent in sized chunks by the server to clients. The default value is 256 bytes.

Figure 4-8 shows the the General configuration page for data source properties. Note that a change to any of these general configuration parameters will be effective only after a server restart or after module redeployment.

Configuring Transactions

Earlier in this chapter, you learned about the two types of WebLogic transactions—local and global. A global or distributed transaction uses the two-phase commit protocol for its transactions.

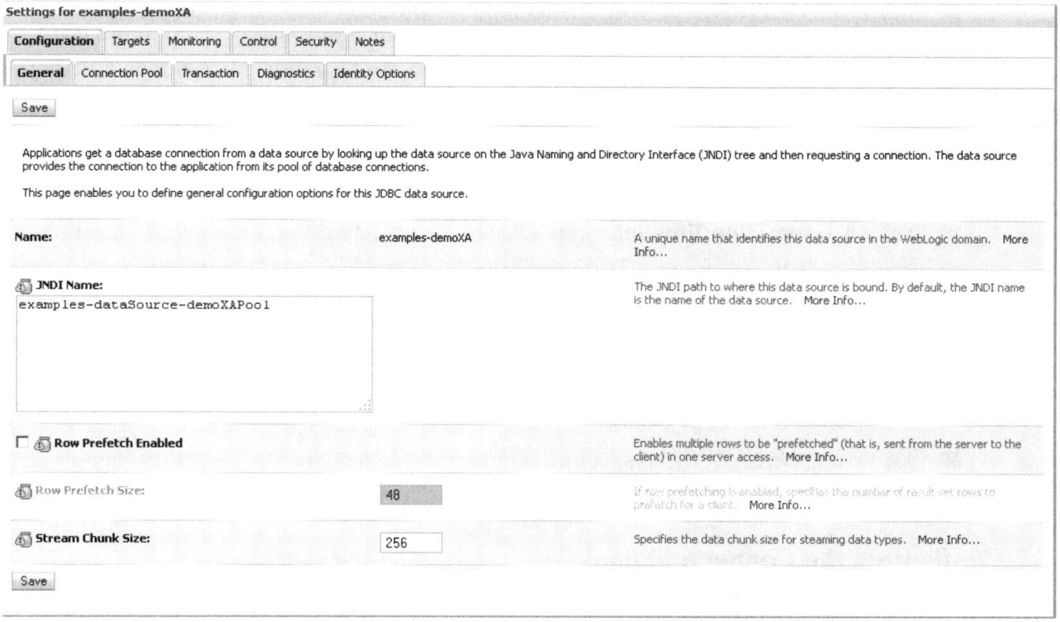

FIGURE 4-8. *Configuring general data source properties*

WebLogic Server supports both local and global transactions. Note that you must configure an XA-aware data source if your application uses EJBs that support container-managed transactions (such as CMP entity beans). You must also make data sources XA-aware if your applications use JTA to update multiple databases within the same transaction or if they use multiple resources such as a database and a JMS service, for example, within the span of a single transaction.

You can create an XA-aware data source by choosing an XA-aware database driver, as I've done here (Oracle Thin XA Driver). When I created a data source earlier, I chose the Global (XA) Transaction Protocol, so this protocol will control the database connections during a transaction. You can also choose to use a non-XA–supporting database driver, in which case, for transactions that span multiple JDBC or JMS connections, you need to specify the (default) transaction option, Supports Global Transactions, during the configuration of a data source through the Administration Console. Once you choose the Supports Global Transactions option, you must select either the Emulate Two Phase Commit or Logging Last Resource option to indicate the protocol for the server to use during global transactions. The Logging Last Resource protocol option performs better and offers greater data safety than the Emulate Two Phase Commit protocol option.

By default, the following four transaction options are preselected when you choose to use an XA JDBC driver:

- **Use XA Data Source Interface** Specifies that the XA interface of a JDBC driver must be used to create database connections.
- **Keep XA Connection Until Transaction Complete** Specifies that the server must use the same database connection until a global transaction completes.
- **Keep Connection After Local Transaction** Lets the server keep the physical database connection open, instead of closing it following a local transaction commit.
- **Resource Health Monitoring** Selecting this property enables JTA resource health monitoring for the data source. If an XA resource fails to respond within the time set by *MaxXACallsMillis*, the server marks the data source as unhealthy and won't accept new calls for connecting to that data source.

In addition, there are other transaction-related configuration properties, some of which I summarize here:

- **Set XA Transaction Timeout** Lets you set a transaction branch timeout based on the values you set for the XA Transaction Timeout property. You set this timeout if you have transactions that exceed the default value on the XA resource.
- **XA Transaction Timeout** Sets the transaction branch timeout, in seconds. In case you set this parameter, its value must be greater than or equal to the global WebLogic Server transaction timeout. If you set the value to 0, WebLogic Server uses the global WebLogic transaction timeout period.
- **XA Debug Level** You can specify the level of debugging for the XA driver with this parameter. The minimum value is 0, which means no logging, and the maximum value is 100.

Configuring the Connection Pool

When the WebLogic Server starts or when you deploy a data source to a new target, the connection pool is registered with the server, meaning that the connection pool and its connections are created at that time. You can configure various settings to control the connection pool size and the way the pool can shrink and grow.

Following are the key connection pool properties that you can configure for a data source. Note that you have to click the Advanced button at the bottom of the page in order to configure some of the properties listed here:

- **Initial Capacity** Lets you specify the minimum number of database connections to create and keep available in the connection pool. The connection pool size never goes below the setting you specify for the Initial Capacity attribute. The minimum value is 0 connections, and the maximum is 2,147,483,647. If you set the initial capacity to 1, only one physical connection is available when you initialize the connection pool. As client requests grow, new connections have to be created on the fly, which will affect your server's performance. It is common to set the initial capacity to a value that handles your estimated average, but not necessarily the maximum number of connections to the database. Ideally, you want to make sure that you have enough initial connections to match the number of concurrent requests that you expect to have running on any given server instance. To be on the safe side, you can set the initial capacity to the same value as the maximum capacity—this way, the connection pool will have all the physical connections ready when the pool is initialized.

TIP
Set the initial capacity of the connection pool to the same value as the maximum capacity to avoid a performance hit for creating new connections to service client requests.

- **Maximum Capacity** Specifies the maximum number of physical connections for this connection pool. The default maximum number of connections is 15 for a development server and 25 for a production server. The maximum should be considered as a mechanism for handling periods of heavy load and configured to allow some expansion during those periods.
- **Capacity Increment** Specifies the number of new connections created by WebLogic Server when it creates additional connections (beyond those you specified with the Initial Capacity parameter) to satisfy connection requests up to the maximum capacity defined. The default is 1 connection.
- **Statement Cache Type** Specifies whether WebLogic Server should use the least recently used (LRU) or the FIXED algorithm to maintain prepared statements in the statement cache. The LRU algorithm removes the oldest prepared statements from the cache to make room for new prepared statements. The FIXED algorithm always caches a specific number of prepared statements in the statement cache.

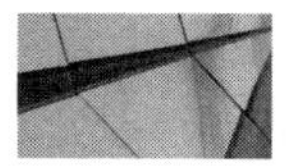

TIP
Statement caching is enabled by default.

- **Statement Cache Size** Specifies the size of the statement cache—a larger cache can cache more prepared statements and help improve performance. If you set the cache size to 0, the server won't cache any prepared or callable statements in the cache. Statement caching enables WebLogic Server to cache the compiled version of a prepared statement, also known as a callable statement. Since the server doesn't have to recompile the prepared statement when it's reused (the server uses the cached compiled statement), it improves the performance of your applications. The default value for the Statement Cache

Size parameter is 10, and the maximum value for this parameter is 1024. You must set this parameter following some experimentation in your own environment.

Note that the statement caching described here is explicit statement caching. There's also statement caching in the Oracle Thin driver that can be configured separately. When you call a *close* method on an *OracleCallableStatement* or *OraclePreparedStatement*, the Oracle driver automatically caches the statement unless you disable caching for that statement. By default, all callable and prepared statements are automatically cached. Experimentation is key with regard to the use of implicit statement caching as well. Although implicit caching only retains the metadata, explicit statement caching retains data, state, and metadata and thus performs better than implicit caching. As to whether to use explicit or implicit statement caching, answering this question in a general way is not easy; the answer depends on your particular situation.

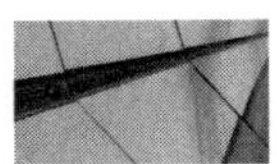

NOTE
Normally the same connection pool is targeted to all of the Managed Servers on which the application is deployed.

Pool connections may sometimes not be valid after a time, so have the server automatically test the connection periodically, and restart any connections that have failed. Following are additional parameters you can specify to configure a connection pool by clicking the Advanced button. These connection pool settings let you specify how WebLogic Server tests a connection before passing it to a client:

- **Test Table Name** If you specify a Test Frequency parameter and enable Test Connections On Reserve, you must specify the name of a test table to test a database connection. Select a table that has few or no rows so the connection test can return fast results. Also make sure that the table is accessible to the database user used in testing the connection. For example, a common test on an Oracle database may be

  ```
  SQL SELECT 1 FROM DUAL
  ```

  In Oracle WebLogic Server 12*c*, you can improve connection testing performance of a data source by setting the *Test Table Name* attribute to *SQL PINGDATABASE*.

- **Init SQL** Specifies the SQL statement the server executes to initialize a new database connection. You can use the Init SQL parameter to specify the SQL to be executed when a new connection is created. This helps prime the JDBC connection when it's initially created. The SQL string you specify must begin with SQL, as shown in the following example:

  ```
  SQL SET LOCK MODE TO WAIT
  ```

  Make sure the Init SQL table exists in the database and also that it contains few or zero rows, to optimize connections.

- **Test Connections On Reserve** Specifies that the server test a connection before handing the connection to a client, thus ensuring that the connection is valid. The downside to selecting this option is that there's going to be a slight delay in conducting the connection test, as well as some overhead in testing the connections. If you're configuring a multi data source with the failover algorithm, this test is required. By default, connections aren't tested by the server.

- **Test Frequency** Specifies the delay between consecutive tests of idle connections (in seconds). If a connection fails this test twice, the server closes the connection. You can set this parameter to the default value of 0 to disable the tests.
- **Seconds To Trust An Idle Pool Connection** During a heavy workload, you can turn off connection testing to improve performance. This parameter lets you specify the length of time for which the server "trusts" that an idle connection is still good.
- **Maximum Waiting For Connection** Sets the maximum number of connections that can wait for reserving connections from the connection pool of this data source. If you set this parameter to 0, connection requests won't wait.
- **Ignore In-Use Connections** Lets the server shut down the data source even if some database connections are still active.

By default, the server doesn't test connections before handing them to a client. The server will test connections if you've configured the Test Table Name parameter and set the test frequency with the Test Frequency parameter. Note that there's a price to pay for testing connections since connections are delayed slightly while they're being tested by the server. The server issues an exception if a connection test fails following a client request to reserve a connection.

By default, WebLogic Server waits for 10 seconds for a connection test result to return, before deciding that the test has failed. Once the assigned period expires, the server closes all connections and disables the connection pool by blocking new connection reservation attempts. The server automatically reenables the pool when it can reconnect to the database. You can change the wait time for the connection test to a nondefault value such as 30 seconds by specifying the following flag at the command line when you execute the *startWebLogic.cmd* (or *startWebLogic.sh*) script to start the WebLogic Server instance:

```
-Dweblogic.resourcepool.max_test_wait_secs=30
```

If you set the wait time to 0 seconds, the server waits indefinitely for a connection test to complete.

When a client requests a new connection, WebLogic Server returns a connection if there are available connections in the pool. If no connections are available, the server will increase the pool size by creating the number of new connections specified by the Capacity Increment setting and returns one of those connections to the client. Note that the server can create new connections only up to the maximum connection limit set by the Maximum Capacity parameter. If the server has reached the maximum capacity limit for connections, it forces the client to wait for a connection, with the wait time determined by the value of the Connection Reserve Timeout parameter. If you've set the Maximum Waiting For Connection parameter to 10, for example, a maximum of 10 requests can wait for a connection. If a new connection becomes available before the client's wait time expires, the server will hand that connection to one of the waiting clients. If not, the client's connection request will fail. In the case of a cluster, this results in the request being attempted on a secondary server.

By default, a connection request from a client times out after 10 seconds. You have to be careful when setting the Maximum Waiting For Connection parameter value because too many waiting connection requests could hurt server performance, predominantly by causing the latency and response times to increase.

When you lose database connectivity, even temporarily, some connections become defunct, and WebLogic Server, during its connection testing process following requests for database connections, tries to replace the defunct connections. This testing of dead connections may lead to long delays on occasion, and to minimize the delays, WebLogic Server data sources consider all connections in a data source as dead if a specific number of connection tests fail consecutively. Following this, the data source closes all connections, and when it allocates new connections to satisfy requests, it doesn't have to test for dead connections.

The Test Frequency setting for a data source determines the number of test failures that can occur before WebLogic Server closes all connections:

- If the Test Frequency setting is greater than 0, the number of test failures before closing all connections is set to 2.
- If the Test Frequency setting is set to 0 (periodic testing disabled), the number of test failures before closing all connections is set to 25 percent of the naximum capacity for this data source.

You can set a connection pool's *CountOfTestFailuresTillFlush* attribute in order to minimize the delay that occurs during the testing of dead database connections on the connection pool. In addition, you must set the Test Connections On Reserve attribute to true.

When a database is unavailable for some reason, data sources keep testing the connection and try to replace the dead connections in their attempt to satisfy new connection requests expeditiously.

Although this behavior is beneficial while the database is up and running, when the database is actually down, it could cause a long delay for clients before they are sent the failure message.

To minimize the delay that occurs for client applications while a database is unavailable, you may want to set the *CountOfRefreshFailuresTillDisable* attribute (default value is 2). For this to work, you must also set the Test Connections On Reserve attribute to *true* and also ensure that the Initial Capacity attribute's value is greater than 0.

Configuring Identity Options

You can specify two security identity options when you map WebLogic Server credentials to database user credentials.

- **Set Client ID On Connection** Lets the server set a client ID for the database connection based on a map of database IDs.
- **Enable Identity Based Connection Pooling** This option lets the server create a database connection with the requested database username based on a map of database IDs and WebLogic Server user IDs. You must specify a credential mapping of the server user IDs to database user accounts.

Database Resident Connection Pooling

Oracle WebLogic Server 12c has introduced Database Resident Connection Pooling (DCRP), which lets you configure multiple web-tier and mid-tier data sources to pool database server processes and sessions that are resident in an Oracle database. The key thing to remember is that DCRP must be designed to return connections to the connection pool when the sessions complete their work with the database connection. Otherwise, configuring DCRP doesn't do you any good!

Configuring a Data Source for DCRP You can configure a data source to support DCRP by doing one the following:

- When creating a new data source on the Connection Properties tab of the data source configuration wizard, under Additional Configuration Properties, enter the DCRP connection class in the *oracle.jdbc.DCRPConnectionClass* field.
- When you're editing an existing data source, select the Connection Pool tab:

- Change the URL to include a suffix of :POOLED or (SERVER=POOLED) for service URLs.
- Update the connection properties to include the value/name pair of the DCRP connection class. For example: *oracle.jdbc.DRCPConnectionClass=myDCRPclass*.

- When creating or editing a data source with a text editor or using WLST, change the URL element to include a suffix of :POOLED or (SERVER=POOLED) for service URLs. For example: *url>jdbc:oracle:thin:@host:port:service:POOLED</url>*. Also update the connection properties to include the value/name pair of the DCRP connection class.

Configuring a Database for DCRP Configuring your applications to use DCRP, as shown in the previous section, is only the first step to using DRCP. The next step is for your database administrator to configure the Oracle database to support DRCP.

You can enable DRCP in an Oracle database by executing the following Oracle supplied procedure:

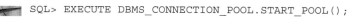

```
SQL> EXECUTE DBMS_CONNECTION_POOL.START_POOL();
```

You must also configure the following parameters for the server pool:

- ***MAXSIZE*** The maximum number of pooled servers in the pool. The default value is 40. You may consider setting the maximum size to the same value as the largest WebLogic connection pool using the DRCP.
- ***INACTIVITY_TIMEOUT*** The maximum time, in seconds, the pooled server can stay idle in the pool. After this time, the server is terminated. The default value is 300.
- ***MAX_THINK_TIME*** The maximum time of inactivity, in seconds, for a client after it obtains a pooled server from the pool. The default value is 120.

Managing Data Sources

You can use the Administration Console or WLST scripts to manage the JDBC data sources in a domain. Probably the most important management tasks are the testing of data source connections and the management of the statement cache for a data source. You can regularly test database connections to avoid connection issues. You can configure automatic connection testing when you create a data source or by configuring it afterward. You can use the JDBC Data Sources | Monitoring | Testing page in the console to test database connections manually. You can clear the statement cache for the data source by clicking the Clear Statement Cache button on the Console's Control page for the data source. You can also clear the cache for individual connections programmatically.

Here are some of the important connection pool management tasks you can perform from the Console's Control page for a data source:

- **Shrinking a connection pool** You can shrink a connection pool after a busy period to free up connections that are no longer needed so you can optimize database and system usage. You can also enable automatic shrinking of the connection pool.
- **Resetting connections** When dealing with faulty data source connections, it may be a good idea to reset a connection pool, especially after you restart a database.
- **Suspending and resuming a connection pool** You can use either the Suspend or the Force Suspend options to suspend a data source. The normal Suspend option is for a graceful suspension of the pool, and the Force Suspend option will destroy all pool connections and roll back running transactions. You can use the Resume option to reenable a suspended data source.

Starting and Stopping a Data Source

You can start or stop a data source from the Administration Console in the following manner:

1. In the left-hand pane of the Console, expand Services and select Data Sources.
2. Click the data source you want to start or stop by selecting the data source on the Summary Of JDBC Data Sources page.
3. Click the Control tab.
4. On the Control page, select the data source you want to start or stop.
5. In the Deployed Instances Of This Data Source table, select the server where the data source is deployed. You have two choices here, depending on the current state of the data source:
   - If the data source is in a shutdown state, click the Start button to start the data source and then click Yes.
   - If the data source is in a running state, click the Shutdown button to shut down a data source. The Shutdown button offers two options: Shutdown and Force Shutdown. If the data source is healthy and there are active database connections, the normal Shutdown command will fail. You must specify the Force Shutdown option to shut down a data source with active connections. Click Yes to confirm the shutdown action.

In addition to starting and shutting down a data source, the Control page for a data source also lets you shrink, reset, suspend, and resume a data source. You can also clear the statement cache from this page.

Configuring Java Messaging Services (JMS)

Oracle WebLogic Server provides messaging services based on the JMS API. A message is simply data exchanged between applications or systems that can consist of queued, transformed, and transmitted messages between these applications or systems. Note that in a two-tier implementation (server and client only), the client communicates directly with the data tier, with no real messaging capabilities. In three-tier architectures, however, the middle tier will often include messaging services as part of the application server's capabilities. In many cases, JMS is used to simply queue requests originated from the web tier to the services tier asynchronously.

WebLogic Server implements and extends the standard JMS APIs through the WebLogic JMS messaging system. As mentioned earlier, a message is simply an exchange of information among processes and could include a request, event, or report. JMS offers a standard API to enable Java applications to create, send, and receive messages. WebLogic Server is compliant with the JMS 1.1 specification. Using the JMS API means that developers can avoid writing low-level code to process the messages at the infrastructure level, and it enables you to use Java to send and receive messages easily.

WebLogic Server supports message persistence, guaranteed delivery, redelivery, expiry, paging, and numerous other services to support enterprise messaging. Clustered JMS implementations help create portable JMS applications that can be migrated across servers.

Message Communication Modes

Messages can use two different communication modes: synchronous and asynchronous. A *synchronous* communication mode is one where the sender of a message has to wait for a response before proceeding. For example, when you swipe a credit card for completing a transaction, the machine dials the authorizing computer and has to wait until it receives an "approved" or "rejected" message. Note that synchronous messaging requires that both parties are active in order to complete the message transaction. With *asynchronous* communication, the sender of a request doesn't need to wait for a response and goes on about its business without any confirmation of the receipt of the message. E-mail messages are good examples of asynchronous communication because you don't have to wait for any confirmation once you send an e-mail message. Asynchronous messages don't require that both parties to a messaging transaction be active—the messages can typically survive hardware and network failures. Asynchronous communication is preferred when a high volume of messages is expected because the responses don't have to be sent immediately after the messages are sent. JMS uses synchronous messaging in only a very limited number of cases—in general, you can handle that type of synchronous messaging better with a direct call to an EJB. Thus, for all practical purposes, you are concerned only about asynchronous JMS messaging.

Structure of a JMS Message

A JMS message always has a header, which is a required component. In addition, a header may optionally include two other components—properties and a message body.

JMS message header fields include the information that identifies and routes messages. Here are some examples:

- JMSMessageID
- JMSDeliveryMode
- JMSPriority
- JMSExpiration

The JMS API allows you to include message properties to further clarify the information in the header fields. Properties can be of various types, such as *Boolean, float, int, long, string,* and so on. You can use the properties and the header field to filter and route messages.

A message body contains the actual information the message is relaying and can have the following formats:

- BytesMessage
- MapMessage
- ObjectMessage
- TextMessage
- StreamMessage

Components of a JMS Messaging Application

A JMS messaging application consists of the following components.

JMS Provider

The JMS provider communicates with the JMS applications and provides the infrastructure for processing messages. WebLogic Server is the JMS provider in our case.

Administered Objects

These are objects created by an administrator, and there are two types: destination and connection factory. The *destination* objects contain the configuration information that's provided by the JMS provider, in this case, the Oracle WebLogic Server. Clients use the destination object to specify the destination for sending and receiving messages. JMS messages can follow one of two different message models. The point-to-point (PTP) message model supports one-to-one messages, and the publish-subscribe model supports one-to-many message types. For a point-to-point model, you use a *queue,* and for a publish-subscribe model, a *topic*.

You must first create a JMS application before you can send and receive messages. Essentially, you must first look up the connection factory (the second type of objects managed by the administrator) in the JNDI tree for a given destination and use that destination to get a physical connection to the messaging system that's anchored by the JMS server. A ConnectionFactory object encapsulates a set of connection configuration parameters that you define and clients use it to create connections with a JMS provider. You can create a set of JMS destinations that will be hosted by the JMS server through the Administration Console. Figure 4-9 shows the steps you must follow to create a JMS application.

In addition to the connection component, there's a separate *session* component, which is responsible for the actual processing of messages. A session creates a *MessageProducer* object to send messages to a destination, which could be either a queue or a topic. When creating the *MessageProducer* object, you can specify the default delivery mode (persistent or nonpersistent), the message priority, and the expiration time for the message.

A session also creates the *MessageConsumer* object to receive the sent messages, and it can do so in either of two modes: synchronous or asynchronous. To process messages in asynchronous mode, you also need to implement a *MessageListener* interface. Clients can also specify a *MessageSelector* object to filter out messages that don't adhere to a specific format, by comparing the message to a string expression.

Sessions coordinate the sending and receiving of messages between message publishers and subscribers. After a subscriber finishes processing a message or set of messages, it notifies the JMS provider that it may delete that message or set of messages. A JMS session lets the subscriber send a message acknowledgment to the JMS provider. There are three distinct acknowledgment modes, as described here:

- **AUTO_ACKNOWLEDGE** Messages are automatically acknowledged one by one by the JMS provider, but because this involves some delay, duplicate messages can be sent.
- **DUPS_OK_ACKNOWLEDGE** The JMS provider acknowledges messages a few messages at a time and leaves open the possibility of sending duplicate messages.

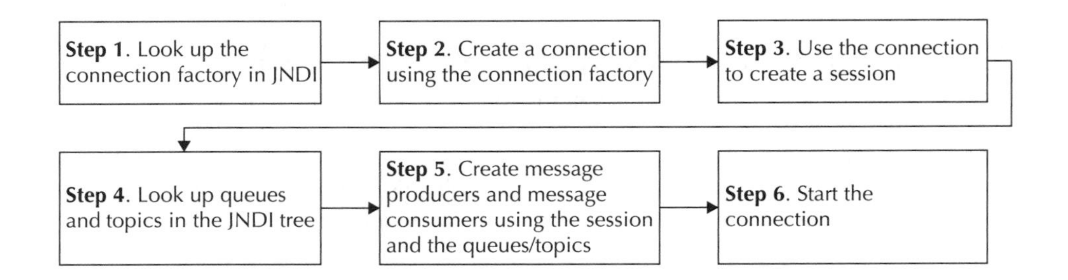

FIGURE 4-9. *Setting up a JMS application*

- **CLIENT_ACKNOWLEDGE** Under this mode, clients are responsible for explicitly acknowledging the consumption of all messages in the current session using the *acknowledge()* method in a message.

Instead of using message acknowledgment, an application can use a transaction session to process groups of messages at once. When a transaction session commits or rolls back its work, it automatically handles message acknowledgment.

Clients

JMS clients are any Java applications that send and receive messages.

JMS Messages

JMS messages contain information exchanged between different applications. As mentioned earlier, JMS supports two basic types of messages—point-to-point and publish-subscribe. The two messaging models are briefly described in the following sections.

Point-to-Point Messaging Under the point-to-point messaging model, the message producer sends messages on a one-to-one basis. The JMS server sends the messages to a destination, also called a *queue*. The messages in the queue are processed on a first-in, first-out basis, with each available consumer or subscriber processing a message exactly once. The message recipient can browse through the queue but can't process recipients in a different order (other than on the first-in, first-out basis). Note that the use of message selectors changes the default behavior, which is for an application to be notified of every message delivered to it. A *message selector,* which can be defined by a SQL statement or XML code, is used to filter out unwanted messages to improve performance by minimizing network traffic. Message selectors thus allow clients to take messages off of the queue in a different order than the order in which they are added.

Following are the steps to process a point-to-point message:

1. Use a JNDI lookup to obtain the *QueueConnectionFactory* object.
2. Use the *QueueConnectionFactory* object to obtain the *QueueConnection* object to the provider.
3. Obtain a *QueueSession* object with the provider.
4. Use a JNDI lookup to obtain the queue.
5. Use the *QueueSession* interface to create a *QueueSender* or *QueueReceive* object for the obtained queue.
6. Send or receive the message.
7. Close the *QueueConnection* object.

Point-to-point messages can be persistent or nonpersistent. Persistent messages stay in the message queue until a consumer processes the message or until the message expires or is deleted. Nonpersistent messages don't survive a server failure or shutdown, whereas persistent messages can be sent even after a server failure or shutdown.

Publish-Subscribe Messaging Applications can use the publish-subscribe messaging model to send and receive messages on a one-to-one or a one-to-many basis. You use the publish-subscribe model to send a message to multiple consumers (also called *subscribers*) simultaneously, such as sending stock prices to multiple traders in a stock exchange, for example. Instead of using a message queue, under the publish-subscribe messaging model, the message producer publishes messages to a destination called a *topic*. A subscriber must subscribe to a topic in order to receive the message—each subscriber to a topic gets an identical copy of a published message.

A subscriber can use a durable or a nondurable subscription model. A *durable* subscription model means that messages are stored when a subscriber isn't online, as is the case when you log off your e-mail service; new messages accumulate in the inbox and are available to you when you reconnect to the service. In a *nondurable* subscription model, on the other hand, if the subscriber isn't connected, the message is still published but is also destroyed afterward, before the subscriber gets a chance to receive the message.

A publish-subscribe mode of communication follows these steps:

1. Use a JNDI lookup to obtain the *TopicConnectionFactory* object.
2. Use the *TopicConnectionFactory* object to obtain a *TopicConnection* object to the provider.
3. Obtain a *TopicSession* object with the provider.
4. Use a JNDI lookup to get the topic.
5. Create a *TopicPublisher* or a *TopicSubscriber* object for the topic.
6. Send or receive messages and close the *TopicPublisher/TopicSubscriber* session and connection.

The JMS provider saves the messages until all consumers process the messages or until the message expires or the topic is deleted. Durable subscriptions end when the subscriber unsubscribes, and nondurable subscriptions end when a subscriber's JMS connection ends.

WebLogic JMS Architecture

WebLogic Server JMS architecture includes the use of JNDI for lookup purposes, a JMS server, JMS configuration modules, and persistent storage. Of course, the architecture includes client JMS applications that produce and consume the messages. Earlier in this chapter, you already reviewed how JNDI helps locate various services provided by WebLogic Server.

A WebLogic Server administrator must understand each of these components and learn how to configure them. There are both domain-dependent and domain-independent configuration items that relate to JMS. Some of the JDBC-related resources, such as JMS servers and persistent stores, are classified as environment configuration, and they are unique to each domain. Environment configuration details are stored, as is the case with the other domain configuration information, in the domain's *config.xml* file. You can configure these through the Administration Console or using WLST commands. The WebLogic Server administrator must also configure the following additional JMS-related resources as domain configuration resources so they can be used by JMS servers and JMS modules:

- Persistent stores
- JMS store-and-forward (SAF)
- Path service
- Messaging bridges

NOTE
Session pools are older mechanisms for processing messages and don't support JTA transactions. Message-driven beans (MDBs) have superseded session pools.

Persistent Stores

WebLogic Server uses a persistent store for two purposes: storing persistent JMS messages and temporarily storing messages sent by a store-and-forward agent. You have some choices regarding the type of persistent store you want to set up. Oracle provides a default file-based persistent store that you can start using right away. Note that this default persistent store isn't just for storing JMS messages—it's for any WebLogic Server subsystem that needs a default storage mechanism. You can also create your own custom file-based or JDBC store for your JMS persistent messages. Chapter 3 explains how to create both a file-based and a JDBC-based persistent store. You must create a custom persistent store on each WebLogic Server instance where you're going to host a JMS server. You can use the default WebLogic Server persistent store to store JMS messages, but creating your own custom stores allows for more flexibility, configuration, and tuning. Also, you can't migrate a default persistent store. If you're setting up a migratable server (more on this in Chapter 7), you must use a custom persistent store.

JMS Store-and-Forward (SAF)

The JMS store-and-forward service is a highly available service that lets the WebLogic Server send messages to distributed destinations. That is, local JMS message producers running on one WebLogic instance can reliably send messages to destinations such as JMS queues or topics running on a remote server. If the remote destination isn't available, the local server saves the messages and forwards them to the remote destinations once they're available. This provides a means for ensuring that an application is not blocked in the event that the hosting server is not available. If a web application were to store an order and then queue a message to a remote server, the application would return to the user even in the event that the back-end system was temporarily unavailable. SAF services are explained in more detail later in this chapter.

Path Service

The WebLogic Server path service maps groups of messages to a messaging resource by pinning messages to a distributed queue member. The path service also pins messages to a store-and-forward path.

Messaging Bridges

The WebLogic messaging bridge is a forwarding mechanism for JMS-based messaging products and offers interoperability between WebLogic JMS and other messaging services. Messaging bridges are discussed toward the end of this chapter.

In addition to the environment configuration, there is other application-related (but not domain-dependent) configuration information that you could include either in a system or an application JMS module. Let's look at the rest of the JMS architectural components in more detail in the following sections.

JMS Servers

The JMS server implements all the WebLogic JMS messaging services. A JMS server serves as the management container for the queues and topics in JMS modules that are targeted to the server. A JMS server hosts destination resources (queues and topics) on a single WebLogic Server instance that are used by the clients that connect to the JMS server. The JMS server provides services to the destination that are targeted to it. The JMS server maintains information on the stores that are to be used for the persistent messages handled by a queue or a topic. The server also maintains statuses of the durable subscribers on the destinations. You can configure and target multiple JMS servers to a WebLogic Server instance. Client applications use the JNDI tree or a naming context to look up a connection factory and use it to connect to the JMS server. A connection factory contains connection properties that apply to all connections that connect to the server.

Each JMS server supports all the requests for various JMS modules that you target to that server. The JMS server receives client requests for queues and topics and forwards them to the appropriate instance. You can control how many messages the JMS server can store in its memory as well as specify thresholds that trigger the storing of messages to the persistent store. You can throttle the rate at which messages are produced when the messages reach a threshold condition. The administrator can also block producers from sending messages, as well as pause destinations such as queues and topics.

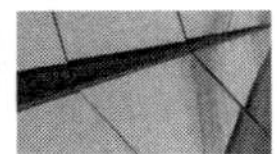

TIP
Use either automatic whole server or service migration to handle failovers, instead of migrating the JMS services manually. Chapter 7 explains both server and service migrations.

JMS servers are at the heart of JMS messaging, and the JMS server must be available at all times so the queues and topics for which it acts as a container are also available. You can use two different failover mechanisms to automatically fail over a JMS server. When a WebLogic Server instance fails due to a machine failure, you can use *whole server migration* to restart the entire WebLogic Server instance on a different machine. You can also use *service migration* to migrate a JMS server and related JMS services to a different WebLogic instance in a cluster. To support high availability, you need to set up a *migratable target list* for the JMS server, which is simply a list of the WebLogic Server instances in a cluster to which you can migrate the JMS server (and all of its destinations). Clusters can also provide load balancing for JMS connections by sending client requests for JMS connections to cluster members that host a connection factory. You'll learn how to perform both whole server and service migration in Chapter 7, when WebLogic clusters are discussed.

JMS servers support both user-defined WebLogic file-based stores and JDBC stores for storing persistent messages. Although JDBC stores are easier to manage, file stores often offer better performance. The choice between the two types of stores is largely a matter of what you have available for local storage and the capacity of your database.

JMS clients connect to remote WebLogic Servers by using JNDI and JMS APIs. The WebLogic Server JMS implementation supports the use of Java, C, and .NET clients, but only the Java clients will support the JTA transaction API. In addition, Java clients support the store-and-forward feature, which allows a client to send messages despite a connection failure.

JMS Modules

While the main function of a JMS server is to keep track of the persistent store for supporting JMS messaging, JMS modules contain the actual configuration of JMS components such as queue and topic destinations, and connection factories. You can configure and manage a system module as a global resource, and you store it as a standard Java EE module.

The WebLogic Server system administrator creates the system modules through the Administration Console. Once created and deployed to a server or cluster, the system modules are available to all applications deployed on that server or cluster. Application modules, on the other hand, are usually available only to the application in which the developer defines them. Although it's easier to package the application modules and move them across environments, it's also easy to mess up a deployment through nondefault targeting of application modules. Also, when you undeploy an application, the JMS destinations are removed and you must redeploy the application to use the administration modules. System modules support all JMS resources, whereas application modules support only some of the resources. Because application modules aren't configurable via JMS, you can't use the Administration Console to configure them. Because of all these drawbacks in using application modules, in production systems, Oracle recommends using JMS system modules rather than JMS application modules.

Each of the following JMS resources is created and stored as a JMS system module:

- **Connection factory** This resource defines connection parameters that enable JMS clients to create a JMS connection. Applications look up the connection factory in the JNDI tree to send and receive messages.
- **Queue** This is a point-to-point destination that allows an application to send messages to another application. A distributed queue is a set of JMS queues that is available as a single logical queue to clients distributed across various servers in a cluster.
- **Topic** This is a publish-subscribe destination that allows an application to send the same message to multiple applications. A distributed topic is a single set of topics available as a single, logical topic to clients spread across the members of a cluster.
- **SAF imported destinations** These are collections of imported store-and-forward queues or topics representing JMS destinations in a remote server or cluster.
- **Destination sort key** This resource specifies the sorting order for messages when they arrive on various destinations.
- **Foreign server** These are third-party JMS providers that allow local servers to reach remote JNDI providers, thus allowing foreign connection factories and destination objects to be available on a single JNDI directory tree.
- **Quota** This resource lets you specify the allocation of system resources to various destinations.
- **JMS template** Templates let you easily define queues and topic destinations with preconfigured settings.

You define the JMS modules in an XML document, either as a system or as an application module. When you create a system module, WebLogic Server creates the module file in the config\jms directory under the domain directory and adds a reference to the XML file that represents the JMS module in the domain's *config.xml* file. You can also use JMS application modules to represent JMS component configuration by including them in a packaged application, such as a jar or ear file, or as a globally available stand-alone JMS module. The key difference between a system and an application module is this: the (WebLogic) server administers the system modules, and they're available to all the applications you deploy in a domain. The application developers, on the other hand, own the application JMS modules, and the modules are usable only by the applications with which the JMS modules are packaged.

TIP
Use system JMS modules instead of application modules in a production system.

Developers can include application information as descriptors in XML files that are part of various ear, war, or jar files, or JMS modules. Unlike the environment configuration items, application-related configuration isn't stored in the domain itself. Rather, it's stored in the module descriptor files, which are XML files. When you, as an administrator, deploy any such prepackaged applications, in effect, you assign various resources to manage the application components supplied by the developers because the application configuration only specifies the actual JMS configuration resources, such as queue and topic destinations, and doesn't specify things such as the JMS server definition. For example, you determine which WebLogic persistent store to use for storing JMS messages based on your environment's configuration of the JMS resources.

TIP
You can't dynamically add or remove an application JMS module as you can with a system JMS module—you must redeploy the entire application.

WebLogic Distributed Destinations

A distributed destination is a logical representation of a set of destinations (queues or topics) that is available as a single destination to a client. Because a distributed destination is transparent to a client, the client uses the distributed destination just as any normal JMS destination. Distributed destinations help make JMS destinations highly available, in addition to providing load-balancing capabilities. You can use distributed destinations only in a WebLogic clustered environment. You must create a JMS server and a custom persistent store on each member of a cluster in order to use distributed destinations.

Configuring WebLogic Server JMS

Configuring WebLogic Server encompasses the configuration of all components of the JMS architecture, such as JMS servers, JMS modules that include destinations, and the persistent store for storing messages. You may also need to configure the JMS store-and-forward mechanism, depending on your architecture. Let's start with creating and configuring the JMS server.

Creating a JMS Server

A JMS server is a container for JMS queue and topic destinations in the JMS modules deployed to the WebLogic Server. It's the JMS server that actually implements the JMS messaging services. It's important to note the following things about a JMS server:

- A JMS server belongs to a single WebLogic Server instance, and the same instance can host multiple JMS servers.
- You can target multiple JMS modules to each JMS server.
- You must configure the JMS server to use a persistent store and target the JMS server to the same target as that for the persistent store.
- Multiple JMS servers can share the same persistent store.

Follow these steps to create a JMS server:

1. Click Lock & Edit in the Change Center of the Administration Console.
2. In the left-hand pane of the console, expand Services and click Messaging. Select JMS Servers.
3. Click New on the JMS Servers page.

4. On the Create A JMS Server page, enter a name for the new JMS server. You also must choose either an existing JDBC store or a custom file-based repository for the Persistent Store parameter. In our case, there's no custom store of any kind, so the Persistent Store drop-down box shows the value "(none)". Note that multiple JMS servers can use the same persistent store, whether it's a database or a file-based store. You can choose to leave the Persistent Store box unfilled, in which case the JMS server will use the server instance's default file-based store. In this example, you want to learn how to create your own store, so click the Create A New Store button.

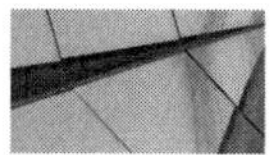

TIP

When you target a JMS server to a migratable target, it won't be able to use the WebLogic Server–provided default store; you must create a custom store and target it to the migratable target.

5. On the Create A New Store page, you must choose between a JDBC data store and a file-based store. Select File Store and click Next.
6. On the File Store Properties page, you must enter three things: a name for the new file store, the server to which you want to target it, and the actual directory in which you want WebLogic Server to create and store the file store. If the directory is new, you must create it before clicking Next.
7. Once the file store has been created, you're brought back to the Messages - JMS Server Properties page (you'll also see the message "File store created successfully" at the top of this page), where you were before you chose to create the new custom file-based store. Now, you can select your new file store from the drop-down list (remember that it showed a value of none before). Figure 4-10 shows the Create A New JMS Server page, with the new file store name (FileStore-1) in the Persistent Store field. Click Next.
8. On the Select Targets page, select the WebLogic Server instance to which you want to target the new JMS server. Click Finish.
9. Activate the changes by clicking Activate Changes in the Change Center of the Console.

Oracle recommends that you target JMS servers to a migratable target. Once you do this, WebLogic Server can automatically migrate a JMS server from a crashed or even an unhealthy instance to a good instance.

You'll now see your new JMS server in the Summary Of JMS Servers page. This section showed you how to create a bare-bones JMS server, but there's a lot to configuring a JMS server, including setting message thresholds and quotas, logging, and many other properties. The upcoming section "Configuring a JMS Server" explains all the JMS configuration options.

Configuring JMS isn't a trivial exercise—it's a labor-intensive and repetitive process. I strongly recommend that you consider recording the session as a WLST script or using the domain generation as a WLST script and then using *Jython,* with loops and the like, to make life easier.

The following section describes the basic steps involved in creating JMS servers and JMS system resources through WLST, and it shows a sample script that follows these steps to create the JMS servers and resources.

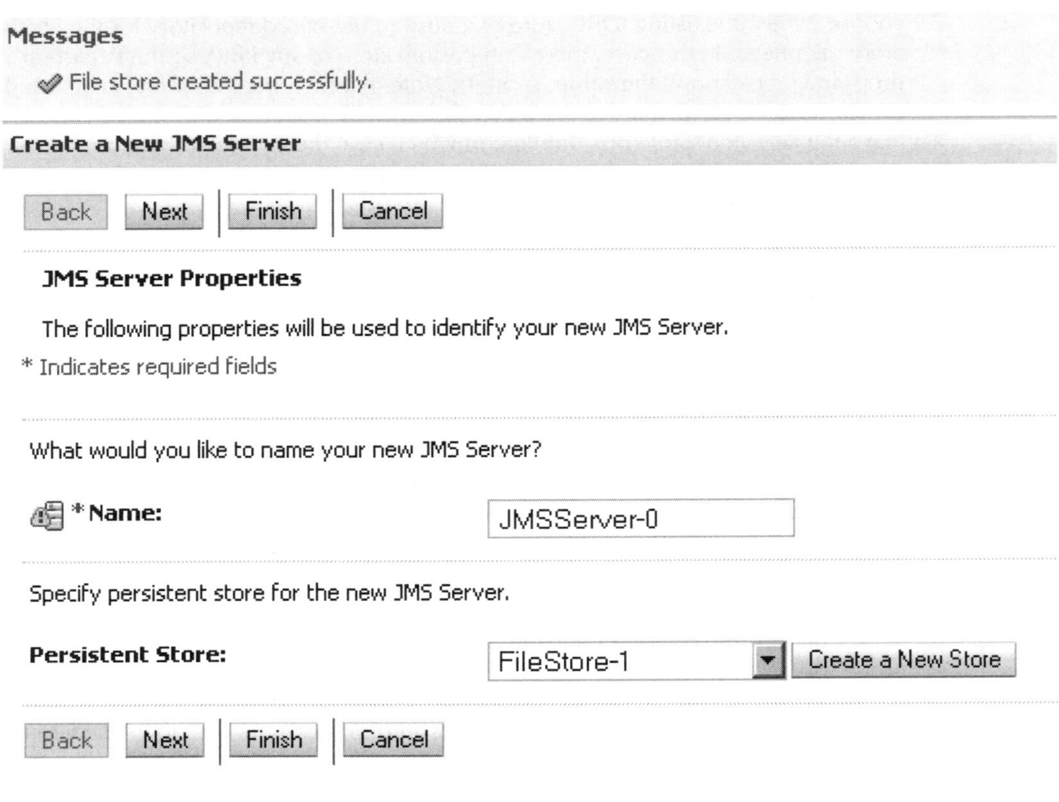

Messages

File store created successfully.

Create a New JMS Server

Back Next Finish Cancel

JMS Server Properties

The following properties will be used to identify your new JMS Server.

* Indicates required fields

What would you like to name your new JMS Server?

*Name: JMSServer-0

Specify persistent store for the new JMS Server.

Persistent Store: FileStore-1 Create a New Store

Back Next Finish Cancel

FIGURE 4-10. *The Create A New JMS Store page in the Administration Console*

Creating JMS Servers and System Resources Through WLST

To create JMS resources with WLST, first start an edit session. You must create a JMS system module that contains systems resources such as queues, topics, and connection factories. You must also create the necessary JMS server resources. Following is a list of the steps you must perform:

1. Retrieve the WebLogic Server MBean object for the JMS server.
2. Create the JMS system resource.
3. Target the JMS system resource to a server instance.
4. Get the system resource object.
5. Create JMS resources (topics, queues, connection factories) for the JMS system module.
6. Configure the JMS resource attributes (names for the queues, topics, and connection factories, for example).
7. Create a subdeployment name for the JMS system resources.

8. Create a JMS server.
9. Target the JMS server to a WebLogic Server instance.
10. Create a subdeployment object using the subdeployment name from Step 7. This will associate a JMS module's system resources to a subdeployment element in the *config.xml* file.
11. Target the subdeployment to a JMS server instance, Managed Server, or cluster.

Listing 4-1 shows a sample WLST script that performs all the steps listed here to create JMS resources. The script creates a JMS server and targets it to a server instance. The script also creates a JMS system module and uses subdeployments to target the queues that are part of the JMS system.

Listing 4-1 *Sample Script to Create JMS Resources*

```
import sys
from java.lang import System

myJmsSystemResource = "CapiQueue-jms"
factoryName = "CConFac"
jmsServerName = "MyJMSServer1"
queueName = "CQueue"

url = sys.argv[1]
usr = sys.argv[2]
password = sys.argv[3]

connect(usr,password, url)
edit()
startEdit()

servermb=getMBean("Servers/MedRecServer")
    if servermb is None:
        print '@@@ No server MBean found'

else:
    jmsMySystemResource = create(myJmsSystemResource,"JMSSystemResource")
    jmsMySystemResource.addTarget(servermb)

    theJMSResource = jmsMySystemResource.getJMSResource()

    connfact1 = theJMSResource.createConnectionFactory(factoryName)
    jmsqueue1 = theJMSResource.createQueue(queueName)
    connfact1.setJNDIName(factoryName)
    jmsqueue1.setJNDIName(queueName)
    jmsqueue1.setSubDeploymentName('DeployToMyJMSServer1')
    connfact1.setSubDeploymentName('DeployToMyJMSServer1')
    jmsserver1mb = create(jmsServerName,'JMSServer')
    jmsserver1mb.addTarget(servermb)

    subDep1mb = jmsMySystemResource.createSubDeployment('DeployToMyJMSServer1')
    subDep1mb.addTarget(jmsserver1mb)
```

Configuring a JMS Server

You can configure various properties for a JMS server once you create the server. Use the Administration Console for the JMS server configuration. Here's what you need to do to configure each of the configuration attributes for a JMS server:

1. Click Lock & Edit in the Change Center of the Administration Console.
2. In the left-hand pane of the Console, expand Services | Messaging and select JMS Servers.
3. On the Summary Of JMS Servers page, click the JMS server you'd like to configure.
4. On the Settings page (Settings For examplesJMSServer, in this example), you'll see several tabs and subtabs—General, Logging, Targets, Monitoring, and Thresholds And Quotas. Click the appropriate tab to configure each area. Figure 4-11 shows the Settings For examplesJMSServer page in the console.
5. Once you complete your configuration change, click Activate Changes in the Change Center of the Console so the server can save the changes.

The following sections summarize the key configuration properties for a JMS server.

Settings for examplesJMSServer

Configuration | Logging | Targets | Monitoring | Control | Notes

General | Thresholds and Quotas | Session Pools

Save

JMS servers act as management containers for the queues and topics in JMS modules that are targeted to them. A JMS server's primary responsibility for its destinations is to maintain information on what persistent store is used for any persistent messages that arrive on the destinations, and to maintain the states of durable subscribers created on the destinations.

Use this page to define the general configuration parameters for this JMS server.

Name:	examplesJMSServer	The name of this JMS server. More Info...
Persistent Store:	exampleJDBCStore	The file or database in which this JMS server stores persistent messages. If unspecified, the JMS server uses the default persistent store that is configured on each targeted WebLogic Server instance. More Info...
Paging Directory:		Specifies where message bodies are written when the size of the message bodies in the JMS server exceeds the message buffer size. More Info...
☑ **Paging File Locking Enabled**		Determines whether OS file locking is used. More Info...
Message Buffer Size:	-1	The amount of memory (in bytes) that this JMS server can use to store message bodies before it writes them to disk. When the JMS server writes the message bodies to disk, it clears them from memory. More Info...
☑ **Hosting Temporary Destinations**		Specifies whether this JMS server can be used to host temporary destinations. More Info...
Module Containing Temporary Template:	(none)	The name of a JMS module that contains a template that this JMS server can use to create temporary destinations. More Info...
Temporary Template Name:		The name of a configured JMS template that this JMS server uses to create temporary destinations. More Info...
Expiration Scan Interval:	30	The number of seconds between this JMS server's cycles of scanning local destinations for expired messages. A value of 0 disables active scanning. A very large scan interval effectively disables active scanning. More Info...

▶ Advanced

Save

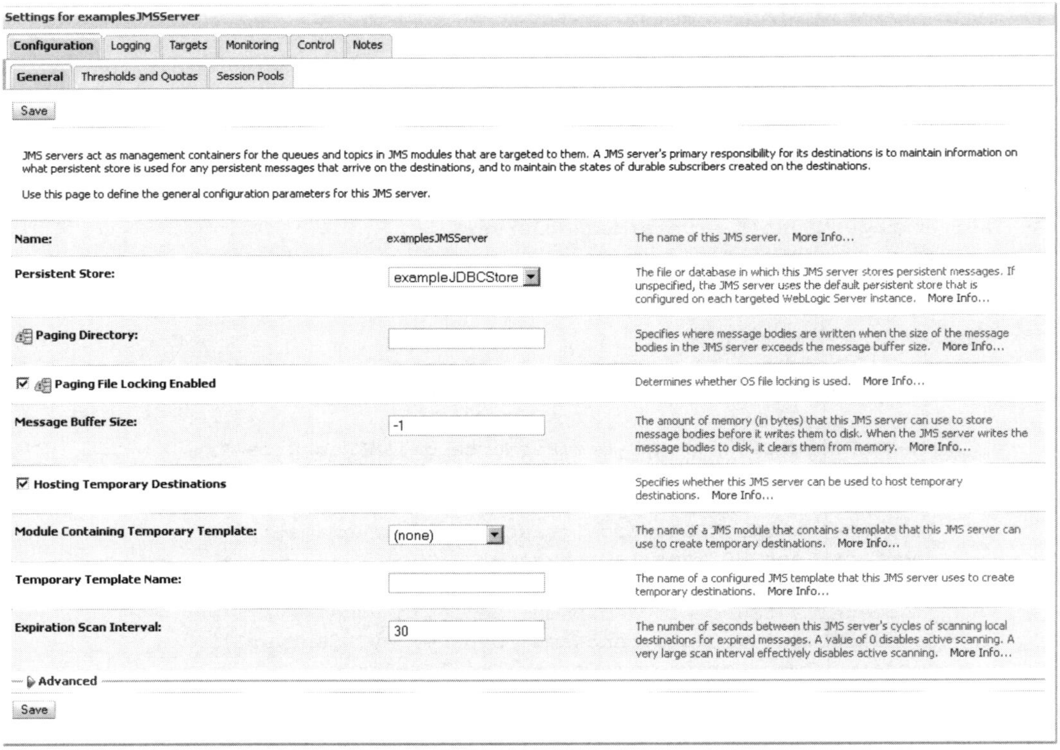

FIGURE 4-11. *The JMS server Configuration settings page*

TIP
It's a good idea to configure message quotas on each JMS server to prevent out-of-memory conditions. Assume that, on average, a message will require 512 bytes of memory.

Configuring General JMS Server Properties Here are the key general configuration properties for a JMS server:

- **Paging Directory** Specifies where the server should write the message bodies when they exceed the message buffer size (this is called *message paging*). Once the JMS server writes the message bodies to disk, it removes them from the message buffer. By default, the server writes these to the DOMAIN_HOME\servers\<*server-name*>\tmp directory of the host server. You can instead specify a separate directory for this, because the \tmp directory can fill up if there are too many large JMS messages.
- **Message Buffer Size** Specifies the amount of memory (in bytes) dedicated to storing message bodies in memory. By default, the message buffer size is one third the maximum heap size of the JVM or 512MB, whichever is larger. The JMS server uses the concept of paging to move messages temporarily from memory to persistent storage when it's faced with too many messages in memory. The server will retrieve the stored messages back into memory when they're needed. WebLogic chooses the lesser of two evils in this case because, although paging increases server overhead, storing to disk also impacts system performance. When the message buffer is full, the JMS server moves messages to persistent storage (disk). Since WebLogic Server keeps both persistent and nonpersistent messages in memory, paging applies to both types of messages.
- **Hosting Temporary Destinations** Specifies whether the JMS server can host temporary destinations. By default, this field is already enabled, and any temporary destinations that are created will use the default destinations. Disabling this field means that the JMS server won't host any temporary destinations.
- **Temporary Template Name** Refers to the configured JMS template that the JMS server uses to create temporary destinations. You can't specify this property if you don't enable the Hosting Temporary Destinations field. If you leave this field unchecked, the server will use default destination values.

NOTE
You must reboot the WebLogic Server instance after modifying the configuration of an existing JMS server. You don't have to reboot the server instance after you initially create and configure a new JMS server.

Configuring Thresholds and Quotas You can configure upper and lower message thresholds for destinations targeted to a JMS server. Exceeding these thresholds will trigger log messages. Quotas specify the upper limits for memory usage, message size, and the number of messages a JMS server can host. You can access the Thresholds And Quotas configuration page by clicking the Configuration | Thresholds And Quotas tab in the JMS server Settings page in the Administration Console. This section covers the key configuration properties related to thresholds and quotas.

When you configure high and low thresholds for messages, WebLogic Server triggers two types of events: log messages, indicating that a high or a low threshold has been reached, and events related to flow control. For example, if a high message threshold is reached, the JMS server requests that message producers decrease the flow of their messages. For configuring thresholds, set the following properties:

- **Bytes Threshold High** and **Bytes Threshold Low** These two properties specify upper and lower thresholds for the number of bytes stored on the JMS server.
- **Messages Threshold High** and **Messages Threshold Low** These two properties specify upper and lower thresholds for the number of messages stored on the JMS server.

The following are the configuration properties for setting message quotas:

- **Bytes Maximum** and **Messages Maximum** These two properties let you specify the maximum number of bytes or messages that a JMS server can store.
- **Blocking Send Policy** Specifies how a JMS server determines whether it should send smaller messages before larger ones when a destination reaches its quota for messages. You have two choices here: the FIFO (first-in, first-out) option specifies that the JMS server deliver messages in the order they were received, regardless of their size—so small messages don't get preference over larger messages. The Preemptive option lets the JMS server send smaller messages before larger messages when it's faced with a situation where destinations have exceeded their message quota.
- **Maximum Message Size** Specifies the maximum size of a message.

JMS producers are forced to wait for a specified time interval when the message quota is reached to see if space is freed up. If not, a timeout occurs, and the producers will receive a Java exception. You must always set quotas to prevent the server from running out of space for storing messages, either in the memory space for the JMS server or in the persistent store. You can set message quotas on individual destinations, such as a queue or topic, or on the entire JMS server. JMS server-level quotas apply only to destinations that don't use named message quotas.

Configuring Message Log Rotation JMS server logs provide useful information relating to the production and consumption of messages. You can configure how the server rotates these logs once you enable server logging on the destinations in the various JMS modules that you target to a JMS server. To configure message logging, click the Logging tab in the JMS server Settings page. You can set the following logging properties on this page:

- **Log File Name** and **Log File Rotation Directory** Specify the name of the file to store the JMS server log messages and the directory for storing rotated log files.
- **Rotation Type** You can choose among three criteria for rotating old logging messages to a new file. Select By Size to specify that the server rename the current log file after it reaches a certain size, By Time to base log rotation on a time interval, and None to indicate that logs are rotated neither by size nor by time. The default value for the Rotation Type is By Size; however, WebLogic Server rotates the log file by default once it reaches a threshold size of 500KB.
- **Rotation File Size** By default, once the JMS server log file reaches 500KB, the server automatically renames the current log file and starts logging events to a new file if Rotation Type is configured to By Size. If you wish, you can specify a much larger value for this attribute.

- **Limit Number Of Retained Files** Specifies the number of log files a JMS server retains before it starts overwriting the oldest log file.
- **Rotate Log File On Startup** Specifies whether the server rotates the log files during startup and in production mode; the default setting is false.

By default, WebLogic Server bases its logging on the Java logging APIs that are part of the JDK.

Configuring Message Logging Once you create a JMS destination such as a queue or a topic, you can enable the logging of message information into a JMS message log file. Make sure you configure JMS server message log rotation, as explained in the previous section, before configuring message logging.

You follow identical steps to configure message logging for a queue or a topic. Here are the steps for configuring message logging for a queue:

1. Click Lock & Edit in the Change Center of the Administration Console.
2. In the left-hand pane of the console, expand Services | Messaging | JMS Modules.
3. In the JMS Modules list, click the JMS module you want to configure. In my example, the JMS system module name is *examples-jms*.
4. The Settings For examples-jms page shows all the JMS resources that have been created for this system module. These resources include queue and topic destinations, connection factories, distributed destinations, foreign servers, and store-and-forward parameters. Select the name of the specific JMS resource for which you want to configure logging. In this example, I chose the queue named *exampleQueue*.
5. In the Settings For examplesQueue page, shown in Figure 4-12, click the Configuration | Logging tab. This page allows you to configure message lifecycle logging options for a destination.
6. On the Logging configuration page, you can configure the following logging properties:
    - **Enable Message Logging** Lets you specify whether to log lifecycle messages for this queue (if this were a topic resource, for a topic instead of a queue).
    - **All Headers** Specifies the inclusion of all JMS Header logs in the log file. You can alternatively choose to log only a subset of the header fields by using the Available and Chosen columns that list the JMS header fields.
    - **All Properties** Lets you include all properties in the log file. Alternatively, you can select specific properties from the list of available properties (User-defined Properties) shown underneath this property box.

Monitoring JMS Servers

You can monitor running JMS servers from the Administration Console. Not only can you monitor the active connections, transactions, and destinations, but also you can kill or pause selected active JMS servers from the Console. To monitor a JMS server, navigate to Services | Messaging | JMS Servers and click the JMS server you want to monitor. Click the Monitoring tab on the top of the page. From here, you can monitor various JMS server data such as the following:

- **Active Destinations** You can view statistics for all active JMS destinations such as queues and topics. You can also "pause" and "resume" a destination for troubleshooting purposes.

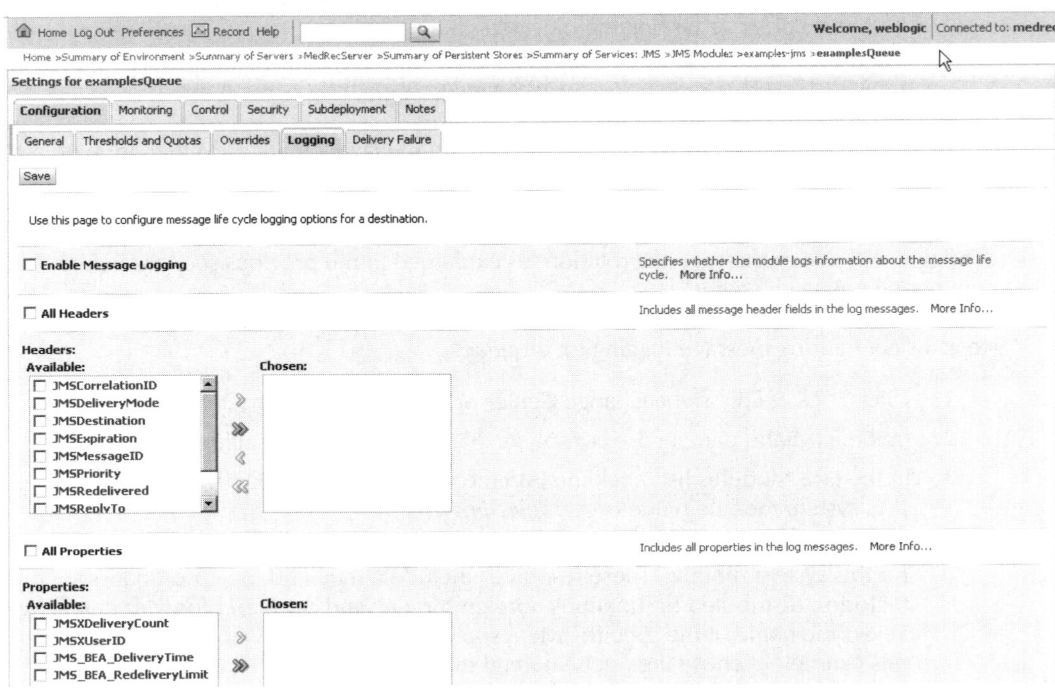

FIGURE 4-12. *The Logging configuration page for a JMS queue destination*

- **Active Transactions** You can view all active JMS transactions and commit or roll back a transaction by force.
- **Active Connections** You can see all active JMS connections for a domain. You can kill a connection by selecting the connection and clicking the Destroy button.

TIP

Because migratable targets offer the restart-in-place capability, Oracle recommends that you use them. Because only a cluster supports a migratable target, you can simulate a cluster by using a cluster of size one to use the migratable targets feature. This also helps you plan for a future migration from a single server to a cluster.

Creating JMS System Modules

As you know by now, you can create various types of JMS system modules to represent JMS resources such as queues, topics, and connection factories. Regardless of the specific system module, you follow the same procedures to create the system module. Of course, after creating the system module, the configuration aspects for that module will vary, based on the JMS resource the module represents. In this section, I show you how to create a simple system module for a JMS queue, which defines a destination for a point-to-point message. The JMS system module creation procedures first let you create a generic JMS system module, with no resources. Once you create the generic system module, you are asked to add resources to that module. In the following example, I'll add a JMS queue resource because I'm creating a module to represent that queue. Here are the steps to create a JMS system module:

1. Click Lock & Edit in the Change Center of the Administration Console.
2. In the left-hand pane, go to Services | Messaging | JMS Modules.
3. On the JMS Modules page, click New.
4. On the Create JMS System Module page, select a name for the new JMS system module. Optionally, you can also specify a descriptor filename and the location where you want to place the descriptor file. If you don't choose any descriptor filename or a location for it, WebLogic Server will use default values for both of these. The server will also automatically add a *jms.xml* extension to the descriptor filename. Click Next.
5. On the Targets page, select the WebLogic Server or cluster to which you wish to deploy the new JMS system module. Click Next.
6. On the Add Resources To The JMS System Module page, check the Would You Like To Add Resources To This JMS System Module? check box because, in this case, you want to add the JMS queue resource to the new generic system module. Click Finish.
7. On the Configuration page, click New.
8. The Create A New JMS System Module Resource page appears next. Since we want to create the queue resource in our new JMS system module, select Queue, and then click Next. The configuration pages that appear next are unique for the queue resource you're adding to the new JMS system module. Other resources may offer different configuration pages.
9. On the JMS Destination Properties page, enter a name as well as a JNDI name for the new queue you've associated with the new JMS system module, MySystemModule1. Click Next.
10. On the next page, you can optionally choose a subdeployment to which to assign the new system module resource by clicking the Create A New Subdeployment button. A *subdeployment* is when you target a JMS resource to a specific server instance or cluster (or a SAF agent). If you don't choose the subdeployment option, the new system module resource will be targeted to all servers. For now, just click Finish.
11. You'll see a message at the top of the page stating that the new JMS queue was successfully created. Save the changes by clicking the Activate Changes button in the Change Center of the Administration Console.

You can view the various resources that are part of a JMS system module by viewing the Settings page for a JMS module.

You can always come back and configure various properties for the new JMS queues (or any other type of JMS resource) later. Note that once you deploy the JMS server that owns the destination (a queue in this case), the destination becomes available in the server's JNDI tree.

Configuring a JMS System Module

You must configure each JMS module that you target to a server, such as system modules for queue and topic destinations, connection factories, and so on. Since I showed you how to create a JMS system module to include a queue resource, let me show you how to configure some of its properties as well. If you need to create multiple queues, you may find it advantageous to create a JMS template to create multiple queues easily. I'm going to briefly summarize the configuration options for a JMS queue, one of the two types of destinations you can configure, with the other being a topic:

- **General Queue Parameters** Lets you specify a JMS template to configure multiple queues.
- **Advanced Queue Credentials** Lets you choose to attach the credentials of message senders.
- **Queue Thresholds And Quota** Lets you define upper and lower thresholds based on the bytes stored in the destination or the number of messages in a queue. You can specify the maximum number of messages (quota) that can be stored in this queue. You can also specify the maximum size of a message from a producer that this queue will accept. Finally, you can enable message paging on the queue to temporarily swap message bodies out of memory when the queue's message load hits a threshold.
- **Message Delivery Overrides** Lets you override values such as message priority that are set by the producers of messages.
- **Queue Message Logging** Configures the logging of messages into the JMS message log file.
- **Queue Message Delivery Failure Options** Lets you configure values such as message redelivery limits and message expiration policies.

Note that you can always temporarily stop a queue from functioning by "pausing" the queue at the server restart time, or dynamically anytime, in case you have a problem with the way a queue is functioning. You can delete a queue by going to the JMS Modules page in the Administration Console and clicking the Delete button under the Summary Of Resources table (after selecting the queue you want to delete).

Using a Connection Factory

JMS clients use a connection factory, which is an object that enables the creation of JMS connections, to obtain a JMS connection to a destination such as queue or a topic. Connection factories contain the configuration details for JMS connections and are hosted on the same server (or cluster) as the actual JMS destinations. Applications access JMS by looking up a connection factory in the JNDI tree and creating a connection from there so they can establish communication with a JMS server. Once created, the connection will have all the attributes of the connection factory through which the connection was created. The client's connection factory instance tracks all active servers in a cluster that have a connection factory. Once the client connects successfully to a specific connection factory, it retains the same host for the duration of that connection. Because a connection factory allows concurrent usage, multiple threads can access the object at the same time. In order to access a JMS destination such as a queue or a topic, messages pass from the client through the connection factory and finally to the actual JMS destination instance that's managed by the JMS server (or SAF agent).

WebLogic Server comes with two default connection factories. You can also create your own custom connection factories. The two default connection factories have the following JNDI names:

```
weblogic.jms.Connectionfactory
weblogic.jms.XAConnectionFactory
```

Note that the default connection factories are hosted on all members of a cluster, whereas you can host a custom connection factory on all or a subset of servers that you specify in a cluster. You can create multiple connection factories, each with a different set of connection attributes.

When the WebLogic Server instance starts, it binds all connection factories targeted to that server to the server's JNDI tree. Although you can just use the two default connection factories, the preconfigured settings of these connection factories may or may not be appropriate for your environment. Thus, one of the important decisions you need to make is whether you want to configure your own connection factories.

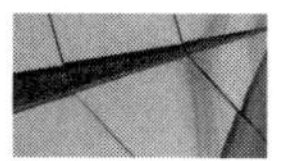

TIP
You can't tune the default WebLogic connection factories. Create custom connection factories for JMS connections.

Targeting a Connection Factory You can target a connection factory to one or more Managed Servers or to all or some of the servers in a cluster. You can also target a connection factory to one or more JMS servers, along with destinations such as a JMS queue or a topic. You can create a group with a connection factory and related stand-alone queues or topics and target it to a JMS server to enhance performance. The grouping also helps during the migration of a JMS server because you can migrate the connection factory along with all the JMS server's destinations such as queues and topics.

Creating a Connection Factory A connection factory is contained in a JMS system module. Therefore, you create a JMS module on which you can configure the connection factory resource. This section explains how to create a connection factory in a system module using the Administration Console. Several of these steps are similar to how you create other system modules such as the one to hold queues described earlier in this chapter.

1. Click Lock & Edit in the Change Center of the Administration Console.
2. In the left-hand pane, expand Services and select Messaging | JMS Modules.
3. On the Module Settings page, click New in the Summary Of Resources table.
4. On the next page, select a name for your new connection factory and click Next.
5. Select a WebLogic Server instance or cluster to which you want to target the new system module. Click Next.
6. Check the Would You Like To Add Resources To This JMS Module check box, and click Finish.
7. Once you see the message stating that the JMS module was successfully created, click New in the Summary Of Resources table so you can add the connection factory resource to the new JMS system module you've just created. The Create A New JMS System Module page allows you to select the type of JMS resource you want to add to the system module, such as queues, topics, or connection factories. Select Connection Factory and click Next.
8. On the Connection Factory Properties page, you can assign a name and a JNDI name for the connection factory. In addition, you can configure the following properties for the new connection factory:
   - **Subscription Sharing Policy** Controls which subscribers can access new subscriptions. You can choose the Sharable policy if you want to allow subscribers created using this connection factory to share subscriptions with other subscribers.

If you select Exclusive as the value for this parameter instead, subscribers won't share subscriptions with other subscribers.

- **Client ID Policy** Specifies whether multiple JMS connections can use the same client ID. If you're sharing durable subscribers, Oracle recommends that you set this parameter to the value Unrestricted.
- **Maximum Messages Per Session** Specifies the maximum number of messages that can be queued for an asynchronous session before the messages are passed along to the message listener.
- **XA Connection Factory Enabled** Determines whether this connection factory can create JTA-aware transactions as well as XA queues and topics. By default, this parameter is enabled.

9. Click Next. You can target the new connection factory to one of the WebLogic Server instances or click the Advanced Targeting tab at the top of the page if you want to use the subdeployment mechanism.
10. Click Finish.

Configuring a Connection Factory Now that you've created a new connection factory, you must configure several important properties for it. Here's how to go about configuring the connection factory:

1. In the left-hand pane of the Administration Console, expand Services and select Messaging. Click JMS Modules in the right-hand pane.
2. In the JMS Modules table, click the JMS module you created to contain the connection factory.
3. On the next page, click the connection factory in the Summary Of Resources table.
4. On the connection factory Configuration (Settings For ConnectionFactory-0 in this example) page, shown in Figure 4-13, you'll see several tabs where you can configure

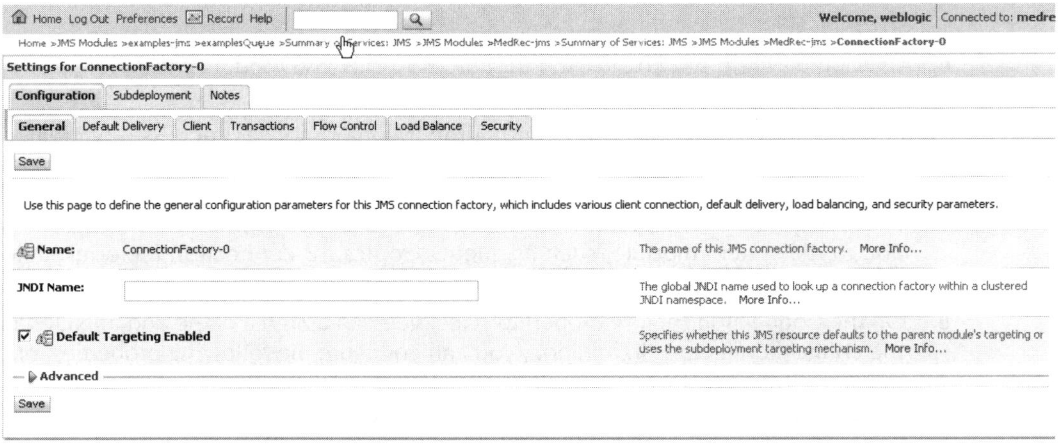

FIGURE 4-13. *The connection factory configuration settings page*

various the attributes of a connection factory, such as Default Delivery, Client, Transactions, Flow Control, Load Balance, Security, and Subdeployment. Several of these configuration attributes affect JMS message delivery, such as throttling messages, for example. The key connection factory configuration items are summarized here:

- **Default Delivery** You can set attributes such as Default Priority, Default Time To Live, and Default Delivery Time to specify message delivery options. The Default Delivery Mode option lets you specify a persistent or nonpersistent delivery mode for all messages sent by a producer through this connection factory.
- **Transactions** You can set transaction parameters such as the time-out value for a transaction created with a JMS connection factory.

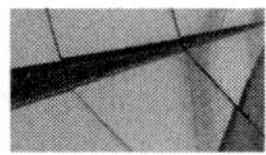

NOTE
You can configure some connection factory options dynamically—the changes you make only affect new messages and not stored messages.

- **Flow Control** You can configure various message flow control parameters to control the creation of messages by producers. For example, you can throttle message production when you determine that the messages are overloading the system. By default, flow control is enabled, which means that message producers will be slowed down automatically if the JMS server reaches its threshold settings, which can be set either on the basis of the number of bytes or messages. You can set parameters such as Flow Maximum and Flow Minimum to control the number of messages per second for a producer that is undergoing a message threshold condition. You can also configure the One-Way Send Mode parameter, which lets producers send one-way messages without waiting for a confirming message from the JMS server. You do this to improve the performance of nonpersistent, nontransactional messages. By default, this feature is disabled.

  Note that although you configure flow control through settings in a producer's connection factory, both JMS servers and destinations also have flow control attributes. However, the default thresholds on JMS servers and destinations are, in effect, disabled, so the connection factory flow control settings are what determine how the server throttles messages. Both flow control and paging are defensive measures used to control message flows, but the best way to ensure that message producers and consumers are in sync is by planning for proper message flow in the application design itself.
- **Load Balance** You can specify load balancing parameters to determine how multiple clients distribute their work to the servers. You can choose Server Affinity Enabled to specify that load balancing will be attempted across any other physical destinations that are running on the same server instance. You can also turn off load balancing by clearing the Load Balancing Enabled box. This setting specifies whether load balance messages are sent to a queue or topic on a per-call basis.

TIP
By default, both load balancing and server affinity are enabled.

Note that you can set message delivery attributes such as Time To Live, Priority, Time To Deliver, and Delivery Mode by setting them in the connection factory, but any settings a developer specifies in the application itself will override the connection factory settings. The message settings you specify in the destination itself, however, such as when you configure a queue, will trump the message delivery settings of the connection factory and even those made through the application code.

System Modules and Subdeployments

You must target a JMS system module to a Managed Server or cluster. In addition, you must target the JMS resources you define in a system module to the JMS server or WebLogic Server instances that are within the scope of the system module's targets. To provide a loose coupling of JMS resources in a domain, you can group the targetable JMS resources in a system module into subdeployments.

When you're configuring the JMS resources in a system module through the Administration Console, you can accept the preselected targets for a resource type, or select an existing subdeployment, or create a new subdeployment from the Advanced Targeting page. When targeting JMS resources, you need to understand what types of targeting are valid. Although you can target a system module to several instances, you can only target a stand-alone topic or queue to a single JMS server. You can, however, target connection factories to one or more server instances or to a cluster. If a member of a subdeployment such as a connection factory is targeted to a cluster hosting JMS servers, you can't associate a stand-alone queue or topic to that subdeployment.

You can collocate a connection factory and a stand-alone queue or topic on a specific JMS server to reduce network traffic. This typical, simple subdeployment strategy also ensures that the connection factory and its connections are migrated along with the JMS server's destinations when the targeted JMS server is migrated to another Managed Server. You must, however, ensure that the connection factory isn't targeted to multiple JMS servers because you can't collocate the stand-alone queues and topics with the connection factory.

The following example shows a system module named *jmssysmod-jms.xml* that has two configured JMS servers: *myjmsserver1* and *myjmsserver2*. If you want to always keep a set of two queues and a connection factory together on just one of the JMS servers (for example, *myjmsserver1*), you can do so by placing the two queues and the connection factory in a subdeployment.

```
<weblogic-jms xmlns="http://www.bea.com/ns/weblogic/91">
  <connection-factory name="connfactory1">
    <sub-deployment-name>myjmsserver1group</sub-deployment-name>
    <jndi-name>cf1</jndi-name>
  </connection-factory>
 <queue name="queue1">
    <sub-deployment-name>myjmsserver1group</sub-deployment-name>
    <jndi-name>q1</jndi-name>
  </queue>
 <queue name="queue2">
    <sub-deployment-name>myjmsserver1group</sub-deployment-name>
    <jndi-name>q2</jndi-name>
  </queue>
</weblogic-jms>
```

NOTE
You can use the Subdeployment management pages in the Administration Console to manage subdeployments for a system module.

The subdeployment targeting to *myjmsserver1group* would be defined in the domain's *config.xml* file, in which a system module is specified within the *jms-system-resource* element, as shown here:

```
<jms-system-resource>
   <name>jmssysmod-jms</name>
   <target>wlsserver1</target>
   <sub-deployment>
     <name>myjmsserver1group</name>
     <target>myjmsserver1</target>
   </sub-deployment>
   <descriptor-file-name>jms/jmssysmod-jms.xml</descriptor-file-name>
</jms-system-resource>
```

The following are the components of the *jms-system-resource* element (MBean):

- **name** The name of the JMS system module.
- **target** The target (server, cluster, or a migratable target) to which you've targeted the system module. (Chapter 7 discusses migratable targets in detail.) In the preceding example, the target is the JMS server *myjmsserver1*.
- **sub-deployment** The name of the subdeployment to which you're targeting a group of JMS resources (connection factories, queues, and topics). The subdeployment name is the name of the subdeployment you have created earlier—*myjmsserver1group*.
- **descriptor-file-name** Location and name of the JMS system module, which is *jmssysmod-jms.xml* in the preceding example.

By default, Oracle targets connection factories to the module and not to the subdeployment. The connection factory will then inherit the module's target.

JMS Server Targeting

You can target a JMS server to an independent WebLogic Server instance or to a migratable target. A migratable target is relevant only to a clustered environment and consists of a set of WebLogic server cluster members that can potentially host the JMS server in case of a failure of the primary WebLogic instance that hosts the JMS server.

Oracle recommends that you avoid default targeting and choose advanced targeting, which involves subdeployment targeting instead. Furthermore, you must make sure that the subdeployment references only JMS servers or SAF agents, regardless of whether the destinations are distributed, nondistributed, or imported. You can use a subdeployment to selectively target a subset of a module's resources. Oracle recommends the following best practices when you use subdeployments to deploy JMS resources:

- Target one JDBC module per each *homogeneous set of targets,* which is defined as a uniformly configured set of clusters, a set of Managed Servers in a cluster, or a single WebLogic Server instance.
- Create one subdeployment per JMS module and target it to the set of JMS servers on the server instance where you targeted the JMS module.
- Target all destinations, such as queues and topics, to the subdeployment.

Oracle recommends that you avoid default targeting (as well as WebLogic Server targeting and cluster targeting) because other applications or third-party products can introduce new JMS servers or SAF agents. Also, over time, your application may require a different set of destinations or JMS servers and SAF agents to simplify administration or for scaling up.

Migrating JMS-Related Services

JMS services run on only a single server in a cluster and not on all server instances. The JMS services are pinned to a single server for data consistency purposes. However, this leaves JMS services vulnerable to a single point of failure. A migratable target lets you avoid this by building in high availability for JMS services. A *migratable target* is one that can move from one server in a cluster to another, taking all the services you host on that target to a different server.

You can configure automatic migration of JMS services with the help of WebLogic Server's Health Monitoring feature. You can also manually migrate JMS services following a server failure or for maintenance purposes. Migratable JMS services include the JMS server, the store-and-forward service, the path service, and custom persistent stores (both JDBC stores and disk-based file stores). Since JMS requires all these services to function, you can treat the JMS-related services as a single group for migration purposes. Chapter 7, which deals with the management of WebLogic clusters, will explain how to configure manual as well as automatic migration of JMS-related services.

TIP
Migratable JMS services can't use the default persistent store.

Store-and-Forward (SAF) Service for Reliable Messaging

JMS messages can fail to be delivered for a number of reasons, such as a network or server failure, a quota failure on a receiving server, or a security denial. WebLogic Server offers the SAF service for reliably delivering messages between distributed applications running on different WebLogic Server remote instances. The reliability is provided through a mechanism whereby the local server saves any messages it can't successfully send to remote JMS queues or topics. Instead of discarding the messages, WebLogic Server saves the messages on the local server instance and redelivers them automatically to the remote server when it becomes available again. SAF services can forward messages to another server, whether it's part of a cluster or not. The service can also forward messages to servers that are part of a different domain.

You can use SAF services with both JMS messages as well as messages that use Web Services Reliable Messaging (WSRM). WSRM uses SAF agents on both the sending and the receiving instances, and guarantees the delivery of messages according to predetermined delivery assurances. If the messages can't be sent, WSRM raises an error. Client applications don't need to be aware of WSRM APIs; they can continue to use normal JMS APIs for sending messages to remote destinations.

WebLogic Server uses SAF service agents to process the storing and forwarding of messages. You configure the SAF service by configuring the SAF service agents. WebLogic applications that send JMS messages, in effect, become SAF clients. When the SAF client encounters a problem on a remote JMS destination due to an issue such as a network failure, the client is disconnected from the remote destination. SAF agents store the messages sent by their clients and forward them to the remote JMS queues or topics once the client is able to reconnect to those remote destinations. The SAF agents work both on the local (sending) side and the remote (receiving) side. You can configure SAF agents to have either sending and receiving capabilities, or just one of the two. The sending agent is used both for JMS messages and WSRM messages. The sending agent stores messages locally before forwarding them to the remote site. It's also responsible for retransmitting messages when the remote server doesn't acknowledge them within the set timeframe. The receiving agents are used only for WSRM and not for JMS messages. These agents eliminate duplicate messaging and ensure the delivery of messages to the intended destinations. For JMS messages, the JMS server takes care of eliminating duplicate messages.

You can configure SAF agents to manage message persistence, paging parameters, thresholds, and queues, just as you would for a JMS server. Note the following about configuring a SAF service before you implement the service in your domain.

- You must configure a SAF agent on the sending-side server instance (or cluster). You can do this through WLST or the Administration Console.
- If you're using WSRM, you must configure a SAF agent on the receiving-side server instance (or cluster).
- You can use the server's default store or create a dedicated store for the SAF messages.

Configuring Store-and-Forward Services

You can set various configuration options for SAF agents, such as the message time-to-live duration and a message delivery failure policy. You can also set the delivery retry attempts for forwarding messages. SAF agents store persistent messages on the local instance until they can forward these messages (or get an acknowledgment) to the receiving side. If the local WebLogic instance reboots for some reason, the SAF agent will attempt to send all messages by retrieving them from the persistent store unless the messages have expired. SAF agents don't store nonpersistent messages that are waiting to be forwarded—these are held in memory on the local instance. Thus, if the remote server isn't available for a lengthy period of time, the local instance could run out of memory due to many nonpersistent messages being stored in memory. You can set message quotas, thresholds, and paging to prevent such a situation. You configure these options similarly to the way you configure them for the JMS server.

Once you configure JMS SAF services, the SAF sending agents start forwarding and retransmitting messages when they don't receive acknowledgement from the receiving side in the specified time. If a failure requires the storing of messages, the SAF agents temporarily store the messages in the persistent store and will attempt sending those messages when connections are restored. You can configure SAF resources just as you would any other JMS configuration resources, such as a connection factory, by using either a system or an application module. The configuration is stored outside the domain in module descriptor files. The following are the key SAF resources that you must configure in order to use SAF services:

- **Imported SAF destinations** SAF agents use local representations of remote destinations such as a queue or topic. These local representations of the remote destinations use an identical JNDI name as the remote destination. All JMS destinations on the remote server are automatically imported, and the set of imported destinations are called *SAF-imported destinations.* When JMS producers send messages to SAF destinations, the SAF agent stores the messages on the imported SAF destination for forwarding them to the remote side.

- **Remote SAF context** This represents the URL of the remote server from which the JMS destinations are imported. A remote SAF context can also define a remote cluster from where the local server will import destinations.
- **SAF error handling** These are optional configuration options that determine how the SAF service handles a failure in forwarding messages to the remote destination. The error handling policy can be configured to discard expired messages both with and without logging information about the messages or move them (using the Redirect option) to an "error destination" you can define for the imported SAF destinations. You can also specify the Always-Forward option to forward messages even after they expire.

NOTE
Because SAF stores nonpersistent messages in memory and not in the persistent store, a server crash can mean the loss of all those messages.

Creating JMS SAF Resources

You can create SAF resources to forward JMS messages to remote destinations through WLST or the Administration Console. Creating and configuring JMS resources involves several steps, which are summarized here. You can find the detailed steps in the Administration Console Help documentation.

1. Create a SAF sending agent on the local sending domain.
2. Create JMS system modules on both the sending and receiving servers to store the JMS destinations.
3. Configure a remote SAF context in the sending-side JMS module so the local JMS agents can import the remote queue or topic.
4. Optionally, configure SAF error handling on the sending side to handle SAF service failures.
5. Configure a SAF-imported destination in the sending-side JMS module. Following this, you must associate this destination with the remote SAF context and the SAF error-handling resources that you've created in the previous two steps in the new JMS system module.
6. You must now create a SAF queue and a SAF topic in the SAF-imported destination to represent the remote queues and topic.

The SAF service always uses the exactly once quality-of-service (QOS) level to forward persistent messages. For nonpersistent messages, you can, in addition to the exactly once mode, configure the at-least-once or the at-most-once mode to specify how many times a message is forwarded by SAF to the remote destinations.

SAF is a pinned JMS service, meaning that it's hosted on a single physical server in a cluster. You can configure automatic or manual migration of SAF agents to a different server in a cluster when the server hosting the SAF service fails. You can set up automatic service-level migration to a *migratable target*, which is a group of JMS services such as JMS servers, persistent stores, and SAF agents. You can use WebLogic Server's Health Monitoring system to decide when to migrate a set of JMS services automatically to a healthy server. You can also manually migrate all pinned services hosted by a migratable target.

WebLogic Messaging Bridge

You can configure a WebLogic messaging bridge to integrate your messaging applications. A messaging bridge lets multiple JMS implementations work together, including messaging products other than WebLogic JMS. The main purpose in creating a messaging bridge is to provide high availability for remote messaging destinations. You can configure a messaging bridge between two WebLogic JMS services from different domains or between the WebLogic JMS implementation and a third-party JMS product such as Oracle JMS or IBM's MQSeries, for example. Oracle JMS is actually JMS queues in the Oracle Database, with Oracle Advanced Queuing (AQ) as its underlying technology.

The WebLogic Server messaging bridge uses a Java EE Connector Architecture (JCA) resource adapter to communicate with source and target destinations. The messaging bridge instance forwards messages between the two destinations. Let's briefly review the components of a WebLogic messaging bridge:

- **Resource adapters** The JCA resource adapters must be present on both the source and target servers, and you configure the adapter JNDI names in the deployment descriptor for a resource adapter (*.rar* file). You must link the source and target JMS destinations with the resource adapter on their server in order for the messaging bridge to communicate with them. You can find the Oracle-provided resource adapters in the WL_HOME\server\lib directory, in a zipped format.
- **Source and target bridge destinations** You must configure a source and target JMS bridge destination instance for each destination you wish to map to a messaging bridge. The messaging bridge connects the two destinations. The bridge destination instance defines the name of the adapter to use in communicating with that destination, as well as properties such as the connection URL and the connection factory JNDI name that it must pass to the resource adapter.
- **Messaging bridge instance** You must configure a separate messaging bridge instance for each mapping you create between a pair of source and target destinations. The messaging bridge instance defines the message filtering selector as well as the quality of service parameters.

You can create a WebLogic messaging bridge through the Administration Console by following this general procedure:

1. Create the source and target bridge destinations.
2. Deploy the resource adapter. (The Console can deploy the appropriate adapter.)
3. Create a messaging bridge instance.
4. Target the messaging bridge.

You can monitor messaging bridges, configure their default execution thread pool size, and suspend and restart them from the Administration Console.

Foreign JMS Servers

A WebLogic messaging bridge links a local destination with a remote destination and forwards messages sent to the local destination to the target destination. Using the WebLogic messaging bridge, however, isn't the only way to connect WebLogic JMS with other JMS providers. You can also set up a foreign JMS server instead of the messaging bridge and make foreign connection factories and destinations directly available to JMS clients. You can make your applications direct clients to a remote JMS server by mapping the connection factories and destinations on the remote JMS server to your local JNDI tree. WebLogic server takes care of the remote JMS connection factory and destination lookups when an application looks up the foreign JMS object in the local JNDI tree. WebLogic Server can use this concept of a foreign JMS server to look up objects owned by a remote third-party JMS provider or another WebLogic JMS server in a different domain.

Foreign JMS providers are outside the WebLogic JMS server, and you can create and configure them in a system module. The foreign server has the necessary information that lets the local WebLogic server instance reach the remote JMS providers. Using foreign JMS providers enables you to create multiple WebLogic messaging bridge destinations since connection configuration details aren't necessary. You just provide the foreign connection factory and destination JNDI names for the objects. Both the foreign connection factory and a foreign destination queue or topic in a JMS module contain the destination JNDI name of the connection factory or destination located in the remote JMS provider. The module also contains the JNDI name that the foreign connection factory and destination are mapped to on the local JNDI tree. Thus, lookups for a foreign destination object on the local server will result in a lookup on the remote JNDI tree in order to return the object from the remote server.

Configuring WebLogic JavaMail

JavaMail APIs provide applications and modules with access to the Internet Message Access Protocol (IMAP) and Simple Mail Transfer Protocol (SMTP) mail servers on the Internet or within your own network. JavaMail APIs offer developers a generic interface for mail network servers, irrespective of the specific mail protocol used by the servers. JavaMail is implemented in the *javax .mail*, *javax.mail.internet*, and *javax.activation* packages. Following are the three most commonly used mail transport protocols:

- **Simple Mail Transfer Protocol (SMTP)** Mail clients use this protocol to send messages to a mail server. Mail servers also use this protocol to send messages among themselves.
- **Post Office Protocol (POP)** Mail clients use this protocol to retrieve incoming messages from mail servers.
- **Internet Message Access Protocol (IMAP)** This protocol is similar to the POP protocol, and mail clients use this protocol to retrieve messages from mail servers. The protocol also allows for clients to review, manage, and delete messages before downloading them.

JavaMail requires access to a mail server. You configure JavaMail by configuring a mail session. Mail sessions in WebLogic Server enable the use of the JavaMail APIs. You can configure mail sessions for a domain through the Administration Console, as explained in the next section.

Creating Mail Sessions

To enable developers to code the sending and receiving of messages, the WebLogic Server administrator must first configure WebLogic JavaMail. You do this by creating and configuring mail sessions. *Mail sessions* contain global mail-related properties that control the mail accounts and network behavior. You can, for example, configure the transport protocols of the mail session and the particular POP server that it must use. Developers can programmatically override the configuration you set up for a mail session. A mail session enables applications to access a preconfigured *javax.mail.Session* object through JNDI. You can create multiple mail sessions to enable different types of applications to connect to multiple mail servers.

Here's how to create a mail session through the Administration Console:

1. Click Lock & Edit in the Change Center of the Administration Console.
2. Go to Services in the left-hand pane and click Mail Sessions.
3. Click New on the Summary Of Mail Sessions page.
4. On the Mail Session Properties page, you must enter a JNDI name for the mail session, such as *MyMailSession*, as well as define the mail properties in the JavaMail Properties box, as described in the next section. Click Next.
5. On the Mail Session Targets page, specify the server instance or the cluster to which you want to attach this mail session. WebLogic Server makes available the mail sessions you create in its JNDI tree. Once it's there, a client session can use the mail session in order to interact with the JavaMail API. Client sessions look up the mail session in the JNDI tree, access the mail session, and use it according to the JavaMail API. Click Finish.
6. Save the changes by clicking the Activate Changes button in the Change Center of the Console.
7. You'll see the new mail session in the Summary Of Mail Sessions page. The next section shows you how to configure a mail session.

Configuring a Mail Session

There are only a couple of things that you need in order to configure a mail session. Click the mail server name you want to configure on the Summary Of Mail Sessions page. You can configure the mail settings in the Settings For *<MailServer_Name>* page (Settings For MailSession-0 in our example), shown in Figure 4-14.

You must first configure a name to identify a mail session. The applications actually use the JNDI name, which you must provide in the JNDI Name box. Most important are the properties you must specify in the JavaMail Properties box. WebLogic Server uses these properties when it returns an instance of this mail server. The mail session uses the configuration options and user credentials you provide here to talk to a mail server. If you don't specify any values here, WebLogic Server uses the default values defined by the JavaMail API Design Specification. You must specify each mail property as a *name=value* pair, as shown here, and separate multiple properties on the same line with a semicolon (;).

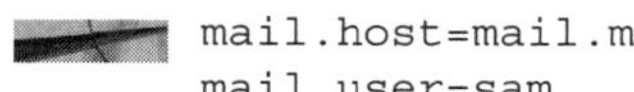

```
mail.host=mail.mycompany.com
mail.user=sam
```

Here are the key JavaMail configuration properties that you can specify:

- ***mail.store.protocol*** Defines the protocol to be used for retrieving mail. The default is IMAP.
- ***mail.transport.protocol*** Specifies the protocol to be used for sending mail. The default is SMTP.
- ***mail.host*** Defines the address of the mail server. The default is localhost.
- ***mail.user*** Defines the mail host for a specific protocol. This is the value of the username Java property.

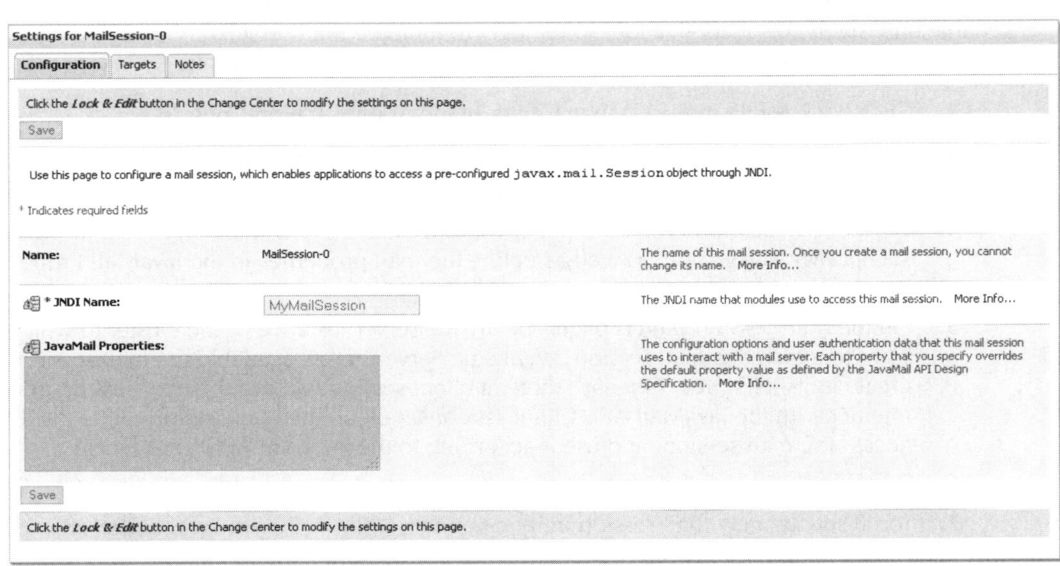

FIGURE 4-14. *The Settings For MailSession-0 Configuration page in the Administration Console*

- ***mail.from*** Specifies the return address of the e-mail. This attribute is required.
- ***mail.debug*** Enables the outputting of debug information to the console. (Set the value to *true* if you want the debug information to be output to the console.) The default value is *false*.

Summary

This chapter provided you an introduction to the key WebLogic Server services—JTA, JDBC, and JMS. You also learned about configuring the JNDI naming services. All these services are going to be highly critical for the performance of your deployed applications. WebLogic Server performance tuning, in fact, involves a great deal of time spent tuning services such as JDBC and JMS, as I explain in Chapter 10.

CHAPTER 5

Configuring the WebLogic Server Environment

This chapter starts off with a description of how WebLogic Server manages its run-time performance. The concept of server thread pools is fundamental to understanding how the server manages requests. Understanding how the server manages overload and how it performs a self-health check is crucial to managing production servers. You'll learn the role Work Managers play in scheduling requests and how to configure them. WebLogic Server lets you create custom network channels for managing complex application needs. This chapter shows you how to create and configure custom channels, as well as how to design them.

WebLogic Server uses Java EE Connector Architecture (JCA) to provide connectivity between enterprise applications and enterprise information systems (EISs). This chapter introduces the WebLogic JCA architecture that uses resource adapters to provide two-way connectivity between web applications and EISs and shows how an administrator can configure resource adapters. While the discussion of JCA in this chapter may seem somewhat unconnected with the rest of the topics, there are several good corollaries in the configuration of JCA and Work Managers. Although these two topics are by no means directly related, this is why JCA is included in this chapter.

Optimizing Application Performance

Understanding how WebLogic Server handles requests by assigning them execute threads is critical to learning how to manage server workloads. In the following sections, let's investigate WebLogic Server thread pools and how the server uses the concept of Work Managers to provide you with a way to control thread utilization. Understanding how the server handles "stuck threads" is also crucial to helping prevent degradation in server performance, and this section discusses stuck thread behavior. You can also configure the server's self-health check mechanism to control how the server handles an overload situation in a production environment.

WebLogic Server Thread Pools

When a client connects to a WebLogic Server instance, the server (actually the socket muxer) places the request in the execute queue, along with the request's security and transaction details. Once a request joins the execute queue, an idle thread will execute the request and return the response to the client. If part of an application, such as an EJB component, blocks an execute thread for a long time, the server has no mechanism to kill that execute thread. If the application blocks many execute threads for any reason, the entire server execute queue slows down and will be unable to accept and process new client requests. The server simply runs out of free execute threads to assign to new requests.

The dedicated socket reader threads will read enough of the message to determine which application component should handle the message. The socket reader thread then schedules that work to a Work Manager. The Work Manager uses a shared internal thread pool manager either to directly execute that work or to queue it up for later processing.

In earlier releases (Release 8.1 and earlier), WebLogic Server used the concept of either a default or user-created execute queue and a thread pool with a fixed number of threads. You could create multiple execute queues, and the server assigned work to different queues based on priority and ordering requirements. Each execute queue had a queue manager, which handed an available thread from its thread pool to a request in the queue using a first-in, first-out criterion. As a system administrator, you controlled how the server used threads by setting the number of threads in WebLogic Server's default queues. You could also create your own queues to ensure applications had enough execute threads. The execute threads from the older releases are often referred to as "8.1-style execute threads." In most cases, the threads were assigned to the queue based on the "dispatch policy" that was defined in the WebLogic Servers–pecific application descriptor and not so much based on priority.

Starting with WebLogic Server 9.0 and continuing with WebLogic Server 12*c*, you can configure Work Managers to manage the application workload. The server uses just a single self-tuning execute queue, which assigns threads to new requests based on either explicit or implicit work priorities. The queue is self-tuning because it changes its size (in number of threads) automatically based on workload to maximize the server throughput. The server tunes the number of threads up or down, based on changing workloads, with the goal of maximizing the throughput. The server assigns a priority to each new request that it adds to the execute queue, based on one of two things: the current server performance and throughput or the parameters you explicitly define with a Work Manager. Setting a priority for a request means that the server doesn't execute requests according to the traditional first-in, first-out fashion. Rather, the server places a request with a higher priority at the head of the request queue, thus making sure it assigns that request a thread ahead of requests with a lower priority.

Since the 9.*x* release, the goal has been to eliminate, or at least minimize, the need for special thread pool tuning. The introduction of a self-tuning Work Manager in the 9.*x* release has greatly simplified the process of managing thread pools. Since then, there has been a single dynamically sized shared pool of threads to which work is distributed to maximize throughput. Tuning is now a matter of providing hints to the server based on higher-level concepts such as "fair share" and specific application targets such as "response time."

NOTE

*Older releases of WebLogic Server let you create thread pools (execute queues) to manage the server workload. WebLogic Server 12*c *supports execute queues, but strictly for compatibility reasons. You should use Work Managers instead of execute queues for more efficient thread management. If you enable execute queues, you lose the functionality of thread self-tuning and all Work Managers are disabled.*

The server changes the size of the thread pool continuously based on its monitoring of current throughput. This means administrators don't need to configure and tune custom execute queues any longer.

Work Managers

Work Managers control the number of threads in the execute queue and the priorities that the server must assign to new and pending requests. Each Work Manager controls the scheduling of requests by the WebLogic Server, by letting you specify a set of request classes and thread constraints. You can specify named Work Managers for applications, web application modules, EJBs, and RMI applications to control how the server manages their work requests. You can create global Work Managers at the domain level, as well as application- or module-level Work Managers.

You may configure Work Managers to assign similar priorities for sets of requests that share common performance and availability requirements. Work Managers let you specify the maximum number of requests from a particular request class that will be allowed to enter the execute queue. If you set the number of maximum requests at the Work Manager level, the server honors either the maximum number of requests you set there or the server's global thread pool value, whichever is lower.

As a server's workload increases, for example, the Work Managers demand more threads to be made available to the execute queue. Work Managers are essentially a set of guidelines to the server as to how it should prioritize work. How many Work Managers should you define? The answer depends on the nature of applications that you host. If you have multiple applications running on the server and each of them has a different workload profile, you may need to configure multiple Work Managers. On the other hand, if all the applications share a similar work profile, you may need just a single Work Manager.

WebLogic Server has a default Work Manager, and all applications for which you don't specify a Work Manager (in the deployment descriptor) will use the default Work Manager. The default Work Manager uses a default fair share of 50; that is, it assigns equal priority for all requests. You can re-create the default Work Manager by configuring a global Work Manager and naming it **default**. Create custom Work Managers if you want to assign a higher priority to one application over others and if you want to implement a response time goal.

NOTE
All applications and modules use the default Work Manager if you don't assign them a custom Work Manager.

Configuring Work Managers

You can configure Work Managers at the domain or the application level either by modifying the appropriate configuration files or through the Administration Console. Here's a summary of the various levels and the relevant configuration file that you need to modify:

- Web application level: *weblogic.xml*
- Module level: *weblogic-ejb.xml* or *weblogic.xml*
- Application level: *weblogic-application.xml*
- Domain level: *config.xml*

A domain-level Work Manager is also called a *global* Work Manager, and you can create it with the Administration Console. A global Work Manager applies to all modules and applications in a domain, so you must be careful before creating one of these Work Managers. Note that each application or module implements a separate Work Manager instance to avoid any adverse impact on the thread management of various applications.

As the following section explains, a Work Manager contains components called request classes and constraints. You can choose to specify one or more components of a Work Manager, such as request class or a constraint, directly in the application's deployment descriptor. Alternatively, you can first define a Work Manager with a specific set of request classes and constraints and then reference the Work Manager in the application's deployment descriptor. In either case, you map a Work Manager, request class, or constraint in the deployment descriptor to a module or an application. Here's an example showing how to define a Work Manager:

```
<work-manager>
  <name>highpriority_workmanager</name>
  <fair-share-request-class>
    <name>high_priority</name>
    <fair-share>100</fair-share>
```

```
  </fair-share-request-class>
  <min-threads-constraint>
    <name>MinThreadsCountFive</name>
    <count>5</count>
  </min-threads-constraint>
</work-manager>
```

In this example, the element *<work-manager>* specifies the name of the Work Manager and defines its components, which include request classes and constraints. In this example, the Work Manager's name is *highpriority_workmanager*. This Work Manager has two components: a request class named *fair-share-request-class* and a constraint named *min-threads-constraint*. Together, these two Work Manager components specify how the server should assign a priority to requests from any application that references this Work Manager in its deployment descriptor.

Let us consider what this case of setting the priority to 100 would mean in the real world. Let's say you have two applications deployed on a server where one of the applications is using the default Work Manager (application A), with a priority of 50, and the other is configured to use the "high-priority Work Manager" (application B), with a priority of 100. In this case, we are expecting that 2/3 (100/150) of the requests will be for application B and 1/3 (50/100) for application A. By telling the system this, we are giving it the opportunity to schedule requests for application B at a higher priority. This will help keep it from getting behind in processing and potentially experiencing greater latency. The decision to make such a change would likely be based on the observation that the response time for application B is suffering (or would suffer) due to the simultaneous processing of application A's requests.

Following is an example that shows how an application component such as a servlet or a JSP references the *highpriority_workmanager* by specifying the Work Manager's name within the initialization parameter in the web application's deployment descriptor, the *web.xml* file:

```
<init-param>
  <param-name>wl-dispatch-policy</param-name>
  <param-value>highpriority_workmanager</param-value>
</init-param>
```

In this example, a web application component, say a servlet, specifies that it will use the Work Manager named *highpriority_workmanager*. To specify a Work Manager for the entire application, you must specify the name of the Work Manager in the deployment descriptor for the application, which is the *weblogic.xml* file. Following is a summary of how a Work Manager becomes applicable to an application or a component based on which deployment descriptor or domain file you use to define the Work Managers:

- ***config.xml*** Because this is a domain-wide file, you can assign the Work Manager to any application or component.
- ***weblogic-application-xml*** You can define application-level Work Managers, as well as assign the Work Manager to a component of an application.
- ***weblogic-ejb-jar.xml*** or ***weblogic.xml*** You can use this deployment descriptor for component-level Work Manager assignment.
- ***weblogic.xml*** You can specify application-level Work Manager assignment within this deployment descriptor.

You can specify the Work Managers directly in any of these files, but it's easier to do so through the Administration Console. Note that multiple applications can share the same global

Work Manager, but the total number of requests among the applications can't exceed the constraints you specify for the Work Manager at the server level.

In addition to request classes and constraints, you can also define a stuck thread component to specify how the Work Manager handles a stuck thread situation. Stuck threads are discussed later in this chapter, in the section "Dealing with Stuck Threads."

Work Manager Components

You can use two basic components—request classes and constraints—to define and use in a Work Manager. The following sections explain the two components.

Request Classes

A *request class* helps to determine the priority the server should assign to a specific request. You use request classes to specify a higher priority to important components of the application's workload. You assign the same request class to similar applications that have the same performance and availability requirements. A request class isn't something that categorizes requests into rigid priority classes, however. A request class is merely a guideline that the server will try to use in determining how it assigns priorities to various requests, but there's no guarantee that the server will, in every single instance, follow the guidelines you specify. A Work Manager can specify one or more request classes, each defining a guideline to the server in assigning priorities for executing requests. You can think of this as giving the algorithm more information about the needs of your application so that it can make better decisions.

There are three basic types of request classes: the *fair-share-request-class,* the *response-time-request-class,* and the *context-request-class*. Note that the request classes and the values you specify for them really come into play only if the number of requests exceeds the number of available threads. If the number of available threads is enough to handle all requests, there's no need to prioritize work—the server can handle the workload simultaneously, without having to keep any requests waiting. The request classes are discussed here:

- ***fair-share-request-class*** This request class is based on thread usage and specifies how the server assigns thread-usage time among modules. The default value for this request class is 50, which means that if there are two modules that are competing for threads, the server allocates 50 percent of the thread-usage time to each of the modules. The server uses the values you set for the *fair-share-request-class* to determine how it allocates server time to a request from a class. It is important to understand that the fair-share values are relative; that is, they determine how the server allocates time to one class compared to other classes. Let's say you configure two request classes, *MyRequestClass1* and *MyRequestClass2,* and assign a fair share value of 20 to the first and 40 to the latter class. In this case, the server will assign a thread to *MyRequestClass1* 33 percent of the time (20/60). Similarly, the *MyRequestClass2* request class will have a 66 percent (40 out of 60) chance of service.

  Here's an example that shows how to specify the *fair-share-request-class* in a Work Manager:

  ```
  <work-manager>
    <name>highpriority_workmanager</name>
    <fair-share-request-class>
      <name>high_priority</name>
      <fair-share>100</fair-share>
    </fair-share-request-class>
    <min-threads-constraint>
      <name>MinThreadsCountFive</name>
  ```

```
    <count>5</count>
  </min-threads-constraint>
</work-manager>
```

- ***response-time-request-class*** This request classes uses response time (in milliseconds) as the criterion on which the server assigns available threads to requests. The server schedules requests such that the average waits for requests within a certain request class are proportional to the request class's response-time goal. The server will always try to keep the average response times for each request class in the same ratio as their response-time goals. For example, you can create two request classes with a response-time goal of 2000 ms and 4000 ms and assign the first request class to module A and the second to module B. The server will then schedule requests to these two modules such that their average response time is always in the ratio of 1:2 (2000 ms to 4000 ms).

  Here's an example that shows how to define a Work Manager that uses a request class based on response time:

```
<work-manager>
  <name>responsetime_workmanager</name>
  <response-time-request-class>
    <name>my_response_time</name>
    <goal-ms>2000</goal-ms>
  </response-time-request-class>
</work-manager>
```

  You want to use this request class, for example, when you are perhaps executing both synchronous work (such as web applications) and asynchronous work (such as JMS). By setting a response-time goal for the web application work, you are providing a hint that the one type of work is latency sensitive and the server should schedule it at a higher priority. Doing this allows a JMS queue to back up temporarily and then be cleared out once the number of web requests decreases. Web users would continue to get good response times during this period because they would get a higher scheduling priority.

- ***context-request-class*** This is a hybrid class that maps a request's context to either the response time– or the fair share–based request class. That is, the server assigns a request class to a request simply based on the request's properties, such as the user or group names.

  Here's an example that shows how to define a context-based request class. Note that the *<context-case>* element specifies the type of context, in this case the client's username. The context request class named *test_context* specifies that the server assign all requests executed by the user system the *high_fairshare* request class. It also specifies that the users belonging to the group *everyone* be assigned the *low_fairshare* request class.

```
<work-manager>
  <name>context_workmanager</name>
  <context-request-class>
    <name>test_context</name>
    <context-case>
      <user-name>system</user-name>
      <request-class-name>high_fairshare</request-class-name>
    </context-case>
    <context-case>
      <group-name>everyone</group-name>
```

```
      <request-class-name>low_fairshare</request-class-name>
    </context-case>
  </context-request-class>
</work-manager>
```

Constraints

Constraints are numerical restrictions on threads. For example, you can specify the maximum number of concurrent threads that can execute requests from a specific application component. Here are the various types of constraints you can specify:

- ***max-threads-constraint*** Specifies the maximum number of concurrent threads that the server can allocate for requests from a specific work set. Once a request type reaches the maximum number for threads, the server won't schedule any more requests from that request type. The server will then use the default or user-specified fair-response time, or it will use a response-time goal to assign threads to this request type.

  Here's how to specify the maximum-threads constraint in a deployment descriptor:

```
<work-manager>
  <name>slow_response_time</name>
  <max-threads-constraint-name>j2ee_maxthreads</max-threads-constraint-name>
  <response-time-request-class>
    <name>slow_response_time</name>
    <goal-ms>5000</goal-ms>
  </response-time-request-class>
</work-manager>
```

  In this example, the *<goal-ms>* element specifies the maximum number of threads to allocate to a web application. Note that you could also specify the name of a data source instead of the number of concurrent threads. You can set either value to ensure that requests that query database connections don't wait for a connection. If you specify a data source instead of the number of maximum threads, the maximum thread value can change based on changes to the database's connection pool.

TIP

A constraint is a type of hint to the server. This type of hint should be used very sparingly. A constraint that uses the connection pool is the one that is the most important and the one you are most likely to use. The other possibility is when you have a nonstandard application that is connecting to a resource that you know has some known limitation that cannot be otherwise represented (such as opening a direct connection to a socket with a nonstandard protocol).

- ***min-threads-constraint*** Specifies the minimum number of threads the server will assign to a request. The default is zero. The minimum value you set here determines the minimum number of threads the server will allocate to resolve deadlocks during server-to-server callbacks. Here's an example that shows how to specify the minimum threads constraint:

```
<work-manager>
  <name>minthreads_workmanager</name>
  <min-threads-constraint>
```

```
      <name>MinThreadsCountFive</name>
      <count>5</count>
    </min-threads-constraint>
  </work-manager>
```

You normally don't need to specify a value for the *min-threads-constraint* unless you notice server deadlocks due to server-to-server callbacks.

- ***capacity*** Sets the limit for all types of requests from a specific work set. The server rejects all new requests once it reaches the capacity threshold (or when the server reaches its global capacity threshold that you set by limiting the maximum queue length, as explained later in this chapter). Note that the capacity constraint takes into account both queued and running requests. The default value for the capacity constraint is –1, which means that WebLogic Server automatically determines the limit for queues or running requests from an application.

Once the server hits the capacity limit, it returns an HTTP 503 error ("Service Unavailable" due to the server being overloaded) to requests or returns exceptions to RMI calls to enable those requests to failover to a different cluster member.

Defining a Work Manager Through the Console

Earlier, you saw how to define Work Managers, request classes, and constraints in various deployment descriptors. You can configure Work Managers just as you would configure any environmental objects such as servers, clusters, virtual hosts, and machines. You can define Work Managers, request classes, and constraints at a global level through the Administration Console. Here are the steps:

1. Click Lock & Control in the Change Center of the Administration Console.
2. In the left-hand pane, expand Environment and click Work Managers.

   You'll see the Summary Of Work Managers page, as shown in Figure 5-1. This page shows all global Work Managers, request classes, and thread constraints that are defined for this domain. Click New.
3. On the Create A New Work Manager Component page, shown in Figure 5-2, you can choose to create a new Work Manager, request class, or thread constraint. In this example, let's create a new request class first. Select Fair Share Request Class and click Next.

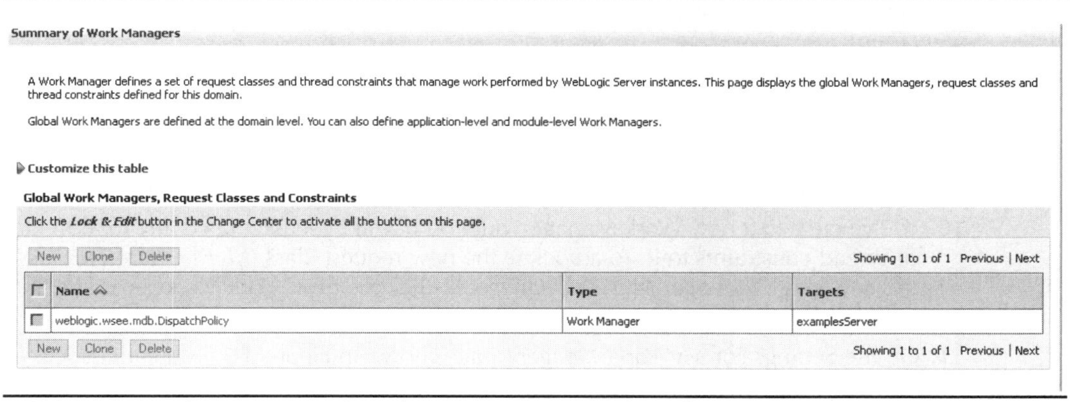

Summary of Work Managers

A Work Manager defines a set of request classes and thread constraints that manage work performed by WebLogic Server instances. This page displays the global Work Managers, request classes and thread constraints defined for this domain.

Global Work Managers are defined at the domain level. You can also define application-level and module-level Work Managers.

Customize this table

Global Work Managers, Request Classes and Constraints

Click the ***Lock & Edit*** button in the Change Center to activate all the buttons on this page.

New Clone Delete Showing 1 to 1 of 1 Previous | Next

	Name	Type	Targets
	weblogic.wsee.mdb.DispatchPolicy	Work Manager	examplesServer

New Clone Delete Showing 1 to 1 of 1 Previous | Next

FIGURE 5-1. *The Summary of Work Managers page in the Administration Console*

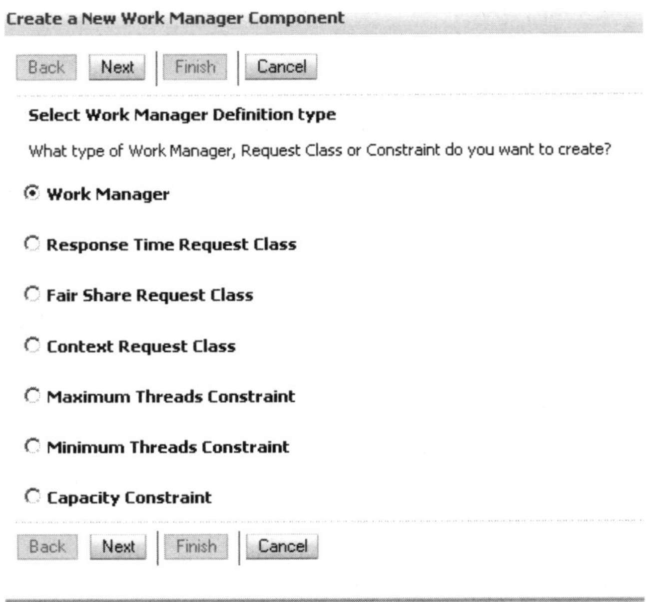

FIGURE 5-2. *Creating a new Work Manager component*

4. On the Fair Share Request Class page, specify a name for this request class. In my example, it's *MyFairShareReqClass1*. More importantly, select a value for Fair Share. The default is 50, which means that the server will treat all requests equally. Choose a value such as 75 for this example. Click Next.
5. On the Select Deployment Targets page, select the WebLogic Server instance to which you want to target this new request class. Click Finish.
6. Your new request class, *MyFairShareReqClass1,* appears in the Summary Of Work Managers page now. To associate this request class to a new Work Manager, click New again on the Summary Of Work Managers page.
7. On the Select Work Manager Definition Type page, select Work Manager as the new component you want to create. Click Next.
8. Type **MyWorkManager1** as the name for the new Work Manager on the Work Manager Properties page and click Next.
9. On the Select Deployment Targets page, select the server instance and click Finish.
10. You've created a new Work Manager, but you haven't yet associated any request classes or thread constraints to it. To associate the new request class (*MyFairShareReqClass1*) to the new Work Manager *MyWorkManager1,* click the new Work Manager in the Summary Of Work Managers page.
11. On the Settings For *MyWorkManager1* page shown in Figure 5-3, you can associate request classes and thread constraints with a Work Manager. Because you want to

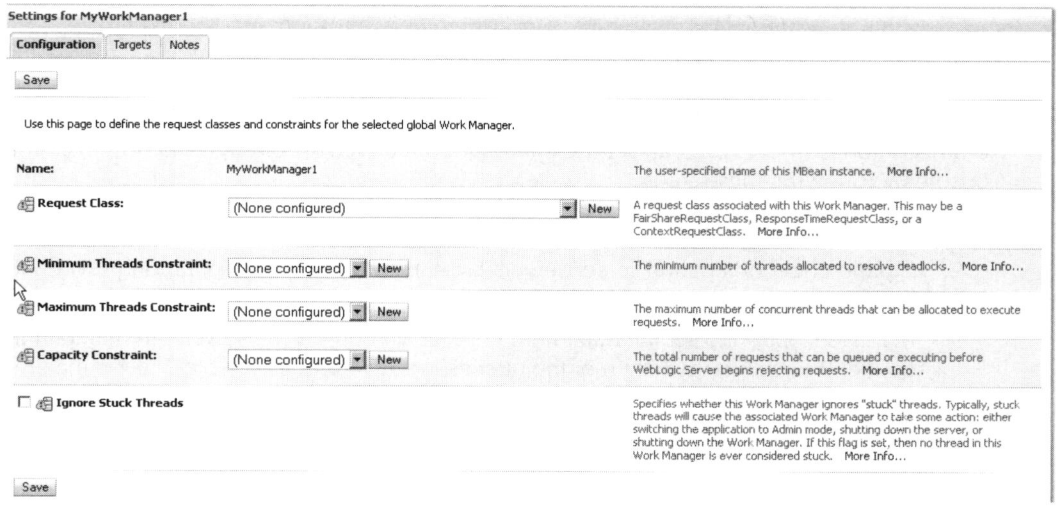

FIGURE 5-3. *The Settings for a Work Manager page*

associate a request class in this example, select the request class *MyFairShareReqClass1* in the Request Class box. Click Save. Don't forget to activate your configuration changes in the Change Center.

This section showed how to create an "empty" Work Manager and then associate a request class with it. You could, of course, associate the Work Manager with a thread constraint as well if you want. However, you can also choose to create a Work Manager and directly associate a request class or thread constraint with it. To do this, select a new, "empty" global Work Manager on the Summary Of Work Managers page. The resulting Configuration tab allows you to configure the request class and the three thread constraints—minimum, maximum, and capacity. Note that, initially, all of the request classes and constraints show the value "(None configured)" against their names because you're dealing with a brand new Work Manager.

Managing Server Work Overload

When a long-running request or faulty application logic blocks execute threads for long periods, new requests could queue up in the server's single self-tuning execute queue. Even if the server starts catching up with the queued requests, you could see degradation in performance and you'll notice a slowdown in the response times of applications. When a WebLogic Server instance is overloaded, as happens when the server reaches its capacity, applications won't perform properly. Under extreme circumstances, the server might even seem totally unresponsive because of the high number of blocked execute threads. WebLogic Server administrators can configure various things to minimize the adverse impacts of heavy workloads. The following sections briefly explain the most important things you need to do to handle an "unhealthy" server state.

Throttling the Thread Pool

Since the server utilizes only a single thread pool, you can throttle this pool by setting a maximum length for the request queue length. Once the server exceeds the maximum queue length, it will reject all new web application requests. You throttle the thread pool (set a maximum limit) by setting the Shared Capacity For Work Managers attribute in the Administration Console. You can set the maximum queue length through the Administration Console by following these steps:

1. Click the Lock & Edit button in the Change Center of the Administration Console.
2. Expand Environment and select Servers | *<server_name>* | Configuration | Overload.
3. On the Overload configuration page, set a value for the Shared Capacity For Work Managers option to set the maximum number of requests the server can maintain in the queue. By default, the length of the queues is 65536 requests. Note that the maximum capacity you set here includes the maximum number of requests, which includes both the currently executing requests as well as those waiting in the queue. Once the server reaches the request limit you set here, it issues a response such as HTTP 503 to indicate that the server is too busy to handle new requests.

TIP
The maximum number of requests you set with the Shared Capacity For Work Managers option includes both requests in the queue and those that the server is already executing.

4. Click Save and click the Activate Changes button in the Change Center of the Console.

Once the server reaches the limit of its request capacity, it handles requests with a higher priority differently from requests with a lower priority. The server will give preference to higher-priority requests over lower-priority ones by executing higher-priority requests first, even if the latter have more seniority in the queue. The server also rejects new lower-priority requests and keeps them from entering the queue.

Note that when a server exceeds the maximum queue length, it rejects web application requests, but it won't reject any JMS and transaction-related requests because they're managed by the JMS system and the WebLogic Transaction Manager.

There's a relationship between this global thread value that you can set and the maximum requests for particular request classes that you define through Work Managers. The server will start rejecting requests when it reaches either the global thread limit or the maximum request limit you set through a Work Manager.

Handling Overload or Failure Conditions

In addition to setting the maximum queue length, there are a number of things an administrator can do to handle overload or server failure conditions. WebLogic Server's self-health monitoring mechanism marks a server as failed when it traps a critical failure condition. You can configure various options as to how the server should react to a failed state. You can access the server overload management page in the Administration Console by going to Environment | Servers | *<server_name>* | Overload. Figure 5-4 shows this page. You have already learned how to set the

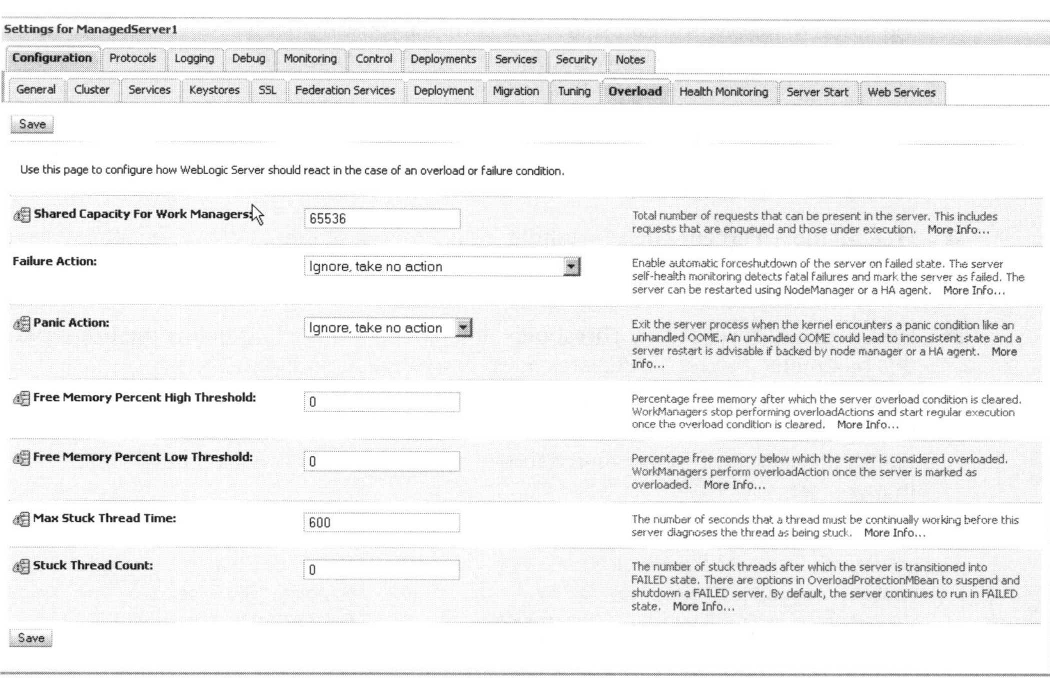

FIGURE 5-4. *Configuring the overload and failure responses of the server*

maximum queue length from this page. Here are the other configuration options you can set on this page to handle overload and server failures:

- **Failure Action** This option lets you specify what actions the server must take when it encounters a failure condition. You have three possible values you can specify for this option:
  - **Ignore, Take No Action** This is exactly what it means—the server ignores the failure condition.
  - **Force Immediate Shutdown Of This Server** The server marks itself as failed when it detects a fatal failure. You can restart the server with the Node Manager.
  - **Suspend This Server For Corrective Action** This option lets you avoid a complete shutdown of the server by merely suspending it. You can correct the situation that led to the server failure condition and resume the server through the *resume* command explained in Chapter 2. One really good reason for doing this is that, in the case of stuck threads, it is often difficult to determine what is going wrong with your application. By causing the server to suspend in this way, it is possible to connect with a tool such as the Administration Console or WLST to get thread dumps or, in extreme cases, even to connect with the debugger to try to diagnose the problem.
- **Panic Action** You can choose between the Ignore, Take No Action and the Exit The Server Process option. When should you choose the Exit The Server Process option? When the server experiences an unhandled out-of-memory exception. For example,

the server state tends to be unstable, and it's a good idea to restart the server through the Node Manager. You can select this choice to ensure that the server quits when it encounters an out-of-memory exception. In the *config.xml* file, you'll see the following elements when you configure this option:

```
<overload-protection>
  <panic-action>system-exit</panic-action>
</overload-protection>
```

- **Free Memory Percent High Threshold** The amount of free memory (in percentage terms) that the server must have before it clears a server overload condition. Normal execution resumes once the server clears an overload condition.
- **Free Memory Percent Low Threshold** If the free memory falls below the threshold set by this parameter, the server declares a server overload condition.
- **Max Stuck Thread Time** Here, you specify how long a thread can work on a particular request before the server classifies it as a stuck thread. The default value is 600 seconds. Here's the server message when a thread bumps against the Max Stuck Thread Time value that you set:

```
<Error> <WebLogicServer> <BEA-000337>
<[STUCK] ExecuteThread: '5' for queue: 'weblogic.kernel.Default
(self-tuning)' has been busy  for "649" seconds working on the request
"weblogic.work.SelfTuningWorkManagerImpl$WorkAdapterImpl@30532a9",
which is more than the configured time StuckThread MaxTime) of
"600" seconds. Stack trace:Thread-61 "[STUCK] ExecuteThread:
'5' for queue: 'weblogic.kernel.Default (self-tuning)'" <alive,
in native, suspended, priority=1,
...
```

- **Stuck Thread Count** Specifies the maximum number of stuck threads after which to mark the server state as FAILED. The default for this property is zero, meaning that a server will continue to run regardless of how many threads are struck. If you specify a value for this property, the server can suspend and shut itself down once it transitions into a FAILED state.

Limiting Active HTTP Sessions

An administrator can limit the number of active HTTP sessions based on the detection of a low memory condition. This is useful in avoiding out-of-memory exceptions. Once the server reaches the maximum number of active HTTP sessions, it won't accept new requests to create an HTTP session. You can configure single server instances to redirect refused requests to other servers. In a cluster, the server redirects those requests to another member of the cluster. You can configure the maximum number of HTTP sessions a Managed Server can handle by specifying the session limit in the deployment descriptor of the application, as shown here:

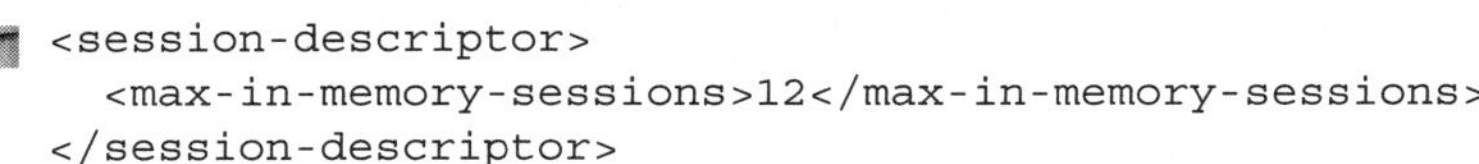

```
<session-descriptor>
  <max-in-memory-sessions>12</max-in-memory-sessions>
</session-descriptor>
```

Dealing with Stuck Threads

WebLogic Server considers a thread to be a "stuck thread" when the thread takes more than a specified amount of time to process a single request. The default threshold for marking a thread as stuck is 10 minutes (600 seconds). When the server encounters a stuck thread situation, it may shut itself down or shut down the Work Manager. It may also switch the application to administrator mode. If you set the *IGNORE_STUCK_THREADS=TRUE* flag, the server won't ever deem a thread as being stuck. Normally, you would not instruct the server to ignore stuck threads unless you know from experience that specific applications hold execute threads for a long duration as part of their normal behavior. To avoid too many stuck thread alarms, you can tell the server to ignore the stuck threads in such a situation.

Note that, in general, the default threshold for marking a thread as stuck (10 minutes) is far too long. If you are experiencing problems with requests that are getting stuck, you will want to reduce this to a much smaller number (on the order of a few seconds). Stuck threads primarily occur in cases such as the following:

- Unresponsive back-end services such as connector resources
- Lockups in the database due to database triggers executed from application logic
- Deadlocks in the application code based on some shared class in the application or a framework library that the application is using

You can specify a shutdown trigger in a Work Manager definition to tell the server that it should shut down the Work Manager once a certain number of threads executing with this Work Manager are in stuck thread status. The following example shows how the Work Manager named *stuckthread_workmanager* uses the maximum stuck thread time you specify within the *<work-manager-shutdown-trigger>* element to shut down the Work Manager when two threads exceed the maximum time specified by the *<max-stuck-thread-time>* attribute:

```
<work-manager>
  <name>stuckthread_workmanager</name>
  <work-manager-shutdown-trigger>
    <max-stuck-thread-time>30</max-stuck-thread-time>
    <stuck-thread-count>2</stuck-thread-count>
  </work-manager-shutdown-trigger>
</work-manager>
```

The previous example specifies that the Work Manager should be shut down if 2 threads are stuck for longer than 30 seconds. You can also specify an admin trigger by including the *<application-admin-mode-trigger>* element in an application's deployment descriptor, the *weblogic-application.xml* file. Instead of shutting down the Work Manager, the admin trigger will place the application in administrative mode once it reaches a certain number of stuck threads.

Note that a single stuck thread could stop an entire application dead in its tracks once the server hits the threshold for declaring that a thread is struck (default value 600 seconds). You can't kill a stuck thread, but you can avoid a potential stuck thread situation by setting the Stuck Thread Max Time parameter. You probably should also take a thread dump when you encounter a stuck thread situation to dig deeper into why the thread was stuck. There are several ways to take a thread dump, including through the Administration Console, and thread dumps are discussed in Chapter 6.

WebLogic Server Self-Health Monitoring

You can use WebLogic Server's self-health monitoring capability to monitor the health status of the server. In addition, subsystems such as JMS and JTA monitor their own health status. Subsystems such as JTA and RMI specify whether the server should deem those subsystems critical for the operation of the server when those subsystems register with the server instance at startup time. The server bases its own determination of server health based on the health of the subsystems. The server continuously monitors each of the critical subsystems, and when any of these fail, the server puts itself in the FAILED health state. You can access the WebLogic self-health monitoring page in the Administration Console by going to Environment | Servers | *<server_name>* | Configuration | Health Monitoring. Figure 5-5 shows the server's Health Monitoring page. The following list briefly describes the various self-health monitoring options you can configure, such as how frequently the server runs an automatic health check and whether the Node Manager should automatically restart a server that reaches a failed health state.

- **Health Check Interval** Sets the frequency (in seconds) with which the server polls each of the critical subsystems to check their health. By default, the server checks the status of all critical subsystems every 3 minutes (180 seconds). If it finds that any of the critical subsystems have a FAILED state during the health check, the server's state goes into the FAILED category as well.
- **Auto Kill If Failed** Specifies whether the Node Manager should automatically kill a Managed Server whose health state goes into the FAILED category.
- **Auto Restart** Determines whether you want the Node Manager to automatically restart a server following a crash.

Settings for ManagedServer1

Configuration | Protocols | Logging | Debug | Monitoring | Control | Deployments | Services | Security | Notes

General | Cluster | Services | Keystores | SSL | Federation Services | Deployment | Migration | Tuning | Overload | Health Monitoring | Server Start | Web Services

Save

WebLogic Server provides a self-health monitoring capability to improve the reliability and availability of servers in a WebLogic Server domain. Selected subsystems within each server monitor their health status based on criteria specific to the subsystem.

Use this page to configure the frequency of this server's automated health checks and the frequency with which the Node Manager application (optional) checks the server's health state. You can also use this page to specify whether Node Manager automatically stops and restarts the server if the server reaches the "failed" health state.

Health Check Interval:	180	The number of seconds that defines the frequency of this server's self-health monitoring. The server monitors the health of it's subsystems every Health Check Interval and changes the Server's overall state if required. More Info...
☐ Auto Kill If Failed		Specifies whether the Node Manager should automatically kill this server if its health state is failed. More Info...
☑ Auto Restart		Specifies whether the Node Manager can automatically restart this server if it crashes or otherwise goes down unexpectedly. More Info...
Restart Interval:	3600	The number of seconds during which this server can be restarted, up to the number of times specified in Max Restarts Within Interval. More Info...
Max Restarts Within Interval:	2	The number of times that the Node Manager can restart this server within the interval specified in Restart Interval. More Info...
Restart Delay Seconds:	0	The number of seconds the Node Manager should wait before restarting this server. More Info...

Save

FIGURE 5-5. *Configuring a server's self-health monitoring*

- **Restart Interval** Specifies the maximum time interval (in seconds) within which the Node Manager can restart a Managed Server.
- **Max Restarts Within Interval** Specifies how many times the Node Manager can restart a Managed Server (within the time interval you specified for the Restart Interval property).
- **Restart Delay Seconds** Sets the number of seconds the Node Manager must wait before restarting a server. The delay ensures that the system has released the ports the server was using when the Node Manager killed the server instance.

Optimal Network Configuration

A network channel defines the attributes of network connections to the WebLogic Server. Each network channel is a unique combination of a port, a listen address, and a connection protocol (for example, t3 or HTTPS). Each WebLogic Server instance has its own network channels for clients to use to communicate with the server. Earlier chapters described how to configure basic WebLogic Server network channels. All you've had to do to set up a basic network channel is to specify a listen address and listen port for it. WebLogic Server comes with two standard network channels for each Managed Server in a domain: a preconfigured default channel and an administration channel, provided you configure a domain-wide administration port. You'll also remember that the network channel and the corresponding network traffic generated are only for administrative requests, and you should configure SSL for this channel. Although the use of an administration channel is purely optional, if you do enable the connection you must use it for all administrative traffic—you won't be able to use the default network channel for administrative traffic once you configure the administration channel.

The default network, consisting of a single port number (another one for secure communications) and a single listen address, works fine for development and test environments. It's also the best way to go if you use just a single network interface card (NIC), and the default port numbers are enough for segmenting network traffic. You can use different network protocols, such as HTTPS and t3s, with the same listen port and listen address combination. In addition to the port address, listen address, and connection protocol attributes, you can define the connection protocols, various connection properties such as the maximum message size, options such as tunneling, and whether the channel can communicate with other server instances in the WebLogic domain. Although you can assign a channel to only a single WebLogic Managed Server instance, you can configure multiple network channels in addition to, or in place of, the default network channel, as long as you configure each of those channels with unique listen addresses, ports, and protocol combinations. You can configure as many network channels as you need for your environment. You can also assign a custom channel to an EJB by first creating the network channel and then specifying it in the *<network-access-point>* element in the EJB's deployment descriptor, the *weblogic-ejb-jar.xml* file.

TIP
Network channels can share the same listen port and listen address, so long as they use a different communication protocol.

Benefits of Using Network Channels

In a production environment, the default network channel isn't sufficient to take care of the complex network traffic requirements, and you'll find that you need additional network channels to support complicated production network requirements. Custom network channels provide several benefits, including the ability to separate different types of network traffic. Multiple custom channels also enable you to specify different connection protocols, such as secure and nonsecure protocols, to meet the needs of different types of applications and their network traffic. You can also create a custom network channel to handle cluster communications.

Generally, you use network channels in conjunction with network router configuration to implement a demilitarized zone (DMZ). A good example of this is to configure RMI connections (used by EJB, JMS, and JMX) on a separate port that is not accessible through the firewall. This means that only web container requests are accessible from outside your internal network. (Make sure to disable HTTP tunneling in this case.)

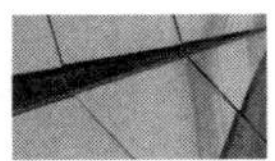

TIP
You can also create a custom administration channel that uses the admin protocol in cases where you may want to bind the channel to different IP addresses.

Creating Custom Network Channels

You can create custom network channels through the Administration Console. Again, although you can create multiple channels for a single server, you can't assign the same network channel to multiple Managed Servers. In addition, SSL and nonsecure network channels must use unique combinations of the listen address and listen port. This section shows you how to create and configure a custom network channel for a stand-alone server instance. To create a custom network channel after enabling the Lock & Edit feature, go to Environment | Servers | *<server-name>* | Protocols | Channels. Figure 5-6 shows the Network Channels page in the Administration Console. On this page, you can view the protocol, listen address, listen port, and allowed connection protocols for all the network channels that are configured for this server.

1. Click Lock & Control in the Change Center of the Administration Console.
2. Click New in the Network Channels table.

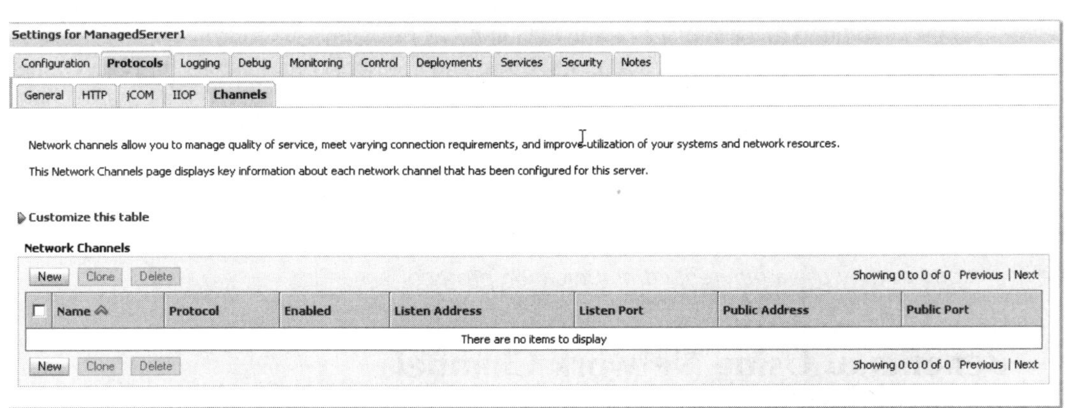

FIGURE 5-6. *The Network Channels page*

3. On the Create A New Network Channel page, select a name for the new channel, as well as a protocol, such as t3, t3s, HTTP, or HTTPS, for example. The complete set of protocols you can choose from includes HTTP, HTTPS, t3, t3s, COM, SNMP, LDAP, and LDAPS. In addition, for a cluster, you also have the *cluster-broadcast* and *cluster-broadcast-secure* protocols. The server uses the HTTP and HTTPS protocols mainly for handling client requests from a web browser. WebLogic Server uses the t3 and t3s protocols for internal and external communications with other servers. WebLogic Server also uses the t3 protocol for RMI. WebLogic clusters route unicast-based cluster messages among cluster members using the *cluster-broadcast* protocol. The secure version of this protocol is *cluster-broadcast-secure*. Click Next.

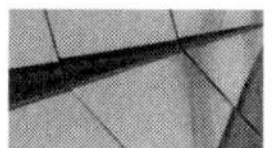

NOTE
All the network protocols are multiplexed over connections that share the same listen address and listen port. That is, you can have both a t3 and an HTTP protocol configured to use the same port and hostname. Clients simply use different protocols to talk to the server. This chapter shows how you can use this capability to separate different types of network traffic.

4. On the Network Channel Addressing page, specify a listen port and listen address for the new network channel. You can optionally specify two other values here: External Listen Address and External Listen Port. WebLogic Server uses these attributes when communicating with clients through channels that support network address translation (NAT) firewalls. Click Next.
5. On the Network Channel Properties page, specify properties such as Tunneling Enabled, Outbound Enabled, and HTTP Enabled. Click Next.
6. On the Secure Network Channel page, you must specify the security configuration for the new channel—you have two options here: Two Way SSL Enabled and Client Certificate Enforced. By default, every server is configured with the Demo Identity and Demo Trust certificates.
7. Click Finish. You'll now see the new network channel in the Network Channels table.

Once you create a network channel, the server starts the channel automatically and you'll see the following in the command console:

```
<Jul 23, 2013 7:21:21 AM CDT> <Notice> <Server> <BEA-002613> <Channel
"MyNetworkChannel1" is now listening on 192.168.80.100:7001 for protocols
t3,http.>
```

Tunneling

Let's say you want to specify the t3 protocol for some types of client traffic. You may run into a problem where your network requires that all client traffic must come through a protocol-filtering firewall that supports just the HTTP protocol. What do you do? You can tunnel the t3 connection requests over the HTTP connections. Tunneling enables a client request using a certain protocol to be sent over a different protocol. In this case, the client traffic using the t3 protocol is tunneled over (or under!) the HTTP protocol. Of course, tunneling will result in slower network communications because of the overhead of HTTP for communicating a client's request.

You can configure tunneling when you select a network protocol, as shown in the previous section, by specifying a value for the Tunneling Enabled property on the Network Channel Properties page. If you enable tunneling, you can specify both a client ping and a client timeout option to control how the server handles tunneling client connections.

Configuring Network Channels

When you create a custom network channel, you specify the listen port and listen address (as well as an external listen address and external listen port, if necessary). You also specify the connection protocol, of course. However, there's a lot more to configuring a network channel than merely specifying the listen port, listen address, and protocol. After you specify these, your new network channel is configured to use the default network settings. This section explains the main network configuration attributes you can then set.

To configure a network channel, go to Environment | Servers | *<server_name>* | Protocols | Channels. In the Network Channels table, click the network channel you'd like to configure. On the network Configuration page, the top portion shows the settings for the listen address, listen port, and protocol that you've already selected for this channel. You can change the settings or even disable a network channel from this page. Note that the Enabled property is checked, by default, meaning that all network channels are started automatically when you start the WebLogic Server instance. This can be helpful when used in conjunction with a load balancer and when a physical machine has multiple physical network devices. You can use various approaches to assigning each server instance to a particular network device to minimize the context switching that might otherwise occur.

TIP

Each network channel you configure for a server must have a unique combination of host, port, and protocol. You can assign different port numbers on a server the same protocol if you're running multiple Managed Servers on a single machine.

Scroll down to the bottom and click Advanced. Here are the main Advanced Network Channel options you can configure in the Administration Console:

- **Outbound Enabled** Lets you specify whether the server can use this channel for server-to-server communications. A server that needs to make EJB calls to another server will use the channel for communicating with the remote server unless you disable the Outbound Enabled setting—by default, this is enabled for all admin channels, meaning the server supports internal server-to-server communications. You can make use of this property to separate external (client) traffic and internal (server) traffic. If your server has multiple NICs, you can dedicate a channel for client traffic on one NIC and use another NIC to support server-to-server communications.

  In a cluster, you'll use internal channels for communications among the cluster members, so you can leave this option unselected.
- **Cluster Address** Specifies the address for RMI communications within a cluster. By default it is false, and you should select it only if you're using this channel for RMI communications.

- **Accept Backlog** Specifies how many backlogged TCP connection requests the network channel allows. The default value is 300 backlogged connections.
- **Maximum Backoff Between Failures** Specifies the maximum backoff time between failures in the acceptance of client connections.
- **HTTP Enabled For This Protocol** Specifies whether HTTP is enabled. Select this option, as binary protocols use HTTP for downloading various resources.
- **Login Timeout** Specifies the maximum time (in milliseconds) the channel waits for a connection before timing out. You can leave it at the default value of 5000 seconds. You can disable the network channel login timeouts by setting a value of 0.
- **Complete Message Timeout** Specifies the maximum amount of time the channel waits to receive a complete message. This attribute is critical because disabling it (by setting it to 0) means that a denial of service attack that launches long messages to the channel could succeed. The default value is –1, and the maximum is 480.
- **Idle Connection Timeout** Specifies the maximum amount of time in seconds that a connection can stay idle before being closed. The minimum value is 0, meaning connections won't time out. Set a value for this parameter or use the default value of –1.
- **Tunneling Enabled** Specifies whether the server should enable tunneling via HTTP for this channel.
- **Maximum Message Size** Sets the maximum message size in a message header. This attribute helps you protect the server against the launch of a denial of service attack, wherein a request tries to use up a vast amount of the server's memory to keep it from servicing other requests. The default value is 100MB, which is also the maximum value for this attribute. You must base the value for this attribute on your application's needs. If the channel is supporting an application sending small HTTP requests that are sized, say, 2KB on the average from a web site, you can set a small value such as 4KB (the minimum value is 4096 bytes). On the other hand, if the channel is supporting web services that are transmitting large requests, go for the default setting instead.

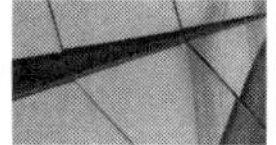

TIP
By configuring the optional administration channel, you can indirectly disable the default network channel. Once you create the administration channel, you must use it for all administrative tasks.

- **Channel Weight** This attribute lets you set a weight or priority for this channel when creating server-to-server connections. You can specify a value between 1 and 100, and the default is 50, meaning that this channel is as equally preferred as any other channel. When a server initiates a connection to another server for the purpose of server-to-server communication, it selects the network channel with the highest weight. It will pick a channel with a lower channel weight if the channel with the highest weight is unavailable owing to a network failure. Thus, the Channel Weight property lets you configure properties for network channels during server-to-server communications. If the server has multiple NICs, you can create multiple channels with different channel weights based on the speed of the channel's NIC.

Designing Network Channels

Real-life implementation of network channels depends on the type of network traffic you anticipate, both for client work and cluster communication needs. You must design network channels to separate the different types of user traffic, as well as your internal traffic. Let's use some simple examples to show how to configure custom network channels. Assume you've already configured an administration channel for the Admin Server, as explained in Chapter 3. Typically, you'll need to configure some custom network channels for satisfying different application needs, as well as a couple of internal network channels for clusters (one to handle the unicast cluster messages and another for replication). Note that you must create each network channel that you configure on each Managed Server in the cluster.

As far as the protocol goes, you must decide among the choices such as HTTP, t3, and so on, based on what that channel supports. If a channel supports just HTTP requests by proxying requests from a web server, you need to use the HTTP protocol. If a network channel supports Java client applications that communicate with the cluster through RMI, you must use the t3 or IIOP protocols. If secure communications are required, you must use the secure versions of the protocol, such as HTTPS, t3s, etc.

For a cluster, to create an internal channel for supporting unicast cluster messages, create a channel with the *cluster-broadcast* protocol. The SSL version of this is the *cluster-broadcast-secure* protocol. You can also create replication channels for clusters to force replication traffic to a dedicated channel. Each Managed Server in the cluster must have a separate replication channel in this case. You must consider creating custom network channels if your Managed Servers are running on separate servers. You can also use custom network channels if your Managed Servers are running on the same machine, as long as the machine is multihomed and the server has multiple NICs. Following are some common criteria to use when designing custom network channels.

Separating Network Traffic

You can separate different types of traffic by assigning different protocols to different ports. For example, you can create a channel that assigns HTTP traffic to port 7011 and t3 traffic to port 8011. This setup separates the t3 and HTTP requests and maintains separate queues for the two protocols. Separating network traffic in this manner offers you quite a bit of flexibility. In this case, you are only exposing the HTTP protocol externally, because that's the channel you dedicated to external HTTP requests.

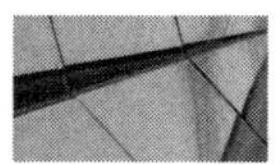

NOTE
You must configure the same custom network channels on all Managed Servers that are part of a cluster.

To implement this configuration of separate network channels, you can set the listen address for the default channel to 192.168.1.10, for example, with a listen port of 8011. You only need a single custom network channel dedicated for the HTTP traffic. You can create a network channel that uses the HTTP protocol with a port setting of 80. Note that the default and custom channels both use the same IP address, 192.168.1.10—that is, they share the same NIC.

Physically Separating Network Traffic

In the previous network setup, you separated network traffic using two different ports for two different types of traffic. However, only a single NIC is handling all the network traffic. You may add additional NICs to the machine and physically separate the network traffic based on the NIC. You achieve the separation of traffic by assigning different protocols to different NICs.

Let's say you have three NICs on a server, each with a different IP address such as 192.168.1.10, 192.168.1.11, and 192.168.1.12. You can configure a default channel with the listen address of 192.168.1.10 for handling t3 traffic. You can then create two custom network channels and assign them the 192.168.1.11 and the 192.168.1.12 IP addresses. You can assign all HTTP traffic to the channel with the 192.168.1.11 address and all secure (HTTPS) traffic to the 192.168.1.12 IP address.

Separating Internal and External Traffic

You can also physically separate the internal server traffic and the external client traffic to provide better security, as well as improve performance. By physically separating network traffic with the help of multiple NICs, you enhance the throughput of both internal and external network traffic. To separate internal server network traffic from external client traffic, use different NICs on the server with a different IP address for each NIC. Configure the two network channels in the following manner.

- You can configure the default channel with the NIC hosting the IP address 192.168.1.10 and enable the Outgoing Enabled attribute (by setting it to *true*) so the server can use this channel to communicate with other servers.
- Create a custom network channel using the second NIC with the IP address of 192.168.1.11. Because this channel is dedicated to servicing external traffic, you can disable the Outgoing Enabled property for this channel. This means the server can't use this channel for server-to-server communications—it uses the default network channel for the internal communications.

Creating an SNMP Network Channel

When you configure SNMP monitoring for a server (see Chapter 6), you'll need to configure an SNMP agent, which requires two channels: one for UDP traffic and the other for TCP traffic. By default, the TCP traffic uses the server's listen port (the default is 7001), but you can separate the SNMP traffic from your business traffic by configuring a custom network channel for SNMP communications. If you decide to create a custom SNMP network channel, you must do so on each Managed Server that hosts an SNMP agent. Configure an SNMP network channel is simple. Navigate to Server | Configuration | Protocols. When you invoke the Create A New Network Channel Assistant, select "snmp" from the protocol list. Once you do this, any SNMP agent you target to this server instance will use the custom SNMP network channel.

The Java Connector Architecture (JCA)

Just as a JDBC driver provides connectivity to a database, resource adapters provide connectivity to an *enterprise information system (EIS),* which can be an enterprise resource planning (ERP) system or a legacy database or mainframe transactional database. WebLogic Server implements the *Java EE Connector Architecture (JCA)* to provide connectivity between the applications you deploy to WebLogic Server and an EIS. In a way, JCA is somewhat like JDBC, which lets a developer write a single set of code to talk to any database using the JDBC API. Similarly, instead of writing custom code to communicate to each of the corporate back-end systems, developers can simply write code that talks to the connectors, which, in turn, will talk to the back-end systems.

Web application components such as EJBs communicate with the resource adapters through the Common Client Interface (CCI), which provides a generic connector implementation. This interface doesn't provide any security management, transaction management, or even connection management. WebLogic Server interfaces with the resource adapter to provide these management services. JCA uses the concept of *system contracts* to manage the transactions and connections between WebLogic Server (or any application server) and the back-end system. Here are the three system contracts that ensure the two systems properly negotiate with each other, thus guaranteeing the integrity of the data the two systems exchange between themselves:

- **Connection management contract** Connection management relies on the use of a connection pool and enables the resource adapter to provide a connection factory and connection interfaces that enable JDBC drivers to align with JCA architecture with minimal impact on existing JDBC APIs. You can create a minimum and maximum number of connections to WebLogic Server.
- **Transaction management contract** Provides transaction support, which includes both support for XA (global) transactions and local transactions.
- **Security management contract** The Connector API propagates the security context from WebLogic Server to the resource adapter.

There are two important types of JCA resource adapters: WebLogic Integration (WLI) resource adapters and WebLogic Server resource adapters. You can deploy the WebLogic Server resource adapters to any Java EE–compliant application server. This section discusses the implementation and deployment of the WebLogic Server resource adapters, which don't use any WLI extensions. There are three types of WebLogic Server resource adapters:

- **Outbound resource adapter** Allows applications to initiate a connection to an EIS.
- **Inbound resource adapter** Allows an EIS to initiate contact with an application. Oracle recommends that the resource adapter use Work Managers to process work instead of creating a thread directly.
- **Bidirectional resource adapter** Allows either the application or the EIS to initiate communications.

In addition, a resource adapter may provide three different transaction levels. The *XATransaction* level lets a resource adapter participate in distributed transactions managed by the WebLogic Server Transaction Manager. Connections using the *LocalTransaction* level can participate only in local transactions and not in transactions involving the two-phase commit protocol. A *NoTransaction* setting prevents the resource adapter from participating in local or distributed (global) transactions.

Although WebLogic Server fully supports both the Java EE 1.0 and 1.5 Connector Architectures, the discussion in this chapter assumes a Java EE 1.5 Connector Architecture.

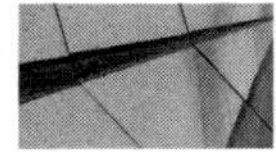

NOTE
WebLogic Server supports the development of resource adapters under both the Java EE 1.0 Connector Architecture and the Java EE 1.5 Connector Architecture. The Java EE 1.5 Connector Architecture offers more capabilities, such as outbound and inbound communications to and from multiple systems.

Oracle WebLogic Server 12*c* uses a Connector container to deploy a resource adapter. For an outbound connection, this container contains the resource adapter and one or more connection pools for the outbound connections. It also contains managed connection objects that represent outbound physical connections to the EIS, as well as the connection handles returned to the application component from the resource adapter's connection factory. For inbound connections, the container includes external message sources such as an EIS that talks to WebLogic Server, as well as a message factory (*MessageEndPointFactory*). It also contains a message endpoint application such as a message-driven bean (MDB), which receives the inbound messages through the resource adapter.

Managing Resource Adapters Through the Console

Once you deploy a resource adapter, you can modify configuration elements of the adapter through the Administration Console. Some changes require a redeployment of the resource module (*.rar*), and others don't. In general, you can dynamically configure JNDI-related properties, such as JNDI names and the creation and deletion of outbound connection pools. In addition, you can configure the following WebLogic Server–specific connection pool parameters (in the *weblogic-ra.xml* file) without having to redeploy the resource adapter:

- *initial-capacity*
- *max-capacity*
- *capacity-increment*
- *shrink-frequency-seconds*
- *highest-num-waiters*
- *highest-num-unavailable*
- *connection-creation-retry-frequency-seconds*
- *connection-reserve-timeout-seconds*
- *test-frequency-seconds*

You can also dynamically configure the following logging parameters for a resource module:

- *log-filename*
- *file-count*
- *file-size-limit*
- *log-file-rotation-dir*
- *rotation-time*
- *file-time-span*

WebLogic Server persists any resource adapter properties that you modify through the Console in the deployment plan for that adapter.

Follow these steps to configure a resource adapter through the Administration Console:

1. Click Lock & Edit in the Change Center of the Console.
2. Select Deployments in the left-hand pane.

3. On the Summary Of Deployments page, click the name of the resource adapter you want to configure.
4. On the Settings page for the adapter, expand Configuration | Properties.
5. Modify the resource adapter properties shown in the Resource Adapter Bean Properties table.
5. Target the resource adapter to a Managed Server or a cluster.
6. Click Save. Click Activate Changes in the Change Center of the Console. The server modifies the deployment plan for the adapter to mark your configuration changes.

In this example, you learned how to configure an existing Java EE connector module. You can also configure a new connector for deployment using the Console by deploying the RAR file for the resource adapter.

Monitoring Resource Adapter Connections

Use the Administration Console to monitor connections made through a resource adapter. You can do this by going to Environment | Deployment | Connector Modules in the left-hand pane of the console. You can then click the Monitoring tab, followed by the Resource Adapters tab to view statistics for all the resource adapters that you've deployed on this server, such as active and idle connections. You can also close a connection from the Console if it's safe to do so—that is, if the connection isn't part of an active transaction and if it has exceeded its maximum idle time limit.

The WebLogic Tuxedo Connector

You can establish connectivity among web applications, Oracle Tuxedo services, and Tuxedo clients through the WebLogic Tuxedo Connector (WTC). You can access WTC by going to Environment | Interoperability in the left-hand pane of the Administration Console. You can also configure Jolt connection pools to enable applications to connect to Oracle Tuxedo domains. Jolt is a client API that manages requests from the applications to Oracle Tuxedo services.

Summary

This chapter introduced you to WebLogic Server Work Managers, which help applications prioritize their work based on rules that you define and the server's run-time performance. Work Managers thus help you to optimize application performance and maintain your service-level agreements. You also learned how to create custom network channels to meet various applications' needs. Finally, the chapter introduced the Java Connector Architecture and explained how to configure a resource adapter.

CHAPTER 6

Monitoring and Troubleshooting WebLogic Server

WebLogic Server offers a powerful diagnostic framework called the WebLogic Diagnostic Framework (WLDF), which consists of diagnostic components that let you instrument diagnostic capture at the server or application level and configure automatic notifications to monitor log messages, instrumented events, and harvested server and subsystem metric data. WLDF also offers a diagnostic archive feature that allows you to store historical diagnostic data. This chapter introduces you to all the important components of WLDF, including the Monitoring Dashboard, which lets you monitor server performance easily. You'll also learn about the integration of WLDF with the JRockit Flight Recorder for run-time or post-incident analysis of diagnostic data.

One of the key tasks for a WebLogic Server administrator is to monitor production environments. WebLogic Server provides several ways for you to monitor a running server instance. You can use the Administration Console, the JMX framework, and the Single Network Management Protocol (SNMP) to monitor servers. This chapter reviews how to monitor running server instances using all these methods The chapter also describes how to configure WebLogic Server to write server, domain, and subcomponent logs and how to view those logs. Dealing with server crashes and with slow-performing applications is, of course, a critical part of any administrator's job responsibilities. You'll also learn how to generate and interpret a thread dump.

The WebLogic Diagnostic Framework

In the latter part of this chapter, you'll learn how to access monitoring information through the JMX interface (directly or through the Administration Console), as well as how to set up SNMP monitoring. You'll be pleasantly surprised to discover that WebLogic Server also offers a powerful and robust monitoring and diagnostic framework called the *WebLogic Diagnostic Framework (WLDF)*. WLDF makes your diagnostic work and analysis of run-time performance of servers and applications much easier by offering you several diagnostic components that allow you to collect, analyze, and archive diagnostic data from the server and deployed applications.

When you configure WebLogic Server with the JRockit JVM, you can use WLDF to access the diagnostic information from the JRockit flight recording file.

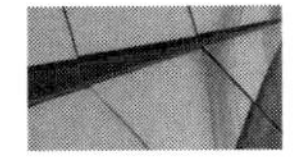

NOTE

You need to download and install the JRockit JVM separately—it's not part of the Oracle WebLogic Server 12c installation. You can download it from: www.oracle.com/technetwork/middleware/jrockit/overview/index.html. Once you download JRockit, install it in your Oracle Middleware home directory. The actual JRockit product I've downloaded is named Oracle JRockit JDK 28.2.7 and JRockit Mission Control 4.1.

Oracle Fusion Middleware's Diagnostic Framework automatically collects WLDF server image dumps and is well integrated with several WLDF features. It integrates with the Watch and Notification as well as the Diagnostic Image Capture component of WLDF.

Following are the major WLDF components:

- **Monitoring Dashboard** Displays both the current and historical states of the server and the applications it hosts by exposing critical run-time performance metrics and tracking changes to those metrics. The Diagnostic Archive component stores the collected metrics that you can view through the dashboard to get an idea about the history of the operating state. You must configure the Harvester component to capture the metrics you want to view from the Diagnostic Archive. In addition to the Monitoring Dashboard, you can also use the Diagnostics Request Performance page in the Administration Console to examine real-time and historical views of method performance information. To view this information, you must configure the WLDF Instrumentation component.

- **Diagnostic Image Capture** Helps create diagnostic snapshots of server performance that you can use to analyze server failures. You can capture diagnostic images on demand by issuing commands from the Administration Console, WLST scripts, or JMX applications. You can also configure image notifications, which automatically capture diagnostic images when a harvester, log, or instrumentation watch rule is triggered.
- **Diagnostic Archive** Stores logs and metrics from both the server and the deployed applications. In addition, the archive stores historical data from the WLDF Instrumentation and Harvester components.
- **Harvester** Captures metrics from the (harvestable) runtime MBeans and provides a historical record of the metrics.
- **Watch and Notification** Enables the observation of specific diagnostic states and automates the dispatch of monitoring notifications sent based on various rules you configure, called *watches.*
- **Instrumentation** Provides ways to embed diagnostic code (called *monitors*) at various well-defined points inside applications and server instances.
- **Data Accessor** You can use the JMX-based access service to access diagnostic data in a running server. You can also use WLST diagnostic commands, and you can export archived data to an XML file so you can access diagnostic data at a later time.

The standard logging features offered by WebLogic Server under the umbrella of the WebLogic Server Logging Services are also technically a part of WLDF. Each of the WLDF components functions at the server level and stores diagnostic data on a per-server basis. For each of the WLDF resources listed here, the server creates an MBean that you can access through JMX or WLST. Although the WLDF architecture and its components seem daunting at first, the way it all works is straightforward: you determine the type and quantity of diagnostic data the server generates by configuring the Harvester, Instrumentation, Diagnostic Image Capture, and Watch and Notification components, which together harvest the diagnostic data and trigger various actions and notifications. The Archive component helps store the diagnostic data, and you retrieve the data with the help of the Data Accessor component.

Here are the main benefits of using the WLDF:

- It is designed for efficient operation with minimal impact on the running server.
- It doesn't require separately starting WLST scripts or JMX programs to interrogate the server.
- It is especially efficient in collecting historical data.
- It properly handles the storing of historical data so you can get to it even after there are problems and a server has been restarted.

The WLDF is also integrated into server components such as the WebLogic Monitoring Dashboard so an administrator can view historical data prior to accessing it. You can configure WLDF using the Administration Console, as you'll see in this chapter. In addition, you can also use WLST scripts to configure WLDF. As with most WebLogic Server configuration tasks, you can also use JMX to programmatically configure WLDF.

TIP

Although you can easily configure WLDF by editing the XML configuration files, Oracle recommends that you do not do this.

You can configure the Diagnostic Image Capture and a Diagnostic Archive at the server level, and when you do so, the server adds the configuration settings to the domain's *config.xml* file. You configure the Harvester, Watch and Notification, and Instrumentation components as part of a diagnostic system module that you deploy to a Managed Server or a cluster. The configuration settings for these components are not part of the *config.xml* file; rather, they are stored in a diagnostic resource descriptor file that you target to a Managed Server or cluster.

Using WLDF with the JRockit Flight Recorder

The JRockit JVM contains a built-in performance monitoring and profiling tool called the *JRockit Flight Recorder (JFR)*. JFR stores diagnostic and profiling data in a file called the *JRockit flight recording file,* which allows you to access the diagnostic data even after a system crash. The JFR file contains JVM events and events from the WebLogic Server, as well as the various Java programs such as servlets that are running in the JVM. The recent integration of WLDF with JFR is a huge step forward in simplifying WebLogic Server diagnostic capabilities, and it greatly reduces the burden of having to configure manually various WLDF modules to capture diagnostic data. Starting with the WebLogic Server 10.3 release, the ability to control the use of instrumentation through the simple setting of the diagnostic volume should be the starting point for those who want to take advantage of WLDF.

WLDF is well integrated with the JFR, and the overhead for configuring the JFR is very low, thus making it a valuable diagnostic tool in production systems. Although your mileage may well vary, Oracle's internal testing with default settings indicate less than a 1 percent performance impact when you use the JFR.

The JFR uses the concept of an *event* to capture diagnostic data, with an event being something that happens in an application at a specific point in time. In addition to the name and time of an event, JFR captures a payload for each event that contains details about the event. For example, for an event that signals a blocked thread, the payload would include the lock holder's ID. You can control the data the JFR captures by both limiting the type of events and setting thresholds for events. For example, you can specify that the JFR collects event information only if the event lasts for a specific length of time—this way, you keep the JFR from capturing too many short-term events that are unimportant. JFR writes event diagnostic data to a circular in-memory buffer first and writes the contents of the buffer to disk when the buffer fills up, thus minimizing expensive disk writes.

JFR data provides the following benefits for problem diagnosis and profiling:

- It is useful for profiling applications by using information such as lock profiles and garbage collection details and by tracing the execution of the Java programs.
- You can use the JFR as a diagnostic store that you can examine after a server crash, for example, just as experts examine the contents of a cockpit "black box" after a plane crash.
- You can use the JFR as a source of data for Oracle Support during diagnostic work.

The JRockit Mission Control Client

You can manage the JFR data collection with the *JRockit Mission Control (JRMC)* client. The JRMC client minimizes performance overhead involved in monitoring, managing, and profiling memory leaks in Java applications. Using the JRMC Client, you can view JVM recordings and run-time parameters as a set of tables that are groupings of performance data. The JRMC client shows the performance event data in the form of various dials, charts, and tables. You can also use the JRockit Memory Leak Detector to analyze the causes of memory leaks in Java applications.

TIP

In addition to the JRMC, you may also want to try out third-party application performance monitoring tools such as CA Wily Introscope.

You access the JRMC client by issuing the following command:

- If the JROCKIT_HOME/bin directory is part of your system path, start the JRockit Mission Control Client by entering **jrmc** at the command prompt.
- If the JROCKIT_HOME/bin directory is not part of your system path, enter the full path to the executable file:

  Windows: JROCKIT_HOME\bin\jrmc.exe

  Linux: JROCKIT_HOME/bin/jrmc
- On Windows servers, you can also start the JRockit Mission Control Client from the Start menu.

Figure 6-1 shows the Overview page, which is the JRockit Mission Control (4.1) home page. You use the Event Types view to select the events you want to analyze. The information the JRockit GUI displays will change as you select different items from the Event Types browser available in

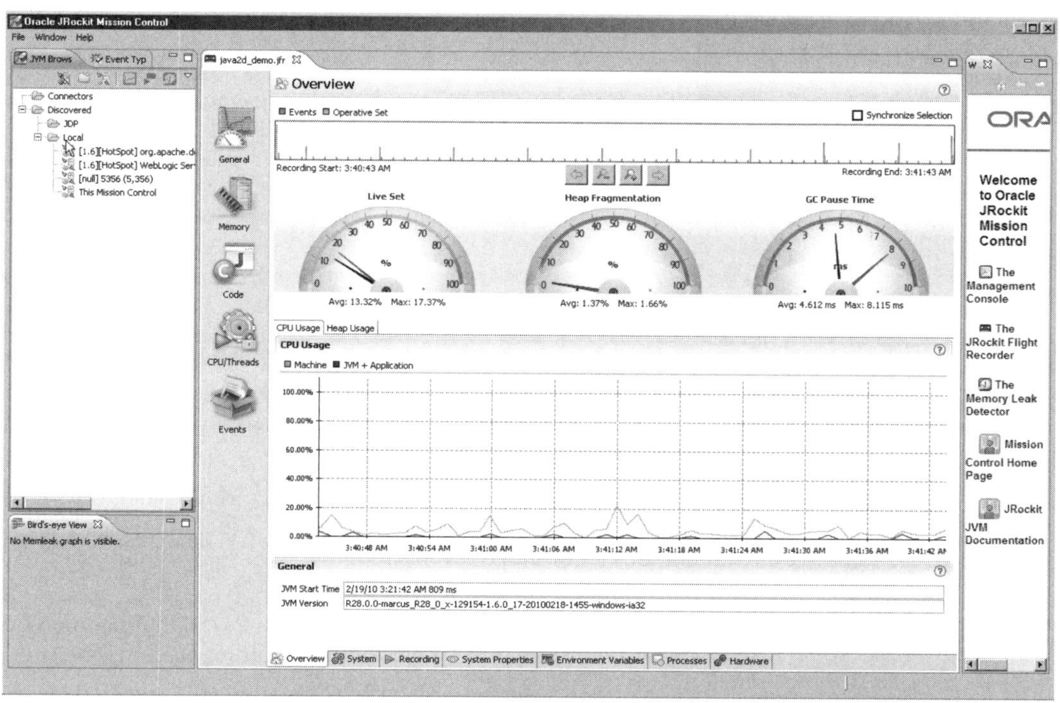

FIGURE 6-1. *The JRockit Mission Control home page*

the Event Types view. For each event type, such as the Servlet event, you can view the events logged by that event by selecting the Log tab.

You can record and view JFR data through the JRMC client, and, in most cases, this is the easiest way. You can start the Flight Recorder from within the JRockit Mission Control client to record the behavior of the JVM process during a specific time period. The JRockit Flight Recorder creates a file to store the recorded data and opens it automatically after completing the recording. Alternatively, you can do the same from the command line. The following sections show the different ways in which you can configure, start, stop, and view JFR event data. An operative set of events is a set of events that you define in the JRockit Mission Control. Once you define an operative set of events, you can analyze the run-time system activity caused by this event set.

Enabling Default Recording By default, the JFR is turned off, but you can configure default recording by setting the default recording option to *true* at the command line:

```
-XX:flightRecorderOptions=defaultrecording=true
```

By default, JFR stores the JFR file in the path specified by the *java.io.tmpdir* property. You can specify a different location with the *repository=<path>* parameter. Similarly, you can specify the *maxsize* parameter to specify the maximum disk space that JFR can use. You can specify *maxsize* in KB, MB, or GB. If you want to specify that the JFR must save event data for a specified maximum time before discarding older data, you can do so with the *maxage* parameter. You can specify the *maxage* in seconds, minutes, hours, or days. Here's an example that shows how to specify various attributes for the default recording:

```
-XX:flightRecorderOptions=defaultrecording=true disk=true repository=
/var/log/jfr maxage=1d
```

This example turns on automatic, continuous JFR recording and stores the JFR file in the /var/log/jfr directory. JFR will retain the data for the past one day (1d) in the JFR file.

Recording JFR Data Through the JRMC Client You start and stop JFR event data recording through the JRMC client by following these steps:

1. Start the client, as shown here:

   ```
   JROCKIT_HOME\bin\jrmc.exe
   ```

   In my case, the JROCKIT_HOME directory is C:\Oracle\Middleware, so I look under the C:\Oracle\Middleware\bin directory for the *jrmc* executable.
2. In the JRockit Mission Control GUI, under the Discovered folder, right-click on WebLogic Server. Select Start Flight Recording from the context menu.
3. Specify parameters for event recording in the Start Flight Recording dialog box. You must select a recording template (prebuilt or custom) and specify a recording time duration. You can specify continuous recording of events, but if you do so, you must specify a value for the maximum size in terms of disk space.
4. To start event recording, click OK. The Remaining column in the Flight Recorded Control view at the bottom shows how much time is left for the recording to complete.
5. You can terminate the recording before the recording time limit you specified by selecting Stop after right-clicking on the recording.

When the recording completes or when you stop it manually, the recording data will appear in the JRockit Mission Control home page.

Recording Data from the Command Line You can start a JFR recording from the command line in two different ways: you can start a recording when you start the JVM or in a running JRockit instance. You can invoke a JFR recording from the command line when you start the JVM, as shown here:

```
-XX:StartFlightRecording=duration=1h,filename=myjfrrecording.jfr
```

You can use multiple options when you start a recording from the command line.

To start a recoding in a running JVM instance, use the *jrcmd* utility (*jrcmd.exe*), which is in the same directory as the *jrmc* executable that I used earlier to invoke the JRockit Mission Control client. You need the PID of the JVM instance to issue the *jrcmd* command. Here's an example:

```
jrcmd <pid> start_flightrecording duration=1h filename=testrecording.jfr
```

This command enables JFR to collect diagnostic data for a period of 1 hour. Alternatively, you can omit the *duration* parameter, in which case the recording will continue indefinitely until you stop it with the *stop_flightrecording* command, as shown here:

```
jrcmd <pid> stop_flightrecording recording=1
```

To check the status of a running recording, issue the following command:

```
jrcmd <pid> check_flightrecording
```

Integrating WebLogic Server Data with the JFR

A Diagnostic Image Capture through WLDF automatically includes the JFR file. You must make sure that you enable the JRockit Flight Recorder in order to generate diagnostic data in the JFR diagnostic image. By using WLDF together with the JRockit Mission Control, you can examine the diagnostic data generated during the occurrence of an event to understand what was happening in the server at that time. Since every Diagnostic Image Capture created through an image notification automatically contains the JFR file, you can examine the captured JFR file to perform real-time diagnosis of problems. To reiterate, the server must be using Oracle JRockit, and you must enable the JFR to do this.

You can specify the amount of server event data that the JFR file records by configuring the WLDF diagnostic volume. That is, you can control the generation of diagnostic data by WLDF that is captured by a JFR flight recording for various WebLogic Server events from components such as web applications; EJBs; web services; and JDBC, JTA, and JMS resources. After you ensure that JFR flight recording is enabled in JRockit (it's enabled by default), set the appropriate WLDF diagnostic volume. You can configure the diagnostic volume by selecting one of four diagnostic volume levels (Off, Low, Medium, or High) by going to Environment | Servers | *<server_name>* | Configuration | General and setting that option for the Diagnostic Volume attribute. The default value for Diagnostic Volume is Low. By selecting Medium or High as the value, you can make the server generate more diagnostic data. Of course, if you select the Off setting for the WLDF diagnostic volume, no WLDF-related data is captured in the JFR diagnostic image.

The server automatically throttles the number of requests it selects for event generation and the recording of that information into the JRF file. As the number of incoming requests changes, the server automatically adjusts the throttling factor by sampling fewer or a larger number of requests to keep the overhead down while providing you with an accurate view of the server activity.

You can use any of the WLST Diagnostic Image Capture commands to obtain the JFR file because the Diagnostic Image Capture automatically includes the JFR file if one is available. Once you retrieve the JFR file from a Diagnostic Image Capture (see the section titled "Using WLST for Capturing Diagnostic Images" later in this chapter), you can view it in the JRockit Mission Control.

Now that you've learned how to integrate WLDF with the Oracle JRockit Flight Recorder, it's time to look into the various components of WLDF itself.

Using the Monitoring Dashboard

Oracle WebLogic Server 12*c* offers you a GUI tool called the Monitoring Dashboard for viewing diagnostic information. You can access the Monitoring Dashboard by going to http://*hostname*:*port*/*console*/*dashboard*. Figure 6-2 shows the Monitoring Dashboard home page. You can view both current and historical performance metrics and how those metrics have changed over time through the Monitoring Dashboard. The dashboard presents run-time server instance information in the form of *built-in views,* a collection of charts that display various performance metrics. In the explorer panel of the Monitoring Dashboard, you can access both the set of built-in views and any custom views you've created. You can also use the Metric Browser to specify the MBean instance attributes whose values you want the dashboard to display in a chart.

The Monitoring Dashboard displays diagnostic data that shows either the current or historical values of runtime MBean attributes. Any value of a runtime MBean attribute that belongs to a runtime MBean instance is called a *metric*. The Monitoring Dashboard shows both real-time *polled metrics,* which are values of active runtime MBean instances, and *collected metrics* from the diagnostic archive, which are the metrics collected by the Harvester component. Thus, you must first configure

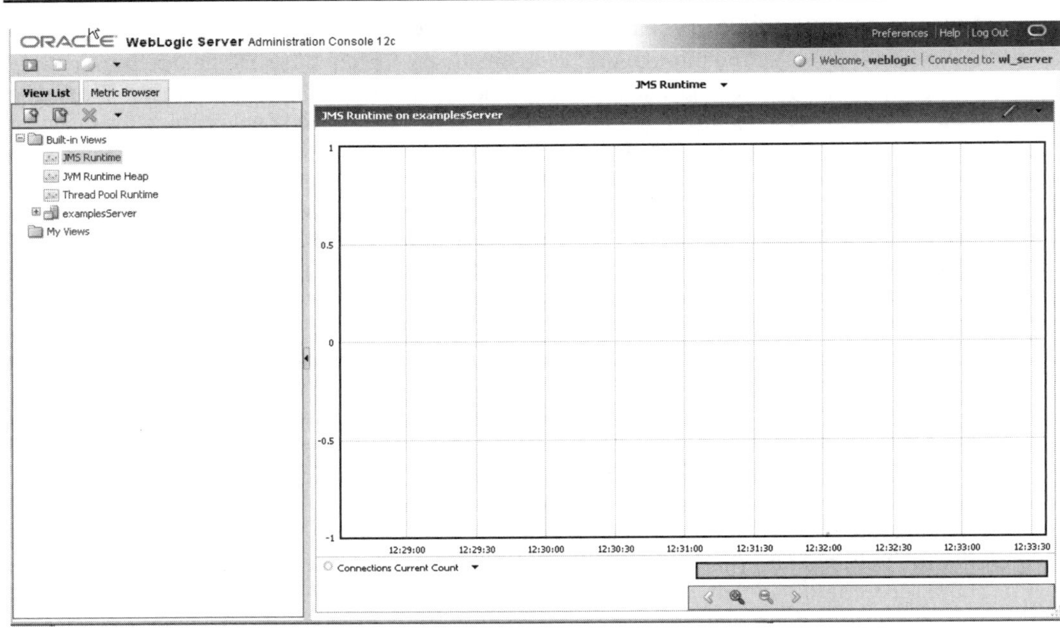

FIGURE 6-2. *The Monitoring Dashboard home page*

the Harvester component, as shown later in this chapter, if you wish to view any collected metrics from the archive. In order to keep the overhead of metric collection to a minimum, the dashboard polls runtime MBean instances only once during each interval to collect the polled metrics.

In addition to the Monitoring Dashboard, WLDF provides another web page to view diagnostic data. This is the Diagnostics Request Performance page of the Administration Console, which requires that you configure WLDF instrumentation first. You can then use this page to view the real-time and historical method performance information captured through WLDF instrumentation. The page shows information about requests that flow through code you've instrumented. The server generates instrumentation events when a request executes an instrumented method. The event information is displayed on the Diagnostics Request Performance page. Each request is identified by a unique ID, the name of the application, and the top-level method executed by the request. You can also view the execution time of the request in comparison with other requests at the same level of method calls.

Before you can request performance data through the Diagnostics Request Performance page, you must configure WLDF instrumentation to use a specific diagnostic action called *ElapsedTimeAction,* because only data from this action is presented in the Performance page. The section "Creating Request Performance Data," later in this chapter, shows you how to configure instrumentation to enable the use of the Diagnostics Request Performance page in the Administration Console. Once you do this and enable instrumentation, you can configure request performance data by following these steps:

1. In the left-hand pane of the Administration Console, select Diagnostics | Request Performance.
2. On the Diagnostics Request Performance page, select the server name.
3. Next, you select a time interval for obtaining request data.

You can choose to display information about specific requests and method invocations. Before you delve into the three main WLDF components (Instrumentation, Harvester, and Watch and Notifications), you need to learn how to use the Diagnostic Image Capture capability and the Diagnostic Archives facility offered by WLDF.

Configuring Diagnostic Image Capture

You can use the Diagnostic Image Capture component of WLDF to get a snapshot of what was happening inside the server and its subcomponents (such as JDBC and JMS) when a failure occurred. You capture the diagnostic images for troubleshooting by Oracle Support personnel. A diagnostic image packages the internal run-time server state information into a convenient diagnostic image file. Diagnostic Image Capture is helpful in performing an analysis of what led to a failure, and it makes it easy for you to send Oracle Support a single zip file that captures all the data necessary to facilitate troubleshooting. You can capture diagnostic images through the Administration Console, using a WLST command, or by configuring a Watch notification. The section "Configuring Notifications," later in this chapter, shows how to configure a notification that captures a diagnostic image, but first this section shows you how to capture a diagnostic image through the Administration Console.

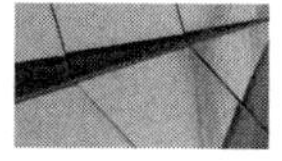

NOTE
If you've configured your server with Oracle JRockit and have also enabled the JRockit Flight Recorder, Diagnostic Image Capture will capture the flight recorder data as well as the server state information.

Follow these steps to configure the capturing of diagnostic images through the Administration Console:

1. Click Lock & Edit in the Change Center of the Administration Console.
2. In the left-hand pane, go to Diagnostics | Diagnostic Images.
3. Select the server on which you want to save the diagnostic image file.
4. In the Destination Directory field of the Settings For *<server_name>* page, enter the details for the directory you want to use for storing the diagnostic image files. The server creates the directory if it doesn't exist. The destination you specify here will be the default location for all diagnostic image captures, but you can specify a different destination for a specific diagnostic image capture. The default directory is logs\diagnostic_images.
5. In the Timeout field, specify the interval between diagnostic image captures. You can use the timeout value to control the frequency of diagnostic image capturing when there are multiple server failure events.
6. Click Save and then click the Activate Changes button in the Change Center of the Console.

The volume or level of diagnostic data that a diagnostic image contains is something that you configure at the server level. Once you create the destination and the timeout for the diagnostic image captures, you must specify the WLDF diagnostic volume settings at the server level by following these steps.

1. In the left-hand pane, go to Environment | Servers.
2. Select the name of the server instance.
3. Select Configuration | General.
4. On the Servers | Configuration | General page, choose one of the following Diagnostic Volume settings:
   - **Off** This setting doesn't mean that no diagnostic data is captured. Rather, it specifies that no diagnostic data be captured for JRockit Flight Recorder diagnostic images.
   - **High** This setting provides detailed error information.
   - **Medium** This setting provides additional information in addition to the basic diagnostic information.
   - **Low** This is the default diagnostic level setting, and it captures basic information for messages with the EMERGENCY, ALERT, or CRITICAL level.
5. Click Save.

Once you configure the Diagnostic Image Capture component, as shown here, the server's *config.xml* file will show the diagnostic capture configuration within the *<server-diagnostic-config>* element, which is a subelement of the *<server>* element. Here's an example:

```
<server>
  <name>myserver</name>
  <server-diagnostic-config>
    <image-dir>logs\diagnostic_images</image-dir>
    <image-timeout>2</image-timeout>
```

```
  </server-diagnostic-config>
</server>
```

Now that you've configured the destination, and the diagnostic volume settings, you're ready to capture a diagnostic image. To capture a diagnostic image, go to Diagnostics | Diagnostic Images and select the server for which you want to capture the image. Once you select the server, you can click the previously grayed out Capture Image button and then click OK. WebLogic Server captures the current server configuration data and state and stores it in the directory you've specified. You'll see the following message in the Console while the image capture process is running:

```
Name=>State=>Start Time=>Duration(ms)=>Remaining(ms)=>Identifier
   WLDFDiagnosticImageRecording_medrec-spring_MedRecServer_Running=>8/15/13
 10:10:34 AM 473ms=>N/A=>N/A=>1
```

If you've configured the JRockit Flight Recorder, you can view the server diagnostic data in the JRockit Mission Control.

The Diagnostic Image Files

When you capture the diagnostic image for a server, the server puts the captured diagnostic image file in that server's logs\diagnostics directory. For example, for the sample server MedRecServer, the file will be in the following format:

```
diagnostic_image_MedRecServer_2013_08_16_20_43_56.zip
```

The diagnostic image file is actually a zipped file containing several files within it, each for a server subcomponent such as configuration, the JDBC data store, the persistent store, a cluster, deployments, and so on. The diagnostic image contains server state information pertaining to the JVM, Work Managers, JNDI, and the most recently harvested diagnostic data. You can view most of these files, though not all, in a text editor. Here, for example, is the image file component for Work Managers, located in the *WORK_MANAGER.img* file:

```
Total thread count   : 17
Idle thread count    : 0
Standby thread count: 13
Mean throughput      : 4.970178926441352
Requests accepted         : 223717
Requests started          : 223717
Requests Completed        : 223716
```

And here's a chunk of the diagnostic file for the persistent storage, located in the *PERSISTENT_STORE.img* file:

```
<Statistics>
  <NumObjects>45</NumObjects>
  <Creates>4</Creates>
  <Reads>27</Reads>
  <Updates>35</Updates>
  <Deletes>2</Deletes>
  <PhysicalWrites>40</PhysicalWrites>
  <PhysicalReads>27</PhysicalReads>
</Statistics>
```

You can examine the JDBC image file, located in the *JDBC.img* file, for details about the server's data sources, as the following excerpt shows:

```
Dumping Resource Pool:MedRecGlobalDataSourceXA
Resource Pool:MedRecGlobalDataSourceXA:dumpPool Current Capacity =
Dumping Resource Pool:MedRecGlobalDataSourceXA complete
Dumping Resource Pool:JDBC Data Source-0
...
Dumping Resource Pool: JDBC Data Source-0 complete
```

You'll notice that some of the captured diagnostic files are in a binary format and that you can't open them in a text editor. Oracle Support uses a special tool called the WLDF Browser to review the diagnostic information from a troubled server. One site where you can download this browser is http://weblogicserver.blogspot.com/2010/02/wldf-browser.html.

Using WLST for Capturing Diagnostic Images

Earlier, you learned how to set up diagnostic image capturing through the Administration Console. You can also use WLST to generate and download diagnostic images.

Generating an Image Capture with WLST Instead of using the Administration Console, you can also use the following set of WLST commands to generate an image capture by including them in a *.py* file:

```
url='t3://localhost:7011'
username='weblogic'
password='welcome1'
server='MedRecServer'
timeout=120
connect(username, password, url)
serverRuntime()
cd('WLDFRuntime/WLDFRuntime/WLDFImageRuntime/Image')
argTypes = jarray.array(['java.lang.Integer'],java.lang.String)
argValues = jarray.array([timeout],java.lang.Object)
invoke('captureImage', argValues, argTypes)
```

Downloading a Diagnostic Image Capture You can use the following WLST diagnostic commands to download diagnostic image captures from a server:

- ***getAvailableCapturedImages*** Gets the list of diagnostic images stored on a server.
- ***saveDiagnosticImageCaptureFile*** Gets a specific diagnostic image capture file.
- ***saveDiagnosticImageCaptureEntryFile*** Gets a specific entry such as the JRockit Flight Recorder diagnostic data for viewing in the JRockit Mission Control.

Configuring a Diagnostic Archive

WLDF offers a diagnostic archiving capability to enable the server to store all the events, logs, and metrics that it collects. You can access the data offline or online using WLST commands. You can configure either a file-based (default) store or one that uses database tables to store the archived data.

If you wish to use a file-based store, you must configure a WebLogic Server persistent store, as explained in Chapter 3. When you choose a file-based store for archiving, WebLogic Server uses a file, of course, to record the data and, by default, uses the *<domain_name>*\servers*<server_name>*\data\store\diagnostics directory. In the *config.xml* file for the server, a file-based store is represented as follows under the base element *<server>*:

```
<server-diagnostic-config>
  <diagnostic-store-dir>data/store/diagnostics</diagnostic-store-dir>
  <diagnostic-data-archive-type>FileStoreArchive</diagnostic-data-archive-type>
</server-diagnostic-config>
```

In the previous example, the *<diagnostic-data-archive-type>* element has the attribute *FileStoreArchive,* indicating that the server is using a file-based repository for archives. If you choose a database for storing the archives, the attribute will have the value *JDBCArchive* instead. If you want to specify a database as the repository, you must create two tables—the *wlst_events* table for storing instrumentation data and the *wls_hvst* table for storing Harvester-generated diagnostic data. You must also configure a valid JDBC data source for the database that hosts the repository.

You can configure the periodic deletion of older diagnostic data from the archives by setting automatic removal of data from the archives, either based on the size of the data or its age. You can set a maximum preferred size for the data store by specifying the *<preferred-store-size-limit>* element within the *<server-diagnostic-config>* element. You can also specify the removal of older data based on how long the data was in the store. Here's a snippet from a *config.xml* file showing how to specify both the size- and time-based deletion of diagnostic data:

```
<server-diagnostic-config>
  <diagnostic-store-dir>data/store/diagnostics</diagnostic-store-dir>
  <diagnostic-data-archive-type>FileStoreArchive</diagnostic-data-archive-type>
  <data-retirement-enabled>true</data-retirement-enabled>
  <preferred-store-size-limit>120</preferred-store-size-limit>
  <store-size-check-period>1</store-size-check-period>
  <wldf-data-retirement-by-age>
    <name>HarvestedDataRetirementPolicy</name>
    <enabled>true</enabled>
    <archive-name>HarvestedDataArchive</archive-name>
    <retirement-time>1</retirement-time>
    <retirement-period>24</retirement-period>
    <retirement-age>45</retirement-age>
  </wldf-data-retirement-by-age>
</server-diagnostic-config>
```

Note that the ability to configure the automatic removal of data from the archives is useful in systems where administrative data might be stored on a shared storage device, in order to separate it from the run-time data for the server.

Let's now turn to the configuration of the three major WLDF components: Instrumentation, the Harvester, and Watch and Notification. Before you learn how to configure these three major WLDF components, however, you first need to learn how to create diagnostic system modules, as you will use these modules for each of these WLDF components.

Using a Diagnostic System Module

Three WLDF components—the Harvester, Watch and Notification, and Instrumentation—require that you use a diagnostic system module to hold their configuration details. You can create multiple diagnostic system modules for a domain, but you can target only one module to each server or cluster. The system module is of the format DIAG_MODULE.*xml*, where DIAG_MODULE is the name of the module. You can optionally provide a name for the descriptor file, an XML file that the server creates, by default, in the <*domain_name*>\config\diagnostics directory.

Once you create a new diagnostic module through the Administration Console or WLST, the server adds a reference to the new diagnostic module in the server's *config.xml* file within the <*wldf-system-resource*> element. Here's an example showing how the *config.xml* file refers to a diagnostic module named *myDiagnosticModule1*. Note that the descriptor file for this module is named *myDiagnosticModule1-1111.xml* in the example:

```
<wldf-system-resource>
  <name>MedRecWLDF</name>
  <target>MedRecServer</target>
  <descriptor-file-name>diagnostics/MedRecWLDF.xml</descriptor-file-name>
</wldf-system-resource>
<wldf-system-resource>
  <name>myDiagnosticModule1</name>
  <descriptor-file-name>diagnostics/myDiagnosticModule1-1111.xml
</descriptor-file-name>
  <description>A diagnostic module with the Harvester, Watch and Notification
 and Instrumentation components.</description>
</wldf-system-resource>
```

The configuration of *myDiagnosticModule1* is stored in its descriptor file, *myDiagnosticModule1-1111.xml,* part of which looks like the following:

```
<wldf-resource>
  <name>myDiagnosticModule1</name>
  <watch-notification>
  ...
  </watch-notification>
  <harvestor>
  ...
  </harvestor>
  <instrumentation>
  ...
  </instrumentation>
</wldf-resource>
```

NOTE
You can only include the Instrumentation component in a diagnostic application module, as opposed to a diagnostic system module, wherein you can also include the Harvester and the Watch and Notification components. You configure application-scoped instrumentation in the weblogic-diagnostics.xml *descriptor file, which you package in the application archive.*

Note that the *<wldf-resource>* element in the preceding example contains all three possible WLDF components—the Harvester, Watch and Notification, and Instrumentation—which you can place in the descriptor file, *DIAG_MODULE.xml*. However, you may configure just one of these three components, in which case you need to include in the file only the component you are configuring.

Creating a Diagnostic System Module

This section describes how to create a generic diagnostic system module. Note that you don't need to create separate diagnostic modules for Instrumentation, Watch and Notification, and the Harvester—you can configure all three WLDF components in the same diagnostic system module. Here are the steps:

1. Click Lock & Edit in the Change Center of the Administration Console.
2. In the left-hand pane, go to Diagnostics | Diagnostic Modules.
3. Click New on the Summary Of Diagnostic Modules page.
4. On the Create A Diagnostics System Module page, enter a name such as **myDiagnosticModule1**, for example, and optionally enter its description in the Description box. Click OK.
5. You'll get a "Module Created Successfully" message and will be taken back to the Summary Of Diagnostic Modules page. Click the new module's name, which is myDiagnosticModule1 in this example.
6. In the Settings For myDiagnosticModule1 page, you can select the following options from the tabs at the top of the page:
   - Collected Metrics (for the Harvester)
   - Watches and Notifications
   - Instrumentation
7. Once you finish configuring some or all of the three WLDF components named here (the following sections in this chapter explain how to configure each of these components), click Save.
8. Click Targets to select the Managed Servers or clusters where you'd like to deploy your new diagnostic system module. Click Save.
9. Click the Activate Changes button in the Change Center of the Console.

Managing a Diagnostic System Module

You can target only one diagnostic module to a server or cluster, although you can create multiple diagnostic system modules to use at different times. You can then choose which module you want to target to a server or cluster at a specific time. You can target the same module to multiple servers or clusters.

Using Built-In Diagnostic System Modules

In Oracle WebLogic Server 12*c*, you have the option of using a set of built-in diagnostic system modules for performing basic health and performance monitoring. The built-in WLDF diagnostic system modules collect data from runtime MBeans that monitor the server components, such as JVM, JDBC, JMS, WebLogic Server run time, and store the data in the Diagnostic Archive.

A built-in diagnostic system module is enabled, by default, in each server instance in WebLogic domains configured to run in production mode. The built-in diagnostic system modules are disabled, by default, in domains running in development mode. You can enable or disable these modules dynamically, using either the WebLogic Server Administration Console or WLST.

You can clone and customize the built-in diagnostic system modules to fit your needs, say by removing or adding individual metrics. These modules come with a set of nonactivated watches and notifications. You can either activate these watches and notifications as they are, or customize them. You can access the data collected by the built-in diagnostic system modules using the Metrics Log table in the Administration Console or the Monitoring Dashboard, as well as through JMX or WLST.

There are three built-in diagnostic system module types:

- **Low** Captures the most important data from key WebLogic Server runtime MBeans (enabled by default in production mode).
- **Medium** Captures additional attributes from the WebLogic Server runtime MBeans captured by Low, as well as data from additional runtime MBeans.
- **High** Captures more verbose data from attributes on the WebLogic Server runtime MBeans than that captured by Medium, and also includes data from additional runtime MBeans.

You can configure a built-in diagnostic system module through the Administration Console by following these steps:

1. On the Administration Console home page, select Built-In Diagnostic Modules in the Diagnostics area.
2. On the Summary Of Built-in Diagnostic Modules page, select the server for which you want to configure the built-in diagnostics module.
3. In the Settings For *<server_name>* page, select the built-in diagnostic system module type you want to configure: Low, Medium, or High.

Once you select a built-in diagnostic system module for a server instance, it is automatically activated and begins collecting the data in the Diagnostic Archive. You can deactivate the module on the Summary Of Built-in Diagnostic Modules page by setting it to None.

Targeting Multiple Diagnostic Modules to a Server/Cluster

In earlier releases of WebLogic Server, you could target only a single diagnostic system module to a server or cluster. You couldn't have two files in the DOMAIN_HOME/config/diagnostics directory with an identical target server or cluster. In Oracle WebLogic Server 12*c*, you can target multiple diagnostic system modules to a server or cluster instance.

Configuring Metric Collection

Server MBeans such as the *ServerRuntimeMBean* contain metrics that are helpful in monitoring system performance. *Metrics* are various simple types of attributes of the server MBeans that the Harvester component of WLDF can collect at a sampling rate that you specify. To "harvest" the metric data, you must configure the harvestable data first. When you start the WebLogic Server instance, the server instantiates all runtime MBean types and thus becomes eligible for the harvesting or collecting of metrics. You can configure the Harvester for collecting server metrics through the Administration Console, WLST, or JMX. You can configure metric harvesting to capture some or all of the harvestable attributes of a named MBean type. For example, if you want to track the number of JDBC connections, you can do so by configuring the Harvester to collect the metrics for the *ActiveConnectionsCurrentCount* attribute of the *JDBCDataSourceRuntimeMBean*. You can also configure harvesting for all or some instances of the specified entity type.

Before you can configure the Harvester, first create a diagnostic system module, as shown earlier in this chapter, for holding the Harvester configuration. Make sure you also target the system module to the server you want to monitor.

NOTE
You can create metrics to monitor all or some attributes of an MBean type, and you can also monitor specific instances or all instances of an MBean type.

Configuring metric collection really means that you must specify which MBeans and which attributes of the MBeans you wish to monitor. Each server metric is based on an attribute value of the MBeans you select. You can configure metric collection through the WLDF Harvester component. As explained earlier, you must first configure a diagnostic system module before configuring the metric collection. Once you create (or select) a previously created module, on the Settings For *<module_name>* page, select Configuration | Collected Metrics. Here, you can specify the MBeans you want to monitor and specify the individual attributes of the MBeans.

For the MBean server location, Oracle recommends that you select the *ServerRuntime* MBean server rather than the *DomainRuntime* MBean server, which is the other available option. You can choose to collect metrics for all or some of the metrics, and you can create new metrics as well. You can enable or disable metric collection for an individual metric.

To collect metrics, you must configure the Harvester inside a diagnostic module. The following example shows part of the Harvester configuration elements in the *myWLDF.xml* file. Note that this configuration harvests metrics from two different runtime MBeans.

```
<wldf-resource>
<name>myWLDF</name>
  <harvester>
    <enabled>true</enabled>
    <sample-period>10000</sample-period>
    <harvested-type>
      <name>weblogic.management.runtime.ServerRuntimeMBean</name>
    </harvested-type>
    <harvested-type>
      <name>weblogic.management.runtime.WLDFHarvesterRuntimeMBean</name>
        <harvested-attribute>TotalSamplingTime</harvested-attribute>
        <harvested-attribute>CurrentSnapshotElapsedTime
        </harvested-attribute>
    </harvested-type>
    </harvester>
<!-- ----- Other elements ----- -->
</wldf-resource>
```

Following is a brief explanation of the key elements you need to configure for the Harvester:

- ***<sample-period>*** Sets the sample period for the Harvester, in milliseconds.
- ***<harvested-type>*** You can include one more of these elements to specify the type of data to harvest, with each element specifying an MBean type. In our example, metrics are harvested from two runtime MBeans; the *ServerRuntimeMBean* and the *WLDFHarvesterRuntimeMBean*.
- ***<harvested-instance>*** An optional element, you specify this to limit metric harvesting to a specific instance of a specific type. You can specify the instance by using its JMX object name in JMX canonical form or by using pattern matching. An MBean server interacts with all MBeans registered with the server by using the MBean object names. Once an MBean is registered with an MBean server, the object name is passed to all MBean server methods pertaining to this MBean. An object name consists of a domain name and the key property list in *key=value* format. For example, a *LogMBean* at the domain level manages the domain-wide log, and the *LogMBean* at the server level manages a server message log. You can indicate scope by specifying the instance of a specific type in the MBean's object name, as shown here:

  ```
  Medrec: Name=MedRecServer, Type=Log, Server=MedRecServer
  ```

  If you don't specify an instance, all instances of the specific type will be harvested.
- ***<harvested-attribute>*** An optional element that specifies that the server must collect metrics only for certain attributes of the specified type.

Configuring WLDF Instrumentation

You can use the WLDF Instrumentation component to insert a diagnostic code into both the server instances and the applications you deploy. Application-scoped instrumentation lets you configure instrumentation at the server level and within the applications you deploy.

The concept of instrumentation is analogous to aspect-oriented programming, which allows generating additional byte code into the application. The term *instrumentation* is often used to refer to the addition of code that uses *System.out.println* to help diagnose functional problems. For performance, *System.out.println* is often paired with timing code that takes the *currentTimeMillis* method both before and after an operation is completed and prints out the time to complete the operation. The WLDF Instrumentation component allows an administrator to integrate such timings into the code without having to go back to the development team and request that they incorporate the instrumentation in their code. It's a powerful tool for dynamically adding code that can quickly help evaluate various issues.

WLDF Instrumentation includes three major features—diagnostic context, diagnostic monitors, and diagnostic actions—and they are described in the following sections.

Diagnostic Context

The *diagnostic context* lets you control when a monitor triggers a diagnostic action. The context is information pertinent to a specific request, such as the IP address or user from where the request originates. The *context identifier* correlates a request through its entire journey. That is to say that the diagnostic context correlates the events generated by a request that starts in a servlet as a web service, uses multiple EJBs, and queues a JMS message, for example.

Diagnostic Monitors

Diagnostic monitors are the actual diagnostic code that you insert into an application or the server instance at specific locations. The definition of a monitor can have a server-wide scope or an application scope. When defining a monitor, you must describe both where you want the code to be injected and what you want that code to do. The following terms are derived from aspect-oriented programming and are how you can describe a specific location in the code:

- **Join point** This is a specific location within a class, such as the entry or exit point of a method.
- **Pointcut** Specifies a set of join points (locations in the code) that generally describe a particular class of work. The join points are generally described in terms of a method signature pattern, which may include wild cards.
- **Diagnostic location** Given that a pointcut defines a method signature, the diagnostic location tells the framework whether the code injection is to take place before, after, or around a particular invocation.

There are three types of diagnostic monitors: standard, delegating, and custom. You can use a standard or delegating monitor at the server or application level, but you can only use the custom monitors for application-level instrumentation. Here's a brief explanation of the three types of diagnostic monitors:

- **Standard** There are two built-in monitors that have predefined behavior and that can only be enabled or disabled. *DyeInjection* is the only server-scoped standard diagnostic monitor, and *HttpSessionDebug* is the only application-scoped standard diagnostic monitor.
- **Delegating** These monitors come preconfigured with their scope and locations, but they require that you specify the action that the monitor will perform. Some interesting code locations where actions can be inserted include getting a JDBC connection from a pool, executing an SQL statement, invoking an EJB, or queuing a JMS message. The full set of delegating monitors along with the actions they can perform are documented with the product as part of the WLDF Instrumentation Library.
- **Custom** These monitors allow you to leverage the full power of the WLDF instrumentation capabilities in your own application code. They are the most flexible type of monitors and allow you to define all aspects of instrumentation.

Diagnostic Actions

For each delegating or custom monitor, you must associate an appropriate diagnostic action. A *diagnostic action* refers to the specific action that a diagnostic monitor will take when the server triggers a diagnostic monitor. Here are some examples of diagnostic actions that you can attach to a delegating or custom monitor:

- ***TraceElapsedTimeAction*** Generates events before and after the execution of an associated join point and computes the elapsed time. This allows you to time specific container or application code without modifying the code itself.
- ***TraceMemoryAllocationAction*** Similar to *TraceElapsedTimeAction*, traces the number of bytes allocated by a thread during a method call.

- ***StackDumpAction*** Generates an instrumentation event at the affected location to capture a stack dump. This action is useful when trying to track down the context in which a particular code path is being executed. Imagine a case in which you know that a particular routine is being invoked, but you can't determine the circumstances in which that is happening. Defining a custom monitor in your application and associating it with a *StackDumpAction* would allow you to obtain this information without modifying your application code to introduce a print stack trace into the code.

A monitor can be classified into one of three types, depending on when it can be called: a *before monitor* is triggered before the application code is called; an *after monitor* fires after the application code is called; and an *around monitor* is triggered both before and after the application code is called. You can, for example, create a monitor named *Servlet_Around_Service* and associate it with the diagnostic action *TraceElapsedTimeAction*. You can also specify a diagnostic location with the *<location-type>* element, with two "around" locations—before and after. The diagnostic actions will be *TraceElapsedTimeAction-Before* and *TraceElapsedTimeAction-After* for those diagnostic monitors.

Configuration Files

You can configure instrumentation at the server or application level, or at both levels simultaneously. A system-level configuration file is stored in the *<domain_name>*\config\diagnostics directory within a diagnostic descriptor file (*DIAG_MODULE.xml*). For each file, you choose the diagnostic monitor to use and the diagnostic actions you want to associate with that monitor. You can create multiple *DIAG_MODULE.xml* files, but you must deploy just one of these files at any given time. Because you can dynamically add and remove monitors as well as enable and disable them, you gain flexibility by configuring multiple *DIAG_MODULE.xml* files to meet different monitoring needs. The *<instrumentation>* element in the server diagnostic module (*DIAG_MODULE.xml* file) contains the instrumentation configuration, within the parent element *<wldf-resource>*, as shown here:

```
<wldf-resource>
  <name>MyDiagnosticModule1</name>
  <instrumentation>
    <enabled>true</enabled>
...
  <instrumentation>
</wldf-resource>
```

You include an application-level instrumentation configuration in an application's archive, inside the *weblogic-diagnostics.xml* file, located under the META-INF directory. Make sure that you enable server-level instrumentation first, because you can't instrument application-level instrumentation without enabling instrumentation at the server level. You configure application-level instrumentation using the same *<instrumentation>* element and the *<wldf-instrumentation-monitor>* subelement within the *weblogic-diagnostics.xml* descriptor file. The *<instrumentation>* module will be identical to that shown for a server-level instrumentation. You can update the configuration of application-level modules through the Administration Console, and you can dynamically update the configuration by using a deployment plan.

NOTE
You must enable instrumentation at the server level before you can enable it at the application level.

Creating Request Performance Data

Once you configure a server or application-scoped instrumentation, you can view the performance data captured by the Instrumentation component on the Request Performance page in the Administration Console. Make sure that you create and configure a WLDF system resource and target it to the server first. You can use either the Console or WLST commands to do this. You must also enable the Instrumentation component. In addition, an application instrumentation descriptor must use the *TraceElapsedTimeAction* diagnostic action attached to an *Around* type diagnostic monitor, as shown here:

```
<instrumentation>
  <enabled>true</enabled>
  <wldf-instrumentation-monitor>
    <name>Connector_Around_Inbound</name>
    <action>TraceElapsedTimeAction</action>
  </wldf-instrumentation-monitor>
</instrumentation>
```

You can make instrumentation changes to a deployed application if you enable the "hot swap" feature before deploying the application and if you use a deployment plan. If you haven't enabled hot swap or if you aren't using a deployment plan, you must redeploy the newly instrumented application.

Configuring System-Level Instrumentation

You can configure system-level instrumentation for a WebLogic Server instance through the Administration Console. The first step is to configure a system-level diagnostic module, as explained earlier in this chapter. Once you have done so, you're ready to configure instrumentation. The next two sections outline the steps you must follow to configure system-level instrumentation.

Adding a Diagnostic Monitor Once you have a diagnostic system module ready, you need to add a diagnostic monitor to that module. When the server invokes a certain location in the server or application code, the diagnostic monitor will execute specific diagnostic actions that you configure. Here are the steps for adding a diagnostic monitor to a diagnostic module:

1. Click Lock & Edit in the Change Center of the Administration Console.
2. Go to Diagnostics | Diagnostic Modules.
3. Choose the module in the Summary Of Diagnostic Modules page.
4. Select Configuration | Instrumentation in the Settings For *<module_name>* page.
5. Add a diagnostic monitor by clicking the Add/Remove button.
6. Select one or more of the predefined diagnostic monitors from the Available list, and select the attributes for the monitors by the moving them to the Chosen list. Click OK.
7. Click Activate Changes in the Change Center of the Console.

You have the diagnostic monitor now, but you need to configure it, as the next section explains.

Configuring a Diagnostic Monitor This section shows you how to configure system-scoped instrumentation in a diagnostic system module. Here are the steps:

1. Click Lock & Edit in the Change Center of the Administration Console.
2. Go to Diagnostics | Diagnostic Modules.
3. Click the name of the diagnostic module in the Summary Of Diagnostic Modules page.
4. Select Configuration | Instrumentation in the Settings For *<module_name>* page.
5. Click the name of the diagnostic monitor you wish to configure from under the Diagnostic Monitors heading in this module section.
6. Use the Settings For *<diagnostic monitor>* page to configure system-level instrumentation. Note that you can add just the predefined diagnostic monitors with their predefined actions for system-level instrumentation. To instrument applications, use the Deployments | *<application>* | Settings for *<app_modulename>* | Configuration | Instrumentation instead. Here, you can create a custom diagnostic monitor or just use a predefined monitor. Here are the configuration options for both system- and application-level diagnostic monitors:
   - **Enabled** Enables instrumentation for this diagnostic module.
   - **Name** Name of the diagnostic module.
   - **Type** You can specify a standard or delegating diagnostic monitor. Note that application-level instrumentation can't specify a standard diagnostic monitor.
   - **Actions** Specifies the diagnostic action for this monitor, such as *ThreadDumpAction* and *TraceAction,* for example. Again, standard monitors have actions, but they're fixed. You can only specify diagnostic actions for delegating and custom diagnostic monitors.
7. Click Save and then click Activate Changes in the Console.

Configuring a DyeInjection Diagnostic Monitor

One of the challenges with using the diagnostics framework on a loaded production system is dealing with the sheer volume of data that is generated. DyeInjection is one of the key tools that WLDF provides for classifying and filtering this mass of diagnostic data. The key idea behind this is to reduce the volume of diagnostic data to a manageable amount, making it easier to classify and correlate the data. The Instrumentation component of WLDF lets you follow request processing as the request flows through the system. A diagnostic context lets you uniquely identify a request by attaching a diagnostic context to a request using request characteristics such as the username or the IP address from which the request originates. You configure a DyeInjection monitor to manage a diagnostic context. The diagnostic context is simple: it consists of a unique context ID and a 64-bit dye vector. The unique context ID lets you determine the specific events and log entries for a request as the request vends its way through the system. The dye vector contains flags that help identify the diagnostic context of the request. Let's say a client makes an HTTP request. As soon as the HTTP request enters the system, the server tags (dyes) the request with diagnostic context and maintains that context through the entire lifecycle of the request, regardless of thread boundaries.

Although the context ID uniquely identifies a request, it's the 64-bit dye vector that lets you capture the request's attributes. Each of the bits in a dye vector is a flag (dye flag) that can be either set or unset to indicate the presence or absence of a specific request attribute. Each dye flag is set if the diagnostic context for a request of the attribute is present—otherwise, that dye flag isn't set. You configure a DyeInjection monitor by assigning specific values to each of the dyes in the 64-bit dye vector. Any dyes you don't explicitly assign values to will simply remain unset, with the exception of the PROTOCOL dye flags. For example, you must assign values for dye flags such as *USERn* and *ADDRn,* but the server will automatically inject the appropriate protocol dye for flags such as *PROTOCOL_HTTP, PROTOCOL_SSL,* or *PROTOCOL_T3*. For example, the server injects all requests that use the SSL protocol with the *PROTOCOL_SSL* dye. Here are some of the important dye flags that the DyeInjection monitor supports:

- ***ADDR1, ADDR2, ADDR3, ADDR4*** Specify the IP address of clients making requests.
- ***USER1, USER2, USER3, USER4*** Specify the usernames of clients making requests to the server.
- ***THROTTLE*** A special dye that determines how often the server dyes a request. The *THROTTLE* dye is set in a diagnostic context if the DyeInjection monitor's *THROTTLE_INTERVAL* and/or the *THROTTLE_RATE* properties are satisfied.

Let's say you configure the dye flag *ADDR1* to represent the originating client IP address of 127.0.0.1 and the flag *USER2* to reflect the user admin@mycompany.com. When the admin user from mycompany.com sends a request from the IP address 127.0.0.1, the dye vector for this request will have the *USER2* and *ADDR1* flags set. The *USER1, USER3, USER4, ADDR2, ADDR3,* and *ADDR4* flags will remain unset. The same goes for the rest of the dye flags.

To create a diagnostic context for requests, you must configure and enable a DyeInjection monitor. To configure a DyeInjection monitor, you follow the same procedures shown earlier for configuring a diagnostic monitor. That is, you must first create a diagnostic system module and then enable instrumentation for that module. When you enable instrumentation in a diagnostic system module, the DyeInjection monitor is automatically enabled and it creates a diagnostic context for all requests made to the server. Create a new diagnostic monitor and follow the steps listed earlier in this chapter for configuring a diagnostic monitor. Once you enable your new DyeInjection monitor, specify the attributes you want to capture in the diagnostic context by specifying values for the various dye flags. For each dye, you must specify a name/value pair, such as the one shown here:

```
ADDR1=127.0.0.1
USER2=admin@mycompany.com
```

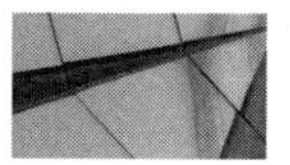

NOTE
If you disable the DyeInjection monitor, the server will not create a diagnostic context for an incoming request.

If you don't set any properties for the DyeInjection monitor, it will contain the unique context ID and the dye vector will have a dye flag set for one of the implicit *PROTOCOL* dyes.

TIP
You can enable only one DyeInjection monitor at any time for a diagnostic system module.

Once you configure the DyeInjection monitor, the *DIAG_MODULE.xml* file will show the following:

```
<instrumentation>
  <enabled>true</enabled>
  <wldf-instrumentation-monitor>
    <name>DyeInjection</name>
    <enabled>true</enabled>
    <dye-mask xsi:nil="true"></dye-mask>
    <properties>ADDR1=127.0.0.1
        USER2=admin@mycompany</properties>
  </wldf-instrumentation-monitor>
</instrumentation>
```

When you enable instrumentation in a diagnostic module, the server turns on all diagnostic monitors, including the DyeInjection monitor (unless you've disabled the monitor individually). The DyeInjection monitor creates a diagnostic context for each request to the server as soon as the request enters the system. You can disable the creation of the diagnostic contexts by disabling the DyeInjection monitor.

Restricting the Triggering of Monitoring

WebLogic Server lets you configure *dye filtering* to restrict the automatic triggering of a delegating or custom diagnostic system monitor. The way you do this is by specifying a *dye mask* for a delegating monitor to specify a selection for dyes from the DyeInjection monitor. This means that you must first create and enable a DyeInjection monitor in order for a custom or delegating monitor to use dye filtering. Dye filtering enables delegating and custom monitors to inspect the dyes injected into the diagnostic context by the DyeInjection monitor and execute diagnostic actions only when the dye vector matches the dye mask. This lets the server proceed with diagnostic actions only for the specific requests that you configure.

You configure dye filtering when you create a custom or delegated diagnostic system monitor or at any time later on. Simply select the diagnostic monitor for which you want to restrict the triggering of monitoring. Check the Enable Dye Filtering check box in the Dye Mask section to turn on dye filtering. Once you do this, select the dye masks from the table.

TIP
You can't add dye filtering to a DyeInjection monitor.

Here's a typical server-scoped instrumentation configuration, described in the *DIAG_MODULE.xml* file that shows a DyeInjection monitor and a custom monitor named *Connector_Before_Work,* which uses dye filtering:

```
<wldf-resource>
  <instrumentation>
    <enabled>true</enabled>
    <wldf-instrumentation-monitor>
      <name>DyeInjection</name>
      <description>Inject USER2 and ADDR2 dyes</description>
      <enabled>true</enabled>
      <properties>USER2=weblogic
```

```
        ADDR1=127.0.0.1</properties>
    </wldf-instrumentation-monitor>
    <wldf-instrumentation-monitor>
      <name>Connector_Before_Work</name>
      <enabled>true</enabled>
      <action>TraceAction</action>
      <dye-filtering-enabled>true</dye-filtering-enabled>
      <dye-mask>USER2</dye-mask>
    </wldf-instrumentation-monitor>
  </instrumentation>
</wldf-resource>
```

Thus far, you've been looking at server-scoped diagnostic monitors. Configuring an application-scoped diagnostic monitor is similar. You define the application-scoped monitors in the *weblogic-diagnostic.xml* file, and a chunk of that file is shown here:

```
<wldf-instrumentation-monitor>
  <name>DyeInjection</name>
  <enabled>true</enabled>
  <properties>ADDR2=127.0.0.1 USER2=admin@mycompany.com</properties>
</wldf-instrumentation-monitor>
<wldf-instrumentation-monitor>
  <name>Servlet_Around_Service</name>
  <dye-mask>ADDR2 USER2</dye-mask>
  <dye-filtering-enabled>true</dye-filtering-enabled>
  <action>TraceElapsedTimeAction</action>
</wldf-instrumentation-monitor>
```

The WLDF monitor library provides the *Servlet_Before_Service* and the *Servlet_Around_Service* diagnostic monitors.

Controlling the Volume of Instrumented Events

You can configure the special dye *THROTTLE* to limit the number of requests a single diagnostic monitor can process. You can configure the *THROTTLE* dye by setting the following two properties:

- **Throttle Interval** Specifies the time (in milliseconds) that the DyeInjection monitor must wait before it dyes a new request with *THROTTLE*. If you set the *THROTTLE_INTERVAL* to 0, the monitor won't dye any requests with *THROTTLE*.
- **Throttle Rate** Specifies the frequency with which the DyeInjection monitor dyes new requests with the *THROTTLE* dye. If you set the Throttle Rate to 10, every tenth request will be dyed with the *THROTTLE* dye.

Note that you need to assign a positive value to only one of the two throttle properties, in order for the server to dye a request with the *THROTTLE* dye.

NOTE
Dye masks and dye filtering enable you to specify which requests the server can pass to the delegating and custom diagnostic monitors.

Configuring Watches and Notifications

Because you need to configure the Watch and Notification component of WLDF through a diagnostic system module, you must first create a new diagnostic system module. If you already have a diagnostic system module, you can also use that module to configure the Watch and Notification component.

A *watch* is any event that you want to monitor by analyzing the logs, data events, and metrics of a running server. You can specify watch rules in the form of alarm settings or expressions to let the server know which event or situation should trigger a notification. A *notification* is the action the server must take when a watch rule expression comes true or the server reaches the threshold of an alarm setting. The server can send notifications through e-mails (SMTP), through JMX, JMS, or SNMP, or through diagnostic images. You configure watches and notifications separately, but you must associate a watch with a notification in order for the server to react to a critical diagnostic event by, say, sending the WebLogic Server administrator e-mails when the server crashes. Watches and notifications offer great flexibility since you can associate a watch with multiple notifications and a single notification with multiple watches.

To set up any type of notification, such as a JMS notification, you must first create one or more watch rules. *Watch rules* are logical expressions that you specify with the WLDF query language. Each watch rule specifies an event that the watch must detect. For example, here's a watch rule for a log watch (one of the watch types) that detects all server messages with the severity level *Critical* and a specified message ID:

```
(SEVERITY = 'Critical') AND (MSGID = 'BEA-149618')
```

The Watch and Notification system can monitor quite a few events in a running server:

- Log watches trigger notifications when they spot a specific message, severity level, or string in the logs.
- Instrumentation watches, also called *event watches,* trigger notifications when an Instrumentation service generates a specific event.
- Harvester watches trigger a notification when a watch rule identifies a performance issue, such as memory usage beyond a specified threshold.

In order to configure a Watch and Notification system, you must specify settings for both watches and notifications in the *DIAG_MODULE.xml* file, which is the WLDF system resource descriptor file. Note that regardless of which WLDF component you're using, such as the Harvester, Instrumentation, or Watch and Notification, you must specify it with the *<wldf-resource>* element. Under the *<wldf-resource>* element, the base element will be the *<watch-notification>* element if you're configuring watches and notifications. You define each watch within a *<watch>* element. Note that each *<watch>* element is followed by one or more notifications within the appropriately named element, such as *<jmx-notification>* for JMX notifications and *<image-notification>* for image watches. The following example shows the structure of the *DIAG_MODULE.xml* file configured with watches and notifications:

```
<wldf-resource>
  <watch-notification>
    <watch>
      <!-- A watch rule -->
    </watch>
```

```
    <watch>
      <!-- A watch rule -->
    </watch>
    <snmp-notification>
    </snmp-notification>
    <image-notification>
    </image-notification>
  </watch-notification>
</wldf-resource>
```

Configuring Notifications

Following are the five types of diagnostic notifications that you can configure with a watch. When a watch rule evaluates to true, the server will trigger the notification. Note that the first four notification types are based on the delivery mode (that is, SMTP, JMX, JMS, or SNMP).

- **SMTP notifications** These are e-mail messages that the server sends when an associated watch is triggered. You must first configure an SMTP mail session, as shown in Chapter 4, before using an SMTP notification. In the *DIAG_MODULE.xml* file, the SMTP mail session you've configured will use the *<mail-session-jndi-name>* element. You can specify the appropriate values for the *<subject>*, *<body>*, and *<recipients>* subelements. Of these three, only the subelement *<recipients>* is mandatory—you must provide at least one e-mail recipient's name for receiving the SMTP notification e-mail message.
- **JMX notifications** WLDF issues a JMX notification when an associated watch rule evaluates to true. The element *<jmx-notification>* identifies this type of notification.
- **JMS notifications** The server posts the messages to the JMS queue or topic you specify in the *<destination-jndi-name>* element. You must also specify the connection factory with the *<connection-factory-jndi-name>* element. The base element of a JMS notification is *<jms-notification>*.
- **SNMP notifications** The server posts SNMP traps when an SNMP notification is triggered. To use an SNMP notification, you must first configure SNMP. Specifying an SNMP notification is easy—all you have to do is provide a notification name, as shown here:

```
<watch-notification>
  <watch>
  </watch>
  <snmp-notification>
    <name>mySNMPNotif</name>
  </snmp-notification>
</watch-notification>
```

- **Image notifications** An image notification lets you create a Diagnostic Image Capture, which is a snapshot of the system state, in response to an event or error. Since a Diagnostic Image Capture automatically includes the JRockit Flight Recording (JFR) file, it is particularly effective in diagnosing fluctuations in application and server performance, as well as occasional errors.

You can enable each individual watch and notification that you configure. You may also turn all watches and notifications on and off. By default, the watches and notifications that you configure and target to a server are enabled and thus will have the *<enabled>true</enabled>* value in the *DIAG_MODULE.xml* file.

Configuring Watches

You can configure three types of watches: harvester, log, and instrumentation watches. The *harvester* and *log* watches trigger notifications based on real-time server events, whereas the *instrumentation* watches wait for the harvest cycle to complete before triggering notifications. Harvester watches harvest monitoring information from the runtime MBean server, whereas log watches monitor the server log messages. The third watch type, instrumentation watches, monitor the events generated by the WLDF Instrumentation component.

Note that you can enable and disable watches at the individual or global watch level. If you disable watches at the global level, this overrides the settings for individual watches so the server disables all watches.

You configure each of the three types of watches in a similar fashion by setting the following configuration options:

- **Severity options** By default, a watch is set to a severity level of *Notice* when it triggers a notification. You can set the severity value to be passed to a notification by using the subelement *<severity>* when configuring a watch.
- **Notifications** When a watch condition becomes true, the watch triggers a notification. You specify the notifications in the *<notification>* element. The preceding section of this chapter, "Configuring Notifications," offers details about the various configuration options for notifications.
- **Watch rule expression** You specify the events the watch must trap by defining a watch rule expression inside the *<rule-expression>* element. You use the WLDF query language to specify a logical expression that specifies when this watch must trigger a notification. Here's a log event watch rule that looks for server messages with the severity level *Critical* and ID BEA-149618:

  ```
  (SEVERITY = 'Critical') AND (MSGID = 'BEA-149618')
  ```

  A watch rule can monitor harvestable runtime MBeans and trigger notifications when a runtime MBean attribute shows a performance issue such as high memory usage, for example. Watch rules can also monitor the messages logged to the server log, as well as events generated by the WLDF Instrumentation component.
- **Alarm options** You can specify whether a watch triggers a notification just once or multiple times using the *<alarm-type>* element. If you set the value of the *<alarm-type>* element to its default value of *None,* the watch will trigger a notification whenever it's possible to do so. Specify the value *ManualReset* if you want the watch to fire only once. You can also specify the value *AutomaticReset* to configure multiple notification triggers.

Creating a Watch You can create a watch through the Administration Console, but first you must create a diagnostic system module as described earlier in the chapter. Follow these steps to create a watch:

1. Click Lock & Edit in the Change Center of the Administration Console.
2. Go to Diagnostics | Diagnostic Modules and click the name of the system module.

3. Select Configuration | Watches and Notifications | Watches and click New.
4. On the Create Watch page, name the watch you're configuring. Select a watch type from the Watch Type list. Select Collected Metrics to set a harvester watch, Server Log to set a log watch, and Event Data to set an instrumentation watch.
5. You can enable the watch at this point by selecting the Enable Watch box. (You can also disable the watch from here later.) Click Next.
6. Construct a watch rule. Click Add Expressions to create an expression or click Edit and manually enter the watch rule. Click Next when done.
7. Select an alarm option on the Create Watch page. The alarm option you set determines when the server reevaluates a watch expression after it evaluates to true the first time. You can specify Don't Use An Alarm, for example, if you want the server to continue to evaluate the watch expression automatically. Click Next.
8. You can assign one or more notifications for your new watch by moving the notifications from the Available list to the Chosen list. The "Configuring Notifications" section earlier in this chapter shows how to configure notifications.
9. Click Finish and activate the watch configuration by clicking Activate Changes in the Console.

Watch Examples Here are simple examples that show the configuration of different types of watches. Here's a typical log watch:

```
<watch>
  <name>myLogWatch</name>
  <rule-type>Log</rule-type>
  <rule-expression>MSGID='BEA-000360'</rule-expression>
  <severity>Info</severity>
  <notification>myMailNotif1</notification>
</watch>
```

And here's an example that shows how to configure an instrumentation watch:

```
<watch-notification>
  <watch>
    <name>myInstWatch</name>
    <enabled>true</enabled>
    <rule-type>EventData</rule-type>
    <rule-expression>
      (PAYLOAD &gt; 100000000) AND (MONITOR = 'Servlet_Around_Service')
    </rule-expression>
    <alarm-type xsi:nil="true"></alarm-type>
    <notification>mySMTPNotification</notification>
  </watch>
  <smtp-notification>
    ...
  </smtp-notification>
</watch-notification>
```

Here's an example that shows a watch that monitors stuck threads and triggers a notification:

```
<August 13, 2013 7:55 AM > <Notice> <Diagnostics> <BEA-320068> <Watch
'StuckThread' with severity 'Notice' on server 'AdminServer' has triggered at
 June 26, 2011 7:55  AM. Notification details:
WatchRuleType: Log
WatchRule: (SEVERITY = 'Error') AND ((MSGID = 'WL-000337') OR (MSGID = 'BEA-
000337'))
WatchData: DATE = August 13, 2013  7:55 AM  SERVER = AdminServer MESSAGE = [STUCK]
 ExecuteThread: '1' for queue: 'weblogic.kernel.Default (self-tuning)' has been
 busy for "600" seconds working on the request
"weblogic.work.SelfTuningWorkManagerImpl$WorkAdapterImpl@121008b4", which is more
than the configured time (StuckThreadMaxTime) of "600" seconds. Stack trace:
Thread-23 "[STUCK] ExecuteThread: '1' for queue: 'weblogic.kernel.Default (self-
tuning)'" <alive, in native, suspended, priority=1, DAEMON> {
```

Accessing the WLDF Diagnostic Data

Thus far, you've seen how to configure the collection of various types of diagnostic data using WLDF components. How do you access all this data? Fortunately, WLDF stores data on a per-server basis and offers the Data Accessor component to provide access to those data stores. The Data Accessor component helps you access diagnostic data (metrics) from harvesters that you configure as well other server log and event records. You can use the WLDF query language to query the Diagnostic Archive through a JMX accessor interface. The Data Accessor can retrieve data from data store types such as *HTTP_LOG*, *SERVER_LOG*, *EVENTS_DATA_ARCHIVE*, and *HARVESTED_DATA_ARCHIVE*. The Administration Console displays the collected data in the Summary Of Log Files page. You can programmatically access the data through the WLDF *AccessRuntimeMBean*. However, WLST offers commands that let you easily access diagnostic data, both offline and online. Following are some of the WLST diagnostic commands you can use:

- ***exportDiagnosticData*** This is a WLST offline command that lets you capture a specific log file's contents to an XML file:

```
wls:/offline> exportDiagnosticData(logicalName='ServerLog', logName='myserver.
log', exportFileName='myExport.xml')

Input parameters: {logicalName='ServerLog', logName='myserver.log',
logRotationDir='.', storeDir='../data/store/diagnostics', query='',
exportFileName='myExport.xml', elfFields='', beginTimestamp=0L,
endTimestamp=9223372036854775807L}
Exporting diagnostic data to myExport.xml ...
< August 13, 2013 9:23:44 PM EDT> <Info> <Store> <BEA-280008>
<Opening the persistent file store "WLS_DIAGNOSTICS" for recovery:
directory=C:\Oracle\Middleware\Oracle_Home\wlserver\common\data\store\
diagnostics requestedWritePolicy="Disabled" fileLockingEnabled=true
driver="wlfileio3".>
< August 13, 2013  9:23:44 PM EDT> <Info> <Store> <BEA-280009>
<The persistent file store "WLS_DIAGNOSTICS" (83d8fc7e-f122-4383-aef8-
d9bd15b189ce) has been opened:blockSize=512 actualWritePolicy="Disabled(single-
handle-non-direct)" explicitIOEnforced=false records=0.>
Exported diagnostic data successfully.
wls:/offline>
```

- ***exportDiagnosticDataFromServer*** This is an online command that lets you retrieve exported WLDF data and save it to an XML file, as shown in this example:

```
wls:/medrec-spring/serverRuntime>
exportDiagnosticDataFromServer(logicalName="HTTPAccessLog",
 exportFileName="myExport.xml")
Connecting to http://MIROPC61:7011 with userid weblogic ...
Exported diagnostic data to myExport.xml
wls:/medrec-spring/serverRuntime>
```

- ***saveDiagnosticImageCaptureFile*** This is an online command that lets you download a specific diagnostic image capture, as shown here:

```
wls:/medrec-spring/serverRuntime> images=getAvailableCapturedImages()
Connecting to http://localhost:7011 with userid weblogic ...
wls:/medrec-spring/serverRuntime> saveDiagnosticImageCaptureFile(images[0])
Retrieving diagnostic_image_MedRecServer_2013_08_15_21_43_56.zip to local path
 diagnostic_image_MedRecServer_2013_08_15_21_43_56.zip
Connecting to http://localhost:7011 with userid weblogic ...
wls:/medrec-spring/serverRuntime>
```

In addition to the WLST commands shown here, in Oracle WebLogic Server 12*c*, WLDF has added the following WLST commands:

- ***listSystemResourceControls()*** Lists all available diagnostic system modules.
- ***enableSystemResource()*** Activates a diagnostic system module.
- ***disableSystemResource()*** Deactivates a diagnostic system module.
- ***createSystemResourceControl()*** Creates a diagnostic system module on-the-fly using a specified descriptor file.
- ***destroySystemResourceControl()*** Destroys a diagnostics system module previously created on-the-fly.
- ***dumpDiagnosticData()*** Dumps the diagnostics data from a harvester to a local file.

Monitoring WebLogic Server Instances

Monitoring a WebLogic server production instance involves much more than the monitoring of a server's run-time events. To manage your deployed applications effectively, you must monitor all the following: the server, the JVM, the JDBC connection pool, the connectors (to EIS systems), JMS, JTA, the network channels, and the EJBs. You can use the Administration Console as well as WLST commands that interrogate various runtime MBeans to perform your monitoring tasks. The following sections introduce you to the various WebLogic Server monitoring techniques.

Monitoring with the Administration Console

Thus far in this book, you've learned how to use the Administration Console to configure various aspects of a WebLogic Server environment. For a WebLogic Server administrator, the console is equally indispensable for monitoring running server instances, including the various subsystems such as security, JTA, and JDBC. Let's quickly review the most important server monitoring features that you can access through the Administration Console.

To access the main monitoring page for a domain, go to Environment | Servers and click the Admin Server link. In the Settings For *<server_name>* page, click the Monitoring tab. The main Monitoring page shows the general runtime information for the server, such as WebLogic Home, Java Version, and OS Version. It also provides a table that shows all the services such as the JDBC and JMS services that are running on this server. You can monitor all aspects of a running server instance by clicking the various subtabs on this page, such as JDBC, JMS, JTA, SAF, and so on, to drill down to the individual services. Following is a brief explanation of the key pages you can reach from the main monitoring page.

Threads

The Threads page shows the thread activity, including the status of the thread pool, the execute queue backlog, the throughput of requests, and details for individual threads. Figure 6-3 shows the Threads page. There are two tables on this page: the first table shows a summary of the Self-Tuning Thread Pool (there's only one of these per server), including the number of total execute threads and the active execute threads. In Figure 6-3, the execute Queue Length is 0, meaning there are no waiting requests because this is a test server—on a production server, you may not find this to be true! You can also check the Completed Request Count and the Pending User Request Count to get an idea about how busy the thread activity is right now. You can also check Throughput numbers and the current Health status (it must be OK).

The second table on the Threads page shows details about individual threads in the thread pool. For each thread, you can find the current request that the thread is handling, as well as whether the thread is in the Idle, Stuck, or Standby status.

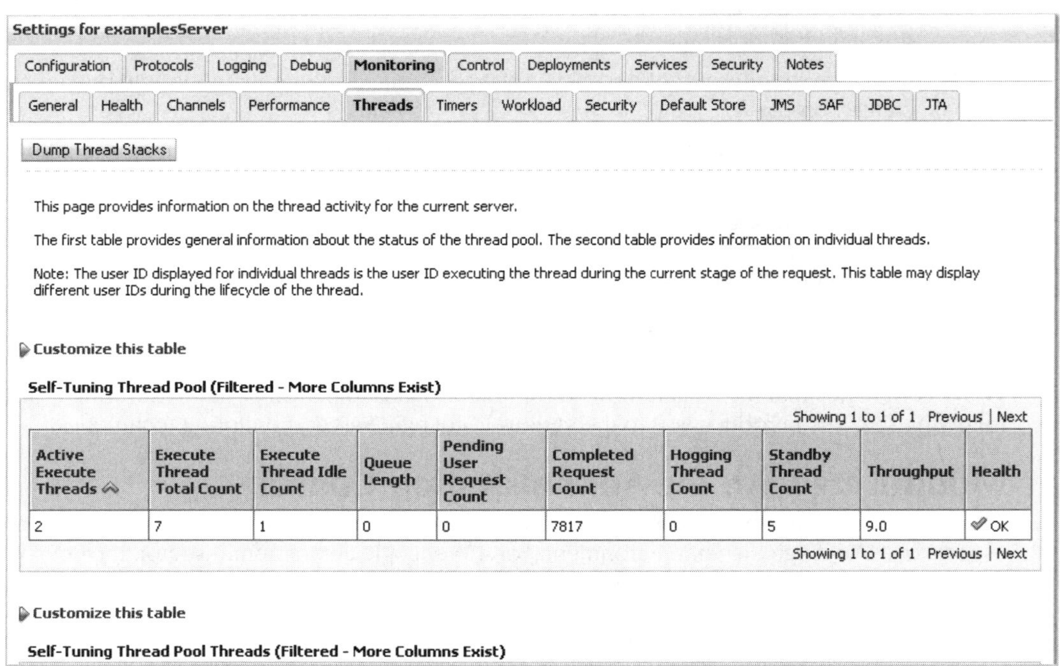

FIGURE 6-3. *The Threads Monitoring page in the Administration Console*

You can click the Dump Thread Stacks button at the top of this page to display the thread stack for each thread. Here's an excerpt from the thread dump:

```
Current thread stacks for server examplesServer
This page displays the current stacks for each thread.

            "[ACTIVE] ExecuteThread: '10' for queue: 'weblogic.kernel.Default
(self-tuning)'" RUNNABLE native
                    java.net.PlainSocketImpl.socketConnect(Native Method)
                    java.net.PlainSocketImpl.doConnect(PlainSocketImpl.java:351)
java.net.PlainSocketImpl.connectToAddress(PlainSocketImpl.java:213)
                    java.net.PlainSocketImpl.connect(PlainSocketImpl.java:200)
                    java.net.SocksSocketImpl.connect(SocksSocketImpl.java:366)
          java.net.Socket.connect(Socket.java:529)
          java.net.Socket.connect(Socket.java:478)
          java.net.Socket.<init>(Socket.java:375)
                    java.net.Socket.<init>(Socket.java:189)
...          "main" waiting for lock weblogic.t3.srvr.T3Srvr@d2b2ce WAITING
                    java.lang.Object.wait(Native Method)
                    java.lang.Object.wait(Object.java:485)
                    weblogic.t3.srvr.T3Srvr.waitForDeath(T3Srvr.java:983)
                    weblogic.t3.srvr.T3Srvr.run(T3Srvr.java:490)
                    weblogic.Server.main(Server.java:74)
```

Performance

The Performance page shows details about the JVM performance by showing performance statistics on the following:

- **Heap Free Current** The current memory that's available in the Java heap.
- **Heap Size Current** Also called "heap size," this is the amount of memory currently allocated to the JVM's heap.
- **Heap Size Max** The maximum memory configured for this JVM.
- **Heap Free Percent** The percent of memory that's free.

Figure 6-4 shows the Administration Console's Performance Monitoring page. You can force garbage collection of unused resources by clicking the Garbage Collect button. You can also do a thread stack dump by clicking the Dump Thread Stacks button. The resulting output shows the current stacks for each thread.

Security (User Lockout)

The Security Monitoring page isn't really about WebLogic Server security itself—rather, it's about monitoring the user lockout management statistics for the server. Here are the main user lockout statistics you can monitor:

- **Locked Users** Shows the current number of locked users (due to too many authentication failures).
- **User Lockout Total Count** Shows the total number of user lockouts.
- **Total Invalid Logins** Shows the invalid login count.

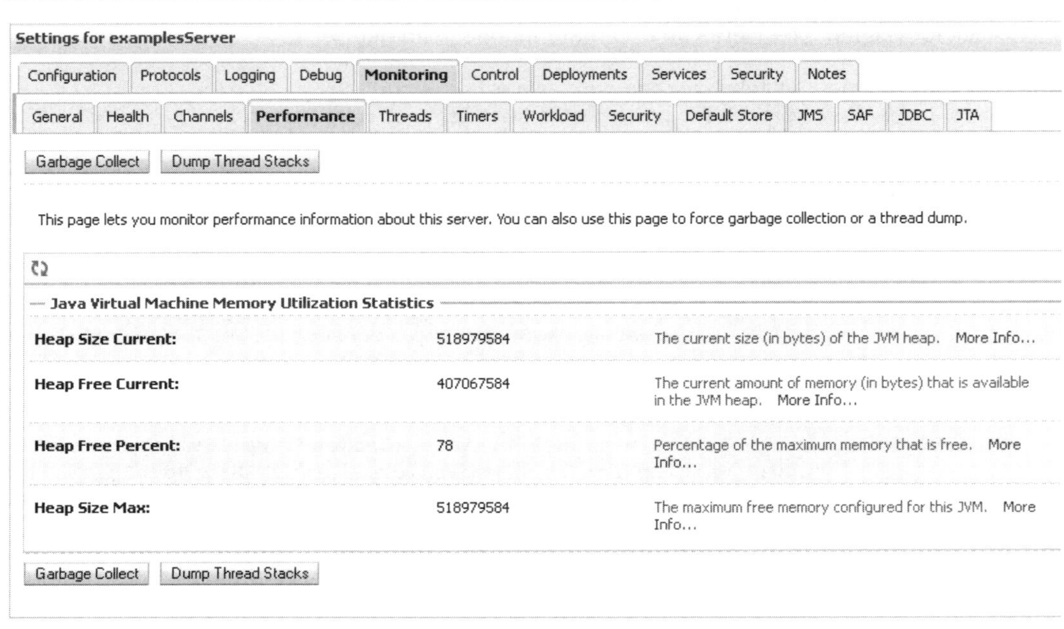

FIGURE 6-4. *The Performance Monitoring page in the Administration Console*

- **Total Login Attempts While Locked** Shows the total number of attempted invalid logins in the server instance while a user was locked.
- **Invalid Logins High** Shows the highest number of users with outstanding invalid login attempts.
- **Total Users Unlocked** Shows the number of times the server's users have been unlocked.

In addition to the main Monitoring pages described here, you can access Monitoring pages for any subsystem you want to monitor. For example, under each data source's Monitoring tab, you can view the database connection pool run-time statistics. You can monitor the value of parameters such as Active Connections High Count, Active Connections Current Command, and Active Connections Average Count from this page to find out how well the JDBC subsystem is functioning. If these parameters show a high value, you may enlarge the database connection pool. The JDBC Monitoring page is quite helpful in analyzing potential contention issues for database connections. Similarly, the JTA Monitoring tab lets you monitor transactions, including active transactions. The JMS Monitoring tab allows you to monitor JMS servers and destinations. You can monitor the Bytes Threshold Time and the Messages Threshold Time to determine how well the JMS server is functioning.

Monitoring with JMX

JMX is the foundation for everything you can do from the Administration Console. However, one can programmatically monitor WebLogic Server by using the JMX interface directly in a Java program or by writing scripts using a tool such as WLST. Programmers can invoke WebLogic

Server's JMX managed beans (MBeans) to monitor various server statistics. MBeans are part of WebLogic Server's implementation of Java Management Extensions (JMX). JMX offers programmatic access to a server's management data, and each run-time MBean represents server management data and operations.

Because this book is primarily for WebLogic Server system administrators and not for Java developers, I won't go into the details of programmatic monitoring through the JMX interface. Let's go through a few examples, however, that show the power of the JMX interface in helping you monitor a server instance. The following example shows how to use the WLST command *threadDump* to get a thread stack dump:

```
wls:/wl_server/serverConfig> threadDump()
Thread dump for the running server: examplesServer
...
The Thread Dump for server examplesServer
has been successfully written to Thread_Dump_examplesServer.txt
wls:/wl_server/serverConfig>
```

In the offline mode, WLST lets you interrogate the configuration MBeans. The configuration MBeans represent configuration information stored in the XML configuration documents. Runtime MBeans contain information about the current run state of the server and the services it runs. The data in the MBeans isn't persisted—when you shut down the server, the run-time statistics and metrics from the MBeans are destroyed. In the online mode, WLST can interrogate the WebLogic Server runtime MBeans. You can query for information about server properties such as the server state and health. You can, of course, use the Administration Console to do the same, but WLST scripts provide an easy way to automate server monitoring.

The runtime MBeans are organized hierarchically. Once you connect to the Admin Server instance through WLST, you can issue the *ServerRuntime* or *domainRuntime* commands to access the runtime MBean hierarchy. The *domainRuntime* command will take you to the root of the hierarchical tree of domain-wide runtime MBeans, the *DomainRuntimeMBean*. You can execute the *domainRuntime* command only for the Admin Server. For any server, the *serverRuntime* command places you at the *ServerRuntimeMbean,* which is the root of the runtime MBeans for that server. The *ServerRuntimeMBean* offers methods to retrieve a server instance's run-time information, as well as for transitioning a server's state. There's also a *ClusterRuntime* MBean that represents a server's view of its cluster. Similarly, the *JMSRuntime*, *JVMRuntime*, and *JDBCServiceRuntime* MBeans, as well as many others like them, get you run-time information about the appropriate subsystem or service. Use the *cd* command to navigate to any child MBean and the *ls* command to display the server and domain runtime MBeans. For example, you can *cd* from the domain run time to the *ServerRuntimeMBean* and use the *ls* command to view all the "running" servers in that domain. Note that you can't edit any runtime MBeans.

The *DomainRuntimeMBean* provides a federated view of all the running JVMs in a WebLogic administrative domain. The *DomainRuntimeMBeans*'s attribute *AppRuntimeStateRuntimeMBean*, for example, lets you determine the state of applications throughout the domain. Here's a simple script that shows how to get the status of all the servers by iterating the *ServerLifeCycleRuntimesMBean*, which is a child MBean under the *domainRuntimeMBean:*

```
cd domainRuntime()
slcs = cmo.getServerLifeCycleRuntimes()
for slc in slcs:
   print slc.getName(), slc.getState()
```

You can use the *AppRuntimeStateRuntime* MBean to check the status of any application. For example, to check the status of an application named *myApp*, deployed on the server MyAdminServer, use the following commands:

```
wls:/wl_server/serverConfig> domainRuntime()
Location changed to domainRuntime tree. This is a read-only tree with DomainMBean

 as the root.
For more help, use help(domainRuntime)
wls:/wl_server/domainRuntime>
cd('AppRuntimeStateRuntime/AppRuntimeStateRuntime')
wls:/base_domain/domainRuntime/AppRuntimeStateRuntime/AppRuntimeStateRuntime
> cmo.getCurrentState('myApp','MyAdminServer')
'STATE_ACTIVE'
wls:/base_domain/domainRuntime/AppRuntimeStateRuntime/AppRuntimeStateRuntime>
```

While we're on this topic, a few notes about Python iteration syntax. The *for* statement starts with a header line that specifies an assignment target or targets, along with the object that you want to iterate. The block of statements you want to repeat follows the header. Here's the general format of a *for* statement:

```
for target in object:
   statements
else:
   statements
```

When working interactively with WLST, adding *()* to the end of the *ls*, *cd*, and *get* commands is annoying at times. The undocumented *easeSyntax* command lets you type in *ls* instead of *ls()* and enter commands such as *get SessionTimeoutSecs* instead of *get('SessionTimeoutSecs')*. Once you turn on easeSyntax (by typing **easeSyntax()** in the WLST online mode), you can also just type ***cd*** instead of ***cd('..')*** each time you have to navigate back to a parent MBean.

Here are a couple of examples that show how to obtain server run-time statistics stored in the runtime MBeans by using WLST navigational commands. When you connect to a server from WLST, you are at the configuration MBean hierarchy (*serverConfig*). To interrogate the runtime MBeans, you must move to the domain run-time hierarchy (*domainRuntime*), or the server run-time hierarchy (*ServerRuntime*), as shown here:

```
wls:/wl_server/serverConfig> domainRuntime()
Location changed to domainRuntime tree. This is a read-only tree with DomainMBean

as the root.
For more help, use help(domainRuntime)
wls:/wl_server/domainRuntime> ls()
dr--   AppRuntimeStateRuntime
dr--   CoherenceServerLifeCycleRuntimes
dr--   ConsoleRuntime
dr--   DeployerRuntime
dr--   DeploymentManager
dr--   DomainServices
dr--   LogRuntime
```

```
dr--   MessageDrivenControlEJBRuntime
dr--   MigratableServiceCoordinatorRuntime
dr--   MigrationDataRuntimes
dr--   PolicySubjectManagerRuntime
dr--   SNMPAgentRuntime
dr--   ServerLifeCycleRuntimes
dr--   ServerRuntimes
dr--   ServerServices
dr--   ServiceMigrationDataRuntimes
-r--   ActivationTime                              Tue Aug 06 08:12:56 CDT2013
-r--   MigrationDataRuntimes                       null
-r--   Name                                        wl_server
-rw-   Parent                                      null
-r--   ServiceMigrationDataRuntimes                null
-r--   Type                                        DomainRuntime
-r-x   preDeregister                               Void :
-r-x   restartSystemResource                       Void :
WebLogicMBean(weblogic.management.configuration.SystemResourceMBean)
wls:/wl_server/domainRuntime>
```

When you move (*cd*) to the *ThreadPoolRuntime* directory tree and issue the *ls* command, you get run-time thread count information, throughput, and many other useful server run-time details. Here is an example:

```
wls:/medrec-spring/domainRuntime/ServerRuntimes/MedRecServer/>
cd('ThreadPoolRuntime/ThreadPoolRuntime')
wls:/medrec-
/domainRuntime/ServerRuntimes/MedRecServer/ThreadPoolRuntime/ThreadPoolRuntime>
ls()
-r--   CompletedRequestCount                       35308
-r--   ExecuteThreadIdleCount                      1
-r--   ExecuteThreadTotalCount                     6
-r--   HealthState
Component:threadpool,State:

HEALTH_OK,MBean:ThreadPoolRuntime,ReasonCode:[]
-r--   HoggingThreadCount                          0
-r--   MinThreadsConstraintsCompleted              299
-r--   MinThreadsConstraintsPending                0
-r--   Name
ThreadPoolRuntime
-r--   PendingUserRequestCount                     0
-r--   QueueLength                                 0
-r--   SharedCapacityForWorkManagers               65536
-r--   StandbyThreadCount                          4
-r--   Suspended                                   false
-r--   Throughput                                  3.494757863205192
-r--   Type
ThreadPoolRuntime
```

TIP
If you've created a WLST file that you are likely to use frequently, you can simply add the set of commands to WLST by storing the .py file in the WL_HOME\common\wlst\lib folder. Let's say you create a file named myLib.py *and define a function called* myCmd *within that file. You can then simply call your command from WLST, as shown here: wlst:/offline>myLib.myCmd.*

You can get details about the JVM by moving to the *JVMRuntime* tree and issuing the *ls* command:

```
wls:/medrec-spring/domainRuntime/ServerRuntimes/MedRecServer> cd('JVMRuntime')
wls:/medrec-spring/domainRuntime/ServerRuntimes/MedRecServer/JVMRuntime> ls()
dr--   MedRecServer
wls:/medrec-spring/domainRuntime/ServerRuntimes/MedRecServer/JVMRuntime>
cd('MedRecServer')
wls:/medrec-spring/
domainRuntime/ServerRuntimes/MedRecServer/JVMRuntime/MedRecServer> ls()

-r--   AllProcessorsAverageLoad                     0.06555242479356185
-r--   GCHandlesCompaction                          true
-r--   GcAlgorithm                                  Dynamic GC, current strategy
-r--   HeapFreeCurrent                              247618928
-r--   HeapFreePercent                              46
-r--   HeapSizeCurrent                              536870912
-r--   HeapSizeMax                                  536870912
-r--   Incremental                                  false
-r--   JavaVendor                                   Oracle Corporation
-r--   JavaVersion                                  1.6.0_22
-r--   LastGCEnd                                    1299949113365
-r--   LastGCStart                                  1299949111793
-r--   TotalGarbageCollectionCount                  77
-r--   TotalGarbageCollectionTime                   6204
...
```

You can redirect WLST information and error messages from the screen to a file by using the *redirect* command after connecting to a server through WLST. Here's an example:

```
wls:/medrec-spring/serverConfig> redirect('../../logs/wlst.log','false')
```

The *redirect* command shown here will send the WLST output to the ../../logs/wlst.log file, relative to where you started WLST. The *false* option disables output from being sent to standard out. To stop redirecting output to the file, issue the *stopRedirect* command.

Using WLST Monitoring Scripts

Entering WLST commands at the command line to monitor various server run-time statistics is tedious. In addition, you certainly want to automate the run-time monitoring. WLST scripts offer a great way to reduce the tedium as well as enable you to schedule monitoring scripts to run at frequent intervals. You can easily create WLST monitoring scripts, which you can run as Python files. There are two basic ways to execute WLST scripts:

- Include the script in the command that invokes WLST and execute the script. You can either specify the full path to the script or execute the script from the directory where it's located, in which case you need to specify just the name of the script. Here's an example that shows how to run a script by specifying it with the *java weblogic.WLST* command:

  ```
  java weblogic.WLST
  C:\Oracle\Middleware\wl_server_12.1\common/templates\scripts\wlst\
  distributedQueues.py
  ```

  Note that the downside to this approach is that you need to make a connection for each script you run, which is fairly expensive.

- The second way to run a WLST script is to first invoke WLST, issue the *execfile* command, and specify your script name within the command, as shown here:

  ```
  wls:offline>
  execfile('C:/MyOra/Middleware/wlserver_10.3/common/templates/scripts/wlst/
  distributedQueues.py')
  ```

TIP

Be careful about indenting code in a Python script. A Python function does not use curly braces to indicate where a function's code begins and ends. The colon (:) and the code indentation itself serve as delimiters. Any code blocks such as functions, for *and* while *loops, and* if *statements must be defined by their indentations. You start a code block by indenting it and end the block by unindenting it. Thus, white space is significant in a Python script! Be consistent with your code indentation. Wrong indentation results in a syntax error.*

WLST scripts can help you monitor virtually any server activity, including various services such as JTA, JMS, JDBC, and the server state itself. Here's a script that helps you quickly find out the current status of all running servers in a domain:

```
username = 'weblogic'
password = 'welcome1'
URL='t3://localhost:7011'
connect(username,password,URL)
domainRuntime()
cd('ServerRuntimes')
servers=domainRuntimeService.getServerRuntimes()
for server in servers:
        serverName=server.getName();
        print '-----------------------------------------------------\n'
        print  serverName
        print '-----------------------------------------------------\n'
        print ' Server Status                    :', server.getState()
        print ' Server Health State          :', server.getHealthState()
```

Note that there's a significant difference between the *ServerRuntime* and *ServerLifeCycleRuntimes* MBeans. The *ServerLifeCycleRuntimes* MBean is there even when the server is not running.

Save the script shown previously in a file called *getServerStatus.py* in the C:\Oracle\Middleware\wlserver_12.1\common\templates\scripts\custom directory, and execute it as follows:

```
C:\Oracle\Middleware\wlserver_12.1\server\bin>setWLSEnv.cmd
C:\Oracle\Middleware\wlserver_12.1\server\bin>java weblogic.WLST
C:\Oracle\Middleware\wlserver_12.1\common\templates\scripts\custom\
getServerStatus.py

Initializing WebLogic Scripting Tool (WLST) ...
Welcome to WebLogic Server Administration Scripting Shell
Type help() for help on available commands
Connecting to t3://localhost:7011 with userid weblogic ...
Successfully connected to Admin Server 'MedRecServer' that belongs to domain
'medrec'.
Warning: An insecure protocol was used to connect to the
server. To ensure on-the-wire security, the SSL port or
Admin port should be used instead.
Location changed to domainRuntime tree. This is a read-only tree with
DomainMBean as the root.
For more help, use help(domainRuntime)
----------------------------------------------------
MyManagedServer1
------------------------------------------------------
 Server Status                : RUNNING
 Server Health State          : Component:ServerRuntime,
State:HEALTH_OK,MBean:MyManagedServer1,ReasonCode:[]
-----------------------------------------------------
MedRecServer
------------------------------------------------------
 Server Status                : RUNNING
 Server Health State          : Component:ServerRuntime,
State:HEALTH_OK,MBean:MedRecServer,ReasonCode:[]
C:\Oracle\Middleware\wlserver_12.1\common\bin>
```

In this example, first WLST connects to the Admin Server and gets the list of servers from the *domainRuntime* MBean. It then iterates through a loop to get the state of each server by interrogating the *ServerRuntime* MBean. In this example, you learned how to get the server status and health state from this MBean, but you can query other server attributes as well. For example, if you want to print out the listen addresses for all the servers, you can use the *ListenAddress* attribute in the server iteration, as shown here:

```
print server.getname(), 'Listen Address = ', server.getListenAddress()
```

The following script gets you the JMS performance information for a server:

```
connect('weblogic','welcome1','t3://localhost:7011')
servers = domainRuntimeService.getServerRuntimes();
```

```
if (len(servers) > 0):
            for server in servers:
             jmsRuntime = server.getJMSRuntime();
             jmsServers = jmsRuntime.getJMSServers();
             for jmsServer in jmsServers:
                 destinations = jmsServer.getDestinations();
                 for destination in destinations:
                     print '  BytesCurrentCount          ' ,
destination.getBytesCurrentCount()
                     print '  BytesHighCount             ' ,
destination.getBytesHighCount()
                     print '  ConsumersTotalCount        ' ,
destination.getConsumersTotalCount()
                     print '  '
disconnect()
```

The example shown here uses cleartext administrator credentials. In a production environment, you should encrypt the credentials when running WLST in an interactive or script mode. Chapter 1 shows how to generate a user configuration file with the help of the *storeUserConfig* command. This command generates both the user configuration file and a key file to encrypt the credentials. Once you do this, you can simply specify the user configuration file (UCF in the following example) and the user key file (UKF in the following example) as follows at the beginning of the script:

```
UCF='/app/scripts/userConfigFile.sec'
UKF='/app/scripts/userKeyFile.sec'
```

As you can see, WLST scripts help you immensely by getting information from all the servers in a domain with a single script. As explained earlier in this book, you can also run WLST scripts by embedding them within Ant build files.

Monitoring with SNMP

The SNMP protocol is commonly used to send monitoring data to enterprise management systems. The popular Nagios network monitoring tool is SNMP based, as are several other monitoring tools. SNMP-based monitoring helps orchestrate interactions with other SNMP-based devices such as load balancers. You can use the SNMP protocol by installing SNMP agents on each of the Managed Servers or systems to transmit data to the management system. The SNMP agents collect the information from the WebLogic Server MBeans. The SNMP management system can poll the SNMP agents for monitored information, or you can configure traps whereby the SNMP agents automatically send data to the managers upon reaching a threshold when the server shuts down unexpectedly, for example. WebLogic Server provides some built-in traps, and you can define custom traps as well. You can configure SNMP agents on both the Admin and the Managed Servers to collect and transmit data to the third-party SNMP managers.

You can configure SNMP agents just on the Admin Server or on all Managed Servers. Configuring the SNMP agents on just the Admin Server means that the server might sometimes be overwhelmed with SNMP messages. In addition, if the Admin Server crashes, you're going to lose the SNMP messages. Therefore, some environments may configure the SNMP agents on all servers in the domain and not just on the Admin Server. A better approach for most environments, however, is to minimize management overhead in the Managed Servers by configuring the SNMP agents on just the Admin Server and letting the Admin Server do all the administrative work.

NOTE
An SNMP agent can automatically communicate with the managers using the SNMPv3 protocol, but you can configure the agent to support the SNMPv1 and SNMPv2 protocols as well.

Note that in addition to responding to a manager's request for information, SNMP agents are also capable of monitoring log messages and sending out notifications to the SNMP managers on their own when a managed resource reaches a threshold for a monitoring threshold or condition. The SNMP agents also automatically inform the SNMP manager when any server instances start or shut down.

The MIB Module

The server uses a *management information base (MIB)* module to specify the managed resource types and the notification types. The MIB is named *BEA-WEBLOGIC-MIB.asn1*, and the WebLogic Server installer places it in the WL_HOME\server\lib directory. The MIB module is hierarchical and contains two distinct hierarchies, one for run-time monitoring of data and the other for configuration data. Here's part of the *BEA-WEBLOGIC-MIB.asn1* file, showing how a server shutdown is represented as an SNMP trap:

```
wlsServerShutDown NOTIFICATION-TYPE
      OBJECTS {trapTime, trapServerName}
      STATUS      current
      DESCRIPTION "This trap is generated when the server has been shut down."
     : : =  { wls 0 70  }
```

WebLogic Server uses tabular objects such as *domainTable* and *serverTable*. Each of the tabular objects refers to a collection of scalar objects, which contain the variables that describe the actual state of a managed resource. For example, the *serverDeployments* scalar object is part of the *serverTable* object and describes the attributes of all deployed applications. The *serverDeployments* object contains variables to represent each of the deployed applications. For each of the managed objects, the MIB assigns a unique object identifier (OID) consisting of a set of integers in a sequence. This sequence uniquely identifies the location of the object in the MIB tree. The server appends additional sets of numbers to an object's ID to identify the variables (object instances). You can view the contents of the WebLogic Server's MIB module by using a third-party MIB browser or a web browser.

You can configure multiple SNMP agents in a domain, and an SNMP agent can also forward or proxy requests to other SNMP agents. Because all agents use the same MIB root, you can't use an SNMP agent as a proxy for agents in other domains. You can create custom MBeans and register them, following which the SNMP agent will send information from those MBeans to satisfy requests from an SNMP manager.

Configuring SNMP Monitoring for a Server

You can configure SNMP monitoring for a server by performing the following steps:

1. Load the WebLogic MIB in the SNMP manager. The WebLogic MIB must be available to both the third-party SNMP manager and WebLogic SNMP agents. The agents already have access to the MIB module, following the installation of the WebLogic Server.

2. Create an SNMP agent.
3. Create a trap destination.

I explain steps 2 and 3 in the following sections.

Creating an SNMP Agent

You can create an SNMP agent by going to Domain Structure | Diagnostics | SNMP in the Administration Console. Click New on the Summary Of SNMP Agents page. You can provide a name for the new SNMP agent and click OK. You can now configure the agent by clicking the agent's name in the Server SNMP Agent's page. Here are some of the key configuration items:

- **UDP Port** Specifies the port number on which the SNMP agent listens for UDP requests from SNMP managers. The SNMP agent uses two ports: a port for UDP traffic and another port for TCP traffic. By default, the SNMP agents can use the server's TCP listen port (the default is 7001). Chapter 5 shows how to create a dedicated SNMP network channel to separate SNMP traffic from other types of traffic. If you assign an SNMP agent to multiple Managed Servers on a host, the server automatically increments the SNMP UDP port value by 1 for the agent on each of the Managed Servers. Thus, if you choose 190 as the UDP port for the agent and you assign the agent to three Managed Servers, WebLogic Server automatically assigns the ports 190, 191, and 192 for the three Managed Servers. Note that the server doesn't configure the UDP ports on a permanent basis—the port allocations may vary, depending on the order in which you start the server instances.

TIP
The SNMP agent uses UDP port 162 as the default port to send notifications.

- **Community Based Access Enabled** Specifies support for SNMP versions 1 and 2. If you disable it, the SNMP agent can process only SNMP version 3 requests.
- **Community Prefix** Specifies the community name or password for the SNMP agent to use during its communication with the SNMP manager to secure SNMPv1 or v2 communications with SNMP managers. If you're using SNMPv1 or v2, you must use community names.

NOTE
Oracle recommends that you set a community prefix value to something other than public when using the SNMPv1 or v2 protocols in order to secure access to WebLogic Server attributes.

- **Trap Version** Specifies the SNMP notification version.
- **Send Automatic Traps Enabled** Specifies whether the agent sends automatically generated notifications to the SNMP managers. The SNMP agent generates the automatic notifications when the server instance starts or stops or when the server hosting the SNMP agent starts. Note that the SNMP agent on the Admin Server sends notifications when any

server in that domain starts or stops, whereas an agent on a Managed Server notifies only the Managed Server's status. The default value is *true*.

- **Engine ID** Identifies the SNMP agent. You must specify this ID when configuring the SNMP manager if you're using SNMPv3.
- **Authentication Protocol** Applies only for the SNMPv3 protocol. You can ensure message integrity by using the authentication protocol. The available options are None, MD5, and SHA. To use the authentication protocol, you must configure the security level of the trap destinations. In order to use the protocol when receiving a manager's request, you must first configure credential mapping in the server's security realm.

Creating a Trap Destination

To send notifications to an SNMP manager, the SNMP agent requires information about the manager, and a *trap destination* contains the information the agent needs. Here is how you create a trap destination.

1. Click Lock & Edit in the Change Center of the Administration Console.
2. In the left-hand pane, go to Domain Structure | Diagnostics | SNMP.
3. Select the name of the SNMP agent on the Summary of SNMP Agents page.
4. Click the Trap Destinations tab at the top of the SNMP Agent: Configuration page.
5. Click New under the SNMP Trap Destinations table.
6. Enter a name for the new trap destination on the Create A New SNMP Trap Destination page.
7. Here are the configuration options you must specify for the SNMP agent:
   - **Community** Refers to the password or community name that the agent sends to the SNMP manager when sending notifications based on the SNMPv1 or v2 protocol.
   - **Host** Refers to the IP address (or DNS name) for the computer where the SNMP manager is located.
   - **Port** Refers to the SNMP manager's UDP port number.
   - **Security Name** Refers to the username the agent uses when utilizing the SNMP version 3 notifications. You must also create a credential map containing a password in the server security realm for this username, and the credentials must match those required by the SNMP manager for this destination.
   - **Security Level** Specifies the security protocol to be used for SNMPv3 notifications.
8. Click the Activate Changes button in the Change Center of the Console.

Using the SNMP Command-Line Utility

WebLogic Server itself doesn't have an SNMP manager—the SNMP agents you configure allow WebLogic to log messages to a third-party SNMP-based enterprise system. However, WebLogic Server does offer an excellent command-line utility that you can use to test the SNMP agents you create.

In order to test SNMP agents, of course, you must first create the SNMP agent as well as a trap destination, as explained in the previous sections. Once you have the SNMP agent in place, run the following command to set the environment:

```
WL_HOME\server\bin\setWLSEnv.cmd
```

Invoke the SNMP command-line utility by issuing a command such as the following:

```
weblogic.diagnostics.snmp.cmdline.Manager SnmpWalk -m BEA-WEBLOGIC-MIB -M
weblogic/diagnostics/snmp/mib applicationRuntimeObjectName
```

In this example, I issued the *SnmpWalk* command to get all managed objects below the node specified in the MIB. The MIB is specified with the *—m* flag (BEA-WEBLOGIC-MIB), and the *—M* flag specifies the resource classpath of the compiled MIB. The *applicationRuntimeObjectName* option specifies that the command must retrieve the names of all deployed applications in a domain.

You can get the usage information for any command, such as the *SnmpWalk* command in the previous example, by using the following command:

```
C:\Oracle\Middleware\Oracle_Home\wlserver\server\bin>java weblogic.diagnostics
.snmp.cmdline.Manager SnmpWalk -?
  USAGE
     SnmpWalk [-?|options] <objectID> [terminationOID]
  DESCRIPTION
     Performs a basic Snmp MIB walk operation starting with the given
     MIB variable and terminating on the specified termination OID.
     If no termination OID is provided, the program will walk all
     MIB nodes contained by the one objectID provided.

  OPTIONS

     -v1|v2[c]|v3                 : snmp version                    [v1]
     -c[ommunity] <community>: snmp community to use              [public]
     -h[ost]      <host>      : snmp agent host                   [localhost]
     -p[ort]      <port>      : snmp agent port                   [161]
     -r[etries]   <retries>   : # of retries                      [3]
     -t[imeout]   <millis>    : message timeout in millis         [3000]
     -maxvbs      <max_vbs>   : max # of varbinds in a single req.[no-max]
     -metadata    <filename>  : metadata file to load             [mib-2]
     -m[ibs]      <mib-list>  : list of MIBs to load from mibdirs [mib-2]
                                (def: SNMPv2-MIB:IF-MIB:TCP-MIB)
     -M|mibdirs   <dir-path>  : directories of precompiled MIBs   [default]
     -list                    : list available MIBs               [false]

     -log         <logfile>   : logfile to store debug output     [none]
     -d[ump]                  : dump debug info to stdout         [off]
                                (note: will not work with -log)
     -pkts                    : display data packets              [off]
     -O outopts               : display output options            [i]
                                n: print OIDs in numeric format
                                l: print OIDs with resolved labels
                                i: print OIDs with formatted indexes
```

```
    -tcp                     : use TCP rather than UDP          [false]

    -nocompat                : disable compatibility mode       [enabled]
    NOTE: You may include a 'dsnmp.conf' file in your classpath  or
          filesystem containing default values for the following:
             mibs=<mib-list>
             mibdirs=<dir-path>
             retries=<retries>
             timeout=<timeout-millis>
             host=<default-host>
             port=<default-port>
             community=<default-community>
          This 'dsnmp.conf' file may be located in any of the following
          directories or JAR file packages:

             .
             /
             /monfox/toolkit/snmp/conf
             /monfox/toolkit/snmp/appl
             /etc/dsnmp/conf
             /etc/dsnmp
  SNMPv3 OPTIONS
    -u[ser] <security-user> : USM username                      [none]
    -A      <auth-passwd>   : Authentication password           [none]
    -a      <auth-protocol> : Authentication protocol (MD5|SHA) [MD5]
    -X      <priv-passwd>   : Privacy password                  [none]
    -x      <priv-protocol> : DES | AES128 | AES192 | AES256    [DES]
    -l      <security-level>: noAuthNoPriv|authNoPriv|authPriv  [authNoPriv]
    -e      <sec-engine-id> : security engine id                [none]
    -n      <context-name>  : context name to use               [""]
    -E      <context-eng-id>: context engine id                 [none]
    -Z      <boots>,<time>  : engine boots, engine time         [none]
    -crypto <provider>      : security provider class name      [...SunJCE]
C:\Oracle\Middleware\Oracle_Home\wlserver\server\bin>
```

Understanding WebLogic Logging Services

WebLogic Server maintains multiple logs to capture both server run-time and application event information, to help you troubleshoot server failures and error conditions, and to help debug applications before cutting over to production. In a domain, the applications, subsystems, and server instances all produce their own separate log messages. Server instances also write log messages to standard out, which is the Console. WebLogic logging services help produce, filter, and view those log messages. Following are the various types of log files a domain generates:

- Domain log files consolidate all the instance logging messages into one domain-wide message log.
- Server logs for each of the WebLogic Server instances.
- Subsystem (JTA, JDBC, etc.) log files.

Note also that standard web server access logs are created on a per-server basis.

NOTE
The domain log provides a consolidated view of the entire domain's status because it contains log messages generated on all the Managed Server instances that are part of the domain.

By default, WebLogic Server utilizes a message catalog to generate log messages and distributes the messages with the Java Logging APIs. An application can send messages to the server log in multiple ways. Application developers can use the message catalog framework to send application messages to the server log. Alternatively, developers can incorporate logging messages directly in the code without using the message catalog. Finally, developers can use the Server Logging Bridge to have the application redirect messages to the WebLogic logging services.

Understanding the Log Files

A WebLogic Server instance maintains a server log (the *<server_name>.log* file in the *<domain_name>*\servers*<server_name>*\logs directory), where it records all messages from each of the subsystems as well as all the applications deployed on that server. It simultaneously sends some of these messages to the domain log file (*<domain_name>.log,* which is located, by default, in the *<domain_name>*\servers*<AdminServer_name>*\logs directory). The server never broadcasts messages with the DEBUG severity level. By default, all servers send messages of severity level NOTICE or higher to the domain log. Later in this chapter, in "Controlling Server Log Messages to Log Destinations," you'll learn how to control which log messages a server writes to its domain log file by configuring custom log filters to override the default filter.

The server log provides you with a wealth of information about run-time events, including the server run-time status, application deployment, and subsystem failures. The log messages are the first thing you check when troubleshooting system performance or a subsystem or server failure. The details provided in the log messages make monitoring or getting to the root of a problem easy. You can also create applications to automatically send e-mails to you if they trap messages regarding serious server conditions such as the failure of the JMS subsystem, for example.

The following output shows how WebLogic Server outputs the server log information on the Console where the server is running.

```
<Aug 18, 2013 3:00:50 PM CDT> <Notice> <LoggingService> <BEA-320400> <The log file
C:\Oracle\Middleware\Oracle_Home\user_projects\wl_server\servers\examplesServer\
logs\examplesServer.log will be rotated. Reopen the log file if tailing has stopped.
This can happen on some platforms, such as Windows.>
<Aug 18, 2013 3:00:50 PM CDT> <Notice> <LoggingService> <BEA-320401> <The log file
has been rotated to
C:\Oracle\Middleware\Oracle_Home\user_projects\domains\wl_server\servers\examples
Server\logs\examplesServer.log00019. Log messages will continue to be logged in
C:\Oracle\Middleware\Oracle_Home\user_projects\domains\wl_server\servers\examples
Server\logs\examplesServer.log.>
<Aug 18, 2013 3:00:50 PM CDT> <Notice> <Log Management> <BEA-170019> <The server
log file
C:\Oracle\Middleware\Oracle_Home\user_projects\domains\wl_server\servers\examples
Server\logs\examplesServer.log is opened. All server side log events will be
written to this file.>
```

Besides viewing the server log files through a text editor on the machine where a server runs or through the Administration Console, you can also create applications that automatically send out e-mail messages to system administrators on occasions such as a subsystem failure. You most likely noticed that when you start an Admin Server there are multiple messages in the command window—these are some of the messages that the server writes to the server log file. By default, the server prints messages with a severity level of NOTICE or higher to the standard out, but you can control this behavior by making the server print messages of a higher or lower severity. You can also redirect the standard out to a different location. If you start a Managed Server through the Node Manager, the server will not output messages to standard out. However, you can view the logs through the Administration Console or in the *<server_name>.out* file in the *<domain_name>*\servers*<server_name>*\logs directory, where *<server_name>* is the name of the server.

Anatomy of a Log Message

In the server log file, each log message contains various attributes, each of which is surrounded by a pair of angle brackets. Here's an example:

```
####< August 13, 2013  3:03:48 AM EDT> <Info> <Server> <MIROPC61> <MedRecServer>
 <[ACTIVE] ExecuteThread: '5' for queue: 'weblogic.kernel.Default
(self-tuning)'> <<WLS Kernel>> <> <e762881ebb876ea1:-63b9f5c8:12edf6f124b:-8000-
00000000000005ad> <1300863828641> <BEA-002635> <The server
"MyManagedServer1" connected to this server.>
####< August 16, 2013 3:03:51 AM EDT> <Warning> <Diagnostics> <MIROPC61>
<MedRecServer> <[ACTIVE] ExecuteThread: '7' for queue: 'weblogic.kernel
.Default (self-tuning)'> <<WLS Kernel>> <> <> <1300863831309> <BEA-320111>
<The elapsed time since the last Harvester cycle (1,250 milliseconds) is
unacceptably short. Skipping this cycle in order to smooth out the responses.>
```

Note that the server log contains all attributes of a log message. The same messages are also shown in the command window (without the #### prefix), but the message includes the message text attribute, which describes the event or condition. The standard out messages don't output attributes such as the server name, machine name, username, transaction ID, or thread IDs.

A server log message contains the following attributes, in this order:

- **Timestamp** Gives you a locale-formatted timestamp that indicates the time and date when the message originated.
- **Severity** Shows the severity of the events reported by the message, such as a WARNING or CRITICAL severity level.
- **Subsystem** Tells you which subsystem, such as JMS, originated the message.
- **Machine name/server name/thread ID** Identify the origins of the message.
- **User ID** Indicates the user ID with which the event was executed.
- **Diagnostic context ID** Shows the context information that helps identify messages coming for a request or application.
- **Message ID** A six-digit message identifier that starts with *BEA* and is in the range 0–400000.
- **Message text** Describes the event that generated the message.

Administrators most commonly use a combination of UNIX shell commands (*cut, awk, sed*) or a Perl script for working with server logs. Of all the message attributes, message severity is, of course, the most important because it shows the potential impact of the error condition or event. Following are the severity levels of log messages listed in decreasing order of seriousness:

- **EMERGENCY** Indicates a severe system failure or panic. When you see this message, it means the server is in an unusable state.
- **ALERT** At least one service is an unusable state, and the administrators need to fix it because the server can't automatically repair the subsystem.
- **CRITICAL** This could indicate a system or service error that either leads to a loss of a service or a performance degradation. The system can potentially recover from this by itself.
- **ERROR** This is most likely a user or application error that doesn't impact the state of the system or services.
- **WARNING** This is usually caused by a configuration setting or an operation, but the setting or operation doesn't impact the server or service availability.
- **NOTICE** This is a high-level informational message.
- **INFO** This is a low-level informational message.

In addition, a DEBUG severity level indicates that the server has generated a debug message. DEBUG is an additional severity level that the applications can use with the WebLogic logging services. If you enable diagnostic instrumentation of server and application classes, any messages from the Diagnostic Action Library will have the TRACE severity level appended to them.

By default, WebLogic Server publishes all log messages to a log destination, starting with the severity level INFO, which is the most basic severity level for messages. You can configure the server to send messages from any severity level you choose by configuring the Minimum Severity To log property in the Administration Console. You do this by going to Settings For *<server_name>* | Logging | General in the Console.

Viewing Logs

You don't have to view the logs by manually opening each of the server, domain, or subsystem log files on the machine where WebLogic Server stores them. The Administration Console provides you with the ability to view the logs through the browser. To view the logs, follow these steps:

1. Expand Diagnostics and select Log Files.
2. On the Summary Of Log Files page, shown in Figure 6-5, select the name of the log you want to view.
3. Click View.

For example, when you select ServerLog, you'll see the latest contents of the server log. You can view the most recent logs at the top of the page. You can search for older log entries by scrolling down and clicking Next at the bottom of the page.

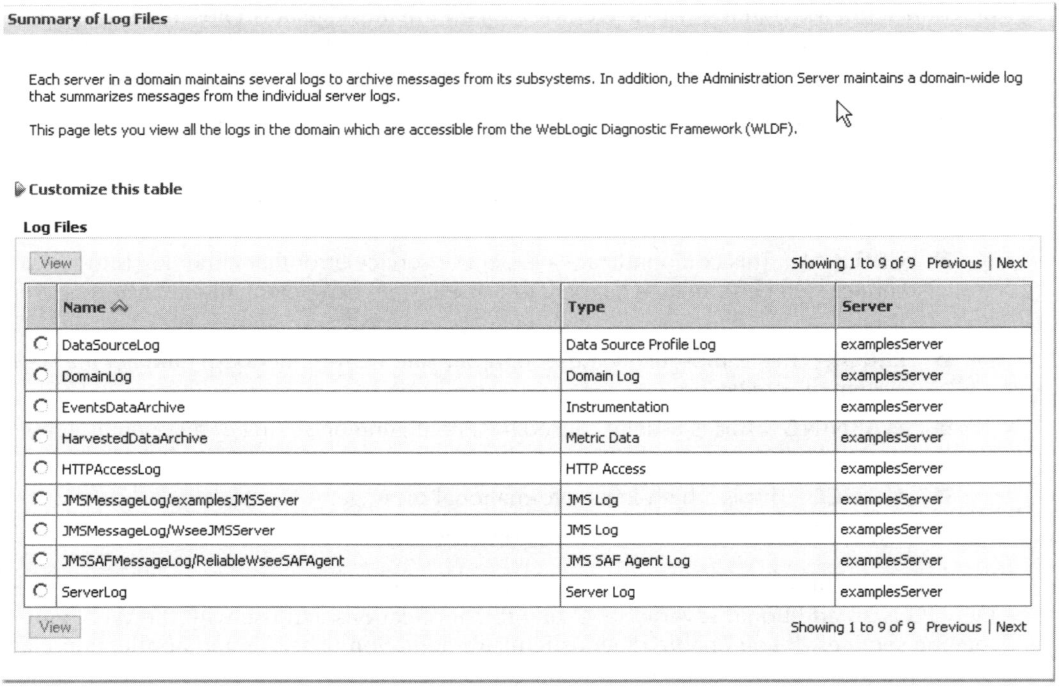

Summary of Log Files

Each server in a domain maintains several logs to archive messages from its subsystems. In addition, the Administration Server maintains a domain-wide log that summarizes messages from the individual server logs.

This page lets you view all the logs in the domain which are accessible from the WebLogic Diagnostic Framework (WLDF).

Customize this table

Log Files

View Showing 1 to 9 of 9 Previous | Next

	Name	Type	Server
○	DataSourceLog	Data Source Profile Log	examplesServer
○	DomainLog	Domain Log	examplesServer
○	EventsDataArchive	Instrumentation	examplesServer
○	HarvestedDataArchive	Metric Data	examplesServer
○	HTTPAccessLog	HTTP Access	examplesServer
○	JMSMessageLog/examplesJMSServer	JMS Log	examplesServer
○	JMSMessageLog/WseeJMSServer	JMS Log	examplesServer
○	JMSSAFMessageLog/ReliableWseeSAFAgent	JMS SAF Agent Log	examplesServer
○	ServerLog	Server Log	examplesServer

View Showing 1 to 9 of 9 Previous | Next

FIGURE 6-5. *The Summary of Log Files page in the Administration Console*

Similarly, you can view the domain log file as well without having to log into the host computer. The Domain Log page shows up to 500 log entries, but you won't be able to view any messages once they have been archived, which is done when the server rotates the log files. You can customize the Server Log and Domain Log pages to show only log entries for a specific time interval. You can also filter the messages so the page shows, for example, only the messages from the JDBC subsystem. You can also select a set of message attributes other than the default set. You do this by clicking the Customize This Table link.

Configuring a Domain Log Filter

By default, server instances use a default log filter that sends messages of severity level NOTICE or higher to the Admin Server, which, in turn, logs those messages to the domain log file. You can control the types of messages sent by a server instance to the domain-wide log by configuring a domain log filter. A *log filter* is a directive to the server to control the messages the server sends to the domain log by specifying a filtering expression. To create a domain log filter from the Administration Console, click the active domain name under Domain Structure in the left-hand plane. Go to Configuration: Log Filters and select New to create a log filter. Enter a name such as myLogFilter1 and click OK. You'll see a message stating that the log filter was successfully created, as well as the name of the new log filter in the Settings For <*server_name*> page.

NOTE
Managed Servers will continue writing to their local log files even when the Admin Server is unavailable. When the Admin Server becomes available again, the Managed Servers will send the messages stored in their local log files to the Admin Server, which writes the messages in the domain log.

Subsystem Logs

In addition to the generation of server log messages in the domain log file and local server log files, most of the WebLogic server's subsystems, such as the JMS and JDBC services, maintain their own log files for monitoring run-time events and error conditions, as well as to enable performance auditing. Here is a summary of the important subsystem log files:

- **HTTP logs** Each server and virtual host maintains a log of all HTTP transactions in the HTTP access log.
- **JDBC logs** These are log messages pertaining to the JDBC subsystem, such as JDBC connections and SQL error messages. You can enable the debugging of JDBC data sources at various scopes by setting any of the following four configuration attributes to *true*:
  - ***DebugJDBCSQL*** Shows information such as arguments, return values, and thrown exceptions for all the JDBC methods that were invoked.
  - ***DebugJDBCConn*** Shows all connection-related information, such as data source connection reservation and release operations and requests for getting or closing connections.
  - ***DebugJDBCRMI*** Shows the same information as the *DebugJDBCSQL* attribute but at the RMI level.
  - ***DebugJDBCDriverLogging*** Enables JDBC driver-level logging.

    You can enable JDBC debugging through the command line, the Administration Console, or WLST. For example, here's how you enable debugging at the *DebugJDBCSQL* scope through the command line:

    ```
    -Dweblogic.debug.DebugJDBCSQL=true
    -Dweblogic.log.StdoutSeverity="Debug"
    ```

    Note that you can do this only at startup time, and you can't turn off the debugging dynamically.
- **JMS logs** JMS server log files record information on message lifecycle events, and the log is located in the *jms.messages.log* file at the following location:

  <domain_name>\servers*<server_name>*\logs\jmsServers*<jms_server_name>*.

  You must enable JMS logging on the message destinations specified in the JMS modules first. You can configure JMS log file rotation through the Console. You should consider the enabling of JMS logging carefully, as it is a debugging-level feature that comes with a great deal of overhead.

Note that most of the time the subsystems generate few critical messages and several INFO messages; you can configure the message level for any subsystem you wish.

Understanding Server Log File Maintenance

In a server running in production mode, the server automatically rotates the server log file when it reaches 500KB in size. When you restart a server running in production mode, it doesn't rotate the local server log. A server running in development mode, however, automatically rotates the log file each time you start the server, as well as when the server log file reaches the 500KB size limit. By default, the server renames log files by attaching a sequentially increasing suffix to the log file. Chapter 3 shows how you can use the Administration Console to change the maximum log file size, as well as the time interval for rotating log files. Check the "Rotate log files" topic in the Administration Console's Help section for the details.

You can use the *LogRunTime.forceLogRotation* command to immediately rotate a server log before it reaches its maximum size limit, as shown here:

```
wls:/offline> connect('weblogic','welcome1','t3://localhost:7001')
wls:/medrec-spring/serverConfig> serverRuntime()
wls:/medrec-spring/serverRuntime> cd('LogRuntime')
wls:/medrec-spring/serverRuntime/LogRuntime> cd('MedRecServer')
wls:/medrec-spring/serverRuntime/LogRuntime/MedRecServer> cmo.forceLogRotation()
```

The preceding command immediately rotates the server log for the server MedRecServer. You can also change the location for the older log files through the Console or by specifying the location at server startup time, as shown here:

```
java -Dweblogic.log.LogFileRotationDir=C:\foo
-Dweblogic.management.username=weblogic
-Dweblogic.management.password=welcome1 weblogic.Server
```

As mentioned earlier, servers running in production mode don't rotate log files on startup. You can also go to the Console (Settings For *<server_name>* page | Logging | General) and set the Rotate Log File On Startup property to *true* (the default value is *false*) to configure the automatic rotation of server log files on startup. On this page, you can also configure the maximum size of a log file (before the server rotates the file), the log file directory, and the number of log files the server must retain by clicking Advanced at the bottom of the page. Chapter 3 shows how to configure various logging properties.

NOTE
By default, the WebLogic Server logging implementation is based on the Java Logging API.

Setting Debugging Flags Using the Console

You can set various server debug settings from either the Administration Console or through WLST. Here's how you define the debug scope and attributes from the Console:

1. Go to Environment | Servers.
2. On the Summary Of Servers page, select the server for which you want to configure debugging.
3. Select the Debug tab.

4. To enable/disable debug for the entire scope, check either the *default* or *weblogic* scope, or both, and click the Enable or Disable button. This effectively enables/disables debug for all attributes within that scope.
5. To enable/disable debug for one or more attributes within a scope, click + to expand either scope and enable or disable any of the attributes by checking the box for that attribute and then clicking the Enable or Disable button.

By default, attributes inherit the debug setting of the scope unless they are manually modified.

You can configure applications to generate the DEBUG severity level messages, but the server doesn't forward those messages to the domain log.

Integrating Application and Server Logging

Server logs record just the server instance run-time data and not the application logs. Application developers can integrate their application logging with WebLogic logging services to simplify application log management. By integrating application logging with the WebLogic Server logging services, you can view your application logs through the Administration Console, filter the logs, and set the log files for automatic archiving and rotation, just as you do for any server log file. Developers can create custom log message catalogs that they can embed in the application code. The server will integrate these application messages with the normal WebLogic Server run-time log messages. Developers have several ways to integrate application log messages with WebLogic logging services:

- Build custom log message catalogs that applications can invoke to generate log messages. Applications generate log messages by invoking the methods of the Java APIs associated with their custom log message catalogs.
- Use the noncatalog logger to generate messages by placing log messages directly in the code.
- Alternatively, developers can enable servlet logging by using the *log* method in the *javax.servlet.ServletContext*.

TIP
Don't use Log4j or any other logging mechanism in DEBUG mode in a production environment—you'll be logging too much information!

If developers don't use any of the previous three options for application logging, they can use either Log4j or the Commons API to produce and distribute log messages. They can also use Java Logging APIs to generate log messages. If you use Java Logging, you must use the Server Logging Bridge Handler to redirect log messages to the WebLogic logging services. Similarly, if you use Log4j, you must define your own loggers and appenders to redirect the log messages to WebLogic Server. You can use Log4j loggers with WebLogic Server logs. WebLogic Server offers built-in bridges to redirect the standard logging-based mechanisms into WebLogic Server logs.

Controlling Server Log Messages to Log Destinations

WebLogic Server instances send messages to the following four destinations: the server log file, standard output, the domain log (through the Domain Log Broadcaster), and finally the memory buffer. You can configure message filtering, such as by specifying a threshold severity level of, say,

WARNING, to control which messages go to each of these four locations. There are several loggers in a WebLogic Server instance, with the root logger being the main one. The first step in configuring message filtering is to create a message filter.

You can configure log message filtering through the Administration Console by navigating to Environment | Servers | *<server_name>* | Logging | General. You must click Advanced on this page to configure message filtering. Here are the key settings you can configure on this page:

- **Logging Implementation** Specifies the logging implementation. The default logging is standard Java Logging (JDK), and you can configure the server to use Log4j logging.
- **Minimum Severity to Log** Specifies the minimum server level for the root logger, which serves as the default severity level of all loggers.
- **Redirect Stdout Logging Enabled** Redirects standard out from the JVM to any of the four log message destinations.
- **Logger Severity Properties** Specifies the properties for any logger to override the settings of the root logger.
- **Filter** Specifies filtering for messages going to the four log message destinations based on various criteria. Note that you can't forward messages with a severity level of DEBUG to the domain log.
- **Buffer Size** Specifies the log message buffer size, which buffers the log messages on the Managed Server and broadcasts them to the domain log in batch when it is full.

NOTE
To reduce performance overhead involved in sending frequent message broadcasts to the domain log, Oracle recommends that you specify at least a value of 10 for the log message buffer in a server running in production mode.

WebLogic Server Troubleshooting

Troubleshooting WebLogic Server instances starts with an analysis of the log files and often a thread dump, as described in this chapter. When contacting Oracle Support for help, be sure to collect enough diagnostic information about the server instances. Probably the most important information will be in the Managed Server's log files. In a clustered environment, the server log files help in diagnosing deadlocks and cluster freezes. The diagnostic image dump is the key artifact that should be used when working with Oracle Support.

Understanding Java Thread Dumps

Java thread dumps play a crucial role in troubleshooting server performance. A *thread dump* is a list of all threads and the full stack trace of code running in each of those threads. It also reveals the state and name of the threads. Thus, a thread dump captures exactly what's happening in the server at an instant in time—it's a snapshot of the current server activity. The *stack trace* is a dump of the current executing stack, and it shows the method calls running in that thread. For example, here is an example of a stack trace for a thread:

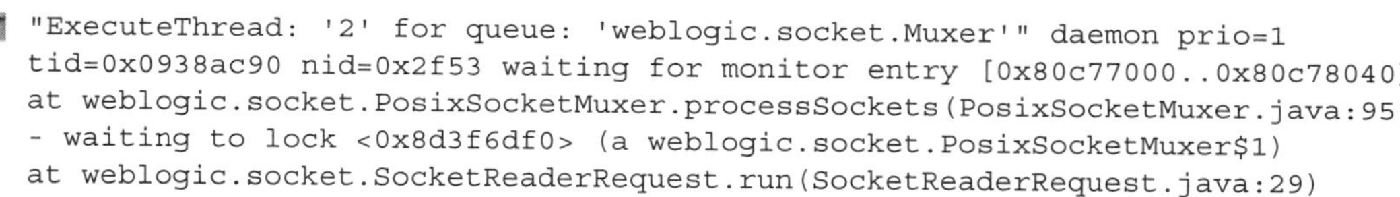

```
"ExecuteThread: '2' for queue: 'weblogic.socket.Muxer'" daemon prio=1
tid=0x0938ac90 nid=0x2f53 waiting for monitor entry [0x80c77000..0x80c78040]
at weblogic.socket.PosixSocketMuxer.processSockets(PosixSocketMuxer.java:95)
- waiting to lock <0x8d3f6df0> (a weblogic.socket.PosixSocketMuxer$1)
at weblogic.socket.SocketReaderRequest.run(SocketReaderRequest.java:29)
...
```

The key thing to understand about a stack trace is that you read it from the bottom up. Thus, in the stack trace being discussed here, the *weblogic.kernel.ExecuteThread.run* method (not actually shown in the output) initialed a call to a method right above it, and so on. Also, the currently running (or waiting) method is always at the top—in this example, the method *weblogic.socket.PosixSocketMuxer.processSockets* is currently waiting on a lock.

These are the threads WebLogic Server has created that are responsible for reading data off the client sockets and translating it into work that is then executed on a worker thread. You will generally see one or two of these always waiting for its turn to execute a select call.

The threads in a thread dump include the JVM's threads for performing tasks such as handling signals and garbage collection, as well as the application threads. Thus, if your application is running slowly, taking repeated thread dumps during this time will reveal exactly where the application is stuck. You must take thread dumps while the application is running—your thread dumps won't affect server or application performance. Note that a stuck thread is a thread that the server has not returned to the thread pool for a specific period of time, which is 10 minutes by default.

TIP
When you are troubleshooting a stuck server, take multiple thread dumps at intervals of 10 to 15 seconds so you can capture the underlying problem.

When you take a thread dump, the individual threads could be in various states:

- **RUNNABLE** In a Sun JVM, the RUNNABLE state means the thread is running or will run once it gets its CPU. In a JRockit thread dump, this state is referred to as ACTIVE. Here's an example:

  ```
  "[ACTIVE] ExecuteThread: '2' for queue: 'weblogic.kernel.Default
  (self-tuning)'" daemon prio=1 tid=0x082e1950 nid=0x2f9d runnable
  ```

- **WAITING ON MONITOR** The thread is sleeping or waiting for notification from another thread. You'll notice the *waitForRequest* keyword in a thread when it's waiting.
- **WAITING FOR MONITOR ENTRY** A thread is waiting to lock an object, but some other thread is holding the lock. You'll also see the "Waiting to lock" message when this happens.

Analyzing a thread dump helps you resolve issues such as poor application response times, a stuck application, and an application crash.

TIP
Collect multiple thread dumps in the server log file for diagnosing problems.

When you are troubleshooting application performance, you need to identify the thread pool that the application code is running in and analyze those threads in the thread dump. You can check the threads marked *weblogic.kernel.Default* to find out what's running in the server. Here's an example:

```
"[ACTIVE] ExecuteThread: '12' for queue: 'weblogic.kernel.Default
(self-tuning)'" daemon prio=1 tid=0x091962f8 nid=0x2f95 in Object.wait()
[0x7cd75000..0x7cd75ec0]
      at java.lang.Object.wait(Native Method)
      - waiting on <0x8ed19d28> (a weblogic.work.ExecuteThread)
      at java.lang.Object.wait(Object.java:474)
      at weblogic.work.ExecuteThread.waitForRequest(ExecuteThread.java:156)
      - locked <0x8ed19d28> (a weblogic.work.ExecuteThread)
      at weblogic.work.ExecuteThread.run(ExecuteThread.java:177)
```

In this example, the *waitForRequest* keyword means that a thread is idle and waiting to process a request. This is fairly typical and indicates that, at the current time, more threads are available than are required to process your workload. The server often allocates threads to handle bursts of work. When work settles back into a normal pace, it holds these threads in reserve so it can more efficiently handle the next round of work. This self-tuning behavior constantly attempts to find the proper amount of concurrency to attain the best possible performance.

If the top line of a thread dump is doing a "socket read," it means that it is waiting on data to come through the network. If you're finding most of the execute threads in a server waiting on socket reads, it usually indicates a bottleneck of some type. For example, inefficient SQL code, a missing index, or insufficient memory allocation to an Oracle database can lead to these kinds of socketRead bottlenecks. The threads could also be waiting on the connection pool for a connection. In general, waiting for any application object indicates contention for that object. The following example shows how a lock caused by a JDBC connection shows up in the top line as a *socketRead* issue:

```
"[ACTIVE] ExecuteThread: '20' for queue: 'weblogic.kernel.Default
(self-tuning)'" daemon prio=1 tid=0x082e1950 nid=0x2f9d runnable
[0x7c96d000..0x7c96dec0]
      at java.net.SocketInputStream.socketRead0(Native Method)
      ...
      - locked <0x8a5b7b38> (a weblogic.jdbc.oracle.OracleConnection)
at jsp_servlet.__my_test._jspService(__my_test.java:108)
```

TIP
You can redirect the standard output of a thread dump to a file.

Here's an example of an error thrown by a deadlock:

```
DEADLOCK DETECTED:
==================

[deadlocked thread] [ACTIVE] ExecuteThread: '12' for queue:
'weblogic.kernel.Default (self-tuning)':
Thread '[ACTIVE] ExecuteThread: '12' for queue: 'weblogic.kernel.Default
(self-tuning)'' is waiting to acquire lock
```

Deadlocks commonly occur when two resources must be acquired under lock (that is, using the *synchronized* keyword in Java or one of the *java.util.concurrent* classes), and the locks aren't always acquired in the same order. In such cases, the two code paths can deadlock as each is holding the resource the other is waiting on. Correcting this means fixing the application code to always obtain the locks in the same order. These locks can be extremely difficult to track down, as they can sometimes occur at infrequent and unpredictable intervals.

If you see the "java.net.SocketException: Too many open files" warning or error message, it means that the server is running out of file descriptors such as sockets. A thread dump will come in handy in analyzing this issue because it can tell you if a backlog of requests has caused a spike in requests for sockets.

Collecting a JRockit Thread Dump

The easiest way to get a thread dump is to use the *jrcmd* command, which was discussed earlier in this chapter. Another important technique is to trigger a diagnostic image dump or thread dump using the WLDF Watches and Notifications component. You can easily write a watch that is triggered when a thread gets "stuck" and automatically trigger a diagnostic image dump that will include the stack trace and generate an e-mail to the administrator. Tracking hogging threads is also a useful thing to configure. You can easily add a watch that will track the hogging thread count and generate an image dump when it exceeds a certain count.

You can also generate a JRockit JVM thread dump using any one of the following methods:

- You can easily generate a dump through the Administration Console: Go to Server | Monitoring | Threads and click Dump Thread Stacks.
- Use the JRockit Management Console if you've enabled the management server by starting the JVM with the *Xmanagement* option.
- Use the WLST *threadDump* command.
- Use the *kill -3 <PID>* command, where *PID* is the ID of the root of the process tree. You can execute the *kill -3<PID>* syntax to kill the session. If the PID is 999, for example, kill that session with this command:

  ```
  $ kill -3 999
  ```

  The server generates a thread dump in the server standard out when you kill the session.

On a Windows server, you can get the process ID (PID) by going to Task Manager | View | Select Columns and checking the PID (Process Identifier) box. You can then get the PID of the *java.exe* process on the Processes tab.

You can also use the JStack utility to take a thread dump. You do this by running the JStack executable from the JAVA_HOME\bin directory, as shown here:

```
$ jstack -l <PID>
```

The best way to view the thread dumps is by using the JRockit Mission Control, which lets you see what's going on inside the JVM at any time. However, the JRockit command-line tool *jrcmd* lets you access remote systems through the command line when you can't use the JRockit Mission Control. You can use *jrcmd* to get information about running JVMs and also control the JVM's run-time behavior. You can use the *jrcmd* utility to create thread stack dumps, but you can also do things such as enabling the management console and using the command line to start the JRockit JVM. Because *jrcmd* is a command-line utility, you can incorporate it in an operating system script. The *jrcmd* tool also lets you execute multiple commands at once by listing those commands one after the other in a file and passing the filename to the *jrcmd* command, along with the process ID of the JVM, as shown here:

```
jrcmd [pid] -f myfile.txt
```

All you have to do to get a thread dump through *jrcmd* is issue a simple command, without having to do a *kill -3* or CTRL-BREAK. Following is a quick introduction to *jrcmd* that also shows you how to get a thread dump with that command:

1. Go to the directory where JRockit is installed and type in **jrcmd** after moving to the bin directory.
2. You can first see the available options for the *jrcmd* executable by typing the following:

```
C:\Program Files\Java\jrockit-jdk1.6.0_45-R28.2.7-4.1.0\bin>jrcmd -h

Usage: <pid | main class> [<command> [<arguments>]] [-l] [-f file]
   or: -p
   or: -h
  <command> is a valid JRockit command. Try "help".
  If the pid is 0, commands will be sent to all JRockit processes.
  The main class argument will be used to match (either partially
  or fully) the class used to start JRockit.
  If no options are given, lists JRockit processes (same as -p).
  -l  display the counters exposed by this process. These counters
      are for internal use by Oracle and are not officially
      supported or documented.
  -f  read and execute commands from the file
  -p  list JRockit processes on the local machine
  -h  this help
C:\Oracle\Middleware\bin>
```

3. You can then type the following command to list all the JRocket processes running on the local machine.

```
C:\Program Files\Java\jrockit-jdk1.6.0_45-R28.2.7-4.1.0\bin>jrcmd -p
7112 jrockit.tools.jrcmd.JrCmd -p
11160 com.jrockit.mc.rcp.start.MCMain
10652 weblogic.WLST
4024 weblogic.Server
9280 weblogic.WLST
8020 weblogic.NodeManager -v
11860 org.apache.derby.drda.NetworkServerControl start
$
```

4. When you issue the *jrcmd* command, it prints out all the currently running JVMs. The command lists the process ID for each running process and the name of the main class. You can view all the available commands for a process by issuing the *help* command

with the process ID as an argument. The process ID for one of the JRockit processes in this example is 4140, so you issue the following command to get all the commands available for that process:

```
C:\Program Files\Java\jrockit-jdk1.6.0_45-R28.2.7-4.1.0\bin>jrcmd help
4140:
The following commands are available:
        kill_management_server
        start_management_server
        print_object_summary
        memleakserver
        print_class_summary
        print_codeblocks
        dump_codelayout
        dump_codelist
        dump_codemap
        print_codegenlist
        exception_trace_filter
        print_vm_state
        print_utf8pool
        check_flightrecording
        dump_flightrecording
        stop_flightrecording
        start_flightrecording
        print_properties
        hprofdump
        print_threads
        datadump_request
        runsystemgc
        runfinalization
        heap_diagnostics
        oom_diagnostics
        print_exceptions
        version
        timestamp
        command_line
        sanity
        verbosity
        set_filename
        help
        print_memusage
        set_vmflag
        list_vmflags
For more information about a specific command use 'help <command>'.
Parameters to commands are optional unless otherwise stated.
C:\Program Files\Java\jrockit-jdk1.6.0_45-R28.2.7-4.1.0\bin>
```

5. The *print_threads* command is the one that prints a thread dump. You can view the various options for the *print_threads* command by issuing the following command:

```
C:\Program Files\Java\jrockit-jdk1.6.0_45-R28.2.7-4.1.0\bin>jrcmd  4140 help
print_threads
```

```
4140:
Print all threads with stacktraces.
        nativestack      - include native frames in the stacktrace (bool,
                           false)
        javastack        - print java stack frames (bool, true)
        monitors         - print lock information (bool, true)
        jvmmonitors      - include the jvm internal monitors (bool, false)
        internal         - print JRockit internal threads (bool, true)
        concurrentlocks  - print java.util.concurrent locks (bool, false)
        compact          - print all threads with the same stacktrace together
                           (will not print nativestack or monitors) (bool,
                           false)
C:\Program Files\Java\jrockit-jdk1.6.0_45-R28.2.7-4.1.0\bin>
```

6. To get a thread dump with all the options, just issue the *print_threads* command without any options. If you take a few thread dumps a minute or so apart, you can figure out if the threads are stuck somewhere in your application code:

```
C:\Program Files\Java\jrockit-jdk1.6.0_45-R28.2.7-4.1.0\bin> jrcmd 4140
print_threads > C:\temp\mythreaddump1

C:\Program Files\Java\jrockit-jdk1.6.0_45-R28.2.7-4.1.0\bin> jrcmd 6480
print_threads > C:\temp\mythreaddump2
```

   The two commands shown here redirect the thread dump output to a directory that you specify. You can now examine the thread dumps and find out what the threads are doing.

If you'd rather view the thread dump in the Console itself, just issue the command *jrcmd <process id> print_threads*. If you don't specify the process ID for any *jrcmd* command, the command will apply to all running processes. If you want to get a thread dump for both a client and server that are running on the same machine, you can do so by executing the command *jrcmd 0 print_threads*.

If you ever wondered about it, no, you can't kill a stuck thread! Earlier Sun Java specifications offered you ways to stop or suspend a thread, but those methods are deprecated. Thus, when confronted by a stuck thread situation, you can just wait for the thread to finish its work or kill the server—that's it. The best thing always is to generate a JVM thread dump when you encounter a stuck thread. As Chapter 5 shows, you can configure a Work Manager to ignore stuck threads.

JVM Crashes

A JVM crash can occur for any number of reasons, including an inefficient garbage collection policy (more on this in Chapter 10), low memory, extensive code optimization, and so on. When the JVM crashes, the operating system usually (but not always) generates a *core dump,* usually a large file that may reach several gigabytes in size and that is, of course, in a binary format, just as any operating system core dump. Core dumps contain the errors and exceptions that crashed the JVM, along with the threads associated with the crash. In a UNIX server, you often find the core dump in the /tmp directory or in the directory from where you started the server. Core dumps usually are specific to an operating system, so you must send those files for investigation by the operating system support personnel, who can analyze those dumps with specialized tools.

When a JVM crashes, it often generates a text file along with the core dump file. In the case of the JRockit JVM, the file is named **.dump,* and for the Oracle (formerly Sun) JDK, the text filename is *hs_err_pid<WebLogicPID>.log*.

You can get the server to generate a thread dump before it crashes by specifying the *-XX:+ShowMessageBoxOnError* option for Sun HotSpot JVMs. This option is more appropriate for a development environment. You can use the *—XX:OnError* option for a production environment, wherein you can specify a set of commands or a script for the server to execute when it encounters a fatal error. Similarly, you can specify the JVM option *—Djrockit.waitonerror* for the JRockit JVM. Doing so will make the JVM prompt you before it crashes, giving you the opportunity to generate a thread dump for the crash event.

You can specify the *—XX:+HeapDumpOnOutOfMemoryError* command-line option to instruct the HotSpot JVM to generate a heap dump when it encounters a Java heap or permanent generation memory error. You can use this in a production system, as there's no overhead to specifying this option. The heap dump you'll get will be in the HPROF binary format, and you can use the *Jhat* tool to perform a basic analysis of the dump.

```
% java -XX:+HeapDumpOnOutOfMemoryError -mn256m -mx512m ConsumeHeap
java.lang.OutOfMemoryError: Java heap space
Dumping heap to java_pid1212.hprof ...
Heap dump file created [491428128 bytes in 11.142 secs]
Exception in thread "main" java.lang.OutOfMemoryError:
...
```

The default location for the heap dump file is the JVM working directory, and the default file name is *java_pid<pid>.hprof*. You can specify an alternative filename or directory with the *—XX:HeapDumpPath* option.

Generating Logs for Troubleshooting

You can redirect standard error and standard output to integrate thread dump information with server error messages to produce a more useful log for troubleshooting purposes. A thread dump displays the current stack in an active thread. Here are the steps for collecting a more useful log with thread dump information to send to Oracle Support personnel:

1. Stop the server and back up the current log files.
2. Restart the server with the following command:

   ```
   % java -ms64m -mx64m -verbose:gc -classpath $CLASSPATH
   -Dweblogic.domain=mydomain -Dweblogic.Name=clusterServer1
   -Djava.security.policy==$WL_HOME/lib/weblogic.policy
   -Dweblogic.admin.host=localhost:7011 weblogic.Server >> logfile.txt
   ```

   The previous startup command turns on the verbose garbage collection switch and redirects all standard error/output to the server's log file. The *—verbose:gc* argument provides a heap image profile that indicates how often the full garbage collection is occurring. During a full garbage collection, the memory heap is compacted to maximize the contiguous free memory in a heap. Chapter 10 provides details about tuning the JVM garbage collection process.

3. Run the cluster (or server) long enough to reproduce the problem.
4. Use the *kill -3* command, or CTRL-BREAK, to create thread dumps if the server hangs. Repeat this multiple times on each Managed Server, at intervals of about 5–10 seconds, to diagnose potential deadlocks.

You can send these log files to Oracle Support for diagnosis.

Using WLST Diagnostic Dump Commands

WLST offers several commands to manage diagnostic dumps. Here's a brief summary of the commands:

- ***describeDump*** Describes a specified diagnostic dump.
- ***executeDump*** Executes a specified diagnostic dump.
- ***listDumps*** Displays all diagnostic dumps that can be executed.

Earlier in this chapter, you learned how to use the *threadDump* command to display a thread dump for a specific server. By default, the *threadDump* command saves the dump in a file with the format *Thread_Dump_<server_name>.txt*, as shown here:

```
wls:/medrec-spring/serverConfig> threadDump()
Thread dump for the running server: MedRecServer
===== FULL THREAD DUMP ===============
Sun Oct 20 10:44:22 2013
.
.
.
.
.
.
===== END OF THREAD DUMP ===============

The Thread Dump for server MedRecServer
has been successfully written to Thread_Dump_MedRecServer.txt
wls:/medrec-spring/serverConfig>
```

If you don't wish to save the thread dump information to a file, specify the *writeToFile='false'* option, as shown here:

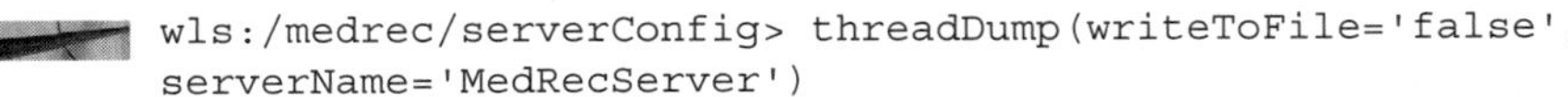

```
wls:/medrec/serverConfig> threadDump(writeToFile='false',
serverName='MedRecServer')
```

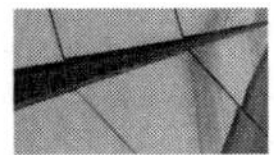

TIP

When reviewing attributes such as "execution time high" and "execution time low," the unit of time is in milliseconds—thus, if a servlet's average invocation time is 5000 ms, it means the average response time is 5 seconds.

Out-of-Memory Errors

Out-of-memory exceptions are some of the most common errors you come across when troubleshooting any JVM. Each Java process uses a memory area called the Java heap, and you set the maximum heap size using the JVM parameter *-Xmx* (*MaxHeapSize*). An out-of-memory error in Java heap condition occurs when the server runs out of memory to allocate for a Java object. This may happen for a number of reasons, such as setting too low a value for the *MaxHeapSize* parameter, memory leaking, or an inappropriate garbage collection strategy.

The following list tells you what the different heap components mean when you're monitoring the JVM memory:

- **Allocated Java Heap** The total memory available to the JVM for placing Java objects and compiled classes.
- **Free Java Heap** Shows the amount of memory the server has available for placing new objects.
- **Used Java Heap** Shows how much memory is taken up by Java objects and classes currently in memory.

If you use a large number of JSPs, you may run into the native out-of-memory condition when the JVM can't allocate enough memory for code optimization and for class and library loading. You'll also see the native out-of-memory errors when you set too small a *StackSize* (*—Xss* parameter) or if the operating system is running low in free memory or swap space. The *StackSize* is the area the JVM allocates to individual threads in its memory. Here's how the error appears:

```
Exception in thread "main" java.lang.OutofMemoryError: unable to create new
native thread …
```

You must analyze the file *x.dump* (JRockit) and the *hs_err_pid.log* (Sun JDK) to analyze the causes of the native out-of-memory errors.

The JVM allocates classes and methods in a non-heap area called the Permanent Generation (PermGen) area. You'll see the out-of-memory error in the PermGen area sometimes when deploying very large applications with numerous classes or when garbage collection doesn't clean up the classes of applications that you've redeployed using the auto deployment method. Setting too low a value for Maximum PermGen Memory (*XX:MaxPermGen*) is also a potential cause of the PermGen out-of-memory errors.

Here's what a PermGen out-of-memory error message looks like:

```
Exception in thread "ExecuteThread:  '1' for queue:'
Weblogic.kernel.Default  (self-tuning) '"java.lang.OutofMemoryError PermGen
Space
```

If you notice an out-of-memory error in Java heap condition, you can include the following Java options in your startup scripts to get details about the garbage collection process:

```
-verbose:gc -XX:+PrintGCTimeStamps -XX:+PrintGCDetails
-loggc:/u01/app/gclogs/gc.log
```

You can instruct the server to generate a heap dump by using the following Java option during startup:

```
XX:+HeapDumpOnOutOfMemoryError
```

The section "JVM Crashes" earlier in this chapter explains how to use the JHat tool to analyze heap dumps.

If you're working with a cluster, check the garbage collection on all the Managed Servers in the cluster. Long garbage collection times for a Managed Server may result in that server failing to inform the rest of the cluster members that it's running. If you find that a server is taking longer than 10 seconds for garbage collection, check the heap allocation parameter.

Summary

This chapter reviewed the essential components of the Weblogic Diagnostic Framework (WLDF), which is a great way to monitor server performance and capture diagnostic information. In addition, you learned how to monitor the database using the Administration Console, JMX, and SNMP. The chapter also discussed the WebLogic Server logging framework, how to troubleshoot server performance, and how to get thread dumps to analyze JVM performance issues.

CHAPTER 7

Working with WebLogic Server Clusters

Although you can develop and test all your applications using a single WebLogic Server instance, in a production setting, you're more likely to use a WebLogic Server *cluster*—a grouping of WebLogic Servers that work together to provide scalability, high availability, and failover capabilities. This chapter introduces you to WebLogic Server clustering. You'll learn about the various recommended architectures such as the basic combined tier, multitier, and proxy tier architectures. The chapter shows you how to create a cluster using different methods, including a sample WLST script provided by Oracle. You'll learn how to configure a cluster, manage the cluster lifecycle, and monitor a running cluster. The chapter explains how WebLogic Server provides load balancing and discusses the various load-balancing algorithms you can use. Clusters provide application failover for various clustered objects such as EJBs, RMI objects, servlets, and JSPs. The chapter shows how WebLogic Server performs failover at the application level. To provide high availability, WebLogic Server can automatically migrate an entire server or just the key services that a cluster hosts. The chapter discusses both automatic and manual whole server migration, as well as service migration.

Introduction to WebLogic Server Clusters

When you create a domain with multiple Managed Servers, all those servers function independent of each other. A cluster, on the other hand, is a group of WebLogic Server instances that work as a single instance from the point of view of a client. The reason you use a cluster is to increase scalability and reliability by taking advantage of a cluster's workload balancing and failover capabilities that you can't have with a single server instance. You manage clustered server instances the same as any nonclustered instance. Of course, to avail yourself of the load-balancing and failover capabilities of a cluster, you must configure a few other things as well.

You use clusters to achieve two important goals: high availability and scalability. High availability includes support for both the failover of applications as well as the failure of a server or an essential service such as a JMS service. A cluster maintains copies of application components (objects), so if a component becomes unavailable, the cluster uses the failed object's copy to complete the processing of the task. WebLogic Server uses session replication to fail over servlets and JSP. Similarly, it uses replica-aware stubs to maintain information about the state of application components such as EJBs and RMIs. Replication allows the copies of the failed objects to finish the job when an application component fails. WebLogic Server also provides for both automatic and manual migration of an entire clustered server instance to a different machine following a server failure. You can use this capability manually for administrative purposes as well.

You can cluster objects such as servlets, JSPs, EJBs, RMI objects, JMS destinations, and JDBC connections. WebLogic Server replicates the HTTP session data for clustered servlets and JSPs. The server uses replica-aware stubs for EJBs and RMI objects to provide load-balancing and failover support for those objects. When you cluster JDBC connections, clients automatically request alternative connections when the initial connection fails. A *pinned* service is one that is active on only one instance at a given time, although it is deployed on all members of a cluster. WebLogic Server maintains only a single copy of a pinned object within the cluster. Certain RMI objects, the JMS servers, and the JTA Transaction Recovery Service are pinned services. WebLogic Server provides for both automatic and manual migration of these services during failures.

Clusters let you scale up easily, either by enabling you to add additional server instances to the cluster on the same set of machines or by adding additional machines to the cluster. A cluster also allows the load balancing of the workload by letting you cluster objects on multiple server instances, thus allowing the cluster to maintain copies of those objects. By clustering EJBs on multiple WebLogic Server instances, for example, you let the cluster distribute the requests for the EJBs among the various members of the cluster. You can specify a load-balancing algorithm to control how the cluster balances the workload. The following points summarize how clustering provides application failover and scalability:

- **State management** Applications often include some state in the middle tier. In web applications, this most often takes the form of an HTTP session state. For EJB-based applications, this often takes the form of a stateful session bean. WebLogic clustering works with either a load balancer or a web server to make sure that a second copy of any such state is maintained, so if a primary server either fails or is intentionally taken down, the user request will be automatically redirected, and the user will not see a disruption in service.
- **Seamless failover of idempotent requests** For a stateless service bean (SSB) that is *idempotent* (executing the operation twice gives the same result as executing it once), an RMI stub will simply retry the request on the secondary server and the caller will not even be aware that the initial request failed. This allows a client (potentially a server in one tier calling another server) to be unaware of these details.
- **Scaling of asynchronous services** Asynchronous services such as JMS are built on WebLogic Server clustering, making it possible to balance the queuing and processing of messages across a group of server instances that can grow and shrink dynamically without having to change the application code.

You can deploy an application to a cluster even when one or more of the cluster members are unavailable. The cluster will initiate the deployment of the application to any unreachable servers once they become available again. You can, however, enforce consistent deployment to all cluster members, if you wish. By doing this, you adopt an all-or-nothing approach to deployment—either the application will be deployed to all the cluster members or it won't be installed to any member. A key concept in clustering is the "homogeneity" of the server instances. This means that all of the servers in a cluster must have access to the same resources and be running the same application code. The WebLogic Server deployment infrastructure is designed with this in mind and performs additional checking to ensure consistency in the cluster.

Relationship Between Clusters and a Domain

Beginning WebLogic Server users sometimes find the relationship between a cluster and a domain a bit confusing. Here are the important points you need to remember about how clusters and domains relate to each other:

- You always want to configure three WebLogic Server instances in order to create a two-node cluster, with the extra instance being the Admin Server, which should not be part of a cluster. You use the Admin Server only for managing the other instances, and if the Admin Server goes down, the cluster will continue running fine—you just need to start a new Admin Server instance. Once you restart the Admin Server, it will automatically discover all the cluster members during its startup.
- A cluster always belongs to a single WebLogic Server domain—you can't create a cluster that spans multiple domains.
- A WebLogic Server instance (Managed Server) can belong only to a single cluster.
- You can't use a configured resource such as a JDBC connection pool for multiple domains.

- You must run the same version of WebLogic Server on all machines that are part of the cluster, except when you do a rolling upgrade from one service pack to another.
- Each of the machines must have a static IP address. You must not assign IP addresses dynamically to a cluster member through DHCP because the members may not be able to communicate with each other if an address changes. This can work in the short term for testing applications locally, but it is not something you would do in a production deployment.

You can build a simple cluster for developing applications by creating a domain with an Admin Server and two nodes (a cluster member is called a *node*), all running on the same physical machine. In a production environment, however, you must deploy the Admin Server and the Managed Servers on different machines for failover purposes.

If a domain has multiple clusters, you use the domain's Admin Server to configure and manage the various clusters. As mentioned earlier in this chapter, it is recommended that you don't include the Admin Server as part of any cluster. The Admin Server manages a domain's configuration, including the configuration of all the Managed Servers in the cluster. Cluster members need the Admin Server to be up so they can connect to it and get the domain configuration information. For stronger security, the Admin Server must be in the same demilitarized zone (DMZ) as the cluster. You start the Admin Server first and start the cluster members after that. Even if the Admin Server fails for some reason, the cluster continues to work fine—all load-balancing and failover capabilities will remain intact.

Deployment in a Cluster

Chapter 8 explains WebLogic Server application deployments in detail. In this chapter, I explain some cluster-specific deployment details. WebLogic Server deploys applications in two phases: in the first phase, it distributes applications to targets and validates the deployment. Once the validation process is complete, the second phase of the deployment begins, in which the applications are deployed on the server instances and made available to the clients. Check to ensure that all cluster members are running and that you can reach them with the Admin Server before you start the deployment process.

WebLogic Server allows you to deploy applications to a partial cluster, when one or more members of the cluster are unavailable. When these servers become available again, WebLogic Server automatically initiates deployment to the servers. However, by setting the property *ClusterConstraintsEnabled* to *true,* you can specify that the deployment should succeed only if all the cluster members are reachable.

CAUTION
Although you can do so, targeting a pinned service (a service such as JTA Transaction Recovery Service) to multiple cluster members is not advisable.

Cluster Architectures

Understanding WebLogic Server cluster architecture is easier once you understand the various application tiers that you host on the cluster. *Tiers* refer to the various ways you can demarcate an application's logical services, such as the presentation and processing of the business logic. The most common application tiers are the following:

- **Web tier** Runs a web server such as Apache, serves static HTML content, and is usually the main interface between the clients and the web application.

- **Presentation tier** Provides dynamic content such as servlets and JavaServer Pages (JSP).
- **Object tier** Provides the business logic through Java objects such as EJBs.

A Java EE application often covers all three tiers. With the advent of JPA and Java EE 5 and 6, these tiers are commonly deployed together.

You can have all three of the application tiers running on the same machine if you want, but in enterprise deployments, they are usually hosted on different physical servers. There are no hard and fast rules regarding how to configure a cluster. It all depends on the design of your application, your security requirements, and your business needs. Oracle recommends three types of architectures: the first is a basic architecture, the second is a multitier architecture, and the third is a proxy architecture where you use a bank of web servers to provide static HTTP content and use one or two WebLogic clusters for hosting the presentation and object tiers.

You can combine all tiers of your application in a single cluster, or you can create a separate cluster for each of the tiers. You can use either a third-party load balancer or WebLogic Server's proxy plug-in for that purpose. Proxy plug-ins also contain information about a client's session state to help during failover of an application. You also must decide how you're going to configure the DMZ in your network, an area of the network consisting of untrusted outside sources that external browser-based clients can access. Again, there are no rules regarding how many firewalls you can use with your DMZ—you may decide one firewall is enough, or you may use two firewalls, one on either side of the DMZ.

Basic Architecture

The basic recommended architecture is one where you combine all three tiers in a single cluster. In this architecture, also called a *combined tier architecture*, you deploy clustered objects such as EJBs in all the WebLogic Server instances in the cluster. Figure 7-1 shows the recommended basic cluster architecture, with the single cluster running all three tiers (web, presentation, and object

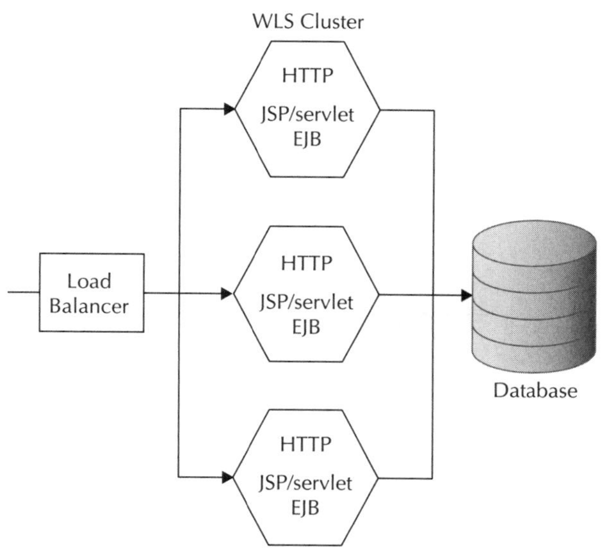

FIGURE 7-1. *The recommended basic cluster architecture*

tiers) of the web application. If most of your presentation-tier objects, such as servlets or JSPs, access EJBs or other objects from the object tier, this architecture works well and even offers better performance than a multitier architecture. It has the benefit of being easy to configure and administer to boot. This architecture allows load balancing and failover between the external clients and the cluster, so it serves the main reason for setting up a cluster.

The disadvantage to using the basic combined architecture is that because you deploy clustered objects such as EJBs to all the WebLogic Server instances in the cluster, you can't load balance the method calls to the EJBs. WebLogic Server simply selects the local EJB object instance to optimize method calls to clustered EJBs, a strategy called a *collocation strategy.* In order to load balance the method calls to EJBs, you must configure a different architecture, with the presentation and object tiers on different physical clusters as offered by a multitier architecture, which is explained in the following section. From a high availability point of view, if one of the WebLogic Server instances in the cluster goes down, it takes away not only the ability to call the EJBs, but also the application's ability to serve static HTTP and servlet content, which is adversely affected. This type of situation usually occurs in the case of applications where one team owns the entire application from front to back.

Multitier Architecture

In the Oracle-recommended multitier architecture, you use a separate cluster for the presentation and object tiers, with the first cluster serving static HTML content and servlets and the second cluster serving clustered EJBs. Figure 7-2 shows the recommended multitier architecture. If your goal is high availability, you should consider using the multitier architecture, as it has fewer single points of failure. For example, if one of the instances in the object-tier cluster goes down, your web application can still continue to serve static content (through HTML and servlets) because this content is served from the presentation tier cluster. You can also provide better security to the object tier by placing just the presentation cluster in the DMZ.

A multitier architecture enhances availability by eliminating the bottleneck of using a single physical server and also increases the scalability of the system. A multitier architecture can't take advantage of the collocation strategy and thus there's the additional overhead of calls to clustered EJBs. However, if

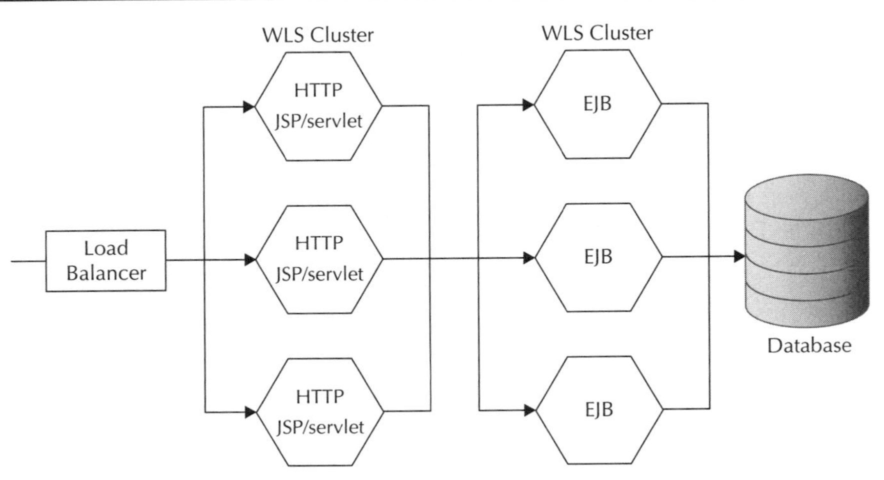

FIGURE 7-2. *The recommended multitier architecture*

your applications access only a few clustered EJBs, this may not be a concern. Another motivation for such a deployment is when there is a natural division of the application by departments or teams. For instance, you may have two applications that provide different views onto the same back-end data. For example, a sales web application and an order-processing application that both reference the same set of back-end data and services would allow each of these to be sized and versioned independently.

Proxy Architecture

In proxy architectures, the web servers aren't part of the WebLogic Server clusters. The web server bank uses either a proxy plug-in or the simple *HttpClusterServlet* to act as a front end to the WebLogic Server clusters that host the presentation and object tiers, as shown in Figure 7-3. Thus, the web tier acts as a proxy cluster consisting of a group of proxy servers that route requests for dynamic content to the WebLogic clusters that host the dynamic content. Users access the web servers directly, and the web servers, in turn, access the presentation and object tiers to respond to the user requests. The web server tier thus merely passes along the servlet and JSP requests to the WebLogic Server cluster. The web tier can use any of the following setups:

- Weblogic Server with the *HttpClusterServlet*
- Apache or Oracle HTTP Server with the WebLogic Server plug-in
- Microsoft Internet Information Services (IIS) or Netscape Enterprise Server with the appropriate WebLogic Server proxy plug-in.

WebLogic Server proxy plug-ins know which WebLogic Server instances host a clustered servlet or JSP, and they forward requests on a round-robin basis. The plug-ins additionally provide

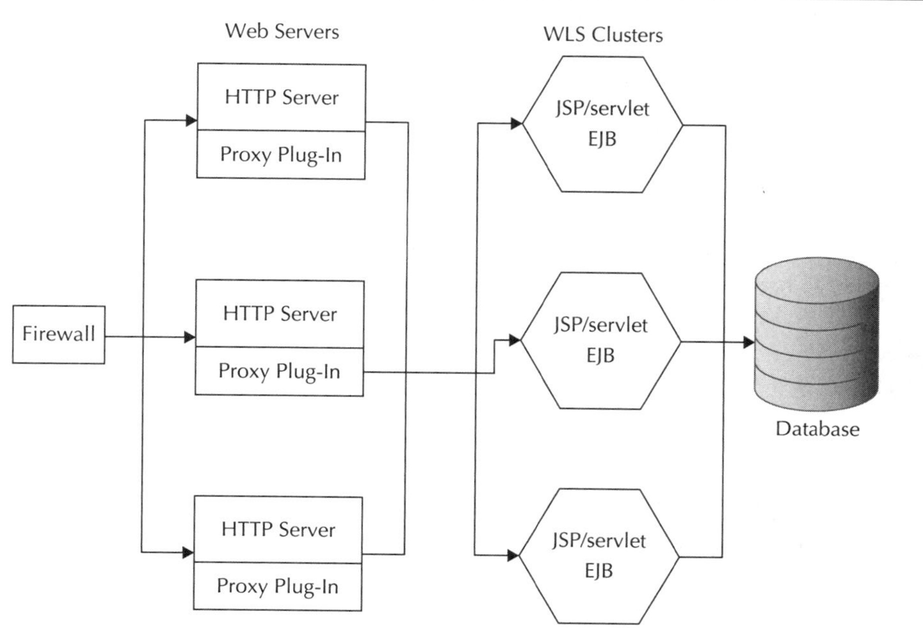

FIGURE 7-3. *A two-tier proxy cluster architecture*

failover support by locating the replica of a client's HTTP session when a server instance fails. Using a proxy architecture with a client-facing web tier, you can combine your presentation and object tiers into one WebLogic cluster (similar to the basic architecture). Alternatively, in addition to the web tier, you can configure two separate WebLogic clusters, one for hosting the presentation tier (servlets) and the other for hosting the object tier (EJBs). You can use the same physical machine or two separate physical machines for hosting the presentation and object tiers.

How Clusters Communicate

The WebLogic Server instances that make up a WebLogic cluster communicate directly with one another so as to coordinate their activities. When each server is started, it advertises that fact to all the other members of the clusters, commonly referred to as "peers." Each of the cluster members keeps track of all of the other cluster members, and they all try to ensure that they have a consistent view of which servers are up and which are not. The members of the cluster combine the cluster configuration information as well as information about the current state of the cluster to negotiate who is the backup for whom. The members of a cluster constantly monitor one another with heartbeats. They use this information to determine when the primary server for a particular piece of state has become unavailable and whether its data needs to be replicated to some other instance.

Instances within a cluster communicate through IP sockets using IP unicast or IP multicast. WebLogic Server cluster members use IP sockets for communicating with other members of the cluster, such as for transferring messages and data between two applications. For example, a clustered instance uses the IP sockets for replicating HTTP session states between a primary and a secondary server. IP unicast or IP multicast messaging is for communications among the cluster members, to announce the availability of services and to broadcast heartbeat messages to show they're alive. IP multicast messaging is offered for backward compatibility—if you're creating a new cluster, use unicast for intra-server messaging. Multicast messaging lets multiple applications listen for messages by subscribing to a given IP address and port number. Multicast messaging requires hardware configuration, whereas unicast messaging doesn't. You also don't have to configure cross-network configuration for unicast messaging. Use multicast messaging only if you have older versions of Weblogic Server clusters. Because you can't mix multicast and unicast, in that case, all servers must use multicast messaging.

For IP sockets, you can use either a pure Java or a native socket reader implementation. Oracle recommends that you use the more efficient native socket reader implementation. By default, each server instance creates three socket reader threads, and you can increase this number to handle peak loads.

NOTE
You can't mix multicast and unicast messaging for the members of the same cluster.

Naming Cluster Instances

When you create a cluster, you must provide the location information for all Managed Servers and the Admin Server. You can use either DNS names or IP addresses for naming the servers. Each of the Managed Servers must have a unique listen address and listen port combination. If your cluster nodes are all on the same server, they can, of course, use the listen address, but you must assign a different listen port to each Managed Server. Oracle recommends that you use DNS names for production environments, as the firewalls may cause translation errors when you use IP addresses. You must use the *ExternalDNSName* attribute of a server instance to define its external DNS name if its internal and external DNS names aren't identical. If remote processes need to access the server instance, you must leave the listen address attribute blank instead of specifying the address as *localhost*. The server will automatically determine the address of the machine when you don't specify a value for the listen address attribute. Also, avoid using *localhost* as the listen address.

When you leave the listen address blank, the server will detect all the available network interfaces on the machine and attempt to create a listener on the listen port on all of them. When you are configuring a cluster that is having requests directed to it through a load balancer or web server, it is best to keep things clear and simple. In that case, you create a fixed or static IP that is configured in DNS to map to one particular network interface on that machine. That name in DNS is then used when defining the listen address for the server and when defining load balancing through round-robin DNS or in the web server proxy.

Cluster Address

You can either define the cluster address during the creation of a cluster or let WebLogic Server generate the cluster address for each request. The dynamic cluster addresses that WebLogic Server generates are in the following format:

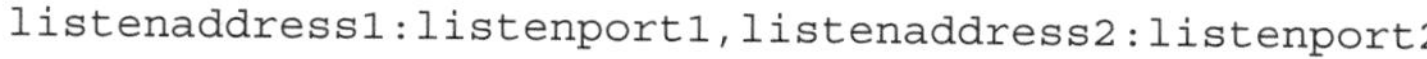

```
listenaddress1:listenport1,listenaddress2:listenport2
```

Each of the listen address and listen port combinations in the cluster address belongs to the particular Managed Server to which the server directs a new request. Note that the requests may be received on a Managed Server's default network channel or a custom network channel. By default, the number of listen address/port combinations you can include in the cluster address is set to 3. You can change the number of combinations by setting the value of the Number Of Servers In Cluster Address setting in the Environment | Clusters | Cluster Name | Configuration | General page of the Administration Console.

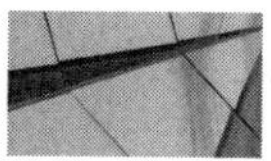

NOTE
The listen address/listen port combination for different requests will appear in a randomly chosen order in the cluster address.

In a production environment, use a DNS name for the cluster address. The DNS name must map to the IP address or DNS names of the cluster members. When you specify the cluster address as a DNS name, each cluster member must have the same listen port number. Instead of simply relying on a DNS round robin, WebLogic Server uses a cached list of addresses, which enables the server to remove unreachable addresses. You can define the cluster address as a list containing the DNS name or the IP address and the listen port of each cluster member:

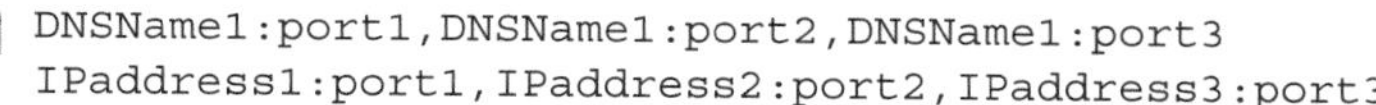

```
DNSName1:port1,DNSName1:port2,DNSName1:port3
IPaddress1:port1,IPaddress2:port2,IPaddress3:port3
```

NOTE
Since you must not include the Admin Server in a cluster, don't include its IP address in the cluster's DNS name.

Creating and Configuring a Cluster

You can use the WebLogic Configuration Wizard, the Administration Console, or WLST commands to create and configure clusters. Oracle recommends that you use the Configuration Wizard to create and configure a cluster. Chapter 3 offers a brief discussion of how to create a domain and configure it using the Configuration Wizard. The Configuration Wizard is a good way to start creating a cluster, but you will almost certainly need to modify the cluster configuration. In this chapter, you learn how to create and configure clusters employing other methods, including using the Oracle-provided WLST script *cluster_creation.py* for quickly getting a cluster up and running in a development environment. Once you learn how to create a basic cluster and are familiar with managing cluster lifecycles and the monitoring of clusters, you can explore the configuration aspects of cluster management, which I describe later in this chapter in the section "Managing a WebLogic Server Cluster" after a review of the cluster creation methods next.

Using the Administration Console

To build a cluster through the Administration Console, you first configure the Managed Servers that are going to be the nodes in the new cluster and then configure the cluster itself. If you are a developer looking to create a simple cluster to test your applications, you can create the entire cluster on a single machine. The basic principles of configuring a cluster are the same whether you use one or many machines. Let's simply use one of the WebLogic Server sample domains (wl_server) to learn how to build a simple cluster whose members are all on a single machine.

You can create a cluster and its members at the same time through the Clusters page. You can also create your Managed Servers separately and then configure them as members of a cluster. You already have an Admin Server for the *wl_server* domain—let's create two Managed Servers (nodes) and configure them into a cluster.

Creating the Cluster Members

To create a simple two-node cluster, you must first create two Managed Servers and configure them into a cluster. Creating the two new Managed Servers is simple. Click Servers in the left-hand pane of the Administration Console and click New. On the Create A New Server page, you must configure just two settings for each of the two Managed Servers: Server Name and Server Listen Port. Type **MyManagedServer1** as the server name for the first Managed Server. You can specify any listen port except the one already used by the Admin Server. Specify **7003** as the listen port for the first server, MyManagedServer1. At the bottom of the page, select the "No, this is a stand-alone server" option, because you don't yet have a cluster. Click Next and after reviewing your choices in the next page, click Finish. Repeat this for the second Managed Server: name it **MyManagedServer2**, and assign it a different listen port, **7005**.

TIP
You can clone an existing cluster through the Administration Console's Summary Of Clusters page.

Creating the Cluster

Once you create the second Managed Server (MyManagedServer2), you can configure a cluster in one of two ways. The first method is to choose the Create A New Cluster option at the bottom of the Create A New Server page. Alternatively, you can select Environment | Clusters to go to the

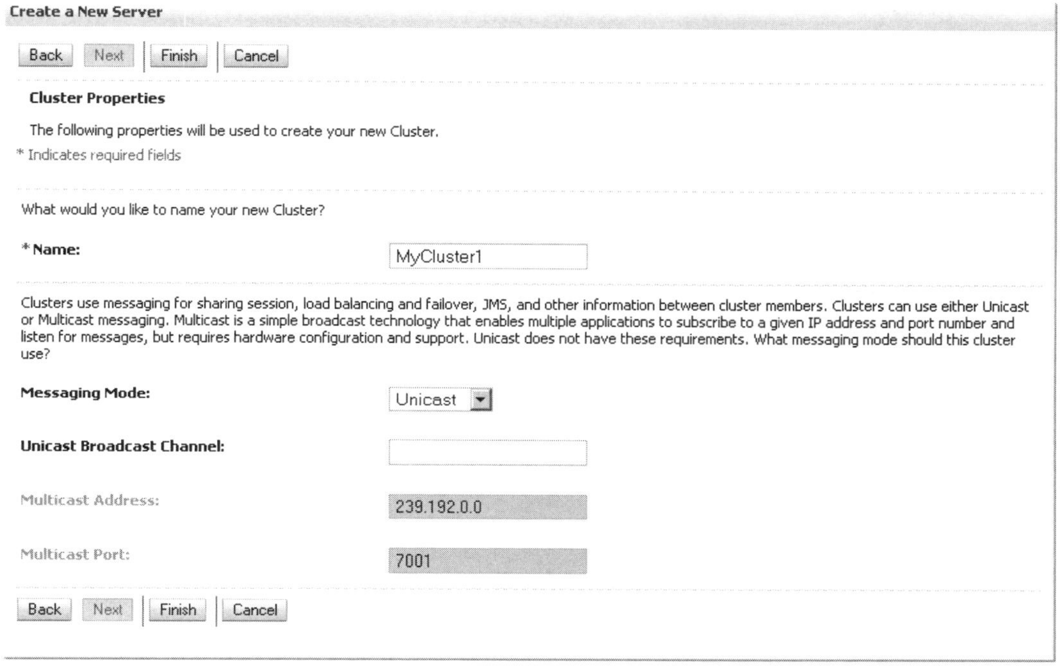

Create a New Server

Back | Next | Finish | Cancel

Cluster Properties

The following properties will be used to create your new Cluster.

* Indicates required fields

What would you like to name your new Cluster?

*** Name:** MyCluster1

Clusters use messaging for sharing session, load balancing and failover, JMS, and other information between cluster members. Clusters can use either Unicast or Multicast messaging. Multicast is a simple broadcast technology that enables multiple applications to subscribe to a given IP address and port number and listen for messages, but requires hardware configuration and support. Unicast does not have these requirements. What messaging mode should this cluster use?

Messaging Mode: Unicast

Unicast Broadcast Channel:

Multicast Address: 239.192.0.0

Multicast Port: 7001

Back | Next | Finish | Cancel

FIGURE 7-4. *The Create A New Cluster page in the Administration Console*

Summary Of Clusters page and click New to create a new cluster (you actually get to choose between a normal Cluster and a Dynamic Cluster. Just choose Cluster for this example). Either way, you get the Create A New Cluster page, as shown in Figure 7-4, which lets you configure various cluster configuration options.

Adding Nodes to the Cluster

The previous two sections showed you how to create the cluster members and the cluster itself. However, the cluster doesn't know about the two Managed Servers you created because they're still stand-alone servers. You must now make the two Managed Servers members of your new cluster, MyCluster1, by assigning the two servers to it. Once you create a new cluster, the cluster name appears in the Summary Of Clusters page. Clicking the cluster name (MyCluster1) takes you to the Settings For MyCluster1 page.

Initially, you'll be on the General section of the Settings for MyCluster1 page, On this page, click the Servers subtab to add servers to the new cluster. Figure 7-5 shows the Servers page. The Servers page lets you configure servers that you want to assign to a cluster. The server table is initially empty because the cluster doesn't have any members yet. Click Add twice (at the bottom of the page, inn the Servers table) to add your two Managed Servers to the new cluster MyCluster1. The resulting Add A Server To Cluster page is shown in Figure 7-6.

On the Add A Server To Cluster page, you must identify the Managed Servers you want to add to the new cluster. Choose the Select An Existing Server, And Add It As A Member Of This Cluster option. You'll notice the first Managed Server, MyManagedServer1, in the Select A Server box.

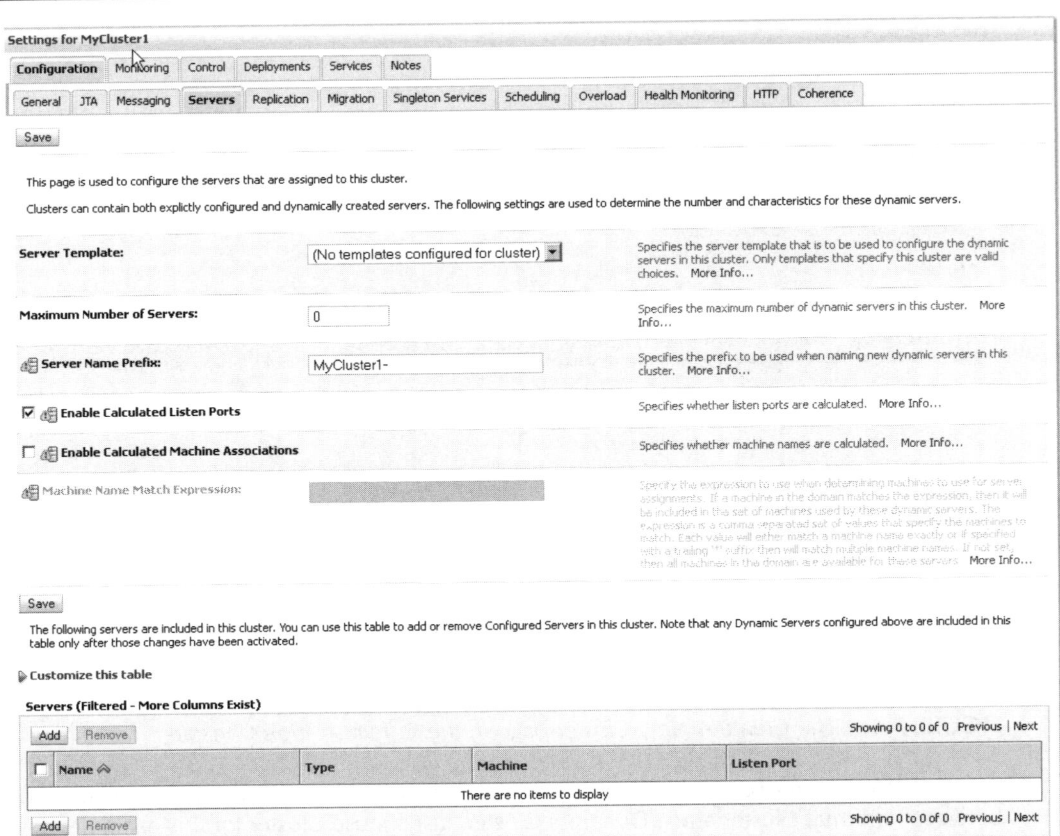

FIGURE 7-5. *The Servers page (Settings for MyCluster1) in the Administration Console*

Click Next. You'll be taken back to the Settings For MyCluster1 page. Click Add again. In the Select A Server box, you will now see the name of your second Managed Server, MyManagedServer2. Click Finish.

Optionally, you can select the Create A New Server And Add It To This Cluster option to create and add nodes to the cluster. If you now click the Servers tab in the Settings For MyCluster1 page, you'll see both cluster members.

Using the WLST Script

Note that you can quickly create a cluster in a development or test environment by using a script such as the *cluster_creation.py* online WLST script provided by Oracle. The *cluster_create.py* script is located in the C:\Oracle\Middleware\Oracle_Home\user_projects\applications\wl_server\examples\src\examples\wlst\online directory. This directory contains a few other useful WLST online scripts as well. The script contains commands that connect WLST to the domain's Admin Server, start an edit session, and create a set of ten Managed Servers. The script then creates one or more clusters

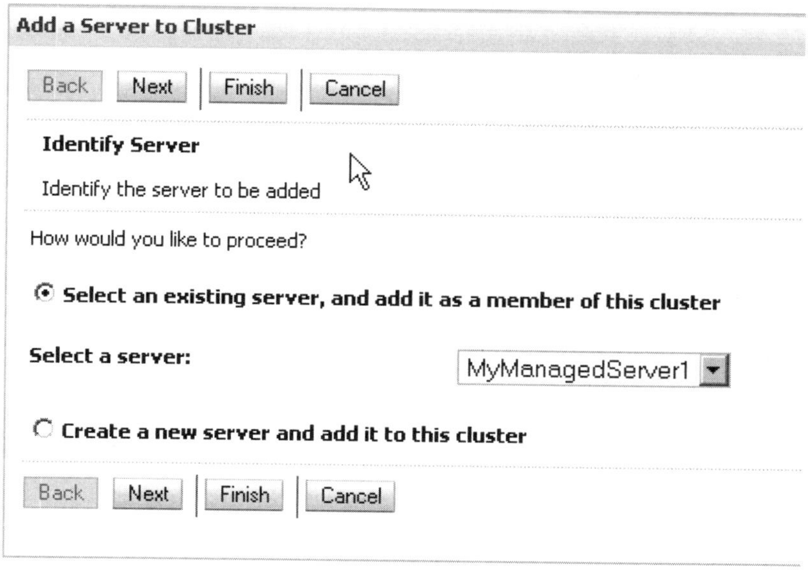

FIGURE 7-6. *The Add a Server to Cluster page in the Administration Console*

and assigns the Managed Servers to the cluster or clusters. Of course, you can customize this script to your heart's content. Here's an example that shows how to use the *cluster_creation.py* script to create a cluster. You need to connect to a running Admin Server to execute this command:

```
C:\Oracle\Middleware\Oracle_Home\wlserver\server\bin> setWLSEnv.cmd
C:\Oracle\Middlware\Oracle_Home\wl_server\common\bin>java weblogic.WLST
wls:/offline> connect()
Successfully connected to Admin Server 'examplesServer' that belongs to domain
wl_server'.
wls:/wl_server/serverConfig/Servers>
execfile('
C:\Oracle\Middleware\Oracle_Home\user_projects\applications\wl_server\examples\src
\examples\wlst\online\cluster_creation.py')
starting the script ....
Connecting to t3://localhost:7001 with userid weblogic ...
Successfully connected to Admin Server 'examplesServer' that belongs to
domain wl_server'.
Warning: An insecure protocol was used to connect to the
server. To ensure on-the-wire security, the SSL port or
Admin port should be used instead.
Location changed to edit tree. This is a writable tree with DomainMBean
as the root. To make changes you will need to start
an edit session via startEdit().
For more help, use help(edit)
Starting an edit session ...
```

```
Started edit session, please be sure to save and activate your
changes once you are done.

creating cluster cluster1
MBean type Cluster with name cluster1 has been created successfully
creating cluster cluster2
MBean type Cluster with name cluster2 has been created successfully
MBean type Server with name managed3 has been created successfully.
creating managed server managed3
MBean type Server with name managed2 has been created successfully.
creating managed server managed2
MBean type Server with name managed1 has been created successfully.
creating managed server managed1
MBean type Server with name managed5 has been created successfully.
creating managed server managed5
MBean type Server with name managed4 has been created successfully.
creating managed server managed4
MBean type Server with name managed10 has been created successfully
creating managed server managed10
MBean type Server with name managed9 has been created successfully.
creating managed server managed9
MBean type Server with name managed8 has been created successfully.
creating managed server managed8
MBean type Server with name managed7 has been created successfully.
creating managed server managed7
MBean type Server with name managed6 has been created successfully.
creating managed server managed6
Saving all your changes ...
Saved all your changes successfully.
Activating all your changes, this may take a while ...
The edit lock associated with this edit session is released
once the activation is completed.
Activation completed
Disconnected from weblogic server: examplesServer
```

Check the status of your new cluster with the *state* command:

```
wls:/offline> connect()
wls:/wl_server/serverConfig> state('cluster1','Cluster')
There are 5 server(s) in cluster: cluster1
States of the servers are
managed1---SHUTDOWN
managed2---SHUTDOWN
managed3---SHUTDOWN
managed4---SHUTDOWN
managed5---SHUTDOWN
```

The cluster creation script *cluster_creation.py* creates the clusters and the Managed Servers that you specify and assigns the Managed Servers to the clusters, but the script doesn't automatically start the Managed Servers in the cluster or clusters you create with the script. Use the *start* command to start the cluster, as shown in the section "Starting and Stopping Clusters with WLST Commands," later in this chapter. You can use the *cluster_deletion.py* script to remove a cluster from the domain configuration. Alternatively, you can delete a cluster from the Administration Console Clusters home page.

Configuring a Cluster

When you create a cluster, you can specify just the name for the cluster as well as the Managed Servers that belong to that cluster, as shown in the cluster creation examples earlier in this chapter. However, you can configure several other cluster attributes. You can configure the new cluster by going to Environment | Clusters and clicking the name of the cluster you want to configure. Following are the key attributes you can configure from the Settings For <*cluster_name*> page:

- **Cluster Address** Clients use the cluster address to connect to the cluster. You can provide either a DNS hostname that maps to multiple IP addresses or a comma-separated list of hostnames or IP addresses. If you don't define the cluster address, WebLogic Server will dynamically generate the cluster address for each new request. It's administratively simpler to let the server handle the cluster address because there's no overhead involved, even in a production environment. The format of the listen address is as follows:

  ```
  listenaddress1:listenport1,listenaddress2:listenport2
  ```

- **Default Load Algorithm** WebLogic Server uses the algorithm you specify for load balancing between replicated services if you haven't specified an algorithm for any of the services. You can choose among the round-robin, weight-based, or random load-balancing algorithms.
- **WebLogic Plug-In Enabled** You must set this attribute to *true* if your cluster receives requests from a proxy plug-in or the *HttpClusterServlet*.
- **Service Age Threshold** This is the time, in seconds, by which two services must differ in order for the server to classify one of the services as the older service.
- **Member Warmup Timeout** Cluster members normally synchronize with other members within 30 seconds. You can specify the maximum time (in seconds) that a cluster will wait to synchronize with the other cluster members. If you set this attribute to its minimum value of 0, the servers will not try to discover any of the running cluster members during their initialization.

While you can certainly use the Administration Console to create and configure the cluster, the Configuration Wizard is the recommended tool for doing this. You can then use the Console for additional configuration and monitoring purposes.

Creating Dynamic Clusters

In the Oracle WebLogic Server 12.1.2 release, you can create dynamic clusters, which are based on a shared server template. A dynamic cluster contains dynamic servers, which are server instances that you don't individually configure, but instead get their configuration from a server template. You use the server template to specify the configuration of the cluster members, thus avoiding having to configure each cluster separately when creating or expanding a cluster.

Configuring a dynamic cluster lets you configure a set of server instances to keep ready for peak load times. When you need additional server capacity, you can easily start the new servers, without having to manually configure each server instance separately and adding it to the cluster.

Creating Dynamic Clusters Through the Administration Console

You can create a dynamic cluster through the Administration Console or through WLST. Follow these steps to create a dynamic cluster in the Administration Console:

1. In the Change Center of the Administration Console, click Lock & Edit.
2. In the left pane of the Console, select Environment | Clusters.
3. In the Clusters table, click New and select Dynamic Cluster.
4. On the Specify Cluster Identity And Properties page, set the following options:
   - **Name** Enter a unique name for your new dynamic cluster.
   - **Messaging Mode** Select the messaging mode you want to use for this cluster.
   - **Unicast Broadcast Channel** If you are using the unicast messaging mode, enter the unicast broadcast channel. This channel is used to transmit messages within the cluster. If you do not specify a channel, the default channel is used.
   - **Multicast Address** If you are using the multicast messaging mode, enter the multicast address of the new dynamic cluster. A multicast address is an IP address in the range from 224.0.0.0 to 239.255.255.255. The default value used by WebLogic Server is 239.192.0.0. This address must be unique to this cluster and should not be shared by other applications.
   - **Multicast Port** Enter the multicast port for the new dynamic cluster. The multicast port is used by cluster members to communicate with each other. Valid values are between 1 and 65535. Click Next.
5. On the Specify Dynamic Server Properties page, set these options:
   - **Number Of Dynamic Servers** Enter the number of servers you need at peak load.
   - **Server Name Prefix** Specify the naming convention you want to use for the dynamic servers in your cluster.
6. Select either Create A New Server Template Using Domain Defaults or Clone An Existing Server Template For This Cluster. If you choose to clone an existing template, select the template in Server Template To Clone. If you don't already have a configured server template, WebLogic Server will automatically generate a template for you. Click Next.
7. On the Specify Machine Bindings page, select the method you want to use to distribute the dynamic servers in your cluster across machines. Click Next.
8. On the Specify Listen Port Bindings page, select how the dynamic servers should be bound to listen ports. Click Next.
9. On the Review Your Cluster Configuration page, check the configuration details for your new dynamic cluster to make sure they are correct. Click Finish.

Once you activate the change, the new dynamic cluster appears in the Clusters table. If you did not apply a previously existing server template, a new server template is automatically created with the naming convention you specified. The Administration Console also displays a message indicating that the cluster was created successfully.

When you create a dynamic cluster by using a server template and specifying the number of server instances, WebLogic Server calculates values for the following attributes:

- **Server Name** Server names use the specified prefix followed by the index number, as in dyn-server-1, dyn-server-2, and so on.
- **(Optional) Listen Ports (cleartext and SSL)** You can set the configuration for the listen ports in the server template or indicate that the default listen ports be used.
- **(Optional) Machines or Vrtual Machines** You can specify the machines to be used for the dynamic servers, and if you don't, all machines in the domain are selected, and the Managed Servers are assigned to those machines using a round-robin algorithm.
- **(Optional) Network Access Point Listen Ports** Same as listen ports.

Creating a Dynamic Cluster Using WLST

Use the following general steps to create a dynamic cluster using WLST:

1. Create a server template with the server attributes you require.
2. Create a dynamic cluster and specify the desired cluster attributes.
3. Set the server template for your dynamic cluster.
4. Set the maximum number of server instances in the new dynamic cluster.

Here's an example that shows how to create a dynamic cluster using WLST:

```
#
connect()
edit()
startEdit()
#
# Create the server template for the dynamic servers and set the attributes for
# the dynamic servers. #
dynamicServerTemplate=cmo.createServerTemplate("dynamic-cluster-server-template")
dynamicServerTemplate.setAcceptBacklog(2000)
dynamicServerTemplate.setAutoRestart(true)
dynamicServerTemplate.setRestartMax(10)
dynamicServerTemplate.setStartupTimeout(600)
#
# Create the dynamic cluster and set the dynamic servers.
#
dynCluster=cmo.createCluster("dynamic-cluster")
dynServers=dynCluster.getDynamicServers()
dynServers.setMaximumDynamicServerCount(10)
dynServers.setServerTemplate(dynamicServerTemplate)
#
dynServers.setServerNamePrefix("dynamic-server-")
#
# Listen ports and machines assignments will be calculated. A round-robin
# algorithm is used to assign the 10 dynamic servers to all machines in this
domain.
#
dynServers.setCalculatedMachineNames(true)
dynServers.setMachineNameMatchExpression("dyn-machine*")
#
```

```
# activate the changes
#
activate()
```

And here's the *config.xml* file for our new dynamic cluster:

```
<server-template>
    <name>dynamic-cluster-server-template</name>
    <accept-backlog>2000</accept-backlog>
    <auto-restart>true</auto-restart>
    <restart-max>10</restart-max>
    <startup-timeout>600</startup-timeout>
</server-template>

<cluster>
    <name>dynamic-cluster</name>
    <dynamic-servers>
      <server-template>dynamic-cluster-server-template</server-template>
      <maximum-dynamic-server-count>10</maximum-dynamic-server-count>
      <calculated-machine-names>true</calculated-machine-names>
      <machine-name-match-expression>dyn-machine*</machine-name-match-expression>
      <server-name-prefix>dynamic-server-</server-name-prefix>
    </dynamic-servers>
</cluster>
```

Limitations When Using Dynamic Clusters

A few important limitations apply to the use of dynamic clusters. Whole server migration and service migration are not supported with dynamic clusters. Because dynamic clusters don't allow targeting to an individual dynamic server instance, you won't be able to use the following with dynamic clusters:

- Deployments that cannot target to a cluster. This includes migratable targets.
- Configuration attributes that refer to individual servers, including JTA migratable targets, constrained candidate servers, user preferred server, all candidate servers, and hosting server.
- Server-specific configuration attributes, including replication groups, preferred secondary groups, and candidate machines (server level).

In addition, there are a few JMS-related limitations on the use of dynamic clusters.

The config.xml File and a Cluster

The *config.xml* file for a domain with a cluster is similar to one without a cluster, except that the *<server>* elements will show the cluster name as well as other information if the servers are designated as migratable targets for pinned services. Here's the cluster-related information from the *config.xml* for the *wl_server* domain in my environment:

```
<cluster>
  <name>MyCluster1</name>
  <cluster-messaging-mode>unicast</cluster-messaging-mode>
</cluster>
```

```
<cluster>
  <name>Mycluster1</name>
</cluster>
<cluster>
  <name>Mycluster2</name>
</cluster>
```

The *<server>* element for each Managed Server in a domain will contain the cluster name, as shown here:

```
<server>
  <name>MyManagedServer1</name>
  <listen-port>7003</listen-port>
  <cluster>MyCluster1</cluster>
</server>
```

Managing a WebLogic Server Cluster

Managing a cluster is, in many ways, similar to managing single WebLogic Server instances. The following sections show how to start and stop clusters, as well as how to monitor them.

Starting and Stopping the Cluster

You can start a cluster in several ways. You can start it with the WLST *start* command, provided the Node Manager is running. Alternatively, you can start each of the cluster members independently, after first starting the domain's Admin Server. You can start the cluster's member Managed Servers from the Administration Console as well, provided you use the Node Manager—this is exactly how you'd manage individual nonclustered servers. The same thing applies to shutting down a cluster—you can either use the WLST *shutdown* command or bring down each of the cluster instances one by one, just as you would any nonclustered WebLogic Server instance.

Note that unlike in the case of nonclustered Managed Servers, for which there's both a Configuration and a Control button on the Summary Of Servers page, the Summary Of Clusters page lets you do only three things—create a cluster, clone an existing cluster, or delete a cluster. You can't stop or start an entire cluster from the Administration Console—you must control the lifecycle of the cluster's member servers by managing them directly from the Summary Of Servers page.

Starting and Stopping with Scripts

Because the Managed Servers are assigned to a cluster, even when you start them one by one, all the cluster members will join the cluster following startup. If you want to start the cluster members individually, you can create start scripts for each server and call them from a cluster startup script. In our examples for the *wl_server* domain, in the WL_HOME\samples\domains\wl_server\bin directory, you'll find a generic *startManagedWebLogic.cmd* command file (Windows) and a *startManagedWebLogic.sh* script (UNIX/Linux). Make copies of this file and name them something like *startMyManagedServer1.cmd* and *startMyManagedServer2.cmd*. You must customize the generic startup command script for each of the Managed Servers. For example, for the Managed Server named MyManagedServer1, you must specify the following values for these attributes:

```
set DOMAIN_NAME=wl_server
set SERVER_NAME=MyManagedServer1
```

```
set ADMIN_URL=http://localhost:7001
set WLS_USER=weblogic
set WLS_PW=welcome1
```

Note that the server name is the name of the cluster member. The *ADMIN_URL* must specify the port number for the Admin Server (7001 in our case) and not the listen port for the Managed Server. The reason for this is that the *ADMIN_URL* is the Admin Server's URL, to which the two Managed Servers will connect once they start. You must specify the same username and password credentials as those you use for the Admin Server. If you don't specify the credentials in the Managed Server startup scripts, the startup process will prompt you for those—placing the credentials here will keep you from typing in the credentials in the command window.

Once you edit the command scripts (one for each Managed Server), just run the scripts in separate command windows. The two Managed Servers will start and automatically join the cluster MyCluster1. Here's the output from the second cluster member's startup process:

```
<Aug 18, 2013 12:22:35 PM EDT> <Notice> <Cluster> <BEA-000197> <Listening for
announcements from cluster using unicast cluster messaging>
< Aug 18, 2013 12:22:35 PM EDT> <Notice> <Cluster> <BEA-000133> <Waiting to
synchronize with other running members of MyCluster1.>
< Aug 18, 2013 12:22:47 PM  EDT> <Notice> <Cluster> <BEA-000142> <Trying to
download cluster JNDI tree from server MyManagedServer1.>
< Aug 18, 2013 12:22:47 PM  EDT> <Notice> <Cluster> <BEA-000164> <Synchronized
cluster JNDI tree from server MyManagedServer1.>
< Aug 18, 2013 12:22:347PM  EDT> <Notice> <WebLogicServer> <BEA-000365> <Server
state changed to ADMIN>
< Aug 18, 2013 12:22:47 PM  EDT> <Notice> <WebLogicServer> <BEA-000365> <Server
state changed to RESUMING>
...
< Aug 18, 2013 12:22:49 PM  PM EDT> <Notice> <Server> <BEA-002613> <Channel
"Default[11]" is now listening on fe80:0:0:0:8b9:1ace:e3d5:ea9a:7005
for protocols iiop, t3, CLUSTER-BROADCAST, ldap, snmp, http.>
```

Starting and Stopping a Cluster from the Administration Console

You can also start and stop a cluster by starting and stopping the Managed Servers that belong to a cluster directly from the Administration Console. Just make sure you first configure a machine and associate the Managed Servers with the machine, as explained in Chapter 2. You must first configure the Managed Server to communicate with the Node Manager and also make sure to start the Node Manager on the machine that hosts the Managed Servers. To start and stop a cluster member, go to Environment | Clusters | Cluster Name | Control. From the Control page, you can start, shut down, resume, and suspend any cluster member. As with a freestanding Managed Server, you must configure the domain-wide administration port to start the server in the standby startup mode.

Starting and Stopping Clusters with WLST Commands

Use the WLST *start* command to start a cluster, after making sure the Node Manager is running. You don't have to connect to the Node Manager, but you must connect to the Admin Server, as this is a WLST lifecycle command. The WLST *start* command (you use this to start a Managed Server as well) has the following syntax:

```
start(name,  [type],[url],[block])
```

At a minimum, you must provide the name of the cluster and the value "cluster" for the type argument—the default value of the *type* argument is *Server,* meaning it will start a single Managed Server that you name. The *url* argument defaults to t3://localhost:7001, and you can provide appropriate listen address and listen port values here. The *block* argument specifies whether WLST should keep you from interacting with it until the cluster is started. The default value is *true,* meaning you can't interact with WLST until it starts the cluster.

Here's an example that shows how to start a cluster with the *start* command. (Note that you don't need to use the *ls* and *cd* commands shown here—they are here just to show how you can find out the name of the cluster from WLST.)

```
C:\Oracle\Middleware\Oracle_Home\wlserver\server\bin\setWLSEnv.cmd
C:\Oracle\Middleware\Oracle_Home\wlserver\common\bin> wlst.cmd
wls:/offline> connect()
wls:/wl_server/serverConfig> cd('Clusters')
wls:/wl_server/serverConfig/Clusters> ls()
dr--   MyCluster1
dr--   cluster1
dr--   cluster2

wls:/wl_server/serverConfig/Clusters> cd('/')
wls:/wl_server/serverConfig> start('MyCluster1','Cluster')
Starting the following servers in Cluster, MyCluster1:
MyManagedServer1,MyManagedServer2
....................................................................
All servers in the cluster MyCluster1 are started successfully.
wls:/wl_server/serverConfig>
```

Note that the cluster start time may be quite long on servers where you don't have plenty of RAM and/or have a lot of other resource-intensive processes running.

If you check the status of the cluster MyCluster1, you should see that all two Managed Servers are in the *RUNNING* state—you're in business!

```
wls:/wl_server/serverConfig> state('MyCluster1','Cluster')
There are 2 server(s) in cluster: MyCluster1
States of the servers are
MyManaged1---RUNNING
MyManaged2---RUNNING
wls:/wl_server/serverConfig>
```

You can use the WLST command *shutdown* to shut down a cluster. Here's the syntax of the *shutdown* command:

```
shutdown([name],[entityType],[ignoreSessions],[timeout],[force],[block])
```

To shut down a cluster, you need to specify at least the attributes *name* and *entityType*.

The *name* attribute refers to the name of the cluster you're shutting down, of course, and you must specify the value *Cluster* for the *entityType* argument. Note that this WLST command also works with a single Managed Server. If you connect to a Managed Server with WLST, you can issue the *shutdown* command without any arguments because the *name* attribute defaults to the Managed Server you connected to and the *entityType* argument's default value is *Server.*

The *ignoreSessions, timeout, force,* and *block* attributes are optional. Here's what these arguments allow you to do:

- The *ignoreSessions* argument specifies whether all HTTP sessions should be terminated immediately when you issue the *shutdown* command or if the sessions should be allowed to complete or time out. The default value for this argument is *false,* meaning the HTTP sessions are allowed to complete or time out.
- The timeout argument specifies the time that WLST waits for a subsystem to complete its ongoing work before shutting down the server. The default value of this argument is 0, meaning there's no timeout period after you issue the *shutdown* command.
- The *force* argument specifies whether WLST should wait for active sessions to complete before terminating the server instance. The default value is *false,* meaning active sessions are allowed to complete before the server is shut down.
- The *block* argument specifies whether user interaction is blocked until the server is shut down. The default value of the argument is *false,* meaning user interaction is not blocked—WLST returns control to the user once the *shutdown* command is issued.

Here's an example showing how to shut down a cluster with the *shutdown* command:

```
wls:/wl_server/serverConfig> shutdown('MyCluster1','Cluster')
Shutting down the cluster with name MyCluster1 ...
Shutdown of cluster MyCluster1 has been issued, please
refer to the logs to check if the cluster shutdown is successful.
 Use the state(server-name) or state(cluster-name,Cluster)
 to check the status of the server or cluster
wls:/wl_server/serverConfig>
```

Starting and Stopping a Dynamic Cluster

You can start and stop a dynamic cluster the same way as you do any other cluster. You can use the Administration Console, WLST, Node Manager, or a start script to start the cluster. Specify the *calculated name* of the server when starting the server.

Now that you know how to start and stop a cluster, the following section shows you how to monitor a running cluster.

Monitoring a Cluster

To monitor the cluster, go to Environment | Clusters and click the name of the cluster you want to monitor, in this case the cluster MyCluster1. In the Settings For MyCluster1 page, click the Monitoring tab. The Cluster Monitoring page, shown in Figure 7-7, lets you monitor the status of all members in a cluster, whether they're running or not.

You can configure health monitoring for a cluster, from the Health Monitoring page, by clicking the Health Monitoring tab in the Settings For <*cluster_name*> page. The idea behind configuring self-health monitoring is to improve the reliability and availability of the clusters. Following are the main configuration options that you can set from the Health Monitoring page:

- **Inter-Cluster Comm Link Health Check Interval** You can set this attribute to control how often a trigger will run to see if the cluster link is restored after it fails. You specify the duration (in milliseconds), and the default is 30,000 ms.

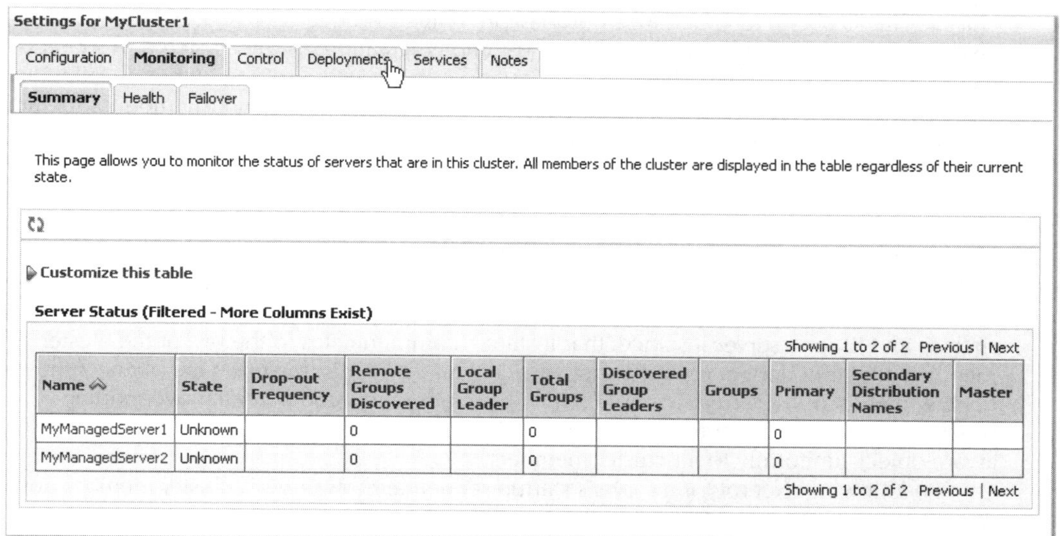

FIGURE 7-7. *The Cluster Monitoring page in the Administration Console*

- **Health Check Interval** Specifies the interval (in milliseconds) for the migratable servers and cluster masters to prove they are alive.
- **Health Check Periods Until Fencing** Specifies the maximum number of periods a cluster member will wait before timing out a cluster master. It also specifies how many periods the cluster master waits before timing out a migratable server.
- **Fencing Grace Period** The amount of time for which the cluster master will wait before declaring a server dead and migrating the server to another server or service during an automatic whole server or service migration.

You can control how the cluster reacts to an overload or failure condition by clicking the Configuration | Overload tab in the Settings For *<cluster_name>* page. The overload and failure attributes you can configure are the same as those you'd set for a nonclustered server. Specifically, you can set attributes such as Shared Capacity For Work Managers, Panic Action, Failure Action, and Stuck Thread Count from the Overload page. Please see Chapter 5 for an explanation of the overload and failure attributes you can configure for a server.

Clustering WebLogic Server Services

Java EE services such as JNDI and JDBC work the same way in a cluster, with a few key differences. The following sections review the nature of a cluster-wide JNDI tree and the JDBC service.

JNDI Naming Service

The big difference between a single instance JNDI naming service and the cluster-wide JNDI tree is that the latter also stores the names of services offered by clustered objects such as EJBs that are hosted on other servers in the cluster. The key to a cluster-wide JNDI naming service is the use of replica-aware stubs for objects. Replica-aware stubs help replicate an object's bindings across the cluster. Clients obtain a replica-aware stub for an object when they access that object. The replica-aware stub contains the list of servers that host implementations of the clustered object and the load-balancing logic for the object. Server instances in a cluster use a cluster-wide JNDI tree to enable clients to access objects and services. Cluster members continuously monitor the unicast (or multicast) address to detect new services offered by other members. Whenever a cluster member binds a service into its local JNDI, it sends the object's stub to the other cluster members.

The replica-aware stub that a client obtains is continuously updated to reflect the servers that currently have bound an implementation of that object in their local JNDI tree. When you start a cluster, the clusters communicate via unicast or multicast addresses about the services they are offering. Once all the cluster members receive the broadcast messages, each member of the cluster ends up with an identical local JNDI tree. Similarly, when you undeploy a clustered object such as an EJB for a server instance, that instance communicates to the rest of the cluster members that it no longer provides that service. Following this, the other members of the cluster update their local JNDI tree. To avoid JNDI naming conflicts and potential overloading of processing on some members of the cluster, Oracle recommends that you deploy all replica-aware objects uniformly to all cluster members.

The following excerpt for a server's startup sequence shows how a cluster member downloads the cluster-wide JNDI tree from the other servers in the cluster so it can synchronize its own JNDI tree with that cluster-wide JNDI tree:

```
<Aug 18, 2013 12:12:45 PM EDT> <Notice> <Cluster> <BEA-000133> <Waiting to
synchronize with other running members of MyCluster1.>
< Aug 18, 2013 12:12:45 PM  PM EDT> <Notice> <Cluster> <BEA-000142> <Trying to
download
cluster JNDI tree from server MyManagedServer1.>
< Aug 18, 2013 12:12:46 PM  PM EDT> <Notice> <Cluster> <BEA-000164> <Synchronized
 cluster JNDI tree from server MyManagedServer1.>
```

JDBC Clustering

You can cluster JDBC data sources and multi data sources for high-availability purposes. When you configure the data sources, you must target them to the entire cluster instead of targeting them to some members of the cluster. Once you do this, the data sources are cluster-aware and the server creates an instance of the data source on all members of the cluster. WebLogic Server handles external and server-side client connections differently. WebLogic Server doesn't automatically fail over JDBC connections when a server instance dies. When the server instance fails, the JDBC connection will die as well and the applications must restart their in-flight transactions. However, by configuring the cluster-aware JDBC multi data source, you can make the server automatically retrieve an alternate data source when a client's current database connection fails. Note that if you're using Oracle RAC databases, you can configure the GridLink data sources.

JMS and Clusters

JMS queues and topics aren't really clustered objects because they're pinned to a specific WebLogic Server instance. Thus, WebLogic Server can't fail over the queues and topics. You can, however, deploy connection factories for a queue or topic on several cluster nodes, thus allowing the load balancing of requests for the queue or topic. You can alternatively create JMS servers on all cluster members and create copies of the queue or topic on those nodes, after which you can target the connection factory to the cluster.

You can also create a distributed destination, which represents a set of destinations, such as queues or topics that a client can access as a single destination. With a cluster, the members of the set of destinations are usually distributed among the various JMS servers, with each member belonging to a different JMS server. Using multiple JMS servers, WebLogic JMS provides load balancing and failover for distributed destination members that you target to a cluster. The best option here is to set up automatic service migration for all pinned services, including JMS services. Key to the automatic migration of services is the configuration of the optional migratable targets, targets that can migrate from one cluster member to another. Pinned services such as the JMS-related services (JMS servers, SAF Agents, path services, and persistent stores) can be configured into a group and deployed to a migratable target, so these services can be moved together. When the migratable target migrates, all services hosted to that target are automatically migrated.

Cluster-Targeted JMS Servers

In Oracle WebLogic Server 12*c*, you can use cluster-targeted JMS servers to simplify the configuration of JMS resources by avoiding the individual configuration of JMS services to each server in a cluster. You can, instead, directly assign the JMS servers and persistent stores directly to a cluster. Using this feature, you can also dynamically scale JMS resources in a dynamic cluster.

WebLogic Clustering Options for JMS

In Oracle WebLogic Server 12*c*, a cluster may contain individual servers, dynamically generated servers, or a mix of both. The following is a summary of the cluster types you can have:

- **Configured** A cluster where each member server is individually configured and individually targeted to the cluster.
- **Dynamic** A cluster where all the member servers are created using a server template. These servers are referred to as *dynamic servers*.
- **Mixed** A cluster where some member servers are created using a server template (dynamic servers) and the remaining servers are individually configured (configured servers).

Simplified JMS Cluster Configuration

The *clustered JMS servers* feature gives you the capability to target a JMS server (and its persistent store if it has one) to the same cluster. When you start the cluster, the cluster starts an instance of the JMS server on each cluster member. When targeting JMS to a dynamic or a mixed cluster, you can also dynamically scale the JMS resources available to the cluster by adjusting the Maximum Number Of Servers attribute on the Clusters | Configuration | Servers tab for the cluster configuration.

Limitations of Using Clustered JMS

Be aware of the following key limitations when considering the use of dynamic clusters and cluster-targeted JMS servers.

- Cluster-targeted JMS servers don't support automatic service migration.
- Whole server migration (WSM) isn't supported.

- Unit-of-order and unit-of-work aren't supported.
- Store-and-Forward (SAF) Agents cannot be targeted to a dynamic or mixed cluster.

WebLogic Server Load Balancing

WebLogic Server tries to balance the workload evenly among the cluster instances. Load balancing works similarly for servlets and JSPs for the most part, and WebLogic Server uses the default round-robin method as the load-balancing algorithm. For EJBs and RMI objects, you have more load-balancing options. Let's briefly review load balancing for these two types of objects.

Load-Balancing Servlets and JSPs

You can configure load balancing either with an external load balancer or by using the WebLogic Server proxy plug-in. You can use the simple *HttpClusterServlet* that comes with WebLogic Server as a proxy plug-in for WebLogic Server. The plug-in maintains a list of server instances that host a clustered servlet or JSP, and it forwards HTTP requests to each cluster member on a round-robin basis. You can use the appropriate proxy plug-in for other HTTP servers. For example, you can use the Apache Server plug-in for Apache Server. To configure advanced load-balancing strategies, you can configure an external load balancer. An external load balancer must support passive or active cookie persistence, as well as SSL persistence. Here's the role played by the three mechanisms involved in maintaining session state:

- **Passive cookie persistence** The load balancer writes session state information to a cookie stored on the client.
- **Active cookie persistence** The load balancer adds its own cookies to a client session.
- **SSL persistence** The load balancer is responsible for encrypting and decrypting data flowing between the cluster and the clients.

Load Balancing for EJBs and RMI Objects

Load balancing is more complex for EJBs and RMI objects. For one thing, instead of being limited to the default round-robin load-balancing algorithm, as in the case of servlets and JSPs, you have a choice of multiple load-balancing algorithms. When you cluster an EJB or an RMI object, WebLogic Server deploys instances of those objects on all cluster members and uses replica-aware stubs to invoke clustered EJBs and RMI objects. Replica-aware stubs that represent an RMI or EJB object can find all the instances of those objects within a cluster. When you send a bean that has a cluster-aware deployment descriptor to the EJB compiler, it automatically generates a replica-aware stub for that bean. You can explicitly create replica-aware stubs for RMI objects during the compilation of the object instance, using command-line options with *rmic,* the WebLogic RMI compiler. The term replica-aware "stub" is a misnomer because the stub is actually a representation of a set of replicas, with each replica representing an object instance.

When a client requests a clustered EJB, for example, the server replaces the EJB's implementation with a replica-aware stub and sends the stub to the client. Replica-aware stubs provide failover capability by automatically sending an object call to a different replica (object instance) when a run-time failure occurs. Similarly, the replica-aware stubs provide load balancing since they're aware of where all the instances of an object are located. The stub uses the load-balancing algorithm built into it to select the specific replica from the multiple replicas located in the cluster.

NOTE
The replica-aware stub is capable of locating an EJB or RMI class on all cluster members where you deployed those objects.

The replica-aware stub maintains the load-balancing algorithm for each clustered object. Thus, when there's a call to the object, the replica-aware stub determines which replica (instance of the object) to call based on the load-balancing algorithm you specify. WebLogic Server uses the round-robin algorithm, by default, for load balancing clustered EJBs and RMI objects. The round-robin algorithm isn't very efficient when one of the servers is much slower than the other cluster members because the algorithm blindly assigns requests to the cluster members one by one, without regard for the actual load. You can specify any of the load-balancing algorithms discussed in the following section for EJBs and RMI objects. You can specify a different load-balancing algorithm by going to Environment | Clusters and selecting an alternative load-balancing algorithm for the Default Load Algorithm setting. Note that you can use the random load-balancing algorithm only for EJBs and RMI-clustered objects and not for servlets and JSPs.

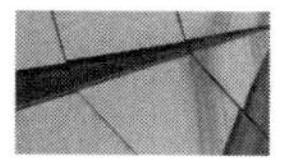

NOTE
You can't specify a weight-based load-balancing algorithm for objects that use the RMI/IIOP protocol to communicate.

All RMI objects, including JMS objects and stateless EJB remote interfaces, can also use the three load-balancing algorithms that provide server affinity: round-robin-affinity, weight-based-affinity, and random-affinity.

Load-Balancing Algorithms

WebLogic Server offers three load-balancing algorithms:

- **Round-robin** The round-robin algorithm load balances requests by simply assigning them to each server instance in a cluster in order. This is the default load-balancing algorithm.
- **Weight-based** This algorithm assigns requests proportionately to server instances based on a weight you assign to each server. For example, by assigning a weight of 50 to server A and 100 to server B, you can make Server A carry only half as much as the load carried by Server B. If all servers in a cluster are homogenous, of course, it doesn't make any sense to use a weight-based load-balancing algorithm. If the processing capacity of some servers in a cluster is different from that of the other servers, however, you can use a weight-based algorithm to advantage.
- **Random** The random algorithm simply specifies that the cluster randomly routes requests to the servers in the cluster. If you have only a few requests, probabilistically speaking, the allocation among servers could be quite uneven. However, as you progress to a large number of requests, the allocation is more or less even among all the members of the clusters. Make sure that all your servers are configured similarly in terms of processing power if you're going to specify the random load-balancing algorithm.

By default, WebLogic Server uses the round-robin load-balancing algorithm. You can configure a load-balancing algorithm with server affinity for JMS objects by configuring the algorithm for the entire cluster. For JDBC connections, you can choose load balancing when configuring a multi data source. If you don't configure load balancing for data sources, the first data source in the ordered list of data sources is always tried; if you load balance the JDBC connections, the server assigns data sources in a round-robin fashion.

Server Affinity

To minimize the opening of IP sockets between server instances and external Java clients, WebLogic Server uses the concept of *server affinity,* which, in essence, turns off load balancing. Note that server affinity only turns load balancing off after the initial request is made. This just means that the state that is required is more likely to be available on the server that the request is directed to. Instead of load balancing requests, the client prefers its current connection to an instance to determine the instance from which it accesses objects. For example, if you configure an RMI object such as a JMS object for load balancing, the client-side RMI stub will attempt to choose a server instance to which it's already connected. When WebLogic Server uses a server affinity algorithm, it doesn't use load balancing for external client connections. Server affinity seeks to keep opened IP sockets between Java clients and the cluster's servers to a minimum. WebLogic Server, however, still uses load balancing for server-to-server connections because server-to-server connections aren't as expensive as external connections in terms of socket usage. Server affinity is always used in combination with one of the three load-balancing methods. Thus, you have a choice among the following types of server affinity:

- Round-robin-affinity
- Weight-based-affinity
- Random-affinity

In each of these three algorithms, server affinity determines the connections with external Java clients, and the load-balancing algorithm specifies how the cluster handles connections among the members. For example, the round-robin-affinity algorithm uses the standard round-robin load-balancing algorithm to assign requests.

NOTE
Server affinity doesn't affect load balancing for server-to-server connections. It turns off load balancing for Java clients, however.

Collocation Strategy

When a server instance in a cluster hosts an EJB, not only do other server instances keep a replica-aware stub of that EJB, but the primary instance will also keep a replica of that object. This replica is called a *collocated* copy of the EJB. It makes more sense to use this local collocated copy of the EJB rather than send the client's requests to the other instances hosting a copy of that object through the network. Thus, collocation optimization doesn't load balance every method call made to the clustered EJB (or other clustered object such as an RMI object). In a single cluster, even though the replica-aware stubs contain a load-balancing algorithm, collocation trumps that and forces the use of the local copy of the clustered object. You must configure multitier cluster architectures to force load balancing of all method calls to an object from a client. To further optimize the choice of the object replicas, WebLogic Server employs a transactional collocation strategy by always using the collocated object's replicas of all objects involved in a transaction. Transactional collocation strategies are even more efficient than the nontransactional usage of local collocated replicas because they lower the network overhead both by avoiding having to send requests back and forth to other servers and by avoiding using a multitier JDBC connection.

Application Failover and Replication

WebLogic Server offers failover capabilities when an application component such as an EJB or servlet fails during the processing of a task. Because a cluster maintains a cluster-wide JNDI tree that provides information about the availability and location of all clustered objects, WebLogic Server uses a copy of the failed object located on a different server to complete the processing that was left incomplete due to the component failure. Making use of an alternate copy of a failed object is called *application failover.* How does WebLogic Server know the state of the job that failed? It uses two types of replication techniques to identify the state of the incomplete job—session replication for servlets and JSPs, and replica-aware stubs to find out where exactly it needs to resume processing of a failed object such as an EJB.

Application failover is competently different from a migration, of which there are two types: server migration and service migration. With *server migration,* you can configure the automatic migration of an entire server to a different machine following a server (machine) failure. You can also manually migrate the server for maintenance reasons. *Service migration* occurs when WebLogic Server migrates a pinned service (a service that can run only on one server at any given time), such as a JMS server or the JTS transaction recovery, when the server that hosts a pinned service fails. This chapter discusses server and service migration in the section "Handling Server and Service Failures."

Detecting Application Failures

Cluster members use IP sockets to detect failures—when a socket suddenly closes during data transmission, the server is marked as "failed" and all the services offered by the server are removed from the JNDI tree. When servers aren't actively communicating via open sockets, WebLogic Server detects failures by monitoring the server heartbeats, which, by default, are sent every ten seconds by every cluster member. Cluster members use the IP unicast (or multicast) to broadcast and revive the heartbeat messages. Once a server misses three heartbeats from a peer server, it marks the status of the other server as failed and updates its local JNDI tree by removing the failed server's services.

In the following sections, let's review how WebLogic Server handles failures of various types of objects, including servlets and JSPs as well as EJBs and RMI objects. The failover of servlets and JSPs depends on the replication of HTTP session state, and the failover of EJBs and RMI objects relies on the cluster-aware stubs.

Handling Servlet and JSP Failures

In order to understand how a cluster manages servlet and JSP failures, you must first understand how WebLogic Server replicates HTTP session state following a failure of one of these components.

Replicating HTTP Session State

You can set up two different ways of handling application failures. You can use a third-party load balancer, or use a proxy plug-in or the *HttpClusterServlet* with a WebLogic instance functioning as a web server. Regardless of whether you use a load balancer or a proxy plug-in (or the *HttpClusterServlet*), WebLogic Server uses two basic methods to replicate HTTP session state in a cluster. You can configure either a file or JDBC-based persistence of HTTP session state information. Alternatively, you can configure an in-memory replication method without persistence, wherein WebLogic Server creates and maintains secondary replicas of session state to use in case a servlet or JSP fails midway through its processing. The following discussion pertains to in-memory replication of HTTP server state.

In-Memory Replication You can configure either a WebLogic proxy plug-in or load-balancing hardware for in-memory replication. If you're using a proxy plug-in, the plug-in doesn't direct the client requests to an alternate server; it simply redirects the client request to a server that has the replicated HTTP session state information. The proxy plug-in knows all the server instances that host a clustered servlet or JSP, and it uses a round-robin strategy to forward the client HTTP requests. You can use WebLogic Server with the *HttpClusterServlet* or a third-party HTTP server such as Apache or Microsoft IIS, with the appropriate WebLogic Server plug-in. For replication to work, you must configure the WebLogic proxy plug-ins the same way on all web servers.

NOTE

*In-memory replication and JDBC persistence aren't your only options for replicating the session state of HTTP objects. If your application is undergoing memory problems because it can't keep up with large HTTP session state objects, you can optionally use Oracle Coherence*Web to maintain the session state information.*

Regardless of whether you use a third-party web server or the WebLogic Server proxy plug-in, the failover process for requests that are proxied to a clustered servlet or JSP is identical. Let's say you configured proxying through the *HttpClusterServlet* on a WebLogic Server instance. The WebLogic Server instance, which is functioning as the web server, will forward (proxy) servlet requests to the cluster through the *HttpClusterServlet*. If the primary server is not reachable due to a network failure, for example, the *HttpClusterServlet* knows which server to send the request to because it maintains a list of all the servers in the cluster. When the client makes the next HTTP request to the unreachable server, the *HttpClusterServlet* automatically redirects the request to the second server, with the switching of servers transparent to the client. By default, WebLogic Server depends on client-side cookies to track the servers hosting the session state, but if a client browser isn't using cookies, WebLogic Server uses *URL rewriting* (using the information in the HTTP request itself) to track primary and secondary servers that maintain the session state.

By default, WebLogic Server chooses a different machine to replicate the session state than the one that hosts the primary session state. However, you can configure replication groups to influence the choice of the alternate machine. WebLogic Server always picks the preferred server you configured in the replication group, regardless of whether it is on the same or a different machine.

If you set up a hardware load balancer instead of a proxy plug-in following the failure of a servlet or JSP, there's no automatic redirection of HTTP requests to a failed server—it is the load balancer that redirects the client request to any of the available servers in the cluster. Note that you must satisfy the following requirements if you want to use a hardware load balancer for replication:

- All session data must be serializable—that is, WebLogic Server must be able to convert the data into a serial form to facilitate its transmission.

NOTE
Large objects may suffer a performance penalty when serializing session data in order to replicate it.

- If your web application uses multiple frames, session attributes could be corrupted or the application's link to an instance could be reset during replication. Oracle advices you to ensure that only one frame manages session data in any frameset.

JDBC-Based Replication You can also set up JDBC-based persistence for maintaining servlet or JSP HTTP session state in a file or a database. Although this is an alternative to in-memory session state replication, JDBC (database) persistence is a requirement for configuring HTTP session state replication in a wide area network, as explained in the next section. To configure file-based replication, in the *weblogic.xml* deployment descriptor file, the element *session-descriptor* lets you specify server properties for JDBC session persistence. Set the *persistent-store-type* parameter in the *session-descriptor* element to the value *file* if you want to use file-based replication. For storing session state data in a database table, set the *session-descriptor* element to the value *jdbc*. You must also specify the name of the connection pool for the *persistent-store-pool* parameter. You can configure the maximum time the database should wait for a JDBC connection to load session data by setting a value for the *jdbc-connection-timeout-secs* parameter.

Once you configure the session state persistence properties, you must also create a table named *wl_servlet_sessions* to configure JDBC-based session state persistence. Here's the DDL for creating the *wl_servlet_sessions* table in an Oracle database:

```
create table wl_servlet_sessions
  ( wl_id VARCHAR2(100) NOT NULL,
    wl_context_path VARCHAR2(100) NOT NULL,
    wl_is_new CHAR(1),
    wl_create_time NUMBER(20),
    wl_is_valid CHAR(1),
    wl_session_values LONG RAW,
    wl_access_time NUMBER(20),
    wl_max_inactive_interval INTEGER,
   PRIMARY KEY (wl_id, wl_context_path) );
```

When the client makes a read-only request, WebLogic Server doesn't update the database table to modify the HTTP session state. However, after each non-read-only request, the server updates the session state so other cluster members can access the database and retrieve an up-to-date session state for a request following a failover. The *cache-size* parameter of the *session-descriptor* element in the *weblogic.xml* file controls how many recently used sessions the server instance must keep in its own cache. By getting session state from its own cache, WebLogic Server can avoid going to the database to retrieve the session state for each request.

Replicating Session State Across Multiple Clusters

You saw how you can configure a session state replication for HTTP requests within a cluster, but what if an entire cluster is unreachable for some reason? For improved fault tolerance, you can configure clusters spread across different geographical regions or even Internet service providers to provide cross-cluster replication capabilities. You must use two load balancers for setting up cross-cluster replication: You configure a global load balancer to balance HTTP requests *across* different clusters (inter-cluster replication) and a local load balancer to balance HTTP requests *within* a cluster (intra-cluster replication). You must also configure a special cross-cluster replication channel, similar to a regular network channel, which the servers in the cluster use exclusively to facilitate replication traffic among (not within) clusters.

You can configure both metropolitan area network (MAN) and wide area network (WAN) session state replication. You must use a hardware load balancer to provide failover in a MAN/WAN environment. WebLogic Server's MAN/WAN failover capability allows failover to occur over large geographical areas as well as across multiple domains. When an entire cluster fails, the local load balancer has no members available to which it can direct an HTTP request, so the local load balancer directs the request to the global load balancer, which then sends the request along to a different local load balancer configured to work with another cluster. From here on, everything works the same way as with intra-cluster replication.

To configure cross-cluster replication, you must specify the value *man* or *wan* for the subelement *cluster-type* under the *cluster* element in the *config.xml* file. When configuring cross-cluster replication, you can either let WebLogic Server take care of the session state replication or use a third-party replication product. Configure both the *jdbc-pool* and the *backup-cluster-address* properties if you're using WebLogic Server to persist data to the remote database instead of locally. If you're configuring a WAN environment, you must configure a JDBC multi data source to store the session state information; this requires creating the special database table named *wls_wan_persistence*.

NOTE
You must use a JDBC data source to configure WAN cross-cluster replication.

Failover for EJBs and RMIs

Whereas HTTP session replication helps failover of servlets and JSPs, it is the replica-aware stubs that do the trick for EJBs and RMIs. When a clustered object fails, the replica-aware stub picks up the client calls to that object and redirects them to a replica of that object on another server. The big requirement for failover to occur in this manner is that the object be *idempotent,* meaning you can call any of the object's methods multiple times with the same effect as calling it once. EJBs work differently from RMI objects here in that they can offer load balancing and failover at two different levels because an EJB can generate two replica-aware stubs, once each for the *EJBHome* interface and the *EJBObject* interface. A client performs a lookup of an EJB object through the *EJBHome* stub, and the stubs make method calls through the *EJBObject* interface. You can specify a home interface for a stateless or stateful session bean, as well as an event bean. A home interface finds or creates bean instances, and you can cluster these interfaces with the *home-is-clusterable* element in the *weblogic-ejb-jar.xml* file.

An *EJBObject* replica-aware stub knows about all available instances of an EJB in the cluster. How the *EJBObject* stub routes requests for EJBs depends on the type of bean:

- **Stateless session beans** If the bean is written with idempotent methods, the stub automatically fails over in the case of a failure. Because there's no state to maintain, the stub can route the call to any of the servers that host the stateless session bean.

- **Stateful session beans** The server handles these the same way it handles replication of HTTP session state—that is, by replicating the state of the primary bean instance to a secondary server. When a failure occurs, the client's EJB stub redirects requests to the secondary WebLogic Server. The secondary server uses the replicated state data to create a new EJB instance.
- **Entity beans** Failover for an entity bean depends on whether it's a read-only or read-write bean. Read-only entity beans don't automatically fail over. However, read-write beans fail over at the home level.

Handling Server and Service Failures

WebLogic Server can fail over most services transparently, but it's unable to do the same when dealing with pinned services. Services such as JMS and JTA are considered pinned services. They're hosted on individual members of a cluster and not on all server instances. You can have high availability only if the cluster can ensure that these pinned services are always running somewhere in the cluster. When a WebLogic Server instance hosting these critical pinned services fails, WebLogic Server can't support their continuous availability and uses migration instead of failover to ensure that they are always available. A whole server migration occurs automatically when a server hosting pinned services is migrated to a different machine with all its services. You can also perform this type of migration manually. In addition, WebLogic Server provides ways to migrate these services through what's known as *service-level migration,* wherein just the pinned services such as JTA and JMS-related services are migrated to a different instance in the cluster. A migratable server is automatically migrated when it becomes unavailable or if it can't be restarted on the same server.

The following sections review key concepts pertaining to service-level and whole server migration, including how to configure automatic migration and perform manual migrations.

Migratable Servers

A *migratable server* is a Managed Server that is eligible for whole server migration. Although a migratable server can host any clustered services, it's really the pinned services the server hosts that make it a migratable server. Both automatic and manual whole server migration depend on the existence of a migratable server, so the first step in configuring whole server migration is to set up migratable servers. By default, WebLogic Server creates all Managed Servers in a cluster as migratable servers. Note that a migratable server uses a floating IP address, which it needs during a whole server migration.

The key point to remember with regard to a migratable server and whole server migration is that all of the resources available to the server need to be available on the machine the server is going to be restarted on. That means the server transaction information and the persistent stores all need to be on shared storage and that it must be possible to "migrate" the network interface to the new machines with some sort of OS-level scripting.

Manual and Automatic Service Migration

You can configure automatic service migration or manually migrate any of the migratable services—JMS-related services, the JTA Transaction Recovery Service, and user-defined singleton services. Note that manual service migration can be in response to a failure or can be for maintenance purposes as well. Manual service migration is the default mode—you must explicitly configure automatic service migration in order for services to be automatically migrated from one server to another when prompted by the cluster's health monitoring system.

Migratable Targets

The concept of a migratable target is crucial to understanding service migration. To configure a JMS or JTA service for migration, you must deploy or target it not to the server as you normally do, but to a migratable target. A *migratable target* is really a logical concept and lets you specify services that should be migrated together. A migratable target specifies one or more servers that can host the target, and only one cluster member can host the migratable target at any given time. Migratable servers ensure that critical services such as the JMS and JTA services are always available. For example, a JMS queue is always available as long as the migratable target is hosted to any cluster member.

A migratable target is a grouping of JMS-related services, namely JMS servers, SAF Agents, path services, and custom stores; and it can be active on only one cluster member. When the original server fails, the JMS server, its destinations, and its persistent store automatically move with their migratable target to a different server. You can configure automatic migration for the migratable target, or you can manually migrate it. By default, when you create a cluster, Oracle creates a default migratable target, as shown in the following excerpt from the *config.xml* file:

```
<migratable-target>
  <name>MyManagedServer1 (migratable)</name>
  <notes>This is a system generated default migratable target for a server. Do not
delete manually.</notes>
  <user-preferred-server>MyManagedServer1</user-preferred-server>
  <cluster>MyCluster1</cluster>
</migratable-target>
```

You must configure and target the default migratable target shown here for the cluster to make use of it.

Leasing and Automatic Migration

WebLogic Server ensures that singleton services such as JMS services run only on a single server in a cluster any time by using the concept of *leasing,* which ensures that only one instance in the cluster owns a service. The key point about a lease is that the owner must periodically renew the lease. Failure to renew the lease allows someone else to "take it over." When the original owner comes back on line, it will, in turn, try to "renew" the lease but will find that someone else now owns it. This is how leasing ensures that only one virtual machine (JVM) is running the service at a time.

There can only be a single lease owner for a resource, and the lease can fail over during a failure, ensuring that the pinned services are always available. Both automatic whole server migration and automatic service migration use leasing. In a whole server migration, the running cluster members use leasing to select a *cluster master,* which is responsible for monitoring other members of the cluster and restarting failed cluster members. The cluster master is always running on one server, and once you enable automatic whole server migration, all servers periodically contact the cluster master to renew their leases. Note that the cluster master need not be a migratable server—any server in the cluster can perform as the cluster master. A migratable server will take over as the cluster master when it notices that the cluster master is not sending regular heartbeat messages. For automatic service migration, leasing helps migratable targets perform automatic service migration. When you configure automatic whole server migration or service migration, you must choose between two types of leasing:

- **Consensus leasing** Servers maintain the leasing information in the server's memory. This requires that you associate a Node Manager for all the servers because it's the Node Manager that monitors the necessary health information to initiate failovers.

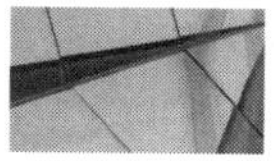

NOTE
You can only configure one type of leasing in any WebLogic Server installation.

- **Database leasing** You must configure a JDBC data source for this type of leasing and create a table in the database to store the leasing information. When you use database leasing, you are not required to associate the Node Manager with each Managed Server. The database that stores the leasing information must be highly available so cluster members can always connect to the database and renew or update their leases. Therefore, database leasing is an ideal strategy if you already have an Oracle RAC database in place. You configure database leasing by creating a leasing table in the database. The leasing table consists of information that associates machines to servers. Execute the Oracle-provided script *leasing.ddl*, located in the WL_HOME\server\db*<db_name>* directory, to create this table (the table name is *ACTIVE*). Ideally, you must assign a separate tablespace and a separate schema for creating the leasing table. You can reset the leasing table by simply rerunning this script.

NOTE
In both manual and automatic service migration, the JTA Transaction Recovery Service can't be migrated from a server when the JTA subsystem reports that it's in an unhealthy state.

Migrating JMS-Related Services

JMS services don't run on all cluster members. Rather, to preserve data consistency, they run on a single service and are thus singleton services. JMS services include the JMS server, the Store-and-Forward (SAF) Service, the path service, and the custom persistent store. For example, when a JMS component such as the persistent store fails, the server notifies the health monitoring subsystem. The server starts the automatic migration of the store from the current server, called the user-preferred server (UPS), to an alternate server in the candidate server list. Note that as long as the server itself is in a healthy running state, the migration framework tries to restart a service and migrates the service to a candidate server only if the server is unhealthy.

For a migratable JMS-related service, you must create a custom persistent store instead of using the default store. You must, in addition, target the persistent store to the same migratable target as the JMS server and the SAF Agent. Oracle recommends that you create a separate migratable target for the path service, with its own custom store.

Configuring Automatic Migration of JMS Services

You can configure automatic migration of JMS services hosted by a migratable target by following these steps:

1. Go to Environment | Clusters in the Domain Structure tree.
2. Select the cluster in the Summary Of Clusters page and click the name of the cluster you want to configure for automatic migration of JMS services.
3. On the Configuration | Migration page, specify choices for the Migration Basis field. If you've created a table in a highly available database that the Managed Servers can use for storing the leasing information, select Database. If all the migratable servers have a Node Manager associated with them, select the Consensus option.

Each server generates a default migratable server automatically. You can see the list of migratable targets in the Administration Console by going to Environment | Migratable Targets and viewing the Summary Of Migratable Targets page, which is shown in Figure 7-8. The migratable targets are named *serverName* (migratable). However, you'll need to configure and target these default migratable targets.

You can also create a new migratable target and configure it, as shown here:

1. Go to Environment | Migratable Targets in the Domain Structure tree.
2. Click New on the Summary Of Migratable Targets page.
3. On the Create A New Migratable Targets page, enter a name for the migratable target and select a cluster for it. Click Next.
4. In the User Preferred Server box, select the preferred server (the best server) with which you want to associate this migrated server.

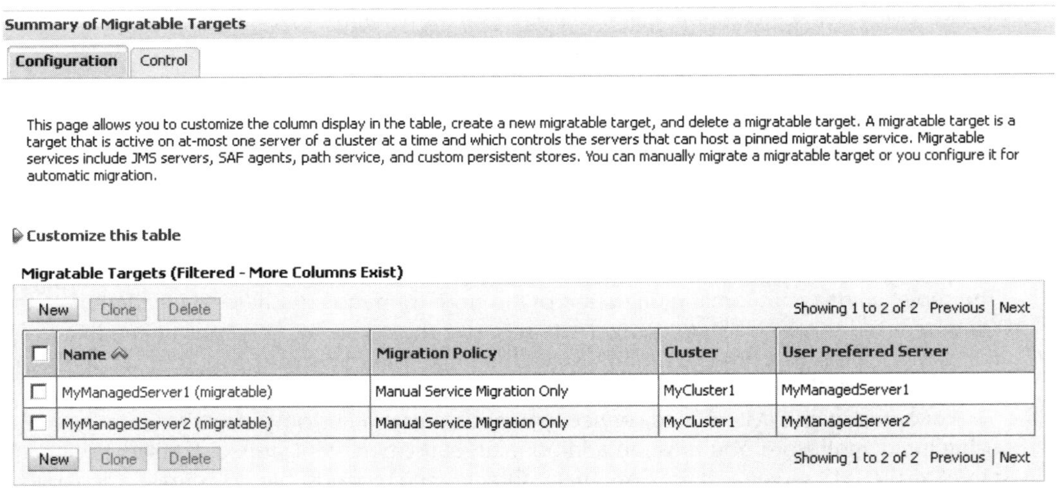

Summary of Migratable Targets

Configuration | Control

This page allows you to customize the column display in the table, create a new migratable target, and delete a migratable target. A migratable target is a target that is active on at-most one server of a cluster at a time and which controls the servers that can host a pinned migratable service. Migratable services include JMS servers, SAF agents, path service, and custom persistent stores. You can manually migrate a migratable target or you configure it for automatic migration.

Customize this table

Migratable Targets (Filtered - More Columns Exist)

New | Clone | Delete — Showing 1 to 2 of 2 Previous | Next

	Name	Migration Policy	Cluster	User Preferred Server
☐	MyManagedServer1 (migratable)	Manual Service Migration Only	MyCluster1	MyManagedServer1
☐	MyManagedServer2 (migratable)	Manual Service Migration Only	MyCluster1	MyManagedServer2

New | Clone | Delete — Showing 1 to 2 of 2 Previous | Next

FIGURE 7-8. *The Summary Of Migratable Targets page in the Administration Console*

5. In the Service Migration Policy drop-down list, specify the type of automatic migration you want the migratable target to support:
   - **Manual Service Migration Only** This is the default value, but you don't want to choose it because you want to configure automatic service migration.
   - **Auto-Migrate Exactly-Once Services** This option guarantees that the JMS service will be active on some server that's in the candidate list, as long as at least one of the candidate Managed Servers is running.
   - **Auto-Migrate Failure Recovery Services** This option specifies that the JMS service should start only if the user-preferred server starts. If the user-preferred server fails, the JMS service will migrate to an alternative candidate server.
6. Restart the Admin Server and the Managed Servers whose migration policies were modified to get ready for automatic service migration.

The cluster's JMS path service should use members in the entire cluster as the candidate servers, but for other services that use the *exactly-once-services* migration policy, limit the candidate servers to no more than three servers. Once the migratable target is created, you can also optionally specify whether you want to provide scripts for running before and after the migration to unmount and mount the custom file store. Oracle provides sample scripts in the *DOMAIN_HOME*\\<*domain_name*>\bin\service_migration directory.

Once the original primary server is back up again, you must manually migrate the automatically migrated JMS services. However, WebLogic Server automatically migrates back the JTA Transaction Recovery Service.

Manually Migrating JMS-Related Services

Even if you've configured automatic migration of JMS services, you still have to manually migrate those services back to the primary server. The steps for configuring manual service migration are essentially the same as for the automatic migration of services, with the following differences:

- **Migration Basis** You don't need to configure this attribute (leasing type), as this is only necessary during automatic migrations.
- **Service Migration Policy** For this attribute, you can just select the default option, Manual Service Migration Only.

You must first configure a migratable target to host the JMS-related services, as shown in the previous section, before you can manually migrate the services. You can migrate the targets individually or all at once. You can manually migrate the JMS services either for maintenance purposes or in response to a server failure. Here are the steps to migrate JMS services manually:

1. Go to Environment | Migratable Targets in the Domain Structure tree.
2. On the Summary Of Migratable Targets page, click the Control tab.
3. Select the migratable targets you want to migrate and click Migrate.
4. Select a new server for the migratable target by using the New Hosting Server drop-down list. Click OK.

Migrating JTA Services

Migrating JTA services is critical when a server fails because transactions may be holding locks on resources, and this adversely affects the performance of your applications. You can migrate a JTA service manually or configure automatic migration. Automatic migration of JTA services will migrate the Transaction Recovery Service (TRS) to a backup server by choosing one from the configured candidate servers. The backup server releases its lease on the TRS once it completes transaction recovery for the failed server. If the backup server itself fails before completing the transaction recovery, its lease expires. In this case, you must manually migrate the TRS to an alternative backup server for the configured list of servers. If you can successfully start the primary server before the backup server completes recovery of the transactions, the backup server will gracefully hand over the lease to the revived primary server.

Regardless of whether you are manually migrating the TRS or configuring it for automatic migration, you must configure the default persistent store. The recommended approach is to use a highly available shared storage solution such as a storage area network (SAN) so the store is accessible to any machine. The reason for this is that the backup server must be able to access the transaction log of the failed server. You can guarantee access to these records, stored in the persistent store, by placing the store on a shared storage system that's highly available as well.

Configuring Automatic Migration of JTA Services

To configure automatic migration of JTA services, you follow procedures that are very similar to those for the automatic migration of JMS-related services. To do this, go to Environment | Servers | Configuration | Migration and select Automatic JTA Migration Enabled in the JTA Migration Configuration section. You must also configure the Migration Basis field for the cluster to specify a database or consensus leasing and enable an automatic migration option by choosing one of the options for Service Migration Policy. Optionally, you can specify pre- and post-migration scripts, just as in the case of automatic JMS-related service migration.

Both manual and automatic JTA service migrations require you to configure the default persistent store on a shared system accessible to all candidate machines. The Node Manager is a prerequisite for consensus leasing, but if you're using database leasing, you'll need the Node Manager only if pre- and post-migration scripts aren't defined.

When the server health monitoring subsystem indicates a primary server failure, the TRS is automatically migrated to the backup server.

Manually Migrating the Transaction Recovery Service

If you're unable to restart a crashed server, you must migrate the Transaction Recovery Service to a backup server so it can take care of the incomplete transactions. Here are the steps to migrate the TRS from a failed cluster member:

1. Click Lock & Edit in the Change Center of the Administration Console.
2. In the left-hand pane, expand Environment and select Servers.
3. Shut down the server if it's not already down.
4. Select the server from which you want to migrate the TRS.
5. Select Control | Migration.
6. Click Advanced.

7. Under JTA Transaction Recovery Service Migration, select the server to which you want to migrate the TRS of the failed server.
8. Click Save.

Whole Server Migration

The Node Manager is the critical player in a whole server migration. You must use the Node Manager to start the migratable servers, and you must use it to shut down the servers as well. While the Node Manager does all the actual work during an automatic whole server migration, it is the cluster master that actually invokes the migration. Note that the Admin Server invokes the Node Manager during a manual whole server migration.

Prerequisites for Automatic Whole Server Migration

You must satisfy several prerequisites before configuring automatic whole server migration, including the following:

- All Managed Servers must use the same subnet mask.
- If the operating systems hosting the cluster members are different, configure *ifconfig* identically on all the servers.
- You can't create custom network channels with a different listen address on a migratable server. You must have a single network channel per server.
- Ideally, you must use a highly available shared storage system, and if you don't have this, you must copy the DOMAIN_HOME\bin directory to each machine.
- You must use the *nmEnroll* command to copy the Node Manager security files to all machines.

Configuring Automatic Whole Server Migration

Configuring automatic whole server migration involves first configuring the availability of floating IP addresses (a unique address and port combination) for all the servers and facilitating communication through Secure Shell (SSH). Before configuring the server, make sure you perform the following tasks:

- **Node Manager** The Node Manager can automatically restart a failed server, along with its services, on a different machine. Therefore, you must ensure that the Node Manager is running and that you've configured it for server migrations. Here are the typical Node Manager properties you must configure in the *nodemanager.properties* file:

```
Interface=eth0
NetMask=255.255.255.0
UseMACBroadcast=true
```

- **IP addresses** Transferring IP addresses from one machine to another is a key part of whole server migration. You must get floating IP addresses for all Managed Servers in the cluster for which you want to enable whole server migration.
- **Privileges** WebLogic Server uses the *wlsconfig.sh* script (UNIX) or the *wlsconfig.cmd* script (Windows) to transfer IP addresses during whole server migration. In UNIX, make

sure you grant super user privileges to this script (*sudo*), so it can invoke *ifconfig*. You can do this by adding the following line to the *sudoers* file in the /etc directory:

```
oracle ALL=NOPASSWD:   /sbin/ifconfig
```

- **Path** In addition, you must ensure that the machine's PATH includes the *wlsconfig.sh* (or *wlsconfig.cmd*), *wlscontrol.sh*, and *nodemanager.domains* files. The first two files are in the WL_HOME\common\bin directory and the last is in the WL_HOME\common\nodemanager directory.
- **SSH** If you're using the SSH version for the Node Manager in a UNIX/Linux environment, make sure that you establish SSH connectivity among the servers.

You can configure automatic restart of a cluster member on another machine by following these steps:

1. Go to Environment | Clusters in the Domain Structure tree.
2. Select the cluster on the Summary Of Clusters page and click Migration. Enter values for the following attributes to configure whole server migration:
   - **Candidate Machines For Migratable Servers** This is the list of machines on which Node Manager can restart a failed server, and it requires you to enable the servers for automatic migration. You can specify the machines where the Node Manager can restart the migratable servers by moving the servers from the Available list to the Chosen list. You can also specify the order in which the Node Manager will start the failed servers. You can specify a maximum of three machines on which a server can restart.

NOTE
You must enable each of the candidate servers for automatic migration.

   - **Migration Basis** You can select the machines for server migration. You can select Database to specify that a database table will store the leasing information. You can also select the Consensus option to store the leasing information in a cluster member's memory instead of using a database.
   - **Data Source For Automatic Migration** This option specifies the JDBC multi data source or GridLink data source the servers will use during the migration. Make sure to configure all cluster members to use this database.
   - **Auto Migration Table Name** This is the name of the table to be used for server migration.
   - **Member Discovery Timeout** This option is the maximum amount of time a server waits during startup to discover other cluster members.
   - **Leader Heartbeat Period** This option specifies the interval for the sending of heartbeats by the cluster leader to transmit cluster-related information to other members for synchronizing purposes.
   - **Additional Migration Attempts** This option specifies the number of times WebLogic Server attempts to bring up a migratable server. If you set the value of this attribute to –1, the server keeps trying the migration until it succeeds. If you have a two-node

cluster and use the default value of 2 for this attribute, the server makes a total of four migration attempts.

- **Pause Time Between Migration Attempts** Here, you set the interval between migration attempts.

Suppose you have a two-node cluster and you configure both Managed Servers as migratable servers and run the Node Manager on a third server—a backup machine that you configure as an available host for a migratable server. You must also run the Node Manager on the machines hosting the two-cluster members. When you start the cluster, the Node Manager running on the two primary machines will start the Managed Servers. The first server to start will become the cluster master. When one of the two cluster members fails, the cluster master first attempts a restart of the failed server. If it can't restart the failed server, the cluster master instructs the Node Manager running on the backup machine to restart the failed Managed Server on that machine. The failed server will now restart on the backup server and cache its configuration after it first contacts the Admin Server to get its configuration information. Note that the Admin Server doesn't really play any role in starting the server except to let the migrated server cache retrieve the configuration with which it originally started.

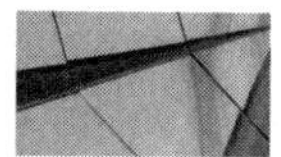

NOTE
You must start a migratable server with the Node Manager for it to be migratable.

When the machine that failed is back in service, the migrated Managed Server isn't automatically started back there. You must first shut down the migrated server on the backup machine and restart the Node Manager and the Managed Server. The clients using the failed server may have to reconnect both times—once during the migration and later when you migrate the server instance back to the original machine.

Performing a Manual Whole Server Migration

You may want to perform a manual whole server migration either following a server failure or as part of a planned outage. The following steps tell you how to perform the migration:

1. Stop the migratable server.
2. In the Administration Console, associate the target machine with the migratable server.
3. Place the target machine at the top of the list of candidate servers for migration.
4. Verify that the target machine is the one you've selected by going to Servers | Control | Migration.
5. Start the server—it should now start on the target machine.

Using WLST to Migrate Services

You can use the WLST command *migrate* to migrate specified services such as the JMS and JTA services to another cluster member. The command can also migrate a migratable server from one machine to another machine. You must be connected through WLST to the Admin Server in order to issue the *migrate* command. You can issue the WLST command *help('migrate')* to learn about this command and see its syntax and a usage example.

You can specify the following arguments for the *migrate* command:

- ***sname*** Specifies the name of the server from which you're migrating the services.
- ***destinationName*** Specifies the name of the server or machine to which you're migrating the services.
- ***sourceDown*** Specifies whether the source server is running. The default value is *true*. For JTA services, the source server must be down.
- ***destinationDown*** Specifies whether the destination server is running. The default value is *false*. The destination server will activate the JMS services once it starts. For JTA services, the target server starts the recovery services once it starts.
- ***migrationType*** Specifies the services that you want to migrate. The default value is *all,* and it migrates both the JTA and JMS services. You can specify the values *jms* or *jta* to migrate only the JMS or the JTA services.

Here's the syntax for the *migrate* command, with the *all* option for migrating both the JMS and JTA services:

```
wls:/mydomain/edit !> migrate('server1','server2', 'true', 'false', 'all')
wls:/mydomain/edit !> migrate('server1','machine1', 'true', 'false', 'server')
```

Summary

This chapter introduced WebLogic Clusters, including their design, creation, and management. You learned how load balancing works in a cluster and how the cluster manages application failures. You also learned how automatic migration works and how to perform a server as well as a service migration. Understanding cluster management and learning how to handle server and service failures sets the stage for exploring application deployment, which is the subject of the next chapter.

CHAPTER 8

Understanding WebLogic Server Application Deployment

The primary purpose of using a web application server such as Oracle WebLogic Server 12*c* is to deploy enterprise applications. So far you have learned about configuring the various services that the application server provides to make it easier to write applications. In this chapter, you learn how to run the code that you develop in the WebLogic Server application server. *Deployment* is the process through which you make your application available to users (and, in some cases, other systems or applications). Once you develop a complete application or a Java EE module, you need to make it available to users. The deployment process involves the packaging and distribution of enterprise applications, web applications, or other modules. The Java EE specification requires you to archive different deployment modules such as EJBs and web applications.

Oracle WebLogic Server 12*c* offers multiple ways of deploying applications—some of these methods are more suitable for development purposes and others for production deployments. You can use the Administration Console to perform any type of deployment and redeployment or to undeploy applications. The same functionality is also available through the *weblogic.Deployer* command-line tools as well. In addition, developers can use the *wldeploy* Ant task, which is equivalent to using the *weblogic.Deployer* utility—actually, *wldeploy* is the Ant task version of *weblogic.Deployer*. As with most things involving WebLogic Server administration, you can use WLST commands to deploy applications as well. Developers can also take advantage of the autodeploy feature to deploy applications automatically, cutting short the development and testing cycle.

This chapter shows how to deploy, undeploy, and update enterprise applications. Note that the same deployment methods apply to the deployment of a web application or an EJB module. You'll also learn production strategies for updating applications that allow you to simultaneously run two versions of an application to avoid downtime or a service interruption.

Introduction to WebLogic Server Deployment

To deploy a WebLogic Server application is to make the application available to users. When we talk about deployment, we usually have production servers in mind, but all environments, including test and development environments, also have applications deployed to them. WebLogic Server offers several ways to deploy applications, and you can employ the various deployment techniques in any environment. However, you can use less stringent deployment methods for your development instances.

During development and testing, applications change more frequently, and WebLogic Server provides alternative deployment tools that minimize the time to redeploy. Developers typically use fewer servers and work with integrated development environments (IDEs). Capabilities such as exploded archive formats, split directories, and fast swap are meant to help with this. Production environments, on the other hand, require greater stability and reliability. Capabilities such as two-phase deployment, archive distribution, and deployment plans are designed to meet these needs.

WebLogic Server implements the required JSR-88 Service Provider Interface, which is a requirement for complying with the Java EE 5 deployment specification. WebLogic Server implements the standard deployment specification API (JSR-88) by generating WebLogic Server configurations and storing them in a deployment plan. The Java EE 5 deployment API offers a standardized way to configure an application with any application server that conforms to Java EE 5, such as the Oracle WebLogic Server 12*c*. More importantly, it provides a mechanism by which application archives can be transitioned between different environments without the need to disturb the integrity of the original archive and offers a way to define cleanly areas that require customization.

Types of Applications You Can Deploy

The Java EE specification outlines how to organize a Java EE application or a standard Java EE module such as an EJB. Each Java EE application (enterprise or web) or Java EE module is called a *deployment unit,* and for each such deployment unit, the Java EE specification states the required files you must include with that unit, as well as where you must place those files in the web application or Java EE module structure. Here's a brief description of the various types of deployment units:

- **Enterprise applications (*.ear*)** These consist of one or more web applications, EJB modules, client applications, and resource adapter modules, with web applications and EJBs being the most common. You can deploy an enterprise application as an exploded EAR directory or as a jar file, with the *.ear* extension, as in *myapp1.ear*. Enterprise applications may include the optional *applications.xml* deployment descriptor. An EAR represents an assembly of other modules together for ease of deployment.
- **Modules that contain code** These are modules such as web applications and EJBs that host the code you develop. They are the modules packaged in an EAR. Web applications provide a web interface for an application or web service and include servlets or JSP pages (along with helper classes), the optional *web.xml,* and the *weblogic.xml* deployment descriptor files. Web applications are denoted by the suffix *.war,* as in *myapp1.war*. Enterprise JavaBeans (EJBs) are reusable Java components that implement your business logic and are packaged as archive files, usually in exploded archive directories. EJB modules are denoted by the suffix *.jar,* as in *myapp1.jar.*
- **Resources that are packaged as part of an EAR** As you can recall from the discussion in earlier chapters, WebLogic administrators create and deploy system modules, but developers own the application modules. You can deploy a JMS, JDBC, or WLDF module as part of a specific application or as a stand-alone module. A stand-alone module is available to all applications you deploy in your domain.
- **Java EE libraries** These are used to augment applications and share classes and libraries. They are stand-alone Java EE modules registered with the Java EE application container as a shared library. Java EE libraries allow multiple enterprise applications to share a Java EE module without actually adding the module to each application. Each application references the shared module in its *weblogic-application.xml* descriptor file and receives a copy of the shared Java EE library at deployment time. These modules aren't deployed as part of an EAR; instead they are dynamically bound into an application at deployment time by reference.

The most common modules that are part of an enterprise application are web applications and EJB modules.

Deployment Targets

You deploy a deployment type such as an enterprise or web application, for example, to a deployment target. *Deployment targets* are the servers and clusters to which you deploy the applications and modules. There are four types of deployment targets, as listed next:

- A single WebLogic Server instance (a Managed Server). The single instance can also be an Admin Server in a development environment.
- A cluster

- A virtual host (Chapter 3 shows how to configure a virtual host.)
- A JMS server

Although you can deploy any of the deployment units described in the previous section (enterprise applications, web applications, EJB modules, resource adapters, Java EE libraries, and JMS, JDBC, and WLDF modules) to a single-server instance or to a cluster, you can only deploy web applications to a virtual host. Of course, you can deploy only a JMS queue or topic defined within a JMS module to a JMS server. You can, however, target a stand-alone JMS application module to a server, cluster, or virtual host target.

The process of deployment simply involves describing which application components are associated with which targets. When deploying an application or a module to a cluster, by default, the deployment is targeted to all cluster members. This type of deployment, called a *homogeneous deployment,* is recommended in general. However, you can deploy a module only on select individual servers of a cluster in special circumstances such as when dealing with pinned services, which can only be operative on a single server.

Deployment Tools

WebLogic Server provides multiple tools to help package and deploy applications. These tools include the *weblogic.Deployer* utility; the Administration Console; WLST commands; and *wldeploy*, an Ant version of *weblogic.Deployer*. The functionality of the various deployment tools is similar for the most part, but each of the tools is suited for a different purpose. Let's look at the functionality of each of these tools:

- ***weblogic.Deployer*** You can use this utility to perform command-line deployment tasks. You can also use it to perform deployment tasks that the Console doesn't support.
- **Administration Console** You can deploy all types of deployment units through the Administration Console. You can change the deployment status of applications, as well as modify the values of deployment descriptors while the application is running.
- **WLST** The WebLogic Scripting Tool (WLST) lets you automate application deployment.
- ***wldeploy*** This is an Ant version of *weblogic.Deployer* that is designed for automating deployment tasks by developers.
- **WebLogic Maven plug-in** This plug-in helps developers deploy applications built using Maven directly from the Maven environment.

Deployment Descriptors, Annotations, and Deployment Plans

Once a developer has written the classes that contain the presentation and services that are the heart of the application, the next step is to provide information to the application server container as to how to interpret those classes. The deployment descriptors and annotations provide these mechanisms.

A *deployment descriptor* contains environment configuration information as well as product-specific configuration details. You can define the deployment descriptor values necessary for a deployment in a domain in several ways: Java EE deployment descriptors, which are historical mechanisms based on external XML files and date back to the origins of Java EE; WebLogic Server deployment descriptors; and a WebLogic Server deployment plan.

In the deployment process, four primary categories of information are specified. The first involves declaring which classes are the main entry points to your application. The second provides the containers with hints about how to interpret the application components. The third involves declaring the relationships among the various components, often referred to as "wiring them up." The fourth and final category of information involves container and environment-specific details.

Java EE 5 and Java SE 5 introduced *annotation-based programming,* which makes it easier for developers to specify application component behavior in the Java class itself instead of developers having to spend time and effort creating deployment descriptors. Older versions of applications (J2EE 1.4 and earlier) required deployment descriptors, but they are optional in Java EE applications. It's important to understand, however, that annotations are not a problem-free alternative. The best strategy is to use annotations wherever possible, ensuring that doing so is not going to reduce the portability of the application. For example, hard-coding environmental configuration details, such as IP addresses, by annotating them in code will affect the application's portability. You can specify any environment-specific information such as IP addresses in a deployment descriptor.

You can use a *deployment plan* to override information specified in the deployment descriptors or through annotations. Deployment plan values override as well as supplement descriptor values in the deployment descriptor files and in annotations, and let you customize a deployment to various environments.

In WebLogic Server, the process of preparing an application for deployment logically involves a three-step process. First, the application descriptors are parsed and read into the document in memory. Next, that information is combined with information stored in the Java EE 5 annotations and applied to the document. Finally, the information specified in the deployment plan is applied to the resulting data structures. The combined descriptors are then used in the application's deployment.

The standard *application.xml* and *web.xml* deployment descriptors are optional with Java EE annotations, which are used for web containers such as EJBs, JSPs, servlets, and web applications. Annotations are an alternative to deployment descriptors and allow the developer to specify the behavior of the application component in the container directly within the Java class. Annotations simplify development of application components, and deployment descriptors can still override values you specify through annotations.

An annotation on a field or method declares that the fields or methods need injection. *Dependency injections,* made possible through annotations, allow components to declare dependencies on external resources and configuration parameters. Once the container reads the annotations, it injects the appropriate external resources or environmental variables into the application components. Thus, dependency injection offers an easier programming alternative to using traditional JNDI APIs to looking up resources.

The WebLogic Server utilities *appc* and *Appmerge* process applications or modules as inputs and produce an output application or module. These applications and modules will contain deployment descriptors with annotation information when used with the *writeInferredDescriptors* option for *appc*. This offers a great way to get a handle on what's actually being deployed.

NOTE
Deployment plans help customize deployments to various environments but require the existence of deployment files.

A deployment descriptor is an XML file that contains the deployment configuration for an application or module. The deployment descriptors describe the contents of the jar or war files, as well as deployment configuration settings. A standard Java EE deployment descriptor, as defined in

Deployment Type	Java EE Deployment Descriptor	WebLogic Server Deployment Descriptor
Enterprise application	*application.xml*	*weblogic-application.xml*
Web application	*web.xml*	*weblogic.xml*
EJB	*ejb-jar.xml*	*weblogic-ejb-jar.xml*
Resource adapter	*ra.xml*	*weblogic-ra.xml*
Web service	*None*	*web-services.xml*
Client application	*application-client.xml*	*client-application-runtime.xml*

TABLE 8-1. *Java EE and WebLogic Server Deployment Descriptors*

the Java EE specification, is required for each Java EE application or module. WebLogic Server also has its own deployment descriptors that supplement the default Java EE deployment descriptors. The WebLogic Server deployment descriptors are used to define the tuning parameters and resource dependencies in the WebLogic Server environment. Table 8-1 describes the Java EE deployment descriptor for each deployment unit and the corresponding WebLogic Server deployment descriptor.

The standard *application.xml* descriptor file for an enterprise application contains basic configuration and deployment information for an application, such as the name and location of each module in the enterprise application and application-wide security roles. The module definitions section of the *application.xml* file contains subelements such as *<ejb>* and *<web>* under the *<module>* element to distinguish the various types of modules in an application. The corresponding *weblogic-application .xml* file includes information such as the custom startup and shutdown classes, Work Manager settings, and the configuration of WebLogic Server application-scoped JDBC, JMS, and WLST modules.

The standard *application.xml* deployment descriptor is optional, and Java EE annotations can provide all of the information. Unless you happen to use any WebLogic Server extensions, the WebLogic-specific application deployment descriptor, *weblogic-application.xml*, is also optional. In the absence of the *application.xml* descriptor file, the container knows the module type (EJB or web application, for example) by looking at the name of the module, which has to follow a convention. For example, a web application should have the *.war* extension, and an EJB module the *.jar* extension. The EJB module must also contain a META-INF*ejb-jar.xml* descriptor or a class with an EJB jar connotation.

Configuring Deployments with Deployment Plans

One of the biggest challenges in developing and deploying Java EE applications is in the transition from development to testing and into production. Each of these environments has its own unique demands and requirements. Fortunately, WebLogic Server provides a sophisticated scheme for isolating the places where customization is needed and defining the environment-specific details.

Developers create Java EE and WebLogic deployment descriptors for configuring applications for the development environment. Developers can export the deployment configuration of an application to a *deployment plan* when they release an application for testing, staging, or production deployment, though this isn't mandatory. The deployment plan, which is an XML-formatted file named *plan.xml,* consists of all or some of the configuration properties contained in the deployment descriptor files. Using a deployment plan makes it easy to configure changes before deploying the application into a different target environment.

Ideally, a deployment plan should include all configuration properties that change in the new environment, such as a testing or production environment. The WebLogic Server administrator can update the deployment or replace it with a different deployment plan after the deployment of the application to a different target environment such as moving from a development to a production environment.

A deployment plan can override properties you've specified in a WebLogic Server deployment descriptor or even provide completely alternative versions of specific descriptors. You can also specify deployment properties in a deployment plan that you haven't specified in a deployment descriptor. You store the deployment plan for an application in a dedicated directory separate from that used for the application archive or exploded archive directory. Oracle recommends that you create a separate *plan subdirectory* in the application's root directory to store the *plan.xml* file. You can specify WebLogic Server tuning parameters in a deployment plan, but this is not mandatory. If neither the deployment plan nor the deployment descriptors define the tuning parameters, WebLogic Server simply uses default values for these parameters.

The WebLogic Server administrator must ensure that the deployment plan for production deployments reflects the production environment. The administrator must ensure that all external resource references in the deployment plan are valid. For example, you must replace all references in the *plan.xml* file to a development or testing data source with an appropriate production data source. Administrators can use the deployment plan created by the developers, modify it, or even use a custom deployment plan. You can also redeploy currently deployed applications with a new deployment plan or update existing deployment plans and redeploy them. The bottom line in all this is that your deployment plan must be valid for the target environment—all external resource references must refer to available resources in the target environment.

You can use either a single master deployment plan or multiple deployment plans. If your environment has only a few target environments, you're better off with a single deployment plan. The application team generally owns the single deployment plan. The master plan must define null variables for resource names that are different among environments, and it's the administrator's job to replace these empty variables with valid resource names before deploying the application. You can leave all valid configuration values alone while updating the deployment plan. If you're dealing with a large number of environments with frequent changes, you should use multiple deployment plans. In these types of situations, you'll find it harder to maintain a single master deployment plan that suits all environments. When using multiple deployment plans, the administrator usually generates custom deployment plans for each target environment instead of depending on the single deployment plan generated by the development team.

Developers can create custom deployment plans and provide those plans to the administrator along with the application deployment files. The main reasons to export an application's deployment configuration to a custom deployment plan are to:

- Specify external resources as null variables in the deployment plan so the deployer can replace the null variables with appropriate values for the deployment environment.
- Expose tuning parameters as variables that the deployer can modify to suit the deployment environment.

You can use the *weblogic.PlanGenerator* tool to create a template deployment plan with null variables for an entire class of deployment descriptors. WebLogic Server deployment descriptor properties fall into four categories:

- **Nonconfigurable properties** You can't change properties such as *ejb-name,* for example.
- **Dependency properties** These are properties that resolve resource dependencies such as data sources, which are defined in the Java EE deployments.

- **Declaration properties** These define resources such as the JNDI name for an EJB which other resources can use.
- **Configurable properties** These include all configurable properties other than the dependency and declaration properties. Configurable properties usually define features and tuning parameters specific to WebLogic Server. Any property other than a nonconfigurable property can be dynamic or nondynamic. You can change the dynamic properties without redeploying the application.

NOTE
You can only remove a value or set a null value for a variable manually; you can't perform these actions thorough either the Administration Console or using the weblogic.PlanGenerator *tool.*

Here's an example that shows how to use the *weblogic.PlanGenerator* tool to create a deployment plan:

```
java weblogic.PlanGenerator -root C:\deploy_dir\prod\testApp\Ver1
```

This command creates the *plan.xml* file in the installation root directory. If you haven't created such a directory, you can specify the location and filename for the plan by specifying the *plan* option with the *weblogic.PlanGenerator* command. If you don't specify a location, WebLogic Server creates the *plan.xml* file in the temporary directory for your environment. By default, the command will create a deployment plan with null variables for all properties that involve external resources the application uses. Oracle recommends that developers use the *weblogic.PlanGenerator* tool just for exporting resource dependencies to minimize the variables in the deployment plan. The administrator can then take this template deployment plan and, using the Administration Console, configure the correct resource names and tuning properties for all the null variables. This allows the administrator to validate the custom deployment plan before deploying the application into a different environment. Note that when you make changes to any deployment properties defined as variables, the changes are stored in a new version of the *plan.xml* file.

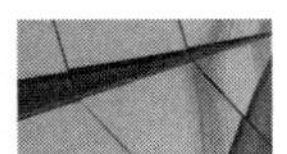

NOTE
Oracle recommends that you store custom deployment plans in a source control system.

Automatically Generating a Deployment Plan

You can automatically generate a deployment plan by creating a plan subdirectory under the application root directory. For example, if your application root directory is C:\deploy_dir\prod\testApp and the current version of the application is Version 1, create two subdirectories under the \Ver1 directory named *app* and *plan*. You'll thus end up with the following directory structures:

```
C:\deploy_dir\prod\testApp\Ver1\app
C:\deploy_dir\prod\testApp\Ver1\plan
```

When you install an application from the app directory using the Administration Console, WebLogic Server automatically creates a *plan.xml* file in the plan subdirectory of the application root directory. Following is the deployment plan that was generated for the sample application *testApp1,* whose installation is described later in this chapter:

```
<deployment-plan xmlns="http://xmlns.oracle.com/weblogic/deployment-plan"
xmlns:xsi="http://www.w3.org/2001/XMLSchema-instance"
xsi:schemaLocation="http://xmlns.oracle.com/weblogic/deployment-plan
http://xmlns.oracle.com/weblogic/deployment-plan/1.0/deployment-plan.xsd" global-
variables="false">
  <application-name>testApp1</application-name>
  <module-override>
    <module-name>jspExpressionEar.ear</module-name>
    <module-type>ear</module-type>
    <module-descriptor external="false">
      <root-element>weblogic-application</root-element>
      <uri>META-INF/weblogic-application.xml</uri>
    </module-descriptor>
    <module-descriptor external="false">
      <root-element>application</root-element>
      <uri>META-INF/application.xml</uri>
    </module-descriptor>
    <module-descriptor external="true">
      <root-element>wldf-resource</root-element>
      <uri>META-INF/weblogic-diagnostics.xml</uri>
    </module-descriptor>
  </module-override>
  <module-override>
    <module-name>jspExpressionWar</module-name>
    <module-type>war</module-type>
    <module-descriptor external="false">
      <root-element>weblogic-web-app</root-element>
      <uri>WEB-INF/weblogic.xml</uri>
    </module-descriptor>
    <module-descriptor external="false">
      <root-element>web-app</root-element>
      <uri>WEB-INF/web.xml</uri>
    </module-descriptor>
  </module-override>
  <config-root>C:\deploy_dir\prod\testApp\Ver1\plan</config-root>
</deployment-plan>
```

The key element in a deployment plan is the *<module-override>* element. It shows the module and deployment descriptor whose values the deployment plan overrides. The *<module-descriptor>* subelement under the *<module-override>* element shows the deployment descriptor (such as *weblogic.xml*) whose properties the plan will override. The *<module-override>* element may have one or more *<variable-assignment>* elements that show where a variable is applied to a deployment descriptor.

Using a deployment plan, you can change the value of a deployment descriptor that is inside an ear file at deployment time. If you have archives that passed through your test and QA process, you can modify the deployment descriptors without having to modify the already tested ear file by using a deployment plan. Deployment plans help you fully externalize application settings and help you override those settings.

If you would rather use an existing deployment plan, you can do so by placing it in the plan subdirectory before installing the application through the Administration Console. When you install the application through the Administration Console, it picks up the *plan.xml* file you placed in the plan subdirectory of the application root directory. Note that the Administration Console can only identify the *plan.xml* file you place in the plan subdirectory. If your application uses multiple plans, you must place each deployment plan in its own plan directory (such as \plan1 and \plan2) and update the *config.xml* file for the domain with the subdirectory information so the Console can identify them.

Modifying a Deployment Plan

You can modify an existing deployment plan for an application through the Administration Console. Follow these steps to reconfigure the deployment plan for an application:

1. Click Lock & Edit in the Change Center of the Administration Console.
2. Click Deployments in the left-hand pane of the console.
3. Click the application (in this example, the application name is *testApp1*) for which you want to modify the deployment plan.
4. In the Settings For testApp1 page, select Deployment Plan.
5. To update tuning parameters, select Tuning Parameters. To update resource dependencies, select Resource Dependencies.
6. Edit the values for the configuration attributes and Click Save.
7. Click Activate Changes in the Change Center.

You can also manually edit the *plan.xml* file to remove a variable or to assign a null value to a generated variable. To remove a variable from the deployment plan, remove the variable definition from the *<variable-definition>* stanza and the *<variable-assignment>* elements under the *<module-override>* element that refer to the variable you've deleted. You can assign a null value to a variable by changing the value in the *<value>* subelement of the *<variable>* element to the following: *<value xsi:nil="true"></value>*.

In order to change the value of a deployment descriptor, first define the variable in the deployment descriptor, as shown here:

```
<variable-definition>
    <variable>
        <name>SessionDescriptor_timeoutSecs_12870427304900</name>
        <value>24000</value>
    </variable>
</variable-definition>
```

Once you define the deployment descriptor, you can then change the value of the deployment descriptor by specifying the name of the deployment descriptor (session timeout) using the *<variable-assignment>* element within the *<module-override>* element, as explained earlier in this chapter.

You can use a deployment plan to deploy the same EJB services with alternate JNDI registrations that point to alternative JDBC connection pools. For example, you can add the following variable definition to a deployment plan to point the data source to the new data source, jdbc/newDS, instead of the original data source, jdbc/myDS:

```
<variable-definition>
    <variable>
        <name>datasource-jndi-name</name>
        <value>jdbc/newDS</value>
    </variable>
</variable-definition>
```

To use a deployment plan to override the values of elements defined in a deployment descriptor such as *weblogic-ejb-jar.xml,* you must set the new values for the *<variable>*, *<variable-assignment>*, and *<operation>* elements in the deployment plan. You must set the value of the *<operation>* element to *replace* in order for the *<variable-assignment>* element to replace the values defined in the deployment descriptor.

Validating a Custom Deployment Plan

When you install a new application through the Administration Console, it automatically validates the deployment configuration. If you export the deployment configuration to create a custom deployment plan, you can validate the plan from the Deployments page. Select Deployment Plan | Resource Dependencies, and verify the validity of the configuration on the Dependencies page.

Preparing Applications for Deployment

You can deploy an enterprise application, which consists of web applications and EJBs, as a stand-alone module by directly deploying the EJBs and web applications. There are several disadvantages to going this route, however, including the fact that the server loads each module with its own application class loader, making it difficult to manage the class loaders in a large deployment. In addition, there's additional overhead to process communications between multiple independent modules. Deployment order of the independent modules is also an issue. In light of these considerations, deploying enterprise application modules directly to the server as stand-alone independent applications is not a recommended approach.

An enterprise or web application consists of several Java classes, static files, and deployment descriptor files, which all must be deployed together. Therefore, before you can deploy the application, you must package all the application or module's components. You can package an application in two ways: you can package it as an archived file or use an exploded archive directory. Both the archive file and the exploded archive directory will contain identical files and directories. If you package the various application modules into an enterprise directory, you use the exploded directory deployment method or you can package the modules into an *.ear* file, which you deploy to the server as a single unit.

Both of these methods of packaging applications for deployment have advantages and disadvantages, as you'll learn in the following sections. The recommended method is to package deployment files in an archive format when distributing applications to different environments.

Deploying an Archive File

WebLogic Server administrators commonly receive the applications from the developers in an archived format consisting of a single file containing all the classes, directories, and deployment descriptor files. The *jar* utility is used to package the various deployment files into a single deployable file. The *jar* tool bundles the application or module files in a directory into a single *Java ARchive (JAR)* file, while maintaining the structure of the application directory. The Java class loader searches a jar file in the same manner it searches a directory. Thus, both the "exploded directory" format and a jar file are equivalent when it comes to deploying modules and applications. The jar files are compact and convenient for packaging and copying, and make distributing applications easier. They also have an additional advantage over exploded directory deployments because the Administration Console can't copy exploded directories to Managed Servers. According to the Java EE specification, you must package an enterprise application as an *.ear* file archive. The file extension of the jar file produced by the *jar* utility may have the same or a different file extension, such as *.jar, .war,* or *.rar,* depending on the type of application. Here are the file extensions for each type of deployment unit:

Web applications	*.war*
Enterprise applications	*.ear*
EJBs and client archives	*.jar*
Resource adapters	*.rar*
Web services	*.war* if implemented by Java classes and *.jar* if implemented by EJBs
Client applications	*.jar*

The *jar* utility is in the bin directory of your JDK. The command works similarly to the UNIX *tar* command. The general syntax for creating a jar file is the following:

```
jar cf jar-file input-file(s)
```

This *jar* command will create a jar file named *jar-file* that contains the files that you list with the *input-file(s)* attribute. If you specify a directory instead of a set of files, the *jar* command adds all the files within that directory (including files in its subdirectories) to the jar file. So, if you want to create an Enterprise Archive (EAR) file for an enterprise application, you first copy the web archives (war files) and the EJB archives (jar files) to your staging directory. You can then create the ear file for the application by invoking the *jar* command in the following way:

```
jar -cvf myapp.ear -C staging_dir
```

To create a war file instead, replace *myapp.ear* with *myapp.war.* Deploying applications using an archive file is the recommended deployment mode for production environments. Note that you don't have to use a deployment descriptor (META-INF*application.xml*) for an archived file deployment, as long as you specify the appropriate type of extension for the archived file.

TIP
You can use either an application's archive jar file (.ear) or the exploded directory structure as an argument when using a deployment tool such as weblogic.Deployer.

Deploying an Exploded Archive Directory

In addition to the ability to package applications into *.ear* archive files, WebLogic Server supports the deployment of archived applications, and this is called an *exploded archive directory deployment.* Using the archive directory deployment method doesn't require that you prepare a single archive file for deployment. Rather, you simply store the files and directories on your file system and make that directory structure accessible to WebLogic Server. Deploying through the exploded archive directory is ideal when you may have to update an application partially after the deployment or the application contains static files such as html files, image files, and css files that you need to update frequently. In both of these cases, you avoid the need to re-create the archive file by simply using the exploded directory deployment method. This approach is most commonly used during development and is ideal for both development and unit testing environments. As explained later in this chapter in the section "Using FastSwap to Shorten the Development Cycle," the FastSwap feature allows the immediate reloading of recompiled classes without having to redeploy an application. FastSwap is a development mode–only feature and works only with an exploded archive directory deployment.

The Java EE specification requires the deployment of archived *.ear* files without deployment descriptors. To satisfy the requirement, if you need to override the defaults you must use annotations instead of deployment descriptors. WebLogic Server not only supports this requirement but also allows the deployment of exploded EAR directories without using deployment descriptors. In the absence of any deployment descriptors, the tools you use for deploying applications should be able to find the application and web modules. You do this by naming the directories with the *.ear*, *.war*, *.jar*, or *.rar* suffix, depending on the type of deployment unit the exploded directory contains.

You can deploy an archive file as an exploded archive directory by using the *jar* utility to unpack the archive file, as shown here:

```
mkdir /myapp
cd /myapp
jar xvf /dist/myapp.ear
```

You should dedicate the *myapp* directory for a single purpose—to serve as the root installation directory for the *myapp* application. Note that you must create an *application.xml* deployment descriptor file to specify the order in which you want to deploy the various modules if the exploded enterprise application doesn't contain a META-INF*application.xml* descriptor.

You can use the *wlcompile* Ant task to compile your application's Java components in a split development directory, as shown here:

```
<wlcompile srcdir="${src.dir}"   destdir="S{dest.dir}"/>,
```

In this example, *<srcdir>* is the source directory and *<destdir>* is the build/output directory. The *wldeploy* task lets you easily deploy an application directly from the split development directory. In order to deploy from a split development directory, all you need to do is to identify the build directory as the location for the deployable files, as shown in the following example:

```
<wldeploy user="${user}"  password="${password}"
              action="deploy"  source="S{dest.dir}"
              name="myAppEar"
```

Naming the Deployment and the Applications

Naming a deployment makes it easy to redeploy or undeploy an application. This is especially true when your WebLogic Server domain contains multiple servers. If you don't specify a name for your deployment, the deployment tool names the application after the archive file. For example, if you name an enterprise application's archive file *newapp.ear*, the deployment is, by default, named *newapp*. In an exploded archive directory deployment, *weblogic.Deployer* uses the name of the top-level directory for the deployment as the deployment name.

The application names must adhere to certain naming conventions: you can use only alphanumeric characters, underscores, hyphens, and periods. Version strings are optional but highly recommended, especially in production environments. The developers provide the version string in the manifest file for the application.

Storing the Deployment Files

Whether you are deploying via an archived file or through an exploded archive directory, always create a special installation directory for the application to make your (and the web app server's) life easier. The purpose behind the creation of the application installation directory is to separate the configuration files from the core application files. The Administration Console will identify your application-related files easily if you create an installation directory. Once you receive all the necessary application files for deploying on the production WebLogic Server, simply create an application installation directory and place all the files there—do this whether you're using the archived format or exploded archive directory method to deploy the application.

NOTE
Oracle recommends that you move all deployments into an application installation directory before deploying them.

Here's an example showing how to create an application directory to store application files under the top-level directory C:\deploy_dir\prod:

1. Create a deployment directory named **C:\deploy_dir\prod**. This top-level directory must be separate from the domain directory and must be accessible by the Admin Server and all the Managed Servers.
2. Create a subdirectory under the top-level directory:

   ```
   mkdir C:\deploy_dir\prod\newApp
   ```

3. Create another directory under the newApp directory to mark the version of the application you're about to deploy:

   ```
   mkdir C:\deploy_dir\prod\newApp\Ver1
   ```

   The Ver1 directory is the version subdirectory, which serves as the installation root directory.
4. You must now create two directories under the Ver1 directory, one for storing the application files and the other for placing the *plan.xml* file(s):

   ```
   mkdir C:\deploy_dir\prod\newApp\Ver1\app
   mkdir C:\deploy_dir\prod\newApp\Ver1\plan
   ```

5. The final step is to copy the source application files into the app directory and the deployment plan files (*plan.xml* files), if you have any, into the plan directory, as shown here:

   ```
   copy C:\backup\newApp.ear C:\deploy_dir\prod\newApp\Ver1\app
   copy C:\backup\Plans\plan1.xml C:\deploy_dir\prod\newApp\Ver1\plan
   ```

Note that the plan directory should mirror the app directory and that for each module there can be a directory that contains descriptors that augment or override the files in the application archive. The previous example shows how to copy the archive file *newApp.ear* into the installation root directory, app. If you're using an exploded archive directory instead, simply copy the entire exploded archive directory into the installation root directory, as shown here:

```
copy -r C:\backup\newApp C:\deploy_dir\prod\newApp\Ver1\app
```

Note that the creation of the dedicated application installation directory, as shown here, is only useful if you're deploying your application through the Administration Console. The *weblogic.Deployer* utility doesn't permit you to specify an application installation directory.

How WebLogic Server Accesses Source Files

The staging mode specifies how the server copies the deployment files from a source on the Admin Server to the Managed Server's staging area during the deployment's preparation phase. You can choose to make the deployment files available to the target servers in three different staging modes: *stage, nostage,* and *external_stage*. In the *stage* mode, the Admin Server distributes the deployment source files for applications to staging directories on each of the target servers. Staging the application files works best when you're dealing with small-sized applications. When dealing with large applications that you're deploying to several targets, you can use the *nostage* option, which requires all servers to use the same physical copy of the application file or files. You must ensure that both the Admin Server and the Managed Servers can access the physical files and reference them with the same declared path on all server instances. You can use shared storage or a networked directory so all targets can access the deployment files.

The *nostage* mode also works well in cases in which you're using an exploded archive directory and wish to redeploy changed applications regularly.

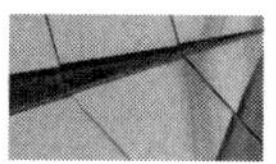

NOTE
Managed Servers use the staging *mode, by default, when you distribute or deploy applications to them.*

The *external_stage* mode is less frequently employed than the *stage* and *nostage* modes. In this mode, a target does use its own copy of the deployment files, but you must manually copy those files to the staging directory of each server that's part of the deployment. This is typically accomplished on UNIX environments with *scp* or is often the case when using an external document management system to distribute content. The Admin Server will still keep a copy of the deployment files for validation purposes, but it doesn't validate the deployment file copies that reside in the staging directories of the target servers.

When dealing with large application migration to multiple servers, use the *external_stage* mode of deployment if you can't use the *nostage* mode for some reason and you also don't have a shared file system. If you leave out the *stage, nostage,* and *external_stage* options when executing the *weblogic.Deployer* command, the server staging mode determines the default deployment mode for a server. You can modify the current staging mode of a server by following this sequence in the console: Environment | Servers | *<Server_Name>* Configuration | Deployment. Figure 8-1 shows the Deployment page for a Managed Server. You can configure three things from this page:

- Staging Mode (select the *stage, nostage,* or *external_stage* mode)
- Staging Directory Name (on the Managed Server)
- Upload Directory Name (on the Admin Server)

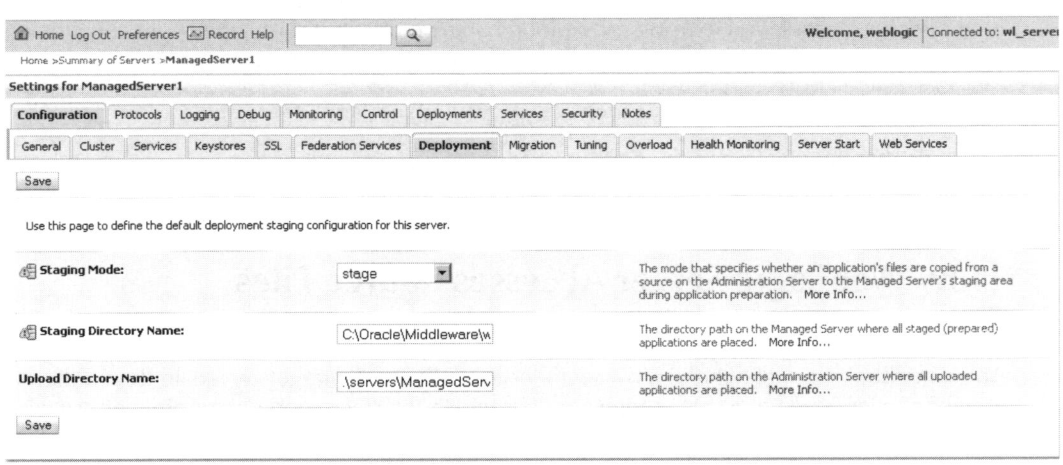

FIGURE 8-1. *Configuring a server's file deployment settings*

The default server staging mode is *stage,* so you don't have to specify the *stage* option when you use *weblogic.Deployer* to deploy an application or module. If you want to use one of the other two staging modes, you need to specify the staging mode with the appropriate option (*nostage* or *external_stage*) when you issue the *weblogic.Deployer* command, as shown here:

```
java weblogic.Deployer -adminurl http://localhost:7001 -username weblogic
                       -password welcome1 -name testApp1
                       -nostage
                       -targets MyCluster1
                       -deploy
                        C:\deploy_dir\prod\testApp\Ver1\app\testApp1.ear
```

Replace *-nostage* with *-external_stage* if you want to use the external stage mode instead.

Staging Deployment Plans

In Oracle WebLogic Server 12*c,* you can stage an application's deployment plan independently of the application archive. This gives you the option of staging a deployment when the application itself isn't staged.

You have three options for staging deployment plans:

- **planstage** Copies the deployment plan to target servers' staging directories.
- **plannostage** Doesn't copy the deployment plan to target servers, but leaves it in a fixed location.
- **planexternal_stage** Doesn't copy the deployment plan to target servers. You are responsible for manually copying the plan (or using a script to do so) and ensuring the deployment plan is copied to the appropriate subdirectory in the target server's staging directories.

By default, a deployment plan uses the value you specify for application staging if you don't specify a staging mode for the plan. For example, if application staging is set to *stage,* the deployment plan staging mode is, by default, set to *planstage*.

If neither the deployment plan nor the application staging is specified, the server setting is used as the default application staging mode. For example, if the server setting is to not stage, then the deployment plan staging mode is set to *plannostage*. In this case, you must explicitly specify the deployment plan staging if it's required.

Deploying Applications

Although the various deployment tools are functionally equivalent, administrators use the Administration Console, *weblogic.Deployer,* or WLST scripts to deploy applications. Developers can use the Administration Console for deployment in a single-server environment, but *wldeploy* is a good alternative for developers because they don't have to go through multiple deployment steps, as required when using the Console. The following sections show how to deploy applications through the Administration Console, WLST, *weblogic.Deployer,* and *wldeploy*. Make sure you start all the WebLogic Server services such as JDBC data sources—some applications may deploy fine even if you haven't started the services, but others will fail to deploy. You also must create any necessary users and groups in the domain's security realm.

Before you start reviewing the various deployment tools, you should understand the order in which WebLogic Server deploys applications and resources upon starting.

Deployment Order

When you are deploying an application on WebLogic Server in development or for the first time in production, you'll necessarily do it in an order in which you deploy resources and applications that are your building blocks first and deploy the dependent resources and applications later. If you are using JMS to communicate between two applications, you deploy the JMS queues and topics first and the applications next. This ordering must somehow be preserved when starting a server instance. As a general rule, there is a well-known order that covers which groupings of deployable entities are deployed in what order. In general, the WebLogic Server deploys applications and resources in the following order:

1. JDBC system modules
2. JMS system modules
3. Java EE libraries and optional packages
4. Applications and stand-alone modules
5. Startup classes

Within the categories of "applications and stand-alone modules" and "startup classes," the Deployment Order attribute controls the order in which each server deploys each deployment unit. You can specify the deployment order in the *application.xml* deployment descriptor or as a parameter when you use the deployment tools. Each deployment unit has a default Deployment Order value of 100. When you boot a server, it first initializes the dependent subsystems and then deploys each deployment unit according to its Deployment Order value. You can change the Deployment Order attribute from the Administration Console. On the Deployments page, click the module for which you want to change the deployment order. In the Settings For *<module_name>* page, enter a new numeric value in the Deployment Order field and click Save. You must first obtain a lock and activate the changes. When the server restarts, the module is deployed in the order you specify. If multiple modules have the same Deployment Order, the server deploys them in alphabetical order.

When the server boots up, it starts everything in the following sequence:

1. The server initializes the JMS and JDBC services.
2. It deploys applications and modules.
3. It performs custom startup tasks (runs the startup classes).

Startup and shutdown classes refer to custom Java programs that the server executes automatically when you start a server or shut it down gracefully to provide system services for the applications you deploy. You can load the same or different startup classes on each cluster member. The server loads the shutdown classes and runs them before a graceful shutdown. Any other server shutdown modes don't let the server run the shutdown classes. To use a startup or shutdown class, you must configure the classes and assign them to a server or cluster. The *examples.jms.startup* API code shows how to establish a JMS message consumer from a WebLogic startup class.

You can create, configure, and alter the startup sequence of startup classes through the Administration Console. Expand Environment in the left-hand pane of the Console and select Startup And Shutdown Classes.

If you want to modify the default startup behavior by, say, having the server execute the startup classes after the JDBC connection pools are activated but before the applications and EJBs are deployed, you can do so by selecting the class name and checking the Run Before Application Deployments check box in the Administration Console. If you want the server to execute the startup tasks after it starts the JMS and JDBC services but before it activates the applications and EJBs, select the class name and the Run Before Application Activations check box in the Administration Console. The server loads and runs the startup classes before it starts the deployment prepare phase. The default behavior is for the server to load the startup classes after the deployment enters the ADMIN state.

Using the Administration Console for Deployment

You can use the Administration Console to deploy applications even if you aren't sure of the target servers or where the various application deployment files are located. The following section shows how to install an enterprise application. The deployment steps are similar when you deploy a web application or an EJB module. In the example, let's install the enterprise application in a domain that's running in production mode. In a production environment, you must perform two distinct steps to deploy an application through the Administration Console: First, install the application, and then start it. Installing the application lets the WebLogic Server access the application files (archived file) or directory (exploded archive directory) and validate the deployment files. Starting the application makes it available to users. In development mode, when you install an application or module, it automatically starts running if the installation is successful, thus installation and deployment are synonymous in development mode, unlike in production mode.

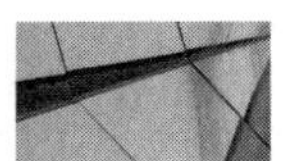

NOTE
Although you can deploy a Java EE application or a Java EE, JMS, JDBC, or WLDF module to a single server (an Admin or Managed Server) or a cluster, you can only deploy a web application to a virtual host.

Installing an Enterprise Application

Installing an enterprise (or any) application means making WebLogic Server aware of the physical archive file or the exploded archive directory under which all the application's files and classes are located. As explained in the section "Types of Applications You Can Deploy," earlier in this chapter, you can install an enterprise or web application as an archived file or as an exploded archive directory. In this example, let's install the application as an archived ear file. Follow these steps to install an enterprise application:

1. Click Lock & Edit in the Change Center of the Administration Console.
2. Select Deployments in the left-hand pane of the console.
3. On the Deployments page, click Install.
4. The Install Application Assistant will guide your installation actions. Locate the application or module in the Install Application Assistant and click Next. You can select a file path that represents an archive file, an application root directory, or an exploded archive directory. If you specify a directory, the server will install all the components in that directory. Note that you must click the radio button to the left of the application name before the Install Application Assistant can proceed. Figure 8-2 shows the deployment location page.
5. On the Choose Targeting Style page, select "Install This Deployment As An Application. Figure 8-3 shows this page. You can also choose to install the application as a library. Click Next.
6. On the Select Deployment Targets page (you'll see this page only if you have one or more Managed Servers or a cluster in the domain), select a cluster or Managed Server(s) from the Available Targets table. In this example, I chose the cluster named MyCluster1. Note that, by default, the server installs the deployment files on all the Managed Servers in a cluster, but you can choose to install the application on only some of the cluster members. Click Next.

   On the Optional Settings page, shown in Figure 8-4, name the deployment (ajaxJSF1 in this example). You can also select a security model, which is a combination of security roles and policies. Select the default option for the security model, which is DD Only: Use Only Roles And Policies That Are Defined In The Deployment Descriptors. You can also choose to use roles and policies that are defined in the Administration Console.

Install Application Assistant

Back | Next | Finish | Cancel

Locate deployment to install and prepare for deployment

Select the file path that represents the application root directory, archive file, exploded archive directory, or application module descriptor that you want to install. You can also enter the path of the application directory or file in the Path field.

Note: Only valid file paths are displayed below. If you cannot find your deployment files, upload your file(s) and/or confirm that your application contains the required deployment descriptors.

Path:	C:\oracle\middleware\wlserver_12.1\samples\server\examples\build\ajaxJSF
Recently Used Paths:	(none)
Current Location:	192.168.56.1 \ C: \ oracle \ middleware \ wlserver_12.1 \ samples \ server \ examples \ build

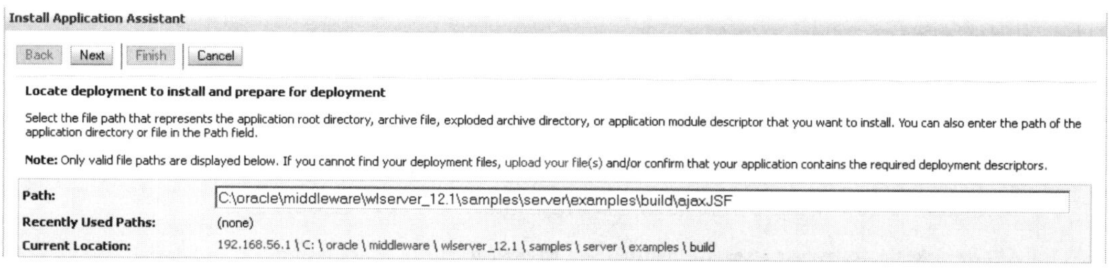

FIGURE 8-2. *The deployment location page*

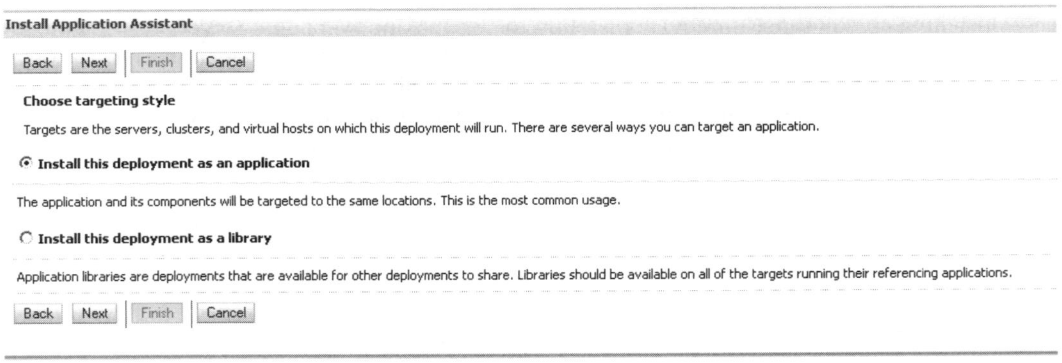

Install Application Assistant

Back Next Finish Cancel

Choose targeting style

Targets are the servers, clusters, and virtual hosts on which this deployment will run. There are several ways you can target an application.

◉ **Install this deployment as an application**

The application and its components will be targeted to the same locations. This is the most common usage.

○ **Install this deployment as a library**

Application libraries are deployments that are available for other deployments to share. Libraries should be available on all of the targets running their referencing applications.

Back Next Finish Cancel

FIGURE 8-3. *Selecting the deployment targets*

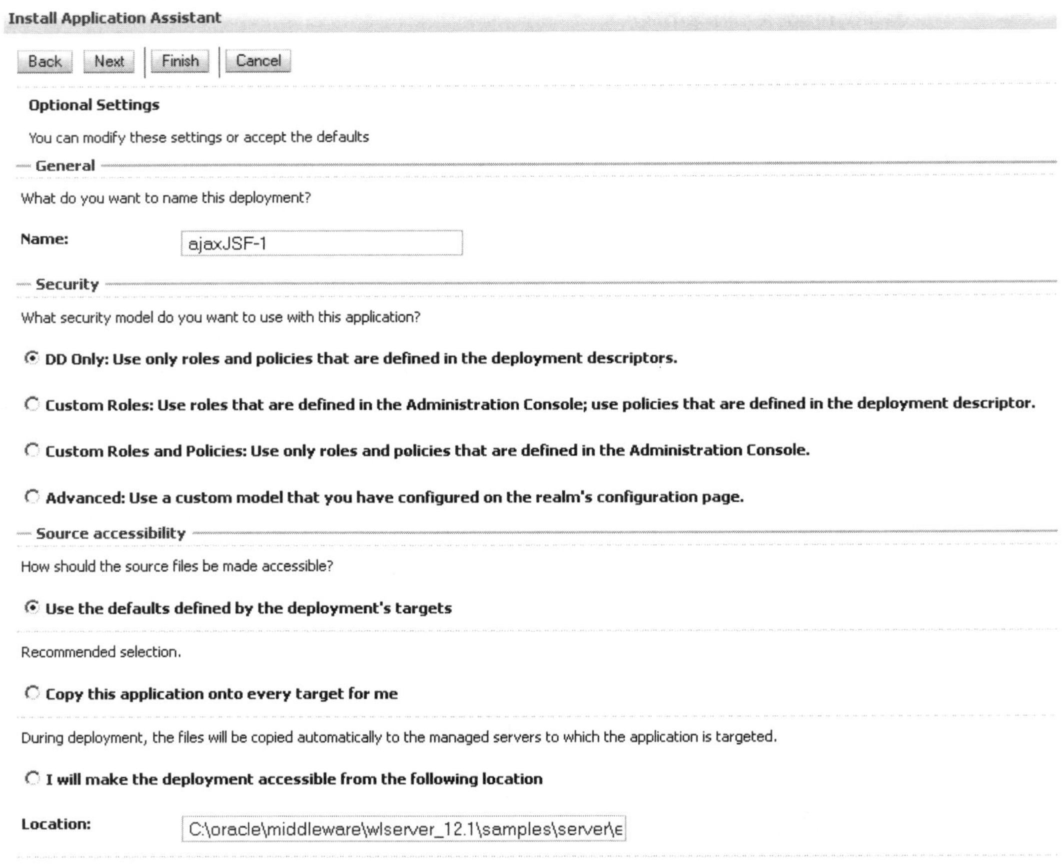

Install Application Assistant

Back Next Finish Cancel

Optional Settings

You can modify these settings or accept the defaults

— **General**

What do you want to name this deployment?

Name: ajaxJSF-1

— **Security**

What security model do you want to use with this application?

◉ **DD Only: Use only roles and policies that are defined in the deployment descriptors.**

○ **Custom Roles: Use roles that are defined in the Administration Console; use policies that are defined in the deployment descriptor.**

○ **Custom Roles and Policies: Use only roles and policies that are defined in the Administration Console.**

○ **Advanced: Use a custom model that you have configured on the realm's configuration page.**

— **Source accessibility**

How should the source files be made accessible?

◉ **Use the defaults defined by the deployment's targets**

Recommended selection.

○ **Copy this application onto every target for me**

During deployment, the files will be copied automatically to the managed servers to which the application is targeted.

○ **I will make the deployment accessible from the following location**

Location: C:\oracle\middleware\wlserver_12.1\samples\server\e

FIGURE 8-4. *The Optional Settings page*

7. In the Source Accessibility section, you must choose how you want to make the application's source files available to the targets. You have three choices:
   - Use The Defaults Defined By The Deployment's Targets
   - Copy This Application Onto Every Target For Me
   - I Will Make The Deployment Accessible From The Following Location

   Selecting the option Copy This Application Onto Every Target For Me will automatically copy the application files to all the Managed Servers to which you target the application. Note that this is equivalent to setting the staging mode to *stage*. If you choose the last option ("I Will Make The Deployment Accessible From The Following Location), make sure that all targets can reach this directory—usually this is a shared directory. This choice is the same as the *nostage* staging mode. Click Next.
8. In the Additional Configuration section on the next page, shown in Figure 8-5, you can choose to configure the application at this point by selecting the "Yes, Take Me To The Deployment's Configuration Screen option. You can skip that step for now by selecting the No, I'll Review The Configuration Later option. Click Finish. You'll see the following message in the Console: "The deployment has been successfully installed."
9. To activate the installation changes you made, click Activate Changes in the Change Center of the Administration Console.

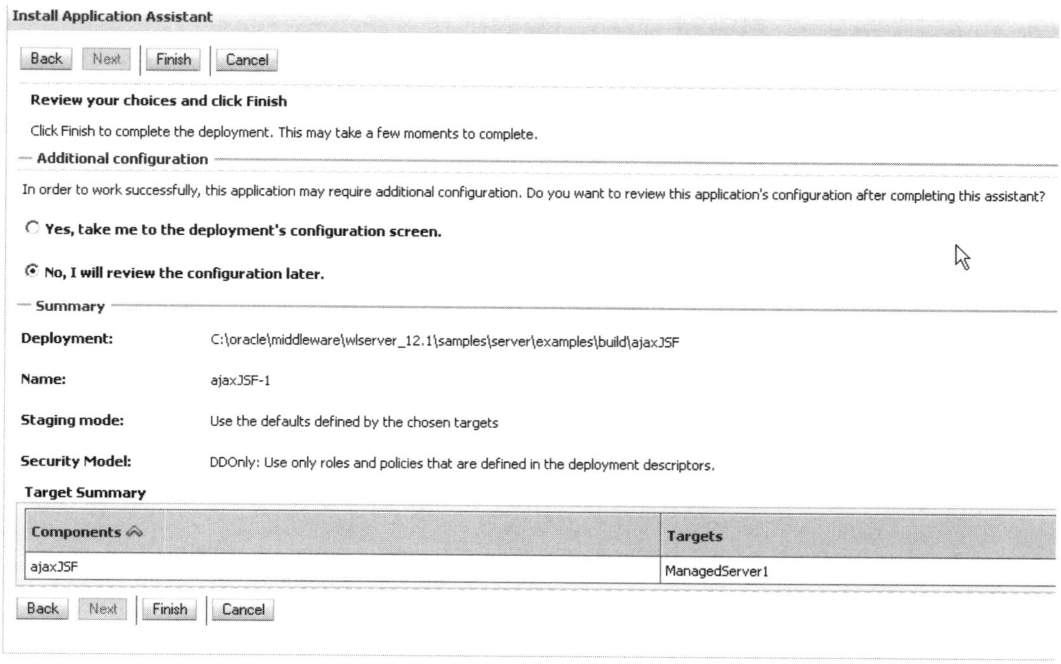

FIGURE 8-5. *Additional Configuration options*

If you follow the Oracle-recommended deployment directory structure (by creating an application root directory with the subdirectories app and plan under it), WebLogic Server automatically creates a deployment plan in the plan directory if there's one there already. If you already have a deployment plan in the plan directory, you'll see the following message in the console:

> "A deployment plan was found for this application at C:\test_dir\plan\Plan.xml. These deployment plan files have been included in this deployment."

Once the installation has finished, you are returned to the Summary Of Deployments page, and you'll now see your new deployment's name, ajaxJSF-1, under the Name column in the Deployments table, which is shown in Figure 8-6. The Type column shows that the application is an enterprise application.

Under the State column, before you activate the changes in the Change Center by clicking the Activate Changes button in step 10, you'll see DISTRIBUTE INITIALIZING (in the case of a single-server deployment, the state will be DEPLOY INITIALIZING instead). Once you activate the changes, the value of the State column changes to PREPARED, indicating that the server has validated the application's deployment files. The value for the State column will change to ACTIVE once you start the application.

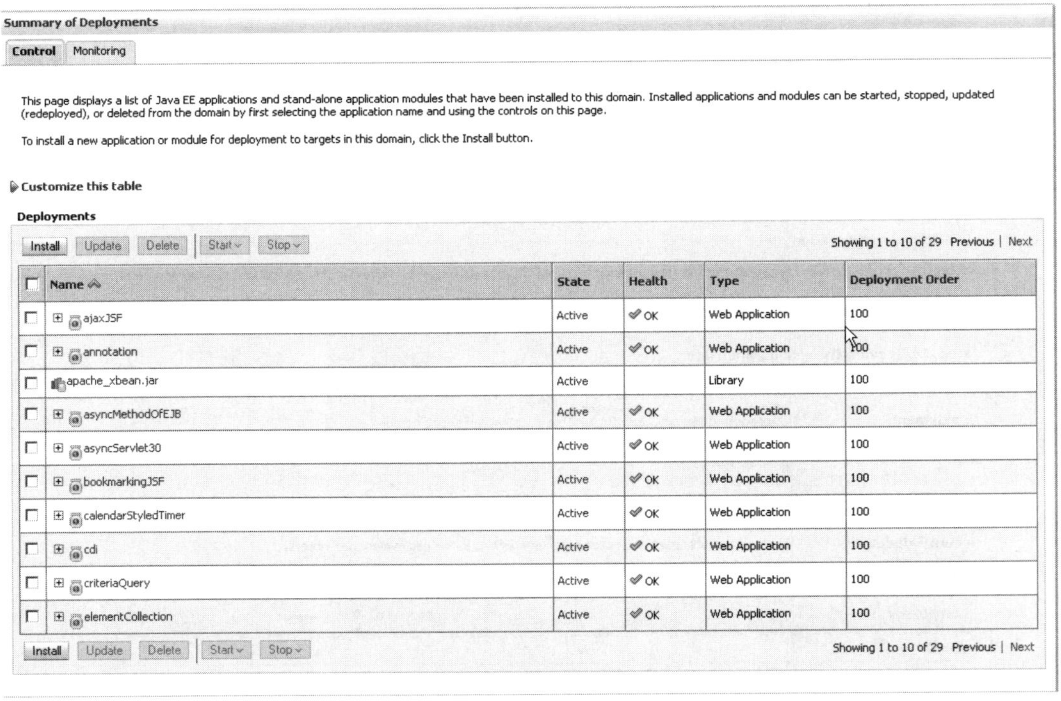

Summary of Deployments

Control | Monitoring

This page displays a list of Java EE applications and stand-alone application modules that have been installed to this domain. Installed applications and modules can be started, stopped, updated (redeployed), or deleted from the domain by first selecting the application name and using the controls on this page.

To install a new application or module for deployment to targets in this domain, click the Install button.

Customize this table

Deployments

Install | Update | Delete | Start | Stop — Showing 1 to 10 of 29 Previous | Next

	Name	State	Health	Type	Deployment Order
	ajaxJSF	Active	OK	Web Application	100
	annotation	Active	OK	Web Application	100
	apache_xbean.jar	Active		Library	100
	asyncMethodOfEJB	Active	OK	Web Application	100
	asyncServlet30	Active	OK	Web Application	100
	bookmarkingJSF	Active	OK	Web Application	100
	calendarStyledTimer	Active	OK	Web Application	100
	cdi	Active	OK	Web Application	100
	criteriaQuery	Active	OK	Web Application	100
	elementCollection	Active	OK	Web Application	100

Install | Update | Delete | Start | Stop — Showing 1 to 10 of 29 Previous | Next

FIGURE 8-6. *The Summary of Deployments page*

When you deploy an application or an EJB module, the deployment goes through three distinct phases:

- **Prepare** The deployment files and the *plan.xml* file are validated.
- **Admin** The server passes through the admin phase before it fully activates the application. However, you can start an application in ADMIN mode for testing the application.
- **Activate** The server starts accepting connection requests for the application.

Once the deployment is completed, the domain's *config.xml* file will show the deployment information for the new enterprise application (*myApp1* in this example), as shown here:

```
<app-deployment>
  <name>testApp1</name>
  <target>MyCluster1</target>
  <module-type>ear</module-type>
  <source-path>C:\test_dir\app\testApp1.ear</source-path>
  <security-dd-model>DDOnly</security-dd-model>
</app-deployment>
```

Note the *<target>* element shows that this application is deployed to the entire cluster MyCluster1.

Deleting an application is easy. On the Summary Of Deployments page, select the application you want to delete from the Deployments table. Click Delete. You must first stop the application before you can undeploy it. If you try to undeploy a running application, you'll receive the following error messages in the console:

> "The application testApp1 is currently running and may not be deleted.
> All of the Deployments selected are currently in a state which is incompatible with this operation. No action will be performed."

When you deploy an application to a target (or targets), the state of the deployment in the Deployments table will show NEW until all the targets are fully started. Once you deploy an application fully by installing and starting it, you don't have to do anything further when you restart the servers. The application will automatically start running after each restart of a target server. You need to start the application only once—the very first time you install it. After that, the application will automatically start when you restart the server.

Starting and Stopping the Application

You can start an application so it goes into an ACTIVE state and starts accepting client connections or start it in administration mode. When you shut down an application, you can either shut it down immediately or bring it down in a graceful manner. The following sections describe the various startup and shutdown options.

Starting an Application Installing an application or module doesn't make that application or module available to the server clients. To make an application available to users, you must start the application, by following these simple steps.

1. Select Deployments in the Administration Console.
2. Select the check box that belongs to the application you want to deploy.

3. Click Start to make the application available to users. When you click the Start button after checking the application's name, you'll see a drop-down list with two choices:
   - Servicing All Requests
   - Servicing Only Administration Requests
4. Select one of the two options to start the application—the first option lets the application start servicing user requests immediately. The second start option will start the server in administration mode so you can test things before releasing an application into the production environment. If you start an application in administration mode, its state in the Deployments table is shown as ADMIN.

You can also start an application by using *weblogic.Deployer*, as shown here:

```
java weblogic.Deployer -adminurl http://localhost:7001 -username weblogic -
password welcome1 -name mymodule1 -start
```

Stopping an Application You can stop an application through the Console, as explained earlier, or with the *weblogic.Deployer* tool by specifying the *stop* command, as shown here:

```
java weblogic.Deployer -adminurl http://localhost:7001 -user weblogic
                       -password welcome1 -name mymodule1-stop
```

You can also take an application offline for maintenance reasons or for troubleshooting by placing the running application into administration mode. Once you place the application in administration mode, you must connect to it using a configured administration channel. Use the *stop* command with the *adminmode* option to place an application in administration mode:

```
java weblogic.Deployer -adminurl http://localhost:7001 -username weblogic
                       -password welcome1 -name mymodule -stop -adminmode
```

The *stop* command, as shown here, will terminate the application without waiting for pending HTTP sessions to complete their work. If you want the server to wait for in-process work to complete, specify the *graceful* option:

```
java weblogic.Deployer -adminurl http://localhost:7001 -username weblogic
                       -password welcome1
                       -name mymodule
                       -stop -adminmode -graceful
```

Once you complete your testing or maintenance work, open the application back up to client requests by using the *start* command, as explained earlier. By default, the server stops the active version of an application if you've deployed more than one version of an application. If you want to stop a version other than the active version, specify the version number of the application with the *appversion* option.

Note that stopping an application is purely an administrative function: it doesn't affect an application's deployment status; it just makes the application unavailable to service client requests. If you undeploy an application, however, the server removes all deployment files generated by WebLogic Server from the domain.

You can stop a running application from the Administration Console by following these steps:

1. Click Stop on the Summary Of Deployments page after first checking the application you want to shut down. You must pick one of the following options when you shut down an application:
   - **When Work Completes** Performs a clean shutdown, where the server waits for the application to finish all pending work and also waits for all currently connected users to disconnect.
   - **Force Stop Now** Stops the application immediately.
   - **Stop, But Continue Servicing Administration Requests** Stops the application once it finishes ongoing work and puts it in administration mode, where only an administrator can access the application.
2. Click Yes to confirm your choice to stop the application.

When you shut down an application, it goes into the PREPARED state before shutting down.

Deploying Internal Applications

WebLogic Server deploys several internal applications, such as the Administration Console, that display a user interface. The server can deploy these internal applications at server startup time or on demand. The on-demand deployment is also called *deployment on first access*. When you run the server in development mode, the internal applications are deployed on demand, and in production mode, they are deployed at server startup time. Starting the internal applications at server startup requires more memory and CPU and leads to a longer server startup time. You can avoid this by configuring the internal applications to start only on demand. Follow these steps to configure this option from the Administration Console:

1. Click Lock & Edit in the Change Center of the Administration Console.
2. Go to the Domain | Configuration | General page.
3. Select the Enable On-Demand Deployment Of Internal Applications check box.
4. Click Save and then click Activate Changes.

Configuring the Enable On-Demand Deployment Of Internal Applications property ensures that internal applications, such as the Administration Console, *uddi*, *wlstestclient*, and *uddiexplorer*, are not deployed automatically during server startup. On-demand deployment is the default in development mode, and you need to configure this for production mode servers in cases where you know you aren't using any of these applications.

Using WLST to Deploy Applications

You can use WLST when you want to automate deployment tasks through scripts. Because the WLST *deploy* command is an online command, you must first connect to the Admin Server. Also, make sure you have the Node Manager running if you are deploying or undeploying from a Managed Server or cluster.

Deploying an Application

The following example shows how to deploy an enterprise application to a target using an archive file:

```
wls:/wl_server/serverConfig>
 deploy('testApp1','C:\deploy_dir\prod\testApp\app\testApp1.ear')
```

```
Deploying application from C:\deploy_dir\prod\testApp\Ver1\app\testApp1.ear to
targets  (upload=false) ...
<Sep 6, 2013  6:15:22 AM EDT> <Info> <J2EE Deployment SPI> <BEA-260121>
 <Initiating deploy operation for application, testApp1 [archive:
C:\deploy_dir\prod\testApp\Ver1\app\testApp1.ear], to examplesServer .>

.Completed the deployment of Application with status completed
Current Status of your Deployment:
Deployment command type: deploy
Deployment State       : completed
Deployment Message     : no message
wls:/wl_server/serverConfig>
```

You can specify several arguments with the *deploy* command, but only two of them are mandatory: *appName* and *path*. If you don't specify a value for the *target* argument, by default, the application is deployed to the Admin Server.

Note that in the examples shown here, the deployment will take the archive file's name (without the *.ear* or *.war* extension, of course). If you want to name your deployment differently, specify the *name* option with the *deploy* command. If you wish to deploy multiple applications, you can simplify things by using a simple WLST script such as the following:

```
connect ('weblogic',welcome1','t3://localhost:7001')
   Target='MyManagedServer1'
f=open(r'./appList.txt','r')
print t
for i in range(3):
         line=f.readline()
         line1=line[ :-1]
         appName='./'+line1
         print '#######################' +appName
         edit()
       startEdit()
       deploy(appName=line1,path=appName,targets=target)
       save()
       activate()
       f.close()
```

You can also use WLST in offline mode to deploy an application, but the process is more complex. Here are the steps:

1. Create an application template using the Domain Template Builder.
2. Open the newly created application template using the *readDomain* command:

```
wls:/offline>
readDomain('C:\Oracle\Middleware\wlserver_12.1\samples\domain\medrec')
wls:/offline/medrec>
readTemplate('C:\Oracle\Middleware\wlserver_12.1\common\templates\domains\
wls_medrec.jar')
```

3. Add the template to the domain:

```
wls:offline/medrec>
addTemplate('C:\Oracle\Middleware\wlserver_12.1\common\templates\applications\
DefaultWebApp.jar')
```

4. Save and close the domain using the *updateDomain* and the *closeDomain* commands:

```
wls:offline/wlwmedrec>updateDomain()
wls:offline/wlwmedrec>closeDomain()
```

One excellent benefit of using a WLST script is that it allows you to automate the creation of servers and resources along with the deployment of the application. Developers can create a simple script embedded in Ant that re-creates a domain for development. Saving that domain as a template for handing off to QA and production is a good use of offline WLST scripts (and the Configuration Wizard).

Undeploying an Application

Use the WLST *undeploy* command to remove a deployed application, as shown in the following example:

```
wls:/wl_server/serverConfig> undeploy('testApp1',timeout=60000);
Undeploying application testApp1 ...
<Sep 6, 2013 8:12:34 AM EDT> <Info> <J2EE Deployment SPI> <BEA-260121>
<Initiating undeploy operation for application, testApp1 [archive: null],
to MyManaged1 .>
..Completed the undeployment of Application with status completed
Current Status of your Deployment:
Deployment command type: undeploy
Deployment State       : completed
Deployment Message     : no message
wls:/wl_server/serverConfig>
```

If the application *testApp1* is deployed to a cluster instead of a single Managed or Admin Server, the *undeploy* command is still issued the same way as shown here for a single-server deployment.

Deploying with weblogic.Deployer

The *weblogic.Deployer* tool is the ideal way to deploy applications in a production environment. The *weblogic.Deployer* tool lets you incorporate deployment commands in shell scripts and batch processes, as well as in administrative environments that use Ant. An important thing to remember before you can start working with *weblogic.Deployer* is that you must configure SSL on the machine where you're executing the *weblogic.Deployer* command if you're accessing the Admin Server through an administration channel. The *weblogic.Deployer* tool offers you all the functionality of the Administration Console and lets you easily integrate deployment commands within shell scripts and batch files.

The following sections show you how to deploy and undeploy an application, as well as perform other deployment-related tasks with the *weblogic.Deployer* tool.

Deploying an Enterprise Application

You use the *deploy* option to deploy an application to a WebLogic Server, whether it be an Admin Server, a Managed Server, or a cluster. Here's an example that shows how to deploy to a WebLogic Server cluster. Make sure that you set the environment first with the *setDomainEnv.cmd* script:

```
C:\>
Oracle\Middleware\Oracle_Home\user_projects\domains\wl_server\bin\setDomainEnv.cmd
C:\Oracle\Middleware\Oracle_Home\domains\wl_server>java weblogic.Deployer
-username weblogic -password welcome1 -name testApp1 -deploy -targets MyCluster1
C:\deploy_dir\prod\testApp\Ver1\app\testApp1.ear
weblogic.Deployer invoked with options:  -username weblogic -name testApp1 -deploy
-targets MyCluster1 C:\deploy_dir\prod\testApp\app\testApp1.ear
<Sep 6, 2013 7:12:27 AM EDT> <Info> <J2EE Deployment SPI> <BEA-260121> <Initiating
deploy operation for application, testApp1 [archive:
C:\deploy_dir\prod\testApp\Ver1\app\testApp1.ear], to MyCluster1 .>
Task 15 initiated: [Deployer:149026]deploy application testApp1 on MyCluster1.
Task 15 completed: [Deployer:149026]deploy application testApp1 on MyCluster1.
Target state: deploy completed on Cluster MyCluster1

C:\Oracle\Middleware\Oracle_Home\user_projects\domains\wl_server>
```

It's important to understand that the *deploy* option doesn't merely make the application files available to the target servers—it actually makes the application available to the users. In other words, the command doesn't stop at the PREPARED stage by installing the deployment files and validating them—it also starts the application. Note that *weblogic.Deployer* doesn't use a deployment plan, even if there's one in the deployment directory. You can make it use a deployment plan by specifying one with the *plan* option.

You can use *weblogic.Deployer* to deploy a module or a set of modules that are part of an ear file. Why would anyone want to package all the modules into a single ear file and then deploy only specific modules to a server? The purpose behind this strategy is that it simplifies the packaging and distribution of complex applications. Note that deploying specific modules from an ear is rare. The normal motivation for doing this is where there's a two-tier application with the web server in the front tier and EJB or web services in the back tier. In such cases, you can have a single ear file and target only parts to various Managed Servers or clusters. Again, this is a pretty unusual case. The following example shows how to deploy three modules, named *module1, module2,* and *module3,* respectively, to three separate servers:

```
java weblogic.Deployer -adminurl http://localhost:7001 -username weblogic
                       -password welcome1 -name testApp1
                       -targets module1@server1,
                        module2@server2,module3@server3
                       -stage
                       -deploy  .
C:\deploy_dir\prod\testApp\Ver1\app\testApp1.ear
```

You can deploy to one or more Managed Servers by specifying the Managed Servers with the *targets* argument, as shown here. This example also shows how to deploy to a virtual host:

```
java weblogic.Deployer -adminurl http://localhost:7001 -username weblogic
                       -password welcome1
```

```
                             -deploy
                             -targets MyManagedServer1,MyManagedServer2
C:\deploy_dir\prod\testApp\Ver1\app\testApp1.ear
```

In the following example, *myHost* is the name of a virtual host you've configured:

```
java weblogic.Deployer -adminurl http://localhost:7001 -username weblogic
                             -password welcome1
                             -deploy -targets myHost
C:\deploy_dir\prod\testApp\Ver1\app\testApp1.ear
```

None of these three examples uses a deployment plan. If your deployment includes a deployment plan, specify the *plan* option along with the *deploy* option.

When you deploy an application to a WebLogic Server cluster, the deployment must succeed on all active members of the cluster or the deployment will fail. However, if one of the members of a cluster is shut down while you're deploying an application, the inactive member will deploy automatically when it's restarted. This is the default behavior. You can override this behavior by specifying the *ClusterConstraintEnabled* option when you start a WebLogic Server domain. Doing this ensures that a cluster-wide deployment fails if any members are unreachable due to a network issue, for example, or even because you brought down an instance for maintenance work. Of course, as explained earlier, a cluster deployment will also fail if you can't deploy the entire set of application files to all the members of the cluster—active or inactive.

Adding a New Module

You can add a new application module to a deployed application without having to redeploy the application. The following example shows how to add a new module named *newmodule.war* to the *testApp1.ear* module, which is already in deployment:

```
java weblogic.Deployer -username weblogic -password welcome1
                             -name testApp1
                             -deploy
                             -targets newmodule.war@myserver
                             -source C:\deploy_dir\prod\testApp\Ver1\app\testApp1.ear
```

This command will deploy just the *newmodule.war* application, without affecting other components in the *testApp1.ear* enterprise application.

Deleting Files from a Deployment

You can delete static content from a deployment by using the *delete_files* option with *weblogic.Deployer,* but only if you have deployed the web application through an exploded archive directory. Here's an example that shows how to delete the file *test.html* that's part of the exploded archive directory named testApp1:

```
java weblogic.Deployer -adminurl http://localhost:7001 -user weblogic
                             -password welcome1
                             -name testApp1
                             -delete_files testApp1/test.html
```

Handle the *delete_files* option with great care. Oracle recommends that you don't use the *delete_files* option in production because it could delete all files in the exploded archive directory if you don't specify a file.

NOTE
A deployment name is associated with the application's deployment files and lets you easily deploy, redeploy, and undeploy applications.

Undeploying an Application

Undeploying an application or a module removes both the deployment name and the application or module's deployment files from a domain. Use *weblogic.Deployer* with the *undeploy* command, as shown in the following example:

```
java weblogic.Deployer -adminurl http://localhost:7001 -user weblogic
                       -password welcome1
                       -name mymodule -undeploy
```

You can undeploy an application or a module from specific targets by issuing the command with the *targets* option:

```
java weblogic.Deployer -adminurl http://localhost:7001 -user weblogic
                       -password welcome1
                       -name mymodule
                       -undeploy
                       -targets MyManagedServer1
```

If you don't specify the *targets* and *submoduletargets* options, the server will remove the application from all targets. It also detargets the JMS submodules.

Whereas the Administration Console doesn't undeploy a running application (when you "delete" an application), the default behavior of the *weblogic.Deployer undeploy* command is to terminate client connections immediately. When you're undeploying an application in a production setup, you may use the *graceful* option with the *undeploy* command, as shown here:

```
java weblogic.Deployer -adminurl http://localhost:7001 -user weblogic
                       -password welcome1
                       -name mymodule
                       -undeploy -graceful
```

The *graceful* option undeploys the application after waiting for the HTTP clients to complete their work.

When you undeploy an application or module, the server doesn't remove the application's source files—it merely deletes the deployment configuration and all deployment files that the server copied during deployment. For example, if you used the *stage* mode during deployment, the server copies the deployment files. Once you undeploy an application, you must perform a complete deployment process to return the deployment files, create a deployment name, and assign targets for the deployment.

Canceling a Deployment

You can cancel an ongoing deployment by specifying the *cancel* command with *weblogic.Deployer*. Specifying a task identifier helps identify your deployment. You can specify a task identifier with the *id* option, as shown in the following example:

```
java weblogic.Deployer -adminurl http://localhost:7001 -username weblogic -
password welcome1
```

```
                         -deploy -targets MyCluster1
                          C:\deploy_dir\prod\testApp\Ver1\app\testApp1.ear
                         -id testDeployment
```

You can then cancel the deployment by specifying the deployment's ID:

```
java weblogic.Deployer -username weblogic
                       -password welcome1
                       -cancel
                       -id testDeployment
```

Listing All Deployments

Use the *listapps* option to view the deployment names for all application standalone modules deployed in a domain, as shown in the following example:

```
C:\Oracle\Middleware\Oracle_Home\user_projects\domains\wl_server>java weblogic
.Deployer
-username weblogic -password welcome1 -listapps
weblogic.Deployer invoked with options:  -username weblogic -listapps
 pubsub [LibSpecVersion=1.0,LibImplVersion=1.6.0.0] <ACTIVE VERSION>
 asyncServletEar
 SamplesSearchWebApp
 xmlBeanEar
 examplesWebApp
 mainWebApp
 weblogic-sca [LibSpecVersion=1.1,LibImplVersion=1.1.0.0] <ACTIVE VERSION>
 ejb30
 jspSimpleTagEar
 ejb20BeanMgedEar
 stockEar
 webservicesJwsSimpleEar
 extServletAnnotationsEar
 testApp1
 apache_xbean.jar
 jdbcRowSetsEar
Number of Applications Found : 16
C:\Oracle\Middleware\Oracle_Home\user_projects\domains\wl_server>
```

As you'll learn in the "Production Redeployment Strategies" section, later in this chapter, the *listapps* command is very helpful in finding the version number of an application.

Using the update Command

The *update* command doesn't update the application; it also doesn't distribute or deploy the application. Rather, it redistributes the deployment plan file and reconfigures the application according to the new plan. Here's an example:

```
java weblogic.Deployer -adminurl http://localhost:7001 -user weblogic
                       -password welcome1
                       -update
```

```
                              -name myTestDeployment
                              -plan
C:\deploy_dir\prod\testApp\Ver1\plan\myNewPlan.xml
```

The production application can remain online for certain types of applications while you're reconfiguring its configuration.

Deploying with the wldeploy Ant Task

You can best put the *wldeploy* tool to use when you're deploying applications in a development environment. However, if your environment uses Ant tasks rather than shell scripts, you can use *wldeploy* instead of the *weblogic.Deployer* tool—the functionality is the same. The *wldeploy* task is primarily for developers to use in their environments. Because this book is primarily for WebLogic Server administrators, I won't discuss the *wldeploy* Ant task in great detail, but you execute it the same way as you execute the *wlserver* and *wlconfig* tasks.

Here are the steps to run the *wldeploy* Ant task:

1. Set the environment:

   ```
   WL_HOME\server\bin\setWLSEnv.cmd
   ```

2. Create an Ant build file (the default name is *build.xml*) with a target that includes a call to *wldeploy*.
3. Type **ant** at the command prompt in the staging directory to execute the Ant task:

   ```
   ant
   ```

Here's an example that shows a target that deploys an application to the Admin Server (development environment):

```
<target name="deploy">
  <wldeploy
    action="deploy" verbose="true" debug="true"
    name="TestDeployment" source="deploy/testdeploy.ear"
    user="weblogic" password="welcome1"
    adminurl="t3://localhost:7001" targets="examplesServer" />
</target>
```

You can undeploy the application by just specifying the deployment name:

```
<target name="undeploy">
  <wldeploy
    action="undeploy" verbose="true" debug="true"
    name="TestDeployment"
    user="weblogic" password="welcome1"
    adminurl="t3://localhost:7001" targets="examplesServer"
    failonerror="false" />
</target>
```

Reducing Deployment Time During Development

WebLogic Server offers a couple of highly useful techniques to simplify development deployments. The first is the autodeploy feature, which lets you deploy applications or modules by placing the deployment files in a specific directory. The FastSwap feature also helps cut back on development time because it allows in-place recompilation of Java classes without the need for redeployment of the application or module. Let's review these two features in the following sections.

Using the Autodeployment Feature During Development

WebLogic Server offers a quick way to deploy applications through its autodeployment option, wherein all you have to do to deploy an application is simply place the application in the *domain_name*\autodeploy directory of the Admin Server. The Admin Server automatically notices any applications you place in the autodeploy directory and deploys them. You can't autodeploy applications through the Managed Servers.

Following are the key things you must understand about the autodeployment feature:

- You can autodeploy an application either as an archived file or through the exploded archive directory method. If you use an archived file, just place it in the *domain_name*\autodeploy directory. If you want to deploy an exploded archive directory, place the entire exploded directory in the *domain_name*\autodeploy directory.
- If you want to redeploy an application that you've autodeployed, place the new version of the archive file over the application file in the *domain_name*\autodeploy directory.
- If the Admin Server is running, the deployment is immediate, and if it's not, the application will deploy when you start the Admin Server.
- You can't set up any roles or security policies, nor can you specify a deployment plan for an autodeployed application.
- The Admin Server won't be aware of any applications you remove when the server is shut down. To ensure that your domain tree remains in sync, remove an application from the *domain_name*\autodeploy directory only while the Admin Server is in the RUNNING state.
- You can remove an autodeployed application anytime by simply deleting the application from the *domain_name*\autodeploy directory.

TIP

If you switch from development to production mode, any applications that you autodeployed will remain deployed—you must undeploy the applications manually if you don't want them to continue to remain deployed.

Although automatic deployment may seem to be a great way to deploy applications quickly, the best way to deploy applications during development is to use *wldeploy* instead. Use autodeployment sparingly, for instance, to check a test application or when you're working in a temporary environment.

Using FastSwap to Shorten the Development Cycle

While developing a web application, a developer is continually modifying, deploying, and testing applications. To speed up this development cycle, WebLogic Server offers the FastSwap deployment feature. You can add new methods to a class at run time and test the result immediately by using FastSwap.

NOTE
The FastSwap deployment feature is disabled in production mode.

The FastSwap feature lets you deploy new application versions without affecting running applications. WebLogic Server makes this possible by dynamically redefining class definitions, thus avoiding the time consumed in the reloading of the classes by the class loader. This is particularly handy when you are debugging the implementation of a class and re-creating the state is time-consuming. With FastSwap, the application is not reloaded, so even the contents of data members remain intact. Using this feature, the developer can make a change while the application is running and let the application recompile on the fly without redeploying the application. The following limitations apply to the FastSwap deployment method:

- You can use FastSwap deployment only in a development environment, not in a production environment.
- You can only deploy applications in the exploded archive directory format (not as archived files)—the feature only picks up the changes you make to class files in exploded archive directories. You must modify Java classes that are in the WEB-INF directory, not the archived jar files in the WEB-INF\lib directory.
- Because FastSwap doesn't compile Java classes, Oracle recommends that you set the *compile-on-save* option in your IDE.

Besides these, there are additional limitations that apply when using the FastSwap feature, such as the nonsupport of adding or removing annotations.

The FastSwap feature isn't turned on by default, but it's very easy to turn it on. Ensure that you're running the WebLogic Server in development mode. If the application you deployed is an EAR file, add the *<fast-swap>* element to the *weblogic-application.xml* file, as shown here:

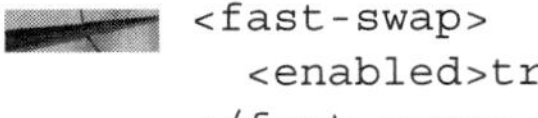

```
<fast-swap>
  <enabled>true</enabled>
</fast-swap>
```

If your application is deployed as a war file instead, you must place the *<fast-swap>* element in the *weblogic.xml* file. Once you set up the FastSwap feature in your application, when a new request comes in to the application, the FastSwap agent will search all directories in the class path for modified classes.

Monitoring and Updating Applications

Once you deploy an application, you need to manage them and, on occasion, update them. The following sections show how to monitor and manage deployed applications, as well as how to sanity test deployments by running an application in administration mode first to ensure the application is performing well before letting external clients access the application. Finally, you'll learn how to update applications.

Monitoring Applications

The Administration Console helps you monitor and manage deployed applications. On the Summary Of Deployments page, click Monitoring. You'll see several tabs under Monitoring. Click the Workload subtab. Figure 8-7 shows the Workload page for all deployed applications and modules in a domain. You can view Work Manager statistics and the constraints you've configured for the deployed applications. This page also lists the pending and completed requests for each deployed application or module.

Clicking the EJB tab will show you statistics for deployed EJBs, including the total count of timeouts and the total number of accesses to the EJBs. By default, the Console shows the statistics for stateless beans, but you can click the Stateful and Entity tabs to view statistics for the other two types of beans.

Clicking the Web Applications subtab shows a wealth of information about all deployed web applications in the domain, including the following:

- State of the web application (active or not)
- Current number of sessions
- Maximum sessions on any server
- Total sessions for each web application

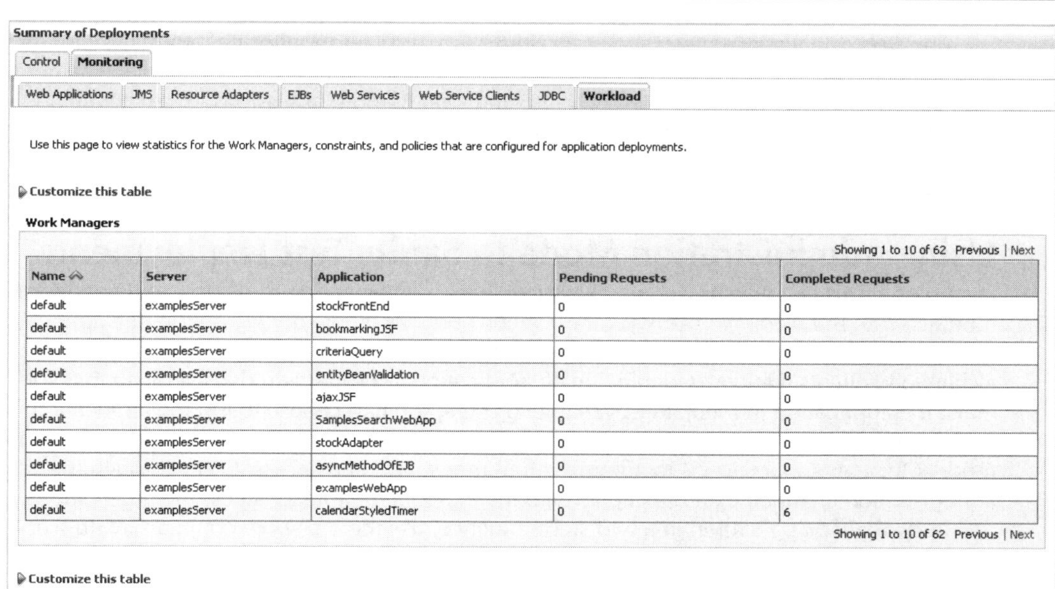

Name	Server	Application	Pending Requests	Completed Requests
default	examplesServer	stockFrontEnd	0	0
default	examplesServer	bookmarkingJSF	0	0
default	examplesServer	criteriaQuery	0	0
default	examplesServer	entityBeanValidation	0	0
default	examplesServer	ajaxJSF	0	0
default	examplesServer	SamplesSearchWebApp	0	0
default	examplesServer	stockAdapter	0	0
default	examplesServer	asyncMethodOfEJB	0	0
default	examplesServer	examplesWebApp	0	0
default	examplesServer	calendarStyledTimer	0	6

FIGURE 8-7. *The deployment Workload page*

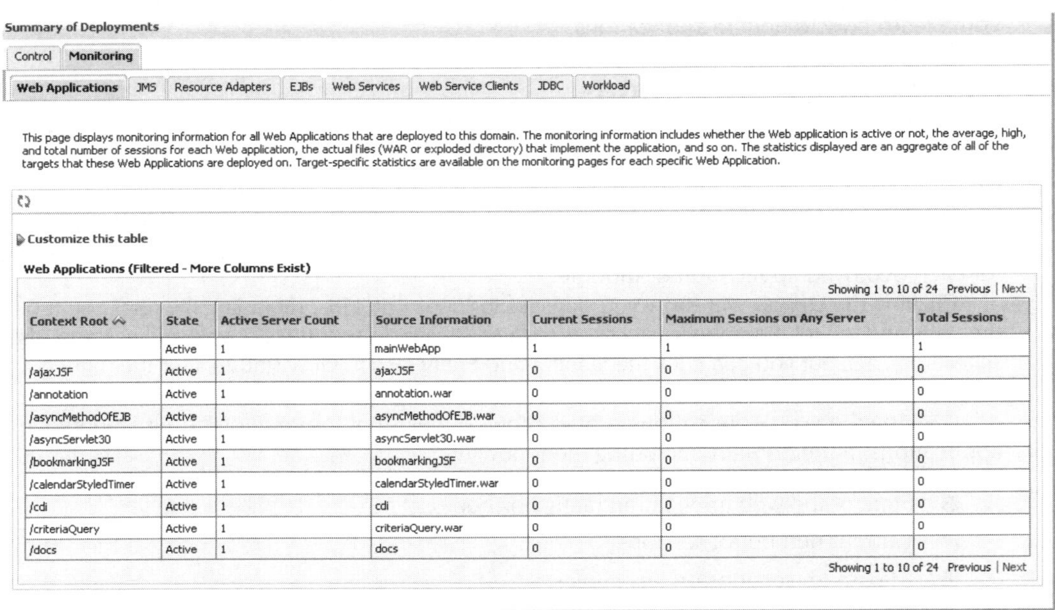

FIGURE 8-8. *The Web Applications page*

The Web Applications page, shown in Figure 8-8, displays monitoring information for all web applications that are deployed to this domain. The monitoring information includes whether the web application is active or not; the current, high, and total number of sessions for each web application; the actual files (war or exploded archive directory) that implement the application; and so on. The statistics displayed are an aggregate of all the targets to which these web applications are deployed. Target-specific statistics are available on the monitoring pages for each specific web application.

Using Administration Mode to Sanity Test Deployments

Examples in this chapter showed you how to use the *deploy* option to deploy applications or modules with the *weblogic.Deployer* tool. When you specify the *deploy* option, the applications are fully deployed to the running server—in other words, the server automatically makes the application available to clients. However, deploying an application to production doesn't mean that you have to make the application immediately available to users. You can choose to test the application first, without allowing clients to access the application by starting the application in administration mode. Once an application is in administration mode, you can access it only through the administration channel; external clients will, therefore, be unable to access the application.

To deploy an application in a two-step sequence, use the *distribute* command with *weblogic.Deployer,* instead of the *deploy* command. The *distribute* command distributes the files to all the targets you specify and validates those files, but doesn't make the applications available to users (or to administrators) because it doesn't start the applications. You must use the *start* command to start an application that you've distributed. You can start a distributed application in administration mode by specifying the *adminmode* option when starting an application with the *start* command.

The following steps show how to first distribute an application and then start it in administration mode.

1. Distribute the application to the target servers (or a cluster):

```
C:\Oracle\Middleware\Oracle_Home\user_projects\\domains\wl_server>java
-Dweblogic.security.TrustKeyStore=DemoTrust weblogic.Deployer -adminurl
t3s://localhost:9002 -username weblogic -password welcome1 -name testApp1
-distribute -targets MyCluster1
C:\deploy_dir\prod\testApp\app\testApp1.ear
weblogic.Deployer invoked with options:  -adminurl t3s://localhost:9002 -username
weblogic -name testApp1 -deploy -targets MyCluster1
C:\deploy_dir\prod\testApp\app/testApp1.ear
...
Task 5 initiated: [Deployer:149026]distribute application testApp1 on MyCluster1
.
Task 5 completed: [Deployer:149026]distribute application testApp1 on MyCluster1
.
Target state: distribute completed on Cluster MyCluster1
C:\Oracle\Middleware\Oracle_Home\user_projects\domains\wl_server>
```

   Note the following about the *weblogic.Deployer* command in this example:

   - I specified the SSL argument *-Dweblogic.security.TrustKeyStore=DemoTrust* because I've enabled the domain-wide administration port. Specifying this SSL attribute makes the server trust the demo CA certificates in the demonstration trust keystore (the *DemoTrust.jks* file in the WL_HOME\server\lib directory). The Admin Server for this domain is using the demo identity and certificates. However, in a production environment, you must not use it. Instead, specify the following pair of SSL arguments in a production environment:

     ```
     -Dweblogic.security.CustomTrustKeyStoreFileName=filename
     -Dweblogic.security.TrustKeystoreType=jks
     ```

     When you supply the two SSL arguments, *weblogic.Deployer* trusts the CA certificates in the keystore located in the directory specified by *filename*. You must use both the SSL arguments in this case.

   - Because the administration port is secured by SSL, you must use either *https* or *t3s,* as these are secure protocols. The example specifies the t3s protocol.

   - The administrator user credentials must ideally be stored in a configuration file using the WLST *storeUserConfig* command. This tells *weblogic.Deployer* to use the stored user credentials instead of using plaintext passwords in scripts and on the command line. You must also specify the *userKeyFile* option, in this case, to specify the location of the key file to be used for encrypting and decrypting the administrator credentials.

   - If you check the status of the application in the Administration Console, it will show as PREPARED, meaning the deployment files are validated and the application is ready to be started.

2. Start the application in administration mode:

```
java weblogic.Deployer -start -adminmode -name testApp1
```

TIP

The Java weblogic.Deployer *tool's* deploy *command will distribute the application and start it, even on a server running in production mode. Use the* distribute *option instead to just distribute the application files. You can start the application in administration mode by specifying the* adminmode *option with the* start *command first to sanity test the application before opening up the application to users.*

Once you start an application in administration mode, as shown in the example, you can test the application through an administration channel, which you configure by configuring a domain-wide administration port. Once you configure the administration port, WebLogic Server will automatically configure an administrative channel for each of the Managed Servers in a domain. Once you're satisfied with the results of your testing, you can allow your clients to access the application by issuing the *weblogic.Deployer* command with just the *start* option:

```
java weblogic.Deployer -start -name testApp1
```

Updating an Application

You update an application by redeploying the application. You update an application when you do any of the following:

- You make changes to the application that you want to make available to the clients.
- You change the deployment plan for the application.
- You want to redeploy a new archive file in a different location.

You can choose to redeploy the original archive file or exploded archive directory, or you can specify a new archive file or exploded archive directory. In addition, you may change the deployment plan for the application. When you update an application, you need to redeploy the application—in essence, you perform another deployment of the application. You can choose either to deploy the old archive file (or exploded archive directory) or deploy a new archive file. You also can modify the original deployment plan during redeployment. In addition, you can update an application if you want to provide the deployment files from a different location.

Follow these steps to update an application:

1. Click Lock & Edit in the Change Center of the Administration Console.
2. Select Deployments in the left-hand pane and select the check box beside the application name from the Deployments table.
3. Click Update.
4. On the Locate New Deployment Files page, click the Change Path button if you want to change the deployment files or the deployment plan.
5. Click Next.
6. Click Finish.
7. Click Activate Changes in the Change Center.

Production Redeployment Strategies

When an application is updated, administrators have to redeploy it. You can do this in a development environment by simply using the *redeploy* option, which immediately undeploys the running application, replaces its deployment files with the updated files, and restarts it. The server immediately replaces the application's class files and libraries in this case. Replacing a running application's deployment files with updated files of either an application or a stand-alone Java EE module is called *in-place redeployment*. In-place redeployment makes the application unavailable until the redeployment is complete, and it will disconnect all existing user connections to the application.

You can schedule an in-place redeployment of a production application during a time when clients don't access the application or during a preannounced downtime period. If you have an alternate set of servers to host the application, you can temporarily point all client connections to the second set of servers. To redeploy the application, issue the following command after placing the new application deployment files in the directory specified by the *source* option:

```
java weblogic.Deployer -adminurl http://localhost:7001 -user weblogic
                       -password welcome1
                       -redeploy
                       -source
                        C:\deploy_dir\prod\testApp\Ver1\app\testApp1.ear
                       -name prodApp
```

If you want to redeploy the application to only some targets, instead of the entire domain, issue the following command:

```
java weblogic.Deployer -adminurl http://localhost:7001 -user weblogic
                       -password welcome1
                       -redeploy
                       -source
                       C:\deploy_dir\prod\testApp\Ver1\app\testApp1.ear
                       -name prodApp
                       -targets server1,server2
```

Note that you can't redeploy an application only to some members of a cluster if the active application has been deployed to the entire cluster. Although the application won't be available during the redeployment process, you can keep the user sessions intact by setting the *save-sessions-enabled* property to *true* in the *weblogic.xml* descriptor file.

The in-place redeployment strategy described here has severe drawbacks in a production environment, where you are often required to keep applications available around the clock. If you can't find the downtime window to update applications in order to support a 24 × 7 environment, you'll be forced to deploy newer versions of applications to an alternate WebLogic Server environment. You also will have to deal with clients accessing multiple application versions and decide when and how you're going to pull the plug on the older version of the application.

Fortunately, WebLogic Server offers a *production deployment strategy,* which lets you deploy new versions of applications in a production environment without affecting the service levels, because you don't have to stop the application first. This strategy provides a seamless way to deploy new versions of applications by letting you run both the old and new versions simultaneously side by side. The new version is termed "active" because it actively receives new connection requests.

The old version continues to run, but it doesn't accept new connections any longer; it merely continues processing current client connections and is called the "retiring" application.

You neither have to perform an in-place deployment, nor do you have to undeploy the older application before putting the new version in place. When you deploy the new version under this strategy, the server doesn't interrupt any existing client connections to the old application. The server allows those clients to continue their work without any interruption, and the administrator doesn't have to worry about managing connections to both application versions. Once you redeploy the application, the server redirects all connections to the new version. When all existing connections to the old application complete their work, or when a configurable timeout period is over, the server retires the old version of the application.

In the following sections, let's review how you perform production redeployment and when you can and can't use this strategy.

Performing a Production Redeployment

You must ensure that both the original version that you're retiring and the new version that's replacing it have a version number. This is very important because you can't perform a side-by-side deployment if either of the applications is nonversioned. Once you version the applications, you can deploy both versions simultaneously until you switch the old version with the new one. You can simultaneously deploy only two versions of an application, however.

Assigning a Version Identifier

You can assign a version identifier to an application by specifying the *appversion* option when deploying or redeploying an application. Because both the old and new versions need to be versioned, issue the *weblogic.Deployer* command as follows when you deploy any application into production:

```
java weblogic.Deployer -adminurl http://localhost:7001 -user weblogic
                       -password welcome1
                       -deploy -name myTestDeployment
                       -source C:\deploy_dir\prod\myApplication\1Beta
                       -targets myCluster -stage -appversion 1Beta
```

Note that you'll have to specify the *appversion* option only if the application's manifest file (*MANIFEST.MF*) doesn't specify a version string. Otherwise, the version number you specify will be ignored. You can confirm the version number of an application by specifying the *listapps* command, as explained earlier in this chapter. The *listapps* command shows the deployed application names and their versions (*<ACTIVE VERSION>*). Alternatively, you can find the version number by looking at the *MANIFEST.MF* file, as shown here for a sample WebLogic Server application with version v920.beta:

```
Manifest-Version: 1.0
     Created-By: 1.4.1_05-b01 (Sun Microsystems Inc.)
     WebLogic-Application-Version: v920.beta
```

WebLogic Server has strict programming conventions that you must follow when specifying version numbers for production deployments.

Redeploying a New Version

Because you can't deploy more than two versions of the same application, first make sure you have only one version deployed to a target. Oracle recommends that you place application files from different versions in separate directories under the application's root directory.

When redeploying an application, you must be especially careful if you're specifying the *nostage* mode to provide the deployment files to the server. The same applies when you specify the *external_stage* mode, because of the potential to overwrite the old deployment files with the new ones. If you deploy with the *stage* mode, you don't have to worry about accidentally overwriting older application files during a redeployment. WebLogic Server will create a dedicated directory for the new version of the application in the server's staging directory. The server will also remove the deployment files from the staging directory once the old version is completely retired and undeployed. By default, WebLogic Server uses the *server_name*\staging subdirectory under the domain directory as the staging directory for application source files.

You're now ready to perform the production redeployment of the application. Following is an example that specifies the *redeploy* command to perform a redeployment of the new application version:

```
java weblogic.Deployer -adminurl http://localhost:7001 -user weblogic
                       -password welcome1 -redeploy -name myTestDeployment
                       -source C:\deploy_dir\prod\myApplication\1Beta
                       -retiretimeout 300
```

Note that in this example there's no need to specify the *appversion* option with the *redeploy* command, since the new version number is listed in the *MANIFEST.MF* file. As mentioned earlier, you don't have to specify the version number at redeployment time in such a case. The *retiretimeout* option (specified in seconds) is optional. By default, WebLogic Server waits for all existing client connections to close before it retires that application. You can set the maximum time the server should wait to retire the application. In the example, the *retiretimeout* option specifies that the server should retire the application after waiting for five minutes for all connections to close, regardless of whether there are connected clients who are processing work. If you omit the *retiretimeout* option, the server will only retire applications gracefully after existing connections complete their work.

Forcing Retirement of an Application

When you deploy an application, WebLogic Server automatically retires the older version of the application. When you find that an older version is stuck in the RETIRING state for some reason, you can forcibly undeploy the application by executing the *undeploy* command and specifying the application's version number. Following is an example that undeploys the application with the version number *1Beta:*

```
java weblogic.Deployer -adminurl http://localhost:7001 -user weblogic
                       -password welcome1 -undeploy -name myTestDeployment
                       -appversion 1Beta
```

Note that you must take care to specify the version number with the *appversion* option. If you don't specify the *appversion* option, the server will deploy not only the older application that is in the process of being retired but also the newer version of the application.

Reverting a Production Redeployment

If you encounter unexpected problems, you can put the older version back in production by issuing the same *redeploy* command, but this time, you specify the version number of the older version, as shown here:

```
java weblogic.Deployer -adminurl http://localhost:7001 -user weblogic
                       -password welcome1 -redeploy
                       -name myTestDeployment
                       -source C:\deploy_dir\prod\myApplication\1Beta
```

The redeployment process works exactly the same as when you redeployed a new version. This time around, however, the newer version will be the one that retires, and the old application will be in the ACTIVE state now.

Redeploying in Admin Mode

Using the *redeploy* option starts the new application immediately and opens it to new client connections. To minimize potential problems, you can redeploy an application by first starting it in admin mode. Because the *redeploy* option doesn't give you a chance to put the application in admin mode, use the *distribute* option instead to redeploy your updated version of the application. Once you distribute the application files, you can start the application in administration mode first. Once you finish your testing, you can start the application in the normal mode. Of course, you can also undeploy the application if your testing warrants it. Once you start the application without the *adminmode* option, the new version becomes the active application and the server starts retiring the existing application.

The big difference between using the *redeploy* command and the *-distribute -start -adminmode* sequence is that the server won't automatically undeploy the retired application—you must do so yourself.

Undeploying vs. Redeploying

Production redeployment lets you avoid stopping a production application and redeploying it. Although production redeployment is a great strategy, if you need to do any of the following, you can't use a production redeployment:

- Change the security model of the application.
- Change the deployment targets.
- Modify the persistent store settings.

Note that in these cases you must first undeploy the application.

When In-Place Deployment Is Safe

You can use in-place redeployment when you change graphics files, static HTML files, or JSPs. The server starts serving the new versions immediately. If you modify any dynamic properties in a deployment plan, the application is updated but retains its version number. If you modify any nondynamic properties, the server creates a new version of the application and retires the active version using a production redeployment strategy.

Summary

This chapter provided an introduction to deploying applications and modules in a WebLogic Server environment. You learned about the exploded archive directory and archive file modes of deployment. You learned the role played by deployment descriptors and annotations and the purpose of a deployment plan. The chapter showed you how to deploy applications using various tools such as the Administration Console, WLST, and the *weblogic.Deployer* and *wldeploy* utilities. The chapter also described how to undeploy and redeploy applications and how to start an application. Developers can benefit from the autodeployment and the FastSwap features, which are designed to shorten application development cycles. You also learned how to use the Administration Console to monitor and manage the applications you deploy. Finally, you learned how to use production deployment strategies that use multiple application versions to avoid application downtime.

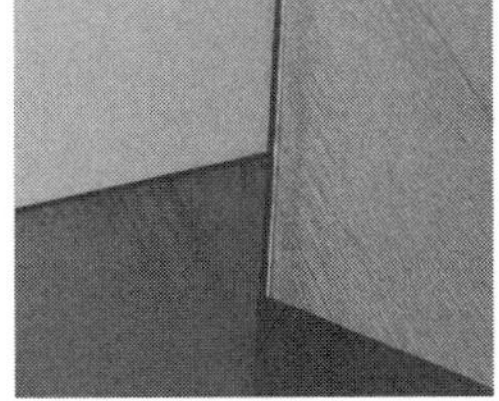

CHAPTER 9

Managing WebLogic Server Security

The common philosophy behind security in Java, Java EE, and WebLogic Server is to separate security from the implementation of the application itself. The goal is that, when building an application for deployment in WebLogic Server, the developer does not include the logic to authenticate the user or determine which users have access to certain web pages or service methods. The security aspects of the application are delegated to the container and managed using a separate and specially designed set of tools that are "plugged in" to the container. The result is a more secure and flexible approach to application security.

This chapter explains how Java security fits in with WebLogic Server security and introduces the Java Security Manager. The chapter reviews Oracle Platform Security Services (OPSS), which provides a standards-based, portable, integrated enterprise security framework for Java applications. The WebLogic Security Service uses a multilayered approach to control access to various WebLogic Server resources such as the administrative resources, server resources, and JNDI, JMS, and JDBC resources. This chapter introduces various WebLogic security topics such as security realms, security providers, and the use of security roles and security policies to control access to domain resources.

Creating users and groups, security roles, and security policies are critical day-to-day WebLogic security administration activities. The chapter explains how to create users and groups and how to use the default WebLogic security roles and policies. You'll also learn how to configure security role and security policy conditions for fine-grained security of WebLogic Server resources.

Security realms are at the heart of WebLogic security management. This chapter shows how to create and configure security realms, and how to manage the embedded LDAP server, as well as how to configure an RDBMS store for storing the user, group, role, and policy information. You'll learn how to export and import security data from one security realm to another. The chapter also explains how to configure two key WebLogic Server security providers—the Authentication and the Auditing provider.

WebLogic Server supports the standard Java EE application model that controls access to web applications and EJBs through the specification of roles and policies in deployment descriptors, but it also offers more flexible application security models. The chapter reviews both the Java EE and WebLogic Server–specific application security models.

You'll learn how to set up various domain-level security features, including cross-domain security, to enable secure communications between local and remote domains. You'll also learn the basics of SSL configuration and how to create custom keystores to store private keys and security certificates. The chapter concludes with a brief review of key Oracle-recommended WebLogic Server security best practices.

Java EE Security and OPSS

Although the focus of this chapter is on WebLogic Server security, it's important to understand how WebLogic Server security fits in with Java EE security. Oracle Platform Security Services (OPSS) is a self-contained security framework designed for securing Oracle Fusion Middleware and is the common security platform for Oracle WebLogic Server 12*c* as well as all Oracle Fusion Middleware components. Let's briefly review Java EE security and OPSS in the following sections.

Java EE Security and WebLogic Server

WebLogic Server supports using Java EE security to protect the web, EJB, and Connector components. The Connector specifications let you specify additional security policies by using the *<security-permission>* tag, and WebLogic Server extends the Connector model. The Connector model supports using the *<security-permission>* tag in the Connector-related *rar.xml* file, but WebLogic Server allows you to specify the tag in the *weblogic.xml* and the *weblogic-ejb-jar.xml* files, thus extending the Connector model to both web applications and EJBs.

The Java Security Manager

You have the option of using the Java Security Manager to provide extra security for resources running in a JVM. You won't normally need to use the Java Security Manager, but it is useful when you're running untrusted classes or when untrusted third parties are using the server. The Java Security Manager uses a Java security policy file that lets you restrict the run-time behavior of the JVM by allowing or disallowing key run-time operations by setting permissions on classes. The Java security file lets you set default security policies for servlets, EJBs, and Java EE Connector resource adapters based on the type of application. You can also set security policies for specific servlets, EJBs, and resource adapters by adding a security policy to the deployment descriptor of the application. You specify the security policies in *weblogic.xml* for servlets, in *weblogic-ejb-jar.xml* for EJBs, and in *rar.xml* for resource adapters.

WebLogic Server provides a sample Java security policy file named *weblogic.policy* that's located in the WL_HOME\server\lib directory. You enable the Java Security Manager by specifying the following attributes when starting the server:

```
java...-Djava.security.manager \
   -Djava.security.policy==C:\weblogic\weblogic.policy
```

The *-Djava.security.policy* argument directs the JVM to use a security policy file, and it specifies the security policy location and name. If you don't specify the security policy file with this argument, WebLogic Server uses the *java.policy* file (located in the $JAVA_HOME\jre\lib\security directory), which contains default security policies.

Oracle Platform Security Services

In multitiered environments, security must be implemented at various levels, such as authenticating requests at the user interface level and providing secure access to databases by the application server. Externalizing security by taking it out of applications lets you centrally manage security, and to modify it you don't have to modify or redeploy applications. Java SE and Java EE do provide server security application programming interfaces and libraries, including Java Authentication and Authorization Service (JAAS). However, these security APIs and libraries are too low level for application developers, they lack management tools, and they don't address the application's lifecycle.

OPSS provides developers and system integrators with a standards-based, portable, comprehensive, enterprise-level security framework for Java applications. OPSS does this by building on Java SE and Java EE security and by providing an abstraction layer to keep developers away from the details of implementing security. OPSS is an independent security framework that provides security for Oracle Fusion Middleware. It offers standards-based APIs for security services such as authentication, credential and policy management, authorization, and cryptography. Developers can use OPSS for both Oracle and third-party environments. The goal is to remove security from applications and centralize it into an external security system that administrators can manage. As with the other components of Oracle Fusion Middleware such as Oracle SOA, Oracle WebCenter, and the Oracle Application Development Framework (ADF), the middleware underlying all these components (Oracle WebLogic Server 12*c*) also uses the OPSS framework.

OPSS is integrated with ADF as well as with all the management tools of Oracle Fusion Middleware to help implement and monitor the security policies for the identity management infrastructure.

OPSS combines BEA System's internal security framework used in Oracle WebLogic Server 12*c* and the Oracle Entitlements Server (OES) with Java Platform Security (JPS), which is Oracle Fusion Middleware's security platform. Note that JPS was formerly known as Java AuthoriZatioN (JAZN).

Developers build security into their applications while building Oracle ADF task flows because OPSS is integrated with Oracle JDeveloper. JDeveloper provides a security wizard for creating the security configuration and also provides an authorization editor to enable the creation of authorization policies. Developers usually first deploy applications to a domain embedded within JDeveloper. They then deploy them to a remote domain using Oracle Enterprise Manager Fusion Middleware Control. Since OPSS is integrated with the Fusion Middleware Control, security policies and credential migration are easily managed during application deployment. Developers can also manage security policies after deployment through Fusion Middleware Control, without making changes to the application. OPSS also provides migration tools to move security policies to a production domain from a test environment.

Following are the key security services offered by OPSS:

- **Authentication** OPSS is integrated with WebLogic Server security for container-managed authentication, which is ideal for many applications.
- **Single Sign-On** OPSS provides a Single Sign-On (SSO) framework and provides support for Oracle Access Manager and WebLogic Server integration through the Security Service Provider Interface (SSPI).
- **Authorization** OPSS provides support for both code-based and subject-based authorization through a Java policy provider. You can use logical, application-specific roles or an advanced policy model that includes elements such as Resource Type and Entitlement that allow the provision of complex authorization policies. You can use either Fusion Middleware Control or the WebLogic Scripting Tool (WLST) to manage an application's authorization policies.
- **Audit** OPSS offers an internal audit framework that allows the use of the OPSS API to maintain audit policies outside the application. You can also view the prebuilt audit reports using the Oracle Business Intelligence Publisher.
- **Credential Store Framework** OPSS provides this framework to allow applications to store credentials to access various services such as databases, directories, web services, and web sites. Applications can use this framework to manage credentials without changing any application code.
- **Cryptography** A set of Java libraries called Oracle Security Developer Tools provides cryptography services that allow developers to include security in applications. Developers can use standards-based APIs to secure message envelopers, public key infrastructure (PKI), Security Assertion Markup Language (SAML), XML Key Management Specification (XKMS), and Web Services Security (WS-Security).
- **Security providers** OPSS offers several security providers that support various identity stores for authentication, including Oracle Internet Directory, Oracle Virtual Directory, Microsoft Active Directory, IBM Tivoli Directory, and Open LDAP.

- **Security stores** OPSS uses a single logical store for storing both policies and credentials, allowing it to support XML, LDAP, and database-based security stores without application code changes. You can start with an XML-based store and migrate to an LDAP store without any changes and without redeploying your applications.

WebLogic Server Security Basics

Let's start the WebLogic Server security implementation by discussing the various WebLogic Server resources that the WebLogic Security Service protects. It's important to realize that you will be protecting two distinct categories of resources. One category applies to the various entities that make up the administrative domain. For these, WebLogic Server provides a complete set of groups and policies. The second category of resources includes the ones you introduce when you deploy your application. Although controlled with the same set of tools, these sets of resources are quite distinct, and unless you keep this distinction in mind, it's easy to get confused. Following that, this section provides a quick introduction to how a security realm helps you manage security for a domain. You'll also learn about the default WebLogic security providers that help you manage various aspects of WebLogic security, such as authentication, authorization, and auditing.

WebLogic Server Resources

When I talk about WebLogic Server security, I'm talking primarily about securing WebLogic Server resources. A WebLogic Server resource is not limited to entities such as a server instance—it also includes actions such as starting a server, for example. You secure the various WebLogic resources from unauthorized access by assigning each resource a security policy—that's why these are called "protected resources." Following are the main WebLogic resources the security infrastructure is designed to secure:

- Administrative resources are entities such as the Administration Console and WLST, and they include the domain and server logs.
- Server resources are operations that control the state of a WebLogic Server instance. This group of services is not made visible outside the server, so you can lock them down. This includes the execution of the *weblogic.Server* and Node Manager commands. Other server resources are JNDI resources such as the nodes in a server's JNDI tree; JMS resources, including JMS modules in an application, JMS destinations, and operations within the JMS destinations; and JDBC resources, including JDBC system and application modules, data sources, and methods within a data source.
- JMX resources are MBean attributes or operations—the attributes are read or written, and the operations are invoked. JMX resources generally relate to the manageability of the server.
- The final set of WebLogic Server resources are those for which access for end users needs to be controlled. These include enterprise applications, web applications, or stand-alone Java EE modules, including JDBC modules and EJB resources. They also include web service resources, URL resources (servlets, JSPs, and EISs), which are the system-level software drivers that WebLogic Server uses to connect to an EIS.

TIP

In a production environment, don't select the option to install the Server Examples component when installing WebLogic Server. You must also delete development tools such as the Configuration Wizard unless you must have them. Also, delete the demo database (the Derby database server) in a production environment.

Security Realms

A security realm is a logical container for the various WebLogic Server security entities such as users, groups, security roles, security policies, and security providers. The security realm provides the authentication, authorization, auditing, credential, and role-mapping services to a WebLogic Server deployment. You can have more than one security realm in a domain, but only one of the realms can be the active (default) realm. A security realm is the mechanism WebLogic Server uses to protect its resources. All resources belong to a security realm, and you must define a user in the active security realm in order for that user to be able to access a WebLogic Server resource. The security realm contains the configuration for all security providers, users, groups, security roles, and security policies. An LDAP server or an RDBMS acts as the actual repository for all the security information. (WebLogic Server comes with its own embedded LDAP server, and you can use external LDAP servers as well.) For each attempt to access a resource, the server checks the user's security role in the realm and the security policy of the resource the user is accessing. If the user has the correct role and the security policy of the resource permits access to this role (or group), the server authenticates and authorizes the user.

The security realm persists security data for all the security providers. For example, it persists user and group data for the WebLogic Authentication provider and security policies for the Extensible Access Control Markup Language (XACML) Authorization provider and security roles for the XACML Role Mapping provider.

Security Providers

Security providers are components that handle specific security functions, such as authorization and authentication. You can use the default security providers that are part of the default security realm, third-party custom security providers, or a mix of the two. Following is a brief description of the WebLogic security providers you can use:

- An *Authentication provider* lets the server validate the identity of users or system processes, and you must have one of these in the active security realm for the domain. You can configure more than one Authentication provider to configure access to a different data store such as an RDBMS or to a different LDAP server other than the embedded LDAP server. WebLogic Authentication providers offer username and password authentication, certificate-based authentication through WebLogic Server, and HTTP certificate–based authentication proxied through an external web server. The login module inside the Authentication provider performs the authentication tasks. Each Authentication provider also relies on a helper provider—the *Principal Validation provider*—which provides additional security protection by signing and verifying the authentication of the principals. You can configure multiple Authentication providers in a domain with a separate Principal Validation provider for each of the Authentication providers. WebLogic Server configures the Principal Validation providers for you.

NOTE
A principal is a user, group, or system process.

- An *Authorization provider* controls access to WebLogic resources based on the security roles granted to a user or group and on the security policy associated with a specific WebLogic resource. You must have at least one Authorization provider in a security realm.
- The *Identity Assertion provider* performs perimeter authentication using client-supplied tokens. Once the Identity Assertion provider validates and maps a token to a username, the provider's login module converts the username to a principal, which can be a user, a group, or a system process.
- The *Role Mapping provider* retrieves the roles granted to a user or group for a specific WebLogic resource and assists the Authorization providers in determining whether a user or group should be granted access to a WebLogic resource secured with role-based security.
- The *Adjudication provider* acts as an umpire by settling authorization conflicts among multiple Authorization providers. You need this provider only if you've configured multiple Authorization providers.
- The *Credential Mapping provider* maps local user credentials to remote system credentials, thus enabling the server to log into remote systems on behalf of previously authenticated users or groups. It provides a mechanism for securely storing and using those credentials.
- The *Auditing provider* does exactly what its name indicates—it stores the audit information for all security requests, successful or otherwise. You can also set up configuration auditing to monitor changes in the server configuration through the Auditing provider.

NOTE
WebLogic Server also supports the Extensible Access Control Markup Language (XACML), which is used to specify authorization and role assignments. The WebLogic Server XACML Authorization provider and the WebLogic Server XACML Role Mapping provider implement the XACML 2.0 Core Specification. You can create XACML documents and add them to a security realm if you want to create complex security roles or policies. You can also use the XACML documents to export and import a realm's security roles and policies.

WebLogic Server provides a default security configuration with the WebLogic Adjudication, Authentication, Identity Assertion, Credential Mapping, CertPath, XACML Authorization, and XACML Role Mapping providers as the security providers in the default security realm *myrealm*. If you create a new security realm, you must configure the following security providers for that realm to be valid:

- Authentication
- Authorization

- Credential Mapping
- Role Mapping
- CertPath Builder

The Adjudication provider is required only if you have multiple Authentication providers. In addition to the required security providers, you can optionally configure the Identity Assertion, Auditing, and Certificate Registry providers. The Certificate Registry provider is a security provider that lets you register the trusted certificates allowed to access WebLogic Server. If you configure the Certificate Registry provider in the security realm, the only certificates that are deemed valid are those registered in the Certificate Registry. The embedded LDAP server stores the Certificate Registry. You can also use custom security providers, in addition to the default WebLogic security providers.

Managing Security Realms

As explained earlier, security realms contain all the users, groups, security roles, and security policies, as well as the security providers. Thus, understanding how to manage security realms is critical to securing WebLogic Server resources. The following sections explain how to create and configure security realms, as well as how to configure key WebLogic Server default security providers.

Creating and Configuring a New Security Realm

The default security realm *myrealm* contains all the required WebLogic security providers and the embedded LDAP server in which the security providers store their security data. To start using the default security realm, all you have to do is define your users, groups, and security roles for the security realm and create security policies to control access to the WebLogic Server resources. In most environments, all you ever use is the default security realm.

You need to change the default security configuration by performing the following types of operations when you want to add new custom security providers or modify existing providers:

- Replace or configure new security providers.
- Add an Auditing provider to the default security realm.
- Modify the configuration of the default security providers.
- Configure an Authentication provider that doesn't use the embedded LDAP server and stores the user and group information in either an RDBMS or an external LDAP server.

So you can easily go back to the default security configuration after performing these types of operations, Oracle recommends that you create a new security realm and make it the new default security realm, instead of customizing the default realm. Once you create a new realm, configure the necessary security providers for that realm and export user and group data from the current default realm to the new realm.

Creating a new security realm is an easy matter—configuring it takes some effort. Following are the steps to follow to create a new security realm:

1. Click Lock & Edit in the Change Center of the Administration Console.
2. Select Security Realms in the left-hand pane under the Services group.

3. Click New in the Realms table.
4. On the Create A New Realm page, enter the name of the new security realm. Click OK.
5. Click Activate Changes in the Change Center.

Once you create a security realm, you must perform the following configuration tasks:

1. Although a security realm can remain without any security providers, you won't be able to set the new security realm as the default security realm without the mandatory security providers. For the new security realm to be valid, you must configure an Authentication provider, an Authorization provider, an Adjudication provider, a Credential Mapping provider, a CertPath Builder, and a Role Mapping provider. You can also define Identity Assertion, Auditing, and Certificate Registry providers, but it's not mandatory.
2. Several of the security providers use the embedded LDAP server, so you must configure the LDAP server settings to enable the new security domain to function.
3. Create users and groups, roles, and security policies in the new security realm. Alternatively, you can export all the security data from the current security realm to a file and import that data to the new security realm. You can also set the lockout attributes to protect user accounts from dictionary attacks.
4. Specify the new security realm as the domain's default security realm in the domain's Security page in the Administration Console.

Various sections in this chapter describe how to perform each of these realm configuration tasks. First, you must confirm some basic security attributes for the security realms, such as the default options for securing web applications and EJB modules. Let's review the basic configuration of a security realm next.

Configuring the Security Realm

Once you create a security realm, you can configure several properties to control how that realm handles security for applications. Selecting a security realm and clicking it on the Summary Of Security Realms page automatically takes you to the Configuration page for that realm, as shown in Figure 9-1.

NOTE
If you use Java Authorization Contract for Containers (JACC) to implement security, you must use the DD Only security model.

Following are the key configuration attributes you can specify on the Configuration page for a security realm:

- **Name** This attribute provides a name for the security realm.
- **Security Model Default** This attribute lets you specify the default security model to be applied to the web applications and EJBs that you deploy in this domain. You normally specify the security model for an application or EJB at deployment time, and the security model you specify at that time will override the default security model for the domain.

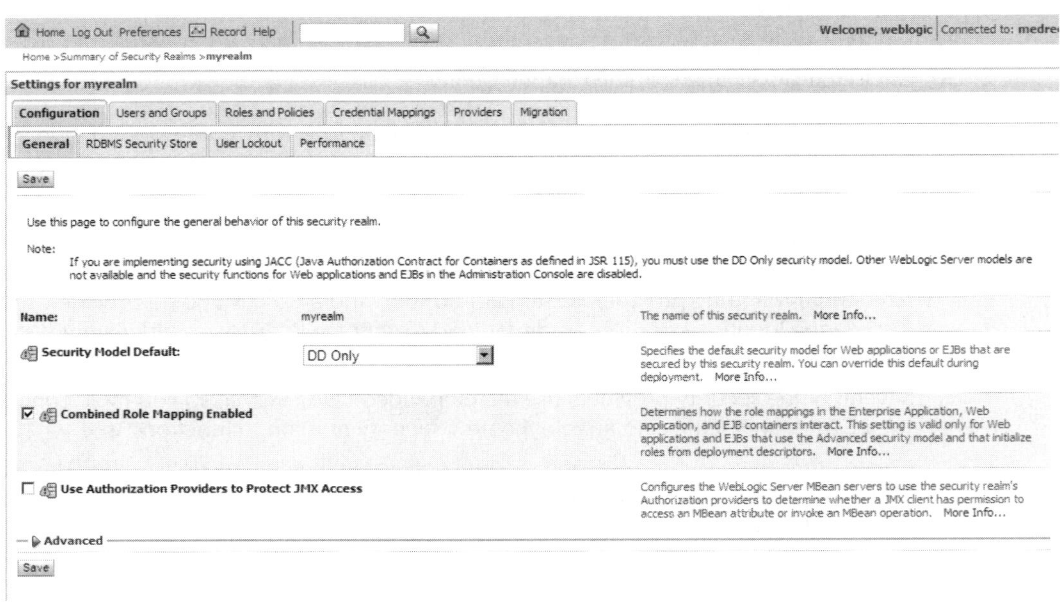

FIGURE 9-1. *The security realm Configuration page*

You can select one of the following security models, all of which are described later in this chapter in the section "Security Models for Web Applications and EJBs":

- Deployment Descriptor Only (DD Only)
- Customize Roles Only (Custom Roles)
- Customize Roles and Policies (Custom Roles and Policies)
- Advanced (Advanced)

Note that you choose a security model for each web application or EJB, and the security model you choose at deployment time will remain in force until you redeploy the application or EJB with a different security model.

- **Combined Role Mapping Enabled** This attribute determines the interaction among the role mappings in the enterprise application, web application, and EJB containers, and the setting affects only those web applications and EJBs that use the Advanced security model.
- **Use Authorization Providers To Protect JMX Access** This attribute enables the MBean servers to use the security realm's Authorization provider to enforce access to MBean attributes and operations by JMX clients. By default, the MBean servers allow access to the four default security roles—*Admin, Deployer, Operator,* and *Monitor*—to the extent allowed by the domain's default security settings.
- **Check Roles And Policies** This attribute determines when the security service checks for authorization to access web applications and EJBs. The setting applies only for web applications and EJBs that use the Advanced security model.

- **Deployable Provider Synchronization Enabled** If the Authorization and Role Mapping providers do not support simultaneous modification of roles and policies, the server can force the synchronization between the work of the two providers by queuing the applications and modules and deploying them sequentially.
- **Deployable Provider Synchronization Timeout** If you set the previous attribute to true, you can set the timeout value for the security provider synchronization operations with this attribute.

Now that you've created a new security realm and have configured the basic attributes of the realm, it's time to turn to the configuration of the security providers, export and import of user data, user security, and other related aspects of a functioning, active security realm.

Configuring the Security Providers

The default WebLogic security providers come preconfigured, but you may have to configure a provider yourself when you create a new security realm. In addition, you must configure a specific security provider when you perform a change in your security realm that affects the security provider. For example, when you want to audit login activity or configuration changes in the security realm, you must configure a WebLogic (or custom) Auditing provider. Similarly, if you want to use an LDAP server (other than the embedded LDAP server), you must configure an LDAP Authentication provider. Note that for most internal applications, users are going to connect the domain to their company's LDAP server. For most commercial production applications, users are going to want to manage users and credentials either in a database or in a third-party LDAP server. For most of the WebLogic security providers, the default configuration is adequate. However, the WebLogic Auditing provider and the WebLogic Authentication provider involve more configuration work than the other security providers. In the following sections, let's review how you configure these two WebLogic security providers.

Configuring the WebLogic Auditing Provider

The WebLogic Auditing provider logs various auditing events such as authentication events, authorization attempts, and the locking of user accounts due to too many invalid login attempts. It's the Auditing provider's job to provide an electronic trail of activity. The Auditing provider also audits WebLogic Server configuration changes. The default security realm *myrealm* doesn't have an Auditing provider configured, although WebLogic Server does include the Auditing provider *DefaultAuditor* as the WebLogic Auditing provider. You can configure this WebLogic Auditing provider or develop a custom Auditing provider. Either way, you need to add the Auditing provider to the security realm in order to audit events and configuration changes. To add the *DefaultAuditor* provider, go to Security Realms | Realm Name | Providers | Auditing and click New in the Auditing Providers table. On the Create A New Auditing Provider page, you must provide the name for the Auditing provider. The *Type* property for the new auditing provider is *DefaultAuditor*. Once you create the new Auditing provider, its name shows up in the Auditing Providers table.

Once you configure the Auditing provider, it starts auditing events (and configuration changes, if you want) and stores the auditing data in the *DefaultAuditRecorder.log* file in the DOMAIN_HOME*<server_name>*\logs directory by default. Whereas the default WebLogic Server Auditing provider writes audit events to its own log file, a third-party or custom provider can write audit events to an LDAP server or RDBMS as well. Each server in the domain records auditing data in its own log file. In order to configure the Auditing provider, click its name in the Auditing

Providers table. You can define provider-specific settings for the Auditing provider by selecting the Configuration | Provider Specific page for the provider.

Exercise caution with the Auditing providers, as the default Auditing providers are synchronous and, therefore, can potentially introduce serious resource contention for high load applications. The auditing output has the potential to be very verbose, and you should be aware of that. However, certain customers and applications, such as those in the financial services industry, need to adhere to very stringent auditing requirements, so this capability of the Auditing provider to provide detailed audit messages can be an answer to their compliance needs.

Figure 9-2 shows the Settings page for the Auditing provider you added to the security domain. You can set the following configuration options for the Auditing provider:

- **Active Context Handler Entries** Each audit event includes a *ContextHandler* that has entries pertaining to various objects or information. By default, the provider doesn't audit any entries in the *ContextHandler*. However, you can select the *ContextHandler* entries

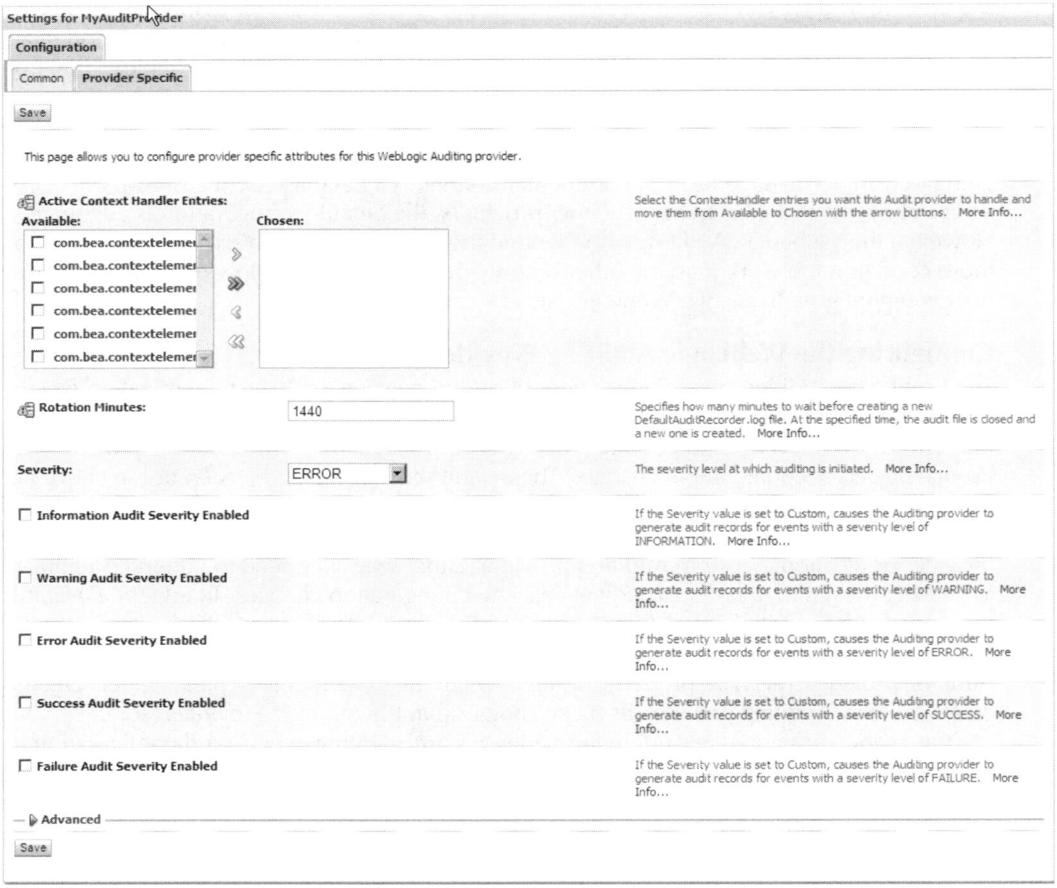

FIGURE 9-2. *Configuring the Auditing provider*

you want to audit from the list of active *ContextHandler* entries. For example, you can select the context element *com.bea.contextelement.servlet.HttpServletRequest* to audit a servlet access request of a SOAP message through HTTP.

- **Rotation Minutes** Specifies the time after which the provider rotates the audit log file by beginning the writing of events to a new log file.
- **Severity** You can specify five severity levels to specify the initiation of an audit event, with each severity level ranked in increasing order of severity:
  - Severity Level 1: INFORMATION
  - Severity Level 2: WARNING
  - Severity Level 3: ERROR
  - Severity Level 4: SUCCESS
  - Severity Level 5: FAILURE

  By default, setting a severity level means that the provider will audit at all lower levels. For example, if you set the Severity Level 5 (FAILURE), the Auditing provider will log all information, warning, error, and success events as well. To avoid this kind of excessive audit logging, you can also set the Custom severity level to specify a specific security level.
- **Information Audit Severity Enabled** Lets the provider generate auditing records for events with a severity level of INFORMATION, provided you set the Severity value to Custom.
- **Warning Audit Severity Enabled** Lets the provider generate auditing records for events with a severity level of WARNING, provided you set the Severity value to Custom.
- **Error Audit Severity Enabled** Lets the provider generate auditing records for events with a severity level of ERROR, provided you set the Severity value to Custom.
- **Failure Audit Severity Enabled** Lets the provider generate auditing records for events with a severity level of FAILURE, provided you set the Severity value to Custom.
- **Success Audit Severity Enabled** Lets the provider generate auditing records for events with a severity level of SUCCESS, provided you set the Severity value to Custom.
  - **Begin Marker** Indicates the beginning of the audit record.
  - **End Marker** Marks the end of the audit record.
  - **Field Prefix** A character that marks the beginning of a field in an audit record.
  - **Field Suffix** A character that marks the end of a field in an audit record

You can modify the default directory for the audit file (the domain-name directory) to a different directory by specifying the location as an option during server startup, as shown here:

```
-Dweblogic.security.audit.auditLogDir=C:\audit
```

Following this, the server will start storing the audit file in the following location:

```
C:\audit\<server_name>\logs\DefaultAuditRecorder.log
```

Enabling Configuration Auditing

Once you enable the WebLogic Auditing provider, you can configure the Admin Server to log all configuration events for domain resources to an additional security log, separate from the domain-wide message log. You can enable configuration auditing by setting one of the following Java options in the *weblogic.Server* command when you boot the Admin Server:

```
-Dweblogic.domain.configurationAuditType="audit"
-Dweblogic.domain.configurationAuditType="log"
-Dweblogic.domain.configurationAuditType="logaudit"
```

The *"audit"* option only emits the audit events, and the *"log"* option only writes configuration audit messages to the Admin Server log file. The *"logaudit"* option does both.

You can also enable configuration auditing through the Administration Console by performing the following steps:

1. Click Lock & Edit in the Change Center of the Administration Console.
2. Select Domain | Configuration | General and click Advanced at the bottom of the Settings For *<auditing_provider>* page.
3. Specify the method for auditing configuration change events in the Configuration Audit Type field. You can choose from among the following four auditing criteria:
   - **None** This is the default auditing criterion and specifies that no configuration events will be written or sent to the Security Audit Framework.
   - **Change Log** The server will write the configuration events to the server log.
   - **Change Audit** The server will send the configuration events to the Security Audit Framework.
   - **Change Log And Audit** The server will write the configuration events to its log as well as send them to the Security Audit Framework.
4. Click Save and then click Activate Changes in the Change Center.

After setting up configuration auditing, the Auditing provider will log audit messages whenever a configuration change is successful or when the attempted change fails due to incorrect user credentials or an internal error. WebLogic Server tags each configuration audit message with an ID between the range of 159900 and 159910. For example, when an unauthorized user attempts to create a resource, the server generates a message with the message ID 159901 and the following message text that identifies the unauthorized WebLogic Server user:

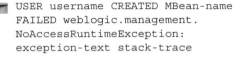

```
USER username CREATED MBean-name
FAILED weblogic.management.
NoAccessRuntimeException:
exception-text stack-trace
```

Configuring Additional WebLogic Authentication Provider Types

The job of an Authentication provider is to verify if a user's credentials exist in the provider's data store. There are many types of Authentication providers you can choose based on the type of data store the provider uses. WebLogic Server provides the WebLogic Authentication provider, called the *DefaultAuthenticator,* which uses the embedded LDAP server as its store. Here are some of the important types of Authentication providers you can use—several, but not all of them, are LDAP Authentication providers.

- Oracle Internet Directory Authentication provider for accessing users and group information stored in the Oracle Internet Directory (LDAP version 3).
- Oracle Virtual Directory Authentication provider for accessing users and groups in Oracle Virtual Directory (LDAP 3).
- LDAP Authentication provider configured for Open LDAP, Sun iPlanet, Microsoft Active Directory, and Novell NDS LDAP servers.
- RDBMS Authentication providers—there are three RDBMS Authentication providers: SQL Authenticator, Read-Only SQL Authenticator, and Custom RDBMS Authenticator.
- An Authentication provider that authenticates users based on Security Assertion Markup Language (SAML) 1.1 assertions. SAML is a language for propagating identity, and Oracle WebLogic Server 12*c* supports both SAML 1.1 and SAML 2.0.

If you use multiple Authentication providers in a security realm, you must set the JAAS control flag in the Administration Console. The values you set for it determine the order in which the various Authentication providers are used during the login sequence. You can configure the settings for the JAAS control flag by going to Security Realms | Realm Name | Providers | Authentication and clicking the name of the provider you want to configure (for example, *DefaultAuthenticator*). Select Configuration | Common and set the Control Flag attribute. There are four possible values you can set for the Control Flag attribute, and the default value is REQUIRED. Here's what each of the four values means:

- **REQUIRED** The login module must succeed—if it fails, the authentication process proceeds to the next configured Authentication provider.
- **REQUISITE** This login module must succeed for the authentication process to proceed down the list of other configured Authentication providers. If it fails, control is returned to the application.
- **SUFFICIENT** The login module is not required to succeed. If it fails, the authentication process continues with the other configured Authentication providers.
- **OPTIONAL** The login module doesn't have to succeed. Authentication proceeds down the list of other configured providers whether the login module succeeds or fails.

When you make a mistake during the configuration of an Authentication provider, the server may not start due to authentication failure (the administrative user can't be authenticated) if the control flag is set to REQUIRED or REQUISITE. Setting the control flag to OPTIONAL or SUFFICIENT, on the other hand, will allow you to start the server in spite of the failure of the Authentication provider and gives you a chance to fix the problem. Therefore, always set the control flag to the OPTIONAL or SUFFICIENT setting until you are sure you've correctly configured the new Authentication provider. For instance, if you configure a new Authentication provider and connect to the corporate LDAP server, it's important that you change the control flag on the *DefaultAuthenticator* and on the newly configured provider to either SUFFICIENT or OPTIONAL. If you leave it as REQUIRED, a failure to find the user in the embedded LDAP server will cause the login to fail.

Let's briefly review the configuration steps for an LDAP Authentication provider. The actual configuration details vary, depending on the LDAP Authentication provider you choose. Follow these steps to configure an LDAP Authentication provider:

1. Create an instance of the LDAP Authentication provider in the security realm.
2. Configure the attributes for the LDAP Authentication provider.
3. Configure communication between the LDAP server and the LDAP Authentication provider.
4. Configure options that specify how the provider searches the LDAP directory.
5. Specify the location of the users and groups in the LDAP tree.
6. Specify how the provider locates the members of a group.
7. Specify the name of the global universal identifier (GUID).
8. Specify the timeout value for the LDAP connections. The default timeout value is zero, but Oracle recommends that you set it to a positive value for enhanced server performance. You can set the timeout value in the *config.xml* file, as shown here:

   ```
   <wls:connect-time>60</wls:connect-time>
   ```

9. Specify the performance options for the LDAP server cache.

The default WebLogic Authentication provider (*DefaultAuthenticator*) comes preconfigured, and you need to configure this only if you want to use this provider in a new security realm. Note that the user and group names are case sensitive. You must also specify a minimum length for user passwords. You can also set user attributes such as *displayname* and *employeenumber,* which conform to the user schema for the *inetOrgPerson* LDAP object calls, as per RFC 2798.

Let's discuss how to configure the *DefaultAuthenticator* provider through the Administration Console. In the Administration Console, go to Security Realms | myrealm. On the Settings For myrealm page, select Providers | Authentication. Select DefaultAuthenticator in the Authenticator Providers table. In the Settings For DefaultAuthenticator page, you can set the JAAS Control Flag to specify how the server uses this provider during the login sequence. Click the Provider Specific tab to configure other properties for the *DefaultAuthenticator*. Figure 9-3 shows the configuration options for this provider, which I summarize here:

- **Keep Alive Enabled** Specifies whether LDAP connections can time out.
- **Propagate Cause for Login Exception** Specifies whether the Authentication provider must propagate the cause of login exceptions.
- **Enable Password Digests** Lets you specify the storage of passwords in an encrypted form to support digest authentication algorithms.
- **Use Retrieved User Name As Principal** Specifies whether the provider should use the usernames stored in the embedded LDAP server as the principal.
- **Minimum Password Length** Specifies the minimum length of passwords.
- **Group Membership Searching** Specifies whether recursive group memberships should be limited.
- **Max Group Membership Search Level** Specifies the levels of group membership to be searched, provided you've set the *GroupMembershipSearching* attribute to unlimited.

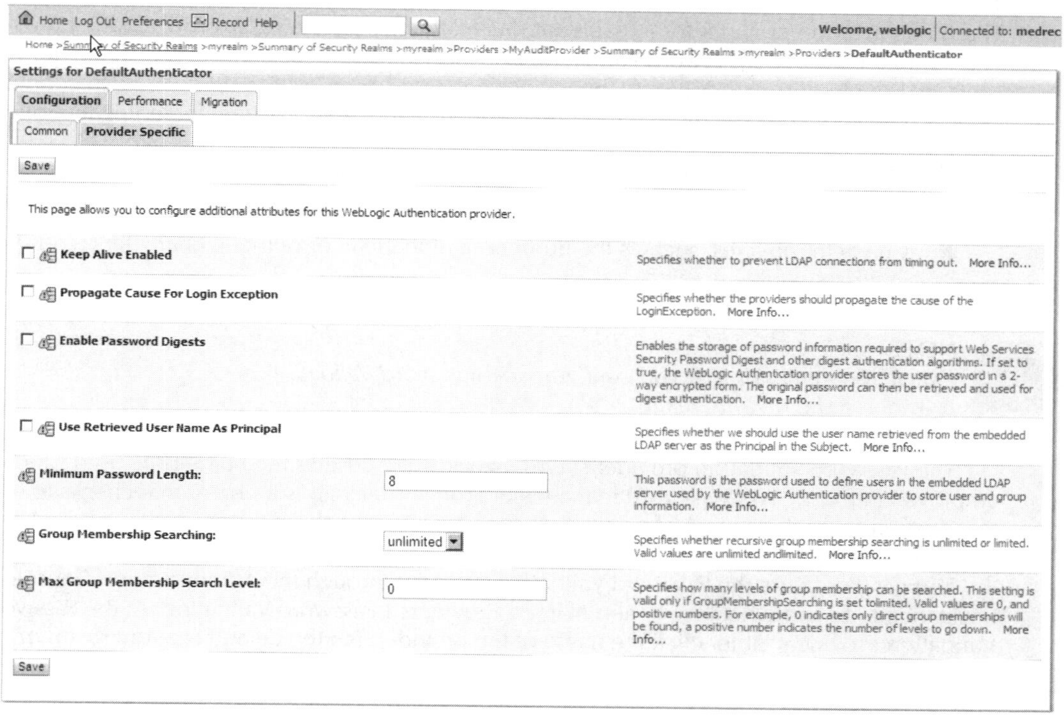

FIGURE 9-3. *Configuring the Authentication provider*

Defining Server Stop and Start Policies

You can use the Server | Security | Policies page to edit security policies that determine who can change the lifecycle state (booting and stopping) of a server. This page has three sections:

- **Providers** The Providers section lets you specify the Authentication provider you want to use. The default Authentication provider in the security realm *myrealm* is named *XACMLAuthorizer*.
- **Methods** You can specify the actions an administrator is allowed to take to modify a server's lifecycle state. You can specify that an administrator is allowed to take one of the following actions:
    - Boot
    - Shut down
    - Lock
    - Unlock
    - All
- **Policy Conditions** You can specify various policy conditions in this section to control access to the server administrative resources. The default policy is the *Admin* or the *Operator* role.

The Password Validation Provider

The Authentication provider for a realm automatically invokes the Password Validation provider if you configure one. The Password Validation provider checks the passwords you supply for new users in order to ensure they satisfy the various password composition rules. You can configure various password composition rules for the Password Validation provider, including the following:

- Password length policies, including minimum and maximum length
- Username policies, such as whether a password can contain the username
- Character policies, such as the number of alphabetic or numeric characters required in a password

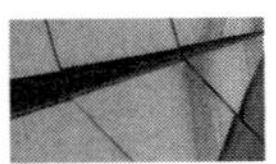

NOTE
Oracle recommends that you configure the Password Validation provider in the security realm.

The Password Validation provider serves the same purpose as the commonly used CrackLib employed in most UNIX password management tools. CrackLib is a library that checks to ensure that passwords can't be cracked easily. It does so by ensuring that passwords aren't based on simple character patterns or on a dictionary word.

You can configure the Password Validation provider through the Administration Console by navigating to Security Realm | Realm Name | Providers | Password Validation. In the Password Validation Providers table, click the name of the provider. For the default security realm *myrealm*, the password validator is named *SystemPasswordValidator*. In the Settings For Password Validation Provider page, click the Provider Specific subtab. Figure 9-4 shows the configuration page where you set attributes for the Password Validation provider.

You can configure Password Validation attributes such as username policies, password length policies, and policies that govern how you can specify characters within passwords. You can configure the Password Validation provider with the WebLogic Authentication provider or other Authentication providers. The Authentication provider automatically invokes the Password Validation provider to make sure the passwords meet the requirements you've configured. Configure the Password Validation provider immediately after you create a new domain.

Improving LDAP Authentication Provider Performance

You can improve the performance of any LDAP Authentication provider, including the WebLogic Authentication provider, through the Configuration | Performance page. You can speed up subsequent searches mainly by configuring the caching of the LDAP subtrees retrieved during a membership lookup. Here are the performance options you can configure on this page:

- **Enable Group Membership Hierarchy Caching** Lets you specify whether the provider should cache group membership subtrees found during a recursive membership lookup.
- **Max Group Hierarchies In Cache** Specifies the maximum size of the Least Recently Used (LRU) cache for storing group membership hierarchies. The default is 100.
- **Group Hierarchy Cache TTL** Specifies the maximum time for which group membership subtree entries remain valid in the cache. The default is 60 seconds.

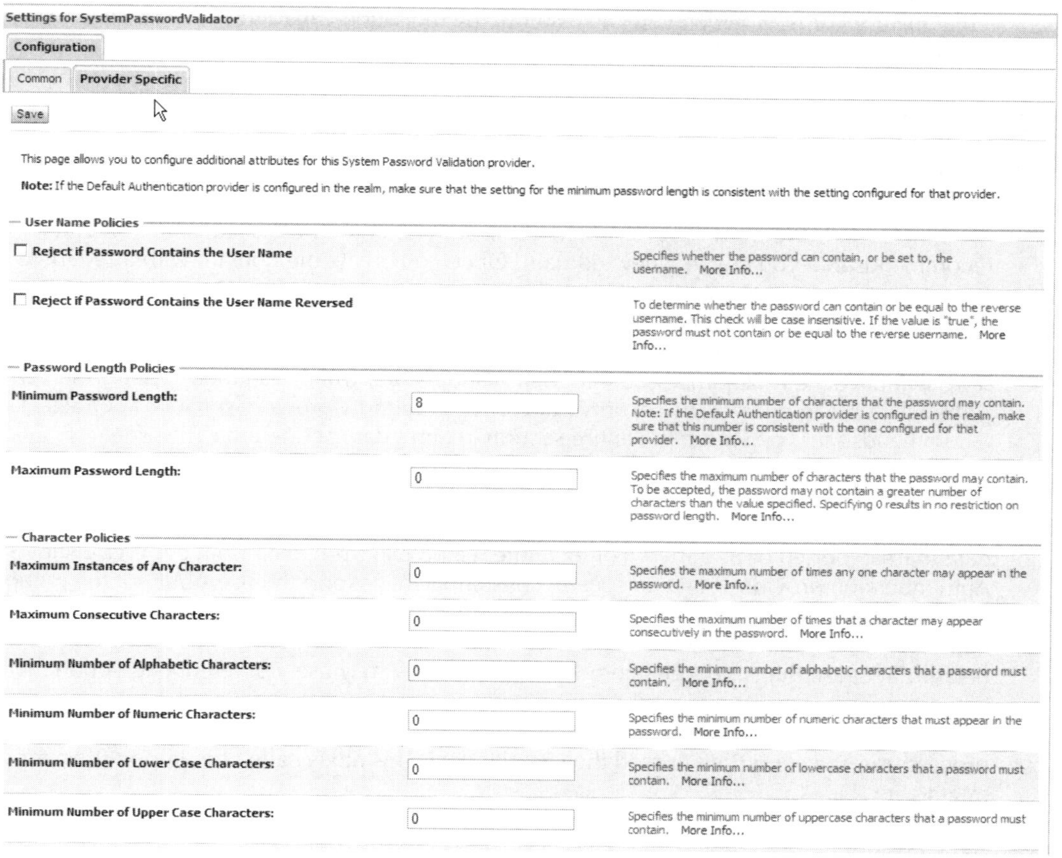

FIGURE 9-4. *Configuring the Password Validation provider*

Exporting and Importing Security Data

When you create a new realm or a new security provider, you can use existing security data in the current default realm instead of re-creating everything, such as users, groups, roles, security policies, and credential maps. To use the current security data, you can export the data from a security realm and import it into another security realm. You can also perform the export and import of security data at the security-provider level instead of the realm level. For WebLogic Server security providers, you export data from the embedded LDAP server. For example, you can export only the users and group data if you want to export data just for the WebLogic Authentication provider. The only requirement for migrating data from one security provider to another is that both providers must use the same data format. One of the main motivations for doing this is so you can incorporate the WebLogic administrative security roles and policies into an existing corporate LDAP store, eliminating the need for the embedded LDAP server. To do this, you copy the schema and policies using *ldif* and then assign administrative roles and policies to the users.

While the ability to migrate security data comes in handy when creating a new realm or replacing a security provider, you can also use the migration capability to move security configurations from one domain to another.

NOTE
You can export security data only from the WebLogic security providers and import the data only into WebLogic security providers.

When you move from the embedded LDAP store to an RDBMS security store, Oracle recommends that you create a new domain. Once you create the domain with an RDBMS security store, export the security data to the domain's security realm. During the import, by default, the security data for all security providers that use the RDBMS security store will be automatically loaded into the RDBMS tables. By default, any providers that don't use the RDBMS store will have their data imported into their default store, which could be an LDAP server. Although you can migrate the security data for each security provider separately, Oracle recommends that you export the entire security realm's data at one time.

To be able to export and import data, the data must be in supported formats—formats that both security providers can understand. Each WebLogic Server security provider has a set of data formats that it supports. You can also specify a list of constraints that restrict the type of security data that's exported or imported. For example, when exporting data from the WebLogic Authentication provider, you can specify constraints that export the users but not the groups. Similarly, you can specify that an Authentication provider (actually the LDAP server or another database) can't import the security policies. Passwords are exported in encrypted format by default. Because the target domain or security provider may use a different encryption method, you can specify a constraint such as *passwords=cleartext* in order to export the passwords in clear text. The export process writes security data to an export file in the specified format. The import process uses the export file to read the security data. This file is called the import file after you migrate it.

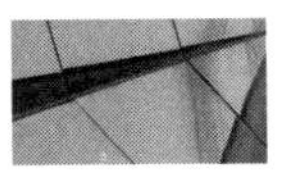

NOTE
Because some of the data formats for the WebLogic Server security providers are unpublished, you can't migrate the data in these formats to a custom security provider.

As mentioned earlier, you can export security from all security providers in a security realm or you can export specific security data from an individual security provider. The following example shows how to export the users, groups, and roles from the default Authentication provider in the security realm *myrealm*. The export writes the security data to a file, which you can use to import the data into another security provider in a different domain.

1. Click Lock & Edit in the Change Center of the Administration Console.
2. Select Security Realms in the left-hand pane. On the Summary Of Security Realm page, select the name of the security realm from which you want to export security data. (In this example, the security realm is *myrealm*.)
3. Click the Providers tab and then the Authentication tab.
4. In the Authentication Providers table, click DefaultAuthenticator.

5. On the Settings For DefaultAuthenticator page, select Migration.
6. You can specify various things on this page to control the export of security data from the Authentication provider's database to a file:
   - **Export Format** Specifies the format of the exported security data—this must be compatible with the import format.
   - **Export File On Server** Specifies the full path to the file where you want the server to store the exported data.
   - **Overwrite** Specifies whether the server should overwrite a preexisting export file.
   - **Supported Export Constraints** All users, security rules, and security policies will be exported by default—you can specify that only a subset of the security data be exported by listing the constraints to be applied during the export (users, roles, and policies).
   - **Export Constraints** Specifies the constraints that apply to the import of the data in a *key=value* format.
7. Click Save and then click Activate Changes in the Change Center.

The import process is very similar to the export process—it takes the export file and loads the security data into the *DefaultAuthenticator*'s data store. You can also use WLST commands to export and import security provider data (but not all of the security realm data) by accessing the run-time MBean for a provider and using the bean's *exportData* and *importData* operations.

Caching Security Information

You can cache security principal information in the security realm to let the security framework perform faster. You can configure security information caching by selecting the Performance tab on the Settings For myrealm page. Following are the two key caching-related configuration parameters:

- **Enable WebLogic Principal Validator Cache** Enabling the Principal Validator Cache lets the server cache all WebLogic principal signatures. By default, this option is checked. Oracle-supplied and custom Authentication providers can use the Principal Validator.
- **Max WebLogic Principals In Cache** Sets the size of the cache in terms of the number of WebLogic principal signatures—by default, the server caches 500 principal signatures.

Configuring Entitlements Caching

Both the *DefaultAuthorizer* (Authorization provider) and the *DefautRoleMapper* (Role Mapping provider) perform better when they cache roles and resource data during entitlement lookups.

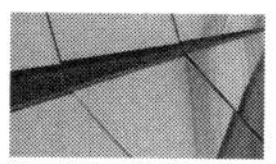

NOTE
You can't configure the cache for the XACML Authorization and Role Mapping providers.

The WebLogic Authorization and Role Mapping providers maintain three caches: the roles, the predicates, and the resources cache. For example, the default number of items stored in the roles cache is 2,000 items. The predicate cache default value is more than enough to cache the predicates of the two security providers. The resources cache stores the name of the resources (with their security policies) that the two providers have already looked up. You only need to increase the size of the caches when a server instance uses more than the default number of roles or resource lookups.

To raise the cache values from their default values, pass the following system properties in the Java startup command when starting the instance:

```
-Dweblogic.entitlement.engine.cache.max_role_count=4000
-Dweblogic.entitlement.engine.cache.max_resource_count=3200
```

The *max_role_count* and *max_resource_count* attributes specify the maximum number of roles or resources the server must cache. It's a good idea to reduce the initial lookup of the entitlement data by specifying that the server instance must load the cache during its startup cycle. If you don't do this and you raise the cache size to a high number, the initial lookup of the entitlement data will take a longer time. You specify the preloading of the cache in the following way when starting a server instance:

```
-Dweblogic.entitlement.engine.cache.preload=true
```

Changing the Default Security Realm

WebLogic Server provides a default security configuration in which the realm named *myrealm* acts as the default security realm in every WebLogic Server domain. The default security realm also contains the WebLogic Authentication, Adjudication, Identity Assertion, XACML Authorization, Credential Mapping, XACML Role Mapping, and CertPath providers as the default security providers, with the embedded LDAP server acting as the data store for the providers. Sometimes you may need to change the default security realm. Following are the steps for changing the default security realm:

1. Click Lock & Edit in the Change Center of the Administration Console.
2. Go to the domain's Settings page | Security | General.
3. If you have created and configured security realms, you'll be able to select one of them as the new default security realm. Click Save. Note that if you have not configured the required security providers for a new security realm, the realm won't appear in the pull-down menu.
4. Click Activate Changes in the Change Center.
5. To set the new realm as the default security realm, restart the server.

You'll now see that in the Realms table the new default security domain has the default realm set to *true*.

Reverting to an Older Security Configuration

If you make a mistake while configuring a security provider or a new security realm, you won't be able to start the Admin Server. You can, however, restore the original configuration files to return to the previous security realm configuration and start the server without a problem. It's nice to know you don't have to back up the previous security configuration—the Admin Server does this for you automatically. The Admin Server saves the last five versions of the security configuration files in the <*domain_name*>\configArchive directory. The jar file with the highest number (ranging from 1 to 5) is the file that contains the configuration for the most recent version of the security realm. In order to revert the security realm to a previous security configuration, copy the *config.jar* file with the highest number to the <*domain_name*>\config\security directory. While reverting to the previous security realm reinstates the configuration of the security providers and the security realm, the users, groups, role, and security policy information is always stored in the embedded LDAP server (or a different LDAP server or RDBMS store).

Users, Groups, Roles, and Security Policies

A WebLogic Server *user* is any entity that needs to be authenticated, so this could include the administrators and other users, as well as clients such as a Java client. To authenticate to the server, you must provision the users with unique identities in a security realm. Although you can manage users individually, you'll find it's far easier to handle large numbers of users by assigning them to groups. A group is scoped to the entire domain. A security role grants an identity to a user, but unlike a group, a user can be scoped to a specific resource. A security policy specifies which user, group, or role can access a WebLogic resource based on conditions that you specify, such as the time of day (time constraints) or membership in a group or role (for example, a user that belongs to a group within the *Admin* role).

Although you can assign a security policy directly to a user, you must not do so because it's not practical to manage a large number of users directly without allocating them into meaningful groups based on job role or function. Here's a simple methodology that helps create and assign security policies to protect key WebLogic resources:

- WebLogic Server provides a default security schema to control access to server, administrative, and JMX resources. Default security policies grant various types of administrative and server access to the set of eight default security roles such as the *Admin* and *Deployer* roles. WebLogic Server also has a set of eight default groups, each of which is assigned one or more of the eight default security roles. All you need to do is assign users to the default groups so they automatically have one or more of the default security roles.
- You can use the standard Java EE security model, where developers define role mappings and policies in the deployment descriptors to control access to web applications and EJBs. Alternatively, you can create security policies and security roles through the Administration Console.
- You must create custom security policies to control access to all other types of resources that you deploy as part of an enterprise application or module. You also need to determine if you need to create root-level or scoped policies for protecting those resources.
- You should assign your administrative users to one of the eight default global roles.
- You should create custom groups and security roles to allow users access to resources for which you've defined custom security policies.

The connection among users, groups, roles, and security policies is as follows:

- You should (you don't have to, but it's highly recommended) assign individual users to groups.
- You should (again, you don't have to, but it's a good practice) create security roles specifying the conditions under which a user, group, or another role should be granted the security role.
- You must create security policies to determine the conditions under which a specific role can access a WebLogic resource. You can simply say, for example, that a user with the *Admin* role can access an administrative resource. However, you can also specify that a user with a certain role can access a specific resource only during a specific period.

- During run time, the WebLogic Security Service performs a role-mapping process to determine whether a user or group should be granted a security role based on the security role's conditions.
- At run time, the WebLogic Security Service determines whether a user, group, or security role can access a specific WebLogic resource.

As you'll see later in this chapter, the simplest way to configure a security policy is to use a *Role condition*—the security policy applies to all users and groups with a role such as the *Admin* role, for example. Using a Role condition makes managing multiple users and groups easy, and Oracle recommends that you use one wherever possible.

In the following sections, let's discuss users, groups, and roles in detail.

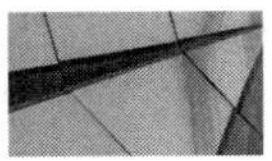

NOTE
You can add groups to another group.

Users

A *user* can be a person such as an end user, a client application, or even another instance of the WebLogic Server. To access the server, users must provide credentials in the form of a password, a digital certificate, or an equivalent means of ascertaining their identity. The Authentication provider of the realm receives the user security credentials through a JAAS login module and associates the user's identity (principal) with a thread for that user to use to execute work. To authorize the user to perform the work, the server checks the security policy of the resource the user is accessing. You can associate an individual user directly with a security role, but the preferred way is to do the association through groups.

Creating a User

You can create users through the Administration Console or WLST. Any users you create through the Administration Console or WLST can only be stored in the WebLogic embedded LDAP server that's configured with the WebLogic Authentication provider or in a database configured with a valid SQL Authentication provider. If you want to use an external LDAP server, you must use the LDAP server's user creation tools instead of the Console or WLST. You can also import users and groups into the embedded LDAP server.

Here's a summary of the steps to follow to create a user through the Administration Console:

1. Select Security Realms in the left-hand pane of the Administration Console.
2. Select the realm in which you want to create the user from the Settings For *<realm_name>* page.
3. Select Users And Groups | Users on the Settings For *<realm_name>* page.
4. Click New to access the Create New User page.
5. Enter the name of the user in the Name field. The username must follow the naming conventions.

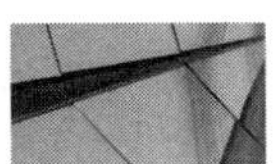

CAUTION
If you create a username with either a pound sign (#) or with double quotations, you may corrupt the domain configuration.

6. You can enter a description of the user, such as the user's full name, in the Description field.
7. If you've configured multiple Authentication providers, you must select an Authentication provider for the user in the Provider drop-down list.
8. Enter a password in the Password field and reenter it in the Confirm Password field.
9. Click OK to save the user configuration.

You'll now see the username in the User table. In the User table, select the name of the new user to set the user attributes. In the Settings For <*username*> page, select Attributes, and for each attribute therein, enter a string in the Values column.

Setting User Attributes

When you create a user through the Administration Console, you're defining that user in the WebLogic Authentication provider. Once you create the user, you can set one or more attributes for that user. When you set the value for an attribute, that attribute is added to the user. You can only choose from the list of attributes offered by WebLogic Server; you can't customize them. You can delete an attribute from a user's definition at any time. Following are some of the user attributes:

```
C: two letter country code
displayname: preferred name for the user
l: name of the locality, such as the city or county
Employeetype: shows the relationship between the employer and the
employee
```

Groups

A *group* consists of a set of users who share something, such as members of a department within a company, for example. WebLogic Server defines several groups in the default realm *myrealm*. Any users you assign to a default group will inherit the default global role corresponding to that default group. Here are the default groups in a realm with preconfigured users:

- ***Administrators*** Contains the administrative user whose information you have to provide during the domain configuration process. A user you add to this group will be granted the *Admin* role by default. Oracle recommends that you add at least one user to this group, in addition to the administrative user created at domain configuration time. Having a second user is helpful if the default administrative user is locked out, for example.
- ***OracleSystemGroup*** Contains the default user *OracleSystemUser* with the default role *OracleSystemRole*.

WebLogic Server also uses two run-time groups that are not visible through the Administration Console: *Users* and *Everyone*. The group *Everyone* contains all users, both anonymous and authenticated, whereas the *Users* group contains the authenticated users. You can't manage these two groups by adding and deleting users, like the default groups. The server dynamically adds users to these two groups during run time.

Creating a Group

You can create groups with either the Administration Console or WLST, but as with users, you're limited to the creation of groups in the embedded LDAP server or in an RDBMS. To create groups in external LDAP servers, you must use tools specific to that LDAP server.

Creating a group through the Console involves steps that are very similar to those for creating users. Just select Users And Groups | Groups on the Settings For *<realm-name>* page and follow the instructions. Once you create a group, you can add users to that group by going to Users And Groups | Users to select the user you want to add to a group and then selecting Groups in the Settings For *<username>* page to add the user to a group (or groups). Note that you can also add a group to one or more groups.

Default Groups

WebLogic Server offers a set of eight default groups. With the exception of the *Administrators* group and the *OracleSystemGroup*, all groups are empty by default. Each default group is associated with a default security role; thus, when you assign a user to a group, that user will automatically be granted the default role associated with that group. Following is a list of the eight default groups and the roles associated with each group:

- ***Administrators*** Contains the default administrative user—this user is the same as the username you provide the Configuration Wizard (for example, weblogic, with the password welcome1) when you configure a new domain. Default security role is *Admin*.
- ***Deployers*** Default security role is *Deployer.*
- ***Operators*** Default security role is *Operator*.
- ***Monitors*** Default security role is *Monitor.*
- ***AppTesters*** Default security role is *AppTester*.
- ***CrossDomainConnectors*** Default security role is *CrossDomainConnector*.
- ***AdminChannelUsers*** Default security role is *AdminChannelUser*.
- ***OracleSystemGroup*** Contains the user *OracleSystemUser*. Default security role is *OracleSystemRole*.

Security Roles

A *security role* is a privilege (or an identity) that the server dynamically grants to a user or group based on specific conditions such as username, group membership, or time of day. The security roles are privileges the server grants to a user or group based on some conditions. Roles restrict access just like groups, but the big difference between a group and a role is that roles are granted dynamically at run time. In addition, you can scope a role to a specific resource, whereas a group is simply a grouping of users that have similar characteristics. A user or group can have more than one role at the same time. Security policies use roles to determine who can access a WebLogic resource. A security role grants defined access privileges to a user or group, as long as the user or group continues to have the security role. During run time, the Security Service dynamically performs a role mapping process to grant roles to users and groups. The Authorization provider then helps make the decision as to whether the user or group can perform a specific operation on a resource.

NOTE
You can certainly grant an individual user a role, but best practice is to create groups and assign roles to the groups.

There are two types of security roles:

- **Global roles** The server can use these with any security policy. You can use the default global roles or create your own.
- **Scoped roles** Security policies can use a scoped role just for a specific instance of a resource such as an EJB method containing sensitive business logic, for example. You can use scoped roles to restrict access to EJBs.

If you have a conflict between a goal and a scoped role, a role with the smaller scope will override the role with the larger scope.

Role mapping is the process of comparing groups against role conditions to determine whether a group and its users should be granted a specific security role.

Default Global Roles

In each security realm, the server defines a number of default global roles, and the default role conditions include one or more WebLogic default groups in each role. The default security policies grant a set of privileges to each global role. Here are the main global roles, the default groups included in the roles by the default role conditions, and the privileges granted to each role by the default security policies.

- ***Admin*** The default security policies allow the user or group with the *Admin* role to view and modify server configuration (including encrypted attributes), deploy applications, and control the server instances (start/stop/resume). The *Administrators* group is in the *Admin* role by default.
- ***Anonymous*** All users are granted this role. The default group *Everyone* is part of this role.
- ***Deployer*** This role permits the following:
  - View server configuration (encrypted attributes limited to deployment attributes)
  - Change web applications and edit deployment descriptors
  - Change startup and shutdown classes
  - Modify JDBC data pool connections

The *Deployer* role includes the default group *Deployers.*

- ***Operator*** This role allows viewing of the server configuration (no encrypted attributes) and starting, stopping, and resuming the server. Includes the *Operator* group.
- ***Monitor*** This role allows viewing of the nonencrypted configuration attributes through the Console, WLST, and MBean APIs. Includes the *Monitors* group.
- ***AppTester*** This role allows access to applications running in administration mode. Includes the *AppTesters* group.
- ***CrossDomainConnector*** This role is used to enable interdomain messaging when you enable "trust" between multiple domains. Includes the *CrossDomainConnectors* group.
- ***OracleSystemRole*** This role is for users whose WS-Security tokens have been authenticated. Includes the *OracleSystemGroup*.

Note that, by default, each of these default roles is linked to one or more of the default groups described in the previous section. Thus, if you assign a user to the *Operators* group, that user automatically gets the *Operator* role.

Security Role Conditions

A role contains one or more conditions to determine when a group or user is assigned that role at run time. The server uses default role conditions to assign a default group to a role. For example, the global role *Admin*'s default conditions include the group *Administrators*—the server automatically places the *Administrators* group in the *Admin* role at run time. Following are the various types of built-in role conditions:

- **Basic** These are simple role conditions such as user or group, which add the specified user or group to the role. For example, you may create a group called *PermEmployees* and specify that only users in that group be granted the *SecretInfo* security role. The other basic role conditions are
  - **Server is in development mode** Tells the server to add a user or group to a role only when a server is running in development mode.
  - **Allow access to anyone** Specifies that all users and groups must be added to a role.
  - **Deny access to everyone** Specifies that the role not be assigned to any user or group.
- **Date and time** A date and time role condition grants a security role to all users for any date and time you specify. For example, you can specify the Access Occurs Between Specified Hours condition to add a user or group to a role only during a specific time. There are different date and time role conditions. You can add other role conditions to a date and time role condition to restrict the users or groups to which you want to grant a security role.
- **Context element** This type of role condition adds a principal to a role based on the presence of a specific parameter or attribute, or on the value of that parameter or attribute. The attributes and values refer to HTTP Servlet Request attributes and HTTP Session attributes. The parameters refer to EJB method parameters.

Configuring Security Policies

You can't consider any WebLogic Server resource a protected resource until you create a security policy for it. A security policy associates a WebLogic resource with a user, group, or security role in order to restrict access to that resource. A security policy helps you control access to WebLogic Server resources by specifying which user, group, or security role can access a specific resource and under what conditions. The WebLogic Security Service uses the roles and policies you create to control access to resources.

By default, no WebLogic resource is protected by a security policy. You can secure multiple resources with a single security policy. To protect a set of resources with a single policy, you can control access to protected resources based on the type of resource or use security policies that protect a hierarchy of resources. The following sections explain the two strategies.

Security Policies Based on Resource Type

You can create a security policy to protect all WebLogic resources of a certain type, such as resources of the Web Service type. These types of security policies are also called *root-level security policies*, and they provide you a way to configure a single, homogeneous security policy for all resources that belong to the same resource type. For example, you can create a security policy that applies to all JMS resources in a domain. The default security realm *myrealm* comes with a set of default root-level security policies, some of which are described in the following list, with each policy designed to control a specific type of WebLogic resource. Here are some of the important WebLogic resource types and the security policies that protect them:

- **Administrative resources** A root-level security policy grants access based on membership in the default global role *Admin*.
- **Application resources** These contain no default security policies.
- **EJB resources** A root-level security policy grants access based on membership in the default group *Everyone*.
- **JDBC, JNDI, and JMS resources** A root-level security policy grants access based on membership in the default group *Everyone*.
- **Server resources** A root-level security policy grants access based on membership in the default global role *Admin* or *Operator*.

Note how certain default root-level security policies grant access to resources based on membership in a group or role.

Hierarchical Security Policies

Whereas a root-level policy applies to all instances of a specific resource type, you can also create a security policy that applies to a specific instance of a WebLogic resource. The security policy you create for a specific instance applies to the hierarchy of the resources included in that instance. You can specify a security policy at any level in the hierarchy of resources, such as the following:

- An enterprise application (EAR)
- An EJB jar file that contains multiple EJBs
- A specific EJB within an EJB jar file
- A single method within a specific EJB

If you create security policies at multiple levels, the policy at the lower level will override policies at the higher level. For example, a security policy for an EJB will override any security policies you specify at the EAR level.

Security Policy Conditions

When you create a security policy, the WebLogic Security Service evaluates the policy "conditions" to determine who can access a protected resource. For example, a security policy for a resource may have a condition based on roles, such as the *Admin* global role, which means that any user that has the *Admin* role can access that resource. WebLogic Server Authorization providers use three kinds of built-in security policy conditions: basic, date and time, and context element policy conditions. These three types of conditions work the same way as the corresponding role conditions discussed earlier in this chapter in the section titled "Security Role Conditions." The basic policy conditions are more extensive than the basic role conditions. Here's a brief description of the basic security policy conditions:

- **User** Allows a user access to a WebLogic resource.
- **Group** Allows a group access to a resource unless a User security policy condition denies the access.

- **Role** Allows all users or groups in a specific security role to access a resource. However, a User or Group security policy condition can override access privileges granted by a role, including the *Admin* role.
- **Server is in Development Mode** Allows the user or group to access a resource only if the server that hosts the resources runs in development mode.
- **Allow Access to Everyone** Allows access to all users, groups, and roles.
- **Deny Access to Everyone** Denies access to all users, groups, and roles.
- **Element Requires Signature by** Controls access only to a Web Service resource. A Web Service operation is allowed only if a specific element in the SOAP request has been digitally signed by the user who you specify as the value for this condition.
- **To Create an Element Requires Signature by** Specifies whether a group or user is required to sign the SOAP element. You must specify the user or group name, as well as the name of the SOAP message element.

Static and Dynamic Security Conditions

As you've learned in this chapter, both roles and security policies can dynamically evaluate a set of conditions at run time. You can specify a security policy that allows access to a resource through a specific role, and you can dynamically assign users these roles as necessary. When you do this, you're controlling authorization based on which user or group can access the resource. Alternatively, you can define a static role and create a dynamic security policy that allows access to the static role depending on the time of day, for example. By adding conditions to a security policy, you're controlling access to a resource based on the resource itself rather than the roles that are allowed to access the resource. For example, you can create a security policy that dynamically grants a user a security role for a specific time (or during a specific period) without adding that user to a different group.

Security Models for Web Applications and EJBs

A security model for an application determines where you specify the roles and security policies and when exactly the server actually performs the security checks (for example, when a client requests a certain URL). In addition to supporting the standard Java EE security model that lets you define role mappings and security policies in a deployment descriptor for the web application or EJB, WebLogic Server offers more flexible security models of its own. Both the Java EE security model and the WebLogic security models are appropriate under various scenarios, as explained in the following sections. Note that once you deploy a web application or EJB, the security model can't be changed unless you redeploy the application or EJB.

The Deployment Descriptor Only Model

The Deployment Descriptor Only (DD Only) security model, which is another name for the standard Java EE security model, only uses the groups, roles, and security policies defined in the *web.xml, weblogic.xml, ejb-jar.xml,* and *weblogic-ejb-jar.xml* deployment descriptors. Developers define the roles and security policies in the deployment descriptors. The developer maps the EJBs and web URLs to roles and maps the roles to principals (users or groups). The administrator ensures that the roles and groups exist and that they are mapped correctly in the realm. Under the DD Only security model, the security framework performs a security check only when clients request a URL or EJB method that is protected by policies specified in the deployment descriptor.

The key thing to understand here is scoping. If the developer doesn't define a role in the deployment descriptor for the application (application-scoped role), the EAR will not have any application-scoped roles—the administrator can't modify the application-scoped roles through the Administration Console under this model. The administrator can, however, create non-application-scoped roles as well as application-scoped *policies* (not roles) for the EAR.

When you use deployment descriptors to grant the security roles and define the security policies, the server loads the role and policy information into the Authorization and Role Mapping providers when you boot the server instance. To enable the server to use the security information defined in the deployment descriptors, you must configure at least one Authorization provider to implement the *DeployableAuthorizationProvider* Security Service Provider Interface (SSPI) and one Role Mapping provider to implement the *DeployableRoleProvider* SSPI. The two SSPIs let these two providers store information from the deployment descriptors instead of having to retrieve them each time they need to authenticate or perform role mapping. Both the WebLogic Authorization and Role Mapping providers implement the SSPIs mentioned here, so you don't have to configure them if you are using these two providers.

The Custom Roles Model

The DD Only security model is probably fine if role mappings are fairly static and developers and administrators work closely together to set up application security. However, in an environment where you need to change role mappings frequently or where developers and administrators work independent of each other, the DD Only security model opens the door to many potential problems, including the need to redeploy the application frequently following a remapping of roles. The Custom Roles security model is better able to handle security in such as environment. Under this model, the developer defines the security policies in the deployment descriptors by mapping the EJBs and URLs to roles in the deployment descriptors. The administrator (or a deployer) is responsible for defining the security roles and mapping them to the principals. You still need to redeploy the application when developers modify the security policies in the deployment descriptors, but the administrator can change the role mappings in the Administration Console without having to redeploy the web application or EJB.

The big advantage of the Custom Roles method is that it offers the ability to configure fine-grained control of specific URL patterns or EJB methods by letting the developer specify these in the deployment descriptors.

You can't create application-scoped security policies for EJBs and URL patterns. The administrator can create application-scoped policies for other resources such as an EAR. Under the Custom Roles security model, the server uses only the security policies in the deployment descriptors for EJBs and URL patterns. If the developers specify any roles in the DDs, the security model ignores them. The administrator is responsible for role mapping.

The Custom Roles and Policies Model

The Custom Roles and Policies security model goes beyond the Custom Roles model by letting the administrator create all roles, security policies, and role mappings, and completely ignores any security definitions in the deployment descriptors. This is a more streamlined approach to managing security, as the administrator defines all security requirements including the roles, security policies, and role mappings centrally through the Administration Console. This centralization of application security configuration makes updating security definitions much easier than in the DD Only or Custom Roles security models.

The drawback with this security model is that it doesn't provide fine-grained security checks based on a client accessing a specific URL or EJB method—the server checks the security permissions following each client request for a URL or EJB method, leading to additional overhead.

The Advanced Model

The Advanced Model is offered primarily for backward compatibility with releases prior to WebLogic Server 9.0. This model lets the server perform security checks for just those URLs and EJB methods the developer has specified in the deployment descriptor or for all URLs and EJBs.

Security-Related Deployment Descriptors

When deploying an application into the WebLogic Server environment, an administrator or security administrator may need to know how to interpret the security configured in an application in order to provide the correct binding to roles in LDAP or in the database. Web application developers can programmatically set up security through annotations or do so declaratively with the help of deployment descriptors. However, many security-related elements in a web application deployment descriptor can't be set through annotations. For this reason, using deployment descriptors for security is more or less a necessity, although Oracle recommends that you use annotations where possible, so it's important for the administrator to understand the basics of how security is configured in Java EE deployment descriptors.

A Java EE deployment descriptor lets you express roles, access control, and authentication rules external to the application. Security-related elements are used in both the *web.xml* and *weblogic.xml* files. In a *web.xml* file, the deployment descriptor for web applications, the *<web-app>* element, contains the security-related elements, which are summarized as follows:

- ***<security-role>*** Contains the security role's definition and, optionally, includes the description and name of the security role.
- ***<security-role-ref>*** Contains the declaration of security role references in the web application code. You specify the same security "role name" here as the security role name coded in the servlet logic, the goal being to configure servlets without changing their code.
- ***<security-constraint>*** Defines the privileges to access a set of resources defined by the *<web-resource-collection>* element.
- ***<web-resource-collection>*** Specifies a subset of resources and HTTP methods on those resources to which a security constraint applies. This is an optional element.
- ***<user-data-constraint>*** Specifies how to secure data passed between the client and the server. Under this element, the *<transport-guarantee>* element is required. You can specify a value of *INTEGRAL* for the *<transport-guarantee>* element to ensure that the data can't be changed in transit. By setting a value of *CONFIDENTIAL* for this element, you can prevent other entities from reading the transmitted data. The server establishes an SSL connection if the user authenticates with the *INTEGRAL* or *CONFIDENTIAL* value for *<transport-guarantee>*.

The *weblogic.xml* file includes the following security-related elements under the *<weblogic-web-app>* element:

- ***<externally-defined>*** Lets you specify that the security roles you define with the *<role-name>* element in the *web.xml* deployment descriptor should use the role mappings you specified in the Administration Console. This element is used within the *<security-role-assignment>* element.
- ***<security-role-assignment>*** Specifies the mapping between a security role and a principal (or principals) in the security realm. The following example shows how to use this element in the *weblogic.xml* file:

```
<weblogic-web-app>
  <security-role-assignment>
       <role-name>PayrollAdmin</role-name>
       <principal-name>Nina</principal-name>
       <principal-name>Sam</principal-name>
       <principal-name>system</principal-name>
  </security-role-assignment>
</weblogic-web-app>
```

- ***<run-as-role-assignment>*** Maps the role name specified by the *<role-name>* element in the *web.xml* file to a valid username.
- ***<run-as-principal-name>*** Specifies the principal's name to use for a security role specified by the *<run-as>* element in the *web.xml* file. This element is used within the *<run-as-role-assignment>* element, as shown here:

```
<weblogic-web-app>
     <run-as-role-assignment>
       <role-name>runasrole</role-name>
       <run-as-principal-name>sam</run-as-principal-name>
     </run-as-role-assignment>
</weblogic-web-app>
```

Configuring the Embedded LDAP Server

The WebLogic security providers such as the default Authentication provider use the embedded LDAP server as the database for storing users, groups, roles, and security policies. In addition, all of the WebLogic security providers, except the Adjudication and Auditing providers, use the embedded LDAP server to store registered end certificates. You can use the embedded LDAP server as a development and testing environment from which you can export security data to an external LDAP server. You can use an LDAP browser to export security data from the embedded LDAP server. If you have a small set of users and groups, you can even use the embedded LDAP server in a production environment because it's a full-fledged LDAP server. The embedded LDAP server lets you access and modify entries, and it grants read and write access to the WebLogic security providers.

The embedded LDAP server stores user, group, security roles, security policies, and credential maps with default values for each attribute. If you use any one of the WebLogic default Authentication, Authorization, Credential Mapping, and Role Mapping providers in a new security realm, you may have to modify the default configuration of the LDAP server. The Admin Server maintains the master LDAP server, and each Managed Server maintains a replicated LDAP server. The master LDAP server replicates changes to the embedded LDAP server running on the Managed Servers. You can configure the refresh properties for replicated data, as well as other configuration properties through the Administration Console, by going to Domain | Security | Embedded LDAP to get to the LDAP server configuration page (see Figure 9-5). Here's a description of the configuration attributes you can set for the embedded LDAP server:

- **Credential** Sets the password to connect to the embedded LDAP server. WebLogic Server uses a default password if you don't specify a value for the Credential attribute. You must specify a value for this attribute if you want to connect to the embedded LDAP server using an LDAP browser and the administrator account (*cn=Admin*).

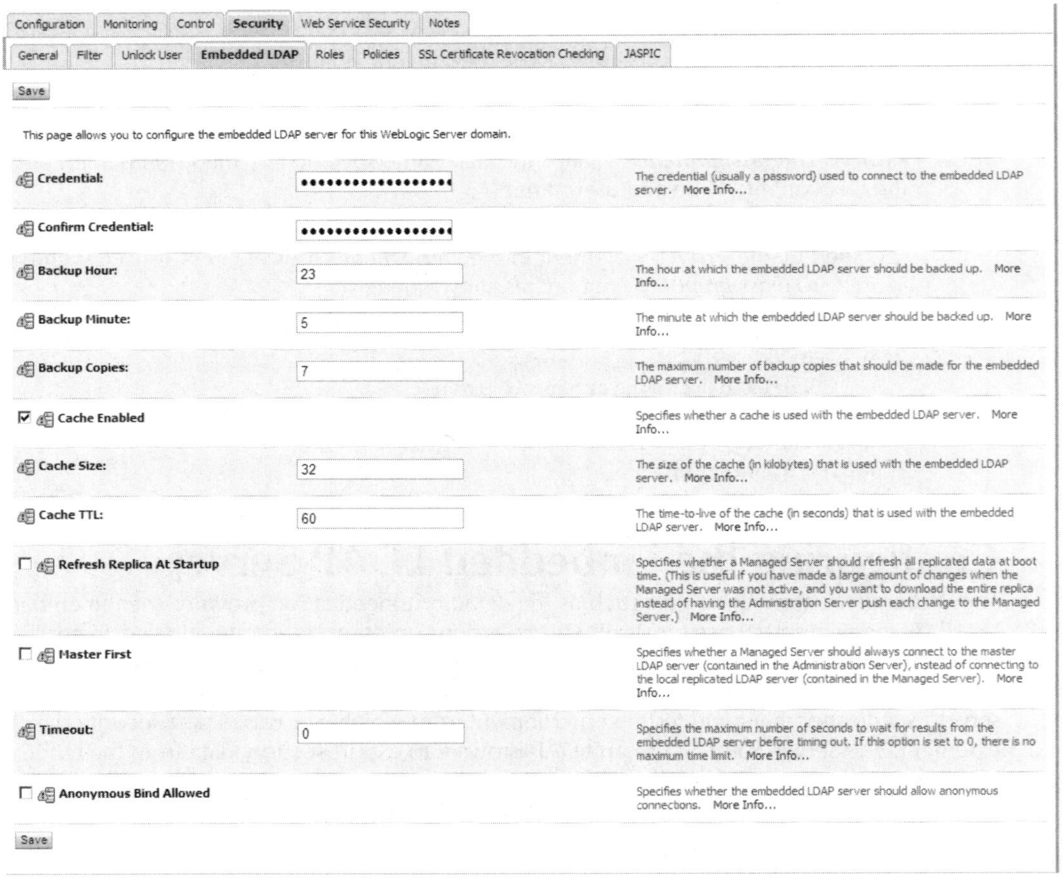

Configuration | Monitoring | Control | **Security** | Web Service Security | Notes

General | Filter | Unlock User | **Embedded LDAP** | Roles | Policies | SSL Certificate Revocation Checking | JASPIC

Save

This page allows you to configure the embedded LDAP server for this WebLogic Server domain.

Attribute	Value	Description
Credential:	••••••••••••••••••	The credential (usually a password) used to connect to the embedded LDAP server. More Info...
Confirm Credential:	••••••••••••••••••	
Backup Hour:	23	The hour at which the embedded LDAP server should be backed up. More Info...
Backup Minute:	5	The minute at which the embedded LDAP server should be backed up. More Info...
Backup Copies:	7	The maximum number of backup copies that should be made for the embedded LDAP server. More Info...
☑ **Cache Enabled**		Specifies whether a cache is used with the embedded LDAP server. More Info...
Cache Size:	32	The size of the cache (in kilobytes) that is used with the embedded LDAP server. More Info...
Cache TTL:	60	The time-to-live of the cache (in seconds) that is used with the embedded LDAP server. More Info...
☐ **Refresh Replica At Startup**		Specifies whether a Managed Server should refresh all replicated data at boot time. (This is useful if you have made a large amount of changes when the Managed Server was not active, and you want to download the entire replica instead of having the Administration Server push each change to the Managed Server.) More Info...
☐ **Master First**		Specifies whether a Managed Server should always connect to the master LDAP server (contained in the Administration Server), instead of connecting to the local replicated LDAP server (contained in the Managed Server). More Info...
Timeout:	0	Specifies the maximum number of seconds to wait for results from the embedded LDAP server before timing out. If this option is set to 0, there is no maximum time limit. More Info...
☐ **Anonymous Bind Allowed**		Specifies whether the embedded LDAP server should allow anonymous connections. More Info...

Save

FIGURE 9-5. *Configuring the embedded LDAP server*

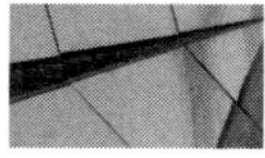

CAUTION
If you specify a value for the Credential attribute, the clear-text password remains in the JVM memory until it's flushed by garbage collection.

- **Backup Hour** By default, the server backs up the LDAP directory once daily. The Backup Hour value (together with the value you specify for the Backup Minute attribute) tells the server when it should back up the embedded LDAP server's data files to a zipped file in the WL_HOME\domains\<*domain_name*>\servers\<*server_name*>\data\ldap\backup directory.
- **Backup Minute** Specifies the minute at which the server should back up the embedded LDAP server.
- **Backup Copies** Specifies the maximum number of backup copies that can be made for the embedded LDAP server. The maximum value is 65,534 copies!
- **Cache Enabled** Specifies whether the server should enable a cache for the master LDAP server from which the Managed Servers can read (or write) the LDAP data.
- **Cache Size** Specifies the size of the LDAP server cache in kilobytes.
- **Cache TTL** Specifies the time-to-live period for the cache.
- **Refresh Replica At Startup** Specifies whether the Managed Server should download the entire replica of the configuration from the Admin Server at boot time. By default, the Managed Servers get incremental updates from the master LDAP servers. You can change the default setting to avoid the sending of individual changes one by one by the Admin Server if you're rebooting the Managed Server after it's been offline for a long time.
- **Master First** Specifies that the Managed Server should connect to the master LDAP server on the Admin Server instead of the local LDAP server on the Managed Server.
- **Timeout** By default, there's no limit on the amount of time to wait for the LDAP server to send results back (*timeout=0*), but you can specify a timeout duration with this attribute.
- **Anonymous Bind Allowed** Lets you specify whether the LDAP server should permit anonymous connections.

The embedded LDAP server's database is in the WL_HOME\domains\<*domain_name*>\servers\<*server_name*>\data\ldap directory. The directory consists of the backup, ldapfiles, conf, log, and replicadata subdirectories. The backup directory contains the daily backups (in zipped format), such as *EmbeddedLDAPBackup.4.zip*. The LDAP server data files are in the ldapfiles directory, and the replicadata directory holds the LDAP data replicated to the Managed Servers.

Configuring an RDBMS as the Security Store

You can use an RDBMS instead of an LDAP server as the security store for the Authorization, Role Mapping, Credential Mapping, and Certificate Registry providers. Oracle strongly recommends configuring an RDBMS security store when using SAML 2.0 services in a cluster. If you create an RDBMS security store in a domain, security providers such as the XACML Authorization provider, the XACML Role Mapping provider, SAML 1.1 and SAML 2.0 Identity Assertion and Credential

Mapping providers, and the WebLogic Credential Mapping provider will use this store rather than the embedded LDAP server.

In the following sections, let's review the main things you must do in order to configure an RDBMS security store.

Setting Up the RDBMS Security Store

You can use the Administration Console to set up a new RDBMS store easily for a security realm. Go to Services | Security Realms | *<realm name>* | RDBMS Security Store to configure the RDBMS Security Store for a security realm. Figure 9-6 shows the Configuration page for the RDBMS Security Store for a security realm.

On this page, the configuration option RDBMS Security Store Enabled specifics whether a subset of the WebLogic security providers uses an RDBMS as its data store. Following are the security providers who may store their security data in the external RDBMS:

- XACML Authorization and Role Mapping providers
- WebLogic Credential Mapping provider
- PKI Credential Mapping provider
- SAML 1.1 providers: SAML Identity Assertion provider V2 and SAML Credential Mapping provider V2
- SAML 2.0 providers: SAML 2.0 Identity Assertion provider and SAML 2.0 Credential Mapping provider
- Certificate Registry

By choosing RDBMS Security Store Enabled on this page, you're specifying that any of the security providers shown in the preceding list will use the RDBMS security store as their repository for security information, instead of the embedded LDAP server. Your choice has no impact on any security providers not in the list. For instance, the Weblogic Authentication provider will use the embedded LDAP server instead of the RDBMS that you've configured as the security store for a security realm.

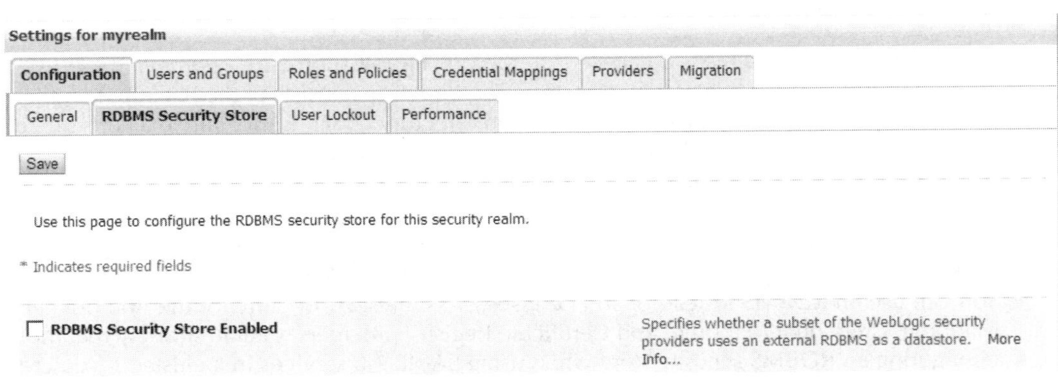

FIGURE 9-6. *Configuring the RDBMS Security Store*

Creating Tables in the RDBMS Store

Once you set up the database store and test the connection, the Oracle (or other database) administrator must execute a SQL script that creates necessary tables in the RDBMS Security Store. Scripts for all supported databases are in the WL_HOME\server\lib directory. For the Oracle 9*i*, 10*g*, 11*g* and 12*c* databases, for example, you execute the *rdbms_security_store_oracle.sql* script. The script creates tables in which the security providers will store the security data. You can remove these tables by executing the corresponding *rdbms_security_store_oracle_remove.sql* script.

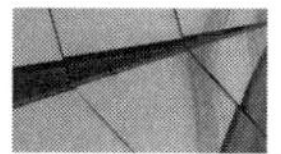

NOTE
Oracle recommends that you create a new domain configured with an RDBMS Security Store versus upgrading an existing domain, if you want to use the RDBMS Security Store instead of the embedded LDAP server.

Setting Up JMS Notifications for Security Changes

Although the final step in configuring an RDBMS Security Store—the configuration of a JMS topic for the use of the store—isn't mandatory, Oracle recommends that you set it up to facilitate the synchronization of security data among the various instances in a domain, including cluster members. Doing this helps you avoid the potential need to reboot the domain's servers to ensure consistency when you make any security configuration or security policy changes. When you set up JMS messaging for the RDMBS store, the WebLogic Security Service notifies all WebLogic Server instances with JMS messages whenever a security provider changes its security data. The WebLogic Security Service running on the server instance synchronizes its local caches with the changes in security data. You can configure JMS notifications for security data updates by going to the Security Realms | *realm_name*> || RDBMS Security Store page in the Administration Console. To do this, you must specify attributes such as JMS Topic, Notification Properties, and JNDI User Name.

Configuring Domain Security

Configuring domain-level security involves setting general domain security properties such as the default security realm, specifying whether anonymous, read-only access to WebLogic Server MBeans should be allowed, and specifying the Node Manager and domain credentials. Domain security configuration may also include enabling trust between a local and a remote domain, enabling connection filters, and protecting user accounts and passwords. Let's review the main domain security features in the following sections.

Configuring Domain Security in the Administration Console

You can configure domain security in the Administration Console by going to Domains | Security. Several tabs on this page enable you to configure various aspects of a domain's security. Let's review the key elements of domain-level security that you can configure on the various security configuration pages in the Console.

General Security Page

When you select Security on a domain's home page, you'll be on the General security configuration page, shown (part of the page) in Figure 9-7. You can define general security settings for the domain from this page. Following is a review of the general security configuration options for a domain. Except for the first four options, all options can be seen only by clicking the Advanced tab at the bottom of the General security configuration page. Following is a description of the key security options you can configure on this page:

- **Default Realm** Specifies the security realm that should act as the default or security realm for the domain. You must configure at least an Authentication provider, an Authorization provider, an Adjudication provider, a Credential Mapping provider, and a Role Mapping

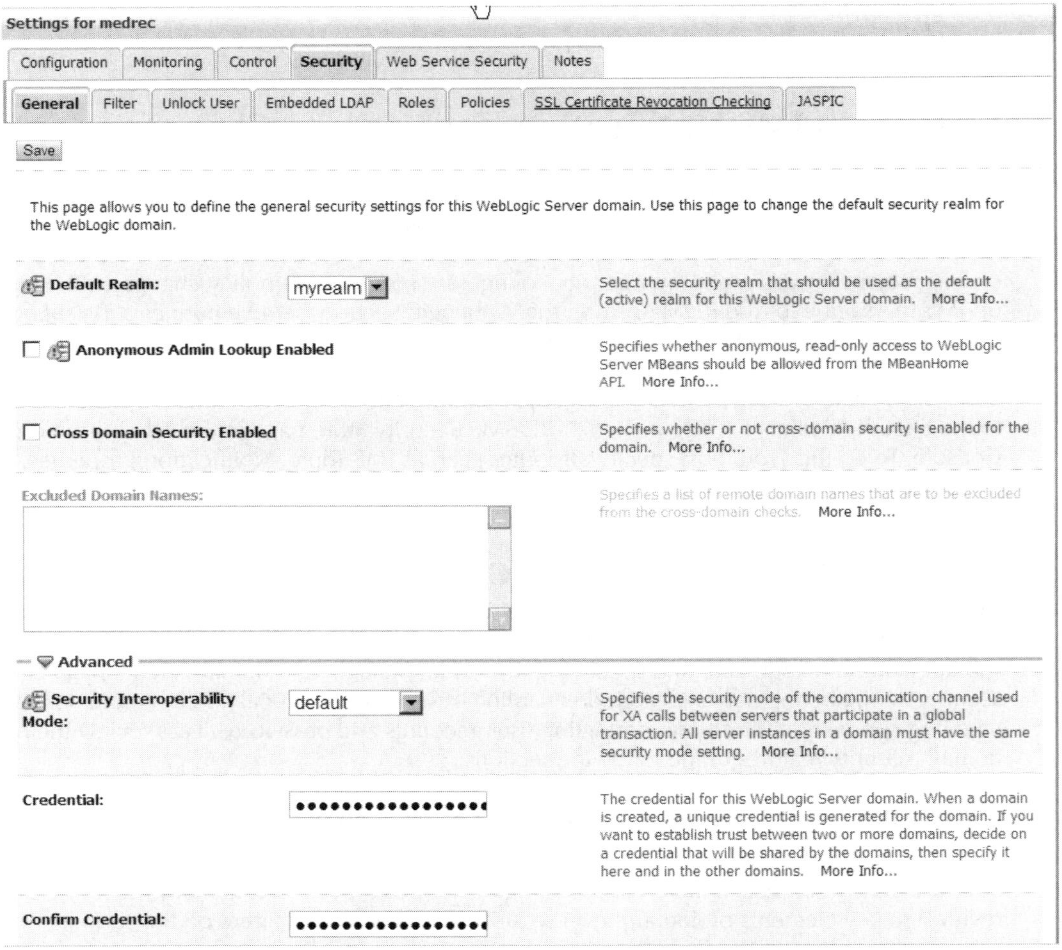

FIGURE 9-7. *The General security page for the domain*

provider for a new security realm before the realm shows up in the menu of security realms. Otherwise, this box is grayed out (with the name of the current default realm).

- **Anonymous Admin Lookup Enabled** Specifies whether the server should allow anonymous, read-only access to WebLogic Server MBeans from the MBean API. By default, anonymous viewing of MBean attributes is not allowed. You must leave anonymous access to MBeans disabled, but you may enable it for backward compatibility.
- **Cross Domain Security Enabled** Lets you enable trust between domains by enabling cross-domain security. The section "Enabling Trust Between Domains," later in this chapter, explains cross-domain security in detail. By default, cross-domain security is not enabled.
- **Excluded Domain Names** Specifies the remote domain names excluded from cross-domain checks.
- **Security Interoperability Mode** Specifies the security mode of the channels used for XA calls between servers participating in a global transaction. There are four different security interoperability modes:
  - **Default** If you enable the administration channel, the transaction coordinator makes the XA calls over that channel—otherwise, it makes calls using *anonymous*.
  - **Performance** The transaction coordinator always uses *anonymous*, which leaves the door open for man-in-the-middle attacks.
  - **Compatibility** The transaction coordinator makes calls over an insecure channel, which potentially could allow an attacker to gain control of the administration channel through the insecure channel. Oracle recommends that you not use this setting unless you have very strong network security controls.
  - **Credential** This is the credential assigned to this domain during domain creation. When you enable global trust between domains, you must specify the credential in the local and remote domains.
- **NodeManager Username** Specifies the username used by the Admin Server to communicate with the Node Manager—the default username is *weblogic*.
- **NodeManager Password** Specifies the password used by the Admin Server during communications with the Node Manager. When you specify a password, the server encrypts the value and sets the value of the *NodeManagerPasswordEncrypted* attribute to the encrypted value. However, the unencrypted password remains in the JVM memory until it's removed through garbage collection. To prevent the exposure of the password, Oracle recommends that you use *NodeManagerPasswordEncrypted* instead.
- **Web App Files Case Insensitive** You can set the URL pattern-matching behavior for servlets, virtual hosts, and others in the *webapp* container and in external security policies. You can set this attribute to *os, true,* or *false* (the default value is *false*). Setting this attribute to *os* means that pattern matching is case insensitive on all platforms except Windows.
- **Enforce Strict URL Pattern** Specifies whether the server should enforce a strict URL pattern ("/") to represent an entire web application.

- **Downgrade Untrusted Principals** Specifies whether to downgrade to anonymous principals that can't be verified. You can consider setting this option when dealing with communications between untrusted domains.
- **Allow Security Management Operations If Non-dynamic Changes Have Been Made** If you make a nondynamic change in the Console, certain security management operations are disabled until you restart the Admin Server—the security pages for those operations won't be available to you until you restart the server. You can make those security pages available by enabling this option.

Connection Filter Page

The Filter page under Security lets you configure connection filter settings for a domain. The section "Using Connection Filters," later in this chapter, explains WebLogic connection filtering. You can set the following attributes on the Filter page:

- **Connection Logger Enabled** Specifies whether the domain should log all accepted connections.
- **Connection Filter** Specifies the name of the Java class that implements a connection filter. A null value means that the domain won't use a connection filter for connections.
- **Connection Filter Rules** Specifies the connection rules for the filter in the Connection Filter Rules box. Use if you specified a connection filter. The format for the connection filter rules is *target localAddress localPort action protocols*.

Unlock Users

In order to protect the user accounts from attacks, the server uses several configuration options that limit things such as the maximum number of login attempts a user can make before the user account gets locked. You can alter the default configuration options by selecting Configuration | User Lockout on the Settings For Realm Name page. You can configure the following user lockout options:

- **Lockout Enabled** Specifies whether the server should lock out users after a set number of invalid login attempts.
- **Lockout Threshold** Sets the maximum number of failed login attempts before the server locks out a user. Once the server locks a user account, the administrator must unlock the user or the user must wait until after the end of the lockout duration before logging in again. The default lockout threshold is five failed login attempts.
- **Lockout Duration** Specifies the number of minutes a user account remains locked out (without the administrator manually intervening by unlocking the user). The default value is 30 minutes. If you don't want a locked user account to be automatically reenabled, set this option to 0.
- **Lockout Reset Duration** Specifies the duration (in minutes) within which multiple consecutive invalid login attempts cause the server to lock the user account.
- **Lockout Cache Size** Specifies the maximum number of invalid login records the server can cache. There's no default for this—the range is 0–99999 records.

- **Lockout GC Threshold** Specifies the maximum number of invalid login records the server stores in its memory. Once the server reaches this threshold, the server's garbage collection (GC) purges expired records. An invalid login record expires when the user account is either automatically or manually unlocked.

By default, the user lockout feature is enabled. Be careful not to turn off the user account security configuration options or make the settings too liberal, as that may increase the vulnerability of your user accounts. The Lockout Threshold configuration option sets the number of invalid login attempts a user can make before that account is locked out.

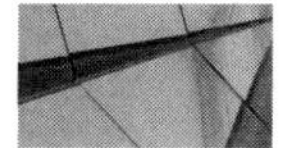

NOTE
If a user is locked out of the Administration Console, that user is not necessarily locked out of applications hosted by the Managed Servers. This also applies in reverse; a user locked out of a Managed Server may still be able to log into the Administration Console. The reason for this is that WebLogic Server manages user lockouts on a per-server basis.

By selecting Unlock Users on the Security page, you can unlock any user who has been locked out due to too many failed login attempts (that is, more login attempts than you've configured). If a user gets locked out of one server instance in a cluster, the user account is automatically locked on all nodes of a cluster. The user lockout attributes you configure apply to the entire security realm and thus to the default Authentication provider as well. If you're using a custom Authentication provider that manages user account locking on its own, you must disable the Lockout Enabled feature.

Once a user's account has been locked due to too many failed login attempts, use the following steps to unlock the user account:

1. Click Lock & Edit in the Change Center of the Administration Console.
2. Select Security | Unlock User.
3. Enter the name of the user account you want to unlock.
4. Click Save.

You can set the user lockout settings at the domain level by configuring the domain's default security realm. Go to the Summary Of Security Realms page and select the name of the security realm. In the Settings For Realm Name page, select Configuration | User Lockout to configure user locking attributes such as enabling user lockout after a set number of failed login attempts.

Protecting User Passwords

The *SerializedSystemIni.dat* file holds the private key used for hashing passwords and signing subjects. If this file is lost, the server cannot verify a password supplied by the user against those in the store. When a subject is created in WebLogic Server, it is "signed" so when two servers in the same domain communicate, they can be assured that the credentials used have not been modified. For example, when a servlet makes a call to an EJB on another server, the signed subject is sent over the wire. The subject is validated with information from the *SerializedSystemIni.dat* file. The need for cross-domain security comes about because the two domains do not share the same secret and cannot vouch for one another's subjects. In the old days, you could create both domains with the same secret and get the same effect. If this file is corrupted or removed by mistake, you have to reconfigure the domain. Therefore, you must protect the *SerializedSystemIni.dat* file by restricting permissions on this file and making frequent backups of it.

Embedded LDAP Server

The Embedded LDAP Server security page lets you configure the embedded LDAP server for a domain. The section "Configuring the Embedded LDAP Server," earlier in this chapter, explains how to configure the embedded LDAP server.

Roles

The Roles page enables you to create new domain-scoped security roles and edit the conditions of the roles. You can use these domain-scoped roles only within the security policies you create on the domain's Security | Policies page.

Policies

The Policies page lets you configure various security policy conditions that control access to various WebLogic resources. Here's the list of resources for which you can stipulate security policy conditions by clicking the appropriate tabs on this page:

- **User Lockout** Manage the user lockout policies from this page. The security policy conditions control access to the Domain Administrative User Lockout resource.
- **Configuration** Manage the configuration security of the domain. The security policies determine access to the Domain Administrative Configuration resource.
- **File Upload (and File Download)** Manage the domain's File Upload and File Download security policies. These policy conditions control access to the Domain Administrative File Upload (and File Download) resource.
- **View Log** Specify the domain's administrative view log policies on this page. The policy conditions control access to the Domain Administrative View Log resource.
- **Identity Assertion** Manage the domain's Identity Assertion security policy. The security policies control access to the Domain Administrative Identity Assertion resource.

Enabling Trust Between Domains

Sometimes a remote domain needs to interact with a local domain. You enable principals in one WebLogic domain to make calls in another domain by setting up trust between (or among) WebLogic domains. Previously, you could enable trust through something known as *global trust*, a feature that's still available in Oracle WebLogic Server 12*c*. When you set up global trust between two domains, you set up the same domain credential for two domains. Once you do this, principals from one domain are accepted as principals in the other domain. Global trust can lead to several problems, however, including authorization problems. In addition, logins to other domains aren't validated. Global trust is transitive, so if you establish global trust between domains A and B and between domains B and C, you're also establishing trust between domains A and C—obviously this could lead to potential problems. In a production setting especially, you must ensure that you have strong firewall protection or a dedicated communication channel to protect against man-in-the-middle attacks when you enable global trust.

Oracle recommends that you establish trust between two domains by enabling what is called *cross-domain security*. The WebLogic Credential Mapping security provider stores the credentials for the cross-domain users. JMS, JTA, MDB, and WAN replication can authenticate and relay the cross-domain credentials. You grant cross-domain users (users who need access to another domain) the *CrossDomainConnector* role and configure credential role mapping. The following discussion shows how to do this.

To configure cross-domain security, you must first enable it by going to Security | General and checking Cross Domain Security Enabled. You can also enter the names of domains for which you haven't enabled cross-domain security in the Excluded Domain Names field on the same page. The default group *CrossDomainConnectors* is assigned the default role *CrossDomainConnector*. You must create a user and add it to the *CrossDomainConnectors* group so the user can inherit the *CrossDomainConnector* security role.

After you enable cross-domain security and create the users with the *CrossDomainConnector* role, you must configure credential mapping for cross-domain security. Credential mapping specifies the credential the user must use in the remote domain that you want the local domain to trust.

Follow these steps to configure cross-domain security credential mapping:

1. In the left-hand panel of the Administration Console, click Security Realms.
2. Select Credential Mappings | Default.
3. Click New.
4. On the Creating The Remote Resource For The Security Credential Mapping page, select Use Cross-Domain Protocol.
5. Enter the name of the remote domain in the Remote Domain field. Click Next.
6. In the Create A New Security Credential Map Entry page, enter the following values:
   - **Local User** The cross-domain
   - **Remote User** The name of the user in the remote domain that you want to authorize for interactions with the local domain
   - **Password** The password for the remote user
7. Click Finish.

Using Connection Filters

Network connection filters allow you to control access to individual servers or an intranet. Connection filters work similar to the way firewalls work because you can configure them to control access based on IP address, protocol, and DNS names. Although the network is your primary protection against attackers, you can further tighten access to administrative resources such as the administration port by specifying that you can access the administration port only through specific servers inside the firewall. You can create custom connection filters or simply use the default connection filter provided by WebLogic Server, named *weblogic.security.net.ConnectionFilterImpl*. You can configure the default (or custom) connection filter by specifying connection filter rules in the Administration Console.

To specify connection filters through the Console, go to Domain | Security | Filter and select the Connection Logger Enabled check box to enable the logging of successful messages. In the Connection Filter field, specify either the default connection filter (*weblogic.security.net.ConnectionFilterImpl*) or, for a custom connection filter, the class that implements the connection filter. Make sure that you specify this class in the CLASSPATH for WebLogic Server. Finally, in the Connection Filter Rules field, specify the connection filter rules syntax.

Configuring SSL

SSL connectivity offers security through both authentication and encryption. You can have both one-way SSL and two-way SSL. In one-way SSL, the server presents a trusted security certificate to the client and the client authenticates the server. In two-way SSL, the server presents a certificate to the client and vice versa. Both the server and the client verify each other's identity. In addition to authentication, the data transmitted over the network is also encrypted. By default, WebLogic Server supports SSL on the default port 7002. Thus, if you want to connect to the Admin Server through the SSL listen port, you must use the HTTPS protocol, as in *https://localhost:7002*. Oracle recommends that you always use SSL in production environments.

Before you can establish either one-way or two-way SSL in a production environment, you must first configure identity and trust, which involves obtaining private key and digital certificates, as well as certificates of trusted certification authorities, and then create the identity and trust keystores (databases to save the keys and certificates—this could be a file in your file system) for storing the private keys and trusted certificates. A keystore helps secure and manage private keys and digital pairs (identity), as well as trusted CA certificates (trust). You can create a keystore and load private keys and trusted CA certificates at the same time when you're creating the keystore. You must then configure the keystores for WebLogic Server before you can set up one-way or two-way SSL.

In the following sections, let's review each of the steps involved in setting up SSL in a WebLogic Server environment.

Configuring Identity and Trust

To establish and verify server identity and trust, SSL uses private keys, digital certificates, and certificates issued by trusted certification authorities. A *certificate* is a digitally signed statement from an entity such as a company that states that the public key (or some other information) of another entity has a particular value. When the certificate is digitally signed, the signature is verified to check the integrity of the data in the certificate and authenticate it. *Integrity,* in this context, means that the data has not been tampered with, and *authenticity* means that the data came from whoever claimed to have created and signed it.

Two concepts—*identity* and *trust*—are at the heart of SSL connectivity. Here's what the two things mean:

- **Identity** SSL uses public key encryption, which requires both a public encryption key and a private key for a server. The public and private keys should correspond to each other. You can decrypt data encrypted with a public key only with a corresponding private key and vice versa. The public key is embedded in a digital certificate. The digital certificate also includes information related to the owner of the public key. Together, the private key and digital certificate pair (containing the public key) provide the identity for a server.
- **Trust** A well-known certificate authority (CA) such as VeriSign verifies the digital certificate and digitally signs it with the CA's digital certificate, thus establishing trust for the server's digital certificate.

Private keys have two formats: digital certificates and certificates from trusted CAs. The Distinguished Encoding Rules (DER) format can be used only for a single certificate, whereas a certificate in Privacy Enhanced Mail (PEM) format can be used for multiple certificates. The preferred format is PEM. The PEM format starts with a *BEGIN CERTIFICATE* line and ends with an *END CERTIFICATE* line. You can select from several formats for the keystores, but the preferred format is Java KeyStore (JKS).

If your company is acting as its own CA, you can use the trusted CA certificates with WebLogic Server, provided the CA certificates are in PEM format. If the trusted CA certificates are in other formats, you must convert them into PEM format before storing the certificates in the keystore.

Before you can configure SSL in a production environment, you must do four things:

1. Obtain private keys and digital certificates from a reputable CA such as VeriSign.
2. Create identity and trust keystores. WebLogic Server is configured with the following identity and trust keystores by default, but you should not use these keystores in a production environment:
   - ***DemoIdentity.jks*** This is the default identity keystore. It contains a demo private key for WebLogic Server and also establishes identity for WebLogic Server.
   - ***DemoTrust.jks*** This is the default trust keystore. It contains a list of CAs trusted by WebLogic Server and also establishes trust for WebLogic Server.

   In addition to the two default keystores, WebLogic Server also trusts the CA certificates in the JDK *cacerts* file. Both of the default keystrokes are located in the WL_HOME\server\lib directory. You don't have to configure these keystores for a test or development environment since they are ready for your use. You must configure separate identity and trust keystores for a production environment, however, because the digital certificates and CA certificates in the demo keystores are signed by a WebLogic demo CA and, therefore, will trust any other WebLogic Server using the demo keystores. Every person who downloads the WebLogic Server software from Oracle has the private keys for the demo digital certificates!

NOTE
Do not use the default demo keystores provided by WebLogic Server in a production environment.

3. Load the private keys and trusted CAs into the keystores you've configured.
4. Using the Administration Console, configure the identity and trust keystores.

The following sections describe how to perform each of these steps.

Obtaining Private Keys and Certificates

To configure SSL, the server needs the following keys and certificates to establish identity and trust:

- A private key
- A digital certificate with a public key that matches the private key
- A certificate from at least one trusted CA

You can obtain the private keys, digital certificates, and trusted CA certificates using the following sources:

- The *CertGen* utility for the demo and testing environment.
- The *keytool* utility.
- The demo key and certificates in the WL_HOME\server\lib directory. (The demo keys and certificates are generated with the *CertGen* utility.)

Using CertGen You must use *CertGen* to generate keys and digital certificates only in a development or testing environment. By default, the digital certificates you generate with *CertGen* contain the hostname of the server on which you generate the keys and certificates and not the fully qualified DNS name. If you use the demo digital certificate (*CertGenCA.der*) and the demo private key file (*CertGenCAKey.der*), you don't need to specify any CA files on the command line when using this tool. Here's an example that shows how to generate certificate and private key files using the *CertGen* utility:

```
C:\MyOra\Middleware\wlserver_10.3\server\bin>java utils.CertGen -
keyfilepass
mykeypass -certfile testcert -keyfile testkey
......  Will generate certificate signed by CA from CertGenCA.der file
......  With Domestic Key Strength
......  Common Name will have Hostname testkey
......
 Issuer CA name is CN=CertGenCAB,OU=FOR TESTING ONLY,O=MyOrganization,
L=MyTown,ST=MyState,C=US
C:\MyOra\Middleware\wlserver_10.3\server\bin>
```

In this example, the *CertGen* command did not specify any CA files on the command line and thus, by default, *CertGen* looks for the *CertGenCA.der* (CA root certificate) and the *CertGenCAKey.der* files in the WL_HOME directory.

You can use the demo public certificate and the demo private key created by the *CertGen* utility in a development environment. Because the *CertGen* utility uses the hostname and not the fully qualified DNS name in the common name (CN) field, SSL connections may fail due to hostname verification issues. To avoid these failures, you can disable hostname verification, as shown here:

```
Set JAVA_OPTIONS=%JVA_OPTIONS% -
Dweblogic.security.SSL.ignoreHostnameVerification=true
```

You should not use demo certificates in a production environment anyway, however, and that means you don't have to turn off hostname verification.

NOTE
Oracle recommends not turning off hostname verification in production environments.

Using Keytool *Keytool* is a key and certificate management utility that stores cryptographic keys and trusted certificates in a keystore. You can use this utility to administer your own public and private key pairs, as well as the associated certificates for self-authentication or data integrity and other authentication services using digital signatures. You can also use the utility to cache the public keys of communicating peers in the form of certificates and administer the secret keys used in symmetric encryption and decryption, such as the Data Encryption Standard (DES). *Keytool* handles X-509 certificates. You can use it to generate a private key, a self-signed digital certificate, and a Certificate Signing Request (CSR). You can submit a CSR to a CA to obtain a digital certificate and use it to update your self-signed digital certificate. You can also use *Keytool* to configure trust and identity in a production environment.

Keytool treats the keystore location you pass to it at the command line as a filename and converts it into a *FileInputStream* to load keystore information. You can view the various *Keytool* command-line options by typing **keytool** (or **keytool -help**) on the command line. Following are a couple of examples to illustrate the Keytool utility.

To create a keystore for managing your public and private key pairs and certificates, you can use the *-genkeypair* option. The option creates a keystore (if you don't have one already) and generates the key pair:

```
keytool -genkeypair -dname "cn=Sam Alapati, ou=marketing, o=mycompany,
c=US"
  -alias regional -keypass mykeypass -keystore C:\identity\mykeystore
  -storepass mystore999 -validity 180
```

Make sure you type any *Keytool* commands on a single line. The command shown here creates a keystore (if one doesn't exist already) named *mykeystore* in the C:\identity directory and assigns it a password. It generates a public and private key pair for the entity whose distinguished name (*dn*) has the common name (*cn*) of *Sam Alapati,* the organizational unit (*ou*) of *marketing,* the organization (*o*) of *mycompany,* and the two-letter country code (*c*) of *US.* By default, *Keytool* creates keys that are 1024 bits long, using the default Digital Signature Algorithm (DSA).

The command also creates a self-signed certificate that includes the published key and other relevant information pertaining to the distinguished name. The certificate will be valid for *180* days. The certificate is associated with the private key, with the password *mykeypass,* and the private key is stored in the *keystore* entry with the alias *regional.*

The *importcert* command, whose syntax is shown here, updates a self-signed digital certificate with a certificate signed by a trusted CA:

```
keytool -importcert -alias aliasforprivatekey
-file privatekeyfilename.pem
-keyfilepass privatekeypassword
-keystore keystorename -storepass keystorepassword
```

Note that, by default, *Keytool* uses DSA as the key-pair generation and signature algorithm. Since WebLogic Server 12*c* doesn't support DSA, you must specify a different algorithm.

Creating Keystores and Loading Keys and Certificates

For WebLogic Server to use the keys and certificates you create to verify identities, you must make the private keys, digital certificates, and trusted CA certificates accessible to the server. You do this by configuring identity and trust keystores for the server. Keystores provide secure storage and easy management of private keys and trusted CAs.

You can use a single keystore for both identity and trust, but Oracle recommends that you use two different keystores—an identity keystore and a trust keystore—because identity and trust have different security requirements. The identity component includes private key and digital certificate pairs, which are classified as sensitive data that you must protect against viewing and modification by unauthorized users. The security component contains only certificates and not private keys, so you configure a less stringent security model for it.

You can create a keystore with either the WebLogic *ImportPrivateKey* utility or the *Keytool* utility. Although both utilities let you create new keystores and load security data into them, the *Keytool* utility lets you generate new private keys and digital certificates and add them to a keystore (or create a keystore if one doesn't exist already). It doesn't allow you to import existing private keys into the keystore. *Keytool* does allow you to import trusted CA certificates from a file into a keystore, however.

The previous section showed how to create new private keys and add them to a new or existing keystore. Let's learn how to use the WebLogic *ImportPrivateKey* utility to create a new keystore and load private keys into it:

1. Generate a certificate file named *testcert* with the private key file named *testkey*:

```
C:\Oracle\Middleware\Oracle_Home\wlserver\server\bin>java
utils.CertGen -keyfilepass
mykeypass -certfile testcert -keyfile testkey
Generating a certificate with common name MIROPC61 and key strength
1024
issued by CA with certificate from
C:\MyOra\MIDDLE~1\WLSERV~1.3\server\lib\
CertGenCA.der file and key from
C:\MyOra\MIDDLE~1\WLSERV~1.3\server\lib\CertGenCAKey.der file
```

2. Convert the certificate file to the PEM format:

```
C:\MyOra\Middleware\wlserver_10.3\server\bin>java utils.der2pem
CertGenCA.der
```

3. Concatenate the *testcert* certificate you've generated with the root CA file:

```
C:\MyOra\Middleware\wlserver_10.3\server\bin>copy testcert.pem
CertGen.pem >>
newcerts1.pem
```

4. Create a new keystore named *mykeystore* and load the private key from the *testkey.pem* file:

```
C:\Oracle\\Middleware\Oracle_Home\wl_server\server\bin>java
utils.ImportPrivateKey
-keystore mykeystore -storepass mypasswd -keyfile mykey -keyfilepass
mykeyfilepass
-certfile newcerts1.pem -keyfile testkey.pem -alias passalias
No password was specified for the key entry
Key file password will be used
<Oct 26, 2013 1:52:51 PM EDT> <Info> <Security> <BEA-090906> <Changing
the default
Random Number Generator in RSA CryptoJ from ECDRBG to FIPS186PRNG. To
disable
this change, specify -Dweblogic.security.allowCryptoJDefaultPRNG=true>
...
C:\Oracle\\Middleware\Oracle_Home\wl_server\server\bin
```

The preceding command imports the private key *testkey.pem* and the certificate *newcerts1.pem* into the keystore you've created, *mykeystore*. Now you can configure this keystore in the Administration Console, as explained in the next section.

Configuring Identity and Trust Keystores

As mentioned earlier, you don't have to configure either the demo identity or the demo trust stores, but you must configure any identity and trust keystores you plan to use in a production environment. Once you configure the two keystores, you can configure SSL for the server. The server's SSL configuration attributes include information about the location of the identity and trust keystores, as you'll see in the next section "Setting SSL Configuration Attributes."

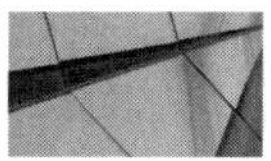

NOTE
When configuring SSL, the deprecated Files Or Keystore Providers option lets you specify either files or the WebLogic Keystore provider for backward compatibility.

You can configure the identity and trust keystores by completing the following steps in the Administration Console (note that you define properties for the identity and trust keystores in separate sections).

1. Click Lock & Edit in the Change Center of the Administration Console.
2. Go to Environment | Servers and select the name of the server.
3. Select Keystores from the Configuration page. Figure 9-8 shows the Configuration page for keystores.

   In the Keystores field, by default, you'll see the demo identity and trust keystores. You can change the server's keystores by clicking the Change button. You can select from the following four options:

   - **Demo Identity And Demo Trust** These are the two demo keystores for use in a development environment.
   - **Custom Identity And Java Standard Trust** Choose this option if you want the server to use a custom identity keystore for identity and use the trusted CAs defined in the *cacerts* file in the JAVA_HOME\jre\lib\security directory.
   - **Custom Identity And Custom Trust** Choose this option if you want the server to use custom identity and trust stores.
   - **Custom Identity And Command Line Trust** Choose this option if you want the server to use your custom keystore. You can specify the command-line argument to specify the trust keystore location.

4. In the Identity section, specify the attributes for the identity keystores you chose in the Keystores field. Of course, you need to specify these attributes only if you choose a Keystores option with Custom Identity in step 3. Here are the attributes you must specify here:

   - **Custom Identity Keystore** The full path to the custom identity keystore.
   - **Custom Identity Keystore Type** The default type is Java KeyStore (JKS), and you can retain this.
   - **Custom Identity Keystore PassPhrase** The passphrase for the keystore. (The passphrase for the Demo Identity Keystore is *DemoIdentityKeyStorePassPhrase*.) Because the passphrase is exposed as plaintext and retained in the Java memory until garbage collection, you should use *CustomIdentityKeyStorePassPhraseEncrypted* instead.

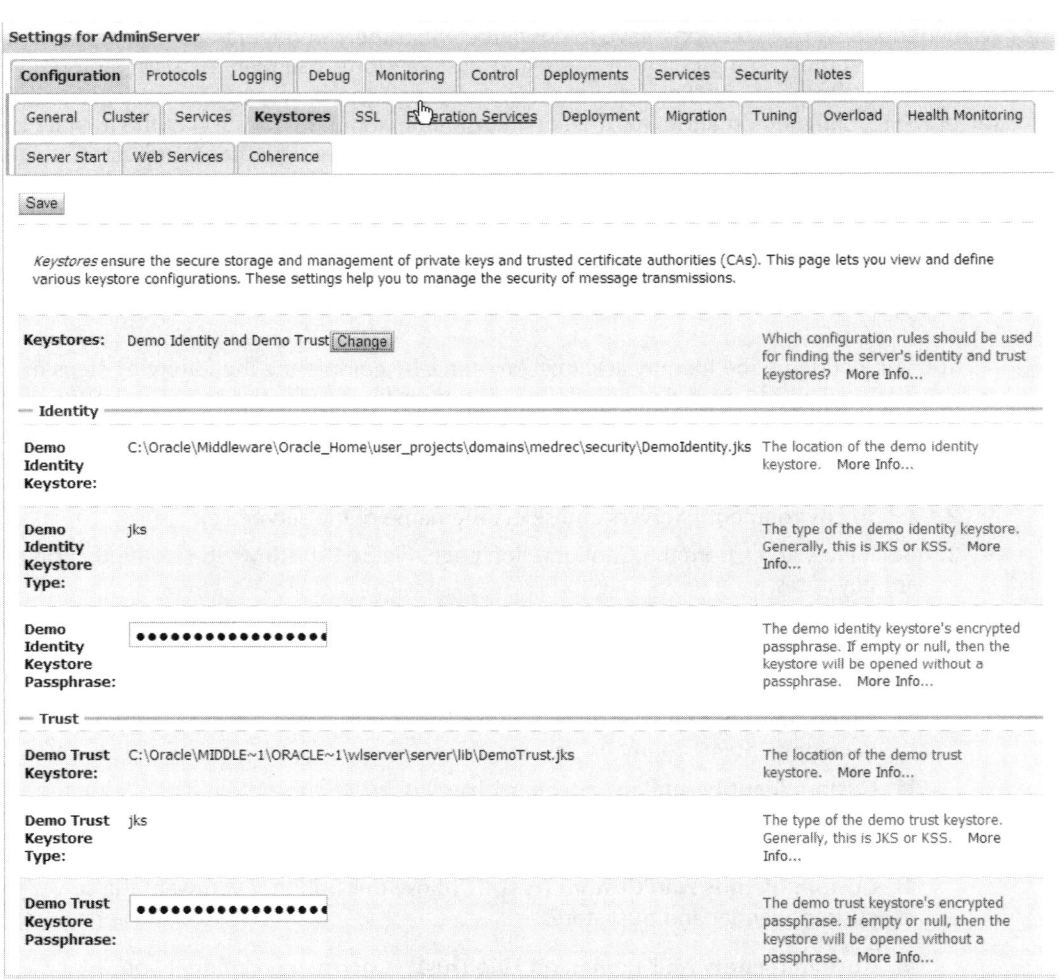

FIGURE 9-8. *Configuring the Identity and Trust keystores*

5. Define properties for the trust keystore in the Trust section.

   If you choose Java Standard Trust as your keystore, you must specify the password you specified when creating the keystore. If you choose Custom Trust, you must supply the path, keystore type (Java KeyStore, or jks for short), and the keystore passphrase, just as you did for the identity keystore.

6. Click Save and then click Activate Changes in the Change Center.

Setting SSL Configuration Attributes

When you enable the administration port for a domain, you must configure SSL for all servers in the domain since the port uses SSL. Because all servers in a domain must enable or disable the administration port at the same time, you must configure the default administration port settings at the domain level. Once you configure the administration port, a command to start any Managed Server in the domain must specify a secure communication protocol such as HTTPS, as well as the administration port, for example:

```
-
Dweblogic.management.server=https://<admin_server>:<administration_port>
```

NOTE

You can find a complete working SSL authentication example in the WL_HOME\samples\server\examples\src\examples\security\sslclient directory. In this directory, you'll find examples that demonstrate how to make an outbound SSL connection and two-way SSL connections from a WebLogic Server that is acting as a client to another WebLogic Server or a different application server.

In the following example, the specification of the SSL attribute *-Dweblogic.security.TrustKeyStore=DemoTrust* makes the server trust the demo CA certificates in the demo trust keystore (located in the *DemoTrust.jks* file in the *WL_HOME\server\lib* directory):

```
C:\Oracle\Middleware\Oracle_Home\user_projects\domains\wl_server>java
-Dweblogic.security.TrustKeyStore=DemoTrust weblogic.Deployer -
adminurl
t3s://localhost:9002
-username weblogic -password welcome1 -name testApp1 -distribute -
targets
MyCluster1
```

The Admin Server for this domain is using the demo identity and certificates in this case. In a production environment, however, you must specify the following pair of SSL arguments instead:

```
-Dweblogic.security.CustomTrustKeyStoreFileName=filename
-Dweblogic.security.TrustKeystoreType=jks
```

In a development environment, once you enable SSL for the domain, the domain uses the two default keystores for looking up the keys and certificates. As the previous section of this chapter explained, in a production environment, you must generate digital certificates, private keys, and trusted CA certificates using the *CertGen* or *Keytool* utility or by acquiring them from a trusted vendor such as VeriSign or Entrust. Following this, you must create custom identity and trust keystores and load the keys and certificates in the two keystores. Once you complete the configuration of the two keystores, you're ready to set SSL configuration attributes for the domain through the Administration Console. As you'll learn, the procedures for configuring one-way and two-way SSL are very similar.

To set SSL configuration attributes through the Administration Console, go to Environment | Servers and select the server for which you want to configure SSL properties. Note that you must configure SSL properties at the server level, so you must do this for each server instance. On the Configuration page, select SSL. Figure 9-9 shows the SSL settings page. You can then configure the following SSL attributes on this page:

- **Identity And Trust Locations** Retrieves the server's identity (private key and certificate) and trust (trusted CA) from the identity and keystores you configured earlier. You must set the value to Keystores to make this happen. The Files Or Keystores option is deprecated. WebLogic Server domains from version 8.1 on default to Keystores.

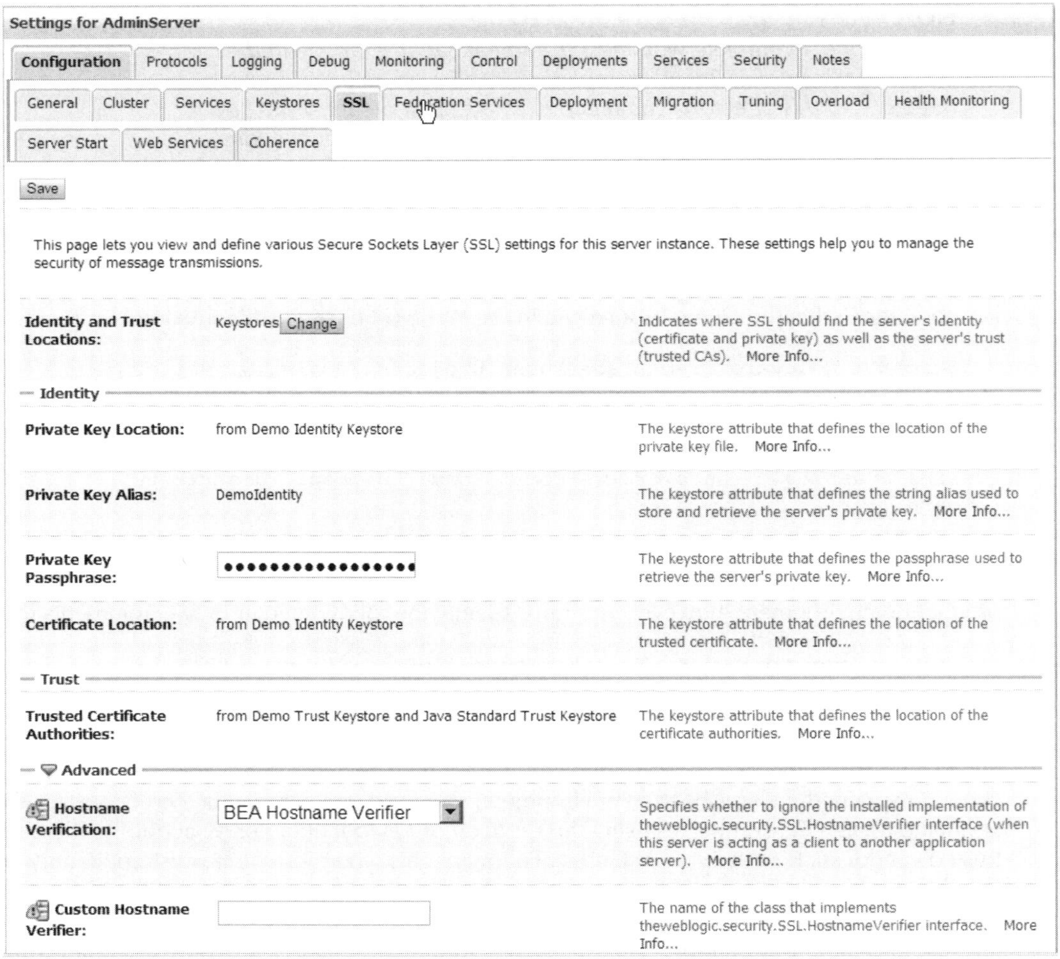

FIGURE 9-9. *Configuring SSL attributes*

- **Private Key Location** Defines the private key file location.
- **Private Key Alias** Defines the alias for the server's private key. (The default value is *DemoIdentity*.)
- **Private Key Passphrase** Specifies the passphrase for retrieving the server's private key.
- **Certificate Location** Specifies the keystore attribute that has the location of the trusted certificate. (The default value is *Demo Identity Keystore*.)
- **Trusted Certificate Authorities** Defines the location of the certificate authorities. (The default value is *Demo Trust Keystore And Java Standard Trust Keystore*.)

You can also set several advanced configuration attributes in this section, including whether you want to enable two-way SSL:

- **Hostname Verification** Hostname verification ensures that both the hostname in the client URL and the hostname sent back by the server in the digital certificate match. By default, hostname verification is enabled, and Oracle recommends enabling this in a production environment to prevent man-in-the-middle attacks.
- **Custom Hostname Verifier** You can specify a custom hostname identifier if you have one—this is the name of the class that implements the *weblogic.security.SSL.HostnameVerifier* interface.
- **Export Key Lifespan** Here, you can specify the number of times the server can use an exportable key between a server and an exportable client. The default value is 500—you can lower this if you want to force the server to generate a new key more often to make the key more secure.
- **Use Server Certs** This option determines whether clients should use the server certificates and key as the client's identity when connecting through HTTPS.
- **Two Way Client Cert Behavior** This attribute has three possible values:
  - **Client Certs Not Requested** This default value, which implies one-way SSL.
  - **Client Certs Requested But Not Enforced** This value implies two-way SSL, without requiring clients to present a certificate.
  - **Client Certs Requested And Enforced** This value also implies two-way SSL, but clients must present a certificate. If the client fails to present a certificate, the server terminates the client's SSL connection request.
- **Cert Authenticator** You can ignore this attribute, as this is a deprecated field meant for compatibility security only.
- **SSL Rejection Logging Enabled** This attribute specifies whether the server should log warning messages in its log when SSL connections are rejected. By default, SSL rejection logging is enabled.
- **Allow Unencrypted Null Cipher** This attribute tests to see if *AllowUnEncryptedNullCipher* is enabled. A *cipher suite* is an SSL encryption method that consists of the algorithms for key exchange, symmetric encryption, and secure hashing. An SSL client with incorrect SSL configuration can potentially specify a cipher suite with null ciphers, which means the data is transmitted in clear text over the network, defeating the purpose of setting up SSL. By default, this control is unset, meaning null ciphers are

disallowed on this server. The SSL handshake fails when an SSL client wants to use the null cipher suite.

CAUTION
Don't allow unencrypted null ciphers.

- **Inbound Certificate Validation** If you're using two-way SSL, this property allows you to set client validation rules for inbound SSL. The two values are Builtin SSL Validation Only and Builtin SSL Validation And Cert Path Validators.
- **Outbound Certificate Validation** This attribute works the same as the previous attribute, but for outbound connections.

Once you configure any SSL attributes, the corresponding SSL server or the channel server restarts with the new configuration settings, but existing server connections continue to run with the previous SSL configuration. If you want all SSL connections to follow the new SSL configuration, you must reboot the server. When you make any changes to the keystore files, you must restart the SSL listen sockets so keystore changes will take effect. You can do this by going to Environment | Servers | Control and clicking the Restart SSL button after selecting the server from the Server Status table.

You can test the SSL configuration by accessing the Administration Console at https://*<server_name>*:*<server_port/console>*. If you can successfully log into the console, you've configured SSL correctly.

By default, WebLogic Server rejects digital certificates that don't have the CA's Basic Constraint extension. That is, by default, the server uses the following setting when starting: *-Dweblogic.security.SSL.enforceConstraints=true*. Don't set this option to *false* because it will disable the strict enforcement of security constraints on digital certificates by the server.

You can view the current SSL configuration option values through WLST, as shown in the following example:

```
C:\Oracle\Middleware\Oracle_Home\wlserver\common\bin>wlst
wls:/offline> connect()
wls:/wl_server/serverConfig> cd('Servers')
wls:/wl_server/serverConfig/Servers> cd('examplesServer')
wls:/wl_server/serverConfig/Servers/examplesServer>
wls:/wl_server/serverConfig/Servers/examplesServer> cd('SSL')
wls:/wl_server/serverConfig/Servers/examplesServer/SSL>
cd('examplesServer')
wls:/wl_server/serverConfig/Servers/examplesServer/SSL/examplesServer>
ls()
wls:/wl_server/serverConfig/Servers/examplesServer/SSL/examplesServer>
ls()

-r--   AllowUnencryptedNullCipher                    false
-r--   CertAuthenticator                             null
-r--   Ciphersuites                                  null
-r--   ClientCertificateEnforced                     false
-r--   Enabled                                       true
-r--   ExportKeyLifespan                             500
```

```
-r--   HostnameVerificationIgnored                       false
-r--   HostnameVerifier                                  null
-r--   IdentityAndTrustLocations                         KeyStores
-r--   InboundCertificateValidation
BuiltinSSLValidationOnly
-r--   JSSEEnabled                                       false
-r--   ListenPort                                        7002
-r--   LoginTimeoutMillis                                25000
-r--   Name                                              examplesServer
-r--   Notes                                             null
-r--   OutboundCertificateValidation
BuiltinSSLValidationOnly
-r--   PeerValidationEnforced                            0
-r--   SSLRejectionLoggingEnabled                        true
-r--   ServerCertificateChainFileName                    server-
certchain.pem
-r--   ServerCertificateFileName                         server-cert.der
-r--   ServerKeyFileName                                 server-key.der
-r--   ServerPrivateKeyAlias                             null
-r--   ServerPrivateKeyPassPhrase                        ******
-r--   ServerPrivateKeyPassPhraseEncrypted               ******
-r--   TrustedCAFileName                                 trusted-ca.pem
-r--   TwoWaySSLEnabled                                  false
-r--   Type                                              SSL
-r--   UseServerCerts                                    false
-r-x   freezeCurrentValue                                Void :
String(attributeName)
-r-x   isSet                                             Boolean :
String(propertyName)
-r-x   unSet                                             Void :
String(propertyName)

wls:/wl_server/serverConfig/Servers/examplesServer/SSL/examplesServer>
```

You configure hostname verification to ensure that the hostname in the client URL matches the hostname in the digital certificate sent back by the server during an SSL connection. If the hostname in the certificate matches the local machine's hostname, the verification of hostnames will pass if the URL specifies the default IP address of the local machine—*localhost* or *127.0.0.1*.

Hostname verification is performed when a WebLogic Server instance acts as an SSL client. By default, hostname verification is enabled for WebLogic Server (with production mode enabled), and Oracle recommends leaving verification on in a production server. You can confirm whether hostname verification is enabled by verifying that the Hostname Verification field is set to BEA Hostname Verifier in the Advanced configuration options on the SSL configuration page (explained earlier in this section). If you don't want to use the default verifier, you can configure a custom hostname verifier.

Note that for some of the SSL configuration options, a "secure value" is configured. For example, for the Cert Authenticator option, the secure value is *weblogic.security.acl.CertAuthenticator*. This class maps the digital certificate of a client to a WebLogic Server user. Similarly, for the Custom Hostname Verifier property, the *weblogic.security.SSL.HostnameVerifier* class verifies whether the server should allow a connection to the host with the hostname from the URL. You can use JMX or the WLST *man* command to view the secure values for a configuration option, as shown here:

```
wls:/wl_server/serverConfig/Servers/examplesServer/SSL/examplesServer>
man('HostnameVerifier')
com.bea.defaultValueNull : true
com.bea.description : <p>The name of the class that implements the
<code>weblogic.security.SSL.HostnameVerifier</code> interface.</p>
<p>This class
verifies whether the connection to the host with the hostname from URL
should be
allowed. The class is used to prevent man-in-the-middle attacks.
The <code>weblogic.security.SSL.HostnameVerifier</code> has a
<code>verify()</code> method that WebLogic Server calls on the client
during the
SSL handshake.</p>
com.bea.dynamic : false
com.bea.secureValue : weblogic.security.SSL.HostnameVerifier
descriptorType : Attribute
displayName : HostnameVerifier
Name : HostnameVerifier
wls:/wl_server/serverConfig/Servers/examplesServer/SSL/examplesServer>
```

Using the weblogic.management.username and weblogic.management.password

Oracle has deprecated the bootname and password system properties *weblogic.management.username* and *weblogic.management.password* in the WebLogic Server 12.1.1 release. In future releases, you won't be able to use these credentials to start WebLogic Server in production mode.

Oracle recommends that instead of using these credentials, you use the *boot.properties* file to specify the boot username and password for WebLogic Server. In a development mode domain, the Configuration Wizard creates a boot identity file (*boot.properties*) in the security directory of the Administration Server's root directory. The boot identity file contains an encrypted version of the username and password. In production domains, the server prompts you to enter user credentials on the command line when booting the server.

Following is a summary of how WebLogic Server uses a boot identity file during startup.

- By default, it looks for the *boot.properties* file in the server's security directory, and if there's a *boot.properties* file there, it uses it.
- You can specify a different location for the *boot.properties* file by specifying the following argument in the startup command:

  ```
  -Dweblogic.system.BootIdentityFile=filename
  ```

  You can specify this argument in the *startWebLogic* script by adding the argument *Dweblogic.system.BootIdentityFile* as a value of the *JAVA_OPTIONS* variable. For example:

  ```
  set JAVA_OPTIONS=-
  Dweblogic.system.BootIdentityFile=C:\Oracle\user_domains\mydomain\myid
  entity.prop
  ```

- You can include the following options in the *weblogic.Server* startup command if you don't want the server to use a boot identity file during startup:

  ```
  -Dweblogic.management.username=username
  -Dweblogic.management.password=password
  ```

  When you add these options, the server ignores the boot identity file.

  Since the previous method means that you store unencrypted passwords in a startup script, Oracle recommends that you use it only when invoking *weblogic.Server* from the command line.

- If the server is unable to access the boot identify file during startup, it displays the username and prompts the user for the password and also writes a message to the log file.

Oracle WebLogic Security Best Practices

Oracle provides several WebLogic Server security best practices. Many of these are somewhat obvious, such as using firewalls, applying the latest security patches, separating development from production environments, and not using unencrypted passwords on the command line. A few key recommendations deserve a close look, however, and this section highlights several of them.

Use Multiple Administrative Users

In a production environment, create an additional system user in addition to the default administrative user created during domain creation. This way, when the first administrative user can't log in for some reason such as a user lockout or a dictionary or brute-force attack, for example, you can still administer the domain by logging in as the alternative system administrator.

Control Access to WebLogic Resources

On each WebLogic host computer, create a special operating system user account to run WebLogic Server–related commands. You must grant strict privileges on the server to this OS user and limit the user's access privileges to the middleware Home directory (the default is Oracle\Middleware), the WebLogic Server installation directory (the default is Oracle\Middleware\wlserver_10.3), and the WebLogic domain directories (for example, Oracle\Middleware\user_project\domains\mydomain). You must also protect sensitive data stored in files such as the JMS SAF files by restricting both read and write access to the files.

Avoid Running the Server Under a Privileged Account

You must not run WebLogic Server as a privileged user. Because UNIX systems don't allow nonprivileged users (users other than root) to bind to ports with a value less than 1025, you must use a strategy to bypass the restriction. However, it's not a good idea to let long-running processes such as those belonging to WebLogic Server run with unnecessary privileges. If you need access to a port lower than 1025, such as port 80, for example, start the server instance as a privileged user, but once the instance binds to the privileged port, change the user ID to a nonprivileged user account. You can start the Node Manager only as a privileged user (root in UNIX systems); therefore, you must configure the Node Manager to accept requests only on a secure port, from a single known host.

You can set the *weblogic.system.enableSetUID* and, optionally, the *weblogic.system.enableSetGID* property to *true* to enable WebLogic Server to switch to a nonprivileged UNIX user account after binding to port 80 as root. The properties *weblogic.system.nonPrivUser* and *weblogic.system.nonPrivGroup* identify the nonprivileged user account and group name under which WebLogic Server will run. You can also switch to the UNIX account "nobody," which is a nonprivileged user present in most systems, or create a special account for running WebLogic Server. Just make sure that the nonprivileged user you create has the necessary permissions to access the WebLogic classes and other files such as log files.

Enable Security Auditing

Oracle recommends that you enable audit logging to trace unsuccessful login attempts as well as file access policy violations. Make sure you've allocated sufficient space for the audit log, which could get pretty large in some circumstances.

Use Connection Filters

Oracle recommends using connection filters in addition to network firewalls. Connection filters act as an additional way to restrict network traffic on the basic protocols and IP addresses. Connection filters are especially helpful when servers in a domain don't have to pass through a network to access other servers in that domain.

Prevent Denial of Service Attacks

To reduce the possibility of denial of service (DoS) attacks, Oracle recommends that you configure the "message timeout" parameter for the server. By default, the server waits for 60 seconds to receive the complete message—the timeout duration is set to a high level to accommodate slow connections. You must lower the message timeout parameter to the lowest possible setting.

Another best practice to prevent DoS attacks is to restrict the size of the message (the default is 10MB) and the message timeout (the default is 480 seconds) on external channels. You can also limit the number of sockets allowed for a server by setting the Maximum Open Sockets option on the server configuration page.

Implement Security for Applications

The following is a summary of some of the best practices that concern application security.

Set the FrontEndHost Attribute

Because it's possible to spoof the host header, set the *FrontEndHost* attribute on the *WebServerMBean* or the *ClusterMBean*. When a request on a web application is redirected to an alternate location, the server uses the host you specify through the *FrontEndHost* attribute instead of accepting the hostname contained in the original request.

Use JSP Comment Tags

If comments in JSP files contain sensitive data, use the JSP syntax for comments instead of HTML syntax, as the JSP style comments disappear after the JSP is compiled.

Use Precompiled JSPs

Consider precompiling JSPs and installing them on the server instead of installing the source code, which opens a security hole. Precompiling JSPs also helps you spot compile-time errors before you deploy the JSPs. Using precompiled JSPs reduces the deployment time. To precompile the JSP files, enable the *precompile* parameter in *weblogic.jar*. You must set *pageCheckSeconds* to –1 to disable run-time page check and recompilation. You can precompile JSPs and EJBs before their deployment by using *weblogic.appc* (*wlappc*), as shown in this example:

```
java weblogic.appc JSP_Example.war
```

Precompiling the JSPs using *weblogic.appc*, placing them in the WEB-INF\classes folder, and archiving them in a *.war* file will help prevent the recompilation of the JSPs during server reboots.

By default, JSPs aren't precompiled. You can turn precompilation on by specifying it in the *weblogic.xml* deployment descriptor, as shown here:

```
<?xml version="1.0" encoding="UTF-8"?>
<wls:weblogic-web-app>
...
<wls:weblogic-version>10.3</wls:weblogic-version>
    <wls:context-root>JSP_Precompilation</wls:context-root>
    <wls:jsp-descriptor>
        <wls:precompile>true</wls:precompile>
        <wls:precompile-continue>true</wls:precompile-continue>
    </wls:jsp-descriptor>
</wls:weblogic-web-app>
```

Setting the *precompile* option to *true* in the *<jsp-descriptor>* element of *weblogic.xml,* as shown here, precompiles all of your JSPs when you deploy or redeploy a web application, or when the server reboots. One other way to ensure that JSPs stay precompiled and keep the server from recompiling them is to use the *JSPClassServlet* instead of the *JSPServlet*. You must also place the precompiled JSPs in the WEB-INF\classes directory to keep them from being recompiled by the server. This way, you remove all JSP source code from the application after the recompilation. The following example shows how to add the *JSPClassServlet* to the *web.xml* file of the web application:

```
<servlet>
    <servlet-name>JSPClassServlet</servlet-name>
    <servlet-class>weblogic.servlet.JSPClassServlet</servlet-class>
</servlet>
<servlet-mapping>
    <servlet-name>JSPClassServlet</servlet-name>
    <url-pattern>*.jsp</url-pattern>
</servlet-mapping>
```

Use HTML Entity or Character References

To avoid the well-known cross-site scripting attacks, scan user data for HTML special characters and replace any HTML security characters with their HTML entity or character references to prevent the browser from executing malicious user-supplied data as HTML code.

Perform JMS Authorization Checks

You must perform an authorization check for all actions performed on a JMS resource by setting the *weblogic.jms.securityCheckInterval* to 0.

Summary

This chapter provided an introduction to various aspects of WebLogic Server security. You learned how to configure the default security realm and how to export security data to a realm. The chapter discussed the role played by security providers and showed you how to configure the Authentication and Auditing security providers. You also learned how to configure SSL in your environment. Finally, the chapter reviewed several key Oracle security best practice recommendations for WebLogic Server.

CHAPTER 10

WebLogic Server Performance Tuning

WebLogic Server performance tuning ranges over an extremely broad area and includes the tuning of the operating system, the JVM, the WebLogic Server instances, databases, transactions, and JMS. It also includes tuning the web applications and web services that WebLogic Server hosts. This chapter is by no means a thorough and complete discussion of the various elements that affect WebLogic Server performance. Topics such as database tuning, operating system tuning, and network configuration are best left to the specialists in that area. The goal of this chapter is to provide a brief summary of the key areas a WebLogic Server administrator should focus on to achieve and maintain high levels of application performance.

This chapter covers the key configuration aspects of WebLogic Server that affect application performance, such as thread management and various aspects of network I/O tuning. Tuning the JVM is a big part of tuning WebLogic Server performance. The chapter explains how the JVM manages memory and how you can tune garbage collection and the compacting of the Java heap to ensure optimal performance. Tuning the JMS container, JMS store-and-forward, and the WebLogic message bridge is critical when dealing with messaging applications. This chapter discusses several ways to tune messaging, such as dealing with large message backlogs, defining quotas, and blocking message senders when quota thresholds are reached. It also shows how to control the flow of messages to JMS servers and destinations. The chapter also reviews key Oracle recommendations for optimizing the performance of JDBC data sources and transactions.

Tuning SQL performance is often a key to improving server performance and the chapter offers several guidelines for improving the performance of SQL statements. You'll also learn about how Oracle's TopLink implements JPA, which is the current standard persistence mechanism for Java EE and SE. The chapter introduces Oracle Coherence, which is a core component of Oracle WebLogic Server that provides a distributed data grid solution to enable the scalability of mission-critical applications.

Tuning WebLogic Server

Two critical areas that relate to the tuning of WebLogic Server are thread management and the tuning of the network communications between clients and servers. The following sections offer a brief explanation of these two tuning areas.

Thread Management

In previous releases of WebLogic Server, the server had a much more static notion of thread scheduling than in Oracle WebLogic Server 11*c* and 12*c*. Previous versions required the user to define separate pools of threads that were defined when the server was configured. Tuning the correct sizes of these thread pools was a time-consuming matter of trial and error. In WebLogic Server releases 9.0 and above, there was only a single, dynamically sized pool of threads. The "self-tuning" Work Manager from the 11*g* release has greatly simplified the effort that it takes to get to the proper number of threads. In certain cases, it may be necessary to configure Work Managers and provide the system with additional hints so that it can achieve optimal results. The general rule is to start with no specific tuning and then configure Work Managers only to address specific problems that might arise. Aggressively configuring Work Managers for a specific environment can end up hurting performance when your application, workload, or underlying system changes.

There are a few common use cases for which Work Manager configuration is indicated:

- If your application is heavily bound by the database and is spending little time in rendering, then you will likely want to create a constraint that is bound to the JDBC connection pool.
- In cases where you have a mixed workload that includes high-priority response time sensitive work alongside batch or queued messaging work, it is often helpful to use "response time" request classes to guarantee responsiveness or "fair share" request classes to lower the priority of background work.
- If your code is using a shared resource other than a connection pool for which you know there is a hard limit, then you can consider using a *MaxThreadsConstraint* to avoid overscheduling.

Tuning the Network I/O

You can configure several things to speed up the network communications between clients and servers. Following are the key network I/O–related aspects that you can configure.

Tuning the Muxers

As you learned in Chapter 1, muxers read incoming requests on a server. There are two types of muxers: native muxers and Java muxers. WebLogic Server recommends using the native muxer, which is the default muxer type. You can configure the server to use native muxers by going to Environment | Servers | Configuration | Tuning and selecting the Enable Native IO check box.

If you're using native muxers, you do not need to configure the number of socket readers—the server takes care of that for you. If you happen to select Java muxers, you can configure the number of socket readers for an instance by going to Configuration | Tuning and changing the Socket Readers setting. The Socket Readers setting determines the percentage of execute threads the server can use as socket readers. The default value is 33 percent, and you can go as high as 50 percent. Note that changing the percentage of execute threads is useful only with the Java socket muxer and is really only for use when tuning for Java clients.

In general, the server will determine the correct type of muxer to use and will use the native muxers by default without your having to make any specific tuning changes. A newer type of muxer implementation that uses the standard *java.nio* package definitely offers better performance on Linux, and you can specify the NIO socket muxer on the command line as follows:

```
-Dweblogic.MuxerClass=weblogic.socket.NIOSocketMuxer
```

The only other option that is generally used is to set explicitly the number of socket readers using the following command-line option:

```
-Dweblogic.SocketReaders=<N>
```

where *N* refers to the number of socket readers. The main reason to do this is that in some releases the number of readers is set, by default, to the number of CPUs available on the system. On some types of hardware, this results in as many as 128 reader threads, which is not so good. In most cases, 3 or 4 reader threads are plenty to get the job done. In some circumstances, not having enough readers will result in work not being read from the sockets quickly enough for the server to process. You must approach all changes with caution and well document the changes you make.

Using Multiple Network Channels

WebLogic RMI is designed such that when a single client JVM makes multiple connections to a single WebLogic Server, all of the requests are carried over a single socket. Although this is generally optimal, there are cases where each thread of a multithreaded client can issue large requests that can cause that socket to become a bottleneck. You can work around such a network bottleneck by configuring multiple custom channels and allowing the multithreaded client to communicate over multiple connections. In order to do this, you must first create multiple custom network channels. You can then configure the client to use multiple network channels by using the JNDI URL pattern that points to multiple network channels. For example:

```
t3://<ip1>:<port1>,<ip2>:<port2>
```

On many multicore systems, multiple network interfaces are also available. In such cases, it is common practice to configure each server to listen on a particular network device and, on NUMA-capable systems, to bind each server to a particular socket in order to minimize context switches.

Tuning the Chunk Parameters

Both the server and client network layers use memory allocated in chunks to read and write data. The server maintains a *chunk pool* to minimize the cost of allocating the memory chunks. The default chunk size is 4KB, and if requests in your application handle large amounts of data, you can increase the value of the chunk size parameter on both the server and the client. Following are the properties you can configure to control the chunk size and the chunk pool size:

- ***weblogic.Chunksize*** If request sizes are large, you can increase the value of this attribute. You must set this attribute to the same size on the server and the client.
- ***weblogic.utils.io.chunkpoolsize*** You can increase the size of the chunk pool with this attribute (the default value is 2048 bytes).
- ***weblogic.PartitionSize*** By default, the server uses four pool partitions. The more partitions there are, the less lock contention there is for those partitions.

The use of memory chunks in WebLogic Server is designed to give the server a cushion that minimizes garbage collection when bursts of network traffic occur. The buffers that are used read incoming requests and are kept in a pool to generate responses. Changing these parameters can be tricky, and the only way to know that you have the right values is to have a reliable benchmark for your application that can help you gauge the impact. Of the three options, the one that is most likely to be useful is the partition size attribute (*weblogic.PartitionSize*). In more recent releases, the number of pools is determined by the number of processors on the machine. This generally eliminates most possibilities for contention, making it less likely you will need to configure the number of pools. The server uses an overflow pool, which takes the form of soft references that can sometimes impact garbage collection. If you see issues in this area, sometimes it can be helpful to increase the pool size. Soft references allow an application to tell the garbage collector that certain objects should be kept around unless memory gets too tight. The garbage collector collects the softly reachable objects only when it really needs the additional memory. The JVM throws an *OutOfMemory* error only after it clears all soft references.

Tuning Connection Backlog Buffering

The server uses a Transmission Control Protocol (TCP) wait queue that holds the connection requests received by the TCP stack as they await acceptance by the server. You can control the number of TCP connections that can be buffered in the wait queue by setting the Accept Backlog parameter. Once the server accepts the number of connection requests you specify with this parameter, it stops accepting further connections. If the client connections are dropped or refused without corresponding error messages on the server, it means this parameter's value is set too low. If you're getting "connection refused" errors when trying to access the server, increase the value of this parameter from its default by about 25 percent. Continue raising it by the same amount (by 25 percent each time) until the messages disappear. You can configure the Accept Backlog parameter from the server's Configuration | Tuning tab.

Tuning the JVM

The JVM executes the byte codes in Java class files, so tuning the JVM significantly affects the performance of applications you deploy on a server. Oracle recommends that, on a Windows or Linux platform, you use the Sun JDK with the HotSpot Client JVM for development work and the Oracle JRockit JDK for production use, owing to its superior performance. You can switch to a different JVM by simply specifying different values for the *JAVA_HOME* and *JAVA_VENDOR* variables and restarting the server. The *JAVA_HOME* variable points to the top directory of the JDK you want to use. You set the *JAVA_VENDOR* variable to the value *Oracle* if you're using the JRockit JDK and to *Sun* if you're using the Sun JDK. In the following sections, you'll learn how you can tune the JRockit JVM.

It's important to understand that most of the JVMs have really good mechanisms for figuring out the best strategies for managing the heap. You should never really try to proactively tune garbage collection. That is to say you should try to explicitly configure the heap only when you're trying to correct a problem you've identified through analysis with a tool such as JRockit Mission Control (JRMC). In such cases, the main options you should tune are the minimum and maximum heap sizes.

Understanding Memory Management

Java objects live in an area called the *heap*. The heap is not the same as the memory used by the JVM—in addition to the heap, the server uses memory for Java methods, thread stacks, and JVM internal data structures. This is why the virtual size of the process reported by the operating system is different from the number you get when you ask the JVM how much heap it is using. The JVM creates the heap when it starts, and the heap size varies while applications are running. Applications written in Java are less prone to memory leaks because they rely on the JVM to manage their memory for them. When Java developers write their programs, they do not explicitly free the memory; instead, they simply stop using it and the JVM is smart enough to detect this. Garbage collection is the process of making room for the allocation of new objects to the heap by removing unused objects from the heap. The server performs garbage collection periodically to remove the unused objects. Without garbage collection, all of the server's memory will be used up and the JVM won't be able to allocate memory to new objects. The problem with Java is that it can even move around the locations of objects the program is referencing. To do this, it "pauses" the application for brief periods. Different applications may benefit from different approaches to garbage collection, emphasizing either short pauses that spread out the work or long pauses that just get it all done in one shot. Each JVM has its own set of garbage collection schemes, and once you understand the nature of your application's workload, in some cases, you'll find it helpful to configure garbage collection to suit your needs.

In all modern JVMs, the heap is generally divided into multiple areas, also called *generations*. Garbage collection strategies that use generations are called *generational garbage collection strategies*. Because most objects are short lived and can thus be removed by garbage collection soon after their allocation, splitting the heap into generations improves performance. The first generation is called the *nursery* or *young space,* and the second generation is simply called the *old space*. The nursery part of the heap is for new objects, and when it gets full, a special garbage collection called a *young collection* will promote the new objects to the old space. This is the moving around of objects that I mentioned earlier. The basic idea is that once an object gets old, it is likely to continue to stick around and, therefore, you don't have to check on it quite as often. This type of garbage collection is designed to make room for new objects in the nursery. There is also a garbage collection process called an *old collection*. Note that a young collection is much faster than an old collection and is also faster than garbage collection in a heap that isn't split into two areas. The JVM uses a *keep area* to store the most recently allocated objects in the nursery. This keep area does not become part of the garbage collection until the next young collection.

The JRockit JVM distinguishes between small and large objects. Generally, a small object is between 2KB and 128KB. The JVM handles the object allocation differently for small and large objects. Java threads are granted an exclusive *thread local area (TLA),* a chunk of reserved area in the heap. TLAs are part of the nursery if there is one. The benefit of the TLA is that for very short-lived objects there is no contention for allocating them from the heap, especially if they don't escape the scope of that thread. The Java thread allocates small objects in its TLA and maintains them independently from the TLAs of the other threads. The JVM allocates large objects directly in the heap if you split the heap into two generations. Allocating large objects, since it's done directly in the heap, requires synchronization among the Java threads.

Garbage Collection

Garbage collection is the process of freeing up space in the heap by removing unused objects from the heap. JRockit uses a garbage collection model called the *mark and sweep model*. Under this model, the JVM first marks the objects reachable from Java threads as "active," with the rest of the objects marked as "garbage." During the sweep phase, the JVM finds free spaces between objects that are active and makes those spaces available for allocation to new objects.

NOTE
Garbage collection reclaims memory no longer referenced by objects.

You can choose between two versions of the mark and sweep model—*concurrent mark and sweep* and *parallel mark and sweep*.

Concurrent Mark and Sweep The (mostly) concurrent mark and sweep model, also called *concurrent garbage collection,* allows the active Java threads to keep running during most of the garbage collection process, with only a few pauses for synchronization. The concurrent part means that garbage collection is running "concurrently" with your application code.

Parallel Mark and Sweep The parallel mark and sweep strategy requires the Java threads to be paused during the entire garbage collection process. This method uses all the available processing power of the server to minimize the time for garbage collection. The parallel part means that as many threads as possible are running in "parallel."

Dynamic (Adaptive) vs. Statically Configured Garbage Collection

You can configure JRockit to use dynamic or static garbage collection strategies. In the dynamic mode, the JVM selects the optimal garbage collection strategy for a specified goal and adjusts it over time, whereas a static mode lets you specify the garbage collection strategy. The following sections discuss the three dynamic garbage collection modes.

Throughput Under the *throughput* garbage collection mode, garbage collection is optimized for maximum application throughput and uses minimal CPU resources during garbage collection. Throughput is the percentage of total time the JVM doesn't spend performing garbage collection. The JVM follows a parallel garbage collection strategy that stops the Java application while garbage collection is on and employs all the available CPUs to complete the garbage collection in the least time possible. If your application requires a high throughput and can withstand occasional long pauses for garbage collection, choose the throughput mode. This type of application is usually a batch-type application or one that is processing requests asynchronously via JMS. You can enable the server to start in the throughput mode by using the following option:

```
java -Xms1024m -Xmx1024m -XgcPrio:throughput
```

Pause Time Mode Under this mode, garbage collection is optimized for short (and even) pause times for the JVM threads during garbage collection. A *pause* is the *time* during which the JVM seems to be unresponsive because it's busy performing garbage collection. This mode tries to keep the garbage collection pauses below a pause target that you specify while maintaining the highest possible throughput. A low pause time means the garbage collection will take longer to complete. As you realize by now, the big tradeoff in memory management is between maintaining the responsiveness of your applications by keeping pause times brief, on the one hand, and maintaining throughput, on the other. If your application requires fast response times, you must keep the pause times short. The pause time mode chooses between the mostly concurrent garbage collection strategy and the parallel garbage collection strategy. Here's how you enable the pause time mode and specify a pause time target in milliseconds:

```
java -Xms1024m -Xmx1024m -Xns256m -XgcPrio:pausetime -XpauseTarget:200ms
```

The command starts the JVM with the pause time garbage collection mode enabled, with a pause target of 200 ms. Note that the *XpauseTarget* command option lets you tune garbage collection per your service-level agreements. You can use the pause time mode for applications that can't tolerate long latencies.

Deterministic Mode The *deterministic* mode ensures very short pause times and limits the total pause time within a target time period, which is referred to as the *pause target*. This mode is available only as part of Oracle JRockit Real Time, the industry's leading solution that delivers superior latency and performance, such as microsecond response performance and guaranteed ("five nines guarantee") maximum garbage collection latency on the order of one millisecond. JRockit Real Time is ideal for environments that are extremely latency sensitive, requiring minimal configuration for instantaneous improvement in performance. Under the deterministic mode, the

JVM uses a special, mostly concurrent garbage collection strategy to minimize pauses during garbage collection. You can enable the deterministic mode in the following way:

```
java -Xms1024m -Xmx1024m -Xns256m -XgcPrio:deterministic -XpauseTarget:40ms
```

This command starts the JVM with the deterministic garbage collection mode and sets a pause target of 40 ms. Note that the shorter the pause target, the more overhead there will be on the memory system. Try to set the pause target to the target period your application will allow. You can control both the maximum pause time as well as the number of pauses within a set time window. Deterministic garbage collection offers fully predictable and short pause times, with minimal manual tuning. Real-time applications that need microsecond latency benefit from the deterministic garbage collection strategy by taking advantage of the guaranteed maximum latency due to garbage collection pauses.

JRockit uses a dynamic garbage collection mode that maximizes application throughput by default. You can select a dynamic garbage collection mode by setting the command-line option *-XgcPrio:<mode>*, with *throughput* and *pausetime* being the possible values for the *mode* parameter. If you use JRockit Real Time, you can use the value *deterministic,* as explained earlier.

Static Garbage Collection Strategies Unlike dynamic garbage collection strategies, static garbage collection strategies don't change during run time. You use static strategies if you want predictable behavior from the JVM. You can choose from four static garbage collection strategies, some with one generation and the others with two generations:

- ***singlepar*** Parallel garbage collection with a single generation. Uses multiple threads and causes longer pause times but provides better throughput for applications with few short-lived objects.
- ***genpar*** Parallel garbage collection with two generations. Uses multiple threads and causes longer pause times but provides better throughput for applications with many short-lived objects.
- ***singlecon*** Concurrent single-generation garbage collection. Performs a concurrent (not parallel) garbage collection using a single thread and minimizes pause times, but throughput is lower because application threads are stopped during garbage collection.
- ***gencon*** Concurrent multigeneration garbage collection. Uses multiple threads for the nursery and a single thread for the old generation. This strategy results in more frequent pauses than the *singlecon* garbage collection strategy, and it's an ideal strategy for applications that need higher throughput but are able to handle short pauses.

Choosing among the static garbage collection strategies is a matter of your application sensitivity to long garbage collection pauses. For example, if long pauses are causing transactions to timeout, you must select a parallel garbage collection strategy such as *singlepar* or *genpar*. If your application isn't sensitive to long pauses, you can select one of the two parallel garbage collection strategies. If your application uses many temporary objects, choose a two-generation strategy rather than a single-generation strategy. You specify a static garbage collection strategy with the command-line option *-Xgc:<strategy>*, with the possible values for the strategy parameter being *singlepar, genpar, singlecon,* and *gencon.*

You can't change the garbage collection mode for an active server if you've specified the static *singlepar* strategy or the dynamic deterministic mode. You can change all other garbage collection strategies during run time by choosing a different strategy from the JRockit Management Console's Memory tab.

Tuning Garbage Collection

The JVM performs a garbage collection whenever the heap memory becomes nearly full. Frequent long-running garbage collections mean that your application response times will get longer. You can use the verbose JVM command-line options or tools such as *jstat* and the JRockit Mission Control to gather detailed heap information during a garbage collection. For example, the JRockit command *-Xverbose:gc,gcpause,memdbg* produces detailed information about the start of the mark and sweep phases and the pause times. Similarly, you can issue the following *jstat* command for the JRockit JVM to get detailed output for the heap size, nursery size, used heap size, and garbage collection times:

```
jstat -gc <pid> 1 1
```

Oracle JRockit Mission Control, the Management Console for JRockit JVM, offers several nonintrusive monitoring and diagnostic tools that help you diagnose and tune garbage collection and the heap size, with minimum overhead of roughly 0.5 percent when you're actively running the tools. JRockit Real Time includes the JRockit Mission Control. Note that you tune several memory-related JVM settings without restarting the server by using the Console. Here's a summary of the main tools offered by JRockit Mission Control:

- **JRockit Management Console** Shows details about real-time CPU usage, memory usage, and garbage collection. You can tune the heap size and the garbage collection strategy dynamically through the Console.
- **JRockit Memory Leak Detector** Lets you track memory leaks and identify the causes for those leaks.
- **JRockit Flight Recorder (formerly the JRockit Runtime Analyzer)** Lets you get recordings of JVM run-time behavior, which shows detailed information about garbage collection and object usage.
- **JRockit Latency Analyzer** Uses the Flight Recorder recordings to show all latency-related information such as threads blocked due to locking, for example. The Latency Analyzer tool can resolve the source of application latency in nanoseconds.

You can influence the garbage collection frequency and the length of garbage collection time by adjusting the heap size. If you leave the various heap size options alone and choose to use the default values, the heap generation defaults may not turn out to be appropriate for your application. To optimize garbage collections and keep pause times low, you must set the heap size options based on the nature of your application. Caching objects rather than re-creating them will also reduce the need for frequent garbage collection.

Manually Requesting Garbage Collection

You can manually request garbage collection through the Console by navigating to Environment | Servers and selecting the server instance from the Summary Of Servers page. Once you select the server, navigate to Monitoring | Performance and click Garbage Collect. Be careful with requesting a garbage collection, as the JVM may have to check every active ("live") object in the heap. Note that depending on the JVM implementation, your manual request may or may not actually trigger garbage collection.

You must also remember that requesting a garbage collection like this is usually pointless because on a running system the JVM is running garbage collections frequently. If the system is loaded and you're thinking about running a garbage collection, it has probably run a few in the time it takes you to navigate to the page and push the button! The number of garbage collection threads depends on the number of available CPUs. If the number of garbage collection threads is too low, garbage collection takes very long and the JVM may have to resort to an emergency garbage collection, with the resulting high pause times. To avoid this, you can increase the number of garbage collection threads as shown here:

```
-XgcThreads:12
```

Compacting Memory

Following a garbage collection, the heap may become fragmented, with numerous small chunks of free space interspersed with "live" objects. The JVM can't use any free chunks smaller than the TLA size. Thus, if the heap becomes too fragmented following multiple garbage collection cycles, the JVM may be unable to allocate contiguous memory to a large object, resulting in an out-of-memory error, even though there is plenty of free memory overall. To reduce fragmentation, the JVM compacts the heap during the sweep phase (of the mark and sweep model), when all Java threads are paused. Compaction, by defragmenting the heap, pushes objects close to each other down in the heap, clearing up contiguous areas at the top of the heap.

After a garbage collection, the heap gets more fragmented because the unreachable objects removed by the garbage collection process don't occupy contiguous space in the heap. If the free space is smaller than the TLA size, the JVM can't use the space until a future garbage collection removes adjacent space to make the chunk of free space at least as large as the TLA. The JRockit JVM compacts part of the heap during garbage collection to create larger chunks of free space at the top of the heap. As mentioned earlier, this occurs during the sweep phase while the Java threads are paused. JRockit uses external compaction to move objects in the compaction area down the heap. The JVM also uses an internal compaction method to move objects within the compaction area itself in order to move objects closer to each other. In order to reduce pause times, only a part of the heap is compacted at any time since the threads that want to access the objects the JVM is moving around have to wait until the compaction is completed. The compaction method the JVM chooses at any given time depends on the current garbage collection mode. The JVM uses sliding windows to traverse through the whole heap in order to compact the entire heap.

In the throughput garbage collection mode, the compaction area size remains constant. In all other garbage collection modes, the JVM attempts to keep the compaction times equal by adjusting the compaction area based on its position. The time it takes to compact the heap depends on the number of objects the JVM needs to move and the number of references to those objects. If the object density is high in certain parts of the heap or the amount of references to objects in that area is high, the compaction area will be smaller. Since object density is higher toward the bottom of the heap, the compaction areas are smaller in the bottom half of the heap when compared to compaction areas in the top half of the heap.

Because the JVM performs a partial compaction during the garbage collection process, this may increase the pause times for garbage collection because all Java threads are paused during compaction. If the JVM doesn't compact enough space in the heap, fragmentation will keep increasing over time, forcing the JVM to perform a full compaction of the heap, which could lead to long garbage collection pauses. The JVM chooses to perform a full compaction when the heap is heavily fragmented—otherwise, the JVM will throw an *OutOfMemoryError* exception. A fragmented heap makes it harder for the JVM to allocate new objects, forcing it to fully compact the heap during garbage collection. Therefore, you will see steady degradation in application performance over time until the JMV fully compacts the heap. Of course, you pay for this full compaction with longer garbage collection pauses.

To avoid fluctuations in application performance due to fragmentation, you must keep fragmentation at a constant level and keep heap fragmentation under control. Instead of depending on the compaction ratio used by the server, you can tune it to reduce garbage collection pauses. Here are the ways to tune the compaction of the JVM heap:

- **Set a compaction ratio** If the heuristics-based compaction ratios used by the JVM are inadequate, you can set a fixed compaction ratio to instruct the JVM to always compact a specific percentage of the heap during each garbage collection. Use the command-line option *-XXCompactRatio* to adjust the compaction ratio from the JVM's default values. The *-Xverbose:memory=debug* option shows the current compaction ratio. You rarely have to adjust the compaction ratio because JRockit does this dynamically.
- **Set the compact set limit** Once the JVM compacts the heap, it must update all references from objects outside the compaction area to objects within the compaction area. Since a larger number of object references leads to higher garbage collection pause times, you can limit the number of references the JVM must update—if there are more references than the limit you set, the JVM aborts the compaction. Use the command-line option *-XXcompactSetLimit:<references>* to limit the number of object references. To reduce pause times, you must decrease the compact set limit. If the JVM is canceling too many compactions, the current compact set limit is too low and you must increase it. Note that you can't adjust the compact set limit when the JVM is using the deterministic or pause time garbage collection mode.
- **Turn off compaction** Although it's unlikely that your application never needs any compaction, you can turn off compaction entirely with the *-XXnoCompaction* command-line option.
- **Run a full compaction** You can manually perform a full compaction if the JVM is not performing garbage collection frequently and you want to increase performance between garbage collections. Remember that this may take a few seconds to complete if the heap is large and contains many objects. Use the command-line option *-XXfullCompaction* to perform a full compaction.

Setting the Thread Local Area Size

To enhance application throughput, you can also tune the object allocation by setting the thread local area (TLA) size. The TLA, as mentioned earlier, is a chunk of free space from the heap or the nursery that the JVM assigns to a thread for exclusive use by the thread. A large TLA enables the thread to allocate large objects in the TLA, but the downside is that it prevents small chunks of free space in the heap from being utilized. Of course, this increases heap fragmentation. JRockit JVM R27.1 and later dynamically adjusts the TLA size based on the chunks of free space available in the heap. The TLA size could be anywhere between a minimum size and a preferred size. Here are some helpful guidelines for configuring the TLA size:

- A higher minimum and preferred TLA size allows the allocation of large objects to the nursery when you're using a two-generation garbage collection strategy.
- You must always set the preferred TLA size to less than 5 percent of the nursery size.
- If threads allocate many objects, setting a larger preferred TLA size is useful. If threads allocate few objects, you do not need a large TLA and you can decrease the preferred TLA size to increase performance.
- If the application uses a large number of threads, decrease the preferred TLA size, since each of the individual threads won't be able to use up the TLA before the next garbage collection.
- Lowering the minimum TLA size reduces the impact of fragmentation.
- Because the JVM ignores free chunks smaller than the minimum TLA size, lowering the minimum TLA size reduces the pause times during garbage collection.

Generally, a minimum TLA size of 2–4KB and a preferred TLA size of 16–256KB work well for most applications. You can adjust the TLA size with the following command-line option when you start the JVM:

```
-XXtlaSize:min=<size>,preferred=<size>
```

The following example sets the minimum TLA size to 1KB and the preferred TLA size to 512KB:

```
-XXtlaSize:min=1k,preferred=512k MyApplication
```

This starts the JVM with a minimum TLA size of 1KB and a preferred TLA size of 512KB.

Configuring the JVM Heap Size

Your goal is to minimize the time the JVM spends in performing garbage collection, ideally keeping it to a very small part of the total execution time. The key determinant of how long the JVM takes to perform garbage collection is the JVM heap size. If you set the heap size too high, the garbage collection is slower but it needs to be performed less frequently. A smaller heap size requires less time for garbage collection to complete, but the garbage must be collected more frequently. When tuning the heap size, you want to minimize the garbage collection time while ensuring that the heap can store the number of objects necessary for supporting the maximum number of clients for the server. Also, remember that if you set the heap size too high, you could run into swapping and paging issues on the server if you run out of free memory. Therefore, you must base the heap size settings on the available memory on the server.

Monitoring Garbage Collection to Determine Heap Size Use the *-verbosegc* option to turn on verbose garbage collection output. This lets you determine the time and resources used by garbage collection during maximum application workloads. Here's the syntax for specifying the verbose garbage collection option:

```
java -ms32m -mx200m -verbosegc -classpath $CLASSPATH
-Dweblogic.Name=%SERVER_NAME% -Dbea.home="C:\Oracle\Middleware"
-Dweblogic.management.username=%WLS_USER%
-Dweblogic.management.password=%WLS_PW%
-Dweblogic.management.server=%ADMIN_URL%
-Dweblogic.ProductionModeEnabled=%STARTMODE%
-Djava.security.policy="%WL_HOME%\server\lib\weblogic.policy" weblogic.Server
>> logfile.txt 2>&1
```

The previous command will redirect both the standard error and standard output to the log file named *logfile.txt*.

Note that if you are using JRockit, it is much, much easier simply to collect a JFR or JRA profile and view that in JRockit Mission Control. Reading through garbage collection logs is somewhat of an unpleasant exercise that should be used primarily when running with HotSpot.

Once you collect the verbose garbage collection output, check the timestamps for garbage collection to see how often the JVM is collecting garbage and how long each garbage collection is taking. Ideally, each garbage collection should take less than 3–5 seconds. If the duration is much longer than this, consider reducing the heap size to reduce the garbage collection duration. Check the free space in the heap after each garbage collection. If the free space is 90 percent or higher after each garbage collection, you can probably lower the heap size safely.

Setting the Heap Size The size of the JVM heap is critical in determining the speed with which the JVM can assign new objects to the heap, as well as the frequency and duration of garbage collection. As long as you don't set the heap size high enough to cause paging and swapping, the extra overhead involved in maintaining a larger heap size is preferable to more frequent garbage collection with a smaller heap size.

The key thing to do when setting heap sizes for production systems generally is to look at the entire system to see how many server instances you are planning to run on a particular piece of hardware. (This is where you get into paging and swapping.) Generally, you want to use up all of the memory available on your physical server and divvy it up across the processes. Enabling large pages on 64-bit hardware is also a really big winner.

You can set the heap size with the parameters *-Xms* and *-Xmx*, with the first parameter setting the initial and minimum heap size and the second parameter setting the maximum heap size. The *-Xmx* parameter indicates the total memory reserved for the JVM, and the *-Xms* parameter shows the memory immediately committed to the JVM. You don't have to make the minimum and maximum heap sizes equal, but Oracle recommends doing so in order to avoid having the JVM frequently grow and shrink the heap.

If you want the heap to maintain two generations, specify the nursery size with the *-Xns* parameter. An optimal size for the nursery area of the heap ensures more garbage collection through a young collection than an old collection. In general, you should set the nursery size to no more than half the size of the heap. By default, the keep area is 25 percent of the nursery, but you can change it using the command-line option *-XXkeepAreaRatio:<percentage>*. The *-XXkeepAreaRatio* parameter sets the size of the nursery's keep area as a percentage of the nursery size. The keep area keeps new objects from being promoted too quickly to the old generation.

Here's an example that shows how to start the JVM with a heap size of 1024MB:

```
java -Xns:20m -Xms:1024m -Xmx:1024m
```

The minimum and maximum heap sizes are set to 1024MB, and the nursery size is set to 20MB.

In Chapter 6, you learned how to use the *jrcmd* command-line utility. You can use *jrcmd's heap_diagnostics* command to get detailed information about how the JVM is using the heap. Note that this command starts a full garbage collection and gives you information about the available memory and heap usage, detailed heap statistics, and information about referenced objects such as how many were reachable and how many were unreachable, making them candidates for garbage collection. You can use the *jrcmd hprofdump* command to output a heap dump to a text file.

Understanding Locking

The JVM uses two types of locks: *thin locks* that are helpful for brief periods and *fat locks* that are held when there's contention for resources. Threads sleep during a fat lock and spin during a thin lock, thus making fat locks less resource-intensive because spinning uses up CPU cycles. You can use the command *-Xverbose:locks* to view information about the JVM locks. You can enable locking instrumentation by using the following command:

```
-XX:UseLockProfiling=true
```

The preceding command shows details about the number and types of locks held by the JVM. You can enable the collection of locking information by the JRockit Runtime Analyzer using the following option at startup time:

```
-Djrockit.lockprofiling=true
```

Using Lock Profiling can be fairly expensive, so be careful when using this on production systems and make sure you adjust the load accordingly by running the profiling option during off times or by adding capacity in the form of additional server instances.

Tuning Messaging Applications

If you use messaging services such as JMS, you can tune several areas to improve performance. These include the tuning of the persistent store, the WebLogic JMS, and the JMS store-and-forward service.

Tuning the Persistent Store

As the earlier chapters in this book explain, WebLogic Server subsystems such as JMS use the persistent store to save their data, such as JMS messages. You can use the default, preconfigured, file-based persistent store, or you can use a custom file store or JDBC store. In addition, each JMS server uses an implicitly created file-based paging store to page persistent as well as nonpersistent messages. Oracle recommends that you share a single persistent store among all the subsystems instead of maintaining a dedicated store for each subsystem.

If you use a file store, you want to make sure you are using a fast disk, because high availability is impacted by your choice. The ability to migrate JMS to a different machine means that the store has to be available at all times. If you place the file store on a network drive, this can impact performance. In cases where the JMS messages are relatively simple and the operations are updating a database anyway, the use of the JDBC store actually can be fairly efficient.

Compacting the File Stores

File stores throw exceptions when the disk on which they're located gets full. However, the store resumes functioning once you clear up space in the disk. You can use Java commands through the persistent store administration utility, *storeadmin,* to perform persistent store administration tasks, including compacting the store to reduce its size. Here's how you invoke the *storeadmin* utility:

```
C:\Oracle\Middleware\Oracle_Home\wl_server>java weblogic
.store.Admin
Type "help" for available commands
storeadmin->
```

The *weblogic.store.Admin* command works only on a store that's currently opened by a running WebLogic instance. You can execute the command from WLST or from the Java command line, as shown in the previous example.

You can compact and defragment the space used by a file store by issuing the *compact* command:

```
storeadmin->compact -dir C:\stores\mystores -tempdir C:\tmp
```

The *-dir* parameter specifies the location of the directory that holds the persistent store. The *-tempdir* parameter specifies the temporary directory with enough space to handle the contents of the uncompacted file store. After compacting of the persistent store, the server will store the original persistent store in a uniquely named directory under the C:\tmp directory.

You can view all the available store administration commands, usage, and examples by issuing the *help* command with the *storeadmin* utility. You mostly use the store administration utility for compacting a file store when it gets too large. You can also use the utility for dumping a JDBC file store's contents (using the *dump* command) to an XML file for troubleshooting. If you just want the statistics for an active JMS store, you can get them by using the persistent store's JMX MBeans.

Tuning the Synchronous Write Policy

You can use any of three transitional safe synchronous write policies:

- Direct-Write-With-Cache
- Direct-Write
- Cache-Flush

In addition, there's a *Disabled* synchronous write policy, but it's not safe for transactions.

NOTE
Oracle suggests that the Disabled synchronous write policy, although it enhances performance, also makes transactions unsafe and could lead to data loss following a system failure.

The goal of the store is to provide a persistent backup in case of a process or machine failure. The trade-off is that a request to send a message must wait until the server actually writes the message to the store. By trading off some level of consistency, it is possible to get dramatically improved results.

The *Direct-Write* policy is the default policy, and it offers better performance than the *Cache-Flush* policy. However, *Direct-Write-With-Cache* offers the best performance of the three of those. Oracle recommends using the *Direct-Write-With-Cache* synchronous write policy, as it offers the best balance between performance and transactional safety of the disk writes. Note that the *Direct-Write-With-Cache* policy uses two sets of files: the first is called the primary set and is stored in the location you specify for the *Directory* attribute when configuring a persistent file store. Temporary cache files are located in the directory you specify with the *CacheDirectory* attribute. Note that you must locate the cache directory on a local file system (the default location is the temp directory) because it's meant for enhancing performance. The primary set of files is for availability purposes, and you should store it remotely for safety. In production environments, the server maintains the cache files automatically.

To improve persistent store native memory usage, you can configure the parameters *MaxWindowBufferSize* and *IOBufferSize*. You can increase the initial size of a store with the *InitialSize* attribute, and you can increase the maximum file size for a single file in the store with the *MaxFileSize* tuning attribute. Oracle recommends that you set the persistent store block size to match the block size of the OS file system.

You can check both the current synchronous write policy for the persistent store as well as its block size by viewing the server log.

Tuning WebLogic JMS

You can configure various messaging properties to improve JMS messaging performance. Following is a quick summary of the main areas you should be looking at.

Tuning Large Messages

You can tune large messages by defining message quotas and tuning the maximum message size, as explained in the following sections.

Defining Quotas on Destinations

Oracle recommends that you always configure message count quotas to prevent message logs from using up all of a server's memory. By default, there's no quota on message counts. Messages continue to consume memory even after they're paged out because paging removes the message bodies, but doesn't page out the message headers. Oracle recommends that you assume each current JMS message consumes roughly 512 bytes of memory. A quota is a JMS module resource and defines the maximum number of messages (and bytes) a destination can have. You can set the following quota parameters in the Administration Console by first going to Services | Messaging | JMS Modules and selecting the JMS module. Once you select the module, click New in the Summary Of Resources table and select Quota on the Create A New JMS System Module page and then click Next. On the JMS Quota Properties page, you can configure the following properties:

- **Name** Creates a name for the quota.
- **Bytes Maximum** Sets the maximum number of bytes that can be stored in the destination using this quota.

- **Messages Maximum** Sets the maximum number of messages that can be stored in the destination using this quota.
- **Policy** Specifies whether smaller messages can be sent out before larger messages once the destination hits its message quota (rather than in the default first-in-first-out sequence).
- **Shared** Specifies whether this quota is shareable among destinations.

If you don't set a quota for a destination, it will share the quota of the JMS server. You can block the sending of messages during quota conditions by defining a send timeout on the connection factory or by specifying a blocking send policy on the JMS server. The *send timeout* policies specify the length of time message producers must wait until space becomes available on a destination. The *blocking send policy* on the server determines the priority the server should accord to smaller versus larger messages when a destination exceeds its message quota.

Tuning the Maximum Message Size You can tune the message backlog between the JMS server and its clients by setting the *MessageMaximum* setting for the connection factory. Oracle recommends that you set this attribute to double the number of acknowledgments or commits. Note that a very high message maximum could potentially lead to exceptions due to large packets. WebLogic Server limits the maximum message size for most protocols to 100MB. If you're receiving "packet too large" exceptions, you must tune the maximum message size on the server for all supported protocols for each of the network channels. You can also set the maximum message size on a client by specifying the *-Dweblogic.MaxMessageSize* command-line property.

Controlling the Message Flow

WebLogic Server uses a flow control mechanism that lets a JMS server or destination slow down message producers when they reach overload conditions. The basic purpose behind the flow control mechanism is to limit the message flow of the producers when the JMS server destination exceeds a threshold set in terms of bytes or number of messages. You can specify a flow maximum and minimum to control the message flow of producers. Message producers adjust their message flow toward the flow minimum when the number of bytes or messages exceeds the value set by the Bytes/Messages Threshold High attribute you set. Similarly, the producers adjust their message flow toward the flow maximum when the number of bytes or messages falls below the Bytes/Messages Threshold Low attribute. You can also configure a flow interval, which determines the period of time within which producers must adjust their message volume from the flow maximum to the flow minimum and vice versa.

Using Unit-of-Order

WebLogic Server lets message producers group messages into a single unit called a Unit-of-Order (UOO) based on their processing order. UOO requires sequential processing of messages in the order in which the messages were created. In applications that have strict message-ordering requirements, UOO can help improve performance.

Tuning Topics

Oracle recommends the following to tune JMS topics:

- Convert singleton topics to distributed topics.
- Leverage MDBs to process topic messages.
- Disable server affinity if messages are not being load balanced evenly among the members of a partitioned distributed topic.

Tuning Distributed Queues

Use the following strategies to tune distributed queues:

- Disable server affinity to improve load balancing among the distributed queue members.
- Oracle also recommends the use of MDBs for evenly balancing the load and recommends the following if you can't leverage MDBs:
  - Force the consumers to perform fresh load balancing by closing and re-creating consumers periodically.
  - Configure the distributed queue to enable forwarding.

Using One-Way Message Sends

Messages from producers are usually called two-way sends because they include an internal request as well as an internal response. Producers must wait for the JMS server's response before applications make further send calls. A one-way send mechanism doesn't involve any waiting. You can configure one-way sends for nonpersistent, nontransactional messages. You can configure both queue senders and topic publishers for one-way message sends. Following are some important things you should keep in mind when using one-way message sends:

- The default two-way send mode offers better QOS (quality of service) than a one-way send mode for topic publishers.
- If the JMS consumer applications are the bottleneck, one-way message sends aren't going to improve performance.
- To accommodate the increased batch size of sends, you may have to increase the JVM heap size on either or both the server and the client.
- Sending applications may not receive quota exceptions because the server deletes the one-way messages that exceed the quota without throwing an exception to the client.

Configuring Message Performance Preferences

By default, JMS destinations don't batch messages for delivery to consumers by pushing out messages to consumers as soon as the messages become available. You can use the Messaging Performance Preference option on a destination to set the length of time for which the destination must wait before grouping batches of messages for delivery. This is an advanced option that you must set with great care in cases where the message consumer doesn't require fast response times. Setting it increases the wait times but requires fewer sends, which improves performance.

Tuning WebLogic JMS Store-and-Forward

JMS store-and-forward (SAF) capability offers high-performance message forwarding to remote destinations. SAF services allow WebLogic Server to deliver messages reliably among applications deployed across multiple server instances. If a remote message destination isn't available for some reason such as a network failure, the local server instance saves the messages and forwards them to the remote destination once it becomes available. However, Oracle recommends using SAF only in situations where the remote destinations aren't highly available. Following are the key SAF-related performance best practices:

- Share a single persistent store between subsystems for increased performance.
- In order to load balance messages among the SAF agents, target imported destinations to different SAF agents.
- If your application uses small messages, increase the default value for the JMS SAF Window Size option, which is set to a low value of 10 messages. You can't set a window size for distributed queues, whose batch size is set internally to 1 message.
- By default, SAF agents forward messages immediately after the messages arrive. You can configure the Window Interval value to a positive value (500 milliseconds, for example) rather than leave it at its default value of 0. By doing this, you ensure the messages are forwarded in batches, which improves throughput and reduces CPU and disk usage. You can't configure the Window Interval attribute for a distributed destination.

Tuning the Applications and Managing Sessions

You can follow several Oracle best practices to tune the web applications and manage sessions. The following sections summarize the best practices for tuning web applications, Oracle Coherence, EJBs, and sessions.

Tuning Web Applications

Application developers can do several things to enhance web application performance, as described in the following sections.

Disable Page Checks

You can disable servlet and JSP page checks by setting Production Mode to *true*. By default, this sets the *page-check-seconds* and *servlet-reload-check-secs* parameters to a default value of –1.

Manage HTTP Sessions Efficiently

Be judicious about what you store in your HTTP session: the less memory you require for each active session, the less heap memory you will consume and the less information that will need to be replicated if you are using high availability. Be careful about indirectly referencing large data structures that will then take up a lot of heap and require extra bandwidth during replication.

Coherence*Web is built on top of Oracle Coherence (introduced later in this chapter) and offers a more efficient way to manage HTTP session state in a WebLogic Server cluster than using WebLogic Server's in-memory HTTP session state replication services. You can install the Coherence*Web session management module in WebLogic Server by using the Coherence*Web Service Provider Interface (SPI)–based installation. Coherence*Web manages sessions by using the

Coherence caches for storing and managing management services data. You may want to consider using Coherence*Web instead of WebLogic Server's built-in session state management services if you're dealing with one of the following situations:

- You're using a Coherence data grid and want to offload HTTP session management to it.
- You want to share session state data across multiple applications.
- Your application handles large HTTP session state objects.
- Storing HTTP session data is leading to memory issues.

Coherence*Web translates Oracle Coherence data grid's scalability, availability, and performance capabilities to in-memory session management. Coherence*Web lets you take advantage of the various caching features available in Oracle Coherence, such as replicated, partitioned, near caching and read-through, write-through, and write-behind caching. It supports the use of fine-grained session and session attribute scoping through the use of pluggable policies. Coherence*Web also allows storing session data outside the server, thus saving on heap usage, and enables a server restart without losing session data. If you're dealing with a large number of clustered production servers, Coherence*Web can provide linear scalability for managing HTTP session data.

Use Custom JSP Tags

You can use the three Oracle-provided JSP tags—*cache, repeat,* and *process*—by including the custom tags within your web applications to make processing faster. You must explicitly reference the tag library description in the *web.xml*'s *<taglib>* element. You use the tag library *.jar* file named *weblogic-tags.jar* to package the three custom tags. To use the three custom tags, follow these steps:

1. Copy the *weblogic-tags.jar* file to the WEB-INF/lib directory of the web application that contains the JSPs.
2. Specify the tag library descriptor (TLD) in the *<taglib>* element of the *web.xml* file:

```
<taglib>
  <taglib-uri>weblogic-tags.tld</taglib-uri>
  <taglib-location>
     /WEB-INF/lib/weblogic-tags.jar
  </taglib-location>
</taglib>
```

3. Finally, use the *taglib* directive to reference the tag library in the JSP:

```
<%@ taglib uri="weblogic-tags.tld" prefix="wl" %>
```

The cache tag caches work done within the body of the custom tag. Here's an example that shows how to use the cache tag:

```
<wl:cache key="request.ticker" timeout="1m">
<!--get current price for whatever is in the request parameter ticker
 and display it, update it every minute-->
</wl:cache>
```

The process tag lets you control the execution of statements specified between the *<wl:process>* and *</wl:process>* tags. The repeat (*<wl:repeat>*) tag lets you iterate over different types of sets, such as Enumerations and Collections.

Precompile JSPs

To avoid having to recompile JSPs upon a server reboot or an application deployment and redeployment, precompile the JSPs by setting the *precompile* parameter to *true* in the *weblogc.xml*'s *<jsp-descriptor>* element. Even better, when you put applications into production, you should run *weblogic.appc* on them so all of the required artifacts are in place. Chapter 9 shows how to precompile JSPs before and during deployment.

Disable Access Logging

You can reduce the logging overhead and thus increase throughput by disabling access logging. You do this by setting the *access-logging-disabled* element.

Some large applications that also include jar files are packaged within the WEB-INF directory. These can take a long time to unpack and perform deployment time processing. If you are deploying into production on a shared device, you can avoid significant processing by creating an "exploded" version of the application, running the WebLogic Server utility *appc* (or its Ant equivalent *wlappc*) on the directory, and deploying in the nostage mode. The *appc* utility processes an application or module and produces an output application or module. Normally, with annotations, understanding what's in the jar, war, and ear files isn't easy. If you use *appc* with the *-writeInferredDescriptors* flag, the output application or module will include the deployment descriptors with annotation information. That is, the tool will generate the equivalent deployment descriptors. Because this will write the *metadata-complete* flag into the replaced descriptors, it eliminates the need to preprocess the annotations at deploy time. Here's how you use the *weblogic.appc* utility:

```
java weblogic.appc -writeInferredDescriptors -output output.war input.war
```

Using Oracle Coherence

The Oracle WebLogic Suite includes Oracle Coherence, a core component of Oracle WebLogic Server. Oracle Coherence is a JCache-compliant, in-memory, distributed data grid solution for clustered applications and application servers. It enhances scalability of your mission-critical applications by providing fast access to frequently accessed data. In addition, it dynamically partitions data in memory among multiple servers, thus ensuring continuous availability of data as well as transaction integrity, even during a server failure. It provides the partitioned data management and caching services on the foundation of a reliable and scalable peer-to-peer clustering protocol. It also performs real-time data analysis and in-memory grid computations, as well as parallel transaction and event processing. Coherence is deployed by many large financial, telecom, logistics, and media companies that require the highest levels of scalability, near-zero latency, and high reliability. If your environment requires very high throughput, high scalability, reliability, and continuous availability, Oracle Coherence is probably going to be of great help.

Coherence is especially useful for large-scale computing grids such as financial trading system grids, where the bottleneck is in loading data and making it available to all the application components. Coherence can potentially speed up aggregate data throughput that is thousands of times faster than what the data sources can provide by themselves. The Coherence data fabric allows you to maintain large data sets in memory and feed the data at extremely fast speeds to all computing nodes.

Oracle Coherence helps you get the most out of your WebLogic clusters by providing the following capabilities:

- **Clustering of data and objects** Oracle Coherence ensures that all of an application's objects and data that are delegated to it by the applications are accessible to all cluster members and that no data is lost when servers fail. Data is synchronously replicated across a cluster, and the clustering protocol used by Coherence detects server failures quickly. Each server is aware of where a replica for a piece of data exists and automatically redirects data access requests to the replicas. Because each data operation is executed in a once-and-only-once mode, executing operations during a server failure won't be accidentally repeated or lost.
- **Automatic management of cluster membership** Coherence automatically adds servers to a cluster when they start and records their departure from a cluster due to a failure or shutdown. Applications can sign up to receive event notifications when members join or leave a cluster. Coherence tracks all services provided by and consumed by each server, using this information to provide load balancing of data and service resiliency in the cluster following server failures.
- **Providing a data grid** Coherence helps create a data grid (also called a *data fabric*) using its partitioned data management service and also provides the infrastructure for applications that use a data grid. If you have large amounts of data spread across many servers in a grid, you can use Coherence to manage that data with near-zero latency. Coherence automatically partitions data across the data fabric, increasing the efficiency of database and EIS connectivity. Its read-ahead and write-behind capabilities reduce latency to a near-zero level and protect your applications from database and EIS failures.
- **Delivering change events** Coherence uses the JavaBean event model to cache events, making it easy to receive events for changes occurring in the cluster. It provides a once-and-only-once guarantee for processing external events. It also uses continuous querying to bring real-time event handling to a server or desktop.

The data fabric architecture of Oracle Coherence, which uses automatic data partitioning and load balancing, ensures that the aggregate data throughput, in-memory data capacity, and aggregate I/O throughput are linearly proportional to the number of servers in a cluster. The high throughput is made possible by the following capabilities of the in-memory data grid:

- A superior clustering protocol that achieves "wire speed" throughput on each server
- Load balancing data management by partitioning the data, thus letting each server handle its fair share of the total data
- Routing all read and write requests directly to the server that manages that portion of the data
- Execution of parallel queries, transactions, and computations against large sets of data, using all servers in the data grid

If your application processes an extremely high number of transactions, the database may become a bottleneck if the application needs to persist the changes. Coherence can eliminate those bottlenecks by making transactions highly efficient—it batches a large number of small changes to various application objects into a single transaction.

You get higher resiliency with Coherence because each server in the data fabric bears only 1/*n*th of the total failover responsibility for a data fabric. When you use Coherence, you don't have a single point of failure—when a server crashes or becomes unavailable, Coherence automatically fails over and redistributes its clustered data management services among the servers. Similarly, when you add a new server or restart a failed server, Coherence transparently fails over services to the new server, thus ensuring that the cluster load is redistributed among all the cluster members. Coherence, therefore, always synchronizes and keeps up to date the data in the various nodes of the data fabric. It also lets each server back up a small portion of data from multiple servers, spreading the impact of a server failure across the data fabric. Coherence also includes network fault tolerance capabilities and allows servers to heal themselves with the transparent soft restart capability.

Tuning EJB Performance

Oracle provides several recommendations for tuning WebLogic Server EJBs. Following is a quick summary of the main recommendations pertaining to the tuning of EJBs and the EJB cache.

Tuning EJBs

It is best to keep state in the middle tier to a minimum. Oracle recommends using stateless session beans where possible instead of stateful session beans because the server doesn't have to maintain state information.

The EJB specification requires that EJB calls are not passed by reference for consistency. As such, in WebLogic Server 8.1 and higher, call-by-reference is turned off by default. You must set call-by-reference to *true* when EJBs call one another within the same application. This also applies when an EJB is called by a servlet or JSP from the same application. Setting call-by-reference to *true* eliminates serialization and the overhead it entails. This is consistent with most modern application development styles that use local JavaBeans.

Choosing the right default transaction properties for beans and methods is an important opportunity to improve performance. The most common case is the one where a servlet will obtain access to an EJB and then make a series of fine-grained getter calls. If a transaction isn't already in process and the *RequiresNew* or *Required* transaction property is set, a new transaction will be started and stopped for each method call, resulting in a great deal of overhead, including the allocation of new database connections. Carefully reviewing these methods and disabling transactions where they are not needed or initiating one wrapping transaction is the best approach.

In a clustered environment, you should deploy all of your EJBs to all available cluster members. A cluster in which you deploy your EJBs in this manner is called a *homogeneous cluster,* and it offers better performance than a heterogeneous cluster when all EJBs aren't deployed on all cluster members. If a single transaction needs to use multiple EJBs, there's less network traffic if WebLogic Server finds all the EJB instances on a single server instance rather than having to use EJBs from multiple servers.

Tuning EJB Caches

You must tune the stateful session bean cache and the entity bean cache to maximize performance, as explained in the following sections. Note that this discussion is targeted at EJB 2.1-style applications.

Stateful Session Bean Cache To maximize performance, you should set the *max-beans-in-cache* parameter in the *weblogic-ejb-jar.xml* file to the number of concurrent users. The EJB container will cache in memory the number of stateful session beans you specify.

Entity Bean Cache By default, an entity bean is retrieved from the cache once it's loaded from the database. However, an entity bean's persistent state isn't cached between transactions. You can enable the persistent caching of entity beans between transactions by setting the *cache-between-transactions* parameter to *true*. Whether caching the state between transactions is safe depends on the concurrency strategy you specify for an entity bean, as described in the following section. You set the size of the entity bean cache by adjusting the value of the deployment descriptor parameter *max-beans-in-cache*. Your objective when setting the cache size is to maximize cache hits. You can instruct the cache not to maintain ready instances of beans if the entity beans have a high cache miss ratio. You can do this by setting the *disable-ready-instances* attribute in the *<entity-cache>* element of the *entity-descriptor* for an entity bean.

CMP Entity Beans

Container-managed persistence (CMP) defines the entity bean instance lifecycle. Entity beans depend on container-managed persistence to generate methods that access persistent data for the entity bean instances. Although you can achieve the greatest performance gain by caching entity beans, you can't do so beyond a particular transaction's scope. You can configure the following EJB container features, however, to minimize the interaction with the database:

- **Eager relationship caching** This allows the container to load related entity beans using a single SQL join statement.
- **JDBC batch operations** By default, JDBC batch operations are turned on in the container, which means the server uses batching to reduce the number of multiple round trips to the database for similar operations.
- **Tuned updates** The EJB container updates the database with only the fields that have changed, which means there's no need for a database call if a bean isn't modified.
- **Field groups** You can group commonly used fields into a single group. Once you do this, if one field of the group is accessed by an application or EJB, the server loads all the fields in the group with a single SQL statement, thus reducing the number of database calls.
- **Concurrency strategy** You can use the *<concurrency-strategy>* deployment descriptors to specify how the EJB container should handle a situation where multiple threads in a server instance want to access the same entity bean simultaneously. The most commonly used value for *<concurrency-strategy>* is *database*, which means the database handles concurrency control and determines whether concurrent access to an EJB should be allowed. The value *exclusive* ensures that all concurrent transactions serially access a single instance of an EJB. Because concurrent access is not possible with the exclusive setting, use this only if the EJB is used infrequently. The *optimistic* concurrency strategy assumes that an EJB is rarely modified. Using this strategy along with caching between transactions could improve performance significantly for such EJBs. The *ReadOnly* concurrency strategy assumes the EJB is nontransactional and turns on caching between transactions, thus improving performance.

You can view EJB run-time performance statistics from the Administration Console by clicking the Monitoring tab for a specific EJB. You can view statistics for things such as the cache miss ratio from this page.

SQL Tuning Best Practices

Although efficient use of statement caching is going to improve performance, the key driver for improved performance is to ensure that you're using efficient SQL queries. Developers must also seek to remove most SQL from the middleware and move it to the back-end database tier, where it belongs. Here are some guidelines for improving SQL performance (mostly generic, but some recommendations pertain specifically to the Oracle database):

- **Use stored procedures** Using stored procedures rather than individual SQL statements is much more efficient in most cases. You can often achieve dramatic performance improvements by taking individual SQL statements out and making them part of a procedure.
- **Use prepared statements with bind variables** Using prepared statements improves performance significantly, and the more complex the query, the greater the performance benefit.
- **Tune the database memory allocation** Ensure that the database administrators have allocated enough memory for the database so it can hold all the prepared statements your application generates.
- **Collect efficient statistics** Every database depends on a set of optimizer statistics to figure out the best query execution plan. Make sure the database objects have fresh statistics and that the statistics are accurate.
- **Avoid expensive queries** If your application includes even one or two bad queries such as the following, your application will be in trouble. Pulling large amounts of data from the database server could lead to a stuck thread situation.

```
SELECT DISTINCT colWithNoIndex from LargeTable;
SELECT * FROM LargeTable ORDER BY colWithNoIndex;
```

If you suspect that some of the application queries are not very efficient, you can ask the DBA to trace the query performance using Oracle's *DBMS_MONITOR* package. The DBA can also run other types of traces, such as the Oracle 10053 event trace, which tracks the optimizer's execution plan. The DBA or the developer can also generate an *explain plan* to trace the query's execution plan without actually executing the query. This can help you (or the database team) generate better-performing queries by using some basic performance-improving techniques such as the following:

- **Use appropriate indexes** Although everyone knows indexes speed up data retrieval, less well understood is the appropriate use of indexes. Make sure the column in a query's *WHERE* clause is part of the index key.
- **Use the right join order** The right join order among a query's tables can make a big difference in performance. Using trace data or an explain plan, developers can improve the query by changing the join order among tables.

- **Perform sorts in memory** Performing sorts in memory as opposed to doing them on disk leads to dramatic performance improvements. The DBAs can allocate memory to appropriate database memory components to ensure memory sorts.
- **Use optimizer hints** The SQL developer can insert appropriate "hints" to override the cost optimizer's choices, such as the use or nonuse of an index, for example.

The suggestions made here are just some of the ways in which the database team can enhance query performance to decrease the load carried by the middleware. The takeaway for WebLogic Server administrators should be that when faced with frequent stuck thread issues and a slow-performing system, often the underlying reasons can be traced to poorly performing SQL statements. Working with the database teams to resolve these performance issues can go a long way toward improving WebLogic Server performance.

Managing Sessions

The key performance goal when configuring session management is to make the server do the least amount of work to handle sessions and session persistence. Following is a summary of the key session management strategies:

- **Manage session persistence** You can configure various session persistence mechanisms to suit your application needs, such as reliability, session failover, and the HTTP session size. If your application requires session failover, you can maintain replicated sessions or JDBC-based sessions. If you have a clustered environment, you can use replicated session persistence, which offers better performance than JDBC-based session persistence. However, you can use JDBC persistence in a single-server environment without a cluster. You can improve JDBC session persistence by configuring the database, JDBC driver, and JDBC connection pool.
- **Minimize sessions** Minimizing sessions is critical to tuning application performance because maintaining a large number of sessions decreases the ability of the server to scale up. In general, do not use sessions for storing state information such as usernames, which you're better off storing on the client. Another strategy you can use to minimize sessions is to store frequently used values in local variables.
- **Aggregate session data** You can avoid serialization, deserialization, and network overhead by separating frequently changing session data and read-only session data into separate session attributes.

JPA and TopLink

The Java Persistence API (JPA) is a Java specification for persisting and managing data between Java objects and classes, and a relational database. JPA is part of the EJB 3.0 specification, is intended to replace the EJB 2 CMP entity bean specification, and is a current industry standard for object-relational mapping (ORM). You can choose from open source and commercial JPA implementations, and a Java EE 5 application server such as Oracle WebLogic Server supports the use of JPA.

Unlike the EJB 2 CMP specification, JPA allows you to define object-relational mappings through standard annotations or XML. JPA includes the object-level query language JPQL to allow the querying of objects from a relational database. It also defines a run-time *EntityManager* API for processing queries and transactions on objects. JPA offers a more portable and less complex persistence standard than EJB 2 CMP.

Oracle's TopLink implements JPA, which is the current standard persistence mechanism for Java EE and SE. JPA 2.0 standardizes advanced ORM features, and EclipseLink is its reference implementation. EclipseLink is open source, whereas TopLink is an Oracle commercial product that offers all the features of EclipseLink along with additional features for integrating with WebLogic Server and the Oracle SOA Suite. TopLink lets you integrate persistence and object transformation in your applications, and it facilitates the building of high-performing applications that store persistent object-oriented data in an RDBMS. TopLink provides an advanced object-persistence and object-transformation layer that supports the following data sources and formats:

- **Relational data** Persists Java objects to a relational database using Java Database Connectivity (JDBC) drivers.
- **Object-relational data types** Persists Java objects in a structured data source representation for storage in an object relational database (such as the Oracle database).
- **Enterprise information systems (EISs)** Uses a JCA adapter to persist Java objects to a nonrelational data source.
- **XML data** Converts in-memory, nontransactional data between Java objects and XML Schema Document (XSD)–based XML documents.

TopLink supports EJB 3 in Java EE and Java SE environments and lets you easily capture and define object-to-data source and object-to-data representation mappings. The TopLink run time lets applications exploit the captured mapping metadata through a simple session façade, providing strong support for data access, querying, transactions, and caching. TopLink lets you take advantage of the best features of object technology and specific data sources by addressing the differences between Java objects and data sources (and seamlessly managing the relational, object-relational data type, EIS, and XML mappings). Since TopLink offers a clear object-oriented view of data sources, you can easily use it even without a strong knowledge of SQL or JDBC.

TopLink provides a flexible, nonintrusive metadata-based architecture that supports Plain Old Java Objects (POJOs), CMP, JPA, and web services provided by EclipseLink. It's optimized for high performance and concurrency, and it offers numerous performance-tuning options and comprehensive object-caching support. It also offers extensive query capability, including JPQL, Enterprise Java Beans Query Language (EJB QL), and native SQL. Finally, it offers optimistic and pessimistic locking options.

Tuning Data Sources and Transactions

As far as tuning the database is concerned, the best policy is to work with the database administrators to ensure that they understand your requirements and configure the database accordingly. Database configuration is a vast topic, and configuration parameters may change over time in new releases. For example, if you let the database administrator know the amount of simultaneous users you expect, they can configure the appropriate initialization parameter. Once the database is configured appropriately, you can focus on the configuration of data sources and transactions.

Tuning Data Sources

Following is a summary of the best practices when tuning data sources.

Configuring the Connection Pool

To avoid connection delays due to on-demand creation of connections, Oracle recommends you set the value of the Initial Capacity parameter to the value of the Maximum Capacity parameter when configuring a connection pool. You can estimate the value of the Maximum Capacity parameter through load-testing exercises. However, beware of oversimplifying and making your application deployment too tightly bound to one particular configuration.

You can use the *<pool-name>* mechanism for setting a *<max-threads-constraint>*, as shown in the following example, which shows part of a *weblogic-ejb-jar.xml* file:

```
</weblogic-ejb-jar>
...
<work-manager>
       <name>test_resource</name>
         <max-threads-constraint>
              <name>pool_constraint</name>
              <pool-name>testPool</pool-name>
       </max-threads-constraint>
</work-manager>

<work-manager>
       <name>test_appscoped_resource</name>
       <max-threads-constraint>
              <name>appscoped_pool_constraint</name>
              <pool-name>AppScopedDataSource</pool-name>
       </max-threads-constraint>
</work-manager>
</weblogic-ejb-jar>
```

This example demonstrates a *weblogic-ejb-jar.xml* file that defines a Work Manager for an EJB with a connection pool–based maximum threads constraint. The EJB will get as many threads as there are instances of a connection pool (or application-scoped connection pool).

Using JDBC Resources Efficiently

Because JNDI lookups are expensive, you must cache any objects that initialize database connections. You can maximize the reuse of connections to eliminate the performance hit involved in the repeated opening and closing of database connections. You can also return connections as soon as you complete the work to minimize the use of resources. The modern way to avoid the lookup of JDBC resources such as connection pools is to use annotations to resolve references to connection pools where possible.

Using the Test Connections On Reserve Feature

If you enable the Test Connections On Reserve feature (see Chapter 4), the server executes a SQL test query to check each connection. In a busy system, you can speed up the creation of connections by telling the server to skip the SQL test if the client successfully connected within a specific time window. The longer the window you specify, the fewer tests the server will make.

Caching Prepared Statements

There are two steps to completing a SQL request: compiling the SQL statement and executing it. By using prepared statements (*java.sql.PreparedStatement*), you can reduce unnecessary compilation, saving time. A prepared statement contains SQL statements that have already been compiled, thus making their execution faster. If you're going to use a SQL statement more than once, you should use a prepared statement. However, when you use a prepared statement or a callable statement (a callable statement object provides a way to call stored procedures in a standard way for all RDBMSs) in an application, there's additional overhead due to the need for communication between WebLogic Server and the database. To reduce resource consumption, you can configure WebLogic Server to cache prepared and callable statements. Caching eliminates a lot of unnecessary work for the database server, reduces CPU use on the database server, and could dramatically improve the statement's performance. When an application or EJB calls a statement stored in the cache, WebLogic Server simply reuses the statement. Any executable statements the server executes repeatedly, such as those inside a loop, benefit from statement caching. The statement cache caches statements from a specific physical connection.

You can enable two types of statement caching: implicit JDBC caching and explicit caching. *Implicit statement caching* is performed when JDBC automatically caches prepared and callable statements using standard connection object and statement object methods. Implicit statement caching doesn't cache plain SQL statements—that is, it caches only *OraclePreparedStatement* and *OracleCallableStatement* objects, not *OracleStatement* objects. The JDBC driver automatically searches the cache for a matching statement when you create an *OraclePreparedStatement* or *OracleCallableStatement* object. Whereas implicit statement caching retains only metadata, *explicit statement caching* retains both statement data (and its state) as well as metadata. Although explicit statement caching is more effective performance-wise, use caution with this type of caching because the data and state are from an earlier execution of a SQL statement, and you don't know for sure what those are. Note that if the JDBC driver doesn't find a statement in the cache, under explicit statement caching the JDBC driver returns a NULL value, whereas under implicit statement caching the driver creates a statement automatically.

The JDBC Data Source Monitoring page in the Administration Console shows various run-time statistics associated with each JDBC data source. Included there are the following statistics related to the use of prepared statements:

- **Prep Stmt Cache Access Count** The total number of times the statement cache was accessed
- **Prep Stmt Cache Add Count** The total number of statements added to the statement cache for all connections
- **Prep Stmt Cache Current Size** The number of prepared and callable statements currently cached in the statement cache
- **Prep Stmt Cache Hit Count** The running count of the number of times the server used a statement from the cache
- **Prep Stmt Cache Miss Count** The number of times a statement request couldn't be satisfied by a statement from the cache

Increasing the Database Listener Timeout

To avoid database listener timeouts in a heavy workload environment, you must increase the listener timeout interval. For example, in an Oracle database you can do this by setting the *INBOUND_CONNECT_TIMEOUT* parameter in the *listener.ora* and *tnsnames.ora* files.

Tuning Transactions

The server incurs additional overhead during two-phase transactions that perform database inserts, updates, and deletes. Two-phase, or X/Open Architecture (XA), transactions in a JMS application involve both the JMS server and the database server. To reduce this overhead, Oracle strongly recommends using the Logging Last Resource (LLR) optimization, as explained in Chapter 4. LLR is a major optimization, and according to Oracle, it can double performance when compared to a nonoptimized XA transaction. In particular, LLR is quite efficient in cases where a transactional JMS destination is used in conjunction with a JDBC resource. LLR uses a table in the same database to turn this into a one-phase transaction and greatly reduce the overhead. Note that this performance improvement is for transactions that perform inserts, deletes, and updates. For transactions that use only *SELECT* statements, the LLR option generally reduces performance.

Summary

This chapter provided an introduction to various aspects of Oracle WebLogic Server performance tuning. Tuning the JVM is a critical part of WebLogic Server performance memory management and garbage collection. The chapter explained the key concepts that underlie memory allocation, garbage collection, and memory compaction, all of which play a critical role in JVM performance. You learned key memory management concepts, including the logging of low memory conditions and the setting of the heap sizes.

The chapter also explained how to tune the persistent store, JMS messaging, and data sources and transactions. It also reviewed the best practices for tuning web application session management. The chapter introduced Oracle Coherence and Coherence*Web. You also learned how to tune EJB performance and reviewed key SQL tuning best practices. Finally, the chapter provided a short review of JPA and TopLink.

A

D

E

F

G

N

O

P

Q

R

S

T

U

V

X

Y

Can I copy Java code to an HTML extension?

I want to improve the performance of my application...

Here's where you can find the latest release.

I coded it this way...

Is the app customizable?

How does restricted task reassignment work?

Just watch the live webcast on virtualization.

The best way to migrate Oracle E-Business Application Suite Tier servers to Linux is...

Where can I find technical articles on logging in Java ME?

Oracle Technology Network. It's code for sharing expertise.

Come to the best place to collaborate with other IT professionals.

Oracle Technology Network is the world's largest community of developers, administrators, and architects using industry-standard technologies with Oracle products.

Sign up for a free membership and you'll have access to:

- Discussion forums and hands-on labs
- Free downloadable software and sample code
- Product documentation
- Member-contributed content

Take advantage of our global network of knowledge.

JOIN TODAY ▷ Go to: oracle.com/technetwork